P9-CMS-788

LAW IN OUR LIVES

LAW IN OUR LIVES

AN INTRODUCTION

THIRD EDITION

David O. Friedrichs

NEW YORK OXFORD

OXFORD UNIVERSITY PRESS

Oxford University Press, Inc., publishes works that further Oxford University's
objective of excellence in research, scholarship, and education.

Oxford New York
Auckland   Cape Town   Dar es Salaam   Hong Kong   Karachi
Kuala Lumpur   Madrid   Melbourne   Mexico City   Nairobi
New Delhi   Shanghai   Taipei   Toronto

With offices in
Argentina   Austria   Brazil   Chile   Czech Republic   France   Greece
Guatemala   Hungary   Italy   Japan   Poland   Portugal   Singapore
South Korea   Switzerland   Thailand   Turkey   Ukraine   Vietnam

Copyright © 2012 Oxford University Press

For titles covered by Section 112 of the US Higher Education
Opportunity Act, please visit www.oup.com/us/he for the
latest information about pricing and alternate formats.

Published by Oxford University Press, Inc.
198 Madison Avenue, New York, New York 10016
www.oup.com

Oxford is a registered trademark of Oxford University Press.

All rights reserved. No part of this publication may be reproduced,
stored in a retrieval system, or transmitted, in any form or by any means,
electronic, mechanical, photocopying, recording, or otherwise,
without the prior permission of Oxford University Press.

Library of Congress Cataloging-in-Publication Data
Friedrichs, David O.
   Law in our lives : an introduction / David O. Friedrichs. — 3rd ed.
     p. cm.
   ISBN 978-0-19-984074-8 (pbk.)
   1. Law—United States.   2. Sociological jurisprudence.   I. Title.
KF380.F75 2011
349.73—dc23   2011026851

For Jessica, Matthew, and Bryan

CONTENTS

PREFACE

WHAT'S NEW TO THIS EDITION

- Material addressing many of the last half-decade's most important news events, including Hurricane Katrina, the Gulf of Mexico oil spill, the election of President Barack Obama, the financial crisis of 2008, and the subsequent economic collapse
- Over 1,000 new sources, many of which are directly cited in the text
- A list of new legal developments pertaining to civil litigation, gay marriage, the 2009 health care bill, technology and privacy rights, and other issues
- Discussions of legal pluralism, constitutional interpretation, and judicial review
- A discussion of post-colonial societies and law
- Current interpretations of Sharia'h law in Islamic countries
- A discussion of the quickly-evolving legal marketplace
- The latest trends on declining support for legal services for the poor
- A discussion of the current status of the environmental law movement
- A discussion of the impact of the internet and social media on the judicial process
- Completely new boxes on a diverse range of topics

The Third Edition of this text went to press in 2011, following the conclusion of the first decade of the twenty-first century. The Second Edition of this text went to press in 2005, in the middle of this decade. The Second Edition had to especially take account of some significant law-related events in the wake of 9/11. In the years since, some dramatic events have occurred, including Hurricane Katrina and the Gulf of Mexico oil spill, the election of the first African-American president, and the financial crisis of 2008, with a broad economic recession and downturn in its wake. The Third Edition of this text attends to some of the law-related consequences of these events, but law is an endlessly dynamic phenomenon, with significant new developments across the board. This edition has accordingly been updated throughout, with relevant scholarship and news stories through much of 2010 (and the deletion of dated and redundant material). More than 1,000 new sources have been consulted for this edition, with a large number of these sources cited. A highly selective listing of new law-related developments addressed in this edition includes those pertaining to avoid repetition to civil litigation, new technology infringing on citizen privacy rights, the controversial health-care bill of 2009, post-financial meltdown legal reforms, gay marriage, medical use of marijuana, and the Employee Free Choice Act. This edition includes new discussions of legal pluralism, constitutional interpretation, and judicial review. It addresses evolving views on punishment, voluntarism, and determinism in relation to law and morality, and conflicts of interest within law. Analytical jurisprudence is distinguished from moralistic jurisprudence, and recent critiques of law and economics jurisprudence are addressed. Giambattista Vico is newly added to the discussion of early forefathers of law and scholarship, and a new section on the methodology of law and society research is included. A new discussion of post-colonial societies and law explores the controversies over the promotion of universal human rights, and new developments relating to American Indians and the law are addressed. The impact of human rights campaigns on law in China, as well as the present role of its Communist Party in relation to law, is discussed, along with current interpretations of Sharia'h law in Islamic countries. The swiftly evolving marketplace for lawyers and some recent trends relating to pro bono worked are discussed. "In-house" lawyers are differentiated from "jailhouse lawyers." And the latest trends on declining support for legal services for the poor, women and minority lawyers, law students and public service careers, and new programs in law schools are all addressed. The operation of the criminal justice system is now affected by such phenomena as Google and Twitter and is taken up in a new section here along with a discussion of the Judge's Advocate-General Corps, among other things. This edition also includes new discussions of cultural context and law, fear and law, ethnic identities and law, and the role played by the media in the recent deregulatory policy law shift. In the final chapter of this new edition, in addition to the most recent legal developments across a wide range of issues, a new discussion of unintended consequences of laws, law and social change in developing countries, and the current status of the environmental law movement are addressed.

In addition to the updating of many existing boxes, the Third Edition of this text includes completely new boxes on: Can Law Promote Happiness?; Animal Law and the Rights of Animals; Texting and Sexting: New Legal Initiatives; The Virginia Tech Shooting Massacre and Privacy Law; The Controversy over Federalism; The Rise of the Conservative Movement in Law; Foreign Law Referrals in American Court Opinions; Criminal Justice, Criminal Injustice, and Cases of Alleged Sexual Misconduct; American Legal Thinking and the Law and Society Movement; Should Jurisprudence be Democratized? Roberto Mangabeira Unger: A Jurisprudential Philosopher and the Future of Brazil; Nudge: An Interdisciplinary Approach to Human Behavior and Legal Policy; A Law and Society Canon?; The International Institute for the Sociology of Law (Onati); Law in Vietnam and Cambodia; Slavery Today; Killing in War: Morality and Law; Harvard Law School's New Curriculum; President Barack Obama as Law Student and Law Professor; Lowering the Bar: Lawyer Jokes; Young Lawyers Sue Bar Exam Prep Company; Cultural Defenses; The Language of Law School: Learning to Think Like a Lawyer; Lex Populi: The Jurisprudence of Harry Potter; Law and Catastrophe: Hurricane Katrina and the Gulf of

Mexico Oil Spill; Immigration: The Optimal Legal Response?; Who Owns the Sky?; and Neuroscience and the Transformation of Law.

LAW IN OUR LIVES: THE ORIGINS AND OBJECTIVES OF THIS BOOK

Law is all over. Law is everywhere. And it may seem to some that law books and books about law are all over and everywhere as well. This book about law was inspired by a certain sense of frustration. I have taught a course titled "Law and Society" for more than 30 years. This course is required for criminal justice majors, and it is recommended that they take the course in their junior year. It is also taken by students in many other majors who have some interest in law, and perhaps especially by those who plan to attend law school. A well-known reader edited by the faculty of the Legal Studies department at the University of Massachusetts-Amherst—John Bonsignore et al., *Before the Law*, Eighth Edition (2006)—serves as a basic source of stimulating articles and cases for this course, but for some years early in my experience of teaching this course, I was unable to find a textbook still in print that provided students with an interdisciplinary framework for understanding law and society. Starting in 1999, I began working on my own textbook for the course.

Several books served as important sources of inspiration for this book. In the late 1960s, as a graduate student and college instructor, I read Edwin M. Schur's (1968) *Law and Society: A Sociological View*, and it made a great impression on me. It certainly inspired in me a deeper interest in the sociology of law and the whole literature on the many challenging questions that arise in this realm. The book was never revised and eventually went out of print. Schur moved on to produce a distinguished list of books on various aspects of deviance, crime (especially victimless crime), gender, and sexuality, among other topics. Then Richard Quinney's (1974) *Critique of Legal Order*, published when I was an assistant professor at City University of New York (Staten Island), was also a seminal influence, as it articulated in a stark form the critical view of law that was so widely promoted during the turbulent era of the late 1960s and early 1970s, and my consciousness of the oppressive and unequal dimensions of law has certainly stayed with me. Quinney also produced many subsequent and original books on various dimensions of crime, spirituality, peacemaking, and personal reflection. Lawrence M. Friedman's (1977) *Law and Society: An Introduction* was fortuitously published about the time I joined the faculty of the University of Scranton and assumed responsibility for the Law and Society course. I assigned that book in the course for many years because it seemed to me that it clearly and concisely identified some elements key to understanding the inter-relationship between the legal and the social. This book also was not revised and eventually went out of print, and Friedman himself has produced a series of landmark books on legal history, the nature of law in American society, and other sociolegal topics.

All of the books mentioned, then, provided me with a perspective on and a mapping of an intriguing and absorbing area of scholarly inquiry. They provided signposts, or starting points, or a window and opening for further investigation. It is my hope that the present text will in some way inspire such an interest in its readers and will at least introduce them to the vast, rich literature on law and society, in its many layers and diverse dimensions.

This book is emphatically not about "black letter law"—the specific content of the different branches of our formal law—although, of course, many references are made to such law. Rather, the book is intended to provide students with a fundamental literacy about law as an immensely important and ubiquitous presence in our social existence. Some of the topics addressed in this book are as follows: the celebration of law and the critique of law; contemporary legal issues confronting society; the definition and meaning of law, the different dimensions or models of law, and the nature of legal reasoning; law in relation to justice, to morality, to religion, and to interests; traditional and contemporary schools of jurisprudence as approaches to understanding law; the law and society movement and the sociology of law as approaches to understanding law; anthropological, comparative, historical, and contextual approaches to understanding law; the legal profession in contemporary society; the basic attributes of the co-existing systems of law, or justice, within our society; some important aspects of legal culture and legal behavior; and the nature of the relationship between law and social change. The chapters of this book are arranged in an order that makes sense to the author, but each chapter is quite autonomous. Instructors who assign this book to their students should be able to re-order the sequence of the chapters on their syllabi to suit the needs of their courses.

The literature pertaining to law is vast. The issues arising in relation to law are endlessly complex. A comprehensive guide to understanding law in all its many aspects would inevitably run to thousands of pages. Any number of sentences in this book could give rise to a long and very detailed footnote or commentary, with elaboration, qualifications, and the like. Again, the intent here is to provide a basic understanding and point of departure for important dimensions of law as a social phenomenon. As do many others, the author has found much of the "technical" literature on law dry and tedious. On the other hand, many of the questions arising out of law have been experienced as endlessly fascinating. Readers of this book will inevitably make some choices on the perspectives, insights, or concepts they find most useful in understanding law. Ideally, readers will be inspired to undertake a lifelong pilgrimage in pursuit of a richer, fuller, and deeper understanding of that remarkable and ever-present dimension of our social existence: law.

A final note to readers: The author of this book welcomes any comments from readers. Any such comments can de directed to:

David O. Friedrichs
Dept. of Sociology/Criminal Justice
University of Scranton
Scranton, PA 18510–4605
friedrichsd1@scranton.edu

ABOUT THE AUTHOR

David O. Friedrichs is Professor of Sociology/Criminal Justice and Distinguished University Fellow at the University of Scranton (Pennsylvania). He was educated at New York University and taught for nine years at City University of New York (Staten Island). He is the author of *Trusted Criminals: White Collar Crime in Contemporary Society* (Cengage Learning/Wadsworth, 1996; 2004; 2007; 2010), and the editor of *State Crime, Volumes I and II* (Ashgate/Dartmouth, 1998). He has published some 130 journal articles, book chapters, encyclopedia entries, and essays on such topics as the legitimation of legal order, legal studies, critical criminology, violence, narrative jurisprudence, postmodernism, white collar crime, crimes of globalization, and crimes of states. His articles have been published in a wide range of refereed journals and in numerous books. He is also the author of well over 300 published book reviews. He served as editor of the Legal Studies Forum between 1985 and 1989, and as president of the White Collar Crime Research Consortium between 2002 and 2004. He has also been active with numerous professional associations and has chaired or served on committees of a number of these associations, and he has served on the editorial boards of various journals. He has been a visiting professor or guest lecturer at a number of colleges and universities, including the University of South Africa (Visiting Professor of Law and Sociology), Ohio University (Rufus Putnam Visiting Professor), Western Michigan University (Kercher Lecturer), Eastern Kentucky University (Distinguished Lecturer), and Flinders University (Visiting Professor of Law). During his 2006 sabbatical in Australia, he gave invited lectures at the Universities of South Australia, Adelaide, Melbourne, Tasmania, and the Australian National University. He has presented more than 100 papers at professional conferences and has participated in international law & society and criminology conferences in Amsterdam, Glasgow, Rio, Jerusalem, Prato, Maastricht, Onati, Utrecht, and Wellington. He has authored the entry on "United States" [Law and Society Activities In] for the *Encyclopedia of Law and Society* (Sage, 2007).

ACKNOWLEDGMENTS

A text such as this is inevitably a collaborative work. My primary debt is to the numerous scholars and journalists whose work is cited throughout this book. I can only hope that I have cited their work accurately and fairly.

My service as editor of the *Legal Studies Forum* (1985–1989), and as an editorial board member in subsequent years, was an invaluable learning experience for me in relation to developing an interdisciplinary understanding of law, and I am especially indebted to Jim Elkins, David Papke, John Bonsignore, and Ron Pipkin for what I learned from this experience. Several of these individuals also encouraged me in connection with this book.

I have benefited from discussions of this project with numerous professional acquaintances and personal friends over a period of many years. Martin D. Schwartz has particularly been a major source of encouragement and inspiration. Graduate courses with the late H. Laurence Ross and with Richard Quinney provided early inspiration for my interest in the sociology of law. I am grateful to John Paul Ryan, for many years director of the American Bar Association Commission on College and University Legal Studies, for writing a Foreword to the first two editions of this book. John was the primary organizer of several stimulating American Bar Association conferences (on law and undergraduate education; law and globalization; and law, morality, and religion) in which I participated.

At the University of Scranton, the Faculty Research Committee, the Faculty Development Committee, and the University Travel Committee provided absolutely crucial support in the form of faculty research grants, support for acquiring essential research materials, student assistance, conference travel grants, and sabbaticals. Since 2006, the annual stipend accompanying my appointment as Distinguished University Fellow has funded many of these research-related activities. Various University of Scranton administrators and colleagues— particularly Harry Dammer, my department chair—have supported my work on this project. Bill Parente of the Political Science Department, an admirer of the legal regime of King Louis XIV, has kept me supplied with daily copies of the *Wall Street Journal* and other sources of useful information.

My current department secretary, Gemma Davis, as well as her predecessors, has provided me with highly competent and efficient service in many areas. University of Scranton students who assisted me with earlier editions of this textbook were acknowledged in those earlier editions. For the present edition, I appreciate the work of Elizabeth Barna and Anthony Policastro on revised versions of Appendices B & C. And I have learned useful things from students in my Law and Society course at the University of Scranton over a period of more than 30 years.

I am grateful as well to Gary Feinberg of the University of St. Thomas—who I first met in graduate school in the later 1960s—for producing the Instructor's Manual/Testing Program for the second edition of this text.

I visited many libraries in connection with doing research for this book and am grateful to librarians at the following law schools for providing access to their collections and assistance on inquiries: Cornell, Fordham, Georgetown, John Jay, New York University, Pennsylvania State University, Rutgers, Toronto, the University of Pittsburgh, and Yeshiva, with special gratitude to Phyllis Schultze of the Don Gottfredson Criminal Justice Library at Rutgers—she is the most outstanding criminal justice information specialist in the country, and a good friend of long standing. The friendly and exceptionally competent reference librarians at the University of Scranton have my thanks for their assistance as well.

Claude (now Julia) Teweles, the original publisher of this textbook with Roxbury Publishing, was encouraging and helpful at all stages, as was his highly professional staff. At Oxford University Press I have much benefited from the enthusiastic support and constructive input I have received from Sherith Pankratz and subsequently Sarah Calabi, as editors, and the conscientious contribution of Richard Beck as coordinating editorial assistant. I also want to acknowledge the excellent work of the copy editor (Angela Wood) and production staff at Newgen Imaging Systems.

I appreciated favorable published reviews, along with constructive suggestions, by John Bonsignore, Mary Kirby Diaz, Linda Maule, and Gerard Rainville. I am grateful, as well, to external peer reviewers of my original prospectus and my manuscript. These reviewers made numerous suggestions, each of which I seriously considered and many of which I adopted. I especially appreciated the exceptionally positive and encouraging comments of many of these reviewers. The reviewers of the prospectus or the manuscript are: Ronald Akers (University of Florida); Mary W. Atwell (Radford University); Steven E. Barkan (University of Maine); James A. Black (University of Tennessee-Knoxville); Sheldon Ekland-Olson (University of Texas-Austin); Gary Feinberg (St. Thomas University); Gilbert Geis (University of California-Irvine); Robert Granfield (University of Denver); Roger E. Hartley (Roanoke College); W. Richard Janikowski (University of Memphis); Robert L. Kidder (Temple University); M. Joan McDermott (Southern Illinois University-Carbondale); Austin Sarat (Amherst College); Ric S. Sheffield (Kenyon College); Matthew Silberman (Bucknell University); and Thomas Franklin Waters (Northern Arizona University-Yuma). The reviewers for the Second Editions were Marshall Derosa (Florida Atlantic University); Elaine Alma Draper (California State University-Los Angeles); Gary Feinberg (University of St. Thomas); Daniel Hillyard (Southern Illinois University-Carbondale); Marla Kohlman (Kenyon College); Matthew T. Lee (University of Akron); Andrea Leverentz (DePaul University); Stephen Light (State

University of New York-Plattsburgh); and Shannon Smithey (Kent State University). The reviewers for the third edition are: Tim J. Berard (Kent State University); Renee Ann Cramer (Drake University); Laura Woods Fidelie (Midwestern State University); Bruce G. Peabody (Fairleigh Dickinson University); Daniel Pontzer (University of North Florida); Charles Putnam (University of New Hampshire); Bobby A. Potters (University of Indianapolis).

In some cases, I have perhaps perversely rejected the advice of these reviewers, as well as that of the copy editor. Any shortcomings or inaccuracies that can be identified in this book are, of course, my responsibility.

A professional involvement with law extends over many generations in my family. An ancestor practiced law in the middle of the nineteenth century; a grandfather wrote about law in the earlier years of the twentieth century; a niece, Natasha Friedrichs is successful corporate lawyer in New York early in the twenty-first century. These associations are one form of inspiration for my own interest in law.

I have been fortunate to have the support and love of many family members over a period of decades, my wife, Jeanne, among others. I owe a special debt of gratitude over the past two years to my brother Martin Friedrichs and my sister-in-law Elizabeth Windle. My two children, Jessica and Bryan, and my son-in-law Matt Fagerburg, by being so successful and well-adjusted in their own lives, have helped make it possible for me to concentrate on writing a book. Accordingly, this book is dedicated to them, with great pride and much love. As for my little grandson Indy—who takes a sometimes dim view of the legal regime of his parents—I hope his turn will come somewhere further down the line.

LAW IN OUR LIVES

CHAPTER 1

INTRODUCTION

Legal historian Harold J. Berman ... once said, "A child says 'It's my toy.' That's property law. A child says, 'You promised me.' That's contract law. A child says, 'He hit me first.' That's criminal law. A child says, 'Daddy said I could.' That's constitutional law." ... [T]here is hardly a time in our lives before ... [we develop] some dim consciousness of law.

—KITTY CALAVITA (2010)

Law isn't just an abstraction or an intellectual exercise ... [It shapes] not just the character of our democracy, but the circumstances of our daily lives.

—PRESIDENT BARACK OBAMA (Hulse 2010)

The life of the law has not been logic: it has been experience.

—OLIVER WENDELL HOLMES, JR. (1881)

Law is all over. Law is everywhere. Law is an enduring presence in our lives. Americans tend to be socialized to think most readily of the police, and more specifically the police in their enforcement or crime-fighting role, when the notion of law is raised. The terms *police* and *law* are sometimes used interchangeably. The police are one conspicuous and important representation of law in our society, but law is a far more pervasive feature of our daily lives (Friedman 2002; Howard 2009). Law is all over for college students and graduate students.

The very building in which you are attending class is governed by legal codes. If, before class, you stopped somewhere for a meal, then you were in a circumstance governed by health codes. If you went to work before class, then you were subject to labor law and possibly occupational and workplace safety standards. If you made a purchase prior to class, then liability law or contract law may have been involved. If you stopped at the library before class to photocopy some research material, then copyright law was involved. If you engaged in some form of search or communication on the Internet, then you were subject to an emerging body of law governing this new medium.

You may encounter law as well if you need to consult a lawyer about such matters as divorce or a dispute with a landlord; if you are called for jury duty; if you do an internship with the probation department; or if you are sued in civil court in connection with an automobile accident. You should also recognize that you are more than likely to encounter law any time you hear the news on the radio or television, read a newspaper, or surf the Internet—you are exposed to accounts of important court decisions, proposed new legislation, alleged violations of international law, polls of public opinion concerning ongoing legal controversies, high-profile trials, and the like.

MAKING SENSE OF LAW

No single framework for understanding law, no one perspective on law, no core thesis about law is adopted here. Rather, law is viewed as many-hued, multifaceted, and often complex and contradictory. Law is everywhere; law is not always visible to us; law matters, and law does not matter; law is beneficial, and law is harmful. In one view, law is only meaningful and understandable within a particular context, not as an abstract concept (Brigham 2009; Nelken 2009). Some dimensions of law are very visible to us; other dimensions are quite invisible and quite incomprehensible (Brigham 2009). When law is mysterious and less visible, the interests of legal professionals claiming special knowledge of law are served. Perhaps Franz Kafka, the celebrated early twentieth-century author and native of Prague, had it right: he formulated several parables about law that suggest that it cannot be fully understood and comprehended by conventional accounts. It seemed to me to be false, then, and a distortion of a complex reality, to attempt to impose a unified framework on the study of how law and society interact. Nevertheless, it will be evident to readers of this book that the author regards some perspectives as more useful and insightful than others and some themes as more central and powerful than others.

Law is studied in different ways. Some of the literature on law is purely descriptive, and prescriptive. In other words, this literature simply states what the law is and what practical procedures to follow to implement the law. Law professors have produced a large volume of commentary on law, commonly described as **doctrinal analysis**. Here, some law or legal ruling is subjected to analysis in terms of its consistency or inconsistency with some relevant set of legal principles or objectives.

Very little of the literature drawn upon in this book falls into the categories of law-related writing just identified. Rather, most of the literature discussed here draws upon one of two traditions of making sense of law.

The **positivistic tradition** looks to the natural sciences for its model. Theories are formulated, and hypotheses are generated and subjected to empirical verification. This approach aspires to dispassionately discover, explain, and make valid predictions about law-related phenomena. The ultimate complexity and variability of the human and legal world, the difficulty of being objective about this world, and the practical or ethical constraints of subjecting humans to scientific tests, however, all act as barriers to the goal of achieving a true science of the sociolegal—that is, the relationship between law and society. Specific methods used within this model include experiments, surveys, observational studies, content analysis, and secondary data analysis.

The **humanistic tradition** looks to the humanities—philosophy, history, and literature—for its model. It adopts the premise that the world of the sociolegal is fundamentally different from the natural and physical world, and accordingly it rejects the positivistic approach. In the humanistic tradition, law and the sociolegal are more likely to be interpreted than explained, and stories about law are preferred to statistical analyses relating to law. Through applying relevant philosophical concepts to the sociolegal, providing a detailed historical account, or looking to literary explorations of it, students can presumably arrive at a rich understanding of how law and society affect each other. The humanistic approach has been criticized for its possible biases, the difficulty of verifying its claims, and its failure to produce helpful generalizations.

Each approach has its limitations. Ideally, a multiplicity of different approaches complement each other, although it seems unlikely that anyone will wholly eliminate contradictions emanating from these different approaches.

One objective of this book is to introduce students to the scholarly literature on law and society, literature from a wide range of disciplines. This literature is vast, and to do full justice to it would require an impossibly large book. The objective here is to provide some preliminary guideposts to this literature and to distill some of its essential themes.

No matter whether our knowledge about the law comes from direct experience or from vicarious experience, each of us is likely to evaluate our images and understanding of law through an ideological prism. We all come to the study of law with a certain set of beliefs. These beliefs may be rooted in such systems as a religious doctrine, a partisan political identification, or a broad philosophy of life and human existence. Individuals' reactions to law and legal phenomena are strongly influenced, then, by a complex of beliefs they hold. Also, people have a tendency to see what they want to see.

Beliefs about law vary over time, and beliefs that inspired specific laws may be much at odds with current beliefs (*see* Box 1.1).

BOX 1.1   IS LAW RATIONAL? THE EVIDENCE OF
ODD LAWS AND LEGAL PROCEDURES

One element of the image of law in a modern, complex society is that law is, or ought to be, a rational enterprise. For our purposes, *rational* means that law is logical, understandable, fairminded, predictable, and sound. There are some, however, who view law as illogical, incomprehensible, discriminatory, arbitrary, and counterproductive. In terms of the substance of law and decisions at law, many examples of "odd" laws can be provided. Listings of **odd laws** have been collected in some books (e.g., Hyman 1977; Napier-Andrews 1976; Shook and Meyer 1995). It has been illegal in Memphis, Tennessee, to drive a car while asleep; in Bexley, Ohio, to install slot machines in outhouses; in Lexington, Kentucky, to carry an ice cream cone in one's pocket;

in Oklahoma, to take a bite out of another person's hamburger; and in New Jersey, to slurp soup in a public restaurant. In Louisiana and in Flint, Michigan, a man can get cited for wearing low-riding pants that reveal underwear or the "cleft of the buttocks." The American Civil Liberties Union opposed such laws as a violation of free expression and as law that would be ripe for selective enforcement by the police (Bennett and Chapman 2008; Koppel 2007).

It has been illegal in London to congregate with Egyptians and in Boston to take a bath. In New York City, a councilman proposed a legal ban on the sale of used underwear (Rutenberg 2005). In London, a Law Commission is charged with sifting out obsolete laws (Scrivens 2008). Some possible candidates for removal include: a law prohibiting entering the Houses of

BOX 1.1 (cont'd.)

Parliament in a suit of armor and another prohibiting Londoners from keeping a pigsty in front of their homes. Numerous other such examples could be cited. These odd, or silly, laws remind us that laws are human creations. Almost anything can be declared against the law. We have to remind ourselves that such laws come into existence in a particular historical context and often spring from a particular circumstance. A decade later, the "particular circumstance" may have disappeared, but the law remains on the books. Some "odd" laws may be seen as having merit. Legislation was introduced in Venezuela prohibiting parents from bestowing unusual names on their children (Romero 2007). Should American parents be prohibited from naming a son "Adolf Hitler," as happened in a case reported out of Pennsylvania (Foderaro 2009)? But who would decide whether a name is unusual enough to be outlawed?

Again, odd laws impress on us the point that laws need not be rational, at least by conventional, contemporary standards. On a more serious note, there is ongoing debate within our society over questions of whether existing laws prohibiting the use of marijuana or some forms of gambling are rational and justifiable.

In terms of the procedures of law, legal cases have not always been resolved by rational means. "Trials by ordeal" and "animal trials" are good examples. The **trial by ordeal** was a basic mechanism for resolving criminal cases in a tradition rooted in ancient Anglo-Saxon law. It was still used in some form in our own system of law into the nineteenth century, and it survives among certain societies in the contemporary world (Custer 1986; Tewksbury 1967). The essence of such trials was that the criminal defendant was subjected to an ordeal to determine guilt or innocence, and for an extended period of time in the English law, an ordeal was the sole means for resolving questions of guilt or innocence. Ordeals ranged from requiring suspected wrongdoers to walk over hot coals to requiring the suspect to touch the victim's corpse.

Trials of animals were held in Europe between the fourteenth and eighteenth centuries and apparently became quite common between the fifteenth and seventeenth centuries (E. Cohen 1986). In France, in 1457, a pig and some piglets were tried for killing a 5-year-old child. The pig was convicted and hung; the piglets were released to their owner on probationary status, insofar as there was no conclusive proof that they actually committed the killing. In France, in 1587, some flies were sued for destroying a vineyard, and a lawyer was appointed to handle their defense. In another French case, when rats failed to appear in court in response to a formal summons, their advocate pleaded their fear of cats as an excuse and requested safe conduct for them. Although these animal trials may appear bizarre by contemporary standards, we should also ask ourselves how some of our own adjudicatory procedures (e.g., trials for young juvenile offenders) will look at some future time.

IMAGES OF LAW

A fundamental tension exists between the idealized image of law and what we may discover about the "realities of law." In our time, it is difficult to sustain an image of law as a source of perfect order, impartiality, and justice. In a person's own experience with law, he or she may witness abuses and cynical trade-offs; such occurrences may be especially likely if the person belongs to a minority group. In the recent era, wrongdoing on all levels of lawmaking and law enforcement has been relentlessly exposed. Films and television dramas have, for the most part, incorporated a gritty, sometimes cynical, realism about law and lawmakers. They have largely abandoned earlier tendencies to portray law enforcement officers and judges in mythic or heroic terms. Law today is a spectacle, a form of entertainment, with real and fictional representations often mixed up or interchangeable.

College students who undertake the formal study of law and legal institutions, as you are doing now, become exposed to the many documented gaps between official standards and actual practices. But a general loss of innocence about law need not be equated with the adoption of a cynical outlook. It is possible to sustain a strong allegiance to "the rule of law" without being naive about the law's biases, abuses, and limitations. Law is indeed all over; law is everywhere.

One other dimension of the image of law must be addressed: What is the nature of the relation between the law and society, or the legal and the social? In one view, law is **autonomous** and must be understood wholly on its own terms, independent of a social context. In an extreme version of this view, law could be seen as equivalent to mathematics. Everyone understands that the laws of mathematics and fundamental mathematical precepts are universals, the same in the People's Republic of China and in the United States. The question of whether it makes any sense to think of law in this way is explored later in this text in various chapters.

In another view, law and society are **homologous**—that is, they correspond in origin and structure and cannot be understood independently of each other. In an extreme version of this view, law is wholly a reflection of a particular social order. Law in the People's Republic of China merely implements the values and objectives of that system, and law in the United States does the same for a very different system. Again, the question of the validity of such a way of thinking about law will be considered later.

There is a third basic perspective on the relation between law and society. In this view, law and society are best thought of in *interactive* terms. This view recognizes that law and society each have some unique and independent dimensions but that they also interact on many levels, with reciprocal influences. Some version of this view is the most widely held, and it informs the perspective adopted throughout this book (*see* Fig. 1.1). Mauro Zamboni (2007) refers to these three models as autonomous, embedded, and intersecting.

The **interactive model** could alternatively be illustrated as in Figure 1.2, with reciprocal influences among social structure (e.g., social class), social processes (e.g., socialization), and law.

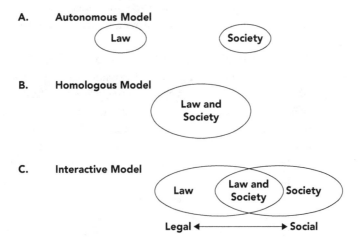

FIGURE 1.1   Relationship of Law and Society

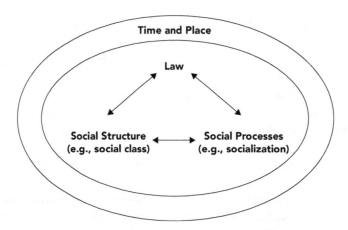

Representation of the interactive perspective on the relation of law and society. It shows that although both law and society have some unique and independent dimensions, they also have reciprocal influences.

FIGURE 1.2   Relationship of Law, Social Structure, and Social Process

THE CELEBRATION OF LAW

In the conventional view promoted by many of our political leaders, taught in high school civics classes, and held by many ordinary citizens, law is not only something "good" in itself, it is the principal means for ensuring that people can enjoy all the good things in life (Bogus 2001; Friedman 1990). Law in this view guarantees the possibility of a civilized existence and contributes to the enhancement of such an existence. Law alone makes freedom possible, along with the choices and rights associated with living in a free society. Law in some form, and the rule of law, is universally embraced by all societies aspiring to an orderly and productive existence. Ideally, and emphatically in the American tradition, law is rooted in democratic consensus. And law in this view is regarded as a profoundly rational entity with an inherent commitment to the promotion of justice and fairness.

In the conventional view, law fulfills some essential functions (Barkan 2009; Ferrari 2007; Vago 2009). Law not only maintains order, it makes order possible. Law provides for the orderly, nonviolent resolution of all manner of conflicts and disputes. More specifically, law allows for social catharsis, or the release of justifiable anger and outrage directed at those seen as willfully engaging in harmful and destructive behavior, and it does so in a form minimizing the potential for further suffering and loss. More broadly, law is an instrument for the realization of justice. Law restores what has been lost—to the extent possible—to plaintiffs and victims, allocates responsibility and costs, and imposes appropriate penalties on guilty and negligent parties.

In the positive view, law should serve as a key element in the fostering and maintenance of a democratic political system. Law provides a fundamental constraint on the exercise of power by the political leadership and is the primary form of protection against tyranny. Law provides the framework for identifying human rights and for protecting those rights. Law allocates power and at the same time supervises the exercise of power.

BOX 1.2   CAN LAW PROMOTE HAPPINESS?

Every American schoolchild learns the following famous words from the Declaration of Independence:

> We hold these truths to be self evident, that all men are created equal, that they are endowed by their Creator with certain unalienable rights, that among these are Life, Liberty, and the pursuit of Happiness.

That the law addresses life and liberty and the protection of these "unalienable rights" is self-evident, although there is some lack of consensus on the meaning of "life" and "liberty." But can the law do anything to promote happiness? Walter Mosley (2009), a member of the editorial board of *The Nation*, argues that prison-like schools, meaningless jobs, unemployment and

underemployment, untreated physical and psychological ailments, and various actions of political leaders and major corporations interfere substantially with our realization of happiness. Many of our habits, from rampant consumerism to empty television-viewing to the pursuit of meaningless sex, compromise this pursuit as well. Although Mosley concedes that some people are naturally happy and some are fortunate enough to find themselves in happy circumstances, too many of us are afflicted with many sources of unhappiness. He calls for the creation of a government department that is focused on the promotion of happiness for all Americans. With all our laws addressing the preservation of life and the protection of liberty, do we also need laws specifically facilitating the "pursuit of happiness," and is this a goal that can be realized by legal initiatives?

Law both creates and promotes desirable social values. Law symbolically defines normative boundaries within society, clearly delineating the differences between right and wrong and between fundamentally acceptable and unacceptable behavior. Law both encourages and compels us to respect the life and personhood of others and to respect the rights as well as the privacy of others. Law tells us to pay our taxes; law tells us not to snort cocaine. Law promotes a healthier environment, better work conditions, and safer consumer products. And law may transcend the symbolic promotion of rights when it becomes the specific means of creating or providing opportunities. Anti-discrimination law and equal opportunity law can be cited as obvious illustrations of this function of law. Affirmative action law, although controversial, is a specific legal initiative to extend opportunities for employment and advancement to members of disadvantaged groups who might not otherwise have enjoyed such opportunities.

Law has some practical and mundane functions. Law provides a structure for, and facilitates, a broad range of private transactions and productive activities. Law defines what constitutes wealth and property and provides opportunities for acquiring wealth and property. Law identifies and distributes all manner of benefits to qualified citizens. Law is a mechanism through which society may formally define relationships—including the most intimate relations between family members—and the obligations attached to such relationships. Law also plays a role in defining and organizing time. Should law be obliged to promote happiness? (*See* Box 1.2.) Although many scholars and legal professionals embrace and propound the positive views of law and its functions discussed here, there is also a body of literature, by other scholars and legal professionals, that criticizes the law.

THE CRITIQUE OF LAW

Law has been characterized as a profoundly negative dimension of the human environment. Thomas Cooper wrote, in 1830, that "the law, unfortunately, has always been retained on the side of power; laws have uniformly been enacted for the protection and perpetuation of power" (quoted in Shapiro 1993, p. 241). The critique of law comes from many sources. In the **radical** or anarchic version of the **critique of law**, it has been portrayed as an instrument of oppression and exploitation (Beirne and Quinney 1982; Travers 2010). In this view, law advances and protects elite interests and values. Law is a mechanism that the powerful use to coerce, dominate, and intimidate the powerless.

THE RADICAL CRITIQUE

In the radical critique, law is inherently oriented toward the preservation of the status quo. Law plays an instrumental role, more specifically, in the preservation of private property—and a grossly disproportionate share of the wealth generally—in the hands of the few. Law is either directly a tool of the ownership class or is "relatively autonomous" but oriented toward the long-term survival of the system. Insofar as law contributes to the maintenance of "order," this purpose is fulfilled on behalf of the interests of the elite class.

In the radical critique, law contributes importantly to the legitimation of domination and the maintenance of hierarchy. In other words, law helps justify the concentration of power in the hands of the few and the privileges of some members of society in relation to everyone else. What law ordains is accepted simply because it is law. Law facilitates "plunder" and exploitation (Mattei and Nader 2008). Law is violence, we are told; law punishes violence but also perpetrates various forms of violence against those accused of crimes, with the imposition of the death penalty as one extreme example (Cover 1986; Sarat 2001). Law legitimates its own violence, then. Law promotes attitudes and actions harmful to people, and it does so through the use of language.

Law in the negative view is seen as promoting conflict rather than resolving it. And rather than eliminating differences between people and bringing them together, law contributes to categorizing people in terms of perceived differences and thereby reinforcing prejudice, discrimination, and misunderstanding (Minow 1990, p. 9). Law all too often, in many different ways, creates confrontations between citizens and the state.

In sum, in the radical critique, law perpetuates injustice, fosters conflict, and promotes selfish interests. Table 1.1 summarizes the positive and negative functions that have been attributed to law.

THE CONSERVATIVE CRITIQUE

A **critique of law** is also associated with the right, or **conservative** forces, going back at least to Edmund Burke's criticism of the legal order established in the wake of the French Revolution (O'Hagan 1984, p. 21). In the modern era, ultraconservative forces and the far right have been especially critical of law being used as an instrument for achieving a liberal agenda and of its ultimate infringement of individual rights. A central thesis of the right-wing critique of law, then, highlights the claim that law interferes with the natural freedom citizens are entitled to enjoy. For example, some rightist critics have attacked tax law and gun control laws as unjustifiable attempts by the state, through the mechanism of law, to confiscate the property of citizens and to deprive them of weapons they are naturally entitled to own. In somewhat less extreme conservative views, law all too often interferes with the natural law of the market and accordingly has a damaging or destructive impact on productive activity and the creation of new wealth. This right-wing critique of law, except at its extreme fringes, is less focused on

TABLE 1.1   THE FUNCTIONS OF LAW

A. Law's positive functions

1. Maintains order

2. Settles disputes

3. Allows for social catharsis

4. Promotes justice

5. Promotes desirable social values

6. Administers practical needs

B. Law's Negative Functions

1. Maintains the status quo

2. Divides people

3. Exploits people

4. Promotes conflict and violence

5. Promotes oppression and greed

6. Extends state power

law as an institution than it is on the perceived misuse and misapplication of law. Although conservative forces typically favor less application of law to the activities of businesses, they favor more vigorous application of law to conventional lower-class offenders.

LAW'S UNFULFILLED PROMISES

The critique of law is not limited to those at the far ends of the ideological spectrum. The rule of law tends to be strongly supported within mainstream ideological thought, but there is much criticism of the perversion of law to fulfill the purposes of special interest groups or to improperly implement the law or to incur waste of time or money.

Virtually all of us can find some specific law, some legal ruling, or some action undertaken by an official of law to be offensive. By its very nature, law cannot fulfill everyone's expectations and perceptions of justice. One of the paradoxes of living in a society that claims to venerate the rule of law is the production of unrealistic aspirations for what law can accomplish. Passage of the Civil Rights Acts of 1964 and 1968 swept away formal barriers to integration and equal opportunity but could not legislate racism *per se* out of existence; it could not obliterate deeply embedded social and psychological patterns of behavior that impeded the realization of equality. Accordingly, there has been much frustration and anger over the gap between the superficial promise of such law and the disadvantaged conditions that too many African Americans and other minority groups have continued to experience.

THE INTERNAL CRITIQUE OF LAW

The critique of law comes not only from those who are "outsiders"—that is, who are not legal professionals—but also from those within the profession of law. Some of these critics rank at the top of their profession. Such **internal critiques**, however, are typically focused not on law as an institution but rather on the way it is used, or abused. Over a period of time, chief justices of the United States, judges, prominent law school deans, and law professors have complained about the cost and inefficiency of the legal system; its imbalances favoring the privileged; its undemocratic dimensions; its perverted worship of legal reasoning; its use of the best and brightest minds for non-productive purposes; and its frivolous lawsuits, delaying tactics, lawyer incompetence, and unseemly behavior by lawyers.

Those who have run for political office in recent American history have often found that criticism of law, judges, and lawyers are popular themes that resonate with many voters. Presidents from Franklin D. Roosevelt to George W. Bush have attacked out-of-touch judges and greedy lawyers, judicial rulings that work against the well-being of the American people and overblown lawsuits that are costly and harmful to professionals. They have complained that we have too many lawyers and too many government regulations made by and promoted by lawyers.

HYPERLEXIS: "TOO MUCH LAW"

Other paradoxes pertaining to law often present themselves. If, on the one hand, we have come to expect law to provide solutions to an exceptionally broad range of social problems and conditions, we also tend to find law overblown and excessively intrusive. The claim that there is "too much law" (and too many lawyers) is commonplace. The term **hyperlexis** refers to the excessive growth of law (Manning 1977). By almost any measure, law has indeed been a growth industry in America (Footlick 1977; Friedman 2002; Howard 2009). Legislative bodies (from local to federal) add more than 150,000 new laws to the books each year. More laws mean more lawsuits, and the number of cases filed (at least in some jurisdictions) has led to a widely perceived **litigation explosion**. The perception of a "litigation explosion" can be found in various English-speaking countries, including Australia (Prest and Anleu 2004). Defining and measuring litigation is more complicated than one might think, but for now, we will say that litigation is a pursuit of some goal by using the courts. Although the perception that Americans are increasingly litigious is quite common, not all commentators agree with it; indeed, at least some focus on American hostility to policies promoting litigation (Burke 2002). And to the extent that Americans engage in much litigation, at least some commentators regard it as something positive, a necessary supplement to government regulation and a form of protection for American consumers (Bogus 2001; Koenig and Rustad 2001). These commentators dispute claims that frivolous lawsuits against major corporations are common. Furthermore, empirical research has challenged a widespread perception that jurors in civil (tort) lawsuits against major corporations are typically hostile to such corporations (Hans 2000). On the contrary, many jurors and prospective jurors seem to be hostile to plaintiffs who sue wealthy corporations. Although jurors may hold corporations to higher standards of responsibility than individuals, it does not follow that jurors will quite uniformly support the claims and demands of civil plaintiffs.

Thomas Geoghegan (2007), in *See You in Court: How the Right Made America a Lawsuit Nation*, argues that the recent "litigation explosion" can be largely attributed to right-wing politicians dismantling an earlier system where contract, trust, and administrative law effectively protected the rights of ordinary people. With the drastic decline of unions and the precipitous decline of the safety net for the poor, workers and disadvantaged members of society see no alternative to the courts to enforce their rights and obtain some measure of justice for themselves.

Robert Bork, a former Federal appeals court judge (and rejected U.S. Supreme Court nominee) was a major critic of the explosion of civil lawsuits (Chronicle of Higher Education 2007). Some commentators found it ironic that he sued the Yale Club after falling off a dais and injuring his leg.

The scope of litigation has broadened; some forms of litigation (e.g., medical malpractice suits) have increased exponentially, and case filings in the federal courts have risen dramatically. Medical errors kill as many as 98,000 patients annually in the United States (Landro 2009). The number of lawsuits filed in federal courts doubled between 1997 and 2002; data on state filings are less available (Glater 2004). Pharmacists in 2009 were anxious over the outcome of a Nevada case where a pharmacy was sued in connection with a customer causing a fatal automobile accident related to abuse of prescription drugs (Merrick 2009). **Class action lawsuits**, in which a large number of plaintiffs (sometimes many thousands) are joined in a legal action, became far more common in the 1970s than earlier; they were certainly a controversial element of the legal landscape in the early twenty-first century (Crier 2003; Hensler et al. 2000; Willing 2004). A critic complains that they are both unconstitutional and undemocratic (Redish 2009). Class action lawsuits have been controversial because they are said to have bankrupted many companies and to have enriched lawyers rather than having adequately compensated plaintiffs (Oppel 2003). But one study reported in 2004 found that average settlements (and lawyers' fees) had held steady over the most recent 10-year period (Glater 2004; *see* the discussion of recent developments pertaining to class action lawsuits in the section on legal developments in the early twenty-first century).

Critics of the litigation explosion contend that the cost of all forms of civil litigation burdens all Americans and that the cost of monetary awards in civil cases has increased significantly. The law of personal injury (tort law) helped give rise to the insurance industry, which in turn gave rise to expanded personal injury liability (Abraham 2008).

It has been estimated that the average civil case can cost between $50,000 and $100,000 to litigate through trial, with the direct annual cost of tort litigation in the United States close to $250 billion a year (Morris 2006). Some lawyers target small businesses and threaten to sue them for some alleged technical violation of law (e.g., failing to post a sign about transaction fees on credit card purchases) if they don't pay a settlement fee (e.g., $1,000) (Morris 2006). Many storeowners—especially if they are immigrants not well-versed in American law—may agree to such extortionate tactics. A study looking at 40 years of data on tort cases in San Francisco and Cook County in Illinois found an increase in average awards (measured by real dollars), but much of this increase could be attributed to changes in the mix of cases (Seabury, Pace, and Reville 2004). The proportion of auto cases has declined, whereas the proportion of medical malpractice cases has increased, and the latter type of cases produce higher-than-average awards. Law professor Tom Baker (2005) has characterized as a "myth" the widespread perceptions that growing numbers of patients are suing their doctors on frivolous grounds, winning multimillion judgments, and that doctors are being driven out of their practices by skyrocketing malpractice awards. He documents that the vast majority of victims of medical malpractice do not sue and that factors other than medical malpractice awards (including losses on insurance company investments) drive increases in malpractice insurance premiums. According to a study reported in 2009, only 2% to 3% of cases of apparent medical malpractice result in a formal legal claim, with the total costs associated with medical malpractice (including insurance) totaling less than 0.5% of medical spending (Leonhardt 2009). It may be true that certain features of the American legal system contribute to relatively higher costs for medical malpractice cases than elsewhere, including jury trials; a contingency fee system; the requirement that each side bear its own costs; and extensive pretrial discovery (Epstein 2009). But the perception of a medical malpractice crisis has not been limited to the United States (e.g., it has arisen in the Great Britain as well; Harpwood 2007). If awards have increased on the average for certain kinds of cases, they have diminished for other types of cases.

If the filing of lawsuits has grown significantly in the recent era, especially in the federal courts, it does not follow that the number of trials has increased. An American Bar Association study in 2003 reported that less than 2% of civil cases in the federal court in 2002 went to trial, compared with more than 11% in 1962 (Liptak 2003c). Similar patterns were apparent in the state courts. The decline in trials could be attributed to negotiated settlements and pretrial dismissals of cases by judges and a growing recognition of the costs and risks of trials. Whether the dramatic reduction of civil trials is a good thing depends on one's viewpoint, with at least some commentators contending that plaintiffs against major corporations fare better with trial jurors than with nontrial settlements. The educational and therapeutic functions of trials can also be considered a loss when they become far less common.

The growth of litigation was accompanied by growth in the size of the legal profession, which almost quadrupled during the second half of the twentieth century and grew at a substantially faster rate than did the population.

Philip Howard (2009), in *Life Without Lawyers* (the latest of a series of books he has produced on the costs of living in a society allegedly "choked to death" by law), claims that Americans avoid all kinds of reasonable activities because of fear of lawsuits.

Some civil lawsuits get much media attention because of their absurdity. For example, a man in Washington, D.C.—an administrative law judge, no less—sued his neighborhood dry cleaner for $50 million for allegedly misplacing an expensive pair of pants he had dropped off there (Sabar and Lee 2007). He lost the case. A man in New York City sued two people for $1 million for allegedly damaging an umbrella he owned (Eligon 2008). This was another lost case. But the attention such cases garner in the media tends to feed a widespread public perception of a civil litigation system that is out of control.

THE PARADOX

In the final analysis, whether people are better off or worse off if they have "more law" today is a matter of ongoing dispute. On the one hand, an argument can be put forth that people's rights are more fully protected, harmful activities are more fully addressed, and inequities and injustices are more likely to be corrected with the extension of law. On the other hand, arguments can be put forth that the law has become too intrusive, that economic inefficiencies and job losses result from excessive litigation, and that the privileged and powerful always have the advantage in the long term when there is more law. On the one hand, Americans collectively have turned increasingly to the formal law and the courts to settle political issues that in the past were often resolved by negotiation and bargaining (Silverstein 2009). On the other hand, the use of trials to resolve criminal cases and civil disputes has declined recently in the United States (Burns 2009). Although trials are time-consuming and hardly error-free, advocates claim that they are crucial for a democratic justice system. Americans typically claim allegiance to the rule of law but not infrequently complain quite bitterly about specific aspects of the law and the legal system (Cass 2001). American law is characterized by many inconsistencies and defects, some of which are quite trivial and some of which are fundamental.

In sum, in America an enduring love–hate relationship with law persists. There are many historical contradictions and cultural sources of ambivalence. The American republic was, after all, founded on a "lawless" rebellion, or revolution; from the outset, nevertheless, the Founding Fathers professed a commitment to a nation of laws. The Constitution is one of the "sacred" objects of American history and an icon of the American rule of law. It is widely venerated and has been a source of inspiration for constitutions in many developing countries. However, in American history, there has been the frontier tradition with its resistance to formal legal controls; this stance is also widely celebrated in the present. The history of American law is more complex and contradictory than common portrayals suggest; however, Colonial America could be quite disorderly, and frontier law was in some respects fairly stable (Ellis 2007; Marietta and Rowe 2006).

In America early in the twenty-first century, an ongoing tension exists between the demand for more and more law in a rapidly growing, exceptionally heterogeneous, and increasingly complex society and vigorous protests by a certain proportion of the citizenry who perceive an expansion and growing oppressiveness of the law. The increasingly broad use of law by overzealous prosecutors and career-minded bureaucrats has been characterized as the "tyranny of good intentions," resulting in a negative impact on personal freedom and the realization of individual justice (Roberts and Stratton 2000). Do we rely too much on law (and litigation) to address a range of complex social and political phenomena that are simply not amenable to legal resolution (Bogart 2002)? This paradox of wanting both more and less law is a source of conflict in American society. It is not, however, the only issue that provokes contention. The following section presents a number of law-related issues around which debate currently swirls.

CURRENT ISSUES BEFORE THE LAW

From all sides, it often seems, we are confronted with contentious debates on law-related issues (Katsh and Rose 2007; Natoli 2006). On some matters pertaining to law, there is broad agreement: that willful homicide or the sexual molestation of children should be forbidden by law is a matter of general consensus. In a large, complex society, however, one can always find some individuals or small groups who dissent from or challenge any law or social norm. An entity known as the North American Man/Boy Love Association, for example, advocates the position that even young children should be permitted to engage in consensual sexual relations with adults (Leo 1983). Such a group is marginalized in the extreme within our society and is subject to condemnation or prosecution. On the other end of the scale, a high level of consensus exists that parents should have the right to establish bedtimes for their minor children and require their participation in household chores and that such matters should not be addressed by governmental laws. Even here one might find extreme proponents of children's rights who would object to the imposition of any such constraints on the freedom of children, but again they would tend to be wholly marginalized within society and devoid of any measurable influence.

Between those issues on which there is a high level of consensus, whether in favor of the law or against it, there are many law-related issues on which members of society are divided. Some of the legal issues identified here have been debated over a long period of time; capital punishment is one such issue. Other issues have surfaced only recently, such as the downloading of copyrighted music and videos. Many issues that were once heatedly debated—including witchcraft trials, slavery, Jim Crow laws (sanctioning segregation), voting rights for women, and the prohibition of liquor—are no longer live issues in American society. And some issues that currently divide people in other countries around the world—including genital mutilation of young girls (in some African countries), religious control over marriage (in Israel), basic rights of women (in some Muslim countries), and the right to dissent (in China, among other countries)—are also not live issues in American society.

SANCTITY-OF-LIFE ISSUES

One set of contentious legal matters can be called **sanctity-of-life issues**. Abortion, euthanasia, and capital punishment are three such issues; each involves the deliberate termination of life in some sense. Those who support capital punishment do not necessarily support the legalization of abortion, and vice versa. A person's position on the sanctity-of-life issues seems to be related to his or her attitudes on such matters as punitiveness (Cook 1998). The stance of the American Constitution on sanctity-of-life issues has been subject to different interpretations during the course of American history (Anastaplo 2009). Some commentators question whether law (and science) can provide answers to questions that arise about the sanctity of life (Palmer 2000). Surely they are difficult to resolve.

The issue of abortion—whether it should be legally available—has been exceptionally contentious in America, with a long and complex legal history (Hull and Hoffer 2001; Woliver 2007). The highly controversial *Roe v. Wade* decision in 1973 struck down laws outlawing abortion as unconstitutional, but in the intervening years, various attempts have been made to reverse this decision or at least impose restraints on the right to abortion. Since a 1992 U.S. Supreme Court ruling that states could impose some restrictions on abortion, more than half the states have adopted some parental consent requirements for girls under 18 years, and more than one-third require some type of waiting period or counseling in connection with abortions (Zernike 2003). Partial-birth abortion bills have been passed in recent years by the U.S. Congress (Woliver 2007). There is often a gap between what the law calls for and its implementation. A study found that state laws requiring parental involvement in abortion decisions of pregnant minor daughters were often poorly implemented, for various reasons, and pregnant minors were not well-served by these laws nor the Supreme Court's ruling on this issue (Silverstein 2007).

The abortion issue entered into the health-care reform bill debate of 2009 when Michigan Congressman Bart Stupak offered an amendment prohibiting people receiving federal health-care subsidies from insurance plans that would pay for abortions (Rosen 2009).

The pro-life movement has led to a decline in the availability and popularity of abortion (Doan 2007). On the other hand, a global study found that abortion rates are similar in countries where abortion is and is not legal; outlawing it in other countries did not seem to deter women from seeking abortions (Rosenthal 2007). Abortion is found to be more dangerous in countries where it is illegal. Altogether, some 67,000 women a year are estimated to die as a consequence of unsafe abortions, principally in countries where it is illegal. Abortion is the second leading cause of death in Ethiopia, where it is illegal. Abortion rates have decreased quite dramatically in countries where contraceptive choices have been made more widely available. But early in the twenty-first century, the issue of abortion remains polarizing, and public opinion in America continues to be sharply divided on the issue (Woliver 2007). No easy resolution is likely.

The status of the human fetus beyond the specific issue of abortion has also raised questions about fetal protection and crimes of mothers against developing fetuses through substance abuse (Daniels 1993; Zerai and Banks 2002; Zivi 2000). Are prosecutions of such mothers a reflection of race and class biases, or are they necessary and effective in protecting fetuses? The rights of pregnant women, in relation to the rights of fetuses, continues to be an issue on which opposing sides adopt especially passionate stances (Scott 2002). Do pregnant women "own" their fetuses, or do fetuses have rights independent of their mothers? There are also complex legal issues relating to troubled pregnancies, wrongful birth, and the rights of those disabled at birth to sue for a diminished life (Mason 2007).

There are many unsettled questions on stem-cell research in relation to law and public policy (Korobkin with Munzer 2007). Although President Obama lifted restrictions on federally financed stem cell research imposed by the previous Bush Administration, complex questions on stem cell policy remain to be addressed by Congress (Stolberg 2009). Is such research an infringement on the sanctity of life or necessary to enhance the quality of humans threatened by devastating diseases?

Questions pertaining to some forms of euthanasia have become increasingly important in conjunction with medical advances that allow for the maintenance of "life" in extreme circumstances (e.g., of the profoundly injured or the terminally ill) (Hale 2003). The issues of physician-assisted suicide, end-of life care, and withholding of treatment have been quite fully addressed in Europe and other countries around the world (Blank and Merrick 2005; Griffiths, Wyers, and Adams 2008). In Germany, in 2008, the assisted suicide of a healthy 79-year-old woman renewed the debate on the right to die (Landler 2008). In the United States, 10 states made euthanasia or physician-assisted suicide illegal during this period. Other states considered such legislation, and an Oregon law legalizing physician-assisted suicide for the terminally ill came under challenge (Smith 2002). "Legal dosing" (providing drugs to dying individuals to alleviate pain, even if the drug dosage hastens death) has long been practiced by American doctors and was acknowledged by the U.S. Supreme Court (Lavi 2005). In a decision reported in 2010, the Montana Supreme Court ruled narrowly to protect doctors who assisted terminally ill patients in dying from being prosecuted (Johnson 2010). For many different reasons, even with living wills, decisions about treatment at the end of life remain complicated (Blank and Merrick 2005). Such cases are likely to become more common in the future, now that we have an enhanced capacity to keep comatose people "alive" indefinitely.

The use of the death penalty has a long history and has gone through many different stages in the course of time (Banner 2002; Sarat 2007; Yorke 2008). Public opinion polls over several decades reported that the majority of Americans endorsed the death penalty. Since 1996, acceptance of capital punishment in the United States has declined, in part resulting from the discovery of innocent individuals on death row and … (Baumgartner, De Boef, and Boydstun 2008). The search for more humane ways of administering the death penalty has also been a part of the ongoing controversy (Essig 2003). Socio-research on the death penalty has addressed such matters as proportionality of punishment and the arbitrariness with which the penalty is adopted, the quality of defense lawyering, racial disparity, the role of mental retardation and mental illness in relation to death penalty defendants, whether commuted capital offenders kill again, prosecutorial discretion in death penalty cases, and whether a medically humane method of execution exists (Lanier, Bowers, and Acker 2009). The U.S. Supreme Court has ruled on some of these issues but has not declared the death penalty itself unconstitutional.

The American Law Institute, which had a major influence on recent American death penalty law—especially the effort to eliminate arbitrariness from the application of this penalty—abandoned these efforts in the fall of 2009 (Liptak 2010a). It declared the capital punishment system irretrievably broken, plagued by racial bias, enormous costs, underpaid and sometimes incompetent defense lawyers, and political pressures. The death penalty today is used principally in Asia, where it suits the purposes of authoritarian regimes (Johnson and Zimring 2009). It remains to be seen whether the United States will follow the path of virtually all other developed nations in abolishing the death penalty itself.

Insofar as positions on these sanctity-of-life issues are likely to reflect deeply felt and often highly personal moral intuitions, they tend to be intractable and difficult to reconcile. Some extremists, a very small number of proponents of the pro-life position on abortion, have committed murders against abortion clinic personnel, and a small number of right-to-die proponents have subjected themselves to criminal prosecution by participating in assisted suicides.

If Americans are beset with some complex legal questions relating to the termination of life, we also face challenging issues relating to the creation of life (Dolgin 1997). Advances in reproductive technology and biogenetics have generated issues about surrogate motherhood, age limitations on motherhood, the ownership of embryos, multiple pregnancies resulting from the use of fertility drugs, genetic engineering, and the possibility of cloning human beings (Pence 2008–2009; Maienschein 2003; Cahn 2009). More specifically, these issues include the question of whether women who serve as surrogate mothers for couples unable to have a child of their own should have a right to renege on the arrangement and keep the child after birth or should at least have some custodial rights; conversely, what happens if the contracting couple no longer wants the child after birth, especially if the child is born with significant defects? Bioethics is engaged with addressing such questions. It has been criticized for failing to make sufficient allowance for the social and cultural context within which bioethical dilemmas arise (Fox and Swazy 2008). But going forward there is sure to be much attention to bioethics issues.

Laws relating to surrogate mothers continue to be somewhat unsettled, generating considerable confusion (Saul 2009).

RIGHTS ISSUES

Human rights issues have become contentious across the globe. The promotion of broad human rights can come into conflict with indigenous legal traditions (e.g., extending rights to women in societies with a strong traditionalist orientation) (Sarat and Kearns 2001). Philosophers have long been concerned about rights to which human beings are entitled, and at least some broad human rights have been encompassed in laws (Griffin 2008). But there is no perfect correspondence between the rights identified in the literature of moral philosophy and the rights recognized by law. In one interpretation, all rights are social, in the sense that they can only be recognized within a social context (Barak-Erez and Gross 2007). Rights are legal entitlements, but sociological research has contributed importantly to the understanding of rights-related issues (Morris 2006). A concern with rights has been a major preoccupation of Americans from the outset of the history of the Republic. The meaning of "rights" to the Founding Fathers was not the same as the meaning of rights to us today (Shain 2007). There has never been a total consensus, whether among U.S. citizens or within legal institutions such as the U.S. Supreme Court, on which rights are "fundamental" and which rights are contestable, or nonessential. The U.S. Constitution identifies some rights quite specifically (e.g., the right to confront witnesses in criminal cases) and other rights by standards subject to interpretation (e.g., due process). Over time, the U.S. Supreme Court has recognized some rights that are inferred from constitutional principles (e.g., reproductive rights or the right to have a family) rather than by any specific recognition in constitutions. The line of demarcation between the public sphere and the private sphere, where rights are concerned, has often been quite blurred. The efforts of the law to regulate intimate relationships have been controversial, in part because of inevitable conflicts among respect for personal autonomy, basic responsibilities to others, and the goal of doing justice to others (Cohen 2002; Eskridge 2008). These issues arise especially in relation to sexual orientation, sexual harassment, and reproductive rights.

One of the principal law-related themes of the latter half of the twentieth century was the dramatic increase in **rights consciousness**. The civil rights movement of the 1950s and early 1960s, challenging segregation and the second-class citizenship of African

Americans, highlighted the fact that some social groups have been systematically deprived of fundamental rights and that through collective action such deprivation could be challenged (Friedman 2002; Kluger 1975). The success of this movement in sweeping away the legal barriers confronting African Americans inspired and influenced other disadvantaged groups. Although some of the legal victories on behalf of African Americans and minority groups generally have been widely accepted by the mainstream of society, other such victories have been the focus of heated, ongoing debate (Bell 2004; Morris 2006). For example, the abolition of official segregation has been widely accepted, whereas court-enforced busing and affirmative action have often been opposed.

An expanding number of groups in the recent era have demanded recognition in relation to claims of rights or denial of rights, including: indigenous peoples; ethnic minorities; women; gay people; victims of crimes; and prisoners (Morris 2006). The final decades of the twentieth century witnessed the emergence of a vigorous women's rights movement, as well as a gay rights movement, and somewhat lower-profile rights movements on behalf of the physically disabled, the mentally challenged and the mentally ill, illegal aliens, prisoners, and children. Each of these movements has encountered resistance in varying degrees, which may range from the highly organized to the subtle and personal. For example, despite the removal of most formal discrimination against women, women continue to experience disadvantages and informal discrimination (Bernat 2007; McColgan 2000). The evolving legal status of people of color, immigrants, women, and gay people is addressed more fully in Chapter 10.

Americans are far from a full consensus on the scope of accommodations that should be made for the handicapped; the right of the mentally ill to reject involuntary treatment; or the specific nature of privileges (such as conjugal visits) to which prisoners are entitled (Hellerstein 2002; Imperato 2002; Morris 2006). Those with mental disabilities—whether or not they are institutionalized, recipients of public services and benefits, or functioning in the mainstream of society—continue to be subjected to various forms of discrimination and harassment, despite the existence of the Americans With Disabilities Act (Stefan 2001; Weber 2007) (*see* Box 1.3).

Finally, any children's rights movement, if it can be truly said to exist, is in its infancy (Bottoms, Kovera, and McAuliff 2002). In one landmark case, a minor child won the legal right to be emancipated from negligent parents, rendering him available for adoption by foster parents (Woodhouse 2008). Perhaps more important, children—even preverbal ones— are supported by groups such as the American Professional Society on the Abuse of Children in having more say on their own behalf in court and more fair investigative interviewing. The adoption by the United Nations of a Convention on the Rights of the Child has had some influence on specific national legal systems to recognize and implement children's rights laws (Ali, Goonesekere, Mendez, and Rois-Kohn 2007). The United States, however, rejected this convention, apparently at least in part on the perception that the expansion of such rights would threaten parental autonomy and family values (Woodhouse 2008). But some commentators argue that fuller recognition of children's rights is a necessary dimension of the broader promotion of human rights.

Age has always been a criterion for certain legal rights, responsibilities, and restrictions, but many issues pertaining to age-related law are unsettled. In the United States, a fundamental

---

BOX 1.3   DISCRIMINATION AGAINST OBESE
AND UNATTRACTIVE PEOPLE

In the late nineteenth and early twentieth centuries, various U.S. municipalities passed so-called ugly laws that targeted "unsightly beggars" for legal prosecution (Schweik 2009). These laws reflected biases against those who were poor, disabled, or simply different by virtue of race, ethnicity, or gender. Although laws proscribing discrimination based on race, religion, ethnicity, and gender are quite widely accepted today, there are questions about the proper scope of anti-discrimination lawsuits. Increasingly, obese people were taking bias claims to the courts (Kirkland 2008). Some of these plaintiffs argued that they were discriminated against because they were disabled, under the meaning of the Americans With Disabilities Act; others, more successfully, argued that they were not disabled as a consequence of obesity, and accordingly employers were not justified in discriminating against them. Insofar as more than one-fourth of all Americans are classified as obese, much was potentially at stake in such cases. A 420-pound man sued McDonald's for reneging on a job offer as a cook, claiming this was based on his obesity.

Some retail companies (e.g., Abercrombie & Fitch) have been accused of discriminating in favor of physically attractive individuals for salesclerk positions (S. Greenhouse 2003a). Although it is not illegal *per se* to hire attractive people, it is illegal to discriminate on the basis of age, sex, or ethnicity, and accordingly, hiring policies favoring a certain type of appearance may in fact be discriminatory on one of these grounds. In *The Beauty Bias* Stanford Law Professor Deborah Rhode (2010) makes a case for prohibiting appearance discrimination. Such laws are on the books in Michigan and several other locales in the United States. Critics, of course, question the wisdom of such laws and wonder whether they will lead to legal protection of the skinny, the bald, and the stupid, among others (Lithwick 2010b). To date, the existing laws have not generated more than a handful of cases.

---

contradiction concerning age long existed—namely, that a young man could be old enough to be drafted, and possibly fight for his country and lose his life, without being old enough to cast a vote for local municipal officers. This contradiction was resolved with the Twenty-Sixth Amendment to the Constitution, which lowered the voting age to 18 years (Lewis and Carlan 2009). On the other end of the age spectrum, the abolition of mandatory retirement continues to be a source of some debate. As the twenty-first century progresses, a larger percentage of older citizens in the population will surely have an impact on this issue.

Changing social values or patterns of behavior have generated new legal standards and new forms of "rights." Until recently in America, no right to a smoke-free environment was widely recognized, but an antismoking movement developed rapidly toward the end of the twentieth century, pushing through legislation that banned smoking in many public places, including some workplaces (Hu 2003; Rabin and Sugarman 1993). In response, some smokers have made claims for recognition of their rights as smokers.

Although sexual harassment has surely existed since time immemorial, the right to be free from such harassment, at least in the workplace, has also gained recent recognition. Sexual harassment laws have been adopted not only in the United States but in other countries as well (Cahill and Horowitz 2007). However, there are those who argue that sexual harassment has been too broadly defined, so it has negative consequences for workplace relationships. Finally, what about the rights of animals? (*See* Box 1.4.)

FREE SPEECH AND PRIVACY ISSUES

Freedom of speech and a free press are among the most sacred tenets of a democratic society such as the United States and are rights guaranteed by the First Amendment to the Constitution (Bollinger and Stone 2002; Feldman 2008; Heyman 2008). It is widely

BOX 1.4 ANIMAL LAW AND THE RIGHTS
OF ANIMALS

Rights issues are thought of primarily in relation to human beings, but for animal lovers the rights of animals are also an important issue. Animal rights activists have long objected to the use of animals for medical research, on the premise that harming and killing animals in that context is a violation of the rights of animals; defenders of such research argue that there are presently no alternatives to animal-related research in the search for cures of harmful conditions afflicting humans and that the well-being of humans has to be privileged over that of animals (Bogle 2003; Pocar 2007). Animal rights activists regard most, if not all, forms of killing animals and other harmful acts relating to animals as serious crimes (Rackstraw 2003; Wise 2001). "Animal law" has become a growing field in law school curriculums, with some 70 schools now offering courses, and within law itself (Monaghan 2007; St. John 2006). Four law schools have journals devoted to animal law (Cadiz 2008). In one law school topics addressed in animal law courses include animal cruelty; hunting; animal fighting; the use of animals in scientific research; and animal sacrifices. Historically, animals as pets have been regarded as property, with few meaningful "rights." But in recent years, both legislative bodies and courts have accorded more recognition to animal rights. A case in which NFL quarterback Michael Vick went to prison for violating dog fighting laws got much attention, especially his complicity in cruel executions of pit bulls that performed poorly (Trosch 2008). Although all 50 states have laws prohibiting cruelty to animals, in 2009 the U.S. Supreme Court was asked to consider an appeal from a prison sentence by a Virginia man convicted of selling videos of dogfights (Liptak 2009f). Was such a video protected by the First Amendment "free speech" right or not protected because no meaningful expression of ideas was involved?

In a different matter involving animals, hotel owner Leona Helmsley left $12 million to her dog Trouble and some $8 billion to a foundation to provide for the care of dogs (Toobin 2008). (She left nothing to two of her four grandchildren; Helmsley had famously contentious relations with most of the people in her life.) The question here was whether the courts had to adhere to such extravagant bequests to animals or could modify the terms of the will.

It remains to be seen whether animal rights activists will succeed in achieving recognition of rights for animals truly comparable to human rights. Many people question whether this would be a good idea.

---

understood that the proclamation of heretical, blasphemous, and thoroughly unpopular ideas cannot be suppressed, but many other issues arise in this context. For example, does the right to free speech encompass such diverse forms of expression as libel of public figures, obscenity, inciting illegal activity, and hate speech? The specific scope of free speech and press rights as protected by the First Amendment has led to a large body of judge-made law (Kalven 1988; Raskin 2002). In the landmark decision *New York Times v. Sullivan* (1964), the U.S. Supreme Court held that critics of official conduct could not be found guilty of libel unless they had disseminated deliberate or reckless falsehoods. In times of war and in the context of a "war" against terrorism, immensely disturbing photographs and images and highly sensitive information can surface (Liptak 2009b). The courts have periodically had to address the question of whether to privilege First Amendment rights versus other considerations. American political leaders have tended to be selective, allowing publication of images or information favorable to their agenda and attempting to block release of images that worked against their agenda. It was widely believed, however, that graphic images of the Vietnam War that were widely disseminated in the United States helped turn the country against the war. More recently, it has been alleged that the publication of American soldiers torturing Iraqi detainees at Abu Ghraib were used by insurgent and terrorist groups for recruiting purposes (Liptak 2009b). Such considerations may have persuaded President Obama to revoke an agreement to release additional images of Americans abusing prisoners in Afghanistan and Iraq. Questions were raised regarding whether such speculation justified suppression of these photographs.

From the middle of the nineteenth century to the middle of the twentieth century, in a series of obscenity trials, the doctrine took hold that art should not be judged relative to conventional standards of morality and that even when art is "sordid" or offensive it may fulfill some legitimate artistic purpose (Ladenson 2007).

Pornography itself is not illegal, unless it is interpreted to be in violation of obscenity standards laid down by the U.S. Supreme Court (i.e., when taken as a whole, lacks artistic, literary, or scientific merit; is patently offensive; or violates contemporary community standards). Pornography today is so widely diffused in the United States, especially on the Internet, that most prosecutors have resisted pursuing such cases, both because of the difficulty of successful prosecution and whether such prosecution is a good application of finite prosecutorial resources (Lewis 2007). However, pornography cases involving children have continued to be widely prosecuted. But questions have arisen about where to draw the line in distinguishing acceptable representations of child models from those that are fundamentally pornographic (Eichenwald 2006). A proliferation of child "model" sites with nearly nude photographs of children raised new challenges for legal controls (Eichenwald 2006). Internet child model sites for paid subscribers are a huge business today.

In a related vein, legal cases in the recent era have arisen over such matters as banning of books from libraries, censoring of student-run newspapers, and the highly provocative act of flag burning. Provocation in another sense arises in connection with speech that wantonly offends or demeans some group (i.e., racist, sexist, homophobic, and so on). "Hate speech" encouraging extreme actions toward minority groups has raised questions about the scope of free speech. Supporters of laws prohibiting hate speech argue that it is really a form of assault, with demonstrably harmful consequences, and accordingly is not protected by the free speech doctrine (Bell 2002; Heyman 2008). The enforcement of the relevant laws is challenging because of the difficulties of discriminating clearly among permissible acts of free speech, ordinary acts of vandalism or assault, and those acts incorporating the extra measure of "hate." Although the Courts have generally held that such speech is protected by the First Amendment, school administrators have often regarded this type of speech as a form of harassment that they should ban (Wolfson 1997). College campuses in particular have grappled with the dilemma of encouraging free speech while acting against speech that has a poisonous influence on the campus environment or that is experienced as harassment (including sexual harassment) (Gould 2001; Shiell 1998). In 2010, the U.S. Supreme Court decided that creating and selling dogfight videos could not be declared a crime because doing so would be too broad a violation of First Amendment free speech rights (Liptak 2010e).

When some form of speech or expression is alleged to be a direct cause of harmful behavior, the issue becomes especially complicated. Indeed, just such a connection is claimed by feminist critics of pornography—that is, that it encourages debasing and violent behavior toward women, including rape (MacKinnon 1993). Over the years, television networks and publishers of action comics, among others, have been sued on the claim that they inspired acts of violence. For some commentators, it is preferable that the media impose their own constraints on forms of free speech that might be harmful rather than that such constraints be imposed by the government (Cohen-Almagor 2001). Nevertheless, the courts have been reluctant to establish precedents that might encourage broad censorship.

At first glance, it might seem difficult to see a connection between political campaign funding and free speech. But from 1976 to 2003, the U.S. Supreme Court consistently held that campaign donations could not be constitutionally limited in amount or source because they represent a form of free speech (Turow 1997). In December 2003, however, the U.S. Supreme Court, in a 5-to-4 decision, upheld the major provisions of the campaign finance law passed by Congress, banning "soft money" to political parties from large and well-funded entities (e.g., corporations and unions) (Greenhouse 2003g). The majority on the Supreme Court justified its decision more in terms of the practical evidence of the corrupting influence of money in American politics rather than on abstract legal principles. But it remains to be seen whether wealthy and powerful entities will find effective ways to circumvent the restrictions of the new campaign financing laws, as they have so often in the past.

Although the defense of free speech has been historically associated with those on the liberal or leftist side of the political spectrum, in the recent era this constituency has sometimes called for restrictions (e.g., on hate speech), whereas conservative and corporate constituencies have called for fewer restrictions, not only on campaign spending but also on advertising for such products as tobacco (Lewis 1998). In contrast, because of their immense economic and political power, corporations are in a position to effectively censor many efforts to engage in free speech in many circumstances (Soley 2002). In a controversial 2010 decision, *Citizens Union*, a divided Supreme Court lifted restrictions on corporate campaign spending (Liptak 2010j). On balance, those with money and power have enjoyed significant advantages in exercising their free speech rights.

The extraordinarily rapid expansion of the Internet worldwide has generated a variety of legal issues about what can be disseminated through this medium and what types of controls, if any, are permissible. How does one balance control and anarchy on the Internet (Chander, Gelman, and Radin 2008; Zittrain 2000)? Some law professors see cyberspace as a new frontier, a new Wild West where freedom is an important source of creative energy and should be promoted (Greene 2000). Technology is developing that will allow for more control over the use of the Internet for business purposes, to access pornography, to exchange copyrighted material, and the like. Can legitimate controls be implemented without significantly limiting access?

The right-to-privacy is another sacred tenet of American society. It is not specifically mentioned in the Constitution, but the Supreme Court has recognized that a general right to privacy is implicit in this document (McWhirter and Bible 1992). The right to privacy issue intersects with other issues, such as reproductive freedom, abortion, and physician-assisted suicide. The legitimate objective of law enforcement agencies to investigate possible criminal activity can clash with privacy rights of individuals, and the right of the press to report news can create the same type of conflict. In the post-9/11 environment, the right to free speech has increasingly come into conflict with legal initiatives adopted in the "war" against terrorism (Liptak 2010d). A specific question arose regarding whether a wide-ranging U.S. law prohibiting any form of "material support" for terrorism was a violation of First Amendment free speech rights.

Lawrence M. Friedman (2007a) has shown that in an earlier time (the nineteenth century), the focus of law was more on protecting the reputation of privileged and "respectable" members of society, but during the course of the twentieth century, a broader constitutional right to privacy for all came to be recognized. But many of the laws on the books were developed in a different time and social context and do not well apply to contemporary circumstances. As to privileged members of society today—public figures and celebrities—many cases have arisen contending that privacy rights are violated with the widespread distribution of compromising or distasteful photographs or information (Mills 2008).

The technological advances that facilitate increasingly sophisticated surveillance now threaten everyone's privacy rights today in multiple ways. The Internet has generated whole new forms of compromising individual privacy by the government and corporations as well as by individuals, and in the views of some commentators, the existing laws in this realm are presently inadequate (Chander, Gelman, and Radin 2008; Keefe 2005; Solove 2007). But different forms of technology today can gather information about a wide range of activities in which people engage. Many car owners are probably not aware that microcomputers or "black boxes" (event-data recorders) are embedded in a growing percentage of new vehicles, and these microcomputers can record data on such matters as speed, braking, and acceleration prior to a crash (Roosevelt 2006). On the one hand, such data can be immensely valuable in determining, for example, whether a driver was illegally speeding prior to crashing; on the other hand, some commentators call for greater clear disclosure to automobile buyers about this form of surveillance.

The different forms of surveillance on citizens engaged in by the government are rarely regulated today. Questions have arisen about whether the National Security Agency's domestic spying program broke laws intended to protect American citizens. But many government entities engage in some form of surveillance. One commentator calls for more legislative protection against government surveillance, which could be based on Fourth Amendment principles, without compromising legitimate criminal investigations (Slobogin 2007). In Great Britain, especially extensive use of closed-circuit television cameras in public places has generated some controversy, with claims on the one hand that such surveillance is a legitimate crime-fighting tool, and on the other hand that it compromises the privacy of ordinary citizens (Goold 2004). European privacy rules are generally much more extensive than those in the United States. As the government's technological capability for surveillance expands, surveillance versus privacy issues are likely to become that much more important.

Both individuals and corporations have concerns about abuses of the massive amounts of information that can be accessed through data banks, although the concerns take different forms. Laws that protect members of the public from "snooping" by corporations are framed in terms of protecting privacy; laws that protect corporations from snooping by members of the public are framed in terms of security (Chander, Gelman, and Radin 2008). Many individuals voluntarily provide all kinds of personal information about themselves within the context of online shopping or to obtain some perceived benefit but then are distressed when this information is used improperly. Much personal information is sold today for profit. And of course some private information is used for various fraudulent purposes.

The growing use of body scanners at airports has generated some concern over invasions of privacy (Rosen 2010). These scanners peer through clothing and produce a graphic, anatomically correct image of an airline passenger's body.

Various controversies arise, then, on where to draw the line between protecting privacy and realizing other legitimate purposes of investigation or information-gathering (*see* Box 1.5).

As standards of private and privileged information evolve over time, controversies inevitably arise. Traditionally, when a woman gave up a baby for adoption, all information about the birth mother was "sealed" and could not be accessed by the child to whom she had given birth. In the recent era, a growing number of adoptees have mobilized to demand access to information about their birth families, for medical history reasons as well as to "reconnect" with this family (Koch 2008). Laws in many states have been modified to facilitate this. Although some birth mothers welcome the contacts, others certainly do not and take offense at laws that now allow the child given up for adoption to track them down.

BOX 1.5   TEXTING AND SEXTING: NEW LEGAL INITIATIVES

In an era when the use of cell phones has expanded exponentially in a relatively brief period of time, some practices associated with cell phones have inspired new legal initiatives. Studies have indicated that using cell phones while driving is as dangerous as drunken driving, and texting (or dialing) while driving is twice as dangerous (Richtel 2009). Yet the legal response to these practices to date in most American states has been quite limited at best. It may be that both the relative novelty of cell phone use in cars and the fact that so many legislators themselves engage in such use have contributed to this limited response. A case in Utah where a college student, while texting, drove into an intersection and killed two scientists led to the adoption in that state of the nation's toughest law against texting while driving, with offenders facing a possible 15 years in prison. Alaska has a broader law with tough penalties for those who cause fatalities while distracted by some technological device; the law was inspired by a fatal accident caused by a driver who was watching a movie while driving. Most European countries ban the use of handheld cell phones while driving, and Great Britain has become especially aggressive on this practice (Rosenthal 2009). Once again, a high-profile case of a young woman killed by another young woman who was texting while driving helped inspire the law. But such laws raise challenges for the criminal justice system, as it is easier to prove drunken driving (through breath analyzer tests) than to prove that a driver was using a cell phone or texting just prior to an accident. Phone records can be subpoenaed, but this is time-consuming and not always possible.

A practice that is apparently quite widespread among teenagers in particular—exchanging nude or semi-nude photos on cell phones—has been labeled "sexting" and has also raised questions for the law (Hamill 2009; Lithwick 2009b; Searcey 2009). It seems evident that many teenagers, some quite young, do not appreciate the long-term possible harm to themselves by putting such photos in cyberspace, where they can become widely disseminated. There are legitimate concerns about the role of sexual predators and purveyors of kiddie porn in all of this. But there has been considerable controversy in the relation to criminal prosecutions relating to texting. About 20 states have now enacted laws addressing teenager sexters, but legislators remain quite divided over whether this is an activity calling for some form of criminal penalties. In a Florida case, an 18-year-old man was prosecuted and required to register as a sex offender for sexting a nude photo of his girlfriend (Richards and Calvert 2009). Did he really merit registration in this category, with all the consequences of such registration? Three young girls in Pennsylvania were charged with disseminating such pornography when they were caught "sexting" their boyfriends. Are they really criminal predators and sex offenders in any meaningful sense or somewhat naive children who may be better viewed as victims of formidable peer pressure to engage in sexting? As one law professor commented, "The whole tawdry episode seems to call for a little parental guidance and a pop-gun approach, not a Howitzer approach with a felony prosecution" (Searcey 2009, p. A17). The family of one of the girls charged in the Pennsylvania case sued the district attorney involved.

FAMILY ISSUES

Early in the twenty-first century, the meaning of the term *family* continues to evolve, with claims for legal recognition from those in *caring* relationships not encompassed by traditional forms of family being more aggressively pursued (Shanley 2001; Wilson 2006). In some important respects, families continue to function as "law makers," and public policy depends on families fulfilling this role (Strach 2007). The legal system favors a particular image of the family and passes laws supportive of families fitting this image (Probert 2007). Although marriage is most typically regarded as a highly personal compact between two individuals, state laws pertaining to marriage—over a long period of time—have had a profound social influence (Friedman 2004; Sclater, Ebtehaj, Jackson, and Richards 2009). New forms of reproductive technology also play a role in expanding options available to those wishing to produce offspring (Jackson 2001; Woliver 2002). The specific scope of rights to take leaves from work for family-related problems are in contention in some states (L. Greenhouse 2003a). The scope and nature of family-related rights and responsibilities remain in flux.

The dissolution of the family is hardly new, although the breakup of families through divorce has increased exponentially in the past few decades. Whether state law can, or should, play a role in fostering or supporting marriage—for example, through Louisiana's "covenant marriage" law that, among other provisions, makes it more difficult to obtain a divorce—continues to be debated (Crary 2001). In one interpretation, legal reforms such as a no-fault divorce were actually introduced with the hope of discouraging divorce, but such laws obviously failed (Friedman 2004). Both the increase in divorces and changes pertaining to gender roles in the context of divorce have produced new and sometimes painful controversies (Brinig 2000). In the recent era, a father's rights movement has emerged in the United States as a backlash against perceived extension of too many custodial and support payment rights to mothers (Crowley 2008). The American Law Institute, in 2002, called for sweeping changes in state laws pertaining to alimony and marital property rights to take into account the realities of recent times (Wilson 2006). For example, a finding of adultery would not affect alimony and marital property rights, and cohabiting domestic partners should also have these kinds of rights. Some other issues arising in the context of divorce include the following: Is reliance on mediation in divorce cases likely to work to the disadvantage of women? Is community property division or some other formula more or less fair? Should divorced spouses who remarry still be eligible for alimony? Should maternal custody of children be privileged over "most qualified parent"? At what age, if any, should minor children be allowed to choose their preferred custodial arrangement? And so on. Although no-fault divorce became the norm in most states in the final decades of the twentieth century, by the century's end there was some backlash against this standard, and there has been a call for making it somewhat more difficult to obtain divorces. It remains to be seen how far this backlash movement will go.

CRIMINAL JUSTICE

Crime and criminal justice are major preoccupations of both the general public and politicians, so they generate ongoing debate on many enduring issues (e.g., gun control and the death penalty) as well as newly raised issues. In the case of gun control, it was far from clear to some students of the issue that any set of policies could be expected to dramatically affect the amount of violent crime (Jacobs 2002).

The American criminal justice system is characterized by inherent conflicts between crime control and the protection of civil liberties, with different segments of the population experiencing criminal justice policies in quite different ways (Zalman 2011). The criminal justice system during the early twenty-first century continues to be characterized by a stress on crime control over due process, and this tendency was enhanced in response to 9/11 (addressed elsewhere in this chapter); but many challenges have arisen to this approach as well. By 2008, some 2.3 million individuals were incarcerated in American prisons, with a total of more than 7 million Americans under correctional supervision (often on probation or parole), at a cost of close to $50 billion for the 50 states (Moore 2009; Webb 2009). This cost was escalating at a much faster rate than expenditures for education, transportation, and public assistance. And these vast correctional expenditures were occurring during a period of falling crime rates and intensifying state budgetary crises. The effectiveness of punitive criminal justice policies and the vast expansion of the American prison population, as a means of addressing the problem of conventional crime, was increasingly challenged (New York Times 2009; Raphael and Stoll 2009; Simon 2007). Various interests have benefited from this expansion, but harmful consequences of the expansion have been identified, and alternative social policies involving education and employment opportunities might just as effectively reduce conventional crime rates.

In 2009, Senator Jim Webb (2009) of Virginia introduced new legislation calling for the establishment of a National Criminal Justice Commission to conduct a top-to-bottom review of the American criminal justice system. This call was inspired by the vast size of the U.S. prison population and the perception that the astoundingly high incarceration rate was both counterproductive and fundamentally unfair to many minor offending inmates from disadvantageous circumstances. As a consequence, many states are eliminating some mandatory sentences, facilitating treatment options, and in other ways attempting to reduce the size of their prison populations.

The police use of racial profiling—focusing especially on minority members for detaining and questioning—has been criticized in New Jersey and elsewhere during this period (Heumann and Cassak 2003; Kocieniewski and Hanley 2000). The transfer of some juveniles charged with homicide to adult court jurisdiction is also controversial; in Florida alone, early in the twenty-first century, some 400 juveniles younger than age 18 years were being held in state prisons (Canedy 2002). The introduction of an ever-widening range of defenses for criminal conduct—including African American rage, parental abuse, premenstrual syndrome, battered-wife syndrome and even obsessed-fan syndrome—has been criticized by some commentators (Crier 2003; Wilson 1997). Although such defenses were typically unsuccessful, it remains to be seen whether they will become more acceptable over time. Controversies have also arisen in connection with such matters as limitations on trying sexual molesters of children because of the statute of limitations, the freeing of molesters who are still perceived to be dangerous from prisons, and the requirement that released child molesters be required to register with their local police (Broder 2003b; Mansnerus 2003; Greenhouse 2002d). And

BOX 1.6   THE VIRGINIA TECH SHOOTING
MASSACRE AND PRIVACY LAW

In April 2007, a Virginia Tech student named Seung-Hui Cho entered a classroom building and shot many of the students and faculty in the building. In addition to two individuals he had killed earlier in the day, and his own suicide, 33 people ended up dead as a consequence of this event (Agger and Luke 2008; Urbina 2007a). Inevitably, many questions arose over whether Virginia Tech could have taken steps to prevent this tragedy or at least diminish its scope. As well, questions arose about the complicity of American law more generally, especially lax gun control laws that made it possible for someone with known mental health issues to easily obtain guns and ammunition. Questions about the legal status of guns on campus also arose.

Court rulings in the recent era have required college administrators to exercise reasonable care to protect people on campus from foreseeable danger (Lake 2007). As is so often the case with the law, the meaning of "reasonable" and "foreseeable" in this context is open to interpretation. In an earlier time, colleges were largely shielded from liability imposed on other businesses, but this is generally no longer the case (Lake 2007). Among other questions, a basic issue of the conflict between privacy and security concerns arose, as it does in various other contexts. The student in question had been seen by mental health professionals, campus police knew of incidents of troubling behavior on the part of the student, and at least one professor had expressed concern about his mental state. But apparently university officials had misunderstood federal privacy laws as prohibiting sharing of information about the student's mental health. Overall, there is a concern to protect the privacy of students when they seek help for mental issues, in part because of a legitimate concern that if they are not assured of such confidentiality, then they will be much less inclined to seek help that they need. But if breaches of such confidentiality must be permitted in some circumstances to minimize chances of a mentally disturbed student injuring others, or himself, just what must occur for such breaches to be permitted? No one should imagine that there are easy answers to this question. If colleges overreact to and report mentally disturbed students or staff, then they face possible lawsuits for breaches of privacy, and if they underreact, then they face potential tragedies.

many other ongoing controversies are associated with the criminal justice system. Some of these controversies are explored in subsequent chapters (*see* Box 1.6).

BUSINESS

A general increase in consciousness of the harmful consequences of some corporate activities conflicts with pro-business claims that interference with free-market activities has harmful economic consequences. Accordingly, there are ongoing debates on product liability law, environmental protection and workplace safety standards, and the criteria for antitrust actions or insider trading prosecutions (Kagan and Axelrad 2000). Product liability refers to a company's responsibility when its products cause harm; antitrust actions refer to efforts to challenge anticompetitive or monopolistic business practices; and insider trading refers to trading on the basis of information not available to the general public, which is prohibited by law. United States courts and legislative bodies were complicit in the corporate takeovers and mergers of the recent era, resulting in many harmful consequences for citizens, consumers, and workers (Sciulli 2001). In *Corporate Irresponsibility*, Lawrence E. Mitchell (2001) argued that legal rules in America are complicit in encouraging corporate executives to pursue any strategies available to drive up stock prices, often at the cost of other objectives that might benefit or protect citizens, consumers, and workers. The series of revelations of massive misrepresentations and outright fraud in the highest echelons of business and finance, beginning with the Enron case, lends some support to this proposition. These developments are discussed elsewhere in this chapter.

Tobacco companies have been successfully sued by states to compensate them for the high health costs associated with tobacco use; gun makers have also faced lawsuits claiming their responsibility for gun-related violence (Higgins 1998; Fried 1999; Rabin and Sugarman 2001). Whether such lawsuits will be initiated against still more types of businesses (e.g., the alcohol industry) (Willing 2004) and whether these initiatives will be supported by both the public and the justice system remains to be seen.

Corporations also increasingly claim to be victims of copyright infringements (*see* Box 1.7).

BOX 1.7   INTELLECTUAL PROPERTY, COPYRIGHT, THE INTERNET, AND FILE SHARING

Copyright is a long-established doctrine in law to ensure that those who produce creative work can maintain basic control over that work and benefit from its distribution outside of "fair use" (e.g., selective quotation). Some commentators argue that the public domain and free access to information and ideas is immensely important for the promotion of innovation and creativity and as a benefit to the culture as a whole (Boyle 2008; Lange and Powell 2009). A new concept of copyright may be needed (Ponte 2009). In this view, the privileging of intellectual property rights is too restrictive and is accordingly socially harmful (Boyle 2008). The First Amendment of the U.S. Constitution can be read, in this interpretation, as imposing limitations on claims of exclusive control over intellectual property. The existing patent system has also been accused of impeding rather than promoting innovation (Bessen and Meurer 2008). Although there may be identifiable benefits to patent ownership in some industries (e.g., the pharmaceutical industry), in many other industries the overall benefits have been challenged. The courts, in this view, have interpreted the patent protection laws too broadly.

The massively ambitious project of Google to scan all books and make them electronically available has generated much discussion and controversy (Darnton 2009; Lessig 2010). On the one hand, it would appear to have the potential to "democratize" access to knowledge in extraordinary ways, making books to date only available to those with access to major research university libraries available to anyone with access to the Internet. On the other hand, of course, publishers and authors have concerns about infringement on their property rights.

China was long viewed as notoriously indifferent to protecting the intellectual property rights of American businesses and individuals, but in the more recent era—at least in part in response to pressure from the United States—it has begun to implement and enforce intellectual property rights laws (Mertha 2005).

In the United States, over the past decade or so, use of the Internet by adults increased from about one-third of this population to more than three-fourths. The Internet today faces immense challenges resulting from spam, viruses, and unreliable connections. Spam is estimated to account for some 75% of all e-mail, with a staggering cost of some $100 billion a year to businesses. There are important technological dimensions involved in the future of the Internet but also many challenges in relation to the optimal form of law necessary to regulate the Internet. In *Wired Shut*, Tarleton Gillespie (2007) claims that big businesses are attempting to achieve wholesale domination over the digital world of the Internet. In this author's view we see increased private ownership of the content available on the Internet and increased commercialization, with pay-per-use becoming more widespread. Increasingly sophisticated surveillance techniques will be adopted to achieve this purpose.

Many controversies have arisen over file sharing on the Internet (Aviv 2007; Seidenberg 2009). People may adopt contradictory positions on this issue. Although many forms of file sharing are perfectly legitimate and legal, including the sharing of material in the public domain, the common sharing of and downloading of copyright music, films, and other such material is regarded as hugely damaging by those corporations and other entities that produce this material. Some of those who want the freedom to share music files without paying protest attempts to subpoena their records—under the Millennium Digital Copyright Act of 1998—as infringements on their privacy. Attempts to limit file sharing are sometimes related to the efforts by private corporations to block the sharing of embarrassing information about them (Schwartz 2003b). For example, the Diebold Election Systems company took action against college students circulating information about their electronic voting machines. Such contentious issues in the realm of free speech and press are likely to persist for some time.

Content producers have sued individuals whom they claim have shared or downloaded their creations in violation of fair use. Of course, the posting of a vast range of privately produced material on YouTube and other such sites has become a huge enterprise today (Seidenberg 2009). But some posters are contending with claims that they are infringing on copyrights—for example, if they use music or a song in their videos. The Digital Millennium Copyright Act of 1998 attempted to achieve some balance between the rights of copyright holders and online businesses as well as those who use them. In contested cases, no uniform outcomes or policy guidelines have developed to date. In 2009, a graduate student at Boston University, despite being defended by a celebrated Harvard Law School professor, Charles Nesson, had a judgment of close to $700,000 imposed on him for downloading and sharing songs (Schwartz 2009a). This challenge to existing federal copyright law interpretation of "fair use" failed. The *Capitol Records v. Thomas* case was an important development in the battle over peer-to-peer file-sharing, because there was a finding that actual dissemination of downloaded material had to be proven to win damages (Ali 2009). Altogether, content producers faced formidable challenges in controlling file sharing.

HEALTH AND MEDICINE

In 2009, a major health-care bill was before the U.S. Congress, to ensure that virtually all Americans would be covered by health-care insurance (Gawande 2009). This legislation, strongly supported by President Obama, was the culmination of efforts by a long line of American presidents, over a period of many decades, to achieve some form of universal health care, which is the norm in most developed Western nations (including Canada). There had been immense resistance to this bill from many constituencies, including private insurance companies, whose interests were threatened by this legislation. Millions of Americans with health-care insurance believed that their health-care choices and benefits would be compromised, and there were legitimate concerns about the ultimate cost of broadly expanded health-care coverage. An especially high level of hysteria attended claims that the legislation would lead to the establishment of "death panels" that would authorize "pulling the plug on Grandma" to save health-care costs (Lepore 2009). Whether over time major new health-care legislation will be viewed as successful in greatly expanding health-care coverage, or unsuccessful because of cost, bureaucratic red tape, and various unintended consequences remains to be seen.

CONCLUSION

Within virtually any branch of law today—tax law, consumer law, environmental law, labor law, welfare law, and so on—we can identify public policy controversies. Also, in a world increasingly described in terms of globalization, issues such as international bans on nuclear weapons and land mines or the desirability of establishing a permanent international criminal court arise.

The identification here of law-related controversies is by no means exhaustive (*see* Box 1.5). Indeed, such a listing might go on almost endlessly. The issues identified in the preceding paragraphs can be, and surely will be, endlessly debated. Many different arguments, from the highly principled to the purely pragmatic, can be and will continue to be put forth on behalf of one or the other side of these issues. These issues should be of special interest to students of law and society because they bring into sharp relief the interaction of legal and social variables; those who acknowledge and work from this point of view have a sociolegal perspective. This perspective allows one to understand the following: What are the primary social factors that influence or shape both the character of an issue (e.g., euthanasia or affirmative action) and the public perception of it or the specific response to it? Conversely, what are the identifiable social (and behavioral) consequences of existing legal policy pertaining to the issue or a hypothetical legal policy at odds with existing policy? Scholars with the sociolegal perspective want to know how the social influences the legal and how the legal affects the social. In the final chapter of this book, at least some of these issues are explored in more depth, specifically within the context of the relation between law and social change.

LAW AFTER 9/11—AND IN THE OBAMA ERA

The 9/11 terrorist attack on the World Trade Center and the Pentagon in 2001 was the largest-scale such action on American soil and profoundly shocking to Americans. Even if these attacks, which caused some 3,000 deaths, appeared to be the most blatant violations of American (and international) law, the terrorists themselves seemed to subscribe to the perverse belief that they were adhering to a higher order of law: Allah's law. Then the question arose whether the subsequent "war on terrorism" could be conducted within the boundaries of existing law or had to be conducted outside those boundaries (Strawson 2002). In the United States, the controversial U.S. Patriot Act was passed within a month of the attacks, greatly expanding the government's powers of surveillance, detention, and prosecution of those suspected of involvement with terrorism (Brown 2003; Lyon 2003). The subsequent invasion of Afghanistan was undertaken as part of the response to the terrorist attack, and "Operation Iraqi Freedom" in 2003 was also launched as part of the war on terrorism.

Many years after 9/11, critics continued to contend that the "war on terrorism" initiatives of the Bush Administration threatened basic constitutional principles as well as the proper balance of power between the three branches of the government (Baker 2006; Pfiffner 2008; Pohlman 2007). More broadly, these initiatives were seen as threatening the rule of law itself (Ball 2007; Fiss 2007; Lichtblau 2008). For one commentator, the problem was not the aggressiveness of the Bush Administration but, rather, its failure to obtain Congressional support for its policies (Wittes 2008). It is widely recognized that the ongoing terrorist threat raises complex moral and legal challenges—for example, on the use of coercion or torture to extract information from suspected terrorists (Dershowitz 2008; Gross 2006; Jaffer and Singh 2007). American military personnel torturing and humiliating Iraqi detainees in Abu Ghraib prison, as documented by widely disseminated and immensely disturbing photographs, was initially blamed on low-ranking soldiers, but subsequent evidence suggested a significant role played by the Bush Administration in fostering conditions leading to the Abu Ghraib abuses (Heurich and Vaugh 2009; Jaffer and Singh 2007). The Bush Administration's establishment of a prison in Guantanamo Bay (Cuba) for suspected terrorists arrested in Afghanistan and elsewhere, and trying them with military tribunals that did not extend conventional due process rights to them, was also quite widely criticized (Glaberson 2008; Rotunda 2008). In 2008 a federal judge ordered the release of 17 of the prisoners held there.

Some commentators defended aggressive security measures and alleged violations of international law as warranted and historically legitimate in emergency circumstances and times of war (Goldsmith 2007; Gross and Ni Aolain 2006; Posner and Vermeule 2007).

Initially, in the wake of the shock of 9/11, such initiatives were quite widely supported by the American public, but this support diminished as fear declined, with no new terrorist attack. The Obama Administration from 2009 on repudiated the use of torture, initiated investigations of Bush Administration lawyers who drafted memos sanctioning such use and other extreme counterterrorism measures, and initially pledged to close the Guantanamo Bay prison, and to try major 9/11 terrorist suspects in New York City under American criminal law, not in Guantanamo Bay under military law (Bruff 2009; Glenn 2009; Savage and Shane 2009). These initiatives were inevitably controversial in some quarters, and were later modified. Much of the larger world clearly viewed the United States during the Bush Administration as contemptuous of international law. The awarding of the Nobel Peace Prize to President Barack Obama, in fall 2009, reflected in part a widespread perception that the new president had a fundamentally different approach to international law.

LAW AND THE FINANCIAL MELTDOWN OF 2008

During the first decade of the twenty-first century, the appropriate role of law in relation to two major financial catastrophes arose. At the very beginning of the decade (in the fall of 2001), the gross misrepresentations of finances at Enron—at that time the seventh-largest corporation in America—were exposed, leading to the bankruptcy of the corporation, losses of billions of dollars for pensioners and investors, and the initiation of criminal prosecutions and civil lawsuits (Fusaro and Miller 2002). Subsequently, financial misrepresentations and other forms of financial fraud were discovered at many other major corporations, including WorldCom, Adelphia, GlobalCrossing, and HealthSouth, with similar consequences. In the wake of these corporate scandals, the Sarbanes-Oxley Act was passed in 2002, holding top corporate executives more directly responsible for financial misrepresentations and imposing tougher penalties for corporate fraud (Lowell and Arnold 2003). Toward the end of the decade, in the fall of 2008, a major global economic crisis and financial meltdown climaxed with the collapse of huge investment banks (e.g., Lehman Brothers), the precipitous decline of the stock market and savings and retirement accounts devastated, millions of homes in foreclosure or "under water" (homeowners owing more on their mortgages than the homes were worth), a sharp increase in the unemployment rate with millions of jobs lost, and a taxpayer-funded bailout to the tune of hundreds of billions of dollars. During the same period, the $65 billion Ponzi scheme of Bernard Madoff was exposed, resulting in a 150-year prison sentence for Madoff (Johnson and Kwak 2010). This was described as the largest-scale such fraud in history, in part made possible by a shocking level of regulatory negligence. At the end of 2009, new legislation was introduced to impose more oversight on financial institutions and instruments and on consumer-related practices, to minimize the chances of another such meltdown. In relation to both the earlier and the more recent crisis, many commentators suggested that the removal of laws and regulations that provided oversight and controls had contributed to these crises in the first place. In both cases, the corporate and financial sector aggressively lobbied to either prevent the adoption of new oversight laws or strip them of various provisions following adoption. Powerful voices always claim that laws and regulations will curtail the global competitiveness of American corporations and financial institutions, cut profits, and cost jobs. The optimal mix of law and regulation for a stable, productive, expanding economy will always be a contentious issue. Some commentators believe the basic "architecture" of the corporate and financial sector must be transformed from the ground up if we are to have any hope of averting future corporate catastrophes and financial meltdowns.

Altogether, newly emerging circumstances in the early years of the twenty-first century reinforced in many different ways the significance of law and legal issues in an evolving, increasingly globalized society.

LAW IN AMERICA TODAY

Law is all over. Law is everywhere. In America an ongoing love–hate relationship with law persists.

On the one hand, Americans generally venerate the tradition of "a nation under law." The Constitution and the Bill of Rights are sacred documents in American history. Key concepts of these documents, including "due process" and "equal protection," are deeply ingrained in the national consciousness. Americans have come to expect **total justice**, as Lawrence M. Friedman (1985) put it—that is, a proper legal remedy for any blameworthy loss or injury. Certainly when Americans are victims of crime or suffer a private injury of some kind, they want the law to be there for them. And if legislators are constantly enacting new laws, it is surely because at least some of their constituents are demanding such laws to address a wide range of perceived problems.

On the other hand, many ordinary Americans also express considerable frustration (or anger) with a nation of lawyers. Most Americans hope to avoid contact with legal authorities and lawyers and may take this into account in planning their daily lives.

The well-off and well-connected and those who belong to the historically dominant group in society are more likely to view law in positive terms than those who are poor and who belong to a minority group.

In their illuminating study of law in the everyday lives of ordinary Americans (*The Common Place of Law*), Ewick and Silbey (1998) found that Americans tend to experience law in contradictory ways: magisterial and remote at some times and all too human at other times. Unsurprisingly, however, most Americans do not spend much time at all specifically thinking about law. In that sense, law would seem to be at best a marginal presence in their lives. Of course, for a minor proportion of Americans (those being processed by the felony courts, those involved in a major civil lawsuit, those engaged in a complicated divorce and child custody case) law becomes, for a time, an all-consuming dimension of their lives. As suggested earlier, law lies invisibly behind many of our mundane daily activities. We can hardly avoid law entirely when it is so pervasively highlighted in our media. But these considerations aside, people in their everyday lives generally prefer to think about things other than law, and most people initiate legal action only reluctantly. According to Ewick and Silbey (1998, p. 196), people are often disappointed in law's inability to address the troubles that plague their everyday lives.

Americans departed the twentieth century and entered the twenty-first, then, with profound ambivalence toward law and many contradictory perceptions of it. In the inevitably complex, dynamic, and expanding society of the future, law will be an unavoidable, and arguably growing, presence. The need to understand law as fully as possible will surely increase. But the traditional American love–hate relationship with law is also sure to endure.

KEY TERMS AND CONCEPTS

autonomous model	interactive model	rights consciousness
class action lawsuits	internal critique of law	litigation explosion
conservative critique of law	sanctity of life issues	total justice
homologous model	odd laws	trial by ordeal
humanistic tradition	positivistic tradition	
hyperlexis	radical critique of law	

DISCUSSION QUESTIONS

1. Explain why it might be difficult to effectively study law following the positivistic tradition. What are the advantages and disadvantages of a humanistic approach to the study of law?
2. Discuss the three views that explain the relationship between law and society—autonomous, homologous, and interactive.
3. According to the radical critique of law, how does law discriminate?
4. Explain America's love–hate relationship with the law.
5. Which legal policy issues are especially difficult to resolve, and why?

CHAPTER 2

LAW: ITS MEANING AND LOGIC

What is law? The word itself is familiar to all literate members of society, but defining the term is more challenging than one might expect. Much scholarship has been devoted to this question, but it has not yet produced either a perfect definition of "law" or a broad consensus on how to best define the term. Indeed, the search for a perfect definition may well be an exercise in futility; rather, those who study law should acknowledge that there are simply more useful and less useful definitions, depending on the context within which the term is invoked (Cohen 1935, p. 835). For some commentators, the central project of jurisprudence has been a quest for a definition of "law" (Letwin 2005; Melissaris 2009; Coleman and Simchen 2003). Jurisprudence, or the philosophy and science of law, is the focus of Chapter 4.

In the course of Western history alone, "law" has had many meanings (Friedrich 1963). It has been equated with the will of God, as a mirror of a divine world order. Law has also been viewed as an expression of human nature, pure reason, general will, and class ideology. Law has been seen as historical fact and as a command. Law is most broadly conceived of as a form, or type, of social control (Davis 1962). It is a universal feature of the human experience that some human beings have always, and everywhere, attempted to exercise control over other human beings. The cross-cultural study of social control, especially in preliterate societies, has been most fully addressed by anthropologists; their work in this realm is addressed in Chapter 6. However, not all observers regard law itself as universal, and one critic declares law to be a "Eurocentric enterprise" to promote Western European values and interests (Nunn 1997). Donald Black (1983) provocatively argued that what we call **crime** is also a form of social control, or self-help, in the sense that crimes are often committed in pursuit of the offender's idea of justice. For example, assassination is defined as a criminal act by society, but the perpetrator may regard his act as appropriate and a necessary way of addressing wrongs against him or his group.

Control has been identified as the central concept of sociology (Gibbs 1989). Social control incorporates attempts by states, organizations, and individuals to regulate human behavior (Chriss 2008). Social control is accomplished by different types of means: normative, utilitarian, and coercive (Etzioni 1968). The normative approach attempts to obtain compliance by fostering belief in the rules of the social order; the utilitarian approach offers some practical rewards or inducements for compliance; the coercive approach threatens or uses force to achieve compliance. Churches rely primarily on the normative, businesses rely primarily on the utilitarian, and prisons rely primarily on the coercive. But most social institutions—including parents attempting to control the behavior of their children—rely on some mixture of these approaches; this is true as well for legal institutions.

THE ORDERS OF LAW AND SOCIAL CONTROL

A person who uses the term *law* may be referring to a social institution, a specific legal system, or some element of a system. The notion of **legal pluralism** enters here. Felix Cohen (1907–1953) is credited with having played a key role in founding American legal pluralism, which came out of his recognition that different orderings of law were necessary for diverse groups with different needs and cultural values (Mitchell 2007). Legal pluralism today reflects "the recognition of the fact that different systems of law may coexist within national boundaries and that national systems of law must coexist with various forms of international law" (Bracey 2006, p. 8). The traditional association of law with state law is challenged, with a sophisticated understanding of law requiring attention to multiple orderings of law (Melissaris 2009). The extent to which the state acknowledges and accepts alternative non-state legal orders varies (Forsyth 2007). In many parts of the world where different ethnic and cultural groups co-exist, the challenge for law is to mediate among these diverse groups, although there is no real consensus on how this is best accomplished (Shabani 2007). For many ethnic or religious groups—for example, Muslims—their interpretation of their own group's law takes precedence over the laws of the state (Yilmaz 2005). Globalization has created circumstances leading to intensification of conflicts between local, national, and transnational laws and legal processes and the redistribution of legal authority (Szablowski 2007). United States courts are increasingly called upon to address cases involving alleged human rights violations that have occurred outside the boundaries of the United States (Davis 2008). The world of law becomes ever more complex.

The term *law* then, is used both very broadly, to refer to a virtually universal form of social control, and very narrowly, to refer to a specific rule or act within a particular legal system. Social control itself exists on many different levels, in many different forms. The term *law* is most typically, but not uniformly, reserved for formal governmental social control. Even with this definition, however, law takes different forms and operates on different levels. Within any society, then, we find co-existing systems of social control and law; which systems of social control are appropriately called *legal* is a matter of controversy (Melissaris 2009; Tamanaha 2006). Laws have been regarded as one subset of the broader category of **social norms**, or rules. Legal scholars are now interested in the complex relationship between laws and other social norms and how social norms influence behavior in relation to law (Etzioni 2000; Posner 2000). More specifically, norms may influence human predispositions. If social norms indeed shape human preferences, the notion of human beings as wholly free to make rational choices is questioned.

TABLE 2.1   LEVELS OF LAW

Universal law	Divine rules (e.g., Ten Commandments)
International	Law treaties (e.g., laws of war)
Regional law	Treaties (e.g., Eurolaw)
Federal law	National legislature; statutes (e.g., law against treason)
State law	State legislature; statutes (e.g., law against larceny)
Local law	City/town council; ordinances (e.g., zoning law)
Organizational law	Formal organization; rules (e.g., rules against cheating)
Community law	Social group; rules and norms (e.g., assignment of chores)

Laws are more difficult to implement and enforce when they are at odds with prevalent social norms. In one interpretation, social norms are signals that people use to encourage others to interact and cooperate with them, and such signaling provides an important basis for law-related behavior (Posner 2000). The state also sends powerful signals when it imposes stigmas on individuals. The use and misuse of social norms in relation to law is an important topic. In an earlier time, *banishment* was a significant form of social control (Coy 2008). For example, in a German city in the sixteenth century, it accounted for 40% of the punishments meted out by the courts. The use of banishment is uncommon in the contemporary era, although deportation represents a form of banishment.

To examine the relationship between law and social control, it is necessary to look at the different levels, or orders, on which the law operates: universal, international, regional, federal, state, local, organizational, and community (*see* Table 2.1).

UNIVERSAL LAW

On a universal level, some laws are taken to be divine in origin, and all human beings are urged to honor them (Golding 1966; Letwin 2005). The golden rule, "Do unto others as you would have them do unto you," is a prime example; the Ten Commandments are also widely regarded as universal laws. Of course, a person's sense of commitment to any such universal law is importantly determined by his or her religious commitments; avowed atheists, for example, may or may not adopt personal codes of behavior that coincide with such universal (and divinely ordained) laws, but they do not experience the same compulsion to obey these laws that religious people experience. In an ultimate sense, obedience to or disobedience of such laws is only sanctioned or rewarded (in some religious faiths) in the next life, through eternal salvation or damnation. A church will also exercise some control here; for example, the Catholic Church venerates those who adhere to divine law in an exceptionally outstanding way and excommunicates those who defy divine law. Such control can only be exercised over those who feel themselves to be believers and followers of the church. (A long history of conflict exists between universal laws identified by a particular church and some secular laws, which will be further explored in Chapter 3.)

INTERNATIONAL LAW AND REGIONAL LAW

Although most law is something created and implemented within the boundaries of a particular state or country, increasingly in the modern era, international law—or global law—is becoming important (Brütsch and Lehmkuhl 2007; Twining 2000; von Glahn 1992). Such law comes into being through international treaties, accords, and other forms of agreement between states. Eric Posner (2009, p. ix), in *The Perils of Legal Globalism*, questions whether international law is "anything more than the sum of states' interests, a useful instrument for cooperation but nothing more." International law faces the challenge that it is unlikely to achieve truly universal support among states, and it is fundamentally more difficult to enforce than is national law. The term **transnational law** has been applied to "all law which regulates actions or events that transcend national frontiers" (Glenn 2003, p. 846). Such law may be religious, commercial, humanitarian, or applied to some other realm of human activity.

In the recent era, both **human rights law** and humanitarian law have become increasingly important elements of the contemporary world. Human rights are rights of individuals simply as human beings, cut across all political boundaries; humanitarian rights are rights that human beings have as members of particular groups or states (James 2007). Courts all over the world are increasingly addressing cases where parties are making claims about their human or social rights (Langford 2008). Human rights tend to receive more attention during times of political stability, whereas humanitarian rights receive more attention during times of political strife and conflict. Proponents of human rights attempt to persuade or pressure political regimes to adopt legal mechanisms to protect the universal rights of all citizens; proponents of humanitarian rights are more likely to promote direct confrontations with states or regimes imposing harm on identifiable groups of people. A study demonstrates that countries with very poor human rights records are as likely to sign international human rights treaties as countries with good human rights records, because leaders in such countries perceive a symbolic benefit in doing so and have the power to act on their inclinations (Hafner-Burton, Tsutsui, and Meyer 2008).

In a noteworthy invocation of international law, the surviving Nazi leadership and other Nazis directly involved in various crimes of war, crimes against peace, and crimes against humanity were tried after World War II at Nuremberg (Rhea 2008). These surviving Nazis were charged with violations of various treaties between various nations, signed at the Hague, Versailles, Locarno, and elsewhere, from 1899 on. Jurisdiction over the Nazi defendants was based on the newly ratified United Nations charter and an agreement between the principal allied World War II victors (the United States, the Soviet Union, Great Britain, and France) (Conot 1983; Rhea 2008). The International Court of Justice at the Hague derives from the Permanent Court of International Justice established in 1923 and is the principal judicial organ of the United Nations (Spiermann 2005).

One of the major challenges for law today is to effectively address crimes committed in the context of war as well as crimes committed by evil regimes that have been toppled. Should war criminals and deposed dictators be tried by courts of their own countrymen or by international tribunals (Bass 2000; Teitel 2000; Lutz and Reiger 2009)? Such challenges are hardly new but have arguably intensified in the context of a globalized, interconnected world. Complex military, diplomatic, and political issues arise here, as do both moral and practical concerns.

In some countries—notably, South Africa in the wake of the collapse of an apartheid regime—"Truth Commissions" have been established that offer a measure of clemency (and forgiveness) to perpetrators of evil acts in the context of the regime, in return for truthful testimony about their actions (Rothe 2009). Such an approach privileges reconciliation and moving forward over vengeance and a focus on the past, but it is inevitably controversial. Some proportion of primary or secondary victims inevitably believes that the perpetrators of evil have escaped full accountability for their actions and that the realization of justice has been subverted.

In the recent era, individuals involved in genocidal atrocities in Bosnia and in Rwanda have been tried by **international tribunals** (Cigar and Williams 2002; Minow 1998). The question of whether a dictator whose principal crimes have been committed against his own people is more appropriately tried by an international tribunal or one constituted by his countrymen arose in the case of Saddam Hussein, the deposed dictator of Iraq, captured in late 2003 (Lewis 2003). Saddam Hussein was accused of a range of crimes, including genocidal actions against Kurds living in the northern part of Iraq.

Some large questions for the twenty-first century are: Will international law become an ever-larger presence in the world? Will a truly effective permanent international criminal court be established? Will nations collectively become more successful in controlling major crimes against peace and humanity carried out on behalf of states or by major political entities within states? The challenges of addressing harm to an increasingly fragile or threatened global environment also confront international law. Many international treaties and international regulatory endeavors have emerged, but there is ongoing debate about their effectiveness (Wotipka and Tsutsui 2008; DiMento 2003). For example, are they mainly symbolic, as opposed to authentic forms of law capable of achieving compliance? A range of institutions is involved in making international business transactions possible, and national law continues to play a significant role (Brütsch and Lehmkuhl 2007). The establishment of entities such as the World Trade Organization (WTO) raises questions about resolving possible conflicts between the rulings of such entities on free trade issues and the laws or policies of specific countries affected by such rulings (Harrison 2007; Francioni 2001). Early in the twenty-first century, tribunals established by the North American Free Trade Agreement (NAFTA) were in some cases attempting to overrule American courts on matters pertaining to transnational trade (Liptak 2004b; He and Murphy 2007). At least some American judges found this objectionable.

Some prominent commentators argue that we are witnessing the emergence of at least an informal global system of international law, or governance, with the potential for the emergence of some form of world governance (Hoffman 2003a; Slaughter 2003; Wotipka and Tsutsui 2008). But an authentic global system of law, if it were ever to be realized, is still far in the future.

The states that compose the continent of Europe can collectively be called a region. At the end of the twentieth century, the formation of a European Union and the establishment of a European Court of Justice (in Luxembourg) and a European Court of Human Rights (in Strasbourg) gave rise to an evolving **Eurolaw** (Cohen 2000; Shaw 2003; Snyder 2007). At the onset of the twenty-first century, European law was increasingly taking precedence over national law on such matters as human rights, the environment, trade, and working conditions. Nations eager to join the European Union (e.g., Hungary, Romania, and Turkey) were influenced to conform to broader European norms on resolving conflicts and on human rights issues, and Europeans in growing numbers appeared to be embracing a European (as opposed to a solely national) identity. Although economic unity and the adoption of a single European currency were the principal objectives of the Maastricht Treaty of 1993, it has followed that European countries increasingly cooperate on cross-border policing and a range of other legal issues. The challenges of legal unification have proven more formidable than those of economic and political unification (Caenegem 2002). But Eurolaw clearly had to be recognized as a form of an emerging regional law, different from both national and international law. It may be that Eurolaw will serve as a model for a movement toward a global legal community (Snyder 2004). The emergence of Eurolaw is a significant milestone in legal history.

FEDERAL LAW

Most people think of law as a creation of states or countries. In many countries—for example, Spain—national law is the single most comprehensive and important body of law to which people are subject. In the United States, however, a federation of states exists, and federal (national) law has had a considerably more limited reach, as state laws and municipal laws also regulate behavior (Feeley and Rubin 2008). Nevertheless, during the course of the twentieth century, the scope of federal law in the United States expanded. Federal law covers, among other matters, violations of U.S. criminal law (including treason, attacks on federal officials, bank robbery, kidnapping, and the like); disputes between states or between citizens of different states; and regulation of a wide range of activities, from interstate commerce to environmental pollution. Federal law is generally more significant in the realm of corporate activity and white collar crime than in the realm of conventional crime and in disputes between corporations than in disputes between individual parties.

STATE LAW

In countries such as the United States, a confederation of states, the principal formal legal order toward which citizens must orient themselves is state law. In some cases, both state and federal law apply (e.g., a business fraud violates state common law and also violates federal anti-racketeering law) (Vandevelde 1996, p. 17). State law in America typically covers such matters as homicide, burglary, rape, arson, auto theft, larceny, and the like, and in civil law it covers disputes between citizens of the state. Most of the lawbreakers in the news have violated state laws and are prosecuted in the name of the state. In the civil realm as well, matters such as landlord/tenant disputes, divorces, estates, automobile accident lawsuits, and the like are governed by state laws.

Although the commonalities among the U.S. states in both their criminal law and their civil law tend to outweigh the differences, some noteworthy differences do exist. All states, for example, have laws prohibiting homicide; not all states, however, have a death penalty for those convicted of homicide. All states have laws prohibiting rape; different states may define rape in different ways. In the recent era, American states were at one point quite evenly divided between those that treated consensual sodomy as a crime and those that did not. All states have laws permitting divorce; grounds for divorce are not necessarily identical across states, and different formulas for the division of marital property exist. All states allow victims of automobile accidents to sue liable parties, but different states have different provisions governing such lawsuits and obligations pertaining to automobile insurance.

Why do variations among laws of states exist? To begin with, such variations reflect different histories. As one especially striking example, law in the state of Louisiana for a long time retained elements of traditional French law, as a reflection of that state's origins and heritage (Herman 1993). Then, different conditions in different states influence the law. As a rather prosaic example, Western states, with their broad expanses and low density of people, have traditionally permitted higher vehicle speed limits than congested Eastern states. Differences of law among states can also reflect successes and failures of lobbying groups and lawmaking coalitions and, in some cases, the power of an idiosyncratic lawmaker.

LOCAL LAW

Citizens must also orient themselves to the requirements of local law. Such law, for the most part, addresses fairly minor matters, such as jaywalking and littering, but it also deals with some consequential matters, such as zoning (e.g., whether a business can be established in a particular neighborhood). It is on the local level that one is most likely to find odd or idiosyncratic laws, insofar as a single influential member of a local council empowered to pass such laws may be able to get a particular personal hang-up or obsession enshrined in local law. For most of us, most of the time, local law is hardly a significant preoccupation.

ORGANIZATIONAL LAW

One of the defining features of contemporary society is participation in formal organizations. All such organizations (or private governments) have rules; whether such rules, and the procedures for administering them, add up to a system of law is a matter of some dispute (Macaulay 1986). In the case of military organizations—which are, of course, a division of the state—there is widespread recognition of the existence of military law and a military system of justice (Bishop 1974). In the cases of corporations and other types of businesses, universities, unions, professional associations, and clubs (or fraternities and sororities), formal rules and adjudicative procedures typically exist but are less likely to be characterized as law of some disputes (*see* Box 2.1).

Organizational rules (and sanctions associated with their violation) can assume great importance for employees, faculty and students, union members, doctors and lawyers, and club or fraternity/sorority members. An employee fired for tardiness, a faculty member stripped of tenure for sexual harassment, a student dismissed for cheating, a union member ostracized for defying a strike call, a doctor stripped of a license to practice medicine or a lawyer disbarred

BOX 2.1　THE NEW ERA OF CAMPUS LITIGATION

Traditionally, American courts have for the most part allowed colleges and universities to govern themselves and have been resistant to applying law to disputes that arise in that setting. But in the recent era, as Amy Gajda (2009) documents in her important and fascinating book, *The Trials of Academe: The New Era of Campus Litigation*, this has changed quite dramatically. She suggests that the lawsuits arising in the wake of the famous 1970 Kent State shootings (National Guardsman shooting anti-war demonstrators on campus, killing several students) helped usher in a new era of campus-related litigation. The adoption of civil rights statutes extending discrimination claims, and broadened extension of free speech and due process rights, have also played a role. As universities and colleges have become progressively more "business-like" in how they operate, they have become progressively more vulnerable to lawsuits. Today, lawsuits are an established fact of campus life, with the number of such lawsuits having tripled in one recent 5-year period. These lawsuits have addressed such matters as alleged discrimination in hiring, promotion, and tenure cases; First Amendment violations when administrative attempts are made to control course content; disputes over the allocation of faculty offices and courses; and student-initiated lawsuits addressing tuition increases, bad grades, and faulty advice.

Cases originating on college or university campuses that have gone to court include: the use of sexual language in classes by instructors; a student claim that performing roles requiring use of coarse language or taking God's name in vain violated religious liberty and free speech rights; a professor challenging a dean's decision to allow failed students to retake an exam; professors' rights not to hand out course evaluations; and professors challenging university policies prohibiting intimate relations with students as a violation of their rights.

Legal battles have also arisen in connection with disputes between universities and businesses using a name associated with a university (e.g., Harvard) for commercial purposes as well as with disputes between universities and professors over patent rights of discoveries or inventions. Lawsuits have also arisen in relation to the question of ownership of classroom lectures (e.g., whether students can take notes in class and then sell them). Confidentiality issues have also been litigated. Universities have been especially concerned that following a U.S. Supreme Court decision, they can no longer assume that the confidentiality of peer evaluations can be protected. Will professors be willing to make candid assessments of candidates for jobs, promotions, and tenure if they cannot be sure their evaluations will be protected from public scrutiny? Confidentiality issues have also arisen when companies have attempted, through legal action, to gain access to research documents relating to studies that produced results harmful to the marketing of their products.

Defamation of character claims were a rarity on campus in the past but have now become quite common. A professor was successfully sued for calling a student a "slut" in class, and some researchers have sued those who have criticized their work.

A law professor who is the author of a leading torts textbook was sued by a female student whom he lightly tapped on the shoulder—ironically, to illustrate the "eggshell plaintiff" tort rule that even such an action could give rise to a tort lawsuit if the specific individual could show injury; the student in question had been raped as a child and claimed that she was traumatized by being touched by a male. Altogether, professors and universities are much more vulnerable today to claims that they have injured students—for example, by awarding them bad grades or exposing them to unsafe classroom conditions. A student at Yale sued successfully when she infected herself with HIV through a needle stick, on the claim that she had been inadequately trained for the procedure involved. Both professors and universities must now be cautious about claims made in course syllabi or catalogs and marketing materials, as a failure to fully satisfy the claims can give rise to a lawsuit. These lawsuits have claimed a violation of a contractual promise.

Amy Gajda (2009), following her exhaustive review of the dramatic rise of campus litigation, argues quite persuasively that this trend has enormous costs for higher education and represents a fundamental threat to academic freedom. She concludes her book with a disturbing case of a writing instructor who threatened to sue students in her class who mocked her feminist interpretation and gave her poor evaluations. When professors contemplate suing students, much harm to higher education can occur.

Although colleges and universities generally assume responsibility for the legal defense of faculty members and other employees in lawsuits that arise in relation to fulfilling work-related responsibilities, the scope of such protection isn't entirely clear (Schmidt 2009). Obviously faculty members are not covered if they initiate a lawsuit against their institution (e.g., in a tenure denial situation), but in other circumstances (e.g., if a professor is threatened with a lawsuit over claims made in a scholarly article) it isn't always clear whether they will be legally supported by their institution. A relatively small number of academics have obtained personal liability insurance to protect themselves in such circumstances.

As of the summer of 2010 federal regulations require colleges to take specific steps against illegal swapping of copyrighted material by their students (Young 2010). Entertainment businesses want colleges to use network filters to detect attempts at illegal downloading or swapping and have filed lawsuits or threatened to do so over such activity. Although many colleges already take various steps to attempt to address this problem, they have also expressed concern over the high costs—and ultimate futility—of expanding any such efforts.

BOX 2.1 (cont'd.)

In 1974 the U.S. Congress passed the Family Educational Rights and Privacy Act (FERPA) to safeguard the confidentiality of student "educational records," but a critic contends that this Act is sometimes invoked in confusing and contradictory ways, and at least sometimes so that institutions of higher education can avoid disclosing information embarrassing to the institution (Lomonte 2010). Colleges tend to adopt a broad interpretation of FERPA and to privilege secrecy over disclosure.

In a series of recent cases, colleges have had to contend with the potential conflict between their obligation to comply with federal and state laws that prohibit discrimination against students on the basis of a disability and their equally important obligation to keep their student population safe by upholding campus disciplinary codes (McKendall 2010). Some students who have been charged with dishonest or dangerous conduct on campus and have been disciplined (or expelled) accordingly have claimed that their behavior was a function of a disability or impairment. Colleges face the challenge of not imposing disciplinary actions

on students because of a disability while also ensuring that they take appropriate measures against students who present a direct threat to members of campus communities.

Colleges and universities have greatly increased the size of their legal staffs over the past two decades and are far more likely to have in-house counsel as full-time employees (Lipka 2005). These general counsels must address a wide range of issues, including but hardly limited to: reviewing and updating university policies (e.g., on sexual harassment) to minimize the chances of lawsuits against the college; responding to lawsuits filed against the college by students, faculty, or other parties; dealing with issues that arise in athletics programs; dealing with a whole range of new challenges arising in relation to the Internet; and the like. Accordingly, some of their work is preventive and some reactive. Universities still hire outside lawyers when especially complex lawsuits are filed that require special expertise not found among the in-house counsel. But even in these cases, the in-house counsel typically collaborates with such outside lawyers.

---

for serious professional misconduct, or a club member ousted for failing to attend to mandated responsibilities may all experience significant personal trauma and shame plus loss of status, income, and possibly livelihood. Of course, aggrieved parties who believe they have been unjustly sanctioned under organizational rules may well turn to the formal civil law system to seek justice. For the most part, the state would prefer not to become involved with the internal rules of organizations, but in a society where people tend to develop a strong sense of their rights, civil courts may have to provide a final resolution of some disputes.

COMMUNITY LAW

Finally, we are all members of social groups and communities. For most of us that means a family, perhaps a wider circle of relatives and friends, and a neighborhood. Such social groups and communities (another form of "private government") have, at a minimum, some generalized norms to which members are expected to conform. Social control in such settings is exercised quite informally, sometimes by no more than a look of disapproval. On the other hand, a neighborhood (or other entity) may have formal proceedings to address rule violations. Homeowners' associations (and co-op boards) have achieved considerable power to impose rules and restrictions on those who own homes in developments or cooperative buildings (Bush 2002–2003; Rich 2003). Some 50 million Americans are estimated to be subject to such associations or boards. These entities can dictate such matters as parking policies, lawn-mowing schedules, and house paint colors and can fine residents who violate rules and foreclose on those who fail to pay dues. They have been criticized as intruding on individual rights and operating without due process.

Ellickson (2008) has explored how one of the core institutions in society—the household—operates in relation to law. He concludes that households generally function quite well with minimal involvement of the formal law. Whether government subsidizing of private ownership of homes and bailing out homeowners who cannot pay their mortgages is a good idea is challenged by Ellickson's analysis of how households work best—that is, on their own resources.

What does any of this have to do with law? This is a question that does not have a single answer; the response to the question depends on one's conception of law. Michael Reisman (1999), in *Law in Brief Encounters*, argued that the complex system of unofficial norms governing our everyday interactions with others—including staring and glaring, standing in line and cutting in, and talking to the boss—constitute social laws, which he calls **microlaw**. And increasingly, questions arise about the lines of demarcation between private rules and public laws. People who visit "virtual cities" on the Internet find themselves contending with a complex list of rules or "laws" (Harmon 2004). In this circumstance, in which the line between reality and fantasy can become quite blurred, when do laws in the larger world apply? What about the case of a teenager who assumes the persona of a prostitute in such an online game or a participant who is banished from the virtual city for expressing critical views? Although Internet game companies have been accorded much freedom in how they operate, parallel to the freedom accorded to private clubs, that could change as boundaries between the real world and the cyberworld erode.

SPECIFIC DEFINITIONS OF LAW

Throughout history, sages and scholars have offered up some specific definitions of law, although these definitions vary considerably (*see* Box 2.2).

As was noted earlier, it may make the most sense for one to adopt a definition of law useful for a given purpose, or in a particular context, rather than to try to come up with a single, all-purpose definition of law. For example, a useful conception of one important form of law, **criminal law**, might include the following elements: It is formal (although some disagreement exists over whether law must necessarily take a written form as opposed to simply being orally proclaimed); it is imperative (that is, it most typically proscribes certain types of conduct); it has sanctions, or "teeth" (i.e., external controls); it is political (it emanates from the state); it is specific (i.e., it does not, as a rule, simply proscribe "bad behavior" but specifies what is forbidden; "disorderly conduct" can be considered one exception to this proposition); it is ongoing (i.e., it is not imposed on an *ad hoc*, or case-by-case, basis, and it is not imposed *ex post facto*, or after the fact); and officials are empowered to enforce and administer it.

The term *law* is also incorporated into many familiar and commonplace expressions. Western democratic nations in particular (and many other nations as well) claim to adhere to **the rule of law** (*see* Box 2.3). This term is generally taken to mean that decisions are made and disputes are resolved in accord with what the law requires rather than by the brute exercise of power or in a state of anarchy. In one interpretation, the commitment to a government of law—not men—was most clearly affirmed in the American experience in the landmark U.S. Supreme Court decision *Marbury v. Madison* (1803) (Kahn 1997, p. 4). In this decision, the Court held that officials of the government's executive branch are subject to correction by the Court when they violate a legal obligation and that the Court has the power to rule on the constitutionality of Congressional acts.

It is important to point out that the rule of law has been invoked in societies with differing legal systems (some repressive) and that the rule of law can be interpreted or applied

BOX 2.2 SOME CLASSICAL DEFINITIONS
OF LAW

Definitions of law by philosophers and sages include the
following:

Law is intelligence without passion.

—Aristotle

*Law is the highest reason, implanted in nature, which
commands what ought to be done and forbids the opposite.*

—Cicero

*[Law] is nothing other than a certain rule of reason for
the purpose of the common good, laid down by him
who is entrusted with the welfare of the community and
promulgated.*

—Aquinas

*The law is the last result of human wisdom acting upon
human experience for the benefit of the public.*

—Samuel Johnson

* * *

From U.S. Supreme Court justices we have the following
definitions:

*The prophecies of what the courts will do in fact, and nothing
more pretentious, is what I mean by law.*

—Oliver Wendell Holmes, Jr.

*We shall unite in viewing as law that body of principle and
dogma which with a reasonable measure of probability may*

*be predicted as the basis for judgment in pending or in future
controversies.*

—Benjamin Cardozo

*Law…[is] the sum total of all those rules of conduct for which
there is state sanction.*

—Harlan Fiske Stone

* * *

From those writing in the tradition of the social sciences, just
two definitional efforts are included here:

*An order shall be called law when it is guaranteed by the
likelihood that (physical or psychological) coercion aiming at
bringing about conduct in conformity with the order, or at
avenging its violations, will be exercised by a staff of people
especially holding themselves ready for this purpose.*

—Max Weber

[Law is] governmental social control.

—Donald Black

* * *

It is evident, then, that law has been conceived of, or
defined, in different ways over time.

Sources: Aristotle, Cicero, and Stone from Shrager and Frost 1986;
Aquinas, Johnson, and Holmes from McNamara 1960; Cardozo from
Shapiro 1993; Weber 1978, p. 34; Black 1976, p. 2.

BOX 2.3 THE RULE OF LAW

Much lip service or rhetorical support is given to the "rule of law,"
even by those who do not in any sense adhere to it. A claimed
allegiance to the rule of law goes far back in history (Tamanaha
2004). It has been associated principally with the notion of a constraint on governmental action, rather than with the promotion
of individual liberty. There is a stress on *formal* legality, and the
impersonal exercise of power. The rule of law has been especially
associated with those wedded to a conservative ideology; radicals, on the other hand, have been more associated with challenging the rule of law. Those who promoted adherence to the
rule of law in American history sometimes did so in the name of
unpopular causes and accordingly put themselves and their own
careers at risk (Gross 2007). In one interpretation, legal institutions increasingly adhere to using law instrumentally—that is, to
achieve specific purposes (Tamanaha 2006). When law is used as
a naked tool by powerful forces for their own purposes, respect
for the rule of law is compromised. In *Plunder*, Mattei and Nader

(2008) argue that the rule of law has been invoked specifically
by Western countries to exploit weaker, developing nations—for
example, in relation to oil extraction and the protection of intellectual property rights. It is clear that the true meaning of the
"rule of law"—on a national and international level—is a matter of considerable debate (Palombella and Walker 2009). In
other countries, the assumption that law has "certainty" or fixed
outcomes is far more pronounced than it is in the United States
(Maxeiner 2008). If the "rule of law" is to be globalized, then it
must be recognized that different assumptions about law exist in
different countries.

The World Justice Forum has developed a "Rule of Law
Index" to measure how well different countries adhere to this
principle (Kole 2008). The factors used to determine the extent
to which a country adheres to the rule of law includes the level
of corruption, government officials' accountability to the law,
respect for property rights, access to essential services, and
whether an impartial judiciary is in place.

in different ways. The rule of law has been attacked as a myth that masks dominance by the power structure; if this is so, a commitment to authentic liberty requires a repudiation of the rule of law (Hasnas 1995; Kahn 1997).

In a parallel vein, a commitment to **"law and order"** (in contrast to "crime and disorder") is commonly expressed in Western societies, but the call for law and order was also one of the rallying cries of the Nazis when they were seeking political power. In at least one sense of the term, the Holocaust (the extermination of some 6 million people) was carried out in the name of law and order (Mueller 1991). Somewhat ironically, Richard Nixon ran for the American presidency in 1968 on a pledge to restore law and order and was then the first president forced to resign as a result of major violations of law by himself and his close associates (Blum 1991).

To what, then, does a claim of support for law and order really refer? It might refer to an institution, a particular system, or a particular regime; more narrowly, it has been an expression of commitment to a particular (conservative) ideology or a particular component (the police) of the justice system. For Diamond, "Law and order is the historical illusion; law versus order is the historical reality" (1973, p. 339). It is indisputable, in any case, that some terrible crimes have been carried out in the name of law and order.

ORIGINS OF LAW

The concept of law has a long history, with many contemporary schools of thought challenging the notion of law as a universal and independent force (Letwin 2005). How did law originate (Davis 1962; Friedman 1975; Shaffern 2009)? Social control on some level has been a part of human experience since the beginning of human existence. In this section, we ask about origins of a more formal conception of law, an officially proclaimed system of rules with associated formal sanctions and officials empowered to administer this system. There are three different views on the origin of such laws: value/consensus, rational/contract, and power/coercion (*see* Table 2.2).

TABLE 2.2   ORIGINS OF LAW

I. Value/Consensus
A. Natural
B. Customary
C. Democratic
II. Rational/Contract
A. Social contract
B. Pragmatic
C. Negotiated
III. Power/Coercion
A. Sovereign
B. Class conflict
C. Interest group

VALUE/CONSENSUS

Law is seen as a formalization of deeply held, widely shared values. This viewpoint has several different versions. First, there is **natural law theory**: that law is, or surely ought to be, based on divinely ordained rules, or the natural rights to which human beings are entitled (Bix 1996). **Natural law**, in this sense, has both a specifically religious and a secular version. In either case, however, the emphasis is on rules or rights that everyone ought to be able to recognize and honor. The Roman Catholic theologian St. Thomas Aquinas is among those identified with the divine version of this form of explanation; the English philosopher John Locke is among those identified with a secular version of "natural rights" (Friedrich 1963). The American Founding Fathers were much influenced by Locke, and the Declaration of Independence specifically invokes the notion of natural rights as the appropriate foundation for American law. For Locke, government comes out of a free contract among people and is legitimate only as long as it enjoys the consent of the governed (Rosenblatt 2003, p. 2140). Shared basic values are implicit in such consent.

An alternative value/consensus view of law regards it as the "crystallization of the mores," or a formalization of customs that emerged within particular societies over a long period of time. A nineteenth-century German student of law, Friedrich von Savigny ([1831] 1986), was an early proponent of this view of law's origins. Stanley Diamond (1973), a contemporary American anthropologist, challenged the view that law (an instrument of state power) reflects a crystallization of customary norms. In his view, law is imposed from above, often at odds with custom.

A third value/consensus view of law has a distinctly modern theme and emphasizes that law is a product of democratization—that is, law reflects the values of the popular majority as expressed through the political process. Of course, any such account is only applicable to laws created in societies that have adopted a democratic system. Jurgen Habermas (1996), a contemporary German social philosopher, is associated with a position that societies should be moving toward the creation of an "ideal speech" situation wherein citizens can in a truly meaningful and well-informed manner engage in a dialogue leading to consensus and the adoption of mutually agreed-upon rules and laws.

RATIONAL/CONTRACT

A second view of the origin of law shifts attention away from values to agreement based on a contract. The English philosopher Thomas Hobbes ([1651] 1958), in his book *Leviathan*, advanced an especially celebrated version of social contract theory. Hobbes held that human beings in a "state of nature" were engaged in a "war of all against all." In such a condition, in Hobbes' further famous formulation, the life of each person would be "solitary, poor, nasty, brutish, and short." Although human beings in a state of nature live like animals, they also have one important faculty, reason, which makes them different from other creatures. And through reason they arrive at the realization that it is in the long-term interest of all individuals to form a social contract with others, wherein they give up certain powers (delegated to the state, or "the Leviathan"), in return for which the state will provide them with a measure of security against their fellow human beings.

In the contemporary context, law may be viewed as a product of pragmatic necessity, or agreement based on practical considerations. In this view, the very conditions of modern life create circumstances requiring an ever-widening net of rules and regulations. Laws that protect people from the dangers of unrestricted operation of various forms of modern technology could be said to fall in this category.

Negotiation can be identified as a specific mechanism closely associated with a contractual conception of the origins of law. In this view, law comes out of a process involving compromises and trade-offs, having a focus on achieving an instrumental objective.

POWER/COERCION

A third basic view of the origins of law adopts a position fundamentally at odds with either a value/consensus or a rational/contract view. In this view law is an expression of the will (and interests) of the sovereign or of the power elite. One classic version of this way of looking at law was advanced by the Italian philosopher Machiavelli ([1513] 1976) in *The Prince*, a famous source for the proposition that the ends justify the means and power makes right. Machiavelli specifically advised rulers to adopt cynical, manipulative means to achieve their political ends, and the law can be a part of this enterprise.

Karl Marx regarded law as a creation of the privileged classes to maintain an inherently exploitative economic system (Cain and Hunt 1979). Marx, with his emphasis on class conflict, highlighted the fundamental conflicts of interest between the ownership class and the wage-earning class, with the law serving the interests of the former. In at least one reading, Marx regarded the very form of law as an inevitable instrument of exploitation, with the strong implication that in a truly communist society, there would be no law (and no need for law). Marx's views of law are addressed in more depth in Chapter 6.

A view of law as a product of the exercise of power and a reflection of conflicts of interest need not be specifically Marxist, or ideological. For example, Austin Turk (1969), a contemporary criminologist, has been a leading proponent of a nonpartisan, interest-group perspective on how law is formed. The perspective holds that these interest groups are not necessarily aligned with the capitalist ownership class and that one can analyze the role of power in lawmaking without choosing to say whether capitalism should be condemned or supported. In the interpretation of some commentators, American law increasingly reflects the interests of economic elites and diminished concern with the interests and needs of the disadvantaged (Carrington and Jones 2006). This trend reflects broader social patterns of increasing social and economic inequality in the recent era.

THE ORIGINS OF LAW: WHICH VIEW IS CORRECT?

This question also lacks a simple answer. First, we can all think of laws that appear to reflect a high level of value consensus. For example, almost all citizens strongly support legal prohibitions on the sexual exploitation of children. Other laws—for example, traffic law—seem to reflect the practical realities of living in a complex, modern society (where people drive cars that are inherently dangerous vehicles unless their movement is regulated). There are also laws (vagrancy law is one classic example) that seem to reflect the powerful imposing their interests on the powerless. Nevertheless, different students of law have put more or less emphasis on one or the other of these forms of explanation for the origins of law, in accordance with their own ideological commitments. Historically, much emphasis has been put on the consensual view of law, despite considerable evidence of the central role of power and the unequal distribution of wealth in shaping law.

MODELS OF LAW

Law clearly has many different dimensions and aspects. To make sense of law, one needs to make a number of distinctions. The **ideal type**, proposed by the great German sociologist Max Weber (1949), provides one starting point for any such distinctions. By ideal type, Weber meant an illustrative type that incorporates essential elements of something that occurs in the real world without necessarily being identical to the real-world phenomenon. For example, many legal decisions are based on "what a reasonable man would do under similar circumstances." This legalistic notion of the "reasonable man" can be considered an abstraction, or ideal type. The reasonable man of the law is not synonymous with any real, living person. Relatedly, dichotomies making sharp contrasts can also be useful in making sense of the law's many aspects (*see* Table 2.3). But reality is more complex and multifaceted than any such ideal types or dichotomies might suggest.

In the pages that follow, ten **models of law** are identified and defined in the form of dichotomies of ideal types. The term *model* is used here to encompass a variety of patterns, conceptions, sources, forms, types, structures, foci, and contents of law. An understanding of and familiarity with these models and the key terms associated with them are necessary for anyone who hopes to claim literacy about our system of law.

FUNDAMENTAL DIMENSIONS OF LAW

The Basic Conception of Law: Principles Versus Practices

One conception of law stresses the abstract in the sense of law as an ideal, law as a statement of principles. Such ideals and principles are then incorporated into written documents, from constitutions to local codes. On the constitutional level, law may take the form of a general principle; statutes and case opinions, on the other hand, tend to be specific. Statutes and case opinions are different forms of written law and are more fully defined later in this section.

In contrast, one can begin with the concrete manifestation of law in behavior, in the practices of those who implement law. Law here is a form of action: what judges do, what parole board members do, what police officers do.

Imagine, for a moment, being approached by an extraterrestrial who has been given the assignment to discover something about this thing called "law," which supposedly exists in your society. On the one hand, you might direct this alien toward the library, with the instruction to visit the "KF" section, to examine copies of the Constitution, the federal code, the volumes reporting case (judge-made) law, and the like; there, law can be found. On the other hand, you might direct this alien toward the courthouse and the police station,

TABLE 2.3 LAW AND THE LEGAL SYSTEM: MODELS AND CONCEPTIONS

I. Basic conception		
Abstract	vs.	Concrete
Law in principle (written)	vs.	Law in practice (action)
Documents/code books/case reporters	vs.	Courts/police/corrections officers
II. Fundamental source		
Natural (divine) (revelation/values)	vs.	Positive (human sovereign) (pragmatism/power)
III. Written form		
Statutory/codes/constitutional	vs.	Case/opinion
IV. Political source		
International	vs.	State-based
Legislative	vs.	Judicial
Executive (Administrative)	vs.	Justice system personnel (e.g., police)
V. Structure (Judiciary)		
Organization: dual	vs.	Unitary
Power: hierarchical	vs.	Horizontal
VI. Form of dispute settlement		
Court model (triad)	vs.	Bargain model (dyad)
Adjudication	vs.	Negotiation
VII. Type of court procedure		
Adversarial	vs.	Inquisitorial
VIII. Foci of law		
Public/criminal (crime)	vs.	Private/civil (tort)
IX. Objective (of criminal law/justice system)		
Crime control	vs.	Due process
X. Content (of criminal law)		
Substantive	vs.	Procedural

with the instruction to observe what transpires in the courtroom and on the police officer's patrol; here, too, law could be witnessed. If these are two different approaches to getting at the essence of law, then it should also be obvious that they complement each other. However, some references to law treat it as essentially a matter of principles, or written rules, and other references to law treat it as essentially a matter of practices, or specific actions.

The Fundamental Source of Law: Natural Versus Positive

Law as natural suggests that human law is (or surely ought to be) rooted in some transcendent order—that is, it reflects divine (God-given) imperatives or natural rights that human beings can discover intuitively. Law as **positive** suggests that human **law** is simply a human creation produced in specific historical circumstances—that is, it is made by sovereigns or other parties who are in a position to make laws. The **natural** conception of **law** tends to stress revelation, in some form, and the intimate relationship between law and moral values. The positive conception of law tends to stress power, in some form, and the practical or instrumental character of law. Of course, it is possible to view some parts of law (e.g., pertaining to homicide) as a reflection of the natural order and other parts of law (e.g., pertaining to business contracts) as a purely practical, human creation. But the basic division between proponents of natural law and those of positive law has been influential in the history of jurisprudence; it is discussed further in Chapter 4.

The Written Form of Law: Statutory Versus Case Law

On the one hand, our written law can be found in such documents as the Constitution and in federal or state codes. Legislative bodies (including a constitutional convention as a special type of legislative body) produce constitutional and **statutory law**. On the other hand, an important part of our written law, **case law,** can be found in appellate court case opinions. Appellate court judges, at least in the common law tradition, produce this type of written law. A sort of ongoing tension about law exists between legislative bodies and judges: Should the will of the legislative body or the interpretation of the judge (or justices) prevail?

POLITICAL DIMENSIONS OF LAW

The Political Source of Law: International Versus State; Legislative Versus Judicial; Executive (Administrative) Versus Justice System Personnel

Most people are socialized to think of law as a product of the state. Within the United States and in some other countries, there is a contrast between federal law and state (or individual state) law. More broadly still, there is the contrast between state (federal or individual state) law and international law. Historically, law has been most effectively legitimated and implemented within the boundaries of a sovereign state. But the world also has a long history of international treaties and accords that have produced a form of international law. As mentioned earlier, some international tribunals have been convened to implement this form of law. If we accept the proposition that globalization is becoming an increasingly dominant feature of our world, then it seems likely that international law will become more important during the course of the twenty-first century (*see* Box 2.4).

Although lawmaking is most readily associated with the legislative and judicial branches, in important respects the executive branch and administrative or justice system agencies linked with it also make law. The executive branch is empowered to issue executive orders, and the president (or governor) can grant pardons, effectively negating law in particular cases. Most important, the executive branch oversees the enforcement of the law, and in its choices about such enforcement, as well as its allocation of enforcement resources, it has an impact on the reality of what law does and does not mean. In the same vein, justice system

BOX 2.4 THE CONTROVERSY OVER
FEDERALISM

As every school child learns at some point, the United States is a federation of states (50 today), with each of the state's having significant powers to make their own laws. There have always been—and continue to be—champions of "state's rights," who resist any new national encroachments on state powers. The "nationalist" views of the influential early nineteenth century Chief Justice John Marshall of the U.S. Supreme Court (as exemplified in the celebrated *McCulloch v. Maryland* case) were deeply resented by many state's rights advocates of that time (Ellis 2007). The Civil War could be described as the apex of claims for state's rights, as the Southern, slave-owning states so opposed federal initiatives toward the elimination of slavery that they opted to secede from the union.

Sociolegal scholars Malcolm Feeley and Edward Rubin (2008) argue that if federalism made sense at an earlier time when states did have quite different cultural identities and outlooks (exemplified by the division between slave states and free states), early in the twenty-first century it no longer makes sense. In their view, the federal government is empowered by the Constitution to make national policy, and to the extent that it does so, the country as a whole benefits. This argument should not be confused with common claims that some government functions are best decentralized.

On the other hand, law school dean Erwin Chemerinsky (2008) argues that although national policy may be appropriate for environmental and civil rights issues, federalism—and state power—allows governments to solve problems and enhance individual liberties and should be strengthened when it comes to issues such as employee protection and consumer privacy. Lisa Miller (2008) argues that currently, national lawmaking works against the interests of the disadvantaged because some single-issue advocates gain great power at this level; the situation during the civil rights era of the 1960s was just the opposite.

For law professor Edward Purcell (2008), the Founding Fathers set forth a form of federalism that intentionally left ambiguous the lines of authority between state governments and the federal government. Accordingly, he argues that the courts today should resolve issues that arise about federalism and this allocation of powers by practical criteria.

The issues of federalism and state rights (or between superior and inferior government units) are hardly unique to the United States (Caravita di Toritto, Kramer, and Schneider 2009). They also arise in such countries as Italy, South Africa, Spain, Great Britain, Germany, Austria, Russia, Australia, and Canada.

---

personnel, down to the police officer on the beat and the corrections officer on rounds, "make" law through their decisions of which laws or rules to enforce and which to disregard. For example, so-called blue laws (prohibitions on doing business on Sunday) remain on the books in many parts of the United States and have been upheld by the courts but are simply not enforced; in this sense, they lack substance as law. In a somewhat more formal way, administrative agencies, such as the Securities and Exchange Commission and the Environmental Protection Agency, have been empowered to make, enforce, and adjudicate many laws or rules in their realm. Accordingly, such agencies represent an important, although somewhat lower profile, source of law.

DIMENSIONS OF LEGAL SYSTEMS

The Structure of the Legal System: Dual Versus Unitary; Hierarchical Versus Horizontal

The American legal system is one with a **dual structure**, with a co-existing federal system of law and state systems of law (*see* Fig. 2.1 and Box 2.4). In some countries, the legal system has a **unitary structure**, with a single system for the entire country.

In terms of judicial power, the United States—and most legal systems in developed nations—has a **hierarchical power** structure, with higher courts empowered to overrule the decisions of lower courts. In some places—for example, in the Ottoman Empire in an earlier time—one might find an essentially **horizontal power** structure, with co-existing courts

A. Dual Legal System:
Federal – State

Unitary Legal System:
Unified National System

B. Hierarchical Legal System:
U.S. Supreme Court
↓
Circuit Court of Appeals
↓
District Court
↓
Magistrate's Court

Horizontal Legal System: Muslim Court · Christian Court · Jewish Court

FIGURE 2.1   The Organization of Legal Systems

for different constituencies (e.g., Christian citizens, Islamic citizens, and Jewish citizens) (Friedman 1977, p. 71). Of course, in the American system of law, different states can be considered to exercise "horizontal" judicial powers within their borders, and different state courts (e.g., civil courts and criminal courts) to exercise horizontal judicial powers in their particular jurisdictions.

The Form of Dispute Settlement: Court Model (Adjudication) Versus Bargain Model (Negotiation)

In the **court model** (exemplified by either the criminal court or the civil court), there are three essential parties: a defendant, a plaintiff or prosecutor, and a judge (and/or jury). The last of these three parties imposes a decision on the other parties. In the **bargain model** (exemplified by labor union/management dealings), there are only two essential parties, who meet on a theoretically level "playing field." The two parties, in the pure version of this model, must arrive at a mutually agreed upon resolution of their differences. In the first model (at least on the criminal court side), a case is adjudicated; in the second model, a dispute is negotiated. Of course, in reality a large percentage of both criminal and civil cases are actually resolved by negotiation between two parties, with a judge's decision a formal declaration of this resolution. And when a labor union and management are unable to resolve their differences by bargaining and negotiating, they may agree to have the matter resolved by bringing in a third party, an arbitrator, who will impose a decision on them. In some cases, they may also turn to the courts to resolve their dispute. So the realities of dispute settlement are frequently at odds with the formal process.

Court Procedure: Adversarial Versus Inquisitorial

In the **adversarial model**, there is what amounts to a contest between two sides, with a judge presiding, or refereeing, and with either a judge or a jury making a determination about who won the contest (in accordance with whatever standard of proof is in effect). In the American criminal justice system, the adversarial model is used in major felony cases. On the plus side, adherents of the adversarial model claim that the truth in a criminal case is most likely to emerge when each side is best able to put forth its case. Furthermore, the defendant in a major criminal case, up against the intimidating resources of the state, has the best chance to put forward a case with the capacity to introduce evidence and witnesses and to challenge the state's evidence and cross-examine the state's witnesses. On the minus side, critics of the adversarial model claim that the whole thrust of such proceedings becomes a contest to win on points, with each side trying to prevent admission of the other side's version of the truth and to present its own one-sided version (Strick 1978). Some critics contend that defendants with substantial resources can win cases on the basis of legal pyrotechnics rather than on the basis of revealing truth (*see* Box 2.5).

The **inquisitorial model** takes the form of an inquiry, with a judge (or panel of judges) interrogating not only the defendant but victims, witnesses, lawyers, justice system personnel, and any other pertinent parties. The civil (or Roman) law courts operate essentially in terms of this approach. On the plus side, a judge (or panel of judges) who is wise and fair-minded can, with considerable efficiency, direct appropriate questions to various parties, focusing on extracting the truth of the matter at hand. On the minus side, such a system may be seen as incorporating an assumption of guilt; it puts the defendant at a considerable disadvantage with no real control over the direction of the inquiry; and when directed by a biased judge, it may simply provide an opportunity for highlighting the judge's own preferred version of the truth.

BOX 2.5 ADVERSARIAL LEGALISM

In a widely discussed book, *Adversarial Legalism: The American Way of Law*, the distinguished political scientist Robert Kagan (2001) offers a thorough critique of the effects of a strong commitment to resolving disputes by lawyer-dominated litigation.

Limitations of such a system are many. It is impractical, slow, inconsistent (i.e., the quality of counsel makes a big difference), expensive, and a promoter of mistrust and ill will. The threat of lawsuits influences much behavior of organizations. Adversarial legalism holds the government and private corporations more accountable than other systems but at a high cost in routine cases. Altogether, the adversarial system favors the "haves" (i.e., those with resources). Despite the landmark *Gideon v. Wainwright* (1963) decision (and subsequent decisions), which extended the right to counsel to all those charged with serious crimes when they are unable to pay for a lawyer, in reality, indigent defendants do not typically enjoy the benefits of an adversarial proceeding (Backus 2008). States have largely failed to provide indigent defendants with truly effective legal counsel. Judges, in one view, are capable of stepping into the breach, and ensuring that the rights of indigent defendants are fully respected. It has high "transaction" costs, which means that a disproportionate share of monetary judgments go to

lawyers, not to plaintiffs, in cases. Accordingly, trial lawyers' associations have a major commitment to the existing system. In other countries, there are more constraints on adversarial litigation.

In the American system, amateurs (jurors) play a central role in the resolution of legal cases. In other countries, legal judgments are more likely to rest with judges, bureaucrats, political authorities, and experts. There are more constraints on adversarial litigation, although adversarial legalism is also increasing in many other countries. Critics raise questions about Kagan's critique of the adversarial system—for example, whether the American system has in fact become more adversarial over the past half-century, whether civil proceedings are indeed more cumbersome in the United States, and whether on balance the effects of the adversarial system are more negative than positive (Kritzer 2004b; Nelken 2003). There is much we do not really know about how the legal systems of other countries operate, and accordingly valid comparisons are difficult. For all their complaints about the costs associated with adversarial legalism, it is far from clear that Americans would accept alternatives. Americans demand much of their legal system, and it is unclear that any other model could effectively fulfill these demands. Alternative legal systems certainly have their own inefficiencies.

France is one of the countries where an inquisitorial system is in effect (Provine 1996). An examining magistrate plays an active role in the investigation of an alleged crime. If a case goes to trial, the judge dominates the process. He or she interrogates witnesses, or must approve questions put to witnesses by others, and interrogates the accused as well, with no cross-examination. The scope of the interrogation is very broad, exploring the past record and character of the accused as well as the case at hand. If a jury is involved, then the judge participates in the jury deliberations.

In the American system of justice, many proceedings—for example, grand jury hearings, Senatorial inquiries, and minor criminal or juvenile delinquency trials—actually take the form of an inquisition as opposed to an adversarial proceeding. Formal inquisitorial proceedings may incorporate some adversarial elements, if lawyers or witnesses aggressively challenge the judge or judges. But the basic differences between these models remain pronounced and consequential.

Basic Focus of the Law: Civil (Torts) Versus Criminal (Crimes)

If we go back to the early stages of recorded history, law, for the most part, took the form of **civil law** (Holmes 1881). That is, one party made a complaint of having been wronged in some way by another party, and the king or whoever administered justice would make a ruling on whether anything, which might include the life of the accused, was owed to the injured party. Civil law is that part of law that addresses private grievances. **Criminal law** is that part of law that addresses "public" offenses. Over time, especially during the Middle Ages, a growing list of harmful acts came to be defined as crimes against the "King's peace" and were ultimately prosecuted in the name of the state (Jeffery 1962). The state administers any punishment imposed on the wrongdoer, and the state collects any fine.

In a civil proceeding, one private party initiates a legal proceeding—say, for a divorce, for a contractual violation, or for compensation in the case of an accidental injury—against another private party. If the plaintiff's case is successful and there are monetary damages, then the award goes directly to the plaintiff. A crime, then, can be thought of as a violation against a person's right as a citizen to be secure in his or her person and property; a **tort** (a civil wrong) can be thought of as a purely private wrong against a person as an individual. But any such broad generalizations require some qualification, and the relationship between crimes and torts is not entirely clear-cut (Melone and Karnes 2003; Gross 1979).

Crimes are not necessarily more harmful or injurious than torts; indeed, some "crimes" (such as possession of small amounts of marijuana or picking pockets) cause minor harm. In contrast, some torts (such as negligence leading to another person's becoming a quadriplegic or the destruction of another person's reputation) cause immense harm.

Crimes are not necessarily intentional acts and torts unintentional; for example, corporations may be held strictly liable for environmental damage under criminal law even if there is no specific intent to do harm; the civil tort of maligning another person's reputation is typically intentional.

Crimes and torts are not necessarily mutually exclusive. In other words, the same harmful action—for example, driving an automobile while intoxicated, causing an accident and injury to another—may give rise to both a criminal prosecution and a civil lawsuit. Indeed, in any case where some party believes itself to have been harmed by another party, a civil lawsuit may be pursued, although not necessarily successfully. People rarely attempt to sue someone who has mugged them, perhaps mainly because even if the lawsuit is successful, there will be no assets to pay damages.

Wealthy offenders—corporations, professionals, or individuals—are often sued in conjunction with criminal prosecutions against them.

The penalties for some criminal convictions are quite minor—a small fine, probation, or some community service—whereas judgments in civil cases may be in the millions of dollars and can cause financial ruin. Finally, the status of an activity as a criminal matter or a civil matter may change over time. In the case of marijuana, some states have, in recent years, decriminalized possession of small amounts (relegating it to the civil law), whereas environmental harm (always potentially subject to civil action) has increasingly come to be defined as a matter of criminal law. In the final analysis, we should recognize that both "crime" and "tort" are social constructs.

The Basic Orientation of the Criminal Justice System: Crime Control Versus Due Process

What is law attempting to accomplish? On the one hand, achieving **crime control** is obviously a primary objective of the criminal justice system. On the other hand, in a democratic system (such as that of the United States), there is also concern with ensuring **due process**, or extending constitutional rights to those accused of crimes (Packer 1968; Roach 2003). Of course, the criminal justice system may have other important objectives as well, such as avenging wrongdoing, imposing just penalties, rehabilitating and reintegrating offenders, and reconciling offenders and victims, while overseeing appropriate restitution. Nevertheless, crime control and due process are commonly regarded as primary objectives, yet they are also inherently at odds with each other. If one's only objective is crime control, one empowers the criminal justice system to move quickly and ruthlessly against any and all suspected offenders. Such an approach, however, will inevitably sweep up many innocent parties as well and will violate the privacy and rights of any number of ordinary citizens. If one insists on adhering fully to all the due process guidelines, a certain proportion of guilty offenders will escape processing or punishment, although this approach is far less likely to compromise the rights of innocent parties. The challenge has always been to achieve the right balance between these objectives. In the 1960s, a series of landmark due process decisions by the U.S. Supreme Court (with Earl Warren as Chief Justice) had given significant momentum to the due process objective (Graham 1970). With the rising crime rate in the 1970s, and the resurgence of political conservatism into the 1980s, the crime-control objective achieved dominance (Beckett 1997). The impact of a declining conventional crime rate early in the twenty-first century remains to be seen.

The Content of the Criminal Law: Substantive Versus Procedural

One part of the criminal law prohibits certain behavior and identifies the penalties for engaging in such activity (Schubert 2004). This is the **substantive law** aspect of criminal law. For example, murder is prohibited, and those convicted of murder are liable for severe penalties. Rape, assault, burglary, larceny, auto theft, and arson are among the other conventional offenses prohibited by the substantive law. One enduring issue for substantive criminal law is this: What is the proper scope of the law? Controversies continually arise. For example, people who call themselves "pro-life" argue that substantive criminal law in the United States fails to include an activity that it should include: abortion. In contrast, many constituencies argue that the substantive criminal law presently includes many activities that it should not include, such as possession and use of marijuana.

The **procedural law** refers to that part of criminal law that governs procedures once an individual (or group) is suspected of a crime, apprehended, indicted, tried, or convicted (Israel, Kamisar, and LaFave 1993). Here, the principal controversies center on whether those accused of crimes have too many—or too few—rights at any of these stages. In the more conservative political environment of the final decades of the twentieth century, many challenges to the accused person's due process rights arose on different levels, and these challenges were often successful.

In a simplified view, the substantive criminal law is intended to protect citizens from those who would do them harm, and the procedural criminal law is intended to protect accused criminals from persecution by the state. However, the substantive criminal law—for example, as it relates to so-called victimless crimes—may be seen as an infringement on the rights of ordinary citizens. The procedural criminal law, meant to protect all of us (insofar as anyone could be mistakenly accused of a crime) has been used in totalitarian societies to empower the police to break down doors, arrest people at will, hold them indefinitely without formal charges, and so on. Accordingly, we should not confuse substantive and procedural criminal law by definition with their character in particular societies.

CONCLUSION

The preceding section, then, defines and distinguishes between a range of concepts essential to the understanding of law—particularly criminal law. Surely the form of reasoning adopted within any system of law is among the most basic elements of that system of law. In the section that follows, then, the matter of legal reasoning is addressed.

LEGAL REASONING

If one of the defining attributes of modern law is its commitment to rationality (as opposed to superstition), it follows that we expect legal decision making to be based on coherent, logical reasoning. Reasoning by analogy (finding connections between cases) and by deduction from rules (identifying conclusions that follow from valid premises) have been identified as two basic forms of legal reasoning (Burton 1985; Levi 1949; Sunstein 1996).

Legal decisions occur on many different levels and in many settings. Not only judges but also prosecutors, probation officers, and police officers may engage in some form of legal reasoning and decision making. In the following paragraphs, however, judges are the focus of attention. In American society, there is a general expectation that an important legal decision (such as that rendered by the U.S. Supreme Court) will be accompanied by some form of justification for the decision. Many lower-level legal decisions are so routine or straightforward that they are not seen as requiring elaborate justifications; in many such cases, a simple rule is cited or is shown to be implicit.

Legal reasoning can refer not only to justification but also to the psychology of choosing (Carter and Burke 2001). On one end of the spectrum, legal reasoning has been regarded as a purely intellectual exercise, akin to the application of mathematical logic to a problem. It follows from this view of legal reasoning that there is a single correct answer to a legal case, and if the appropriate legal principles are applied in an accurate way to a particular case, then the appropriate decision will be produced. At the other end of the spectrum, legal reasoning has been regarded as a purely subjective phenomenon, a product of social, psychological, or ideological influences (Lammon 2009). In this view, two judges who are looking at the same case may arrive at opposite conclusions, and no case has a single inevitable outcome (*see* Box 2.6).

In the **traditional view of legal reasoning**, then, judges apply the relevant law (L) to the relevant facts (F) and arrive at a decision (D) (i.e., $L + F \rightarrow D$). In the alternative, **modern view of legal reasoning** (or its extreme version), the judge is biased (for social, psychological, or ideological reasons) in favor of a particular decision and then selects legal rules and facts to justify that decision (i.e., $D \rightarrow L + F$) (Frank 1930). The first view has been associated with legal formalism and positivism, and the second with legal skepticism or realism and critical legal studies. Chapter 4 devotes more detailed attention to the schools of jurisprudence associated with these different views.

Appellate court justices and trial court judges render decisions that can have a profound impact both on individual lives and on social groups or even on society as a whole. They

---

BOX 2.6 LAW AND EMOTIONS

The claim that law is a rational enterprise has been mentioned at various points in this text, but emotions (e.g., disgust and shame, revenge and remorse, and love, forgiveness, and cowardice) can influence law and legal decision making (Bandes 1999; Polletta 2001). In many complex ways, an interplay between law and emotions often occurs. Legislators, judges, and lawyers can claim that their actions in relation to law are made independent of emotions, but such claims can be challenged. Chief Justice C. E. Hughes instructed a new justice, William O. Douglas, in this way: "At the constitutional level where we work, ninety percent of any decision is emotional. The rational part of us supplies the reasons for supporting our predilections" (Douglas 1980, p. 8). U.S. Supreme Court Justice Clarence Thomas introduced an emotional critique of "cross burning" into a case considering whether such a provocative act was protected under First Amendment speech rights (Lithwick 2002). This inspired considerable discussion: Was this an inappropriate personal intervention

in a case that should be determined by legal reasoning, or was this an appropriate acknowledgment that some legal questions cannot be resolved dispassionately? On the lower court level, legal matters ranging from sentencing decisions in cases of mass murder to the awarding of custody in divorce cases engage the most intensely experienced emotions. Emotions such as disgust have experienced a revival in law, according to some commentators (Nussbaum 2004). But disgust as a basis for lawmaking, or imposing sanctions, carries with it the danger that it will validate biases (e.g., against women, against homosexuals) and enhance the stigmatization of certain classes of people. Philosopher John Deigh (2008) views support for law as rooted in the emotional connection of children to parents and their acceptance of parental authority. But he distinguishes between the primitive emotions that can be triggered by experience and "tutored" emotions that take into account values and can be shaped by reason. In this account, emotion and reason are not necessarily and always at odds with each other.

are compelled to make decisions, typically choosing between competing options, and these decisions can be influenced by many factors. All justices, or judges, adopt or internalize a judicial philosophy that serves as one important basis for their decisions (*see* Table 2.4). Some judges have a specific, fully developed judicial philosophy that they identify in the context of their judicial opinions or in books and articles they write (*see* Box 2.7). Other judges may choose not to articulate a judicial philosophy and may even claim to have no such philosophy, deciding each case before them on its own merits, but this approach itself can be characterized as a perspective on how cases should be decided. Appellate court justices, in rendering their decisions, may look to what was done in the past, what is called for in the present case before them, and what impact their decision might have on society, law, and individual persons in the future. It is far from clear, on the basis of the evidence, that appellate court justices who are former judges are more likely to decide cases objectively and without bias than those justices that do not have this background (Liptak 2009a). Are some judges truly more objective than others? Whether judges themselves are deluded about the basis of their judging—that is, whether they really believe that they apply rules objectively and without bias—is a matter of dispute (Tamanaha 2009). Chief Justice John Roberts of the U.S. Supreme Court has characterized judges as "umpires" who apply rules but don't make them (Weber 2009), but this claim has been characterized as disingenuous. Federal Judge Richard Posner (2008), in *How Judges Think*, criticizes "legalism" or "legal formalism"— that is, the idea that judges rely on law and legal precedent only in deciding cases. Posner concedes that this may be true in routine cases but is not true in the more important, atypical cases. His book confirms what many academic students of judicial decision making have long claimed: judicial decision making is importantly influenced by politics, ideology, and strategic concerns. Altogether, for Posner, we need to recognize the very complex set of processes that enter into judicial decision making. The law school curriculum itself should be reformed to integrate more attention to the findings of the social sciences, to counterbalance the traditional bias of legal education in the direction of legal formalism.

Ronald Dworkin (2006), in *Judges in Robes*, argues that judges neither can nor should disregard their own values in making legal decisions but are obliged to work out their best estimate of which decision is most just and corresponds most fully with enduring principles that have been applied in earlier cases.

TABLE 2.4 THE BASIC TYPES OF JUDICIAL PHILOSOPHY AND THEIR CHARACTERISTICS

I. Judicial restraint
Originalism; strict construction
II. Judicial interpretation
Conceptualism; historical/referential
III. Judicial activism
Functionalism; pragmatism

BOX 2.7   JUSTICE WILLIAM O. DOUGLAS AS
A JUDICIAL ACTIVIST

William O. Douglas ([1898]–1980) served for more than 36 years on the U.S. Supreme Court, longer than any other justice in American history. He was appointed by Franklin Roosevelt in 1939 to succeed Justice Louis Brandeis, and he resigned in 1975, some time after suffering a debilitating stroke. Douglas was also one of the most controversial justices in the history of the Court, owing to his arch-liberal and libertarian views, his outspokenness, and his unconventional personal life (Murphy 2003; Simon 1980). He was an uncompromising defender of the First Amendment right to freedom of expression; he wrote for *Playboy* magazine; he was married four times (his last wife was 44 years his junior). Several attempts were made to impeach Douglas; all failed.

Douglas was a supremely American type: a rugged individualist, immensely energetic, strong-willed, stubborn, a demanding taskmaster, and a convivial companion. Although many justices have come from privileged circumstances, Douglas and his siblings were raised by their widowed mother in more modest circumstances. He rode the rails from his native Washington State to New York City to enroll at Columbia University Law School. Douglas was a self-made man who claimed throughout his life a strong empathy for humble people at the bottom of the social order. He also believed that judges who failed to engage fully with life became "dried husks." Douglas was a dedicated mountain climber and outdoorsman; he traveled widely, wrote numerous books, and spoke out on controversial matters.

Douglas was wholly committed to individual freedom and to social justice. Although Douglas (originally a law professor at Yale and then Commissioner of the Securities and Exchange Commission) was regarded as a legal genius by some of his peers, he was devoid of pedantry. His characterization of the purpose of the Constitution ("to keep the Government off the backs of people") is clear even to a young child.

Douglas has been described as an "anti-judge" because he was almost indifferent to precedent and judicial convention; he was result-oriented in his votes and written case opinions on the Court (Murphy 2003; White 1988). His decisions and case opinions were based on intuitions, as well as on a romantic affinity with the natural environment and his dedication to its preservation (Ray 1999). Douglas was an important participant in the landmark due process decisions of the Warren Court of the 1960s. He was an activist in every sense of the term, both on and off the bench.

Judges in contemporary times increasingly find themselves addressing complex issues requiring expert knowledge, so in many kinds of cases their decisions are influenced by the expertise provided by social, behavioral, biomedical, and physical scientists (English and Sales 2005). Some law professors are using sophisticated computer programs to analyze how legal decisions are made (Hayden 2009). Clearly the process of judicial decision making has many different dimensions.

CONSTITUTIONS AND CONSTITUTIONAL INTERPRETATION

Constitutions serve as a basic foundation for law in democratic societies. But constitutions, including the American Constitution, require interpretation. The adoption of the U.S. Constitution required many compromises (Berkin 2002; Purcell 2008). It is most commonly characterized in positive terms, providing the framework for the structure of our government and for individual liberties. The doctrine of **judicial review** (the review of laws passed by legislative bodies and executive branch entities on the basis of their constitutionality) allows for an ongoing dialogue on what the Constitution should really mean (Dorsen 2002; Seidman 2001). Prominent legal scholar Cass Sunstein (2001), in *Designing Democracy*, argued that constitutions ideally foster a "deliberative democracy" in which citizens are encouraged to seek a successful resolution of contentious issues. In one interpretation, the Founding Fathers also incorporated their imperial ambitions in the American Constitution, and from the outset harbored the ambition to build an American empire (Wilson 2002). The meaning of the Constitution evolved over time (Currie 2005; Magliocca 2007; McGinty 2008). Presidents Andrew Jackson and Abraham Lincoln adopted particular understandings of the Constitution and constitutional law that came to be very influential, with Congress also playing a role in the interpretation of the Constitution during the first half of the nineteenth century. The Constitution, and its judicial interpretation, serve as a constraint, in a democratic society, on pure rule by the majority (Eisgruber 2001). A critique of constitutionalism argues that these documents protect elite interests from democratic politics (Hirschl 2004). Law professor Sanford Levinson (2007) argues that the U.S. Constitution is fundamentally undemocratic and at odds with the needs of Americans in the early twenty-first century. Accordingly, a Constitutional Convention should be convened to produce a constitution that better reflects both the aspirations and the needs of contemporary Americans. The ultimate purpose of constitutions is certainly open to debate.

Many constitutional scholars (across the ideological spectrum) have adopted a "foundationalist" belief that it is possible to find one master key to interpreting the U.S. Constitution, or an "idealist" meaning to it. Other commentators argue that this is a futile endeavor, that justices must develop principles out of specific cases and engage in pragmatism and compromise in the interpretation of constitutional doctrine (Cooter 2000; Strauber 2002). Harvard law professor Laurence Tribe (2008) is a highly regarded constitutional law professor who in a recent book has argued that the text of the Constitution itself does not provide clear answers to many of the most fundamental issues that arise in relation to constitutional law. Jefferson Powell (2008) also argues that the most controversial legal issues do not have a single constitutionally defensible resolution but require humility and good faith on the part of judges who render constitutional opinions. Robert Spitzer (2008) argues that advocacy scholarship and sloppy scholarship by law professors addressing legal issues all-too-often distort constitutional meaning. This approach can be applied to environmental law, pornography, and flag-burning, among other contentious legal issues. Over time, Supreme Court justices have interpreted the Constitution in different ways (Shaman 2001). Because the Constitution could not anticipate changing circumstances, justices who produce "landmark" decisions on important issues play a key role in the production of a "living" constitution (Lipkin 2000). Judicial review of the Constitution has extended fundamental rights to certain people (e.g., women and minorities) not directly granted such rights by the Constitution itself (VanBurkleo, Hall, and Kaczorowski 2002). The Constitution, however, can be seen as empowering some parties to determine the rights of others (Aleinikoff 2002). For liberals, a "shadow Constitution" imposes an affirmative obligation on the government to alleviate inequality, protect citizens from harm by government officials, and extend broad rights to those accused of crimes. This constitutional vision has never been fully implemented.

In the more recent era, since the 1980s presidency of Ronald Reagan, the Supreme Court has adopted a constitutional philosophy with the guiding principle that the government is quite limited in the problems it can be expected to address (Tushnet 2003). The U.S. Supreme Court, early in the twenty-first century, was a generally conservative Court, especially on criminal justice issues (Belsky 2002; Maltz 2003; Schwartz 2002). But it was often divided (5-to-4) on issues, and many conservatives were unhappy with the Court's unwillingness to overturn the liberal decisions of an earlier era, especially those of the Warren Court (L. Greenhouse 2003b). However, at least some liberal decisions were overturned, and decisions on new issues often reflected a conservative ideology (Teles 2008). The Court's judgments were unlikely to fully satisfy any one political constituency.

Constitutional interpretation is dynamic, subject to changing circumstances and judicial personnel. And one should bear in mind that significant constitutional interpretation occurs in the state supreme courts as well, with important consequences for public policy (Langer 2002). Federal and state supreme courts influence social behavior of citizens on many different levels.

JUDICIAL RESTRAINT

In view of the importance of appellate court decisions, especially on constitutional questions, the judicial philosophies of U.S. Supreme Court justices have received much attention (Carter and Burke 2001; White 1976). First, there is **judicial restraint**, which is typically regarded as a conservative judicial philosophy. United States Supreme Court Chief Justice John Roberts claimed to be an adherent of judicial restraint during his confirmation hearing (Stolberg and Rosenbaum 2005). Adherents of this philosophy tend to hold the view that the Court is "the least democratic branch of [the federal] government" and should defer to the will of the people's elected representatives in the legislative branch. Accordingly, the justices should scrupulously avoid making new law and should restrict themselves to fairly narrow questions that may arise in cases brought before them. For example, did a defendant's actions violate or fail to violate a legislatively produced statute, according to the statute's specific language or the intentions of the legislative body that produced it? Is a legislatively produced statute in conflict with a constitutional clause or amendment?

On constitutional questions specifically, adherents of judicial restraint favor the position that a judge should not interpret or apply a constitutional provision in a manner that goes beyond the "original intent" of the framers or the specific language of the provision (Burgess 2001; Jaffa 1994; Lichter and Baltmanis 2009). An enduring debate has focused on the issue of whether the framers themselves meant for the Constitution to be read in this way; whether, even if they did, it is in fact possible to correctly identify a specific intent (indeed, exactly whose intent should count—that of the framers or that of the ratifiers of the Constitution?); and whether, in any case, it makes sense to attempt to apply constitutional provisions formulated in an earlier and very different time to circumstances in today's world.

The conservative approach called **originalism** locates constitutional authority in the meaning of the Constitution's provisions at the time of its authorship and enactment.

It is certainly difficult to reconcile one of the most widely respected twentieth century U.S. Supreme Court decisions, *Brown v. Board of Education* (which invalidated segregation), with an "originalist" reading of the Constitution, as some of the key drafters of that document owned slaves. In a parallel vein, the term **strict constructionism** refers to the position that the application of a law (or constitutional provision) must not go beyond the literal meaning of the wording of the law. But justices who claim to be adherents of such views appear to be less persuaded by arguments focusing on the text of a statute than by its consistency or inconsistency with their beliefs (Howard and Segal 2002). Ideology seems to play an important role here.

JUDICIAL INTERPRETATION

A second judicial philosophy, which can be called **judicial interpretation**, adheres to the view that justices should interpret the Constitution while remaining true to, and constrained by, an evolving tradition of such interpretation (some confusion on terms is possible here, as *interpretivism* has been used to describe the originalist position discussed previously). In this view, typically identified with those with a liberal or moderate outlook, justices should be respectful of the interpretations of constitutional concepts adopted by their judicial predecessors. The Constitution is viewed here less as a document than as an interpretive tradition rooted in a document. Perhaps the principal matter of controversy is the specific principles that should guide such interpretation. One version of judicial interpretation (historical/referential) stresses the historical evolution of public and judicial understanding of constitutional doctrine; another version (conceptualism) focuses on a valid and coherent notion of constitutional concepts, such as due process.

JUDICIAL ACTIVISM

A third judicial philosophy, known as **judicial activism**, has been most commonly associated with liberals but has also been adopted by justices with a conservative orientation. Adherents of this judicial philosophy believe that it is wholly appropriate for justices to declare law in accordance with the perceived needs of the times. Such justices essentially believe that constitutional doctrine should provide a fundamental point of departure for creating legal doctrine that is specifically responsive to the dominant values and practical necessities of the present. For Stanley Fish (2005), because texts cannot declare their own meaning, all judicial interpretation is "activist." The roots of judicial activism (or judicial power) have been traced to the eighteenth-century French social philosopher Montesquieu (Carrese 2003; Kirby 2004). A great expansion of judicial activism occurred in the late nineteenth and twentieth centuries, despite the apparent contradiction with a growing commitment to democratic principles.

The terms **functionalism** and **pragmatism** have been applied to the activist approach, with its stress on a currently useful interpretation. Any such judicial philosophy is bound to be controversial, and adherents of judicial activism have been bitterly attacked for arrogantly implementing their own value preferences and applying them to the rest of the citizenry (Powers and Rothman 2002). Critics of judicial activism claim that it occurs when judges or justices inappropriately allow their personal views on policy issues to affect their judgment. Judicial activism has also been defined in terms other than subjective and ideological, focusing simply on the extent to which justices have been willing to overturn legislative and executive branch action (Lindquist and Cross 2009). Conservative critics of judicial activism have charged that it has led to the extension of a broad range of rights (e.g., to prisoners) not supported by the Constitution or statutory law or has led to interpretations of policies (e.g., affirmative action) going beyond the intent of the legislative lawmakers (Ponnuru 2009; Rosen 2008). But conservative justices have also been activists in interpreting the Constitution in line with their ideological beliefs. Harvard Law School Dean Martha Minow (2005) has noted that it is misleading for conservatives to claim that liberal justices are activists when they protect individual rights but conservatives are not activists when they cut back on such rights. Conservative justices tend to characterize case opinions that they oppose as "activist" but can actively advance their own preferences in their case opinions (Lund and Kopel 2009). One study found that the more conservative U.S. Supreme Court justices in the recent era voted to overturn Congressional legislation significantly more often than did the more liberal justices; overturning the legislative actions of the duly elected representatives of the voters could be called the most activist choice for a justice (Gewirtz and Golder 2005).

PHILOSOPHY VERSUS ACTION

The association of a judicial philosophy with a particular political outlook has to be qualified here. Historically, conservatives have tended to interpret legal doctrine quite flexibly, or actively, when it has suited their purposes—for example, to extend more power to the executive branch, the police, and employers. Liberals have tended to read the Constitution quite strictly, or with restraint, when an amendment is in line with their beliefs—for example, the First Amendment stipulation that Congress shall make no law restricting freedom of speech. However, judicial restraint and judicial activism are not inherently conservative or liberal.

The Constitution contains both **rules** and **standards** (Sunstein 1996). The interpretation of rules (e.g., people younger than age 35 years cannot be President) has been quite straightforward and uncomplicated. It is the standards (e.g., equal protection of law or unreasonable search and seizure) that have given rise to an immense body of case law.

The application of standards (or principles) versus rules arises in other legal contexts as well. John Braithwaite (2002b) is a leading authority on regulation and has argued that precise rules work best for much that has to be regulated; but in the case of complex phenomena, principles deliver more consistency than rules. The lesson here is that one should recognize that different circumstances may call for different types of responses in relation to principles and rules (*see* Box 2.9).

Some appellate court justices choose to rule broadly, using the case before them to attempt to formulate general legal principles. In the final years of the twentieth century, the U.S. Supreme Court avoided broad, wide-ranging rulings; rather, it focused on deciding specific cases correctly. On the appellate level, **judicial review** is one of the most important functions of the court. The notion of "judicial review" originally referred to nothing more than the duty of judges to ensure that cases were decided in accord with the law, but in modern times it has increasingly become a basis for judges declaring new law (Hamburger 2008). United States Supreme Court opinions throughout the history of the Court have been found to be quite aligned with the views of the ruling regime during the time of the opinions

BOX 2.8   THE RISE OF THE CONSERVATIVE
MOVEMENT IN LAW

The Warren Court of the 1960s was widely regarded as an activist liberal court and famously issued a series of decisions relating
to the rights of the accused that were seen by many as protecting criminals during a period of rising crime rates. Over a period
of several decades, from the 1970s on, conservatives began
to organize a countermovement against the perceived liberal
dominance of the highest courts, and in the recent era there
is much evidence that they have been successful (Teles 2008).
Conservative entrepreneurs challenged the liberal legal network
on intellectual and political grounds and shifted from an allegiance to judicial restraint to promotion of an activist agenda to
promote a libertarian agenda and the restraint of government
intervention in a wide range of matters. These conservatives
specifically believe that individual economic rights are inviola-
ble, and they challenge the constitutionality of various government regulatory agencies (e.g., the Environmental Protection
Agency) and programs (e.g., Social Security) (Rosen 2005a).
Several conservative Republican presidents (Ronald Reagan and
both George Bushes) were able to appoint conservative justices
in large numbers to the U.S. Supreme Court as well as the federal courts. By 2008 conservative Republican judges were in the

majority on the federal appeals court (Savage 2009). Their decisions tended to favor corporations over regulators and plaintiffs,
and the government over various parties claiming discrimination or infringement of their rights. Harvard Law Professor Cass
Sunstein (2005) has characterized these judges as "Radicals in
Robes" in his book of that title. The controversial 2010 U.S.
Supreme Court decision in *Citizens United v. Federal Election
Commission*, which accords corporations much broader freedom
in funding political candidates, has been interpreted as a specifically activist conservative decision most likely to favor conservative Republican candidates and interests (Dworkin 2010).
It overruled both legislation such as the McCain-Feingold Act
and earlier decisions on the issues. Of course whether or not this
conservative judicial movement is something to be celebrated
or castigated is likely to be determined by commentators' own
ideological commitments.

President Barack Obama was quoted as favoring justices
who understand that "justice isn't about some abstract legal
theory or footnote in a casebook; it is also about how our laws
affect the daily realities of people's lives" (Rosen 2009a, p. 53). It
remains to be seen whether the judicial appointments made by
him during the course of his presidency will lead to a measurable
shift in the orientation of federal justices and judges.

(Power 2009). Interest groups have influenced Supreme Court decisions, through the filing
of *amicus curiae* ("friend of the court") briefs. There is also evidence that the U.S. Supreme
Court takes public opinion into account in its decision making and that court opinions that
are generally in line with public opinion tend to be more enduring than those that are not
(Marshall 2008). In *The Will of the People*, Barry Friedman (2010) argues that public opinion
is the principal determinant of Supreme Court decisions and that the justices' opinions
reflect the evolving views of the American public. If judicial review was originally intended
to offer a check on the popular will, in recent times it actually implements the majority view.
This author contends that the American people are collectively the highest court in the land.
But a critic of this claim argues that Supreme Court decisions are still quite often at odds
with prevailing public opinion and can still be shown to shape rather than simply reflect
the views of the American public (Driver 2010). For example, the Supreme Court ruled that
someone could not be executed for the crime of raping a child, although both the majority
of the American public and major political leaders didn't support this view. Altogether, U.S.
Supreme Court decisions reflect a complex mix of factors.

The nature of judicial opinions reflects both the professional legal culture and the political context of a particular time in history; the character of judicial opinions has evolved over
time to incorporate increasingly personal interpretations of judges (Popkin 2007). But for
one commentator, during the course of its long history, the U.S. Supreme Court has more
often than not ruled for the advantaged over the disadvantaged (LaMarche 2009). What is

BOX 2.9   FOREIGN LAW REFERRALS IN
AMERICAN COURT OPINIONS: AN
ONGOING CONTROVERSY

In recent years, some U.S. Supreme Court justices have cited foreign courts in their opinions, but this practice has been highly controversial and strongly opposed by other justices on the Court (Feldman 2008c; Finkelman 2007; Rivlin 2009). Foreign legal reasoning and judgments have been invoked in decisions striking down executions of juveniles, on gay rights, and affirmative action in university admissions, among other matters (Althouse 2005; Rivlin 2009). This approach, associated with liberal and centrist justices, has been designated as "comparativism" (Bazelon 2005). Rationales for the citation of foreign law judgments in American cases include the notion that it is efficient to learn from and draw on the reasoning of foreign justices who have worked through issues now appearing in American courts, they may provide new solutions to shared legal problems, and empirical data in such foreign case opinions may aid American justices (Finkelman 2007; Rivlin 2009). Justice Kennedy, who has invoked foreign law in his opinions, notes, "[W]hile not controlling our outcome, [foreign opinion] does provide respected and significant confirmation for our own conclusions" (Rivlin 2009, p. 6). Commentators who favor this approach note that the U.S. Supreme Court has a long history of citing foreign legal opinion, although ironically in the past it was often cited to justify restrictive and discriminatory policies (such as protecting bondage, taking land from Indians, suppressing certain religious practices, and expelling certain classes of immigrants), whereas today it is more often invoked to expand liberties and equal protection (Finkelman 2007). Conservative justices such as Scalia, Thomas, and Roberts claim that citation of foreign law is at odds with the "original intent" of the founders, is highly selective and subjective, and has no place in American legal opinions. They objected with special vehemence to the notion that an international court could instruct lower American courts on whether its procedures for addressing the rights of foreign nationals were acceptable or not, and on this issue they prevailed (Feldman 2009). Other critics suggest that invocation of foreign court opinions can compromise the supremacy of the U.S. Constitution and American popular sovereignty—ultimately, the judgment of the American people—on how important legal issues should be decided (Feldman 2008; Larsen 2009; Paulsen 2009). One commentator suggests that such citation is neither intrinsically good nor bad, but its appropriateness depends on how the law is cited and for what particular purpose (Rivlin 2009). The controversy on this issue is sure to continue.

In the past, judges in other countries have often cited U.S. Supreme Court opinions, but that practice seems to be waning at present (Liptak 2008d). The recently established European Court of Human Rights is more often cited today by foreign courts. The declining citation of the U.S. Supreme Court opinions has been attributed to the diminished reputation of the United States around the world, reaction against the rejection of foreign court influences by some American justices, and the perception that the court itself is too conservative (foreign courts tend to be more liberal). But it does seem that in an increasingly globalized, interconnected world, both American and foreign courts will have to be more attentive to each others' legal judgments and reasoning. Ultimately, the nature of the role of the United States in an evolving international legal order is at stake.

needed, in this view, is a Supreme Court that is empathetic toward those who are marginalized in society. Although the U.S. Supreme Court receives a great deal of attention, an argument can be made that the federal appellate courts have a greater impact on American law simply because so many more legal issues are addressed and resolved on that level (Cross 2007). Lower federal and state courts—not just the U.S. Supreme Court—contend with the challenge of correctly interpreting legislative and statutory laws (Cross 2009). In some cases that come before appellate court justices, they choose to rule narrowly on the specific issues arising in the case itself. In other cases the justices rule broadly, using the case before them to attempt to formulate general legal principles (Friedman 2009; Sunstein 2009a). It is a matter of ongoing controversy whether it is appropriate and constructive for the appellate courts to rule broadly on legal issues, especially when they are issues on which the public is quite divided.

Justices and judges make profoundly important decisions that affect the lives of many people, often in dramatic ways. Whether one gets better justices and judges through an appointive or an elective system has been a matter of historical debate, with each form of selection having both merits and drawbacks (Bybee 2007; Streb 2007). There is a broad consensus that there is much at stake in selecting the best possible people for judicial vacancies.

The lifetime tenure of U.S. Supreme Court (and federal appellate court) justices has been questioned (Greenhouse 2005). The original rationale was that it would ensure greater judicial independence. On the other hand, justices in the recent era have sometimes served into their 80s and longer (on average) than previous justices, and among other issues (including the onset of the infirmities of age) this does not allow for appropriate turnover in the membership of the Court and a perception that at least some aging justices are out of touch with the times.

STARE DECISIS AND THE RULE OF PRECEDENT

In the common law tradition, the doctrine of *stare decisis* (literally, "let the decision stand") has prevailed, and the rule of **precedent** has been adopted (Carter and Burke 2001; Gerhardt 2008; Llewellyn [1930] 1951). In their decisions in appellate court cases, then, judges look back to how other such cases were decided and seek guidance from these earlier rulings. Two principal rationales exist for this practice. First, if the courts rule as they did in the past in the same type of case, they achieve consistency. Such consistency would certainly seem to be one means of achieving justice—that is, the same type of case produces the same type of outcome. Second, such consistency should also more easily allow people to orient their conduct toward the law and should enhance respect for the law and the legal system. After all, if the courts constantly handed down decisions that contradicted earlier decisions, people would likely become both confused about and disillusioned with the law. In addition, the invocation of an earlier decision fulfills the goal of efficiency. If the same kinds of cases arise, with the same kinds of issues, the court does not have to go back to ground zero and painstakingly work its way through all these issues. Rather, once it has been determined that the case before the court fits into a particular category, the court can apply the reasoning and ruling of the earlier cases.

On the other hand, the doctrine of *stare decisis* has some definite drawbacks. First, and perhaps obviously, no two cases are truly identical. In relying on precedent, the court may not be sufficiently attentive to unique features of the present case (or defendant) and may accordingly impose an unjust, inequitable, or unfair decision in the present case. Second, the earlier decision itself may have been a bad or erroneous decision, and invoking it in a present case simply perpetuates injustice. More generally, social circumstances, values, and interests tend to change over time, so a decision that may have seemed appropriate in an earlier time may no longer be suitable or appropriate at the present time. In *Law and the Limits of Reason* Harvard Law Professor Adrian Vermeule (2009) argues that the courts, including the U.S. Supreme Court, play too central a role in American lawmaking. Their reliance on precedent serves as a constraint on needed changes in the law. The claim that American courts play a key role in "common law" countries is at odds, in this view, with the reality that the United States has increasingly moved away from the common law model and is dominated by legislatively produced statutes. Vermeule favors empowering Congress to enact statutes that would clearly define those parts of the Constitution that are ambiguous, rather than relying on the U.S. Supreme Court to interpret the Constitution.

A court of appeals is not bound by its own precedents, although in the interest of maintaining consistency and respect, courts have tended to be reluctant to overturn their earlier decisions. In one famous exception, in *Brown v. Board of Education* (1954), the U.S. Supreme Court ruled against segregation. In so doing it effectively overruled the precedent of *Plessy v. Ferguson* (1896), which had found no constitutional barrier to segregation. In 2003, the U.S. Supreme Court, in *Lawrence v. Texas*, overruled an earlier decision, *Bowers v. Hardwick* (1986), which had upheld the criminalizing of consensual sodomy. One of the justices in the majority in that earlier case later concluded that the Court had decided that case wrongly. But in a 1992 case, the Court rejected the position that a decision should be overruled merely because it was wrongly decided (Yoshino 2002). The Court identified four factors to be considered in connection with overruling an earlier decision: the workability of the rule, the extent to which the public had relied on the rule, relevant changes in legal doctrine, and changes in facts or perceptions of facts.

Although the more conservative justices of the early twenty-first century U.S. Supreme Court are not favorably disposed toward the Warren Court due process decisions of the 1960s, they have not specifically overruled them. Rather, in a series of decisions, the Court narrowed somewhat the scope of these decisions, recognizing various circumstances in which they do not apply. During his confirmation hearings for appointment as Chief Justice of the United States, John Roberts affirmed his commitment to the doctrine of precedent—including 32 years of precedent behind the controversial *Roe v. Wade* (1973) abortion decision—noting that it was a "jolt to the legal system" when a precedent was overturned (Toner 2005). But fairly early in his term as Chief Justice, Roberts was part of 5-to-4 majorities that overturned some significant precedents (Greenhouse 2007). Justifications for overturning a precedent include its alleged erosion over time through disuse, experience proving it has not worked, or confusion generated by the precedent. Courts sometimes overturn precedents without directly acknowledging that they are doing so. In the recent era, the U.S. Supreme Court has overturned many precedents (one or two a year).

United States Supreme Court justices throughout the history of the Court have mainly been guided by adherence to their own outlook rather than by unreflective adherence to the doctrine of *stare decisis* (Spaeth and Segal 1999; Spriggs and Hunford 2002). Some students of the U.S. Supreme Court focus on strategic considerations, or how individual decisions are influenced by the desire of justices to realize particular outcomes in cases (Brenner and Whitmeyer 2009). This understanding of judicial decision making is in line with a widely accepted "attitudinal" model of justices as policy makers (Bloom 2001). The **attitudinal model** is deemed incorrect when it dismisses the influence of precedent, but the invocation of precedent by the U.S. Supreme Court is complex. The U.S. Supreme Court's adherence to precedent is at least a part of its need to have its decisions viewed as legitimate by the American public, as well as those who specifically implement its rulings (Hansford and Spriggs 2006). When Supreme Court justices uphold a precedent, it does not necessarily mean that they personally agree with the precedent.

Lower courts within the jurisdiction of a higher court of appeals are in fact bound to uphold the precedent established by the higher court. As a practical matter, such courts may have some leeway in determining whether the present case raises issues resolved in an earlier appellate court decision. District court judges seem to be influenced by the policy preferences of the Supreme Court and tend to affirm or uphold lower court decisions consistent with those preferences as well as their own (Haire, Songer, and Linquist 2003; Klein and Hume 2003). Although ideology and a concern with avoiding reversal by the higher court play a role, other factors enter as well, such as efficiency and commitment to reaching sound legal judgments (Cohen 2002).

In their briefs setting forth their argument on one side or the other of a legal dispute, lawyers will also cite earlier cases in support of their argument. However, as the celebrated law professor Karl Llewellyn ([1930] 1951) demonstrated, the doctrine of *stare decisis* is "Janus-faced." If a previous decision is in line with the case a lawyer wants to make (a welcome precedent), then the lawyer will claim that the principle enunciated in the earlier case is also applicable to the present case, even if some factual differences exist between the two cases. On the other hand, if a lawyer finds that the ruling in an earlier case does not support the present case (an unwelcome precedent), then the lawyer will argue that the facts in the earlier case render it fundamentally different from the present case and that the precedent is not applicable. Clearly, then, some interpretive leeway exists in the application of precedents.

JUDICIAL DECISION MAKING AND INTERPRETATION, IN SUM

Judicial decision making is complex, and the influences on such decision making are often difficult to clearly identify (Duxbury 2001). Although judges are ordinarily regarded as obliged to apply rules, should they do so when the application of rules produces an unjust result in a particular case (Alexander and Sherwin 2001)? This is one of the dilemmas confronting judges. They must also contend with tensions between achieving fairness and efficiency (Cohen 2002). Justices must often contend with conflicts among liberty, equality, and democracy and between the rights of individuals and the rights of groups (Huscroft and Rishworth 2002). Owen Fiss (2003) and Charles Fried (2004), prominent law professors, have both argued in different ways that judges should be guided by reason. For Fiss, the principal obligation of judges is not to adjudicate disputes but to give meaning to the public values embodied in law.

CONCLUSION

Law is endlessly complex, because it has many different aspects, dimensions, and levels and its origins are explained in quite different ways. A basic assumption of this chapter holds that if people are to be literate about law, they must recognize and understand the many manifestations of law and implications of the various accounts of law. Whenever you encounter the term *law* or related terms such as *the rule of law* and *law and order*, you should attend to the context in which these terms are invoked. The *models* of law identified in this chapter should be helpful toward recognizing basic aspects of law.

Law in the Western tradition is intimately linked with a process of reasoning. An understanding of legal reasoning, then, is central to understanding law in contemporary society. Sociolegal scholarship has served as one source of challenge to the notion that judges operate as some type of "legal scientists," objectively and dispassionately applying law to cases. In an alternative reading, judges make decisions reflecting the various social and psychological influences to which they have been exposed or the beliefs and policy preferences they hold. In a more moderate view, legal reasoning combines objective and subjective dimensions, insofar as judges are strongly constrained by traditions and peer pressures from within the legal system but also are responding to other, external influences. It is important to recognize, as well, that no consensus exists on whether one gets better justice if judges are simply expected to apply the law logically and objectively or if they are expected to apply some discretionary judgment based on their own experience and knowledge. Some of the implications of this last point are explored in Chapters 3 and 4.

KEY TERMS AND CONCEPTS

adversarial model	human rights law	negotiation
attitudinal model	ideal type	originalism
bargain model	inquisitorial model	positive law
case law	international tribunals	precedent
civil law	judicial activism	procedural law
court model	judicial interpretation	social norms
crime	judicial restraint	*stare decisis*
crime control	judicial review	statutory law
criminal law	legal reasoning	strict constructionism
dual structure	microlaw	substantive law
due process	models of law	tort
Eurolaw	modern view of legal reasoning	traditional view of legal reasoning
hierarchical power	natural law	transnational law
horizontal power	natural law theory	unitary structure

DISCUSSION QUESTIONS

1. What are the basic limitations of universal law, international law, and regional law?
2. Why is it that the repercussions associated with violating occupational laws can at times be worse than the penalties that might result from a conventional criminal offense?
3. When specific events occur on college campuses (e.g., date rape), is it best for the situation to be handled internally? Why or why not? Who would tend to benefit the most in a college campus date rape incident that was resolved by the college disciplinary board?
4. Compare and contrast the adversarial model of court procedure to the inquisitorial model. Is one procedure more fair than the other? Explain.
5. Explain how both judicial philosophies and the doctrine of *stare decisis* are a reflection of, or application of, partisan and instrumental purposes.

CHAPTER 3

LAW, JUSTICE, AND THE MORAL ORDER

You live in a world where you are constantly confronted by choices. You must make choices in relation to law, and law itself reflects choices of some values over others. Law co-exists with, and is interrelated with, other systems of values. It is a common assumption that law is linked with justice, but the specific character of the relationship between law and justice is not simple; it is explored in the first section of this chapter. Many people also see law as intertwined with morality. The second section of this chapter examines the relationship of morality to law. Also, at least some part of the American legal code has important points of origin with religion, so the third section of this chapter considers some of the ways in which religion has either influenced or been in conflict with law. Finally, law is also interrelated with and shaped by considerations independent of justice, morality, and religion. These considerations are here classified under the term *interests* and include everything from facilitating safe movement of automobile traffic to the promotion of efficient business practices. A brief final section of this chapter discusses such interests in relation to law.

JUSTICE AND LAW

The terms *law* and *justice* are sometimes used interchangeably. We speak of the legal system and the justice system, of the rule of law and the principles of justice, of issues of law and of justice. "Law," then, is sometimes treated as a synonym for "justice."

Alternatively, law may be considered an instrument either for achieving justice or for subverting justice. But law and justice have also been seen as independent of each other.

The great Associate Justice of the U.S. Supreme Court, Oliver Wendell Holmes, Jr., has been quoted as responding to a plea to "Do justice" by stating, "That is not my job. It is my job to apply the law" (Bork 1990, p. 6). What is lawful has not always been in accord with what is just. The death sentence imposed on Socrates in ancient Athens may have been lawful, but it was not necessarily just. Socrates was indicted, tried, and condemned to death by a jury of his peers because they believed that his teaching was corrupting the city's youth. Although Socrates regarded the verdict as unjust, he refused an opportunity to escape because the verdict was lawful and one is ethically obliged to comply with law. He believed that society was harmed when people disobeyed the law (Harris 2006; Parsons 1998, p. 184). We can probably all think of contemporary examples where the lawful and the just failed to coincide. Civil rights protesters in the South in the early 1960s were jailed for violating laws supporting racial segregation; the jailing may have been legal, but few today would argue that it was just. The relationship between law and justice is complex. Some of the questions posed about the relationship are as follows:

> Do we believe the law good because it is just, or is it just because we think it is good? To what degree or under what circumstances should the law be judged by a standard external to the community that creates it? To what degree is our understanding of justice determined by the laws under which we live? Is there a body of laws, a way of life regulated by law, that is simply the most just? Are there certain universal requirements that any tolerably just law or constitution must follow? (Rubin 1997, p. vii)

The challenge of arriving at a wholly satisfactory definition of justice is considerable. Edmond Cahn, a law professor at Columbia University for many years, adopted a creative approach to this challenge. In *The Sense of Injustice*, Cahn (1949) began with the observation that if justice is the ultimate end of law, we should recognize that the ultimate meaning of justice is also beyond our reach. It may then be useful to think of justice as an active process of remedying or preventing what would create a sense of injustice. Cahn thus lays out the following criteria for avoiding the creation of a sense of injustice: First, inequalities of law, where they exist, must make sense; second, law must give people what they deserve; third, law must operate in a manner consistent with maximizing human dignity; fourth, procedural proprieties must be exercised when law is implemented; fifth, governmental powers must not be exceeded; and sixth, insofar as society experiences changing needs over time, the sense of injustice must also necessarily vary over time and space.

Cahn's general criteria are certainly helpful, but they leave us with many difficult issues to resolve. Examples are questions like the following: Is the requirement that welfare mothers accept job assignments or lose their benefits just or not? Do people who commit murder deserve the death penalty? Are strip searches necessary security procedures or an affront to human dignity?

To add to the difficulty of definition, the sense of injustice is not experienced uniformly, and in the same circumstance, one individual may believe the legal system has achieved justice and another, injustice (*see* Box 3.1). Ultimately, justice and the absence of justice is experienced subjectively (Lazar 2007).

The desire to see justice realized seems in some sense to be universal. Some scientists (naturalists) suggest that there is evidence of a biological (or evolutionary) basis for the desire for justice (Masters 1990). In one traditional view, humans are naturally selfish, aggressive, solitary, and competitive; but in an alternative view, humans have evolved to be predisposed toward empathy and mutual care toward others (O'Manique 2002). The great nineteenth-century novelist Charles Dickens, in *Great Expectations*, noted that in the world of little children, nothing is as finely felt as a sense of *in*justice (Sen 2009).

BOX 3.1   JUSTICE DEFINED

"...[J]ustice is equality."
—Socrates, in Plato's *Gorgias*

"This...is what the just is—the proportional; the unjust is what violates the proportion."
—Aristotle, *Ethics*

"There is no more ridiculous opinion than to believe that all customs and laws of nations are inherently just."
—Cicero, *Laws*

"Revenge is a kind of wild justice; which the more man's nature runs to, the more ought law to weed it out."
—Bacon, *Of Revenge*

"...[W]hen a covenant is made, then to break it is unjust; and the definition of injustice is no other than the not performance of a covenant. And whatsoever is not unjust is just."
—Hobbes, *Leviathan*

"Under a government which imprisons any unjustly, the true place for a just man is also prison."
—Thoreau, *Civil Disobedience*

"Perhaps we shall even find that when talking about justice, the quality we have to mind is charity."
—Cardozo, *The Growth of Law*

"To take appropriate measures in order to avert injustice even toward a member of a despised group is to enforce justice."
—Felix Frankfurter, *Dennis v. U.S.* (1950)

"There is no such thing as justice—in or out of court."
—Clarence Darrow, *Interview*, 1936

"One receives only imperfect justice in this world: only fools, children, left-wing Democrats, social scientists, and a few demented judges expect anything better."
—Walter F. Murphy, *The Vicar of Christ*

Sources: Socrates, Aristotle, Cicero, Bacon, Hobbes, and Thoreau from Adler and Van Doren 1977. Cardozo, Darrow, Murphy, and Frankfurter from Shapiro 1993.

Social psychological study has provided us with the notion that people want to believe they live in a **just world,** where all get their just deserts (Lerner and Lerner 1981). The just world concept has provided a point of departure for much research, exploring how such a belief influences people's behavior in a wide range of circumstances (Ross and Miller 2002). Cross-cultural studies undertaken by anthropologists find that people attempt to settle disputes justly (Nader and Todd 1978). Of course, the specific content of just deserts and justly settled disputes varies among individuals, groups, and whole cultures. Is probation, imprisonment, or the amputation of a hand the just penalty for theft? Is a person who has been crippled through the negligent actions of another entitled to $10,000, $100,000, or $1 million? Is a homemaker wife entitled to half the wealth of a successful entrepreneurial husband she is divorcing or less?

The specific content of an individual's sense of justice may have various sources. In developmental psychology, as pioneered by Jean Piaget (1932) and Lawrence Kohlberg (1981), moral development (and an attendant sense of justice) is a matter of logically ordered sequences of cognitive development. In the earliest stages of life, human beings have a "premoral" orientation, where what is good is equated with pleasure and what is bad is equated with pain. As young children experience the socialization process, they are likely to acquire a conventional orientation, where moral evaluations are guided by what is approved of and disapproved of by one's most important reference group. Only a minority of individuals move on to a "principled" orientation, where moral evaluations are based on some coherent philosophical perspective on the proper grounds for morality and justice. Developmental psychology, accordingly, provides us with one way of understanding the basis of our sense of justice, although Harvard psychologist Carol Gilligan (1982), in her book *In a Different Voice*, criticized the Kohlberg interpretation as based only on studies of males. Gilligan made a case for the view that females tend to use a different form of moral reasoning from that favored by males.

Over a period of thousands of years, philosophers have set forth conceptions of justice. Several different such conceptions can be briefly identified (*see* Table 3.1). First, there is an **intuitionist conception of justice**. The eighteenth-century German philosopher Immanuel Kant ([1785] 1998) advanced the view that people know justice, or the good, *a priori* (before experience). His **categorical imperative** is a test of the good, or just; it calls for acting on such principles as you would want to be adopted as universal law, or acting as you would have all others act.

The late-eighteenth-century British philosopher Jeremy Bentham ([1789] 1970) is associated with a **utilitarian**, or pragmatic, **conception of justice**. In this view, people determine what is good, or just, by a calculus: Does the action in question serve the greatest good or benefit the largest number?

A late-twentieth-century American philosopher, John Rawls (1971; 2001), is especially associated with a **contractual conception of justice**. The guiding principle here is the equation of justice with fairness. Justice is achieved by implementing rules in society to maximize fairness. The question we must ask about the governing rules of society is this: If we were in the original position of not knowing, from behind a "veil of ignorance," whether we would end up among the advantaged or disadvantaged, what rules would we choose?

Finally, the nineteenth-century social philosopher Karl Marx ([1867] 1962) advanced an **egalitarian conception of justice** that at least implicitly equates justice with equality. A contemporary American philosopher, Jeffrey Reiman (1990), has derived from the Marxist conception the following principle for evaluating justice within a society: conditions under which humans are not subjugated. For Marx, in one common interpretation, the rhetoric of justice and rights is an artifact of a capitalist society and irrelevant to a truly communist society (Buchanan 1982). In this sense, a society that has eliminated the conditions producing socioeconomic inequality is inherently just.

When the notion of justice is invoked in relation to law, we must recognize that different conceptions of justice may be involved (Feinberg and Gross 1977; Grana 2010). At different times and places, different conceptions of justice have tended to be dominant. What was regarded as just in the Middle Ages is unlikely to be regarded as just today, and the standards of justice in some other country (e.g., North Korea) might be seen as very much at odds with ours. Even within one society, lawmakers and judges vary in their specific conceptions of justice. Law professor Robin West (2003) called for embracing a vision

TABLE 3.1   PHILOSOPHICAL CONCEPTS OF JUSTICE

Intuitive	Known *a priori*; universal principle
Utilitarian	Practical calculus; greatest good
Contractual	By agreement; as fairness
Egalitarian	Organization of society; as equality

of justice through law, putting less emphasis on freedom and more on a broader concern for humanity.

Although discussions of justice tend to be most readily associated with theologians, philosophers, and judges, ordinary members of society also form ideas of justice and are concerned to see justice realized. The concept of "unfairness" is a familiar one in relation to perceptions of justice and injustice, but this concept has meant different things in different historical, religious, legal, and psychological contexts (Chew 2001; Christodoulidis and Veitch 2001; Finkel 2001). Justice and fairness may also have a different meaning to men and women.

Some current research has shown that people's judgments about justice influence their attitudes and behavior toward others on such matters as accepting decisions of others, helping a group of others, and their willingness to support authority figures (Tyler 2007; Tyler and Huo 2002). This social justice research suggests that people's beliefs and attitudes may be more influenced by a sense of justice than by pure self-interest, and people will support just policies or processes even if they do not directly benefit from them. Furthermore, when people are in a position to render actual verdicts in cases, they may be guided more by their sense of justice than by the formal requirements of the law (Robinson and Darley 1995, p. 212). The concept of **jury nullification** refers specifically to a circumstance in which a trial jury returns a verdict that it believes to be just, even if the verdict is arrived at through reasoning at odds with what is called for by the formal law. Paul Robinson (1999) recounted the details of a series of cases that pose such questions as the following: Does law punish having a guilty mind? Can committing a crime be doing the right thing? Are we responsible for who we are? Such questions—and the cases in which they arise—bring into especially sharp relief some of the fundamental inconsistencies in the law's assignment of responsibility and imposition of punishment, and the "gap" that sometimes emerges between following the law and doing justice.

Scholars have identified principles of justice applicable to the resolution of legal cases (*see* Table 3.2) (Dreisbach 2009; Sanders and Hamilton 2001). First, **commutative principle of justice** (or legalistic, corrective, and restitutive) criteria can be adopted. This formula calls for restoring "balance" following some wrongdoing or making redress in accordance with formal entitlement. Second, **distributive principle of justice** (or primary, moralistic, and equitable) criteria can be adopted. This formula calls for resolution through proportional merit or in accordance with a moral calculus. Third, **retributive principle of justice** criteria can be adopted. This formula calls for resolution through the imposition of suffering on those who have done harm.

To illustrate the differences among different conceptions of justice, we can consider examples in the form of a criminal case and a civil case. First, in a case of white collar crime

TABLE 3.2 APPLIED CONCEPTS OF JUSTICE

Commutative	Formal, legal entitlement
Distributive	Equal division
Retributive	In relation to blame or fault

(e.g., fraud), a commutative resolution would emphasize making restitution to the victim or victims; a distributive resolution would settle the case according to who could best afford the losses; and a retributive resolution would impose punitive damages on the offender. Second, in a case of property division arising out of a divorce case, a commutative resolution would assign property in terms of formal ownership (traditionally favoring husbands); a distributive resolution would adopt the "community property" standard and would divide marital assets equally; and a retributive resolution would compensate the wronged party with a larger share of property. Of course, in many cases the resolution may combine, in varying degrees, these different criteria for resolution. Historically, the legal profession has been biased in favor of commutative criteria for the resolution of cases, but other social forces (the public or special interest groups) have succeeded in promoting legal reforms based on other criteria of justice.

INDIVIDUAL JUSTICE AND SOCIAL JUSTICE

The distinction between individual justice and social justice is clear, at least conceptually. If society is to implement **individual justice**, it must ensure that individuals receive what they are entitled to, merit, or deserve. To implement **social justice**, society must ensure that groups receive what they are entitled to, merit, or deserve, or that the general social welfare is advanced. Historically, legal justice has been defined in terms of doing justice in specific cases and ensuring justice for the individual parties in these cases. Can legal justice be differentiated from social justice (Sadurski 1984; Sanders and Hamilton 2001)? Some argue that true legal justice is inseparable from social justice and not independent of it. Others hold that legal justice only pertains to the individual case at hand and must be separated from issues of social justice. In particular cases, it is sometimes difficult to reconcile individual with social justice.

The policy of **affirmative action** brings the conflict between individual and social justice into sharp relief (Shuck 2007; Skedsvold and Mann 1996; Sterba 2009). Affirmative action policies have as their principal rationale the advancement of social justice. By making certain concessions to increase the representation of traditionally disadvantaged groups (e.g., women, African Americans), society is addressing historical injustices and benefiting all its members by diversifying various professions and enterprises. If the policy facilitates the admission of African Americans to law school or to the police force, the society is atoning for their past exclusion, compensating them for possible disadvantages caused by racism and discrimination, and providing itself with more African-American lawyers and police officers, who are likely to work for underserviced communities or provide more empathetic law enforcers.

Hiring more female professors or business executives can fulfill similar purposes. Because women have been discriminated against historically, they may face some enduring disadvantages in the socialization process; also, they are much-needed role models for female students and business employees.

Society as a whole may be said to benefit from affirmative action policies. But it should be obvious that injustice is done to individual White males who are accordingly excluded from admissions or positions, despite their superior formal qualifications. It could be said that these White males are expected to pay the price for past practices in which they had no part and for future social benefits that may exclude them. There is no formula that can ensure maximizing both individual and social justice in all cases, and the proper balance between these objectives is always going to be somewhat contentious. For much of American history, however, White males have benefited from a form of affirmative action; custom had long excluded African Americans and women from even competing for many opportunities (e.g., joining professional athletic teams or entering a university). Also, in many cases, special connections (e.g., an alumnus parent or father who is the boss)—rather than talent and aptitude—gained White men admission to programs and career opportunities. In the recent era, however, a significant backlash to affirmative action has developed in America. This topic is discussed more fully in Chapter 10.

In a democratic society such as the United States, an inherent conflict exists about whether the rights of individuals or the needs of the community should be given precedence (Selznick 1992; Wellman 1995). **Libertarians** are associated with the position that individual rights (and freedom) must be preserved above all other objectives (Nozick 1974). **Socialists** are identified with the view that choices must promote a humane, egalitarian community over the rights of individuals (Harrington 1973). In the more recent era, **communitarians** have argued that the challenge today is to achieve a better balance between individual rights on the one hand and duties to the community, or society, on the other hand (Elshtain 1995; Van Seters 2007). Accordingly, Americans are likely to engage in an ongoing debate over which specific allocation of rights and duties produces a truly just society.

PROCEDURAL JUSTICE AND SUBSTANTIVE JUSTICE

Procedural justice refers to achieving fairness in the legal procedure (Sadurski 1984; Sanders and Hamilton 2001). **Substantive justice** refers to achieving a correct or appropriate outcome in a legal case. Obviously, one hopes that fair procedures will result in appropriate outcomes, but this is far from guaranteed. In our system of law, procedural fairness is especially associated with the notion that the accused, or the defendant, should enjoy the fullest measure of due process and have every opportunity to raise a reasonable doubt or challenge evidence. In the American system, the appropriate outcome should be one consistent with truth, imposing deserved sanctions on wrongdoers and providing satisfaction or resolution for authentic victims, while also protecting or appropriately compensating the larger community.

Supporters (typically conservatives) of a crime control model have held that the more emphasis the system puts on ensuring procedural fairness (for the accused and defendants), the less likely it is to achieve substantive justice for authentic victims and society (Uviller 1999). In recent decades, the U.S. Supreme Court and other appellate courts have issued opinions that, on balance, have strengthened the hand of prosecutors and sent record numbers of people to prison (*see* Box 3.2).

The debate over the **exclusionary rule** highlights this fairness dilemma (Siegel 2009, pp. 231–232). This rule requires the exclusion of improperly (or illegally) obtained evidence

BOX 3.2 CRIMINAL JUSTICE, CRIMINAL INJUSTICE, AND CASES OF ALLEGED SEXUAL MISCONDUCT

If it is one of the core purposes of the criminal justice system to administer justice, then there is a long history of criminal trials that result in *injustice* (Harris 2006). The revelation of large numbers of wrongful convictions in American criminal cases can be taken to demonstrate fundamental, organic problems with the criminal justice system itself, rather than inevitable but isolated errors (Ogletree and Sarat 2009). An endless range of ethical questions arise in relation to the broad operation of the criminal justice system: Which policies and practices advance, and which subvert, the pursuit of justice (Kleinig 2008)? Countless odd or disturbing cases could be considered. As one example, in 2007 a man who shot and partially paralyzed a police officer in 1966 (and served some 20 years in prison for the crime) was charged with murder when the officer died from an infection said to be related to the shooting (Urbina 2007b). A question was raised here on whether justice was properly realized by charging someone with a death that occurred more than 40 years after the crime in question.

Although injustices can arise in connection with the whole range of criminal cases, here attention is directed at alleged injustices that arise in cases involving sex-related charges, with unusual or atypical dimensions to them. In a high-profile case in 2006, three White male Duke University students, members of its LaCrosse team, were formally accused of sexually assaulting a young African-American woman who had been hired to perform a striptease at a team party (Seigel 2009). A "race to injustice" occurred, as it emerged that the charges were clearly false and the prosecutor had engaged in clear-cut misconduct in pursuing the charges. This case brought into especially sharp relief a whole range of complex criminal justice issues. But certainly one dimension of it was an attempt to overcompensate for indisputable historical injustices to African-Americans through uncritical acceptance of the accuser's story and unwarranted assumptions of the guilt of privileged White males. That historically underprivileged African-American males have been and continue to be far more often victims of injustice in cases involving sexual assault allegations is indisputable.

Few forms of crime are more widely reviled than sexual predation directed at minors and trafficking in child pornography. Harsh sanctions are directed at those who engage in these forms of crime. Accordingly, claims that such offenders may themselves be treated unjustly are somewhat surprising (Zilney and Zilney 2009). A popular NBC investigative television show, "To Catch a Predator," involved confronting men trolling the Internet to connect with and arrange meetings with teenagers for sex (Stelter 2007). Some critics claimed that the show was engaged in entrapment and led to ruined lives, even suicide. The men arrested often had no criminal record and were typically granted probation by the courts. And an increasing number of judges have now questioned guidelines calling for long prison sentences (in the range of 20 years) for those who download child pornography but have no record of inappropriate conduct with children, no past record of criminal behavior, who express remorse, and who are evaluated as low risks for re-offending (Hansen 2009; Sulzberger 2010). The guidelines treat such offenders with a severity equivalent to that directed at murderers, rapists, and child molesters. The possession of even a single image of child porn is punishable by up to 10 years in prison. More than 80% of those charged with this offense had no prior felonies of any kind (including any involving children; only a small minority of those charged—about 5%—had engaged in the production of child porn) (Hansen 2009). In many cases, those who are caught committing the offense of downloading child porn are naive about the possible penalties for doing so. Those who support the harsh penalties for this offense argue that such downloading contributes to severe harm to children who are exploited for this purpose.

---

from a trial; if such evidence has been used to obtain a conviction, then the conviction must be overturned. An example of improperly obtained evidence could be a confession secured without providing the accused with a recital of his or her rights as a suspect (a *Miranda* warning) or physical evidence seized without a proper search warrant. The rationale for the exclusionary rule is that criminal justice personnel should fully adhere to the requirements of the law in making cases against criminal suspects. Inevitably, many people will experience a sense of outrage if an obviously guilty criminal obtains a reversal of conviction on the basis of the exclusionary rule and ends up avoiding punishment. This happens rarely. Nevertheless, the argument is made that the exclusionary rule, in the name of procedural justice, subverts or blocks the realization of substantive justice. On the other hand, if one wants to absolutely minimize the chances that the guilty will escape justice, then one is likely to compromise standards of procedural justice.

It is difficult, then, to develop in practice a balance between attention to procedural justice and substantive justice that will satisfy all. According to Garth and Sarat (1998a, p. 1), scholars who have focused on the relation between law and society have shifted their attention in the recent past to procedural justice, from an earlier concern with substantive justice. For example, an earlier generation of scholars had focused more on such matters as the complicity of law in producing poverty and segregation; subsequently, more scholars studied unfair legal procedures, such as denying bail or allowing the introduction of tainted evidence. A primary focus on substantive justice may well be coming back, however. In the recent past, the inequities between the principles underlying procedural law and actual practices were especially glaring (e.g., illegal searches, lack of counsel, coerced confessions), but since the time of the Warren Supreme Court of the 1960s, case law has made some progress in addressing these inequities. Perhaps relatively less progress has been made in addressing many of the substantive inequities that still separate the privileged and the underprivileged.

JUSTICE AND THE CRIMINAL JUSTICE SYSTEM

The realization of justice is a key objective—arguably, the principal formal objective—of the criminal justice system (Dubber 2006a). Much controversy exists over how this objective could be best realized (Beckett 1997; Dreisbach 2009; Shelden and Brown 2003). Do we need more laws, or fewer, to achieve justice? Do we rely more on law as a formal means of social control or on alternative, informal means of social control? With regard to the police, do we need strict controls on their activities or should we extend broad discretion to them? In the courts, do we get better justice when we rely on judges or on juries? Is it better to impose sentencing guidelines on judges or to give them a broad measure of discretion? Is justice more likely to come out of plea bargaining (when defendants waive their right to trial and plead guilty to a charge in return for some form of leniency) or out of a formal trial? And when we have trials, do we get closer to just outcomes when we have an adversarial model, involving a contest between the prosecution and the defense, or an inquisitorial model, involving an inquiry by a judge or panel of judges? Finally, in the realm of the corrections system, is justice accomplished when the system is based on retribution, incapacitation, and deterrence or when it is based on rehabilitation and restitution (*See* Box 3.3). Punishment in some form is a universal feature of human societies, but justifications for punishing people have varied over time and between different cultures, and arguments for the inherent irrationality or injustice of punishment are put forth by some contemporary philosophers (Smith 2008; Zaibert 2006). A recent study found that people typically favor the realization of multiple goals—and not simply the punishment of offenders—in response to findings of wrongdoing (Gromet and Darley 2009). A celebrated supporter of capital punishment, Ernest van den Haag, argued that unequal justice is preferable to equal justice—that is, society should privilege unequal application of deserved punishments (unequal justice) to abandoning deserved punishment and just deserts for

BOX 3.3 RESTORATIVE JUSTICE

In recent years **restorative justice** has been quite widely promoted as an alternative to traditional models of criminal justice that have focused primarily on punishing, incapacitating, and deterring criminal offenders. Calls for the use of restorative justice in international criminal law cases have been put forth (Combs 2007). This approach focuses more on addressing harm done to victims and communities, calling on offenders to assume responsibility for their actions, and seeking ways to both "repair" the harm done and reintegrate the offender back into the community (Braithwaite 2002a; Olson and Dzur 2004; Sullivan and Tifft 2001). Restorative justice is a form of informal justice, which requires participation from the offender, the victim, and the community toward the resolution of the harm done in a constructive way, with reconciliation and closure as ultimate goals. It remains to be seen whether the restorative justice approach will replace traditional approaches to the administration of justice, including retaliatory justice.

heinous offenders (equal injustice) (Laufer and Hsieh 2003). This position can be applied in some form to a range of criminal justice issues, including racial profiling.

The questions posed in the preceding paragraph constitute ongoing controversies about, and within, the criminal justice system. This system contends with many tensions and conflicts: justice for the victim versus justice for the perpetrator; justice for the accused versus justice for society; individualized justice versus uniform justice; and so on. It is in the operation of the criminal justice system that we can witness the inevitable dilemmas surrounding issues of justice in especially sharp relief.

LAW, VIOLENCE, AND JUSTICE

The meaning of justice is inevitably influenced by the political context. To put this more directly, those in power have a disproportionate say in how justice is defined. The state declares its own violence as necessary to ensure order and justice and considers the violence of individuals and anti-state groups criminal. However, throughout history, revolutionary and anti-state violence has often been carried out in the name of achieving justice (Coblentz 1970). Such violence includes the acts of American revolutionaries, vigilantes, early labor unionists, and oppressed racial minorities.

The idea of challenging unjust institutions can be traced far back in America's political history. The English philosopher John Locke ([1690] 1965), who greatly influenced the Founding Fathers, held that in a democratic society, people had the right to alter or abolish institutions found to be detrimental to justice. The twentieth-century philosopher Herbert Marcuse (1966) argued that revolutionary violence was really a form of counterviolence carried out against the existing violence of the state. The Algerian psychiatrist Frantz Fanon (1968), in *The Wretched of the Earth*, advocated violence in the struggle against colonial oppressors as necessary both to overthrow the oppressors and to liberate the oppressed (through a cathartic release from their experience); this thesis was endorsed by the French existentialist philosopher Jean-Paul Sartre (1968). Some of the radicals and African-American militants of the 1960s era called for violence against the state in the name of realizing justice (Gitlin 1987).

Political assassinations have long been justified as a form of **alternative justice** (Ben-Yehuda 1997). In the present era, terrorism is a particular concern, but terrorism too has typically been justified as a necessary response to existing injustice and as a necessary means to achieve authentic justice (Oliverio 1997). The 9/11 attack on America, as well as the subsequent American actions in response (e.g., invading Afghanistan), were forms of violence carried out in the name of someone's conception of justice (Calhoun, Price, and Timmer 2002). And even conventional lawbreaking, including homicide and assault, is at least sometimes driven by a moralistic impulse, aimed at avenging some injustice or pursuing some notion of justice (Black 1983).

The call for vengeance is less widely supported today than it was in the past, but the ancient desire to avenge wrongdoing is hardly extinct (Jacoby 1983). If the state is seen as failing to avenge some wrongdoing, then groups or individuals may take this form of pursuing justice into their own hands. Altogether, the relationships among law, violence, and justice are more complex than sometimes portrayed (*see* Box 3.4).

This issue arose after World War II in connection with the defeat of Nazi Germany and militarist Japan, when somewhat controversial trials were held by the victors rather than by new regimes (Douglas 2001). In the more recent era, this issue has arisen in some Latin American countries (e.g., Bolivia, Argentina, and Chile), some Eastern European countries (e.g., Hungary, Poland, and East Germany), and in South Africa. In some countries (e.g., France and Cambodia), the efforts to achieve justice with regard to the wrongdoing of officials of past regimes was addressed only decades after the fall of the earlier regime. In other countries (e.g., Bosnia and Rwanda), these issues have arisen while atrocities, conflict, and governmental instability were still ongoing. In the case of the former Yugoslavia, in particular, deep-rooted historical antagonisms led to warfare and brutal "ethnic cleansing," or genocidal actions, and to many unresolved questions at the outset of the twenty-first century. In 2005, Iraq in recent years had to contend with the challenge of trying Saddam Hussein and his associates for their crimes while trying to move forward with creating a new, democratic regime.

Different approaches to the problem of transitional justice have been adopted in the various countries. The fundamental challenge is often seen as one of finding the right balance between outright vengeance and total forgiveness, between extracting the truth of what happened and responding to the suffering of surviving victims, and between achieving reconciliation and doing justice. An overly aggressive pursuit of wrongdoers from past regimes may frighten and anger many citizens who have at least some ties to those regimes, and in extreme cases it could precipitate terrorism or civil war. Furthermore, new regimes must often choose between devoting time and resources to challenges of the present and future or to resolving

BOX 3.4   LAW AND TRANSITIONAL JUSTICE

One complex issue that arises when considering the relationship between law and justice is this: How is it possible to realize justice when dealing with fallen regimes under which many injustices occurred? More specifically, the term **transitional justice** has been used with reference to the process undertaken by new democracies attempting to resolve past human rights abuses by former authoritarian or totalitarian regimes (Kritz 1995; McAdams 1997; Teitel 2000). Researchers have identified some 70 countries that have, in the recent era, experienced a form of transitional justice following civil war, genocide, or the fall of a dictatorship (Karstedt 2009; van der Merwe, Baxter, and Chapman 2009).

issues of the past. Such regimes must also address the question of how the rule of law can be applied retrospectively to what was often lawful or condoned during past regimes. Some specific cases of transitional justice are addressed elsewhere in this book.

CONCLUSION

Perfect justice, as the nineteenth-century U.S. Supreme Court Associate Justice Joseph Story once observed, is an aspiration. Certainly we should have no illusion that it is possible to achieve perfect justice through law. Our legal institutions have sometimes been more concerned with fostering the appearance of justice than with achieving justice *per se*. Any number of failures to realize either procedural justice or substantive justice are identified at various points in this book. Law has clearly been an instrument complicit in the realization of some of the worst cases of historical injustice, including slavery in America and the Holocaust in Nazi Germany. More broadly, some claim that law is complicit in sustaining conditions of fundamental, ongoing inequality and injustice in society.

The call for promoting justice through law certainly endures. It encounters many challenges. The preceding section has documented the existence of different conceptions of justice, or criteria for accomplishing just outcomes in legal cases, and it seems highly unlikely that members of a society can ever achieve a full consensus on matters of justice. Even where people are agreed on their perception of justice and injustice, there is what Judith Shklar (1986) called **passive injustice**, or the unwillingness of people to intervene because it is too much trouble and too disruptive. Also, there is the fact of human fallibility: Human beings, even the wisest and most intelligent of judges, make mistakes. In addition, some human beings will always be among us who are not interested in doing justice and who choose rather to do that which is unjust. And still another challenge confounding the realization of justice through law is this: In some legal cases, equally valid rights, precepts, or objectives are in conflict. For example, citizens are entitled to enjoy a pollution-free environment, but some productive business enterprises cannot operate without producing a certain level of pollution. In a free society, some individuals will argue that they should have the right to smoke, but others will claim that their fresh air is contaminated by cigarette smoke. Citizens are entitled to privacy, but the state has to collect taxes and may infringe on citizens' privacy rights to do so. In the case of affirmative action, as mentioned earlier, rights of specific individuals cannot be satisfactorily reconciled with the realization of some desirable social goals.

Finally, there is this: As long as socioeconomic and other forms of inequality persist, a certain level of injustice will be inevitable. Those who have more resources will more often have advantages before the law than those with more modest resources. Any number of poor but innocent people have been convicted of crimes and punished, and sometimes executed, because good legal counsel was not available to them. Wealthy criminal defendants have been able to hire teams of top-rated attorneys and overcome substantial evidence of guilt. Individuals engaged in civil lawsuits with wealthier, more powerful businesses tend also to be at a substantial disadvantage. In the absence of a level playing field, the hope of realizing justice for all is necessarily an illusion. The pursuit of justice is one challenge confronting the law. Another is reconciliation of the legal and the moral.

LAW AND MORALITY

According to W. G. Sumner ([1906] 1960, p. 89), an early twentieth-century sociologist at Yale University, you can't legislate morality. Is this familiar proposition true or not true? The answer to this question has to be explored in some depth.

First, what is morality; what is moral? There is no broad consensus on morality and no uniform conception of the moral. Different general standards of morality can be identified if we make cross-cultural comparisons (between different cultures or societies); historical comparisons (between past and present within a culture or society); and intrasocietal comparisons (between different segments, or subcultures, within a particular society). One of the most enduring principles for establishing morally defensible practices and policies — and one most young children learn — is the "Golden Rule" (i.e., Do unto others...) (Duxbury 2009). Whether the application of the Golden Rule allows for the imposition of personal preferences or is most correctly invoked in support of more uniformly defensible policies has been a matter of some discussion. Are there any **moral universals**, forms of behavior that are considered immoral in all societies, in all times, and among all segments of a particular society? Homicide, rape, and incest might easily come to mind as possible examples of such moral universals. In each case, however, one can find circumstances in which homicide, rape, and incest are tolerated or even expected.

Traditional anthropological scholarship tended to emphasize cultural diversity with regard to morality (Westermarck 1906). Accordingly, anthropologists identified societies that condoned ritual killing, cannibalism, sex with children, and many other practices outlawed by developed Western societies. Some contemporary scholarship, however, has stressed uniformities of morality across many different cultures. For example, Newman (1976) examined public perceptions of deviant behavior in six countries (India, Indonesia, Iran, Italy, Yugoslavia, and the United States) and found considerable uniformity in perceptions in these different countries.

In sociology there is the contrast between ethnocentrism and cultural relativity. **Ethnocentrism** is the belief that one's own culture, encompassing its system of moral beliefs, is superior to other cultures. **Cultural relativity** refers to the practice of evaluating a culture, including its moral beliefs, in its own terms. Ethnocentrism is obviously one form of the various types of chauvinism (including racism and sexism) that have been complicit in much human oppression and discrimination, with genocide, imperialism, slavery, and wife battering as some of the more extreme manifestations. It thus appears that we should want to separate ourselves from an ethnocentric outlook and attempt to understand the moral order of another culture in its own terms. If we do so, does it follow that we make no moral judgments about the practices of this culture? For example, it is one thing to try to understand why the practice of genital mutilation of young girls has been adopted by some African cultures; it is another thing to say that we cannot express moral repugnance at this practice (Dugger 1996). We should recognize, of course, that some of our own cultural practices, such as imposing the death penalty on some convicted murderers, are viewed as immoral or barbaric by people in many other countries.

Moral beliefs profoundly influence the law. They influence the making of laws, their enforcement, and—if it comes to that—the repeal of laws. In a democratic society, a certain tension exists between the view that the law should simply reflect the morality and will of the majority and the view that law should reflect substantive moral principles that protect minorities and dissidents. For example, should broad legal rights be extended to homosexuals on the principle that minorities should enjoy the same rights as other members of society, or should homosexuals be denied certain rights (e.g., the right to marry a same-sex partner) because the majority of society's members regard same-sex marriages as morally repugnant or untenable? Should abortion be outlawed because it can be regarded as at odds with a sanctity-of-life principle, or should abortion be legally available because the majority of society's members favor that status either on practical grounds (to prevent death from illegal abortions or the birth of unwanted children) or on the moral principle that the pregnant woman's right to choose should prevail? Legislators and other elected officials charged with making and implementing laws must sometimes confront the dilemma of following either their principles or the will of their constituents (the voters); to make the principled choice may cost them their office the next time they are up for election. Historically, it seems fair to say that practical political considerations have more often taken precedence over moral principles when such dilemmas have arisen.

Law and morality are not necessarily synonymous (*see* Box 3.5). Dennis Lloyd (1970, pp. 68–69) identifies three basic models for understanding the relationship between the legal and the moral. First, they may coincide if morality dictates the content of law or if morality is fully reflected in the law. Second, they may be seen as separate, but with the moral judgment, there is a higher form of law by which the manmade law can be evaluated. And third, they may be viewed as quite separate spheres, with each evaluated in accordance with its own criteria. Lloyd's three models provide a useful point of departure for more narrowly focused discussions of law and morality.

Judith Shklar ([1964] 1986), the late Cowles Professor of Government at Harvard University, made some concise and useful comparisons in her book, *Legalism*. First, Shklar reminds us of the basic thesis that for natural law, the moral and the legal intersect, whereas for positivistic law, the moral and the legal are separable. More narrowly, law is concerned with external action, whereas morality is directed at the inner state of the mind; law demands mere conformity of behavior, whereas for morality action is motivated by the voice of conscience; law is social, objective, and coercive, while morality is individual, subjective, and

---

BOX 3.5 A CASE OF CONFLICT BETWEEN LEGAL AND MORAL DUTY

The moral and the legal are not synonymous. In a much publicized case in 1997, a 19-year-old man, David Cash, witnessed a good friend initiating an attack on a 7-year-old child, Sherrice Iverson, in the bathroom of a Nevada casino and did nothing to interfere, seek help for the child, or subsequently report the crime to the police (Terry 1998). The child was sexually assaulted and strangled, and her killer was convicted of the crime, but no criminal prosecution was initiated against Cash. All reasonable people would surely agree that his behavior was immoral and reprehensible; under existing law, it was not illegal.

voluntary; law calls for abstention from the forbidden, whereas morality calls for fulfillment of positive duties; law is subject to fairly quick change, whereas morality is more enduring. These generalizations seem valid, for the most part, but also may call for some qualifications. For example, one might argue that laws proscribing fornication (or voluntary sexual relations outside marriage) remained on the books long after the moral center of American society had shifted toward at least grudging tolerance of premarital sex.

LEGALISM, MORALITY, AND RESPONSIBILITY

"Legalism" can be regarded as an attitude or belief holding that compliance with rules is a moral way of being in the world. Robin West (2003) has raised questions about the appropriateness of this attitude for addressing the immensely complex political and moral challenges we face in the world today (e.g., in connection with America's preemptive invasion of Iraq). Should American policy be driven by purely moral and strategic arguments or by adherence to international law and legal principles?

Thane Rosenbaum (2004) argued that our legal system itself is organized to strip away moral, emotional, human dimensions and to transform disputes into bloodless contests on purely logical grounds, on winning at all costs, and on meeting the needs of bureaucratic organizations. But if we are to transform our legal system into a more empathetic, morally oriented system, whose morality would we adopt? Would such a system intrude even more into people's private lives? Would it raise false expectations of the law's capacity to alleviate human pain and suffering?

One of the central conundrums for law centers on the question of the attribution of responsibility, which has a moral dimension, to those charged with violations of the criminal law or sued under the civil law (Cane 2002; Glenn 2008a). Many complicated issues arise in this context. The criminal law and the civil law have taken different approaches to the attribution of responsibility. The question of whether human beings have a free will (voluntarism) or that their behavior is driven by various influences acting upon them (determinism)—or some complex mix of these alternative possibilities—is one of the enduring questions of philosophical inquiry. To this day, our law and legal system incorporates a voluntarist assumption—that is, that human beings freely choose to engage in actions (or refrain from doing so) and can accordingly be held legally accountable for their choices and actions. The law does allow for exceptions to this assumption, most famously in the case of insanity. But for well over a century, scientific research (particularly in the disciplines of psychology and sociology) has produced a vast amount of evidence documenting the powerful influence of a wide range of factors on human behavior. This has profound moral implications for law and the legal process. If the deterministic position is correct it would appear to be unfair (and immoral) to hold people responsible for their choices and actions and to punish them for behavior or activities that they cannot help or control. Accordingly, some commentators are calling for law to attend more fully to including "environment, nurture, society, genetics, neuroscience, addiction, poverty, gender, and culture" (O'Hanlon 2009, p. 425) as among the key dimensions that undermine the law's assumption of a free will and to embrace "behavioral realism" acknowledging how the human brain operates and how

BOX 3.6 SUICIDE, HOMICIDE, AND THIRD-PARTY RESPONSIBILITY

Under what circumstances, if any, should third parties be held responsible for suicides and homicides? In a Connecticut case in 2003, the mother of a 12-year-old boy who committed suicide was criminally prosecuted and convicted of a felony count of putting her child at risk (Santora 2003a). The mother had not only failed to take steps after learning that her son was being bullied at school but had also failed to address the cluttered and chaotic conditions of her home. One commentator expressed concern over a precedent wherein the condition of a home could be seen as complicit in a suicide. In 2006 the Connecticut Supreme Court overturned the conviction of the mother in this case, on the basis that the prosecution had not established objective standards for determining when the mother's poor housekeeping put her son at risk for suicide (Salzman 2006).

In another Connecticut case, a man whose severely depressed wife killed herself with a gun shortly after being released from a psychiatric hospital agreed to plead no contest to a second-degree manslaughter charge, with a suspended sentence (Cowan 2004). Charges were brought against this man because he had been specifically advised to remove all guns from the home prior to her release and had failed to remove a loaded gun from their bedroom.

This man had also made statements prior to his wife's suicide that he would not spend money for her treatment, and he had suggested she could kill herself with pills if she chose to do so.

Colleges and universities have faced civil suits, although not criminal prosecutions, following some on-campus suicides. The family of an M.I.T. student who committed suicide sued the university on the grounds that university personnel were aware of the severely depressed state of the young woman who committed suicide and had failed to take appropriate steps or inform her parents (Tavernise 2003). One of the dilemmas facing colleges and universities in this situation is that they feel compelled to respect the privacy rights of students who seek counseling but may then face legal action from parents when something along the lines of a suicide occurs.

In an Illinois case, a young woman was convicted and sentenced to 37 years in prison when her boyfriend murdered her 3-year-old daughter while she was sleeping (Liptak 2002b). In the view of the prosecution, the mother in this case should have anticipated the killing in light of her child's many bruises and scrapes prior to the murder. The Illinois Supreme Court ultimately overturned the conviction, stating that the prosecution's approach in this case had no basis in law; the mother involved had already served 7 years in prison following her conviction.

choices are made (Glenn 2008a). And this issue arises not just in relation to alleged law-breakers but also in relation to the assumption that legal decision-makers (including judges and jurors) can make purely rational and fair-minded choices, rather than risk influence by unconscious (and conscious) biases (Glenn 2008a). But in relation to alleged law-breakers, some commentators have cautioned against confusing the moral responsibility set forth by law with responsibility in a purely scientific sense, arguing that we must continue to pursue the right balance between holding most people responsible for their actions and not excusing these for a wide range of excuses, while excusing those who can be shown to lack the fundamental capacity for moral reasoning (Hoffman and Morse 2006). Despite ongoing significant advances in neuroscience on the working of the brain, we are still a long way from being able to read minds or provide a comprehensive, definitive account of human behavior and choice (Sasso 2009). In this account, the criminal law can continue to hold people responsible for their actions in the face of neuroscience findings but should more clearly articulate the basis for doing so. Sometimes third parties have been held at least partially responsible for the actions of others (e.g., suicide) (*see* Box 3.6 for a sampling of cases involving issues of **third-party responsibility**).

LAW AND MORALITY: PHILOSOPHICAL DIMENSIONS

Philosophers have long grappled with a range of questions pertaining to the relationship between law and morality. One set of questions focuses on whether it is an appropriate function of the law to dictate moral conduct. In the case of some forms of immoral conduct, such as willful homicide, there is no real controversy. In the case of other forms of conduct viewed by many as immoral (e.g., gambling, promoting prostitution, engaging in consensual homosexual relations, selling pornography, purchasing and using marijuana, and the like), there is considerable controversy, although the degree of controversy varies by the issue. The nineteenth-century British philosopher John Stuart Mill ([1859] 1963) made a celebrated argument on behalf of the view that the state has no business criminalizing activities that are not demonstrably harmful to others. Some argue, however, that although the harm done by so-called victimless crimes is far less obvious than the harm done by predatory crimes, they cause real and identifiable harm and should retain criminal status.

Another set of fundamental issues on the relation between law and morality addresses such matters as these: Is an immoral law still law? Does one have an absolute duty to obey law, even when law is immoral? These aspects of the relation between the moral and legal are certainly important and are discussed at length in Chapter 9.

The relation between the legal and the moral is complex, and we should not imagine that there are any simple formulas for defining either the actual nature of this relationship or what it could be. Basil Mitchell (1970, pp. 134–135), in *Law, Morality, and Religion in a Secular Society*, has made one stab at delineating the parameters of the relationship. He puts forth the following propositions:

1. The function of the law is not only to protect individuals from harm but to protect the essential institutions of a society.
2. The law should not punish behavior solely on the ground that it is—or is generally thought to be—immoral. But it cannot be, in all respects, morally neutral.
3. The morality that law presupposes is not beyond criticism and ought to be open to informed discussion and debate.
4. The protection of institutions—and legitimate concern for the ethos of society—may justify the reinforcement of morality.

If lawmakers endorse the proposition that law may appropriately play a role in reinforcing morality, Mitchell (1970, p. 135) suggested that they can be guided by the following principles:

1. Respect human privacy, wherever possible.
2. Recognize that it is undesirable to pass unenforceable laws.
3. Recognize that it is undesirable to pass laws that are unlikely to be respected by reasonable people.
4. Avoid passing laws that will cause suffering or fail to prevent it.
5. Avoid passing laws that punish people for things they cannot help doing.

No one should imagine, of course, that any such set of propositions or principles can resolve the many complex issues arising out of the relation between law and morality, but they at least provide a point of departure for further discussion. And it is at the least implicit in these propositions and principles that sociological and psychological research must be undertaken if we are to successfully identify the prevailing moral values and needs of society, the nature of laws likely to be enforceable and respected, and the capacity of people to comply with particular laws.

LAW AND MORALITY IN AMERICAN HISTORY

Although morality has been a major influence on the substance of American law, one still has to ask: whose morality? After all, American society over time has become increasingly heterogeneous and has long included numerous groups and subcultures subscribing to radically different moral belief systems. The morality reflected in American law has surely been disproportionately the morality of White Anglo-Saxon Protestants (WASPs) of middle- and upper-class social status; it has also been disproportionately a patriarchal, male-oriented morality as well as a morality of middle-aged and older people. Throughout American history those whose belief systems have been different from or directly at odds with this dominant morality have contended with formidable pressures to conform or to face ostracism, persecution, and formal legal prosecution. On the one hand, moral dissidents have included abolitionists and civil rights workers, suffragists and feminists, free love proponents and gay activists, Mormons and Moonies; a number of these groups have been legitimized, or at least many Americans believe they should be tolerated. On the other hand, moral dissidents include Ku Klux Klan members, skinheads, Satanists, and survivalists, for whom the society offers far less sympathy (Zellner 1995). An ongoing tension exists, then, between a certain level of tolerance for moral dissent and widespread intolerance for some specific forms of moral dissent.

The moral values of the politically dominant classes naturally shape the law when these laws are made, enforced, and administered by WASP, middle- or upper-class, middle-aged or older males. According to one historian, state constitutions empowered legislators to adopt laws reflecting their moral commitments, and early in the history of the United States many legislative bodies did just that (Miller 2008). But morality also becomes a force shaping law when "moral entrepreneurs" consciously lobby for laws reflecting their moral belief system and succeed in getting them enacted (Becker 1963, p. 147). **Moral entrepreneurs** are crusaders who hope to enlist the law as one means of stamping out some condition they regard as evil. Prohibition of alcoholic beverages in the early part of the twentieth century was one of the most dramatic cases of moral entrepreneurism shaping American law (Gusfield 1963; Pegram 1998).

PROHIBITION OF ALCOHOL

A temperance movement calling for the prohibition of alcohol had long existed in America and was quite successful in many states in securing laws against alcohol (Peck 2008; Valverde 2007). But in the period immediately following World War I, a series of circumstances came together allowing the temperance movement to achieve its long-standing dream of a national prohibition on the sale and distribution of alcohol. The circumstances included the disproportionate representation of legislators from rural and small-town jurisdictions, who were more favorably disposed toward Prohibition than the underrepresented big-city jurisdictions, and the nation's receptivity to such an initiative in the wake of the successful resolution of World War I. This victory for the temperance movement has sometimes been interpreted as the last triumph of a traditional, agriculturally based moral ethos over the rapidly encroaching forces of a modern, urban-dominated society. The Volstead Act and the Eighteenth Amendment, both implemented in 1920, were the specific mechanisms that put Prohibition into effect. The hope of those who promoted Prohibition was that in the face of legal prohibition, Americans as a whole would embrace the view that the consumption of alcohol was an inherently immoral activity, and people would voluntarily and happily comply with the law.

Much has been written about the failure of the "Noble Experiment." Millions of Americans, including President Harding and any number of other high-level government officials, simply did not comply with the law, and flagrant violation was widespread. Organized crime, including Al Capone's operation in Chicago, thrived in an environment where high demand for alcohol persisted despite the absence of a legal supply; organized crime cartels, as well as independent bootleggers, enriched themselves, and "speakeasies" (or camouflaged bars) emerged all over. Ironically, the 1920s eventually came to be known as "the Roaring Twenties," characterized by a rejection of many aspects of the Victorian, pre–World War I moral order, with changing styles, tastes, and habits.

Over time, disenchantment with Prohibition grew among various segments of society. Many citizens became alarmed over the amount of crime and violence seen as one consequence of the competitive, lawless market in alcohol. Corruption of many enforcement agents and politicians on all levels was also a concern. Legitimate businesses believed that they were paying a disproportionate part of the tax burden because the hugely lucrative liquor trade, being illegal, could not be taxed. Also, political reapportionment began to give a stronger measure of political power to big-city jurisdictions, which had never been especially supportive of Prohibition. If the "drys" who were still actively engaged with the temperance movement had been willing to consider compromise measures (e.g., controlled legalization of beers and other such liquors) they might have preserved at least a partial prohibition, but the most active "drys" were somewhat fanatical and uncompromising. Accordingly, in 1933, the "Noble Experiment" ended, and Prohibition was repealed with the Twenty-First Amendment.

From one point of view, the failure of Prohibition to realize its stated goal of obliterating alcohol from American life has been tragic. The costs of alcohol in terms of its complicity in a high percentage of crimes (especially violent crimes), in accidents (including automobile accidents), in domestic abuse and discord, in school- and job-related failures, in premature death resulting from cirrhosis of the liver and other illnesses aggravated by alcohol, and in personal unhappiness and suicide is literally incalculable.

If the legal prohibition on the sale and distribution of alcohol obviously did not come even close to eliminating alcohol consumption, there is some evidence that overall levels of such consumption declined during the Prohibition era; for many decades after repeal, levels of alcohol seemingly rose quite steadily (Goode 2008, p. 127). If such data are accurate, it suggests that one may, in fact, not be able to legislate morality, as Sumner proposed. Laws prohibiting the sale and distribution of alcohol, however, did deter a certain proportion of citizens who might otherwise drink from doing so and may have reduced somewhat the level of drinking of other citizens. Moral condemnation of alcohol-related excesses has persisted in the face of broad support for the legal availability of alcohol for social drinking. We continue to experience some cultural ambivalence about alcohol; drunkenness is the focus of much humor, along with bitter attacks on it. Consumption of alcohol on some level is too deeply engrained in our culture for anyone to seriously imagine that it could be prohibited in the foreseeable future. Since the 1970s, however, a more limited movement against alcohol, promoted by a new generation of moral entrepreneurs such as Mothers Against Drunk Driving (MADD), has led to tougher penalties in cases where a driver is charged with driving under the influence of alcohol; to broader liability in connection with alcohol-related accidents; and to a higher age for legal drinking (Gusfield 1996; Jacobs 1989; Peck 2008). Whether the new laws have had a substantial impact on drinking and driving has been questioned.

RECENT CONTROVERSIES

The relationship between behavior that is viewed as generally acceptable even if deviant and a specifically illegal status for such behavior is complex, with some acceptable deviance illegal and some not (Edwards 2006). Over time, some activities that were outlawed and widely viewed as "immoral" have become increasingly legalized and "normalized" (Dombrink and Hillyard 2007). In the United States, gambling is one clear-cut example of this. Are use of marijuana, gay rights, and physician-assisted suicide following in this path? In recent decades we have witnessed many fierce confrontations between those who believe the law must reflect and incorporate traditional (or conservative) moral values and those who have campaigned for broad legal tolerance of deviant lifestyles and practices and for individual choice over socially imposed morality. In the latter part of the 1960s and into the 1970s, the emergence of a "counterculture" and both a feminist movement and a gay rights movement contributed to an environment where abandonment or repeal of traditional legal proscription of some forms of sexual deviance could occur (Goode 2008). During much the same period, millions of Americans began experimenting with or using various illicit drugs—especially marijuana—and many opposed or simply disregarded the legal prohibitions pertaining to such drugs. In one view, the moral momentum in the United States since the end of the Cold War has been toward greater tolerance, with the moral force in favor of this norm more potent today than that supporting greater equality (Fagelson 2006).

The immensely controversial 1973 U.S. Supreme Court decision in the case of *Roe v. Wade*, which struck down state laws prohibiting abortion, contributed to the unleashing of an ongoing, large-scale moral battle over this issue. Subsequent developments led to the intensification of debate on legalized euthanasia, such as physician-assisted suicide. On some of these issues, liberal or progressive moral forces have tended to prevail—for example, on the general legal availability of pornography and of abortion. On other issues, people more aligned with conservative or traditional moral forces have been more successful—for example, the ongoing illegal status of illicit drugs and of euthanasia. On still other issues, such as the rights of homosexuals, results in the recent era have been mixed, with victories for both sides.

Clearly, many different forces can come into play in determining the legal outcome of these battles over morality. On at least some of these issues, unusual coalitions are formed. For example, in the campaign to criminalize the sale and distribution of pornography, conservative fundamentalists and at least some feminists find themselves on the same side, calling for censorship of pornography, although they object to it on different grounds. Of course, traditionalists and feminists are at odds on other issues. But good timing, the effectiveness of moral constituencies in their lobbying efforts, the particular makeup of the U.S. Supreme Court and other appellate courts, and various other factors can determine the character of law and legal reform on such issues. Some of these issues tend to be especially difficult to resolve insofar as people's most heartfelt moral beliefs are involved. Abortion is surely one such issue. Some other contentious issues are discussed in Chapter 10 in the context of an examination of law and social change.

LAW AND RELIGION

Law and religion are separate but interrelated realms (Barzilai 2007; Greenawalt 2008; Berman 1974, 1993). Concerns with obligation, order, responsibility, and restitution are common to both law and religion; legal concepts such as crime, contract, rehabilitation, and justice parallel religious concepts such as sin, covenant, redemption, and righteousness (Witte 1996, pp. 5, 7). A distinction between the sacred (religious) and the secular (law) has been a core theme in the development of the modern Western world, but the relationship between the sacred and the secular in this world is ultimately complex (Sarat, Douglas, and Umphrey 2007a). In past societies, law and religion were sometimes inseparable. In Western European society, for a long period of time, the canon law of the Roman Catholic Church was a dominant force; indeed, the **canon law** of the Church has been described as the first modern Western legal system (Berman 1983). The Protestant Revolution also had a formidable impact on the development of Western law (Berman 2004). In America, the Puritan society of early colonial Massachusetts largely took the form of a theocracy. Religious leaders also served as lawmakers and judges, and much of the law was taken directly from the Bible (Erikson 1966, pp. 54–64). Over time, as the colonial society evolved and became more heterogeneous, the dominance of religion declined. But we can certainly identify societies in the modern world—for example, Iran—where religious forces are the core feature of the legal system.

The substantive content of law, including American law, has been profoundly influenced by religion. At least some of the Ten Commandments—for example, "Thou shalt not kill" and "Thou shalt not steal"—are key elements of our criminal law. Of course, there are large bodies of law, such as commercial law, where there is little or no religious dimension. Much law in modern society is a reflection of the practical realities of such a society. But for many people, the core values of the law are seen as rooted in religious doctrine. Although American law has been especially influenced by various strains of the Protestant faith as it evolved in Europe (and especially England), various other religious traditions have shaped American law (Cochran 2008). New immigrant faiths are likely to have an increasing influence on American law going forward.

CONFLICTS

Conflicts between religious principles and law inevitably arise in some circumstances (Kephart and Zellner 1991; Moon 2008; Thierstein and Kamalipour 2000). In the nineteenth century, for example, Mormons in America found themselves in conflict with the larger legal system because of their practice of polygamy, or marrying multiple wives (Daynes 2001). The official Mormon leadership repudiated this doctrine to enable Utah to become a part of the United States. The resolution of the conflict over polygamy had an enduring impact on American constitutional law, clarifying the difference between a freedom to believe and a freedom to act on beliefs (Gordon 2002). Some Mormons have continued to advocate and practice polygamy into the present time, coming into conflict periodically with legal authorities (Krakauer 2003). Accordingly, polygamy is defended by some Mormons as a valid manifestation of their religious beliefs, but most people view it as a form of oppression (and enslavement) of women at odds with broader American legal principles and moral beliefs. In increasingly multicultural societies, the co-existence of secular law and religious law is challenging and complex (Petersen, Mehdi, Woodman, and Sand 2008). Many challenges persist if one is to respect religious pluralism and the rights of women, when religious identity clashes with other forms of identity or rights (Ahdar 2000; Peach 2002). Conflicts between religious beliefs and equal rights for women now arise in many parts of the world.

Christian Scientists have been opposed to the application of modern medicine; this opposition has sometimes come into conflict with the expectation within our law that parents will provide proper care for their children (*see* Box 3.7). Jehovah's Witnesses, Quakers and the Old Order Amish are opposed to warfare on religious grounds and have, in the past, come into conflict with the draft laws. In this case a resolution of the conflict has been achieved by allowing those who object to military service on the basis of religious belief to provide alternative forms of service. Traditional Catholics, as well as some of those affiliated with other religions, regard legal abortion as an abomination, fundamentally at odds with their understanding of divine law. The ongoing battle over the abortion issue is at least in part a conflict between religious and secular values.

Some Native American religious groups have claimed the right to smoke marijuana in accord with their traditional ceremonial practices, although this use of an illicit drug is at odds with the law. Within prisons, conflicts have sometimes arisen when inmate demands to be allowed freedom of worship on constitutional grounds are seen as compromising prison security or other institutional objectives. Tolerance of diverse religious practices need not be equated with acceptance of all religions as equal and worthy of the same level of respect (Cookson 2001; Oliver, Scott, and Tadros 2000; Smith 2001). Religions sometimes endorse or even require behavior that is at odds with the law.

The question of what constitutes an authentic religion is significant here as well, insofar as religious organizations are entitled to certain state-ordained benefits, such as immunity from taxation. The Church of Scientology, for example, is regarded by many people as a somewhat bizarre and sinister enterprise that is more of a cult and profit-making business than an authentic religious organization (Wright 2011). The Church of Scientology

BOX 3.7   RELIGIOUS BELIEF AND THE STATE'S
LEGAL OBLIGATION TO PROTECT
CHILDREN

If tolerance of diverse religious beliefs is a long-standing American cultural value, in recent years American law has become proactive in relation to protecting children from harm. What happens when religious practices come into conflict with the legal obligation to protect children? In 1890, the Church of Latter Day Saints (Mormons) rejected the practice of polygamy that had been introduced by its founder, Joseph Smith, to enable Utah to become a state (Gibbs 2007). But a branch of the church, the Fundamentalist Church of Latter Day Saints (FLDS), practices polygamy to this day. In recent years this practice has obtained a higher profile as government prosecutors have pursued sexual abuse and accomplice to rape charges against FLDS leaders. Warren Jeffs, a "prophet" with some 10,000 followers, was convicted in 2007 of accomplice to rape charges on the grounds that he coerced a 14-year-old girl to marry her first cousin and have sex with him, despite her pleas against this. On similar grounds, more than 400 children were seized at a polygamist ranch in 2008 on the grounds that they had been subjected to or were especially vulnerable to sexual and other forms of abuse (Blumenthal 2008). But a Texas appeals court subsequently ruled that the seizure was illegal.

Some religious communities—notably Christian Scientists—believe in faith healing (through prayer) and are opposed to medical treatment. There is now a fairly long history of criminal prosecutions of parents who failed to seek medical treatment for a seriously ill child, with the child dying as a consequence (Peters 2008). An advocacy group, Children's Healthcare Is a Legal Duty (CHILD), specifically addresses this issue. In a 2009 case, a Wisconsin couple was convicted of charges relating to the death of their 11-year-old daughter, who died of untreated diabetes. They were sentenced to spend a month in jail each year for 6 years, to be followed by probation. Historically, the penalties for parents in such cases have been relatively mild. Such punitive mildness may reflect respect for religious faith, an assumption of no intent to do harm on the part of parents, and possible uncertainty whether the death of the child was indeed preventable by medical treatment.

Religious faith and commitment also plays a role in a historical tendency of religious groups to cover up or avoid reporting cases of sexual and other forms of abuse of children surfacing within their community. Although in such cases the abuse itself is not sanctioned by religious faith, the privileging of protecting the church from scandal (and litigation) over protecting young children has been harshly condemned. The long-standing scandal of sexual abuse of children by Roman Catholic priests achieved a high profile again in 2010 when Pope Benedict XVI was being accused of having failed to take appropriate steps against priests who had been accused of sexual abuse over a long period of time (Bruni 2010). Other religious groups (e.g., Orthodox Jews) also have a tradition of keeping cases of sexual abuse against children away from the criminal justice system (Vitello 2009). But tolerance of resolving such cases by religious authorities has been diminishing.

engaged in many years of litigation with the Internal Revenue Service before receiving some recognition, for tax purposes, as a religious entity.

The conflicts and tensions between commitment to religious principle and commitment to law are not easily resolved. Many people have gone to prison rather than compromise their religious principles. The Jesuit priest Father Daniel Berrigan and his brother (a former priest) Phillip Berrigan endured prison sentences at various times during the final decades of the twentieth century because their understanding of their religious duty led them to engage in illegal actions such as the burning of draft board records (during the Vietnam War era) and attacks on nuclear facilities (Berrigan 1970; Dear 1997). The Reverend Martin Luther King, Jr. (1963) engaged in acts of civil disobedience during the civil rights era, leading to his being sent to jail (Branch 1988, 1998). His famous "Letter from Birmingham City Jail," in response to criticism from some Baptist ministers who felt he was setting a bad example as a religious leader by breaking laws, reminds us that those who share the same religious faith may interpret their moral obligations in different ways.

The ongoing controversy on the abortion issue has generated a considerable dilemma for at least some of those who regard themselves as law-abiding citizens but regard the legal status of abortion as profoundly immoral and at odds with their most deeply felt religious convictions.

In the most extreme cases, those opposed to legalized abortion have carried out violent attacks on abortion clinic personnel or have firebombed such facilities (N. Friedrichs 2002; Papke 1998). Many have engaged in attempts to block entrances to abortion facilities or harass those attempting to enter. Still others have undertaken less intrusive forms of protest. In the view of foes of legal abortion, the seven justices in the majority in the landmark U.S. Supreme Court decision *Roe v. Wade* (1973), which struck down state laws prohibiting legal abortions, were imposing their (secular) morality on the American public and were effectively making bad law. Of course, supporters of the decision tend to believe that the Supreme Court justices recognized that decisions about abortion fall in the realm of private, not public, morality and should be left up to individual consciences. The extension of mercy (and forgiveness) is one of the central doctrines of many religious faiths practiced in the United States. In the recent era, American criminal justice policies (e.g., harsh sentences and high rates of incarceration) appear to be more driven by vengeance and control than by mercy (Rothchild, Boulton, and Jung 2007). This state of affairs raises questions about the role religion can and does play in influencing criminal justice policy in a more merciful direction.

DOCTRINE DECLARING SEPARATION OF CHURCH AND STATE

The United States has a long history, stretching over hundreds of years, of unresolved tensions and conflicts between religion and law (Feldman 2005; Fish 1997; Saunders 1997). This tension is experienced too by those who teach or practice law (Cochran 1997). In America the doctrine of separation of church and state was adopted by the Founding Fathers. Some of the earliest settlers were escaping from religious persecution sponsored by, or condoned by, a European state. By the late eighteenth century, at the time of the writing of the Constitution, various religious groups co-existed in America. The Founding Fathers were concerned with preventing a circumstance in which the state would engage in the persecution of religious minorities.

The exact meaning of the doctrine separating church and state, and the prohibition of state "establishment" of religion, however, has been a source of ongoing tension and conflict throughout American history (Allen 2006; Dreisbach 2002; Miller 2003). In one interpretation, this doctrine became part of Constitutional law in the nineteenth century—mainly because of American anti-Catholicism—and was not invoked earlier in our history (Hamburger 2002). The **establishment clause** of the First Amendment of the Constitution reads as follows: "Congress shall make no law respecting an establishment of religion, or prohibiting the free exercise thereof." Some have interpreted this to mean that the national government should refrain from involvement with or support of religion in any form. Others say that this clause only prohibits the national government from literally establishing a state religion, but it allows for individual states to provide support for churches and religions in whatever form the state chooses. In *The Godless Constitution: The Case Against Religious Correctness*, Isaac Kramnick and Lawrence Moore (1996) (of Cornell University) argued that evidence from the Constitutional ratification debates supports the view that the framers wanted to maintain a godly nation but believed this could be best done by defining religion as a private pursuit, not subject to governmental policy. Brooke Allen (2006), in *Moral Minority*, argues that the key Founding Fathers were "deists" oriented toward rationality, whose secular practices were often at odds with their public acknowledgment of God and religion. Vincent Munoz (2010), on the other hand, argues that the views of key Founding Fathers—Washington, Jefferson and Madison—were quite diverse on religion and its proper role in public life.

CONTEMPORARY ISSUES

In the United States and elsewhere, there is an ongoing tension between support for freedom of expression and respect for religious sentiments: In other words, should the mocking and insulting of religious beliefs and sacred symbols be tolerated in the name of free expression (Kapai and Cheung 2009)? In different countries, different approaches have been adopted in response to this dilemma. In the contemporary era, then, religion has become a basis for divisiveness and conflict, with at least some religious fundamentalists calling for the establishment of a Christian state and some ardent secularists opposing any form of state support for religious activities. In the recent era, some conservative Christian public interest law firms have challenged laws and court decisions offensive to those of fundamentalist religious beliefs, and these law firms have had some measurable impact on public policy (Hacker 2005). The question of whether prayer in some form should be allowed in public schools is just one issue that has led to acrimonious debate and to a number of landmark cases. In the case of *Abington School District v. Schempp* (1963), the U.S. Supreme Court ruled that schools could not require students to pray (Solomon 2007). This decision to the present day angers many of those who subscribe to fundamentalist religious beliefs, in particular.

Yale University law professor Stephen Carter (1993), in *The Culture of Disbelief: How American Law and Politics Trivialize Religious Devotion*, made a provocative argument that many major institutions, including the courts, have been complicit in denigrating religion and banishing it from public life. He observed that the separation of church and state was originally intended to protect religion from state interference and persecution, but contemporary legal rules take the form of protecting the state from religion! The doctrine of separation of church and state in one view discriminates against religious faith (Eisgruber and Sager 2006). A principle of "Equal Liberty" would ensure that people with religious faith are not disvalued. A critic of the claimed neutrality of the U.S. Supreme Court in law and religion cases argues that such "neutrality" fails to take account of differences in religious practices that could be more fully acknowledged by different legal principles (Ravitch 2007). In this view, law should not take a form that specifically discourages religious practices.

In the recent era, some presidential initiatives, legislative acts, and U.S. Supreme Court decisions had recognized, in modest ways, the need to accommodate religious expression more fully (Cloud 1999). In relation to challenges to the constitutionality of faith-based rehabilitation programs in American prisons, Winifred Sullivan (2009) argues that the separation of church and state issue has become more complicated because religion is increasingly a matter of individual choice rather than a matter of religious institutions. Early in the twenty-first century, the U.S. Supreme Court was called on to rule on the constitutionality of the phrase "under God" in the Pledge to the Flag (it chose not to do so on a legal technicality) (Greenhouse 2004d). It ruled that states cannot be required to subsidize religious

BOX 3.8 A CROSS IN A PUBLIC PLACE?

In a case that came before the U. S. Supreme Court in 2009, the question arose of whether a large cross in a remote part of a national park was a violation of the constitutional (First Amendment) ban on the government's establishment of religion (Liptak 2009e). Because the cross was erected by a veteran's group, and not the government itself, an argument was set forth that it was not in violation of the constitutional ban. Associate Justice Scalia, conservative and Catholic, during oral argument of the case, took offense at the claim that a cross only honors the Christian war dead. Scalia has insisted, however, that his Catholic faith has no bearing on his judicial decisions (O'Reilly 2007). But the resolution of the case also hinged on whether the Court focused on narrow issues relating to the legality of a transfer of the cross site to private hands or the broader constitutional issues about separation of church and state. In a 5-to-4 decision handed down in 2010, the majority held that the cross could remain where it was (Liptak 2010f). The court was especially divided over whether the cross was exclusively a Christian symbol.

training despite the fact that the states provided scholarship money for studying nonreligious topics (Greenhouse 2004a). The Court set aside a lower court's ruling that allowed a city to charge a religious group for municipal services provided to other groups for free (L. Greenhouse 2001b). Other courts dealt with questions such as the following: Should Amish farmers be granted an exception to laws prohibiting child labor, in light of their dependence on children working in their shops? Do chaplains belong in the secular institution of a firehouse? Should a woman of the Muslim faith be required to remove her veil for a driver's license photograph (Broder 2003a; S. Greenhouse 2003c; Rothstein 2003)? The satisfactory resolution of issues involving religion in any way is difficult to accomplish if people feel that their heartfelt religious convictions are threatened by a judicial ruling. The ultimate meaning of the establishment clause would clearly continue to be a contested terrain (*see* Box 3.8).

LAW AND INTERESTS

The preceding sections have considered how values—in terms of conceptions of justice, in terms of morality, and in terms of religious beliefs—intersect with the law. But much of law is also shaped by, or interacts with, other types of considerations that fall outside the realm of values as conventionally defined. These considerations can be called "interests." *Conflict of interest* is a central and enduring issue in political life and in relation to the making of laws (Trost and Gash 2008). Indeed, Plato recognized this dilemma in *The Republic*. In the twentieth century, a number of European and American students of law put forth a view that placed the promotion (and conflict) of interests as central to understanding law (Herget 2007). Some discussion of this jurisprudential perspective can be found in the next chapter. Roscoe Pound (1942), a celebrated dean of Harvard Law School, put forth a view of law as a mechanism for adjudicating (or settling) conflicts between competing interests. In all realms of law, there are competing interests in the sense that different parties are attempting to realize different specific goals. The problem of conflict of interest produces a considerable challenge for law in many realms. An especially obvious conflict of interest arises when a legislator supports legislation that benefits his or her private interest (e.g., taking a bribe) but works against the public interest. Those who hold public office, which comes with a fundamental obligation to act in the interest of the general public, all-too-often favor special interests, such as major campaign donors (Trost and Gash 2008). Legislators quite uniformly support laws and legislation that benefits their constituents but are not necessarily in the interest of society as a whole. At what point should such legislative action be defined as an unacceptable form of conflict of interest? The decisions of the U.S. Supreme Court are not influenced by legal reasoning and the belief systems of the justices alone but also by "friends of the court" (amicus curiae) briefs filed by various interest groups (Collins 2008). These interest groups are diverse, including for example both business organizations and labor unions. In the criminal law and criminal justice system, some of the competing interests include the following: avenging wrongdoing (retribution); protecting society (incapacitation); discouraging lawbreaking generally and the repetition of lawbreaking by specific offenders (deterrence); transforming lawbreakers into constructive, law-abiding citizens (rehabilitation); and returning to victims of lawbreaking what they have lost (restitution). Obviously, priorities among these competing interests or objectives may be said to reflect in some part particular conceptions of justice—some scheme of morality, religious beliefs, and purely practical concerns. So interests can hardly be separated from values or the moral order. But the emphasis on interests, as here defined, is on outcomes as opposed to underlying principles. When different parties want to maximize their material gain and minimize their material loss, then we typically think of these objectives as practical interests. Examples might include a corporation's interest in achieving maximum economic efficiency and profit or a husband's interest in minimizing financial responsibility for a wife he is in the process of divorcing.

If competing interests are the norm in legal issues, whose interests prevail? If it comes down to might versus right—or power on the one hand versus a more persuasive moral entitlement on the other hand—many students of law will argue that might has all too often prevailed. However, three basic models of the relationship between interests and law, or public policy, can be identified (Olson 1970). First, there is the **power elite model**. In this model the interests of the power elite prevail; in C. Wright Mills' (1959) famous analysis, in American society the top people in the government, the military, and the business community constitute a power elite with various ties. A second model is the **pluralist model**. In this model, competing interest groups vie for influence, and different groups are successful at different times. A third model is the **democratic model**. In this model, law and public policy reflect principally the will of the majority of the public, as implemented by the public's representatives. Altogether, American law reflects a complex mix of interests. The last of these models has been especially celebrated in American culture, yet much evidence suggests that a mix of the first two models is more relevant to understanding whose interests are translated into law. American law has disproportionately reflected the interests of White people of European extraction, of males, and of people over age 21 years. American law has disproportionately reflected the interests of property owners over renters, of businesses over environmentalists, and of wealthy taxpayers over welfare recipients.

The relation of interests to law has been discussed only briefly here. However, these connections are explored more fully in particular contexts addressed by subsequent chapters.

CONCLUSION

Law is intimately entangled with questions of justice, morality, and religious belief. This chapter has attempted to identify some of the principal parameters of this entanglement and some of the critical issues involved. The ongoing tensions and conflicts arising in this context should be evident. The final brief section of the chapter acknowledges the significance of interests reflecting practical objectives in relation to law. Although the pursuit or promotion of such interests can be viewed independently of purely normative questions, in the long term we have to recognize that there are connections between the promotion of specific interests and a conception of justice.

KEY TERMS AND CONCEPTS

alternative justice
canon law
categorical imperative
commutative principle of justice
contractual conception
    of justice
cultural relativity
democratic model
distributive principle
    of justice
egalitarian conception of justice

ethnocentrism
exclusionary rule
individual justice
intuitionist conception of justice
jury nullification
just world
moral entrepreneurs
moral universals
passive injustice
pluralist model
power elite model

procedural justice
restorative justice
retributive principle
    of justice
social justice
substantive justice
third-party responsibility
transitional justice
utilitarian conception
    of justice

DISCUSSION QUESTIONS

1. Do you think that affirmative action policies are just? Should they continue to exist? Why or why not? What stand would libertarians, socialists, and communitarians each take on affirmative action issues?
2. The exclusionary rule exists as one way of protecting accused persons' rights to due process. Is such a rule really fair? Is it more important for our legal system to put an emphasis on achieving procedural or substantive justice?
3. Can violence ever be justified as a way of achieving justice? Should a mother be prosecuted for attempting to kill the man who molested and took the life of her 6-year-old, if in her mind she was "doing justice?"
4. There is no law that says an ordinary citizen has a legal duty to save the life of a drowning person. Should laws be created that criminalize the act of "doing nothing" in a situation in which one has the capability of coming to another's aid? In your answer, include comments on the 1997 David Cash case, as well as the example here.
5. In *The Dissent of the Governed: A Meditation on Law, Religion, and Loyalty*, Stephen Carter (1998) calls for some form of protection for those who break laws out of religious conviction. Do you agree or disagree with his belief? What problems might occur if this became a regular practice in our system?

CHAPTER 4

JURISPRUDENCE AND THE STUDY OF LAW

Law is rules. Law is principles. Law is practices. Those who have studied and taught law want to be able to explain what the rules are based on, what the principles are or should be, and what those who practice law in some sense look to when they make their decisions or what it is that influences those decisions. Making sense of law in this way is the work of jurisprudence.

JURISPRUDENCE

The term **jurisprudence** is derived from Latin, as is true of so much legal terminology. *Juris prudentes* can be translated as "wise in the law." In broad terms, jurisprudence encompasses general forms of intellectual inquiry about law (Coleman and Shapiro 2002; Davies 2008; Hutchinson 2009). It may refer to legal philosophy or to a science of law. Although no one would dispute the notion of a philosophy of law, the claim that a science of law is also possible is a matter of contention. The term **analytical jurisprudence** has been applied to an approach suggesting that jurisprudential analysis is scientific and objective. The term **moralistic jurisprudence** has been applied to jurisprudential work that specifically promotes policies and practices that are in accord with a set of moral principles. The term *jurisprudence*, then, is applied to different types of inquiry and practice. Some approaches to jurisprudence are "internal" (tied closely to the practice of law) and some are "external" (linked more with the larger political and social world) (Nobles and Schiff 2006). Analytical jurisprudence has often been sterile and has worked against understanding law in cultural and economic terms (Hutchinson 2009). Contrary to the claims of analytical jurisprudence, law has no real meaning independent of social, economic, and political context; analytical jurisprudence has not been attuned to the realities of how power works (*see* Box 4.1).

Jurisprudence may focus on legal principles or on the actual practices of legal institutions; on what the law ought to be or on what the law as implemented actually is; on law as a system of rules with its own internal logic; or on law as a social institution shaped by outside influences. Jurisprudence has sought to identify the underlying principles that

BOX 4.1 AMERICAN LEGAL THINKING AND THE LAW AND SOCIETY MOVEMENT

Harvard Law professors David Kennedy and William W. Fisher III (2006) have compiled an anthology of the 20 most influential articles for *The Canon of American Legal Thought*. Although some of these articles are almost exclusively focused on "internal" legal, doctrinal issues (legal principles and rules), quite a number of the articles intersect with and have been influential in the law and society movement, including: Llewellyn on legal realism; Coase on social costs and law; Galanter on why the "haves" come out ahead in legal proceedings; and MacKinnon on the feminist critique of law.

BOX 4.2 SHOULD JURISPRUDENCE BE DEMOCRATIZED?

Allan C. Hutchinson is a professor at the Osgoode Hall Law School of York University (Canada). In *The Province of Jurisprudence Democratized* (2009), Hutchinson attacks historically dominant *analytical jurisprudence* as an internal product of law professors and judges and as fundamentally undemocratic. In its premise that law and legal logic is independent of social and political influences, it has perpetuated a pernicious myth. It has disguised the central role of power (and its maldistribution) in shaping law and legal decisions. A progressive and realistic jurisprudence should promote widespread political engagement of ordinary citizens in the fundamental issues of law and public policy, with democratic consensus rather than legal professionals shaping the ultimate direction of legal policies and decisions that are so central to contemporary social existence. A critic wonders whether Hutchinson takes sufficient account of the capacity of highly motivated special interests to promote legal initiatives that reflect their values but impact negatively on historically oppressed groups, from immigrants to gay people (Fraser 2009). Does recognition of the many limitations of analytical jurisprudence necessarily translate into support for a democratically based approach to jurisprudence?

should inform specific bodies of law, such as contract law, property law, and criminal law (Coleman and Shapiro 2002). Some broad themes of concern to contemporary jurisprudence include the following: law in relation to communities; freedom in relation to necessity; the proper reach of the law (e.g., in relation to the abuse excuse; in connection with warfare); formal law in relation to informal "law"; and law in relation to morality (Collier 2000). Globalization has presented jurisprudence with new challenges, insofar as many traditional forms of legal theory have limited usefulness for understanding complex global legal issues.

All justices who render legal decisions and issue legal opinions adopt a jurisprudential philosophy, whether or not they specifically acknowledge it. But there has been significant disagreement on how justices arrive at their decisions. The term **mechanical jurisprudence** suggests that judges are judicial scientists who, if they apply the appropriate legal principles correctly in a particular case, will arrive at the right decision (Pound 1908). The term **nihilistic jurisprudence** suggests that judges are idiosyncratic individuals who arrive at decisions according to their political biases or personal inclinations (or hunches) and that one should not pretend law itself dictates correct answers (Stick 1986) (*see* Box 4.2). These terms present a stark contrast and do not necessarily capture the complex mix of considerations that enter into judicial decision making. But this dichotomy should be kept in mind as you read about different schools of jurisprudence, some of which are clearly aligned with one or the other of these two ways of thinking about what judges do.

TABLE 4.1   TRADITIONAL SCHOOLS OF JURISPRUDENCE

I. Natural law: B.C., Ancient Greece and Rome
Law as a reflection of the moral/divine order.
II. Positive law: Early nineteenth century
Law as the will of the sovereign; law as science.
III. Utilitarianism: Early nineteenth century
Law as the greatest good for the greatest number; pragmatism.
IV. Cultural/Historical: Nineteenth century
Law as a reflection of historical circumstances; of particular cultures.
V. Sociological jurisprudence: Early twentieth century
Law in relation to social reality; social engineering through law.
VI. Legal realism: First half of the twentieth century
Social and psychological influences on legal decision making; focus on trial courts.
VII. Process theory: Mid-twentieth century
Emphasis on procedural consistency in law; legal process.

SCHOOLS OF JURISPRUDENCE

Law is an inherently contentious enterprise. Accordingly, the fact that there are many competing schools of jurisprudence, each incorporating premises starkly at odds with many of the premises of the competing schools, should hardly be surprising. In this chapter, seven traditional schools of jurisprudence and seven contemporary schools of jurisprudence are identified and briefly described. These schools of jurisprudence are discussed in roughly chronological order, in terms of when they were first introduced. **Traditional,** in this context, refers to **schools of jurisprudence** originating early in history or by the mid-twentieth century; of course, many of these schools of jurisprudence, in some form, have vigorous adherents today (*see* Table 4.1). **Contemporary schools of jurisprudence** refer here to jurisprudential perspectives originating, for the most part, in recent decades, principally from the 1970s on. The number of schools identified here, and the classifications themselves, may be somewhat arbitrary, but they should at least provide a good appreciation of the diversity of jurisprudential approaches. In the context of the sociolegal focus of this book, some attention will be directed toward the relationship of each particular school of jurisprudence to social context and social variables.

TRADITIONAL SCHOOLS OF JURISPRUDENCE

NATURAL LAW

The oldest and most enduring school of jurisprudence, with origins among classical Greek and Roman philosophers, is **natural law** (Charles 2008; Kries 2007; Oakley 2005). Contemporary proponents of natural law insist that its way of understanding fundamental issues of law, morality, and justice remains superior to competing approaches (Finnis 2003; George 1999). The key attribute of this school of thought is that the human law is (or ought to be) rooted in a transcendent law of divine origin or as part of nature itself. One tradition of natural law theory holds that the will of God is the only truly legitimate standard for morality; the other holds that human beings on their own have the capacity to discern universal and unchanging standards of right and wrong that should form the basis of law (Oakley 2005). Among the ancient philosophers, the Greek Aristotle and, to a lesser extent, Plato and the Roman Cicero are viewed as progenitors (Budziesewski 2008; Morrison 1997).

The jurisprudence of the great Roman Catholic theologians, especially St. Thomas Aquinas ([1266–1272] 1993), is also regarded as part of this tradition. In the natural law approach of Aquinas, the validity of law depends on its relation to some higher law or principle; a specific law must be in accord with this higher law (which emanates from God), or it is not valid. In natural law thinking, there can be no separation between law and morality. The seventeenth-century English philosopher John Locke ([1690] 1965), for example, proposed that human beings possess certain fundamental rights in a state of nature, and when they are members of a civil society they are entitled to these rights. If the state infringes on these natural rights of citizens, then the authority of the state is nullified. These ideas of Locke's were, of course, immensely influential with the framers of the Constitution of the United States. The famous reference in the Declaration of Independence to "unalienable rights" reflects Locke's version of natural law theory. Although the commitment to this core concept has remained strong, over time various other schools of jurisprudence described here have been embraced.

In the contemporary era, natural law jurisprudence takes a number of different forms. Traditional Catholics continue to identify with a version of natural law theory rooted in Aquinas (Oakley 2005). A philosophically oriented natural law jurisprudence is based on work by the German philosopher Immanuel Kant ([1785] 1998) and his categorical imperative (calling for laws based on principles that can be applied universally) for its basic point of departure.

A sociological version of natural law jurisprudence suggests that one can empirically investigate issues of human needs and draw upon these data to formulate laws that might contribute to the filling of such needs. One prominent contemporary proponent of natural law, John Finnis (1980, 2003), argued that "human" (positive) law, although it has some important functions, must ultimately be reconciled with the criteria of natural law. In Finnis' conception, natural law integrates ethics with political philosophy and may be defined as "the set of principles of practical reasonableness in ordering human life and human community." Basic human goods such as life, knowledge, play, aesthetic experience, friendship, and religion must, in this view, be reconciled with "practical reasonableness." Also in the natural law tradition, Robert Clinton (1997) called for a return to a God-centered Constitution because he saw the secularist interpretation of the Constitution as having various undesirable consequences.

On the whole, natural law jurisprudence is leery of social science, as opposed to theological or philosophical texts, as a basis for law. Natural law tends to be associated with an ideologically conservative perspective. In the famous *Lochner v. New York* (1905) case early in the twentieth century, a predominantly conservative U.S. Supreme Court invoked natural law in upholding the "right" of employers to be free from laws limiting the number of hours in an employee's workday. Although natural law has been cited to support free enterprise and property rights, it has probably more often been associated with fundamentalist religious belief and the position that state law is obliged to proscribe morally offensive and decadent activity while promoting biblical virtues.

Natural law also provided one foundation for the Nuremberg Trials and the prosecution of surviving Nazi leaders and perpetrators of the Holocaust. The crimes of the Nazis were interpreted as contrary in the extreme to long-recognized, widely accepted principles of natural law. During the civil rights era in the United States (in the 1950s and 1960s), Martin Luther King, Jr. (1963) also referred to natural law as providing grounds for disobeying inherently immoral laws perpetuating segregation.

A fundamental problem with natural law has to be acknowledged, then. The substantive content of such law is open to interpretation. Although natural law has been invoked against genocide and segregation, it has also been invoked, historically, to vindicate slavery and the apartheid system (denying people of color basic rights) in South Africa and to discriminate against women (Margolick 1990; Shea 1997). It is far from clear that a single natural law position on the death penalty exists. In a defense of natural law, Daryl Charles (2008) argues that it provides an essential moral compass in an increasingly dehumanized world. Identification with a natural law jurisprudence, then, is seen as attractive to some on the grounds that it is principled and maintains a strong connection between the moral and the legal, but the specific principles called for are open to ongoing debate (*see* Box 4.3).

BOX 4.3   LON FULLER AND LEGAL NATURALISM

Legal naturalism is a term sometimes applied to the views of Lon Fuller (1940, 1969, 1981), a twentieth-century professor of law at Harvard University. For Fuller, law is the enterprise of subjecting human conduct to the governance of rules. Law has an **external morality**. In other words, one can ask the question of whether the substantive content of law is in accord with some defensible scheme of morality. For example, can laws permitting abortion or mandatory sterilization or physician-assisted suicide be defended on moral grounds? Of course, as we have seen elsewhere, heated debate in response to such questions is the norm.

In his book, *The Morality of Law*, Fuller (1969) put forth the novel argument that law also has an **internal morality**, which is indifferent to the substantive content, or aims, of the law. This internal morality is one of duty and aspiration and is a precondition for valid law. To illustrate what he means by the internal morality of law, Fuller tells the story of King Rex, a fictitious monarch who attempts to establish a system of law in his country. Without going into the details of Fuller's fable, one can simply note that King Rex encounters a series of frustrations and failures with each new tactic

he adopts in this effort to create a system of law, and each of these failures generates a principle that is a critical element of a valid system of law. In brief, these principles are as follows:

1. There must be general rules, or laws.
2. These laws must be made known.
3. Laws must not be retroactive.
4. Laws must be clear and understandable.
5. Laws should not be contradictory.
6. Laws should not require the impossible or the extremely unreasonable.
7. Insofar as possible, laws should be reasonably constant through time.
8. Laws and the administration of laws should not be in conflict.

It should be immediately evident that these eight propositions tell one nothing about the substantive morality of laws or whether laws permitting abortion, enforced sterilization, or physician-assisted suicide are moral or immoral. Rather, they identify the basic attributes of a valid system of law. For Fuller, a system of law that fails on any one of these eight criteria is

BOX 4.3 (cont'd.)

not really a valid system (Wueste 1986). On the one hand, Fuller rejects the formalist position (associated with legal positivists) that any command of the sovereign constitutes law. But Fuller also rejects the natural law position that a law whose content is at odds with natural law principles is not law. Rather, Fuller's "legal naturalism" may be viewed as a compromise perspective that emphasizes the form as opposed to the content of law. Yet Fuller clearly believed that a legal system encompassing his procedural criteria was also highly likely to adopt good and defensible substantive laws.

Following World War II, Fuller engaged in a famous debate with H. L. A. Hart, a leading proponent of legal positivism, on whether Nazi law was really law (Minda 1995, p. 50). For the legal positivists it was law, even if it was bad law. In the view of traditional adherents of natural law, who were influential in identifying grounds for trying the surviving Nazi leadership after the war, Nazi law was not law because of its inherently evil content (at odds with the moral criteria of natural law). But for Fuller, Nazi law was not really law for a different reason: It was procedurally defective, insofar as it did not meet the criteria for a valid system of law. In other words, whatever its failures in terms of external morality, it was also internally immoral and therefore was not law. Such ideas have been controversial, but at a minimum Fuller has provided a provocative alternative to the traditional viewpoint on the relationship between the legal and the moral.

LEGAL POSITIVISM

Legal positivism is often represented as an approach to law in stark contrast to the approach taken by natural law jurisprudence (Davies 2008; Hutchinson 2009; Zamboni 2008). This jurisprudential school of thought is of much more recent vintage than natural law, with principal early contributions made in the nineteenth century. Legal positivism, in contrast to natural law jurisprudence, treats the legal and the moral—the "is" and the "ought"—as separate realms. In this approach, the validity of law is determined by its source, as opposed to its content. Law is a human product of a political system, and valid law is accordingly produced by appropriate procedures. Legal rules are part of a formal, logical, closed system. The English legal philosophers Jeremy Bentham ([1776] 1960, [1789] 1970) and John Austin ([1832] 1954), writing in the late eighteenth and early nineteenth centuries, are considered to be the founding fathers of legal positivism. For Austin, law is the command of the sovereign (or the head of the state). Commands, in this view, are orders backed by threats. The citizen's duty to obey the law is linked with the legitimacy of the source of the command rather than a moral evaluation of the command. Such moral evaluation may be important and appropriate in some contexts, but it is separate from the legal question of a command's, or law's, validity.

In the United States, after the Civil War in the mid-nineteenth century, positivism was quite widely embraced and natural law was more commonly rejected (Feldman 2000). In the late nineteenth century, Christopher Columbus Langdell became dean of the Harvard Law School. Langdell adopted a version of legal positivism that became exceptionally influential in legal education. For Langdell (1871), law was a complete, formal, and conceptually ordered system. Accordingly, law could be considered a form of science, and the student of law could take on the role of a scientist of law. Langdell believed that the appropriate way to educate law students called for the analysis of appellate case opinions. Students could arrive at the correct solution to a particular case—even if the justice or justices who actually wrote the opinion had failed to do so—by identifying the right legal principles underlying the particular case and by applying a rigorous form of legal analysis to the case. This approach to legal education was widely adopted on the premise that it would teach students to "think like lawyers," but it also came to be subjected to increasing criticism. (Such criticism is discussed more fully in Chapter 7.)

In the twentieth century, law professor Hans Kelsen ([1934] 1967), a refugee from Nazi Germany, developed a version of legal positivism that begins with the characterization of the legal system as a hierarchy, or pyramid, of norms. Kelsen labeled the basic, or foundational, norm the **"grundnorm"**; other norms must be understood in their relation to this norm and in terms of how they derive authority from such fundamental norms (Bindreiter 2002; Zamboni 2008). Accordingly, a pure science of law is regarded as possible by Kelsen, with laws understood as logical outcomes of fundamental principles.

The English legal philosopher H. L. A. Hart's (1961) *The Concept of Law* is regarded as a major statement of modern legal positivism (Hutchinson 2009; Mayes 1989; Orrego 2003). In Hart's view, law (a self-regulating system rooted in social fact and convention) has both primary and secondary rules. The secondary rules (of recognition) are the basic sources of the validity of primary rules, or rules pertaining to individual rights and obligations (Minda 1995, p. 48). For example, the federal law prohibiting bank robbery is a primary rule, and Article I of the Constitution, granting the power to Congress to legislate, is a secondary rule.

The emergence of legal positivism as a school of jurisprudence can be seen as reflecting the aspiration of some students of law to emulate the obvious success of the physical and natural sciences in the realm of the law. It could also be regarded as reflecting the modern drive toward imposing rationality and order on life and social existence. In its most extreme form, it seems to suggest an image of law virtually analogous to mathematics. In this view, even if law originates with human commands and norms, it then seems to take on a life of its own and operates almost independently of the social context.

Critics of this approach to law have found it unrealistic and morally offensive and have noted that any such approach inevitably tends to endorse or legitimate the status quo and the authority of the power elite who create, interpret, or apply law (Hutchinson 2009; Ross 2001). Despite such criticism, legal positivism has persisted and by the end of the twentieth century may even have experienced a revival. One defender of legal positivism disputes the widely held view that it is indifferent to moral principles (Sebok 1998). Two other proponents (Schauer and Wise 1997) have argued that legal positivism alone is capable of differentiating clearly between law and other categories of knowledge.

HISTORICAL/CULTURAL JURISPRUDENCE

During the nineteenth century another school of jurisprudence—most commonly called **historical jurisprudence**—also emerged. At odds with legal positivism, this school of jurisprudence strongly emphasized the interdependence of law and the social world. In this view, law can only be properly understood in a particular historical and cultural context. Law is regarded as a dependent variable, or a product of social forces. In the interpretation of the nineteenth-century German law professor Friedrich Karl von Savigny ([1831] 1986), a leading early proponent of historical jurisprudence, law is best understood as the slow, organic distillation of the spirit of a particular people (*Volkgeist*). The validity of law, then, is not linked with its emanating from a legitimate "sovereign" but, rather, depends on whether it accurately reflects this spirit, or national character.

Because the "spirit" of a people and its moral belief system are intimately interconnected, the positivist separation of the legal from the moral is not really applicable here. But the notion of a folk spirit has not lent itself to easy measurement and has been criticized on a number of grounds. If law reflects, or ought to reflect, a national cultural outlook, it is not easy to explain obvious variations in the law that arise between different jurisdictions within a particular nation. Also, the notion of "folk spirit" that was proclaimed by romantic nationalists in the nineteenth century was embraced and then transformed for pernicious purposes by some of the demagogues and tyrants of the twentieth century.

The nineteenth-century English legal historian Sir Henry Maine ([1861] 2001) is also associated with this school of jurisprudence. In his celebrated book, *Ancient Law*, Maine explored the historical development of law out of political conditions existing in early societies, with special attention to the origins of Roman codes of law (Scala 2007). He identified as a basic trend a movement from law oriented toward status to law oriented toward contract. In other words, in ancient legal systems, one's status (in terms of social class, gender, and so on) determined one's standing before the law and the law's treatment. In modern, developed societies, a contract (a free agreement between two or more parties) was at the center of legal matters. Maine celebrated this perceived movement from status to contract as a sign of progress.

Maine's view of contracts, however, has been criticized as somewhat starry-eyed and naive. In many—perhaps most—contracts, one party has significant advantages over the other, and the contract itself ends up favoring that party. Although Maine was attuned to long-term social changes, he was somewhat insensitive to the immense consequences of social inequality in many legal matters in the modern world. It is perhaps ironic that the growing recognition in the modern world of the fundamental unfairness of social inequality has led to the re-introduction of status as an important element in the legal order. Now, however, social status as a disadvantaged person (e.g., as a minority group member or a woman) may translate into a legal advantage under affirmative action law. Maine was right in recognizing that law must be understood in a socio-historical context and that the tenor of law may evolve and change significantly over time. At the same time, students and scholars have to be leery of sweeping generalizations about the changing character of law, insofar as that character is often complex and contradictory in certain respects.

UTILITARIANISM

All students who have taken an introductory philosophy course are likely to have been introduced to the core ideas of **utilitarianism**. This school of philosophy, emerging in the late eighteenth and early nineteenth centuries, became very influential, especially in the practical realm of legal reform (Schofield 2006). The British philosopher Jeremy Bentham ([1789] 1970), although he has been identified as a founder of legal positivism, is best known for espousing utilitarianism. The core principle here is that utility should govern. More specifically, that which promotes the greatest happiness, or good, for the greatest number is what society should strive for. It should be a primary objective of philosophers of law to determine which laws or policies would best promote this outcome. Bentham was a somewhat eccentric personality, and much of his work may seem dated or naive by contemporary standards. But he was immensely influential in promoting the criteria of social utility for legal reform, and his ideas challenged in a fundamental way the abstract or superstition-ridden ways of interpreting the world still common in his time. One of his best-known disciples, John Stuart Mill ([1859] 1963), produced the celebrated essay "On Liberty," with the core argument that the government should only make criminal laws proscribing identifiably harmful behavior toward others.

The eighteenth-century Italian nobleman and economist Cesare Beccaria ([1764] 1988), typically identified in criminology textbooks as the founder of a "classical" school of thought, developed ideas somewhat parallel to those of utilitarianism. Beccaria is especially associated with the notion of introducing rationality into the criminal justice system and imposing punishments that fit the crime. In Beccaria's view, rational punishments would both deter people from committing crimes in the first place and deter convicted offenders from repeating their offenses. Both Beccaria and Bentham adopted a fundamental assumption about human nature as being rational, self-interested, and naturally oriented toward maximizing pleasure and minimizing pain. Their basic stress on the capability of humans to make rational choices is incorporated in modern law and has been adopted by at least some prominent social philosophers and criminologists.

The whole tenor of the utilitarian way of thinking about law inevitably tips it toward the notion that law must not be interpreted independent of the social context within which it arises and of social consequences. This pragmatic, policy-oriented approach to law is clearly reflected in some contemporary schools of jurisprudence. It has been criticized as being based on a simplistic and distorted view of human nature, having excessive emphasis on practical consequences as opposed to support of higher principles, and showing insufficient concern with the rights of minorities.

SOCIOLOGICAL JURISPRUDENCE

With the emergence of a **sociological jurisprudence**, principally in the early decades of the twentieth century, the connections between the legal and the social came to be even more sharply highlighted (Banakar 2007; Deflem 2008; Kalman 2002). This school of jurisprudence is most readily associated with the Austrian scholar Eugen Ehrlich ([1913] 1936) and the American Harvard law professor (and dean) Roscoe Pound (1907, 1910). During the period that Ehrlich and Pound wrote, sociology was emerging as an autonomous, clearly recognizable discipline. In the United States, in particular, early sociologists were concerned with developing sociological knowledge that could provide guidance for social reform. Ehrlich and Pound came to believe that sociological knowledge also had a specific role to play in reforming the law.

They recognized that law co-existed with other social rules and norms and that social order depends on a high level of acceptance of such rules. Ehrlich emphasized that the formal law was most effective when it was in accord with the living law, or the complex of rules and norms by which members of society actually lived. Accordingly, students of law must not remain content to simply study legal treatises but must turn to the real world in which people live to understand law as a part of that world. Roscoe Pound called for the study of "law in action" to determine the extent to which a correspondence existed between the formal law and the rules that people actually tried to follow. In addition, Pound directed attention to the frequent discrepancy between claims about what legal institutions were doing and what in fact they were doing. Empirical sociological research could be applied to the investigation of such questions as these: Are the formal proclamations of the courts in conformity with the actual decisions or practices of the courts? Are the specific aims and objectives of legislative statutes realized through the process of implementing these statutes?

Pound (1942, 1943, 1945) is also associated with a theory of interests. For Pound, it is important to identify the specific social interests underlying laws and to expose some of the inevitable conflicts between these interests. Inevitably one has to recognize that individualistic (legalistic) justice is not always in accord with social (humanistic) justice: For example, even if the formal law does not require that workers injured in the workplace be compensated, social justice does require such compensation. In this view, the formal law should be adapted to the prevailing standards of social justice. A sociological (or social) jurisprudence, according to Pound, should identify the most important social interests and the crucial values of a modern society, and law reformers (as social engineers) should devise a scheme to realize these values. The influence of utilitarianism and pragmatism is evident here in the view that the law as a social institution should play a central role in enabling society to fulfill its aspirations (*see* Box 4.4).

LEGAL REALISM

The repudiation of the abstract manner of viewing law, which was characteristic of the earliest schools of jurisprudence, reached a climax of sorts with **legal realism** (de Been 2008;

BOX 4.4 THE BRANDEIS BRIEF

Some judges and other legal actors, influenced by the sociological jurisprudential school, became more attuned to the realities of the societal environment. The so-called **Brandeis Brief** reflects this influence (Schur 1968, p. 42; Urofsky 2009). A brief is a written argument highlighting facts, laws, legal principles, and opinions of respected authorities relevant to and in support of a lawyer's application to a court of law to take some action or render a particular decision. As a Boston lawyer, Louis Brandeis prepared a brief in an early twentieth-century case (*Muller v. Oregon*, 1908) about the hours of working women. His brief highlighted many forms of evidence demonstrating the pernicious effects of long workdays on the health of women. This type of brief, drawing on social data, represented an important break with traditional legal arguments, which were framed wholly in technical legal terms. Brandeis himself became a distinguished justice of the U.S. Supreme Court, and that court and other courts came to accept the type of evidence highlighted in the Brandeis Brief as relevant to their decisions. One famous example is the landmark desegregation case, *Brown v. Board of Education* (1954). The unanimous opinion of the U.S. Supreme Court in this case did not rely simply on internal legal doctrine. Rather, social science evidence of the harmful consequences of prevailing segregation practices was taken into account in the opinion, which determined that segregated schools were in violation of the Constitution. For one commentator, a disturbing trend in the current era for legal decisions to be shaped by special interests, with indifference to factual evidence, renders the Brandeis Brief all the more important (Cohen 2006).

Zamboni 2008). This repudiation has been labeled "the revolt against formalism." Legal realism disputes the notion that abstract, foundational concepts resolve legal cases and holds instead that extralegal considerations are dominant (de Been 2008). Although legal realism is clearly related to, and sometimes confused with, sociological jurisprudence, it has a somewhat different emphasis and focus (White 1972). Legal realism challenged a traditional view that judges simply identify what the law is by "finding" what has been recognized as the law; it insisted on recognizing that judges make new law when they render their opinions.

The celebrated Associate Justice of the U.S. Supreme Court, Oliver Wendell Holmes, Jr. (1881, 1897) is typically identified as a major source of inspiration for legal realism. The utilitarianism of Bentham and the historical jurisprudence of Maine were clearly important influences on Holmes. Although he also incorporated some aspects of Austin's positivistic approach—for example, on the fundamental difference between the legal and the moral— Holmes differed with the positivists on where one should look to discern the essence of law. Holmes said to look to human practices, whereas positivists relied on formal principles. Holmes was also influenced by a pragmatic orientation toward law, with special attention to results as opposed to general principles. In the most famous of his Supreme Court dissenting opinions, in *Lochner v. New York* (1905), Holmes took exception to the majority's view that New York could not pass a law limiting the working hours of bakers (on the pretext that it violated a Fourteenth Amendment due process right to freedom of contract); for Holmes, the majority view was simply a reflection of the majority's economic conservatism and also was inconsistent with earlier court rulings.

In *The Common Law* (1881, p. 1), Holmes set forth, on the first page, his oft-quoted observation, "The life of the law has not been logic: it has been experience." Holmes was here urging students of law to turn away from a treatment of law as an exercise in abstract reasoning and to focus rather on law as it was in the real world. For Holmes, the substance of the law inevitably reflected the "felt necessities" of the times and other social and practical influences, rather than abstract legal logic. In his landmark *Harvard Law Review* essay of 1897 (pp. 460–461), "The Path of the Law," Holmes offered up a provocative assertion that "the prophecies of what the courts will do in fact, and nothing more pretentious, are what I mean by the law." If this is so, Holmes suggested, then we have to look at the law as the "bad man" does. The bad man, in this view, is really not concerned with abstract principles and moral reasoning. The bad man is simply interested in the actual decision of the court and ideally in being able to predict what the courts will do. It follows from this reasoning that the judicial process, and the decision making of judges, should be an important focus of jurisprudential analysis, as indeed has been the case since the time of Holmes (*see* Box 4.5).

The legal realist movement thrived mainly during the 1920s and 1930s. It was more of a movement than a unified school of jurisprudence. A varied group of law professors adopted the Holmesian attention to practices, as opposed to principles, as a fundamental point of departure. Karl Llewellyn ([1930] 1962), a law professor at Yale (and later at the University of Chicago), was among the most respected of this group. Llewellyn provided one vivid demonstration of the realist perspective in his discussion of the doctrine of *stare decisis*, or precedent. The citation of precedents—or the lending of an aura of authority to the present

BOX 4.5 OLIVER WENDELL HOLMES, JR. AS
A LEGAL ICON

Oliver Wendell Holmes, Jr. is a towering figure in American legal history, arguably the most frequently cited of all legal writers and perhaps second only to John Marshall among the most famous U.S. Supreme Court justices (Schnayerson 1986; Schwartz 1974; Voss 1989). To his admirers, Holmes was a great legal stylist and original thinker, a champion of judicial restraint, legal realism, and free speech. He was also a controversial figure, regarded by some commentators as a cold man, a nihilist, a glorifier of war, and someone contemptuous of losers in the struggle to survive (Alschuler 2000; Hoffman 2001). Holmes was born in 1841, fought (and was wounded) in the Civil War, and lived to witness the New Deal, dying only in 1935. His father, Oliver Wendell Holmes, Sr., was a physician, celebrated wit, and well-known writer, but in time the son's fame came to overshadow that of the father. Holmes was related to a number of prominent American families; growing up, he knew his father's friend Ralph Waldo Emerson. Among his own contemporaries, he knew the psychologist William James and his brother, the writer Henry James. During the course of his long life, Holmes knew and corresponded with many leading figures of his time.

Holmes was educated at Harvard and practiced law for some years. In 1881 his famous book, *The Common Law*, was published; this work emphasizes the influence of external forces on the formation of the common law and the need to see law in terms independent from morality. In 1882 Holmes was appointed Professor of Law at Harvard.

In the same year, however, he was appointed an Associate Justice of the Massachusetts Supreme Court, becoming Chief Justice in 1899. Holmes was 61 years old when Theodore Roosevelt appointed him to the U.S. Supreme Court in 1902; he then served as Associate Justice for almost 30 years, retiring from the bench when he was older than 90 years. Although he produced some 2,000 opinions, he is especially famous for his dissenting opinions, which, although few, were influential and earned him a reputation as "the great dissenter." Holmes observed that "great cases like hard cases make bad law." Accordingly, in such cases, he felt that a dissenting opinion served a useful function. Holmes was especially uncompromising in his opposition to any efforts to limit free speech and is known for his tough-minded insistence on tolerance of dissenting viewpoints. For the most part, Holmes argued that judges should defer to the will of the people's representatives in the legislative branch, even if much of the resulting legislation was "humbug." As Holmes famously observed:

> About seventy-five years ago, I learned that I was not God. And so, when people want to do something that I can't find anything in the Constitution expressly forbidding them to do, I say, whether I like it or not, Goddamit, let 'em do it. (Schwartz 1974, p. 191)

case opinion by reference to a similar opinion in an earlier, parallel case—has always been a core feature of the common law. Llewellyn demonstrated that the doctrine of precedent is actually two-sided: If judges find that precedents are inconsistent with the favored opinion in the case under study, then the precedents are read narrowly (or strictly) by emphasizing basic factual differences; if precedents are consistent with the favored opinion in the case under consideration, then they are read broadly (or loosely) by emphasizing the general principle involved as applicable to a category of cases. In other words, Llewellyn sought to show that precedents are not applied in a mechanical fashion but rather are interpreted by judges who have a good deal of discretion in this regard. Altogether, for Llewellyn, law students must learn that any substantive body of law can only be understood by focusing on the procedures through which it is produced and the human actors (e.g., judges) who produce it.

Jerome Frank (1930, 1949), a lawyer and Yale law professor who eventually became a federal judge, is another leading figure in the legal realist movement. Frank called for more attention to the trial courts and the judges who sit on them; traditionally, most attention had focused on appellate courts. Although students of jurisprudence sometimes promoted skepticism about rules and the process of making rules, Frank stressed the importance of skepticism about facts or, rather, attention to how facts are determined in legal cases. Frank advanced the proposition, which most people today take for granted but which was heresy in the view of traditional jurisprudence—that judges are human. Accordingly, he called for attention to the social and psychological factors that influence or determine judicial decision making. Traditional jurisprudence suggested that judges apply legal rules to case facts to produce the proper legal outcome (or decision); Frank argued, provocatively, that judges often decide first and then seek to identify rules and facts that support their opinions.

Legal realism has had considerable influence. The Yale Law School, from the 1930s on, pioneered the incorporation of realist principles into the legal education curriculum (Kalman 1986, 2002). Legal realism led to more attention by at least some legal scholars to social and behavioral dimensions of law; it provided one important foundation for the Law and Society movement, or the interdisciplinary study of sociolegal phenomena, as well as for some contemporary schools of jurisprudence (de Been 2008). As a practical matter, legal realism has promoted far greater attention to what actually goes on in courts of law and to the need to adopt any available strategies to minimize the improper influence of bias within the law. Many of the tenets of legal realism have simply become part of the conventional wisdom in law, with the result that legal realism as an identifiable intellectual movement is less evident today. The primary contribution of legal realism, in the view of most commentators, has been the exposure of limitations and distortions inherent in traditional forms of jurisprudence. But if legal realism has been successful in injecting a measure of realism in the understanding of law, it has its own inherent limitation in not providing any clear foundation for discriminating between good and bad laws and for dismissing too fully the role formal law plays in constraining the abuse of judicial discretion.

PROCESS THEORY

In the 1940s and 1950s, a number of law professors at Yale (Myres McDougal and political scientist Harold Lasswell), Harvard (Henry Hart and Albert Sacks), and Columbia (Herbert Wechsler), although strongly influenced by legal realism, were concerned with re-establishing a more objective and neutral grounding for legal decision making (Duxbury 2003; Grey 1996, pp. 502–505). The so-called **process theory** emanating from their approach also reflects the specific influences of utilitarianism and sociological jurisprudence. These legal scholars argued for the importance of attending to the specific functions and responsibilities of the different branches of the government, with special emphasis on the formal process through which decisions were reached. In this view, reason is again elevated to an important status, because it should guide the legal decision-making process. Judges should not make decisions based on their personal or ideological preferences but should dispassionately analyze the competing interests in particular cases and arrive at judgments based on procedural consistency (establishing by sound reasoning that the present case is being decided in a manner logically consistent with that applied in earlier cases). Principled decision making and appropriate respect for legal procedures should produce socially desirable outcomes. Associate Justice Ruth Ginsburg, of the U.S. Supreme Court, has been identified as one of those strongly influenced by the legal process approach. On balance, this jurisprudential school has not had an especially enduring influence, other than in the realm of international law (Arend 2003). Perhaps the faith of process school adherents in the possibility of neutral decision making in law has been largely rejected by more skeptical subsequent generations.

CONTEMPORARY SCHOOLS OF JURISPRUDENCE

The term *contemporary* is applied here to schools of jurisprudence that emerged principally in the final decades of the twentieth century. Of course, the traditional schools of jurisprudence have survived, with varying degrees of influence. Students of law continue to identify strongly with a natural law or a positivist law tradition, for example, and utilitarianism and pragmatism in some form remain influential. The contemporary schools of jurisprudence typically take the form of modifications or extensions of a traditional school of jurisprudence, as opposed to a entirely new set of premises. They have in common an especially pronounced interdisciplinary character, integrating many elements from a wide range of disciplines (Minda 1995). The social sciences—particularly economics, sociology, and political science—have been especially important, but such disciplines as philosophy, history, and even literature have also exerted a significant influence. These contemporary schools of jurisprudence also tend to be oriented more toward intellectual challenges pertaining to meaning (i.e., not assuming that terms and concepts have a single, fixed meaning), the sources of knowledge (i.e., exploring where one's knowledge of legal phenomena comes from), and the proper grounds for morally defensible choices than with the practical problems confronting lawyers. At least some of these schools of jurisprudence differ from the traditional schools in their focus on special questions within the realm of law, such as the standing of women or people of color before the law (*see* Table 4.2).

TABLE 4.2 CONTEMPORARY SCHOOLS OF JURISPRUDENCE

I. Law and economics: 1960s

Economic analysis of law; economic efficiency and wealth maximization.

II. Interpretive jurisprudence: 1970s

Law as principle; faithfulness to evolving interpretation.

III. Critical legal studies: 1970s

Law as politics, as hierarchy; indeterminacy of law.

IV. Critical race theory: 1980s

Law as racist; integrating concerns and views of people of color into law.

V. Feminist jurisprudence: 1970s

Law as patriarchal; integrating concerns and views of women into law.

VI. Narrative jurisprudence: 1970s

Law as storytelling; literature and law.

VII. Postmodern jurisprudence: 1990s

Law in an emerging postmodern world; challenging truth claims of law.

LAW AND ECONOMICS

The **law and economics** school of **jurisprudence** is one contemporary extension of the utilitarian tradition. It emerged principally in the 1970s, with the University of Chicago as an important center of activity (Cooter and Ulen 2008; Friedman 2000; White 2009). Several prominent economists at that university began developing innovative recastings of classical free-market economic theory, and some law professors began to pay attention to these developments. Among the economists, Ronald Coase was especially influential. In a famous article, "The Problem of Social Cost," Coase (1960), who eventually won a Nobel Prize for his work, proposed a theorem (thereafter known as the **Coase theorem**) challenging conventional assumptions about governmental regulation of economic activity. The essence of his theory is this: Legal regulation of private economic activity, such as the government's compelling private parties to bear costs for harmful conditions they cause, can produce "transaction costs" that can be avoided, in many cases, if private parties are allowed to negotiate their own arrangements with each other. In other words, if some economic activity of mine is imposing costs on you, then it is likely to be more efficient to allow us as private parties to negotiate a solution than to have the government impose a solution and costs on the first party. This theorem provided inspiration for a law and economics jurisprudence stressing that economic considerations should take precedence in the resolution of legal cases.

Law and economics jurisprudence assumes that human beings are rational creatures (Friedman 2000). It argues that traditional ideas of abstract individual rights should be abandoned in favor of the principle of achieving economic efficiency or maximizing wealth. Although it is conceded that there are circumstances requiring legal intervention, judges should defer, whenever possible, to the free market or some other consideration promoting economic efficiency. In other words, the law and economics school of jurisprudence adopted Adam Smith's celebrated laissez-faire principle and applied it to the realm of the law. In its early arguments, such principles were applied inflexibly, but in the work of one of law and economics' leading lights, Richard Posner (1990, 1995a, 1998), the emphasis shifted from economic efficiency to wealth maximization (i.e., favoring legal decisions that can be affected to increase monetary wealth in society) and from purely economic considerations to more pragmatic, broader considerations of what works best in maximizing human goals and aspirations (or helps people achieve appropriate objectives that do not impinge on the rights of others) (*see* Box 4.6). Cost–benefit analysis of law and social policy is a central project for law and economics jurisprudence (Adler and Posner 2001; Revesz and Livermore 2008). Other strands of law and economics jurisprudence emphasize such factors as the impact of legal rules on individual incentives, the collective consequences of individual choices, and the economic significance of how institutions (e.g., administrative agencies) are organized (Scheppele 1994, p. 389). Law and economics analysis has been applied to a range of issues (e.g., marriage and divorce) (Dnes and Rowthorn 2002). Yale law professor (and former dean) Guido Calabresi, in *The Cost of Accidents* (1970) and in *Tragic Choices* (Calabresi and Bobbitt 1978), addressed such matters as shifting attention away from fault to focusing on ways to best avoid accidents and negotiate responsibility and how to reach decisions to maximize public benefits and minimize losses.

BOX 4.6   RICHARD POSNER AND PRAGMATIC
              JURISPRUDENCE

Not all jurisprudential approaches can be easily classified by schools identified here. Federal judge Richard Posner (1990), for example, is a prodigiously prolific writer on jurisprudential topics who identifies pragmatism as the key to an alternative approach (MacFarquhar 2001; Parisi 2007). Posner (b. 1939), a native of New York City, graduated first in his class at Harvard Law and then served as a clerk for U.S. Supreme Court Associate Justice William Brennan. Posner has also worked as a government lawyer and has been a professor of law at the University of Chicago. He was appointed to the U.S. Court of Appeals, 7th circuit, by President Reagan in 1981. He is one of the founders of law and economics jurisprudence and the author of one of its leading texts (1998). Posner has published almost 40 books and hundreds of articles, not only on law and economics but also on jurisprudence, moral philosophy, law and literature, sex and reason, aging, and the Clinton impeachment case, among other topics (Posner 1988, 1990, 1992, 1995a, 1995b, 1999a, 1999b). Since 2003, Posner has published books on intellectual property law (2003), responding to catastrophe (2004), post-9/11 intelligence (2005; 2006), plagiarism (2007), terrorism (2007), and the failures of capitalism in the wake of the financial meltdown of 2008 (2009). Posner is highly contentious and provocative. For example, he suggested at one point that legalizing the sale of babies could be a market-driven solution to the glut of unwanted children; he has also applied a purely economic approach to the sensitive topics of abortion and rape. Posner's (1995a, 1999a, 2003) **pragmatic jurisprudence** holds that law is an activity (as opposed to a set of rules) and that judicial decision making should be guided by attention to consequences and by the objective of achieving sound and defensible solutions, based on practical knowledge or science. Other prominent writers on law also favor some version of a pragmatic approach. Cass Sunstein (2009a), arguably the most prolific and influential law professor today, calls for a jurisprudence that focuses on consequences—not abstract principles—and favors "minimalism" on the part of justices as opposed to making bold new law. Aharon Barak (2005), President of the Supreme Court of Israel, calls for a "purposive" interpretation of law—that is, an approach to law that focuses on purpose more than principle.

The law and economics position was very influential during the Reagan/Bush I era of the 1980s and the Bush II Administration of the 2000s, for the obvious reason that its outlook on legal matters was in accord with the conservative economic ideology of these administrations. A disproportionate percentage of judges appointed to the federal bench (including Posner) were identified with this school of thought, as were several nominees to the U.S. Supreme Court. Economic theory has been applied to the major Microsoft antitrust case, in an effort to demonstrate that the litigation against Microsoft did not serve consumers well (Page and Lopatka 2007). Unsurprisingly, much criticism has been directed at the law and economics school. In a critique of law and economics analysis, it is accused of cloaking itself under the impartial guise of science when in fact it often promotes a particular ideological agenda (Hackney 2007). Some critics specifically claim that too much of the economic analysis of law underestimates the benefits and overestimates the costs of regulation and accordingly has a pro-free-market and anti-regulatory bias (Revesz and Livermore 2008).

But not all attempts to impose economic analysis into the understanding of law are linked with free market fundamentalism or conservative perspective; it has also been applied to addressing how law can foster development (Trubek and Santos 2006). Critics allege that it embraces a questionable view of human beings as rational creatures. Law and economics scholars, in this view, should attend more to how social forces shape views of what is rational in the first place (Edelman 2004). Critics note that law and economics jurisprudence slights many noneconomic interests and values with which law is or should be concerned. They say that it tends to favor the status quo and those who have the advantage in terms of wealth and power and that it incorporates an unrealistic view of the free market, with inadequate consideration of the possibilities for fraud and exploitation within such a market.

INTERPRETIVE JURISPRUDENCE

At least one version of liberalism survives within jurisprudence in the work of the remarkably prolific law professor Ronald Dworkin (affiliated with both Oxford University in England and New York University), among others (Hershovitz 2006; Duxbury 2003; Ripstein 2007). Dworkin has been described as "our leading public philosopher." Dworkin has also been described as "the last judicial idealist," a major challenger of legal positivism (Romano 2006), and "the most original, provocative, and prominent American legal philosopher" (Kress 1987, p. 834; McCaffery 1997, p. 1043). His **interpretive jurisprudence** approach (sometimes referred to as rights and principles) has been strongly influenced by certain developments within philosophy, especially the work of Harvard University philosopher John Rawls (1971). Rawls sets forth a scheme upon which social ethics can be grounded and calls for a social contract based on a principle of fairness, with rules determined on the basis of maximizing opportunity for the least advantaged. Interpretive jurisprudence also parallels some developments in literary interpretation, carried over to the realm of law.

Dworkin (1977, 1985, 1986, 1993, 1996, 2000, 2006) has produced a series of works in which he has both set forth a distinctive jurisprudential philosophy and applied this philosophy to an understanding of a range of challenging contemporary issues (including abortion, euthanasia, pornography, homosexuality, affirmative action, and free speech). Dworkin's approach rejects the positivists' claim that legal rules dictate legal outcomes, but it also rejects a nihilistic claim that law is nothing more than subjective opinion. For Dworkin, law is about policy and principle as well as about rules. Arguments of policy are goal-oriented, in the spirit of Bentham's utilitarianism, and try to show that the community would be better off, on the whole, if a particular program were pursued. Arguments of principle are rights-based, in the spirit of Kant's idealism, and claim that particular programs must be carried out or abandoned because of their impact on particular people, even if the community is worse off.

When judges decide cases on principle, they are not necessarily applying rules. Dworkin illustrated this point through the oft-cited case of *Riggs v. Palmer* (1889). In this case, the central question was whether a young man who poisoned his grandfather should nevertheless inherit his grandfather's estate, as called for in the grandfather's will. A judge following the standard *rule* in probate cases would indeed allow the grandson to inherit, insofar as that rule calls for respecting the wishes of the person who made the will. However, a judge applying the widely recognized *principle* that people should not benefit from their evil acts would deny the grandson his inheritance, as was the outcome in this case. Principles, then, may take precedence over rules in legal cases.

For Dworkin, jurisprudence can play a useful role in identifying the enduring principles that have evolved within a legal tradition. One must first identify fundamental background rights (e.g., "Equal concern and respect for each other" and "Freedom of political speech") and find the appropriate balance between individual rights and the communal sense of justice or needs. Judges should neither apply rules mechanically nor base judgments on their personal preferences; rather, they should feel constrained to decide cases in ways consistent with the principles that have evolved within a legal and political community. A right to privacy is one example of such a principle. Dworkin invokes the metaphor of the **chain novel** to make this point. In a chain novel, each chapter is written by a different author, but all of the authors have to remain faithful to the narrative line of the book to provide it with coherence and consistency. Analogously, in legal cases, each judge must be faithful to the shared decisions, structures, conventions, and practices of the legal community within which he or she functions. In this sense, if these guidelines are followed, then Dworkin believes that "right answers" in particular cases can be identified.

Dworkin's interpretive jurisprudence has been criticized on many grounds (e.g., Burley 2004; McCaffery 1997; Posner 1990, 1995a). If indeed there are "fundamental rights," can one really obtain a consensus on the criteria for identifying such rights? Is this approach too wedded to traditional values and interests, and accordingly is it aligned with the status quo and the rights of dominant groups? Does it have any relevance for the everyday practice of most lawyers, who in many cases apply, rather than interpret, straightforward legal rules? Does an interpretive approach ultimately create a philosophical hall of mirrors that leaves practitioners bereft of any firm grounding for discriminating between good and bad legal rulings?

CRITICAL LEGAL STUDIES

Surely no school of jurisprudence has been at the center of more controversy than **critical legal studies** (Bauman 2002; Duxbury 2003; Kairys 1998; Kelman 1987). The first Critical Legal Conference was held in 1977, organized by a group of younger law professors. Critical Legal Studies (CLS) became a conspicuous presence throughout the 1980s, with annual well-attended conferences, a steady stream of law review articles and provocative books, and symposium issues of reviews featuring heated exchanges between adherents and critics. It also was at the center of a number of high-profile law school battles over hiring and tenure cases, with CLS law professors claiming ideologically based discrimination against fellow adherents and mainstream law professors flinging back parallel charges.

Critical Legal Studies law professors had been influenced by the radicalizing events of the late 1960s and early 1970s and were disenchanted with the inherent conservatism of much jurisprudence and the law school curriculum. Critical Legal Studies also reflected the intellectual influences of legal realism, neo-Marxist theory, and some strains of continental European (predominantly French) critical theory, especially postmodernism (Milovanovic 2003). "Law is politics" may be identified as a basic premise of CLS (D. Kennedy 1997; Zamboni 2008). One mission of CLS scholarship, then, is the deconstruction (or trashing, in more colloquial terms) of mainstream legal doctrine, to uncover the political agenda (and fundamental contradictions) beneath the formal, purportedly neutral legal rhetoric. Indeed, CLS adopted an especially uncompromising repudiation of legal "formalism" and of "false necessity" (i.e., the notion that legal rules objectively dictate certain outcomes) (Hutchinson 2000). Claims of objectivity and a neutral form of "legal logic" are challenged in case law (or judge-made law) as well as statutory law.

The proposition that the law—and law school—is oriented toward the maintenance of hierarchy, privilege, and the status quo is a central claim of CLS scholarship. Accordingly, a certain percentage of CLS scholarship has been devoted to challenging (or promoting the delegitimation of) mainstream claims about the appropriate focus of legal education and the role of legal professionals. The promotion of egalitarianism, or equality on all levels, is one of the key objectives of the CLS program. In one celebrated critique of the CLS program, Paul Carrington (1984) then dean of the School of Law at Duke University, argued that CLS scholars had no business teaching in law schools because they had a "nihilistic" orientation toward law—did not believe in law, as it were—and if the principal mission of law schools is to prepare their students for careers as lawyers, CLS-oriented professors could not contribute to that mission. The CLS response to this critique, in the most concise form possible, is that the exposure of traditional myths about law is a necessary and constructive dimension of the law student's education, and ideally it will open these students to the possibilities of law careers more consistent with the realization of authentic social justice (Gordon 1985).

Through the 1990s, the original energy of the CLS movement dissipated somewhat; some fragmentation took place in the form of alternative critical perspectives on law developing their own identity; and some conflict surfaced between the original group of CLS scholars and a younger generation of such scholars (Bauman 2002; Minda 1995). Despite some of its excesses, CLS continues to provide an immensely provocative challenge to the tenets of mainstream jurisprudence and legal education (Anderson 2004). It has been applied to such matters as assisted suicide, affirmative action, and gay rights (Mootz 2006) (*see* Box 4.7).

CRITICAL RACE THEORY

The leading lights of critical legal studies have been, for the most part, White males, although from the outset women and people of color were better represented among CLS scholars

---

BOX 4.7 ROBERTO UNGER: A JURISPRUDENTIAL PHILOSOPHER AND THE FUTURE OF BRAZIL

Roberto Mangabeira Unger, a scion of a prominent Brazilian family on his mother's side, was for many years a prominent Harvard Law professor and a leading figure in the critical legal studies movement, the author of a series of highly original and widely discussed books. While at Harvard Law he taught unusual courses such as "Aquinas, Kant and Hegel." When Harvard Law's dean asked if he would change the title of the course to "Aquinas, Kant, Hegel and Law," Unger reports, "I said no because of the code of honor that kept me from saying yes to a figure of authority...And he just laughed and shrugged his shoulders, and that was that" (Romano 2008, p. B8). Unger's three-volume *Politics* (1987) and other books called for a basic transformation of the foundation of contemporary society—an alternative mode of human existence—eliciting both high praise

and withering contempt. For Unger, the critique of traditional approaches to law cannot be separated from the larger project of a critique of the social order. He has promoted efforts to "destabilize" conventional social existence, to expand universal freedoms, to extend "immunity rights" against governmental coercion, and to redistribute wealth in fundamental ways (Romano 2008). Such an unorthodox jurisprudential and political philosopher would typically be discussed by academics and students and have no "real world" influence. In 2007, however, Unger accepted the invitation of Brazilian President "Lula" da Silva to oversee a newly established "Secretariat for Long-Term Actions," taking a dramatic cut in income to relocate to Brasilia, the country's capital (Romano 2008). It remains to be seen whether Unger's appointment will influence a fundamental reorganization of Brazilian society in line with his utopian jurisprudential and political philosophy. In 2009 Unger returned to his tenured position as a Harvard Law School professor.

than in the ranks of traditional or mainstream schools of jurisprudence (an overwhelmingly White male enterprise throughout most of history). **Critical race theory** emerged, principally in the 1980s, on the premise that people of color bring a unique perspective to the legal system, and this perspective can advance people's understanding of some challenges confronting the system of law as well as society generally (Delgado 2003; Minda 1995; Parks, Jones, and Cardi 2008). The principal impetus for critical race theory has been the realization that the experience and perspective of people of color has either been absent from or inaccurately represented in traditional jurisprudence, and even in critical legal studies. Derrick Bell (2004), the first tenured African-American professor of law at Harvard, is one spokesman for this theory. Bell (1987, 1992) has used narrative and storytelling as a device for representing the experience of law endured by African-American women.

Other critical race theory scholars in law include Richard Delgado of the University of Colorado and Charles Lawrence and Mari Matsuda of Georgetown Law School. These scholars have campaigned for greater diversity on law school faculties, have attempted to devise new approaches to enduring civil rights challenges, and have sought new ways to express the voice of people of color in legal scholarship (Goldberg 1992). They support affirmative action as a necessary corrective to various injustices against people of color (Delgado 2003; Lawrence and Matsuda 1997).

Although the First Amendment doctrine of free speech is among the most venerated principles in American law, critical race theorists (Matsuda et al. 1993) argue that it has been used (in the form of hate speech) to keep minority students from participating fully on campus. This concern with the misuse of the First Amendment parallels the concern of some feminist law scholars with First Amendment protection of pornography.

Kimberle Williams Crenshaw (1989), of the University of Pennsylvania School of Law, has made the argument that the experience and circumstances of African-American women are fully captured neither by the experience of women generally nor people of color generally. The term **intersectionalism** is invoked to capture some of the unique dimensions and circumstances of being both a woman and a person of color. For Crenshaw and other adherents of this position, a just system of law finds ways to acknowledge this uniqueness (Wing 2000). **Critical Race Feminist Theory** attends especially to the special experience and vulnerability of women of color, before the law (Wing 2007). **Critical Race Realism** attempts to draw upon the social sciences to expose racial bias in law and document its harmful consequences (Parks, Jones, and Cardi 2008).

The critical race theorists have been criticized for too often being indifferent to truth in the name of advancing their agenda (Farber and Sherry 1997). They have been criticized as well for wholly disparaging merit, conventional standards of fairness, and tolerance for alternative points of view. These are contentious claims, of course, but at a minimum the critical race theorists have challenged the dominance and complacency of White people in the world of law.

FEMINIST JURISPRUDENCE

The contemporary feminist movement that emerged principally in the 1970s has had an immense influence in many different disciplines and fields, and law is certainly among these

(Chamallas 1999; Levit and Verchick 2006; Olsen 1995). One basic premise of **feminist jurisprudence** is that law is predominantly a product of males and therefore has a patriarchal character. A feminist jurisprudence is dedicated to exposing the patriarchal bias of law and legal principles and to identifying and articulating the perspectives, needs, and rights of women (Chamallis 2007; West 1997). More specifically, feminists say, within the Anglo-American jurisprudential and legal tradition, doctrine based on liberal notions of individual rights, freedom, and reasonableness, although purporting to be value-neutral and objective, actually favors the interests of men and reinforces male domination (Anleu 1992, p. 423). Historically, as one dimension of such dominance, the law has restricted the entry of women into the public sphere and has done little to hinder or intervene with male dominance (and abuse) in the private sphere. Women, in their experience with law, have been represented—in actual cases, and in literary accounts—differently than men (MacPherson 2007). Although feminist jurisprudence is not a monolithic enterprise and adherents are divided on some important issues, the general neglect by male-dominated jurisprudence of the values, fears, and harms experienced by women is one shared premise.

Feminists are divided on the significance of common experiences of women and the appropriate response of law to the difference between women and men (Baer 1999; Dowd and Jacobs 2003). Should feminists emphasize the commonality of the female experience, or should they stress the varieties of such experience? Does the difference between women and men require special treatment for women or simply truly equal treatment with men? And if women are different from men, why is this so and what are the significant manifestations of this difference?

Harvard University psychologist Carol Gilligan (1982) provided one influential answer to the "difference" question. According to her research, a young boy and a young girl respond differently when presented with the hypothetical dilemma of a man considering whether to steal a drug he cannot afford to save his wife's life. The boy relies on the legal system to provide a just result; the girl goes beyond the confines of the narrow legal question and looks at the matter in terms of a broader network of relationships. Gilligan labels the male response a "justice approach" and the female response an "ethics of care" approach. One of the implications of these different ways of looking at such cases is that women are more amenable than men to mediation for the resolution of legal cases, although there is some controversy over whether women are really better off or worse off with mediation (e.g., in domestic dispute cases).

For feminists who embrace the view that women are fundamentally different from men and have different experiences, it follows that laws should be reformed to take these differences into account and that the judicial process should be changed as well. For example, in the realm of contracts, the way in which women are socialized should be taken into account, as opposed to reliance solely on the traditional "reasonable man" standard, and damages should attend to relational losses, not simply monetary losses. For example, a woman defrauded by a man with whom she had both a personal relationship and a business contract has lost more than just money. In the realm of torts (or personal injury), feminine values of caring and concern should be more fully integrated, as opposed to reliance on traditional male standards oriented toward efficiency and profit (Bender 1990).

A feminist law professor who teaches a seminar titled "A Feminist Revisit to the First-Year Curriculum" reports that she incorporates into this course discussion of elements of a "missing curriculum," including seduction as a tort, marital rape, battered women's syndrome, prenuptial agreements, division of marital property, and exclusion of women from jury service (A. Bernstein 1996, p. 219).

At least some influential feminists have attacked the application of the free speech doctrine to pornography (*see* Box 4.8). In addition to the issue of pornography, feminists have been concerned with and have influenced legal developments on many issues. They have played a role in the reform of rape law and in the introduction of laws pertaining to sexual harassment in the workplace (MacKinnon and Siegel 2004). They have been involved in the defense of battered wives who have killed their husbands, or abused women who have killed their partners. They have, of course, been concerned with the many forms of gender discrimination that still affect women in the workplace and elsewhere. Law schools have not been immune to the charge of gender discrimination (Rhode 2003). Indeed, all forms of

---

BOX 4.8 CATHARINE MACKINNON AND THE FEMINIST WAR ON PORNOGRAPHY

Catharine MacKinnon (of the University of Michigan School of Law) is arguably the best-known (and most controversial) promoter of feminist jurisprudence (*Current Biography* 1994; Jackson 1992). MacKinnon was born in 1946; her father was a Republican politician and federal appellate court judge. In 1974, prior to receiving her law degree from Yale, MacKinnon became involved in an early sexual harassment case and wrote a pioneering work on the subject (MacKinnon and Siegel 2004). In the 1980s, she shifted her attention to the pornography issue. Despite outstanding academic credentials and many widely discussed articles and books, MacKinnon was unable to secure a full-time faculty appointment for many years and was a visiting professor at various law schools. She only received a tenure offer from the University of Michigan in 1988. She is an intense and dynamic speaker who has given lectures in numerous forums.

MacKinnon rejects biological determinism and the notion that gender is basically a difference rather than a hierarchy. MacKinnon (1987) characterizes the modern liberal state as an entity organized on behalf of men; the law of such a state reflects the rule of men over women and male-oriented norms. Furthermore, sex and the sexual relation is at the core of a society where men dominate and women submit. MacKinnon (1993), with the feminist writer Andrea Dworkin, has been a leading feminist advocate of the legal banning of pornography, on the grounds that pornography is a key means of "actualizing" the dynamic of social inequality and sexual domination. In other words, pornography turns sex inequality into sexuality and turns male dominance into sex difference. Pornography, in

this reasoning, should be banned because it contributes both to the ongoing dominance of women and to the actual practice of males inflicting physical harm, including rape, on women.

Feminists have been divided on the issue of pornography, with some arguing that it is a mistake to become aligned with conservative fundamentalist groups on this issue, because these groups, although opposed to pornography, are opposed to equality for women. They argue that a precedent on behalf of censorship can ultimately provide a basis for censorship of work or representations supported by feminists.

Some argue that it is counterproductive to the feminist agenda to portray women principally as victims, as opposed to active agents in their own destiny. Finally, some say there are more important issues confronting women than pornography (Ellis et al. 1986; Lacombe 1994). MacKinnon has been widely criticized by law professors and others with a range of ideological commitments, including some feminists. She has concisely summarized this criticism: "My work is considered not law by lawyers, not scholarship by academics, too practical by intellectuals, too intellectual by practitioners, and neither politics nor science by political scientists" (*Current Biography* 1994, p. 366). Her importance in the debate on law and feminism is not in dispute, however. In *Women's Lives, Men's Law* MacKinnon (2005) forcefully reiterates her uncompromising views on pornography as a cause of violence; rape as a crime that occurs even with consent by the adult female, if she is less powerful than the male; and females as generally still subordinate to males in fundamental ways in contemporary American society. One recent book (2006) was titled *Are Women Human?* In 2007, Mackinnon was a visiting professor of law at Harvard.

economic discrimination against women, subtle and not-so-subtle, are matters of concern. For example, feminists have exposed some of the specific disadvantages confronting women under traditional legal standards and practices pertaining to divorce. Feminist lawyers have played a key role in gaining a wider audience for domestic violence toward women and as advocates for battered women (Schneider 2000). Feminists have generally been advocates of all forms of expanding options and choices available to women, including the right to legal abortion. They have exposed and opposed laws that in various ways impose disadvantages and liabilities on pregnant women. A specifically *lesbian legal theory* argues that legal scholarship has explicitly or implicitly denigrated lesbians and has paid little attention to many issues of importance to lesbians, including same-sex marriage, lesbian mothers' custody rights, and lesbianism and violence (Robson 1998). Altogether, for many feminist students of law, conceptions of gender, the role of women, the status of motherhood, and the meaning of privacy, autonomy, and equality remain contested arenas and require the exposure of standards and practices unfair to women, as well as reforms effectively addressing such unfairness.

NARRATIVE JURISPRUDENCE

Narrative jurisprudence emerged in the 1970s and became increasingly conspicuous in the late 1980s and into the present era (Elkins 1990; Hanafin, Geary, and Brooker 2004; Sanders 2007). On the one hand, narrative jurisprudence has been concerned with law-in-literature; on the other hand, it is also concerned with law-as-literature (Ferguson 1984; Weisberg 1984). In other words, proponents look to the treatment of law and justice in literature, and they also recognize that law is a form of literary activity that can be analyzed like any other literary activity (Aristodemou 2000). Literature (e.g., the work of Harriet Beecher Stowe) played a role in exposing law's support for the social evils of slavery and racial oppression (Crane 2002). Various contemporary legal problems (e.g., capital punishment sentencing) can be usefully analyzed through reference to specific works of literature (Heald 1998). The narrative form—storytelling—is a way of conveying important truths about law.

James Boyd White ([1973] 1985, 1984) has argued that the study of literature should be part of legal education and that literary studies have something distinctive to say about law. Richard Weisberg (1992) promoted the view that the study of literature can influence lawyers to be more ethical in their professional conduct. Shakespeare's *The Merchant of Venice*, Herman Melville's *Billy Budd*, Dostoyevsky's *The Brothers Karamazov*, and Kafka's *The Trial* are just a few of the great works of Western literature that address, in some profound way, issues of law and justice.

Some critics have questioned whether literature can promote deeper ethical sensitivity in lawyers; these critics have also insisted that law and literature are different forms with different purposes, and, accordingly, the lessons they might learn from each other are limited. Even Judge Posner (1988), however, who expressed critical views of the law and literature movement, conceded that lawyers and judges can benefit from exposure to great literature if it encourages them to write legal opinions with an enhanced sense of style, clarity, and human empathy. Anthony Amsterdam and Jerome Bruner (2000)—a prominent law professor and a prominent psychologist, respectively—have argued that storytelling tactics play a key role in the decision making of the U.S. Supreme Court.

James R. Elkins (1985a) of West Virginia University School of Law has been a leading promoter of narrative jurisprudence, with special emphasis on its role in legal education. Elkins observed:

> Lawyers are, by profession, storytellers: we relish a good tale and tell stories as a fundamental and functional part of our craft....Law and legal education surround us with stories....Law is a compendium of stories about how we use and abuse rules to manage our social relations and resolve both our differences and commonality....(1990, p. 1)
>
> It is the story of law (as it is set alongside other stories) that locates us in relation to others: to family, community, work. We use legal narratives, as we use other stories, to give meaning to social existence, to ourselves as women and men, as people of color, as persons the culture welcomes or fears.

David Ray Papke (1987, 1998), of Indiana University–Indianapolis School of Law, has, in particular, applied narrative jurisprudence to recovering and understanding just those who are especially feared by mainstream, law-abiding society: conventional criminals, ideological heretics, and militant radical groups. Papke did this by recounting the stories of such legal heretics as the abolitionist William Lloyd Garrison, the suffragist Elizabeth Cady Stanton, and the socialist Eugene Debs. The prominent philosopher Martha Nussbaum (2006) argues that exposure to literature can help lawyers (and judges) develop three important humanistic abilities: to lead the examined life; to understand a global, interconnected world; and to cultivate "narrative imagination" or empathy for others. In *Memory, Imagination, Justice: Intersections of Law and Literature*, David Gurnham (2009) demonstrates how the literary work of Shakespeare, Dickens, Kafka, and others can illustrate how past wrongs are "remembered" and accordingly can be applied to a range of legal and ethical issues, including child pornography, crimes of passion, and life sentences. In *The Affective Life of Law: Modernism and the Literary Imagination*, Raavit Reichman (2009) seeks to show how intuitions and emotions so richly expressed in literary work by Virginia Woolf, Rebecca West, and others can provide us with a richer and deeper understanding of the pain experienced in some noteworthy legal cases and helps us to imagine a world not as it is but as it should be.

Adherents of feminist jurisprudence and of critical race theory have been especially receptive to using the narrative form as a means of bringing the different voices of historically marginalized people—women and people of color—into the dialogue about law and legal issues. In American literature, women have often acted in accordance with their own moral code and at odds with law (Pagnattaro 2001). Robin West (1988, p. 65) has argued that women in law must "flood the market" with their stories to counter the traditional dominance of stories coming from men, as there are significant differences between female and male stories. Perhaps women have been more willing than men to bring honest autobiographical accounts of their experiences into their accounts of law and legal matters. In a landmark article on rape law, Susan Estrich began this way:

> Eleven years ago, a man held an ice pick to my throat and said: "Push over, shut up, or I'll kill you." I did what he said, but I couldn't stop crying. A hundred years later, I jumped out of my car as he drove away. (1986, p. 1087)

This is not a conventional opening for an article in a major law review. The author goes on to examine essential elements in the existing legal response to rape and to offer an alternative to deficient aspects of this response. Does the introduction of her own story and experience with rape make a difference? Does it enhance or diminish the impact and validity of her analysis? Or is it utterly irrelevant? Susan Estrich, the author, stated that she has made a conscious decision to invoke her own story:

> I cannot imagine anyone writing an article on prosecutorial discretion without disclosing that he or she had been a prosecutor.
>
> I cannot imagine myself writing on rape without disclosing how I learned my first lessons or why I care so much. (1986, p. 1089)

Perhaps one need not have experienced rape personally to be able to write cogently on its legal dimensions. One may even write empathetically without having experienced rape. But if the experience is in fact part of one's story, then telling the story would seem to be the honest thing to do, leaving it to the reader to decide whether it is relevant. An emphasis on the relevance of personal experience, then, is certainly one central theme of a narrative jurisprudence.

Derrick Bell (1987), a critical race theorist, used the narrative form to expose the harsh realities of the struggle for justice by African-Americans. Specifically, he created an imaginary character, Geneva Crenshaw, to explore the strategies that African-American people have used in this struggle as well as the means used by the dominant White forces to deny the struggle. Clearly, Bell (1992, 2004) believes that storytelling is a more powerful way of addressing these issues than through some form of dispassionate legal or historical analysis.

Narrative jurisprudence, then, challenges the traditional tendency within law to engage in dry, dispassionate, and disengaged forms of analysis, all too often with more attention to technical, formal legal questions than to raw human consequences. It has been criticized as introducing a wholly subjective dimension into discussions of law and legal issues, which interferes with rigorous analyses and open-minded argumentation (Farber and Sherry 1997). Narrative jurisprudence attempts to fully reintroduce the human dimension into the study of law, to make connections between legal issues and the larger questions of the meaning of human existence, and to facilitate the dialogue between law and the humanities.

POSTMODERN JURISPRUDENCE

The last of the contemporary schools of jurisprudence to be considered here is the most recent to surface and the most difficult to clearly define (Litowitz 1997; Stacy 2001; Arrigo, Milovanovic, and Schehr 2005). Indeed, some of those associated with critical legal studies, critical race theory, and feminist jurisprudence incorporate themes and terms associated with postmodern thought, and accordingly, there are no sharp boundaries between these jurisprudential perspectives and a **postmodern jurisprudence** (Minda 1995). Nevertheless, the distinctive themes associated with the postmodern merit some attention independent of any discussion of other perspectives.

Postmodern thought and jurisprudence reject claims of anyone's exclusive possession of "truth" and of the notion of a stable, fixed meaning in the world; they reject totalizing concepts (e.g., the state) and totalistic visions (e.g., that of communism, or liberal democracy) that claim to wholly capture human experience; they celebrate difference and multiculturalism; they emphasize the local and are profoundly skeptical of the potential of collective action to transform society; and they repudiate positivism, or the scientific method, as an appropriate methodology for understanding human existence (Rosenau 1992; McVeigh 2007).

In postmodern jurisprudence, then, there can be no single, solid foundation for law or for legal opinions. When judges and lawyers act as though law is objective and culturally neutral, they are deluding themselves and others. One mission for a postmodern jurisprudence is the exposure of how law as an enterprise systematically excludes many voices and experiences in a culturally diverse society. A postmodern jurisprudence seeks to open law up to a multiplicity of interpretations and to liberate law from the myth of determinacy.

Boaventura de Sousa Santos (1995), of the University of Coimbra, Portugal, provided us with one vision of a postmodern jurisprudence. Santos made the provocative argument that in our time, mainstream science no longer provides a framework for understanding our world and we must therefore look to other sources upon which we can establish a decent human life. In the context of increasing globalization, Western standards of human rights are hypocritical and insufficient, and we must learn to recognize new rights (including the right to bring historical capitalism to trial in a world tribunal!). For Santos, postmodern critical theory must displace the dominant, traditional forms of power, law, and knowledge and must provide us with a new map for making sense of our world.

Unsurprisingly, postmodern thought and postmodern jurisprudence have been strongly criticized (Handler 1992; Litowitz 1997; Patterson 1996a). Proponents have been attacked for being nihilistic, or denying belief in anything; for failing to provide a vision for transforming society and law in a progressive direction; and for being pretentious in their use of arcane and obscure terminology. It remains to be seen whether postmodern jurisprudence will be discredited as a passing intellectual fad or will broadly transform our way of understanding law and human existence in relation to law.

CONCLUSION

It may seem bewildering to the novice student of law to be confronted with such a diversity of jurisprudential perspectives. Figure 4.1 shows roughly how the perspectives discussed in this chapter are related to each other. The different schools suggest very different bases for understanding what law is, what it ought to be, and what legal decision making is based on, as well as what it ought to be based on. Some schools of jurisprudence clearly treat law as relatively autonomous. For other schools of jurisprudence, law can only be understood in relation to a social context or in terms of particular variables (e.g., wealth, power, gender, or race). In the more recent era, there has been a strong tendency within jurisprudence to look to disciplines outside of law—including economics, history, philosophy, and literature—but the field of law is divided, and many law professors continue to adopt a jurisprudential

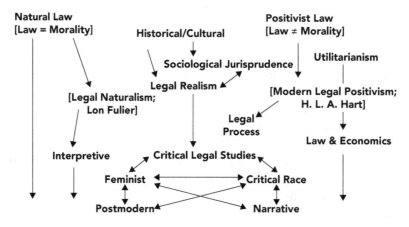

The relationship between the different schools of jurisprudence is complex, and accordingly can be diagrammed in different ways. The relationships suggested here are approximate and provisional.

FIGURE 4.1 Schools of Jurisprudence: An Approximate Genealogy

---

BOX 4.9 JURISPRUDENCE IN A GLOBALIZED WORLD

If *globalization* is one of the buzzwords of the current era, what impact should this have for jurisprudence? A prominent student of jurisprudence, William Twining (2009), has noted the need for jurisprudence to acknowledge globalization and its implications for thinking about law. Other commentators recognize that an understanding of law today must increasingly orient itself toward a global, as opposed to a national or state, framework (Dauvergne 2003; Kalir 2001). More specifically, law must be understood on many different levels, "including global (e.g., global environmental issues), international (e.g., relations between nation-states), regional (e.g., the European Union), transnational (e.g., rules for multinational corporations), intercommunal (e.g., the relations between ethnic or religious groups), territorial (e.g., the law of subnational jurisdictions, such as Quebec), substate (e.g., religious law, officially recognized in a plural legal system), and

nonstate (e.g., the laws of subordinated peoples)" (Kalir 2001, pp. 788–789). The perspectives of disciplines outside of law become especially important in a **globalized jurisprudence**, as there is a need to understand law in many different economic, political, cultural, and human circumstances. A globalized jurisprudence seeks to develop concepts and a language that can be applied most broadly and generally across borders. Such a jurisprudence must also integrate the innovative new forms of technology into an understanding of how to resolve complex legal issues, crossing many borders. The spread of free market forces and pressures toward democratization around the world, along with such technological developments as the Internet, must increasingly be incorporated into a globalized jurisprudence. A globalized framework has to be applied to current developments in international business, labor, nationality, immigration, and crime. Such phenomena can no longer be adequately understood by a jurisprudence rooted in a national, or even a Western, framework.

---

perspective that emphasizes the internal concerns of law. The world of legal scholarship itself has been characterized as divided between those who engage in "committed argument" and those who engage in "detached observation"; those who engage in doctrinal analysis (or the technical analysis of legal principles found in judicial opinions) and those who engage in analysis driven by social science; and those who engage in lawyerly advocacy and those who engage in the scholarly pursuit of truth (Underwood 1981). Early in the twenty-first century, it has been increasingly recognized that jurisprudence will have to take fuller account of globalization in an interconnected world (*see* Box 4.9).

The "mainstream" of legal scholarship is criticized by many of the adherents of emerging schools of jurisprudence as reinforcing conventional legal thought, taking the world we live in as a given, and being boring. The adherents of the new schools of jurisprudence are criticized in turn by mainstream scholars as elitists, engaged in pretentious wordplay, utterly out of touch with the real world, and promoters of a nihilistic, destructive orientation toward law (Duxbury 2003; Schlag 1987). This standoff between very different approaches to making sense of law endures. Despite the many attacks, from any number of vantage points, legal positivism survives, and by some measures it has even been reinforced. Arguments for pragmatism and practical reasoning staying close to the particulars of actual cases, as well as the traditional logic of law and legal rules, have been advanced against the efforts to bring the perspectives of various other disciplines upon matters of law (Dickstein 1999; Patterson 1996a).

In the final analysis, the different schools of jurisprudence impress on us recognition of the ultimate complexity of law and its many dimensions. Any school of jurisprudence can be challenged on some grounds, and this is true of the contemporary schools as well as the traditional schools. But law and economics, interpretive jurisprudence, critical legal studies, feminist jurisprudence, critical race theory, narrative jurisprudence, and postmodern jurisprudence all sensitize us, in provocative and fruitful ways, to dimensions and aspects of law not readily visible through the perspective of traditional schools of jurisprudence. As you encounter particular issues within law, and particular legal cases, it is surely valuable to ask yourself how these perspectives might enrich your understanding of the issue or case. A diversity of jurisprudential perspectives will certainly prevail in the future. New schools of jurisprudence are likely to emerge, and some of the existing schools are likely to become marginalized or largely discredited. If the postmodern premise is correct, then the search for "truth" about law is an open-ended process that will continue in some form indefinitely.

KEY TERMS AND CONCEPTS

Brandeis Brief
chain novel
Coase theorem
contemporary schools of
  jurisprudence
critical legal studies
critical race theory
external morality
feminist jurisprudence
globalized jurisprudence
grundnorm

historical/cultural jurisprudence
internal morality
interpretive jurisprudence
intersectionalism
jurisprudence
law and economics
  jurisprudence
legal naturalism
legal positivism
legal realism
mechanical jurisprudence

narrative jurisprudence
natural law
nihilistic jurisprudence
postmodern jurisprudence
pragmatic jurisprudence
process theory
sociological jurisprudence
traditional schools of
  jurisprudence
utilitarianism

DISCUSSION QUESTIONS

1. An understanding of law can come from any number of sources. Which of the schools of jurisprudence, in your opinion, most accurately explains, or attempts to explain, law in our society today?
2. Compare and contrast sociological jurisprudence with legal realism. Give reactions to the specific quotations

and suggestions made by Oliver Wendell Holmes, Jr. Would Ehrlich and Pound tend to agree or disagree with his views?

3. Discuss some of the major contributions feminists such as Carol Gilligan and Catharine MacKinnon have made. Why is it important to have such a school of jurisprudence? Will women ever have an equal voice in the law?

4. What can narrative jurisprudence bring to the study of law? Do you think law can accurately be portrayed through literary works?

5. Discuss the major premise of postmodern jurisprudence and whether or not this school of thought has the potential to become a major influence on future legal studies.

CHAPTER 5

THE LAW AND SOCIETY MOVEMENT

The **Law and Society Movement** is not a unified enterprise; it encompasses the work of historians, literary critics, anthropologists, political scientists, economists, psychologists, sociologists, and others who study some dimension of the interrelationship of the legal and the social (Abel 2010; Galanter 2006; Tomlins 2000). Much crossing of boundaries occurs among these disciplines and between the traditional realms of the legal and the social (Reichman 2008; Sarat et al. 1998b). At least some law professors have become involved with the law and society movement by drawing heavily on one or more of the various disciplines in their study of law and legal issues and by focusing on law as a social phenomenon (Dickinson 2007; Kalman 2002; Macaulay, Friedman, and Stookey 1995). But the law and society movement is best thought of as an endeavor to make sense of law from a vantage point outside of the professional study of law; jurisprudence (the focus of Chapter 4) is the work of law professors making sense of the law from within the context of legal education and practice (*see* Box 5.1).

Those engaged in **sociolegal scholarship** adopt diverse methods. The methods range from interpretive critical analyses to detailed case histories to highly quantitative empirical studies (Shram and Caterino 2006). Students of law and society tend to share a general assumption that law must be understood as a product of sociohistorical, cultural, political, economic, and psychological forces and that law, in turn, has an impact in each one of these areas.

Law has been characterized as "the oldest social science," as it precedes the establishment of social science disciplines but has come to increasingly draw upon these disciplines (Goodrich 2009). A growing recognition of the ultimate complexity of social existence—and law as a dimension of social existence—has led to more interdisciplinary study of law (Reichman 2008). Neuroscience and behavioral genetics, for example, play an increasing role in the study of law-related behavior (Farahany 2009). Altogether, the empirical study of law and legal phenomena has steadily increased (Galanter 2006). Legal rights and how people come to develop "rights consciousness" and choose to invoke their legal rights has been one focus of sociolegal research (Dickinson 2007).

BOX 5.1 NUDGE: AN INTERDISCIPLINARY
APPROACH TO HUMAN BEHAVIOR
AND LEGAL POLICY

Nudge: Improving Decisions about Health, Wealth, and Happiness,
a book co-authored by Richard Thaler and Cass Sunstein (2008),
may be taken to represent one interdisciplinary approach to law
and society issues. Thaler is a professor of behavioral science and
economics at the University of Chicago, and Sunstein is a professor of law at Harvard. Their book adopts an approach to designing public policy that takes full account of knowledge of human
cognitive limitations developed out of research in psychology
and behavioral economics (Goldstein 2008). The book challenges
a common economic model of humans as rational decision-
makers. Rather, humans are often quite irrational, error-prone,
impulsive, and distracted. It also challenges those who advocate *laissez-faire* government policies and those who advocate
imposing government preferences on citizens. In an approach
described as "libertarian paternalism," Thaler and Sunstein advocate public policies that allow people free choices while "nudg-
ing" or influencing them to make choices from which they will
benefit in terms of altogether better, healthier, and longer lives.
For example, laws can be designed so that they increase levels of
savings by individuals while allowing them to opt out of savings
programs.

Cass Sunstein, when he was appointed to the Harvard Law
School faculty in 2008, was described by its dean as "the pre-
eminent legal scholar of our time—the most wide-ranging, the
most prolific, the most cited, and the most influential" (*Current
Biography* 2008, p. 85). It is worth noting, then, that Sunstein's
work draws upon a broad range of disciplines and has been of
interest to law and society scholars in many different fields. He
served for many years as professor of both law and political
science at the University of Chicago. He is the author of more
than a dozen books and countless articles and has addressed
major issues in constitutional theory, administrative policy, family
law, and environmental law, among other areas, and has written authoritatively on animal rights, gay rights, the impact of
the Internet and numerous other topics. A recent book is titled:
*On Rumors: How Falsehoods Spread, Why We Believe Them,
What Can Be Done* (2009). He has been an advocate of "judicial
minimalism," arguing that the courts should proceed cautiously
about changing laws and should avoid ruling broadly in the cases
before them. He was appointed administrator of the Office of
Information and Regulatory Affairs by President Obama.

An interest in the relationship between the legal and the social goes far back in history.
The emergence of a recognizable law and society movement is much more recent (Reichman
2008; Garth and Sterling 1998). The founding of the Law and Society Association in 1964
signified a formal recognition of interest in interdisciplinary sociolegal scholarship. Other
associations fostering an interdisciplinary approach to the study of law include the American
Law & Economics Association, the American Psychology and Law Society, and the Association
for Political and Legal Anthropology. The law and society movement brought together scholars from many of the disciplines referred to earlier who had developed a special interest in
law and legal phenomena, as well as law professors who were drawing upon one or more of
these disciplines in their own studies of law. These objectives are sometimes at odds with each
other. Despite the involvement of a growing number of law professors in the law and society
movement, it has continued to occupy a somewhat marginal status in law schools, with most
law professors focused on internal issues and questions of legal policies and practices. Austin
Sarat (2004) is among those who have argued forcefully that the study of law is too important
to be left to law schools but requires full engagement by the liberal arts and law as part of an
undergraduate college curriculum. In the recent era, sociolegal scholarship has expanded in
many countries around the world, and the law and society movement has become increasingly
transnational, with international meetings in Amsterdam (1991), Glasgow (1996), Budapest
(2001), Berlin (2006), and a joint meeting in Vancouver in 2002 with the Canadian Law and
Society Association. Although this movement has been dominated by the United States, this
dominance is likely to be increasingly challenged (Reichman 2008; Mather 2003). The law
and society movement is now more global in its focus and concerns (*see* Box 5.2).

BOX 5.2　A LAW AND SOCIETY CANON?

A canon is essentially an authoritative set of works quite broadly recognized to have shaped some realm of scholarly inquiry. These works are widely cited over a long period of time, and all serious students of the area in question will be familiar with these works. Attempts have been made to collate and identify the law and society canon: for example, Austin Sarat (2004) edited *The Blackwell Companion of Law and Society*, and Carroll Seron (2006) edited *The Law and Society Canon*. We also have collections such as Javier Trevino's (2006) *Classic Writings in Law and Society: Contemporary Comments and Criticisms*.

But any listing of or discussion of "canonical" works will be open to criticism for having neglected some clearly influential work and highlighting other work not yet tested by time. Elizabeth Loeb (2008), commenting on Seron's "canon" volume,

notes that those represented are principally White males associated with the dominant views of law and jurisprudence during the mid-twentieth-century period. The contributions of and perspectives advanced by those associated with critical legal studies, critical race theory, Chicano studies, Third World theory, disability studies, radical feminism, and Queer theory are largely, if not wholly, absent. Amnon Reichman (2008) argues that contemporary law and society scholars are more conscious of the ultimate complexities of social reality and the limitations of social sciences than the legal realist founders of the law and society movement. These contemporary scholars are less focused on "nuts and bolts" of legal decision making than on the social uses of law, its effects, and its limits. The law and society movement is increasingly interdisciplinary, transnational and global, and attuned to the transformative effects of a digital era.

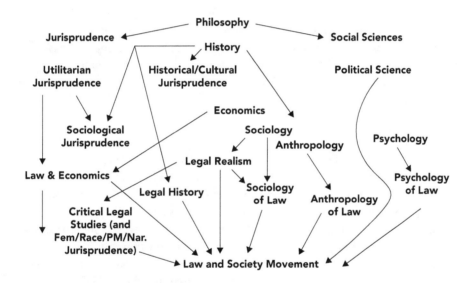

The relationship between the different disciplines and the Law and Society Movement is complex, and accordingly can be diagrammed in different ways. The relationships suggested here are approximate and provisional.

FIGURE 5.1　The Law and Society Movement: An Approximate Genealogy

DISCIPLINES CONTRIBUTING TO THE LAW AND SOCIETY MOVEMENT

Various humanistic and social science disciplines in many countries contribute to our understanding of law and legal phenomena (*see* Fig. 5.1). The perspective of several of these disciplines is briefly reviewed in the paragraphs that follow. Two significant disciplinary perspectives—anthropology and history—are discussed more fully in Chapter 6.

PHILOSOPHY

Philosophers are concerned with the meaning of justice and law and with the relationship between them (Adams 2000; Coleman and Shapiro 2002; Patterson 1996b). Ethics as a branch of philosophy is concerned with formulating principles for identifying goodness and morality; of course, ethical questions intersect with legal issues at many points. Philosophers grapple with the complex relation between morality and law. Metaphysics as a branch of philosophy is concerned with such matters as the nature of reality and of human beings. The enduring question of whether human beings have a free will (voluntarism) or human behavior is a product of various forces acting upon people (determinism), or some mixture of voluntarism and determinism, obviously has major implications for law. Still another dimension of philosophy is concerned with principles of logic and the role of language in making sense of the world. Again, logic is intimately involved in legal reasoning, and issues of language usage and interpretation are critically important in legal opinions.

Indeed, all those who engage in the study and practice of law come into contact at various points with the kinds of philosophical questions just mentioned. All such study and practice involves the adoption of explicit or implicit assumptions on such matters as the nature of justice, morality, reality, and human nature itself. Many of these philosophical matters have already been mentioned in the first several chapters and will inevitably show up at other points in this text. But precisely because philosophy is in some respects so central to the study of law, and so intertwined with jurisprudence, it is not a major component of the law and society movement, other than in the sense of being part of the background and context of this movement.

POLITICAL SCIENCE

Law in one interpretation is an expression of power, and the use of power is one major preoccupation of political science. The use, as well as the abuse, of power in connection with law is studied by political scientists (Jacobs and Jackson 2010; Jacobs, Novak, and Zelizer 2003; Vincent 1996). Law both imposes constraints on the use of political power and serves as a means of exercising political power. Furthermore, political power is most effective in promoting law and persuading people to comply with it when the power holder is viewed as legitimate, or entitled to respect and obedience. The legitimation of law is studied by political scientists, among others; this topic is more fully discussed in Chapter 9.

Some political scientists apply quantitative, mathematical techniques to the analysis of law and legal institutions, whereas others use qualitative methods and case studies (Schram and Caterino 2006).

In developed nations it is the formal political institutions (in the American system the legislative branch, the judicial branch, and the executive branch of government) that make, administer, and enforce the laws. Political scientists are interested in both the formal processes for the making, administration, and enforcement of law and the informal political pressures and behind-the-scenes negotiations involved (Neubauer and Meinhold 2004; Porto 2001; Renteln 2007). In the United States there are especially strong links between the political and the legal realms. Political officials greatly influence the legal system through the appointment of judges and prosecutors. Elected judges, in particular, can be influenced in their decision making by political considerations and public opinion. The decisions of the courts can also have an impact on the political process in many ways. Political scientists have increasingly had to concern themselves with international law, and the impact of globalization on law, and legal institutions (Renteln 2007).

Crime and crime control are major issues in American political life; accordingly, the courts can be subjected to unusually intense attention and pressure from officials and from the public, while crime-related decisions in turn help determine the response of political officials. Although the criminal justice system has received a disproportionate amount of attention, political scientists have also become interested in how the legal system resolves civil cases (Jacob 1996; Renteln 2007). Divorce law, automobile insurance cases, product liability, and many other civil matters have become important political issues.

Americans are especially likely to turn to the courts to resolve political controversies (most famously, in the recent era, to resolve the Bush vs. Gore election of 2000) (Jacob 1996; Neubauer and Meinhold 2004). These controversies range from abortion to zoning and everything in between. The American courts play an important role in formulating public policy and accordingly can become entangled in political disputes. The Warren Court of the 1960s, for example, was widely denounced, especially by political conservatives, who claimed that it broadened the rights of criminals and handcuffed the police and consequently fueled a rising wave of crime (Graham 1970). The most conspicuous policy making takes place on the appellate court level. Political scientists have played a key role in the study of the U.S. Supreme Court: the process involved in the selection and confirmation of justices; the role of political ideology in the decision making of individual justices; factors influencing the response in the larger American community to landmark Supreme Court decisions; and many other such issues. Political scientists have studied patterns of lower court compliance with higher court decisions (Benesh and Reddick 2002; Renteln 2007) and tensions between following law or following political beliefs in higher court decisions (Richards and Kritzer 2002). Increasingly, political scientists have recognized and studied the political dynamics of the lower courts as well.

Many political scientists have judged the law—and the institutions of law, such as the courts—as inherently conservative, with a strong vested interest in the established order and the maintenance of orderliness and compliance. They have declared that historically, the poor and the powerless have been at a major disadvantage in the legal systems, and they have documented some of the political ramifications of this disadvantage. Political scientists have explored the political factors leading to some increase for the disadvantaged in accessibility to the courts, as well as ongoing limitations of this accessibility. Altogether, political scientists have had to sort out the relationship between beliefs about law and such other factors as the political organization of the system in determining who litigates, and why.

ECONOMICS

The existence of a law and economics school of jurisprudence was discussed in Chapter 4, and the connections between economists who study law and law professors who adopt economic analysis are especially pronounced (Edelman 2004; Markovits 2008; White 2009). Economic approaches to the understanding of law often include complex quantitative analyses and mathematical formulas, and in this sense economic analysis is closest to the rigor of the physical and natural sciences (Kitch 1986). Game theory, which focuses on calculations of payoffs by "players" engaged in some form of activity, is one form of economic analysis that has been applied to law (Rasmusen 2007). Originally, the economic analysis of law addressed such legal areas as taxation, regulation, and antitrust matters, for which economic dimensions are central and obvious, but in the more recent era this analysis has been extended to other matters, including contracts, torts, property rights, and crime (Goldberg 2006; Landes and Posner 2003; Shavell 2004). In one sense, this new interest reflects a return to the concerns of pioneering political economists in the eighteenth and nineteenth centuries, although the contemporary focus tends to be narrower and more technical.

An economic analysis of law might focus on the interrelationship between a particular type of economic system and law. Capitalism as an economic system can be shown to shape the legal system in many ways (e.g., with laws favoring free markets and free enterprise); it can also be shown that a particular type of legal ideology (i.e., that of the European bourgeoisie) helped promote the growth of capitalism (Tigar and Levy 1977). The ideological orientation of contemporary economists (e.g., conservative or leftist) may influence whether they attempt to identify legal rules and procedures compatible with the efficient expansion of capitalist growth or expose legal rules and procedures that contribute to economic exploitation and inequality.

From an economic perspective, one seeks to identify ways in which law provides incentives (or disincentives) for productive economic activity and growth. This type of analysis has been applied to the problem of pollution, where the challenge has been to identify the legal response that minimizes pollution without producing unacceptable economic costs. It has also been applied to the problem of drug abuse, where the challenge has been to identify the legal response that raises the cost of such abuse to a level discouraging it without imposing excessive economic costs on society. Will government officials adopt policies favoring the public interest when market forces fail? Critics have seriously considered this notion, offering promotion of self-interest and special interests as an alternative (Tullock, Seldon, and Brady 2002). Although economic efficiency and wealth maximization is a central theme in the economic analysis of law, some recent work has focused more neutrally on the character of different types of transactions and the impact of different types of institutional arrangements on these transactions.

The economic approach to understanding law is often insensitive to human values and considerations that are independent of economic efficiency (e.g., realizing justice and fairness). This approach has been especially controversial when applied to the realm of the personal, such as sex, family relations, and consumer behavior (Hill 2004). The economic analysis of law can also be criticized on the basis that it is inherently conservative, is theoretically impressive but impractical, and adopts the questionable assumption that human beings act rationally, choosing the means (on the basis of what is known) that most efficiently realize their ends (Edelman 2004). On this last point, the alternative view is that many factors other than rational calculation determine human behavior, and much human behavior is not rational in the sense identified by economists.

PSYCHOLOGY

The individual and the dynamics of individual behavior are the primary focuses of psychology. The impact of groups on individuals, and of individuals on the group, is the province of social psychology. Because decision making is obviously one key element of legal behavior, it follows that psychological factors play an important role in law (Castanzo 2004; Kapardis 2004; Canter and Zukauskiene 2008). First, do people who violate laws do so with an understanding of the wrongness of their actions and with the capacity to control their conduct? And by what criteria should people be deprived of their liberty and committed to mental institutions? Psychology has been intimately involved with the assessment of sanity in cases of lawbreaking and with a broader range of legal issues arising out of the problem of mental illness (Williams and Arrigo 2007). **Forensic psychology** focuses on investigating (and testifying about) patterns of criminal behavior (Bartol and Bartol 2004). Psychological evidence has played an important role in some landmark Supreme Court decisions (Jackson 2001). Psychologists are interested in understanding the psychology of both law making and law breaking and in assisting legal decision makers in understanding cases in psychological terms.

Psychology has also studied factors influencing the behavior of bystanders and witnesses in legal cases. Various personal attributes as well as situational factors influence how people respond when they witness a crime, accident, or some other event that has legal repercussions. Psychological studies have established that past traumas, perceptual deficiencies, memory gaps, and emotional stresses can interfere with or distort memories of past events for witnesses in legal cases (Kapardis 2007; Marshall 1966; Memon 2003). The reliability of the testimony of child witnesses is especially questionable (Bottoms, Najdowski, and Goodman 2009; Kapardis 2007). Such findings are in conflict with the general expectation in courts of law that witnesses are capable of providing accurate and reliable testimony.

Psychologists have investigated the relationship among a range of psychological factors, including personality type, and decisions made by judges, jurors, police officers, and other legal actors (Lloyd-Bostock 1988; Winter 2002). They have recognized the need to account for race and cultural differences in the interpretation of law-related behavior and decision making (Barrett and George 2004). Many studies have addressed the social psychology of jury decision making, as well as the various sources of bias in judicial decision making. In some cases, psychologists have produced profiles of jurors most likely to be sympathetic to one side or the other in a legal case, although some observers are uncomfortable with this type of direct involvement in jury selection. Psychologists have also investigated the psychological impact of being subjected to the legal process, as one of the accused, a plaintiff, or a witness. The need for psychological counseling of such parties was established, in part, through such investigations.

Finally, Tyler and colleagues (e.g., Tyler, 1998; 2007; Tyler and Yuen 2002) have been especially active contributors to the sociolegal literature with studies of such psychological

TABLE 5.1   A SUMMARY OF SELECTED DISCIPLINARY PERSPECTIVES ON LAW

Philosophy	Fundamental assumptions (e.g., on human nature) and law; law and justice; law and morality.
Political science	Law and the use of power; the role of formal institutions of law (e.g., the legislative branch); law and politics.
Economics	Law and the economic system; legal policy and economic principles; law and economic costs.
Psychology	Law and individual behavior and mental processes; psychological dimensions of legal decision making and testimony; perceptions of law and legal institutions.
Sociology	Law and society; social and group dimensions of legal behavior; the social organization of legal institutions.

issues as how people perceive and respond to the procedural justice of the legal system (e.g., do they experience it as fair or unfair) and why people choose to obey or disobey the law. Some of these issues are addressed more fully in Chapter 9. Table 5.1 summarizes the disciplinary perspectives on law discussed here.

THE ORIGINS OF A SOCIOLEGAL PERSPECTIVE

Although the formal emergence of a law and society movement and a sociology of law is quite recent, an interest in the relation between the social and the legal goes far back in history. In the sections that follow, some of the principal stages in the evolution of this interest are identified and discussed. The review here is limited to work emerging in the Western European tradition. This limitation reflects constraints of space as well as of the author's own knowledge.

THE CLASSICAL GREEK PHILOSOPHERS

It is always remarkable to realize how much contemporary thought has its roots in the ideas of a relatively small number of philosophers living in Greece thousands of years ago (Ewald 2007b; Rubin 1997). References to law and justice can be found in the thought of the Sophists, Plato, and Aristotle. The Sophists (late fifth and early fourth centuries B.C.) were divided between those who regarded human laws as being at odds with the superior laws of nature and those who believed law could fulfill some worthwhile purposes for human society.

Plato's (427–347 B.C.) *The Republic* and *Laws* introduce ideas and issues with which we are still contending (Gouldner 1966). He was concerned in these works with the kinds of laws needed to govern human society and to avoid anomia, or a sense of confusion about the rules to be followed. Plato viewed law as a necessary constraint on human nature. For Plato, law educates, and law has the capacity to create a sphere of equality (which was not, however, to be extended to all). Plato called for the rule of the philosopher/king.

Aristotle (384–322 B.C.) also regarded the rule of law as an absolutely necessary element in the survival of the state (Ewald 2007a; Rubin 1997). Aristotle believed that the law should promote the common welfare of the citizenry. He recognized the role of popular will in the making of law but especially emphasized the responsibility of well-trained legislators.

Aristotle believed that a certain amount of judicial discretion was inevitable and desirable and that customary laws sometimes took precedence over formal, written laws.

The ideas of the Greek philosophers provided one starting point for subsequent efforts to understand the relation between the social and the legal.

EUROPEAN SOCIAL PHILOSOPHERS

Observations about the relation between law and society can be extracted from the works of social philosophers throughout the ages, but attention to this relation intensified during the Enlightenment in the seventeenth and eighteenth centuries. Although it is difficult to apply broad generalizations to the diverse social philosophers of this period, the Enlightenment is associated with an emphasis on the powers of reason, the potential of science, and the prospect of progress toward a more advanced society and way of life. The English philosopher Thomas Hobbes (1588–1679), in the early stages of the Enlightenment, is credited with having directly raised the question of social order or how it is possible for human beings to live together in a state of relative harmony. In *Leviathan*, Hobbes ([1651] 1958) answers this question by asserting that in a "state of nature" human beings live in a situation of a "war of all against all." However, human beings differ from other creatures in that they have the power of reason, and reason leads them to recognize that it is in their interest to delegate power over themselves to the state (the Leviathan) in return for security. This is the essence of Hobbes' social contract, and it has influenced one way of thinking about the basis of law in human society.

For another English philosopher, John Locke (1632–1704), writing some decades after Hobbes, humans are naturally inclined to form social bonds with each other. Locke expressed the view that human beings have certain "natural rights," and the social contract is formed to ensure that a government's primary mission is the promotion and protection of these rights. As every American schoolchild learns, these ideas greatly influenced the Founding Fathers of the new American republic and were incorporated into the formative document on American law: the Constitution.

The French/Swiss philosopher Jean-Jacques Rousseau (1712–1778) also made an important contribution to the idea of the social contract, although his views were at odds with those of both Hobbes and Locke. Rousseau's thought was original, and he is not easily classified; the romantic strain in his work, for example, is at odds with the Enlightenment celebration of reason. For Rousseau, human beings in the original state of nature lived freely and harmoniously; civilization has had a corrupting and oppressive impact on human existence. The social contract, then, should be based on the "general will" of the people, expressed through the state—not the government—which only enjoys delegated power. This centralized power of the state should be absolute, once the general will has been expressed. These ideas have been interpreted as supportive of both totalitarianism and democracy. Rousseau's thought was influential during the French Revolution (reflected, some would say, in the reign of terror), but it also inspired the utopian aspect of Marx's vision of a society of liberated and equal human beings, working together cooperatively. The eighteenth-century Italian philosopher Giambattista Vico (1688–1744) promoted the notion of law as a human creation (Luft 2007; Mootz 2008; Sullivan 2008). Vico was a proponent of an approach to human history highlighting progressive stages and cycles. He regarded the origins of law as rooted in primitive social practices that became formalized over time. We should look to the historical development of jurisprudence, not abstract reasoning, to identify fundamental moral principles that should guide law. Vico anticipated contemporary issues of law in relation to society and the character of legal education.

Baron Charles de Montesquieu (1689–1755), the French essayist, is considered an important forefather of the sociology of law specifically. Montesquieu (who had studied law as a young man) challenged the core assumption of natural law, that the source of law lies outside human experience, and argued instead for a view of law as a product of history, custom, the climate, and the environment human beings live in. He was concerned with identifying the totality of factors that account for the laws people live by (divided into civil, or family-related, criminal, and political law). For Montesquieu, laws are only understandable in a particular social context. Laws vary between different societies, in different climates, and during different periods. Each society, in this view, should have the laws most suited to its needs.

Another Frenchman, Alexis de Tocqueville (1805–1859), produced a famous account ([1835–1840] 1945) of his visit to the new American republic early in the nineteenth century. The official purpose of his visit, in 1831, was to examine and report back on the prison system being developed in the United States, but the book he produced described and analyzed many dimensions of the dynamic new country he toured. Montesquieu was living in a time of, and writing about, traditional monarchical republics, but Tocqueville was addressing an emerging modern type of society. Tocqueville, also a law student in his youth, admired and was greatly influenced by Montesquieu. His book, *Democracy in America*, has been an enduring classic in part because Tocqueville's observations about the essence of the new republic were remarkably astute. He recognized that the federal Constitution provided many benefits to American citizens and that law generally played a central and influential role in American life. He was especially interested in the way that the legal structure in the United States provided some balance between the will of the general population and the capacity of the political leadership to govern with some authority. Tocqueville also observed that lawyers had moved into the power vacuum created by the repudiation of an aristocracy as one consequence of the American Revolution. Altogether, he produced an inspirational model of analysis for later students of the relation between the legal and the social.

During the nineteenth century, other social historians set forth interpretations of the social basis and the changing nature of law with the evolution of society. In Chapter 4 (focusing on jurisprudence), Savigny's thesis of law as an expression of the national spirit (or *volkgeist*) was discussed, as well as Maine's thesis on the shifting character of law from status to contract.

FOUNDING FATHERS OF SOCIOLOGY

The most influential contributions to sociological theory were made during the latter part of the nineteenth century and the early years of the twentieth. The **founding fathers of**

TABLE 5.2   FOUNDING FATHERS OF SOCIOLOGY: KEY IDEAS

Karl Marx	Law as a reflection of the political economy; law as complicit in oppression and exploitation.
Herbert Spencer	The application of Darwinist principles to the understanding of law; survival of the fittest.
Emile Durkheim	Law as a social fact; changing forms of law as society evolves; law and social cohesion.
Max Weber	Law defined in social terms; law and legitimation; the growing import of rationality and law.

sociology (*see* Table 5.2) clearly recognized the importance of law as a dimension of society, perhaps more so than many later sociologists.

Karl Marx

Karl Marx (1818–1883), although best known as the principal critic of capitalism and the leading exponent of communism, has also been influential within the social sciences, including sociology. Marx studied law early in his career as a university student, although he found the study of law unrewarding. His personal encounters with law, principally in the form of experiencing censorship, were negative. Indeed, he specifically criticized censorship laws as wholly at odds with the notion of freedom. Of course, many later followers of Marx—including Stalin, Mao, and Castro—adopted their own censorship laws. Although Marx and his collaborator, Friedrich Engels, did not produce a systematic treatise on law as an aspect of society, they made various observations on law throughout their work (Cain and Hunt 1979; Travers 2010). Since Marx's views on some matters changed over time and some of his work was unfinished, it is possible to come up with different interpretations of law in his work.

Marx came to regard law as epiphenomenal, or a reflection of the material conditions of society. Marx exposed the contradiction in bourgeois (or capitalist) law, which claims to protect rights and promote justice when it actually is complicit in preserving privileges and denying the majority of members a fulfilling life. He was specifically critical of laws depriving peasants of common use rights in forests. These laws served the interests of wealthy members of society. In the *instrumentalist* interpretation of Marx's work, law is viewed as directly controlled by the ownership class and an important instrument in the maintenance of social inequality and the exploitation and oppression of the working classes. In the *structural* interpretation, the state and the law are principally oriented toward the long-term survival of the system, and the law is therefore relatively autonomous. This second interpretation, which is more sophisticated and persuasive, allows one to account for laws prohibiting especially outrageous capitalist activities (e.g., monopolistic practices and polluting the environment) while not denying the basic role of law in maintaining an inherently unjust system. For Marx, there should be no need for law in an authentically communist society, where people would live cooperatively and the motivations for predatory conduct would have disappeared. In its broad outlines, then, Marx's conception of law has been an influence on social theories that address the negative role of law in modern societies. Some aspects of Marx's views on law are explored further in Chapter 6.

Herbert Spencer

Although Herbert Spencer is little read today, he had a large influence in his own time, and some of his core ideas have been revived in contemporary society. Herbert Spencer (1820–1903) was an Englishman who, despite relatively little formal education, produced a series of works on the basic principles of ethics, biology, psychology, and sociology. Writing in the wake of the introduction of Darwin's theory of evolution, Spencer (1898) applied the Darwinian perspective on human evolution to whole societies; just as the individual organism evolves, so analogously can society be regarded as an organism that evolves over time. Law itself evolves from an orientation stressing individual interests and privileges to inherited custom, divine orders, the will of leaders, and finally consensual, contractual equality before the law.

Spencer's ideas were adopted by **Social Darwinists** to support the notion that law should not interfere with the process of natural selection; the government's role should be confined to the protection of personal safety and the enforcement of contracts. On this view, the law should not specifically discriminate against the disadvantaged, but it should also refrain from "social engineering" in an effort to improve their circumstances. In the late twentieth century, American conservatives, without necessarily invoking Spencer, embraced some of the premises of Social Darwinism in their successful campaign to reduce the scope of welfare law and other law-based programs to aid the disadvantaged.

Emile Durkheim

Still another Frenchman, Emile Durkheim (1858–1917), provides us with an influential approach to understanding law and its role in society (Cotterrell 1991; Deflem 2008; Lukes and Scull 1983). Durkheim (who wrote a dissertation on Montesquieu) occupied the first professorship of sociology in France and has been considered the ultimate sociologist, insofar as he attempted to explain human activities almost wholly in sociological (as opposed to psychological) terms. For example, in his famous book, *Suicide* ([1897] 1951), Durkheim sought to demonstrate that this most "individualistic" of human acts is in fact best understood in terms of sociological factors, such as the relative absence of ties to social groups or supportive others.

In his first book, *The Division of Labor in Society* ([1893] 1984), Durkheim identified law broadly defined as an important social fact worthy of study (by ethnographic means), both in terms of its origins and its functions for society. On the origins of law, Durkheim held that in primitive societies, a repressive form of law was the norm, but in modern society law took on a restitutive form. Repressive law stresses control of people, whereas restitutive law stresses the equitable settlement of conflicts. Much criticism has been directed toward this familiar Durkheimian dichotomy. First, it is simplistic in its contrast between primitive and modern societies, with no consideration of the intermediary stages in the evolution of society. Second, much evidence suggests that Durkheim is simply mistaken both in regarding primitive societies as having a uniformly repressive law and in regarding modern societies as having a law that lacks this character and is restitutive (Spitzer 1975). Indeed, the contrary argument has been made that law becomes more controlling and severe in modern societies and is more flexible and reconciliative in so-called primitive societies. Nevertheless, Durkheim was among the influential early promoters of a comparative approach to the understanding of law.

Throughout his career, Durkheim was preoccupied with the nature of social solidarity, or the forces binding members of society together. For Durkheim, law could be regarded as an expression of the collective sentiments of society and the nature of social solidarity. Law, through the administration of punishment to those who deviate from society's norms, promotes social cohesion, in this view. Crime itself is declared to be both normal and inevitable—normal in the sense that it exists in every society, and inevitable in the sense that the needs of society and of individuals will never be wholly in accord. Crime is functional as well, insofar as the societal response to crime clarifies society's standards and reinforces social solidarity.

Here, again, Durkheim's interpretation has been justly criticized, although it has been very influential. First, Durkheim naively assumed that law expressed the will of society as a whole, when in fact there is much evidence that the powerful and privileged disproportionately determine the content of the law. Second, Durkheim neglected the many ways in which conflict occurring in connection with law and law itself can promote social conflict and divisiveness. In spite of these serious limitations of Durkheim's interpretation of law, he articulated one influential way of understanding law and its functions.

Max Weber

The German sociologist Max Weber (1864–1920) has been called the last universal genius of the social sciences. Weber, like Marx, was the son of a lawyer who himself studied law as a university student; some of his earliest published work addressed issues in legal history, and he taught law at the outset of his academic career. But, also like Marx, Weber ultimately assumed an immensely ambitious project of making sense of the modern world. It has been said that Weber engaged in a lifelong dialogue with the ghost of Karl Marx, because Weber's whole approach to understanding the modern world, and his interpretation of it, both paralleled and was at odds with Marx's on many key points (Loewith 1960). Weber viewed history and human society as more complex, contradictory, and pluralistic than did Marx.

Weber's work is immensely erudite; it is also difficult and subtle, and it does not lend itself readily to concise summaries. He is associated with the position that the social scientist must assume a "value-free" approach to the study of social phenomena; in other words, the social scientist should strive for objective analysis in his or her work, as opposed to taking sides and advocating social reforms. Weber also promoted the use of the "ideal type"—abstractions through which social reality can be categorized—in his study of society and law.

In his massive unfinished work, *Economy and Society*, Weber (1978) explored many aspects of law in relation to the nature of freedom, authority, secularization, bureaucracy, and the rise of capitalism. He identified the basic attributes of the bureaucracies that assumed such central importance in modern societies and in the operation of the legal system itself. A bureaucracy has a hierarchy of authority (or chain of command), specialization (or a division of labor), reliance upon a system of rules, and impersonal, formal criteria for advancement.

Weber's definition of "law" can be cited again here: "An order will be called *law* if it is externally guaranteed by the probability that coercion (physical or psychological), to bring about conformity or avenge violation, will be applied by a *staff* of people holding themselves specially ready for that purpose" (Weber 1978, p. 34). The notion that in the course of the evolution of Western society, rationality becomes an increasingly important attribute of law can be identified as a central theme in Weber's sociology of law. Although the term *rationality* was used in different ways by Weber, here it refers to a movement away from superstition and spontaneity in social control to reliance on an orderly, logical legal system.

Weber argued that a rational orientation was becoming increasingly important in the modern world, relative to tradition or personal charisma as a ground for legitimation (people's belief that they have an obligation to comply with a system of authority) (Boucock 2000; DeFlem 2008; Travers 2010). On the other hand, a legal system emphasizing formal justice and guaranteed rights, in Weber's interpretation, both facilitated the rise of a capitalist economic system and was in turn reinforced by such a system. Capitalism and formal, rational legal systems, then, have important affinities (Ewing 1987). Although for Weber these developments were inevitable in certain respects and a reflection of the general evolution of society, they could also be regarded with some ambivalence. Disenchantment with modern law occurs when people become increasingly reliant on the technical expertise of bureaucrats of the legal order, and in Weber's famous metaphor people develop a sense of being imprisoned in an "iron cage." Law in modern society, then, contributes to a sense of alienation.

Although critics tend to acknowledge the breadth of Weber's knowledge, his specific interpretations of the evolving character of law in society have been challenged on many grounds. Indeed, the understandings of law of all the founding fathers of sociology discussed here have been criticized (e.g., *see* Deflem 2008; Sheleff 1997), but they have nevertheless been influential and widely cited (*see* Box 5.3).

BOX 5.3   CONTEMPORARY EUROPEAN SOCIAL
PHILOSOPHERS AND LAW

In the final decades of the twentieth century, several European social philosophers produced work that was widely discussed and quite influential. Michel Foucault and Jurgen Habermas are two of the most important of these social philosophers (Tuori 2002; Wickham and Pavlich 2001). Much of their work is exceptionally dense and difficult, and it is unlikely to be comprehensible to most undergraduates. In light of how often their names and ideas are invoked, however, it seems worthwhile here to summarize a few key themes of their work as they relate to the sociology of law.

Michel Foucault (1926–1984), born in Poitiers, France, was a social philosopher and cultural historian (Turkel 1990, 1996). Foucault challenged the conventional idea that the modern era represented progress toward a more rational legal order, with broader rights and more freedom for individuals. Rather, in Foucault's interpretation, the state and other social institutions in the modern era are oriented to achieve greater and more efficient control over human beings. The law plays a key role in this process by cataloging and imposing judgment on individuals. Foucault's work seems to argue both for the greater penetration of law in society, through surveillance and discipline, and the possibilities of invoking law to challenge state oppression (Golder and Fitzpatrick 2009). In his celebrated book, *Discipline and Punish* (1977), Foucault sought to document the transformation of punishment from the traditional forms of public spectacles with direct punishment of the body to the modern form of imprisonment and therapeutic control over the mind. In the modern capitalist society, law, power, and knowledge are concentrated in the hands of a relatively small elite who achieve an ever greater capacity to watch over people, intrude on their privacy, and control them.

BOX 5.3 (cont'd.)

Jurgen Habermas (born in 1929 in Dusseldorf, Germany) is an immensely erudite and prolific social philosopher, whose work has been widely discussed and debated in intellectual circles (Baxter 2002; Rosenfeld and Arato 1998; Salter 1997). In his book, *Between Facts and Norms* (1996), Habermas described modern society as fragmented and ridden with cynicism and moral relativism, which leads to political disenchantment. In these circumstances, society faces a formidable challenge to regenerate social solidarity and heartfelt belief in law and other social institutions. Liberalism puts too much emphasis on individual rights, with a commensurate cost in terms of social solidarity; collectivism puts too much emphasis on social solidarity, with a resulting denigration of individual rights. The most effective response to the circumstances of contemporary society, then, requires a movement toward a radical form of democracy, where citizens can freely and fully communicate with others (the "ideal speech" situation). Law based on mutual understanding and a rational, democratic consensus is most likely to be supported and legitimated.

JURISPRUDENTIAL, HISTORICAL, AND ANTHROPOLOGICAL INFLUENCES ON SOCIOLEGAL SCHOLARSHIP

In Chapter 4 some attention was devoted to sociological jurisprudence and legal realism as early twentieth-century schools of jurisprudence. The call for more attention to sociological factors, social and behavioral science research, and social policy had an impact on the development of jurisprudence, but it also encouraged sociologists and other social scientists to attend to the relationship between the social and the legal.

Historical scholarship on law traditionally took the form of a narrative account of legal doctrine and decisions, with a stress on appellate court opinions and great cases, but James Willard Hurst (1950) directed attention to the impact of social and economic factors on the law and the operation of less conspicuous legal institutions and ordinary cases. Hurst was a major inspiration for and influence on some of the leading sociolegal scholars of the recent era.

Morton Horwitz (1977) exemplified the critical approach to sociohistorical analysis, with its thesis that in the nineteenth century, American judges ruled on many issues in ways that benefited the wealthy and powerful while having negative impact on other citizens. Laura Benton (2002) has ambitiously studied the historical movement from diverse or plural legal orders to state-dominated legal orders. Historians and lawyers have quite different projects, but both draw inferences from evidence (Twining and Hampsher-Monk 2003). The historical perspective is considered more fully in Chapter 6.

An anthropological approach to the study of law and society has been influential as well (Bracey 2006; Goodale and Mertz 2007; Nader 2002). In the nineteenth century, Sir Henry Maine ([1861] 2001) claimed that the nature of law was transformed in the movement from simpler to more complex modern societies. In the twentieth century, anthropologists such as Bronislaw Malinowski (1926) and E. Adamson Hoebel ([1954] 1967) explored what law meant in the world of preliterate peoples. In the recent era, some anthropologists (e.g., Merry 1990; Yngvesson 1993) have studied the meaning of legal consciousness and legal culture in contemporary American communities. The anthropological perspective on law is also explored in more depth in Chapters 6 and 9.

THE SOCIOLOGY OF LAW AND THE LAW AND SOCIETY MOVEMENT

The **sociology of law** is principally a development of the post-World War II era, although earlier contributions can be identified (e.g., Eugen Ehrlich's [1922] "The Sociology of Law" and Nicholas Timasheff's [(1939) 1974] *An Introduction to the Sociology of Law*). It is best described as a subdisciplinary field within the discipline of sociology; the American Sociological Association, for example, has a Sociology of Law section (Cotterrell 2007a; Halliday et al. 2002). The related law and society movement, which has blossomed since the founding of the Law and Society Association in 1964, is a more broadly interdisciplinary movement, including not only sociologists but psychologists, historians, economists, and political scientists, as well as law professors; all are drawn together by a common interest in the interrelation between the legal and the social, broadly defined (Barkan 2009; Munger 1998; Tomlins 2000). The term *sociolegal scholarship* is also sometimes used to describe this interest.

The development of general theories that explain social processes in which law is involved is one mission of a sociology of law (Banakar and Travers 2002; Sutton 2001; Trevino 1996). Some such theories are aligned with the functionalist approach, which views society as a system and focuses on the functions fulfilled by different aspects of the system; some theories are aligned with the conflict approach, which views society as a contested terrain and focuses on the maldistribution of power and resources; and some theories are aligned with an interactionist or constructionist approach, which views society as a symbolic creation of interacting humans and focuses on the production of social meaning. There are other specific theoretical approaches—from feminist to postmodernist—aligned in some degree with these broader theoretical approaches.

The **empirical study** of and analysis of interrelations between legal and social factors and variables is another mission of the sociology of law (Baumgartner 2001; Mertz 2008; Vago 2003). Scholars ask, how do social factors affect and shape the law and legal institutions, and how do the law and legal institutions influence and shape society or social behavior? (*See* Box 5.4.) Elizabeth Mertz (2008) distinguishes between an "insider" approach — social science as a "tool" for legal use – and an "outsider" approach – social science and sociology applied to an understanding of law and legal phenomena. There is also a "language of law" approach which involves a linguistic analysis of the language of law.

BOX 5.4 THE JURISPRUDENTIAL AND THE
SOCIOLOGICAL

Although the concerns of the sociology of law parallel (and sometimes intersect with) the concerns of jurisprudence, there are significant differences of emphasis. The sociologist Donald Black (1989, p. 21) has compared the two approaches concisely (if somewhat artificially):

	Jurisprudential	*Sociological*
Focus	Rules	Social Structure
Process	Logic	Behavior
Scope	Universal	Variable
Perspective	Participant	Observer
Purpose	Practical	Scientific
Goal	Decision	Explanation

A POSITIVIST APPROACH

Sociologist Donald Black (1995) is a proponent of the **positivistic approach**, or the application of the perspective and method of the natural sciences to the sociology of law. His work is very much in the tradition of Durkheim. Such an approach calls for the formulation of hypotheses that can be systematically tested by empirical means. Black (2007) now describes his theory as "legal relativity," insofar as it addresses variations in law in relation to social variables. It challenges the common fiction of legal universalism: that all are treated equally before the law. Black (1976) defines law, quite simply, as governmental social control. Law is a quantitative variable: law is arrests, cases, trials, decisions, complaints, and accusations. Law is a dependent variable and can be measured. Law increases and decreases from one setting to another.

Some specific empirical hypotheses formulated by Black include the following:

- Law varies inversely with other forms of social control (in other words, the more law you have, the less you need other forms of social control, and vice versa).
- More stratification produces more law (in other words, the more social and economic inequality in a society, the more law).
- Downward law is greater than upward law (in other words, more law is produced by the powerful and wealthy that has impact on the powerless and poor).
- Law increases as intimacy decreases, but law declines when people are wholly unconnected to each other (in other words, there is a curvilinear relationship, and there is little law between people intimately connected with each other and between people so removed from each other's lives that they have no contact, with the most law between people who have regular contact with each other without intimacy).

Black (2000, 2007) has continued to put forth striking, if controversial, claims. Black (1989) argued that the field of law has largely neglected legal sociology. Contrary to the traditional view of legal formalism that law is a matter of rules and that cases are resolved by the logical application of these rules, law is in fact socially relative. This means that the social attributes of the parties involved in a case—not only victims and perpetrators, but judges and jurors as well—predict how a case will be handled and how it will turn out. Here, too, Black formulated some basic propositions, for example:

- Third parties socially superior to the adversaries in a legal case are more likely to invoke rules than those closer in social status.
- The more equal and intimate parties in legal cases are, the less likely they are to use rules.
- Rules become more prominent as society grows and becomes more complex.

Black believes that his approach here, and the propositions he has generated, have important implications for both legal education and legal reform. Law students should learn to assess the sociological as well as the legal merits of a case; even if a case seems strong on legal grounds, it may be weak on sociological grounds. He argues that legal sociology exposes more clearly the discriminatory way in which the law operates in the real world; such exposure may promote the adoption of reforms that diminish the effects of social inequality.

Black's contribution to the sociology of law has inevitably been controversial, with some commentators hailing it as a major advance in the field and others criticizing it on the grounds of an absence of logical connections between the propositions and the failure of empirical testing to support the propositions (e.g., Baumgartner 2001; Gottfredson and Hindelang 1979; Greenberg 1983). Other research has claimed to find at least limited support for Black's propositions (e.g., Borg and Parker 2001; Lessan and Sheley 1992; Phillips 2003). Black's work is also attacked on the grounds that it misses the important and interesting questions of how and why people behave and believe as they do and how law itself is a "linguistic practice" through which various moral choices are justified (Frankford 1995). Black, then, provides a stimulating if controversial approach to making sense of the relation between the legal and the social.

A NORMATIVE APPROACH

Philippe Nonet and Philip Selznick ([1978] 2001) promote a normative sociology of law. This **normative approach** is influenced by the natural law tradition and accepts Lon Fuller's notion of an internal morality of law (*see* Chapter 4). For Nonet and Selznick, the task of the sociologist of law is to study the nature of legality and the conditions that encourage its development. Legality is equated with "the rule of law," or the reduction of the arbitrary element in the formation and administration of the formal law. Legal systems, then, can be evaluated in terms of how well they are in accord with such standards. The ideal is to foster a society where citizens have the "civic competence" to participate effectively in the legal order, which should lead to "rational consensus," or agreement on the restraints that states must adhere to and the degree of freedom citizens should enjoy. In such circumstances, authentic legality may be said to exist.

Philip Selznick (1992) builds on some of these ideas. His basic proposition holds that the sum of morality is that all social practice should serve human needs, discovered in the course of human experience. He promotes a form of communitarian justice that reconciles competing interests in society without eliminating all differences. Selznick identifies some specific principles consistent with this idea, such as the protection and integration of minorities, government advancement of communal well-being, and political participation rooted in social ties. The ideal social order, then, serves the needs of individuals in the context of a vibrant, supportive community. Selznick (2008), in his last book, continued to argue in favor of a sociological approach that incorporates values and ideals rather than separates them from analysis. His ideas have made an impression on many students of law and society (Cotterrell 2004; Kagan, Krygier, and Winston 2002). Critics ask, however, whether this approach provides answers to the many specific conflicts that arise between individual and community needs.

AN IDEOLOGICAL APPROACH

A third approach to making sense of the relation between the law and society can be called the **ideological approach**. Many sociolegal scholars, reflecting in part the influence of Marx, have attempted to expose the political basis and agenda of law (Beirne and Quinney 1982;

Chambliss and Seidman 1982; Hunt 1993). An ideological perspective on law is exemplified by Richard Quinney's ([1974] 2001) *Critique of Legal Order*. Quinney begins with the query, can we imagine a world not regulated by law? The "rule of law" tends to be treated as a moral absolute, but Quinney here suggests that law may not be necessary and is not necessarily good. Law is produced by special interests, representing the goals of the ruling (or capitalist) class. Law in a capitalist society fulfills a number of functions. First, law mystifies through its pretence of autonomy and disinterested commitment to justice, obscuring the actual power relationships within society. Then, law legitimates by suggesting that legal forms of power are available to all, when in reality only the elite classes are in a position to fully use that power. Law also oppresses, insofar as it exercises control over the powerless and administers punishment to them far more than it protects their rights. Finally, law exploits, because it is used by the elite classes to maintain and extend their power, property, and privileges. If all this is so, Quinney concludes, we would be better off abolishing law, or retaining law simply for guidelines and for symbolic reasons, to represent desirable behavior. Also, in view of the functions of the existing law just identified, the obligation to obey law is problematic.

Quinney, then, provides us with one striking version of an ideological interpretation of law as a part of the social order. One part of Quinney's (1991) later work took the form of a call for a peacemaking criminology—making peace on crime—as an alternative to the mainstream "war on crime" approach. Quinney's work has inevitably been criticized as blatantly ideological, either implicitly supportive of existing communist regimes or utopian and out of touch with reality.

This section has reviewed some theoretical perspectives on law and society. Such perspectives enrich our understanding of the complex relationship between the legal and the social, as do some of the jurisprudential perspectives considered in Chapter 4. But sociology is strongly committed to generating empirical knowledge, or knowledge based on systematic, direct observation.

EMPIRICAL RESEARCH AND THE SOCIOLOGY OF LAW

How should one go about studying the relationship between the legal and the social? The positivistic approach adopts the methods of the natural and physical sciences. Hypotheses are generated from theories and then subjected to systematic observation, testing, and analysis. A positivistic approach claims to be objective. Its purpose is to discover, explain, and predict. Quantitative data play a central role in this approach. Much sociology of law research adopts some version of this model. On the whole, however, positivistic research in the sociology of law (and on social phenomena generally) has been less successful in producing lawlike propositions and patterns leading to reliable predictions than has been true in the natural and physical sciences (see Box 5.5). This difference has been explained on a number of grounds.

Ultimately, sociolegal phenomena tend to be more complex than natural phenomena, with many more variables in the social environment and variations between human beings involved (Halliday and Schmidt 2009). The hypothetical capacity of human beings to choose their actions by will, as opposed to in response to forces acting upon them, further

BOX 5.5   A POSITIVIST SOCIOLEGAL STUDY:
THE EFFECTS OF SEVERE PENALTIES
FOR DRUNK DRIVING

In the 1980s, a judge in the Ohio community of New Philadelphia decided to impose severe penalties on those convicted of drunk driving. Penalties called for jail time, excluded plea bargaining, and provided for license-plate identification of offenders. Social scientists H. Laurence Ross and Robert B. Voas (1989) undertook an empirical study of the impact of these severe penalties: Did they deter people from drinking and driving? Arriving at an accurate answer to this question is difficult. A traditional approach has measured patterns of traffic-related fatalities following the adoption of the new drunk-driving policies, but this method is unreliable because the number of such deaths is relatively small in any given community and because the role that drinking alcohol has played cannot always be clearly established. Ross and Voas chose to carry out, with the cooperation of local police, a stop-and-question survey of drivers in the New Philadelphia area and in another Ohio community, Cambridge, where the judge had not adopted this tough approach to drunk drivers. Were a higher proportion of drivers in the "control" community, Cambridge, driving after

drinking; were New Philadelphia drivers aware of and deterred by the prospect of severe penalties? The researchers also compared post-conviction drunk driving records in both communities.

Perhaps disappointingly, neither measurement supported the proposition that severe penalties could deter drinking and driving. Although Ross and Voas found some evidence of community awareness of the severe penalties in New Philadelphia, they concluded that drivers focused on the relatively low likelihood of being caught rather than on the severity of the penalties. Accordingly, deterrence of drunk driving may depend more on proactive police activities than on the policies of judges.

Ross and Voas acknowledge that their stop-and-question survey may not have been able to detect differences in deterrence between the two communities studied. Because they felt that it was necessary to announce in these communities that the survey would be undertaken on two weekends, the study itself may have affected the drinking and driving patterns on those weekends. The relatively small size of the survey sample, and the fact that it was conducted only during two brief periods of time, may also have limited the conclusions that can be drawn from this study.

complicates the explanatory challenge on an organizational level. "Neo-institutionalists" explore how law is shaped by interactions between many different public and private organizations (Edelman and Suchman 2007). Insofar as sociolegal research calls for human beings studying other human beings, and matters that may intersect with personal experiences and beliefs, it may be more difficult to maintain objectivity. And both practical and ethical constraints often make it more difficult to systematically test sociolegal hypotheses than hypotheses in the natural and physical sciences.

An alternative approach to the study of sociolegal phenomena can be described as the **humanistic approach** (Banakar and Travers 2002; Cotterrell 2006b). This approach looks to humanistic disciplines such as philosophy, history, and literature rather than to the natural and physical sciences for guidance and inspiration (*see* Box 5.5). One core assumption is that the human world is fundamentally different from the natural and physical world and accordingly cannot be studied in the same way. Objectivity is less likely to be claimed in this approach, and it may be specifically disavowed. Indeed, at least some proponents of the humanistic approach affirm the need to make commitments to the advancement of an agenda of reform or social transformation (Calavita 2002; Munger 2001). Interpretation based on analysis and observation and qualitative data, as opposed to systematic testing and quantitative data, is at the heart of a humanistic approach (Ewick and Silbey 1995). Work in this tradition explores how law and legal institutions differ among societies and different segments of a society; how meanings and understandings of law and legal institutions are constructed; and how our understanding of law in our lives can be enriched and deepened by attending to narratives, or stories, about law.

The humanistic approach to the study of law has been criticized as subjective and impressionistic and accordingly filled with unverifiable or unrepresentative observations about law and society.

THE METHODOLOGY OF LAW AND SOCIETY RESEARCH

The range of empirical methods used to study law include "econometics" (statistical methods to test the effects of new legal initiatives); time-series studies (systematic evaluations of an individual or organization at different points of time to evaluate patterns of change); cross-sectional studies (multiple subjects during a particular point in time, for comparative purposes); and panel studies (tracking subjects over a period of time, measuring change). Polls and surveys are widely used to explore such public beliefs and attitudes about law and legal institutions, although many methodological challenges arise in constructing valid surveys (Schuman 2008). Ethnographic research, on the other hand, involves direct observation of human practices in relation to law, and to the plurality of legal orders (Darian-Smith 2007). But in the face of all these applications of social science to law, one commentator suggests that law itself is more like theology than the social sciences, because it makes assertions independent of social scientific evidence (Samuel 2009). Students of law vary greatly in the extent to which they attend to the work of social scientists.

The Journal of Empirical Legal Studies (and the Conference on Empirical Legal Studies), first published in 2004, specializes in applying rigorous social science methods to the study of legal phenomena and legal issues (Myers 2008). This approach to law can document the gap between common perceptions and demonstrable realities: for example, civil rights cases are less common than imagined, as are escalating class action awards. Such research has established that while trials are in decline summary judgments are increasing, and that juries make higher awards in financial injury cases but judges do so in bodily injury cases. The premise here is that knowledge about law and legal proceedings should be based upon data, not speculation.

A book of interviews with some prominent law and society researchers who produced landmark studies in the field highlights the complexity, creativity and serendipity involved in such research (Halliday and Schmidt 2009). Researchers in this field of inquiry have long had to choose between scientific and humanistic approaches, between detached objectivity and values-driven agendas, between empirical observation and critical interpretation, and between quantitative and qualitative approaches (Partington 2008). The tension between scientific and humanistic approaches to law endures.

TOPICS OF RESEARCH

A wide range of empirical and interpretive studies have been carried out by students of law and society, especially since the mid-twentieth century (*see* Box 5.6).

STATUS DIFFERENCES

The study of law and society has attended to law in relation to differences of power, wealth, race, gender, age, and other such variables, as well as differences of cultural traditions and values

BOX 5.6   THE INTERNATIONAL INSTITUTE FOR
THE SOCIOLOGY OF LAW (ONATI)

The International Institute for the Sociology of Law is housed in a beautiful eighteenth-century building on the campus of the University of Onati, in an ancient city in the heart of Basque country in Spain (Feest 2007). It was founded in 1988 by the International Sociological Association's Research Committee on Sociology of Law, with the support of the Basque government. The Institute offers an international master's program, with both faculty and students drawn from a wide range of countries and different disciplines, and also sponsors a series of workshops on a wide range of sociolegal topics. Participants in these workshops come from countries all over the world, and the papers presented have often subsequently been published in books. Despite the "sociology of law" title in the institute's name, it is best viewed as exemplifying a global, interdisciplinary approach to promote deeper understanding of sociolegal issues. The author of this text was pleased to participate in one of the Onati workshops in the summer of 2008.

TABLE 5.3   JOURNALS FEATURING SOCIOLEGAL RESEARCH

Australian Journal of Law and Society
Canadian Journal of Law & Society
Crime, Law & Social Change
International Journal of the Sociology of Law
Journal of Empirical Legal Studies
Journal of Law & Society
Law & Contemporary Problems
Law and Human Behavior
Law & Policy
Law & Social Inquiry
Law & Society Review
Social and Legal Studies

(Barkan 2009; Sarat 2004; Vago 2003). Sociologists of law who adopt a progressive, conflict, or critical perspective, in particular, have sought to demonstrate how law both reflects and reinforces the interests of the wealthy and the powerful, how it discriminates against and oppresses women and minorities, how its formal processes (e.g., trials) often have a political agenda, and how legal institutions in socialistic countries differ from those in capitalist countries. Within American society, access to law, then, is found to differ significantly between the various strata or layers of society. How do people, or groups of people, mobilize law or initiate legal action and legal reform? When and why do people turn to the courts and the formal institutions of law, as opposed to alternative, more informal processes, to resolve their disputes?

ACQUIRING ATTITUDES ABOUT LAW

The process of being socialized about law and acquiring attitudes toward legal issues has also been studied. Sociologists have studied the "legal culture" and the values people hold that relate to law, the views people form on law-related issues, and the impact of law or law-related actions on people's attitudes. Under what circumstances do people feel obliged to comply with law, and why do people fail to comply? For example, studies have been undertaken identifying reasons why most people comply with tax law and why laws designed to deter drunken drivers often fail (Ross 1992a; Smith and Kinsey 1987). Patterns of compliance and noncompliance with law have been linked with the nature of legal authority and with the degree to which people regard the law as legitimate (Tyler and Yuen 2002). These matters are addressed in more depth in Chapter 9.

RULES OF LAW VERSUS ACTUAL PRACTICES

The "gap" between the formal rules of law and the realities of how law operates has been a persistent topic of interest to sociological students of law (Nelken 2009; Stinchcombe 2001). The concept of "discretion" in decision making has also been central here, insofar as it suggests that legal decision making is not mechanical or programmed (Sarat 2004). Sociologists of law have been especially interested in identifying social and situational factors that influence the exercise of discretionary decision making within legal institutions. Sociologists of law, then, have carried out research on what goes on behind closed doors within such institutions. Jerome Skolnick's (1966) *Justice Without Trial* is a contemporary classic exploring the actual practices of police officers in a large city police department; these practices are often at odds with the formal guidelines for policing. Harry Kalven and Hans Zeisel's (1966) *The American Jury* was a pioneering study of how juries actually arrive at their decisions (and how jury decision making varies from that of judges). Still another book, Arthur Rosett and Donald R. Cressey's (1976) *Justice by Consent,* was an influential study of plea bargaining, in which informal negotiations between prosecution and defense result in a guilty plea in return for some consideration (e.g., a lesser charge) for the defendant. Contrary to many people's perspective that plea bargaining is an improper procedure that extends excessive lenience to criminals, Rosett and Cressey found it to be both an inevitable feature of contemporary court operations and a defensible device for tailoring justice to the particulars of each case (*see* Box 5.7).

BOX 5.7 SOCIOLOGISTS IN COURT

Sociologists sometimes testify in legal cases on such issues as nuisance suits, toxic torts, capital sentencing hearings, spousal abuse, and civil rights violations (Jenkins and Kroll-Smith 1996). Sociologists can influence legal opinions by giving a deposition, testifying in a legal proceeding, helping to prepare a legal brief, or serving as consultants. The insights of sociology are seen in the following areas: sociologists may contribute to an understanding of the complexity of determining guilt or innocence in legal cases and may challenge premises derived from medicine or psychology that have been adopted in a legal case; sociological testimony may help "humanize" defendants in criminal cases by portraying more fully environmental influences that contributed to their criminal conduct; and sociologists may assist the court in understanding the accurate meaning of social statistics and surveys (Jenkins and Kroll-Smith 1996, p. 4).

Sociologists have specifically testified on surveys indicating what a particular community does and does not regard as morally unacceptable in a pornography case, how members of a community are affected by the presence of pollution in their environment, and how members of a community attempting to block the building of low-cost housing were driven by racial bias. The author of this book was a witness in a criminal case, testifying on social science research revealing the effects of racial bias in jury decision making.

Courts are required to arrive at specific verdicts in legal cases. The testimony of sociologists can complicate this task by raising questions about conventional assumptions adopted by the courts. But sociologists should also be able to contribute to the objective of doing justice by applying sociological knowledge to legal cases.

In recent years there has been also been a dramatic increase in psychologists appearing as expert witnesses in both criminal and civil court cases (Costanzo, Krauss, and Pezdek 2007). Because these expert witnesses are well-paid, there is a legitimate concern that their testimony is principally tailored to suit the objectives of the lawyers who hire them and does not necessarily reflect objective scientific criteria and established findings.

THE LEGAL PROFESSION

The legal profession is obviously a central element of our legal system and accordingly has been extensively studied by sociologists of law. These studies have looked at lawyers who service the poor and lawyers who service the rich (e.g., Jerome Carlin's [1962] *Lawyers on Their Own* and Erwin Smigel's [1964] *The Wall Street Lawyer*) and lawyers within particular specialties (e.g., Arthur Wood's [1967] *Criminal Lawyer*, Welsh White's [2005] *Litigation in the Shadow of Death: Defense Lawyers in Capital Cases*, and Lynn Mather, Craig McEwen, and Richard Maiman's [2001] *Divorce Lawyers at Work*). There are studies of the process of becoming lawyers (e.g., Robert Granfield's [1992] *Making Elite Lawyers*) and of lawyers who are distinctive because of some attribute, such as gender (e.g., Cynthia Epstein's [1993] *Women in Law* and Jean Leiper's [2006] *Bar Codes: Women in the Legal Profession*). There have been studies of lawyers involved in advancing specific causes (e.g., Austin Sarat and Stuart Sheingold's [2008] *The Cultural Lives of Cause Lawyers*) and how lawyers contend with conflicts of interest (e.g., Susan Shapiro's [2002] *Tangled Loyalties*). There are also studies of the bar in a particular city (e.g., Chicago, in J. P. Heinz and Edward Laumann's *Chicago Lawyers* [1982]); within a country (e.g., the United States, in Richard Abel's [1989] *American Lawyers*); and comparing the work of lawyers in different countries (e.g., Jerry Van Hoy's [2001] *Legal Professions: Work, Structure, and Organization*). Some of the findings of these studies are drawn upon in Chapter 7.

Sociologists of law also recognize that as society changes over time, law changes as well, and conversely, changes in law can have an impact on aspects of society. Law has been studied, then, as both a dependent variable and an independent variable. The specific relation between law and social change is addressed in the final chapter of this book.

COMPARATIVE STUDIES AND THE GLOBALIZATION OF LAW

Many of the founding fathers of sociology discussed earlier in this chapter (e.g., Marx, Durkheim, and Weber) were concerned with the comparative study of different types of societies. Much of the early American sociological research on law, however, focused on law and legal institutions in the United States. In the more recent era, there has been a substantial increase of studies of law, legal institutions, and legal processes in other countries (e.g., Germany; Brazil), the expansion of law and society research in many countries (e.g., Poland; Korea), and work that is increasingly comparative in nature (Clark 2007; Friedman, Perez-Perdomo, and Gomez 2011; Trevino 2001). A study comparing attributions of legal responsibility in the United States and in Japan (Sanders and Hamilton 1992) exemplifies the comparative approach to law and society. A study of law and legality in Cuba (Zatz 1994) is a good example of an in-depth exploration of law in a noncapitalist society.

The growth of law and society scholarship in many countries, as well as growing interest in comparative approaches, is signified by International Law and Society meetings attended by scholars from all over the world. Although law cutting across national boundaries has been important for a long time, especially in connection with international commercial transactions, it has increasingly expanded into other areas; the explosive growth of concern with human rights law is an example (Friedman 1996a). In a world of increasing inter-dependence of people in many different countries, traditional borders have become less important. The emergence of a European community and European law (discussed briefly in Chapter 2) is one obvious example of the eroding status of traditional national borders.

The traditional Western and Anglo-American dominance of sociolegal scholarship is diminishing somewhat with scholarship emerging from many countries. The specific social and law-related impact of globalization, or the spreading web of worldwide interconnections (facilitated by new forms of communication and transportation), can be interpreted in differ-ent ways. Susan Silbey (1997), in a presidential address to the Law and Society Association, provocatively characterizes globalization as a form of **postmodern colonialism**, insofar as it facilitates the divide between the rich and the poor and the concentration of power in the hands of few, through the domination of increasingly larger numbers of people by those who shape and control law and communication in first-world countries. During the course of the twenty-first century, the attention of sociologists of law to transnational law and the impact of globalization will surely expand.

KEY TERMS AND CONCEPTS

empirical study	law and society movement	Social Darwinists
founding fathers of sociology	normative approach	sociolegal scholarship
humanistic approach	positivistic approach	sociology of law
ideological approach	postmodern colonialism	

DISCUSSION QUESTIONS

1. It seems ironic that sociolegal scholarship has expanded in many countries yet only occupies a marginal status in law schools. Do you think that the law and society movement should be given more attention, especially in law schools that are supposedly preparing men and women for careers in which they will be serving society? Explain.

2. Discuss Herbert Spencer's application of the Darwinian perspective on human evolution to whole societies. What is the main idea of his Social Darwinism? How could this have an impact on welfare laws as the author suggests?

3. Compare and contrast the theories of Karl Marx with those of Emile Durkheim. In what ways do their ideas differ the most, especially in their view of law?

4. Examine the three approaches explaining the relationship between the legal and the social (i.e., empirical, normative, and ideological). How does each approach add to a greater understanding of the law and society movement?

5. Do you agree with Susan Silbey when she characterizes globalization as a form of postmodern colonialism? Do you feel that as we move through the twenty-first century, the expansion of transnational law and the concern of globalization will do more harm than good?

CHAPTER 6

COMPARATIVE AND HISTORICAL PERSPECTIVES ON LAW AND SOCIETY

Is law universal, and do all human societies have law? In particular, what has *law* meant in the world of preliterate and indigenous peoples, and specifically what role has law played in the history of American Indians? How does the form and nature of law differ *among* the developed nations of the world, and how should one classify the different "families" of law? In particular, how has the law of nondemocratic communist nations differed from American law? And how did law in the past, within the Western tradition of which America is a part, evolve over time? What forces and influences shaped American law, and specifically what was the significance of the African-American experience with law? Finally, what does law mean in the context of war, or specific wars such as those that occurred in Vietnam and Iraq? These are some of the fundamental—and endlessly fascinating—questions explored in this chapter. Those who wish to acquire a deeper and richer understanding of the relationship between the legal and the social must address such matters. The disciplines of anthropology and history are especially useful in the search for answers to the questions raised here.

THE ANTHROPOLOGICAL PERSPECTIVE ON LAW

Social and cultural anthropology has as its focus the understanding of the whole of human cultures, but it is especially associated with the study of preliterate (primitive, in past terms) societies (Bracey 2006; Donovan 2007; Nader 2002). Contemporary anthropologists have increasingly focused on people living in industrialized or developing nations, and they have abandoned some of the traditional assumptions and methods of earlier anthropologists (Darian-Smith 2004; Griffiths 2009; Scheffer 2008). With surviving preliterate cultures, anthropologists used an **ethnographic approach** to research, which calls for intensive, extended fieldwork among the people being studied. Analysis of the findings produces a rich descriptive account of the culture as a whole and of the interrelationship of its different parts and aspects. The principal legal issues are these: Is law universal? What are the means of social control among preliterate peoples? What does law have in common with, and how does it differ from, other means of social control?

Although social philosophers and historians, including Sir Henry Maine ([1861] 2001), have long speculated about the differences between law and social control in primitive and modern societies, cultural anthropology is principally a twentieth-century enterprise. Because the question of whether law is a universal feature of human societies is one of the important issues investigated by twentieth-century cultural anthropologists, the challenge of coming up with an acceptable definition of "law" arises; in fact, anthropologists have adopted quite different definitions. In *Crime and Custom in Savage Society*, Bronislaw Malinowski (1926) rejected the notion that law is necessarily a product of the state. Preliterate tribes in the Trobriand Islands (located in the South Pacific) did not have formal, state-based laws, but they did have rules governing proper human conduct, rights of individuals, and obligations, and they had mechanisms by which people were induced to conform to these rules and expectations. For Malinowski, this was a system of law, and such a system could be found in all human societies. Other anthropologists have criticized this conception of law as too inclusive or broad.

Another landmark study was carried out by law professor Karl Llewellyn (discussed in Chapter 4 as one of the leading figures in realist jurisprudence) and anthropologist E. Adamson Hoebel among the Cheyenne Indians of the Great Plains of North America in the 1930s. This work used interviews and drew upon earlier published accounts to recapture the traditional ways of these people, which led to publication of *The Cheyenne Way* in 1941. This book is widely acknowledged as a classic and influential contribution to the anthropological study of law, although its methodology and conclusions have been criticized (Conley and O'Barr 2004; Mehrotra 2001). Hoebel ([1954] 1967), on his own, subsequently published a more general work on legal anthropology. The approach pioneered by Llewellyn and Hoebel looked at **trouble cases** to identify the law of the Cheyenne; these cases arise when some traditional rule within the tribe has been infringed and the tribe's leaders come together to deliberate and resolve the dispute at hand. For Llewellyn and Hoebel, law is not defined in terms of rules or institutions but is rather identified with the process of social control. According to Llewellyn and Hoebel, this process seldom results in a winner and a loser. Rather, because members of these small tribes are so dependent on one another for survival and have to continue to associate with each other after resolution of a dispute, a compromise permitting both parties to win a little is the resolution most conducive to ongoing harmonious relations.

In the decades following these pioneering studies of dispute resolution among preliterate peoples, cultural anthropologists traveled to many remote parts of the world to study this process among indigenous people and other preliterate tribes—in Africa, the South Pacific, Latin America, and elsewhere (Nader 2002; Nader and Todd 1978; Sack and Aleck 1992). Anthropologists have embraced diverse conceptions of law (Boyle 2005; Snyder 1996). Some have followed the lead of Malinowski, viewing law in broad and inclusive terms to include "rules," customs, and any identifiable means of social control. Others have adopted a view that says a systematic application of explicit rules is the minimum criterion for an identifiable system of law. The most conservative approach to this issue limits the notion of law to a system in which a political state, courts, and written legal codes exist.

TABLE 6.1   FROM NO LAW TO FULL LAW

Level of law	No law	Minimal law	Medium law	Full law
Character of law	Spontaneous; informal; social control	Established norms; informal "courts"	Specific codes/compensation; popular tribunals	Written codes; courts
Setting	Andaman Islanders	Zuni Indians	Yurok Indians	United States

The claim that law in some sense is a cultural universal, found in some form in every human culture, has been challenged. Among the Andaman Islanders, for example, there was apparently no agreed-upon means of settling disputes and no specific sanctions for acting contrary to norms (Radcliffe-Brown 1922); this would indeed be a culture with no law. Among many other preliterate people or indigenous tribes, law could be described as minimal (e.g., where public pressure is imposed on disputants to resolve their differences) to rudimentary (e.g., where a code exists that one party who has done harm to another must provide compensation) (Redfield 1967).

Table 6.1 summarizes the nature of "law" known to be practiced by various cultures—from no law to full law. The **Eskimo Drum Song "Court"** is an especially remarkable procedure for settling disputes (Hoebel [1954] 1967). When a dispute between Eskimos developed, a drumming contest would be arranged. This contest, which could extend over years, took the form of an exchange of accusations and insults and sometimes included head-butting and wrestling. Spectators would ultimately signify which contestant had won the contest in the sense of getting the better of, or shaming, the other contestant. The loser might be exiled, or some form of reconciliation might occur. Other cases of such song contests among preliterate peoples have been reported in parts of the South Pacific and Africa. Indeed, in contemporary society, the inner-city ritual called **the dozens**, in which disputants hurl insults at each other while being egged on by onlookers, bears a close relationship to this singular process for resolving disputes.

Whether one calls the various means of dispute resolution used by preliterate people "law" or something else depends on one's definition of law. The relationship between customs and laws has been characterized in different ways. For Paul Bohannon (1967a), law is best seen as **double institutionalized** customary rules—that is, rules that have first become adopted naturally within a culture and then are formalized with specific institutions and procedures. Anthropologist Stanley Diamond (1973), however, has argued that customs and laws are fundamentally different: Customs are the natural reflection of the beliefs and values of a tribe or social group, whereas law is imposed on people by the state, at least sometimes, to achieve the purposes of the state and powerful interests. However one views this issue, it is indisputable that most Westerners who moved into underdeveloped countries—even those well beyond the preliterate stage of cultural development—did not regard the indigenous means of dispute settlement as law. And concepts of such matters as property among indigenous peoples have typically been quite different from those of people in developed societies (Buck, McLaren, and Wright

2001). Accordingly, in the traditional view, Western law was largely imposed on people in colonized third-world countries (Foster, Berger, and Buck 2008; Ivison, Patton, and Sanders 2000). The claim that no system of law existed among indigenous people was used to justify the imposition of law. Although the rationale for this imposition of law was that it would enable these traditional societies to advance and join the family of civilized nations, it is also obvious that Western law became a critically important means for controlling and exploiting indigenous people in many parts of the world (Hussain 2003). Colonial regimes (e.g., in India) imposed on indigenous business practices forms of law that advanced Western capitalist interests (Birla 2009). Traditional cultural practices also shaped colonial rule, and recent research suggests that local elites sometimes played a significant role in colonial legal developments (Benton 2002; Foster, Berger, and Buck 2008; Merry 2004). But, traditional means of dispute settlement typically also survived in these third-world countries, co-existing with and sometimes in conflict with the formal, Western legal system. The term *legal pluralism* was formulated by cultural anthropologists in recognition of the fact that formal systems of law typically co-exist with one or more other systems of social control or dispute settlement (Griffiths 1986; Bracey 2006; Weisbrod 2002). In developing countries (e.g., Malawi, in Southern Africa) calls for fuller adoption of legal reforms consistent with respect for "the rule of law" are made (Kanyongolo 2006). In post-colonial societies, a melding of colonial and customary law sometimes occurred (Santos et al. 2006). But these developing (or post-colonial) societies often experience rising rates of crime and violence, with a complex relationship between the increasing adoption of laws and regulations and disorder and disobedience (Comaroff and Comaroff 2006). The extent to which such conditions can be attributed to the legacy of colonialism continues to be debated.

The promotion and protection of universal human rights has been a major project since the middle of the twentieth century. So has the worldwide promotion of Western "neo-liberalism" (or free market economics). But some anthropologists have explored how these projects can come into conflict with indigenous kinship norms in cultures in developing and post-colonial societies (Comaroff and Comaroff 2006; Goodale 2009; Merry 2006; Speed 2008). Accordingly, the attempt to impose universal human rights norms and free market economic policies on traditional societies in various parts of the world, however well-intended, can be viewed as an extension of the Western imperialist, colonialist project of an earlier time. Law and the adoption of legal strategies is both an instrument for the continuing domination of people in such countries and part of the resistance response to this domination by people in these countries (Fitzpatrick 2008; Foster, Berger, and Buck 2008). Anthropologists continue to explore the many complex dimensions of the interaction of Western law with indigenous legal norms in developing countries (Anderson 2009; Goddard 2009; von Benda-Beckmann et al. 2009a, b, c). This is sure to be an ongoing project. But in the case of cultural practices condoned by some order of law in developing countries, how far should our tolerance extend? (*See* Box 6.1.)

BOX 6.1   HONOR KILLING, STONING TO
DEATH, AND GENITAL MUTILATION:
THE LIMITS OF CULTURAL TOLERANCE

How does one find the right balance between tolerance for the cultural and religious values of people different from ourselves and rejection of repellent and harmful practices? For example, a traditional practice in India—sacrificing widows on the funeral pyres of their husbands—was never acceptable to Americans. The notion of protecting personal or sexual honor has sometimes led to violence that is at odds with the law and with American cultural values (Whitman 2007). But legal systems have differed in terms of the extent to which they acknowledge the claim of honor as a valid justification for certain acts of violence. "Honor killing" has been characterized as an extreme form of policing female sexuality and perceived threats to traditional notions of masculinity (Welchman and Hossain 2005). Thousands of women worldwide—especially in predominantly Muslim countries—are victims each year of honor killings, not infrequently carried out by their fathers or brothers who believe they have brought dishonor to their family. The murder of a 16-year-old rape victim in Syria, by her older brother, led to some heated dialogue in that country regarding honor killing (Zoepf 2007). Some 300 girls or women in Syria alone die each year from honor killings, which are not classified as murders under Syrian law. In a high-profile case in India in 2010, a mother was charged with murdering a daughter who wanted to marry outside her caste (Yardley 2010). Especially in the northern part of India, honor killings have occurred when a young woman violates potent, traditional cultural values proscribing marriage outside one's caste, although Indian law specifically protects such marriages. Tougher penalties for honor killing were under consideration in India.

In some Islamic countries—for example, in Nigeria and Iran—sentences of death by stoning are on the books and are sometimes pronounced, along with calls for flogging and mutilation, although the stoning and mutilation sentences are rarely carried out (Polgreen 2007). However, in Somalia in 2008, a 13-year-old rape victim was stoned to death (Reuters 2008). She had been raped by three men, and when her family attempted to report this, she was arrested, charged with adultery, and then sentenced to death by stoning.

Female circumcision—or female genital cutting and mutilation—has existed for some 2,500 years and is practiced in some 40 countries (mainly in Africa). More than 140 million females are affected, and about 2 million are at risk each year (Sussman 2011). The principal objective of this practice is to diminish the possibility of female premarital sex and sexual infidelity by removal of the clitoris and stitching together the genital lips. Although female genital cutting has been outlawed in such countries as Guinea, there is much evidence that customary tribal law takes precedence, and the practice continues (Sussman 2011). Most Americans support a law criminalizing circumcision of females younger than age 18 years, but this practice is still carried out in some immigrant communities. A question arose in American courts on whether a 16-year-old female could be granted political asylum in the United States, if deporting her to her predominantly Muslim country would mean that she would almost certainly be subjected to genital mutilation (Bernstein 2007). American courts have traditionally been reluctant to broaden the notion of "political asylum" to cover such matters. Altogether, there is a conflict between progressive women's rights laws and traditional customary law in many countries.

INDIGENOUS PEOPLES AND THE LAW: THE CASE OF AMERICAN INDIANS

The issues surrounding American Indians (or Native Americans) and the law are related to the broader problem of law and "indigenous" or "aboriginal" peoples. This term refers to descendants of the original inhabitants of a particular geographic area. About 4% of the world's population, or approximately 200 million people, are considered to belong to this category, with some 3,000 indigenous nations within some 200 nation-states (Rosen 1992; Lauderdale 1997, p. 140). Most of these indigenous peoples—whether in Africa, Asia, Australia, the Americas, or elsewhere—have had outsiders (or colonizers) come in, conquering, exploiting, and in some cases virtually exterminating them. The colonizers then imposed on survivors the outsiders' own law and legal system. This imposed legal system then typically became a mechanism for controlling and further exploiting the indigenous people. In the modern era, in response to outside pressures, demands of indigenous militants, and some acknowledgment of past injustices, questions on the rights of indigenous peoples have arisen. Here, we examine questions that arise in connection with American Indians and the law.

INDIAN LAW

First, what was the nature of the "law" of American Indians prior to their contact with Europeans? We cannot come up with a definitive answer to this question, partly because there is no written history among American Indians. Furthermore, the term *American Indian* encompasses peoples with very different histories, identities, and practices. Through oral history and observational reports, scholars have gathered accounts of traditional American Indian law, although the reported forms of American Indian law may already have been affected, in some ways, by contact with European and American government agents, soldiers, and settlers. Indeed, one scholar believes that "so-called customary law is a product of colonization" (Sierra 1995, p. 228). Many different regimes of "law" existed in early America among the indigenous peoples, and inevitable conflicts arose from the outset between these regimes and those of European settlers (Tomlins and Mann 2001). In the end, the Europeans had the upper hand.

The work of Llewellyn and Hoebel (1941), referred to earlier, on the Cheyenne of the Great Plains is one of the most famous accounts of indigenous law. Hoebel (1960), in a brief summary, noted that among the Cheyenne the law was collectively declared by the tribal leaders. Its purpose was primarily to define relations, allocate authority, address conflicts of interest, and take appropriate action against crimes such as murder or threats to the communal hunt, upon which the Cheyenne were so dependent. When a member of the tribe violated important tribal norms, the leadership class would meet and effectively resolve the matter, sometimes imposing a temporary banishment of the offender. Typically, the ultimate objective of this juristic process was to rehabilitate the offender and reintegrate him into the group.

In a parallel vein, "traditional justice among the Navajo tends to be swift, direct, personal and emphasizes the restoration of harmony and reacceptance by the community rather than punishment and ostracism" (Armstrong, Guilfoyle, and Melton 1996, p. 51). In a contemporary idiom, this is justice-as-peacemaking.

Although American Indian law primarily seems to have emphasized justice-as-healing and to have avoided repressive punishment, it may be a mistake to romanticize the original Indian cultures as uniformly reconciliatory (Lauderdale 1997). There were great differences in the legal practices and penal attitudes of Indian groups; the Aztecs and Mayans, for example, had laws and punishments similar to those of traditional European cultures. In the modern era, the law administered within Indian communities can sometimes be harsh and oppressive (Garrow and Deer 2004; Richland and Deer 2009). Early in the twenty-first century, some Indian tribes revived the ancient penalty of banishment in response to a plague of substance abuse, gambling, and violence with which they were contending (Kershaw and Davey 2004). Although harsh, this penalty is defended as consistent with traditional tribal community values. Ironically, in at least some cases, members of the Indian community may look to the law of the larger society to protect them from some aspects of their own community's law. However, some Hopi Indian community members in the American Southwest are calling for the Hopi tribal courts, modeled on American law, to more fully integrate Hopi cultural values and traditions (Richland 2008). Ongoing tensions between American law and tribal law persist.

TAKING LAND AND THE LAW

A second question that must be asked with reference to American Indians has to do with the law of colonizers: By what legal (or jurisprudential) theory was the expropriation of Indian lands carried out or justified? Was the "conquest of paradise" (i.e., the European settlement of North and South America) the greatest crime in Western history? Was it genocide on a monumental scale? On the first of these questions, Western explorers and colonizers justified what they did in terms of a right of discovery, the need to save the souls of irrational heathens, and the divine right of entitlement to develop and control the underutilized land occupied by indigenous peoples (Williams 1990). Certainly from the perspective of American Indians, the conquest of their lands is considered a crime on a very grand scale. The native people of the Caribbean islands—the Caribs and Arawaks—were largely exterminated; many massacres continued against Indian populations for hundreds of years, culminating in the Wounded Knee massacre in 1890 (Brown 1971). Millions of Indians died from diseases contracted from Europeans, in battle, and from the loss of traditional sources of food. In the modern era, American Indian communities have had extraordinarily high rates of unemployment and such pathologies as alcoholism, child abuse, and suicide, linked with the conditions imposed on them (Egan 1998a, 1998b; Garrow and Deer 2004). Obviously, American Indians have also had many positive achievements and experiences, but in historical terms the law and the legal system are more readily associated with negative experiences, which are accordingly emphasized here.

The continued oppression of American Indians through the present era has been characterized by Indian activists and their sympathizers as a war against the Indian nations; the dramatic overrepresentation of Indians among prison inmates is seen as one outcome of this war (Nielsen 1996; Weyler 1992). The **American Indian Movement (AIM)**, founded in 1968, is a militant group dedicated to challenging this oppression and the historic theft of Indian lands. Inevitably, this movement has found itself in conflict with the laws and agents of the federal government. In one especially celebrated confrontation at the Pine Ridge Reservation in South Dakota in June 1975, an exchange of gunfire between AIM members and the FBI resulted in the death of one Indian and two FBI agents (Davey 2004; Matthiessen 2009). As of this writing, Leonard Peltier, an AIM leader, is still in prison in connection with this incident, although many questions have been raised about both his culpability in the original incident and his treatment at the hands of the justice system and the penal system in the years since. In one interpretation, this case is an especially high-profile incident in a long history of an American FBI war on American Indian activists (Hendricks 2006).

Every American schoolchild learns at some point that various treaties were signed by American Indians and representatives of White American society. But what was the understanding of American Indians of these treaties and other agreements with White people?

Did the Indians who "sold" Manhattan to Dutch settlers (for the equivalent of $24 worth of trinkets and implements) have the same understanding of property law that the Europeans did? It is generally recognized that they did not, and they certainly did not understand that they were giving up for all time the right to hunt, fish, and settle on Manhattan island. One can note, however, that some students of American Indian history challenge the commonly held notion that indigenous cultures had a communal orientation toward the ownership of property and promoted stewardship of the environment (Anderson, Benson, and Flanagan 2006). In this view, private property rights were in some forms recognized by Indian groups.

Did the White Americans, who had every advantage in drawing up the treaties in the first place, comply with the terms of these treaties? On the contrary: Despite the principle embedded in Article VI of the Constitution (that treaties backed by Congress are the law of the land), provisions of treaties were systematically violated by the American state and White settlers, and reservation land promised to Indians was taken away from them and opened up to White homesteaders (Egan 1998a; Wilkins and Lomawaima 2001). Historically, contests over the ownership and control of law have been at the center of relations between White people and Indians, with different resolutions in different settings but most typically settlements that favored White people over Indians (Banner 2007). One might say that the European colonizers and White American settlers violated natural law by expropriating Indian lands in the first place and then violated the conditions of their own positive law. Stuart Banner (2005), in *How the Indians Lost their Land*, argues that this story is more complicated than the traditional narrative that they were simply tricked out of this land by White colonists and settlers who did not acknowledge their basic rights and claims (Kades 2008). In this reading, a movement toward more coercive land seizures from Indians evolved over time, and Indians sometimes had a reasonably clear understanding of the conditions of treaties and land transfers. In 2009 the federal government announced that it had agreed to pay some $3.4 billion to settle a longstanding lawsuit claiming federal mismanagement of Indian lands (Savage 2009). This lawsuit was characterized as one of the largest and most complicated class action lawsuits involving the federal government.

In a series of early nineteenth-century decisions (*Johnson v. McIntosh*, 1823; *Cherokee Nation v. Georgia*, 1831; *Worcester v. Georgia*, 1832), the U.S. Supreme Court, under the leadership of John Marshall, asserted the basic right of the United States over the Indians through discovery and conquest, although the Court also acknowledged the duties of the central government toward the Indians and the right of Indians to manage their own affairs (Egan 1998a; Rosen 1992, pp. 367–368). For much of the subsequent history, the "duty" aspect (if it was acknowledged at all) was interpreted in a paternalistic manner, providing modest forms of support in return for submissiveness on the part of Indians.

A leading authority on American Indian law argues that American law pertaining to Indians has always incorporated racist assumptions about Indians and continues to do so in the present era (Williams 2005). In the nineteenth century the legal system in Southern California was used to harass Indians in that part of the country (Gunther 2006). American law in the recent era has often been confused and contradictory, sometimes promoting tribal self-governance and separation and sometimes promoting forced assimilation and disenfranchisement (Vinzant 2009). Altogether, this is a complicated story.

From the 1880s through the first part of the twentieth century, the dominant policy, known as **allotment**, broke up many of the Indian reservations into private holdings, with the principal objective being integration of Indians into the larger society and assurance that non-Indians would not be subjected to control by Indians (Bordewich 1996; Castile 2006; Fixico 2008). The practical effect of these policies—supposedly intended to challenge paternalistic policies of the past—was cuts in programs for Indians (Castile 2006). And they failed to lead to assimilation or integration of American Indians into the larger society.

TRIBAL SOVEREIGNTY

The allotment policy began to change significantly in the 1970s, when the federal government adopted a policy favoring **tribal sovereignty**, or more direct control by Indians over their own affairs (Davies and Clow 2009; Wunder 1996). Over a long period of time, state and territorial governments, and not just the United States government, played a role in policies defining the parameters of Indian citizenship and sovereignty (Rosen 2007). What is the basis of tribal sovereignty? In one interpretation, tribal sovereignty is preconstitutional and extraconstitutional (Clinton 2002; Duthu 2008a; Wilkins and Lomawaima 2001). This means that the sovereignty of Indian tribes existed prior to the adoption of the American Constitution, and under principles of international law, the United States was never entitled to preempt the original sovereignty of the indigenous peoples of the Americas. The new policy has generated a host of complex questions. First, what is a *tribe* and exactly who belongs to the tribe (Tsosie 1997)? The term has had a dual meaning in American law, referring sometimes to an ethnologically defined group of people who share a common heritage and community and sometimes to a legally recognized political entity (Goldberg-Ambrose 1994). *Tribe* and *tribal membership* have been defined by outsiders and by Indians themselves. The issues involved in defining racial and tribal membership have a long and contentious history (Basson 2008). In recent years, growing numbers of people have claimed tribal membership in the hopes of sharing the bounty from Indian casinos, whereas on the other side tribes have purged their rolls of members to limit sharing this bounty (Bazar 2006; Hitt 2005). Many factors and different motivations can enter into this process and into specifying the criteria for tribal membership.

If American Indian tribes have sovereignty over their own domain, which law should prevail when a conflict arises between state law and tribal law? For example, how much authority should the state have to regulate tribal gaming enterprises and environmental protection and to impose sales taxes (Belluck 2003; Valencia-Weber 1994)? In a case that went before the U.S. Supreme Court, *Peyote v. the State*, a criminal prosecution of an American Indian for using peyote was contested on the basis that peyote use was part of his tribe's religious practices, and accordingly the prosecution violated his First Amendment rights (Epps 2009). In an extreme case, if an Indian community sanctions the assassination of alleged witches, should the state intervene and prosecute the matter as a violation of state laws pertaining to homicide (Sierra 1995)? Indians, as American citizens (a status formally recognized by Congress in 1924), are subject to the same laws as other citizens with the exception of minor crimes and some civil matters occurring on reservations, where tribal courts have jurisdiction (Davies and Clow 2009; Garrow and Deer 2004). Because of the jurisprudential confusion, many cases where Indians (especially Indian women) are victimized by outsiders, on tribal lands, are never prosecuted (Duthu 2008). Federal law prohibits tribal courts from prosecuting outsiders, but federal and state prosecutors often lack either incentives or resources to do so.

The doctrine of tribal sovereignty has in some cases led to Indian demands for the return of sacred lands, ancestral bones, and artifacts; local economies, non-Indian landowners, and museums have felt threatened by such demands (Bell and Napoleon 2008; Brown 2003). The resulting litigation has sometimes had unintended consequences: It has produced conflict between American Indians concerned with maintaining traditional cultural identity and those concerned with practical gains—sometimes within the same tribe (Kempers 1989). By the late 1990s and early 2000s, a backlash against tribal sovereignty had developed, in response to the anger of non-Indians increasingly affected by this sovereignty (e.g., through attempted imposition of taxes on them if they reside on Indian lands); jealousy over the new casino-based wealth of some Indian tribes; and increasing unease in Congress and on the Supreme Court about the creation of parallel nations within the United States (Belluck 2003; Dudas 2008; Light and Rand 2008). The pursuit of treaty rights by American Indian groups has encountered increasing resistance from the political "new" right (Dudas 2008). This "counter-mobilization" initiative objects to claimed "special rights" for Indians. In Canada as well as the United States, there is a long history of conflicts over granting indigenous "first people" special rights and privileges and respecting their cultural traditions, and other objectives pursued by the Canadian legal system, on behalf of all citizens (Harris 2008; Law Commission of Canada 2008). Altogether, the relation between American law and the American Indian community has been filled with injustice, contradiction, and ambivalence.

A growing number of law schools in the United States (between 12 and 20) now have Indian law programs, and a surge of interest in such programs has been reported (Mangan 2008d). This interest may well reflect both growing economic and political power of American Indians, as well as growing numbers of jurisdictional disputes relating to tribal law. Indian law topics have been incorporated in the bar exams of some Western states.

THE COMPARATIVE PERSPECTIVE ON LAW

Whether or not law is a universal phenomenon in the sense that it can be found in some form among all human societies, it is indisputably an aspect of all developed nations and of all societies more complex than tribal societies. Looking around the world, one also becomes conscious that there are diverse legal traditions and systems and that law exists on many different levels. A comparative, or cross-cultural, perspective on law is important for several reasons. Such a perspective enables one to overcome **ethnocentric tendencies** toward glorifying one's own system of law, and it reinforces one's appreciation of the fact

TABLE 6.2 THE MAJOR FAMILIES OF LAW

Civil law	Legal system in which legislative codes are central; statutes rather than judicial opinions are dominant; of continental European origin.
Common law	Legal system in which judicial finding of law is central; legal precedents rather than legislative statutes; of English origin.
Socialist law	Legal system in which socialist practices and objectives provide fundamental guidance; popular justice; Communist countries.
Sacred law	Legal system in which sacred (religious) texts—e.g., the Koran—provides fundamental guidance; religious laws enforced; countries where religious fundamentalism is dominant.

that law does not emerge in a social vacuum but rather both reflects and influences the society of which it is a part. Also, in a world of increasing international contacts, eroding borders, and globalization, a comparative perspective is necessary to promote greater cooperation and understanding (Dammer and Albanese 2011; Reichel 2010; Smits 2008).

There are "families" of legal traditions; then, within these traditions, there are different legal systems in particular nations; within nations, there may be differences between states; and within states, there may be differences between local (e.g., city or town) legal systems or laws. The understanding of law as a social phenomenon is necessarily comparative, then, and must begin with identifying the major families of law. As is always true with such classifications, no full consensus exists on just how many such families can be identified and how to divide up the world's legal systems. Furthermore, any typology of legal families inevitably distorts the reality that specific legal systems are rarely pure types but incorporate in varying degrees elements of different families of law and specific legal systems. Some legal systems with distinctive attributes, such as the ancient Egyptian and Mesopotamian systems, essentially became extinct with the passing of these cultures, although elements survived in later systems of law (Reichel 1999, pp. 80–83). It is quite difficult to make valid comparisons among legal systems in different countries, insofar as features of legal systems are not always directly comparable (Nelken 2009). In any case, despite inherent limitations, a typology of legal families is a necessary starting point for the comparative study of law. For our purposes, we identify civil law, common law socialist law, and sacred law families (*see* Table 6.2).

CIVIL LAW

The oldest, largest, and most enduring legal family within the Western tradition is called the **civil law tradition**, also sometimes known as Roman law or continental law.

The term *civil law* is somewhat unfortunate here because this term is also used for the U.S. system of private law, which inevitably causes some confusion. The so-called civil law family derives from various continental European sources, including elements of classical Roman law, customary law, the canon law of the church, judicial decrees, the law of merchants, and monarchical law. A centerpiece of the civil law tradition is **codification**, or the absolute primacy of written codes of law. (Codes, however, are not unique to civil law legal systems, nor are they central to all legal systems so classified.) As an example of such codes, there is the ancient code—and for some the true starting point of civil law—called the "Twelve Tables," set forth in about 450 B.C. in Rome. This code was not the only source of law for Romans, however, as various legislative bodies, magistrates, and judges also promulgated laws applicable to different classes of people and different circumstances (Watson 1995).

In the sixth century A.D., the Institutes of Justinian (an emperor) attempted to address the inevitable confusion and conflicts created by multiple sources of law. Through creation of a comprehensive code, this notion became central to the civil law tradition. In the early nineteenth century in France, the Napoleonic Code (1804) was another influential effort at comprehensive codification, as was the German Civil Code (1896) later in the century, following the unification of Germany.

Much earlier in Western European history, with the emergence of a Catholic church of growing influence, a legal system known as **canon law** emerged. Although its origins go back at least to the fourth century, the publication of the *Concordat of Discordant Canons* by Gratian in about 1150 extended its influence (Caenegem 1992, pp. 60–62; Shaffern 2009). Canon law, claiming its roots in divine law as decreed by the Pope and other church authorities, and administered by ecclesiastical courts (presided over by officials of the Church), was intended to apply in cases involving Christians, especially in matters pertaining to moral issues (Berman 1983). (It is principally, although not exclusively, associated with the Roman Catholic Church.) Inevitably, over time, conflicts between the law of the state and of the Church developed, and much of the jurisdiction of the Church was co-opted by emerging national states. Canon law had an important influence on secular Western laws of marriage, inheritance, property, contracts, and crimes and torts, as well as on rules of judicial procedure (Berman 1983, pp. 225–254). It has survived into the present to govern matters purely within the province of the Church, such as the granting of marriage annulments.

Judges in the civil law tradition are generally expected to defer to the will of the legislative bodies that produce the codes and to apply (rather than broadly interpret) relevant provisions of codes in specific cases; in the recent era, however, they have also been influenced (but not bound) by earlier judicial rulings (Merryman 1969, pp. 54–55; Schauer 2009). At the same time, this tradition is associated with an inquisitorial system, with a judge (or panel of judges) exercising fairly direct control over the inquiry into the facts of cases before them (as in France), as opposed to lawyers directing this process (as in the United States). Judges are typically civil servants who specialized in training to become judges early in their legal education, which is not an option in common law countries. The pretrial investigation by prosecutors is especially important in determining guilt or innocence in criminal cases, and the accused generally have more limited rights; indeed, they do not have a right to bail, do not necessarily enjoy a presumption of innocence once their case has reached the trial stage, and have more limited options on appeal. Juries either are not used at all or have a severely limited role. This civil law tradition is dominant in Western Europe, among the Scandinavian countries and continental European countries such as Germany, the Netherlands, France, Italy, Spain, and Portugal; it also shaped the legal systems of most of the countries colonized by these European countries, especially in Latin America, Asia, and Africa.

COMMON LAW

The **common law tradition** is specifically a product of English history. Its roots go far back in the law of the Anglo-Saxon tribes, an amalgam of compilations of customs, royal proclamations, early statutes, and manuals on practices (Caenegem 1988; Schauer 2009). After the conquest of England by the Normans under William I in 1066, this law was largely preserved, and it was formalized during the reign of William's descendant, Henry II, in the twelfth century. The common law became the law of the royal courts, common to all citizens (as opposed to local law, which applied only to local citizens). Starting with prominent judges such as Glanvill during Henry II's reign, with his listing of writs available in the king's courts, and Henry de Bracton in the thirteenth century, with his articulation of fundamental common law principles in *De Legibus*, and culminating with the great commentary by Oxford law professor William Blackstone in the middle of the eighteenth century, attempts were made to identify and bring together some of the core elements of the common law.

The term *common law* has had quite different meanings—that is, "shared" law, customary law, and judge-made law (Glenn 2005). The common law principally emerged out of case law rather than from legislatively produced codes of law. In this tradition, the judge plays a much more central role, because judges "find" the law in what has come to be recognized as law in the tradition of the community; they seek the law in findings of judges in earlier cases (precedent, or the principle of *stare decisis*). Because judges have considerable interpretive leeway in this tradition, it is sometimes claimed that, for all practical purposes, judges make law and that the notion of "finding" law in past decisions is a fiction. On the other hand, the common law tradition is also associated with an adversarial system where the lawyers (prosecutors and defense counsel in criminal cases) take the lead in questioning witnesses and other parties to the case and engage in a contest over the evidence. The judge presides over this contest, especially by ruling on procedural issues. The use of a jury to determine guilt or innocence, at least in cases with serious charges and claims, is also a central feature of this system. Defendants are generally regarded as having more rights within this tradition, including a fairly extensive right of appeal.

The common law tradition is especially associated with England and its former colonies, but at least elements of common law can be found in other countries. The United States is regarded as a common law country in the sense that the U.S. Supreme Court, with its power to produce important law through its interpretations and decisions, operates in this tradition. But from the country's earliest history, written codes of law have been a conspicuous and, over time, an increasingly important source of law. Furthermore, although in the nineteenth century in some frontier states it was still possible to be charged with "common law" violations, or violations of what was understood to be the law, through the twentieth century and into the present century Americans can only be charged with violations of written laws. Elements associated with the common law in the American tradition include: allegiance to precedent, but also adaptability; being attuned to community norms, but also mindful of "natural rights"; use of trial juries; and privileging of judicial opinions over codes (Scott 2007). In the United States, by some interpretations, there has been an erosion of commitment to common law traditions, exemplified by the increasing reliance on legislation and statutes. For one observer, the diminished common law dimension of the American legal system is a regrettable development because this tradition historically contributed to building consensus between different constituencies (Scott 2007). On the other hand, for another observer, the common law tradition has been fundamentally elitist and undemocratic and is less necessary in a world where statutes increasingly address matters that require some formal resolution (Vermeule 2009).

SOCIALIST LAW

The **socialist law tradition** is the most recent of the families of law and is a product of the revolutionary establishment of communist or socialist regimes in the twentieth century. The status and character of law in such countries has been a matter of considerable dispute (Cowling 2008; Shichor and Heeren 1989). In one view, no valid system of law exists in communist countries, insofar as "legal procedures" and "legal decrees" are cynically used simply to serve the purposes of the regime. In this view, as there is no recognized constitutional basis for state power, such systems are really "anti-legal." In a second view, what exists in socialist countries that have systematic legal provisions is a system of law, but it is best classified as being within the civil law tradition, with some socialistic elements incorporated. A third view recognizes a system of law that is socialist and has such distinctive features that it cannot be considered simply a version of a civil law system. Which of these views is correct? The answer depends at least in part on one's ideological outlook and in part on the specific country and period (e.g., the Soviet Union under Stalin or during the Gorbachev years). The view adopted here is that for the most part, legal systems do exist in communist and socialist countries and that their socialist features do set them apart from nonsocialist legal systems.

One dimension of law in socialist countries is the **idealistic view of law**, in the sense that the law incorporates Marxist, socialistic, or revolutionary principles (e.g., profit-making private enterprise may be declared illegal) (Berman 1966, p. 205). A second dimension is the **traditional view of law**, in the sense that the indigenous legal norms and traditions of the country in question have not been abolished but have been adapted by the new regime (e.g., Russian secret police became Soviet secret police). And a third dimension is the **pragmatic view of law**, because the conditions of modern industrialized nations—capitalist or communist—and international commerce impose demands for certain legal norms and procedures (e.g., traffic law in the People's Republic of China).

The status of law in communist countries has inevitably been influenced by the views of Karl Marx, although these views have by no means been uniformly adopted. Marx's basic stance was one of general hostility toward law. Marx and his lifelong collaborator, Friedrich Engels, did not produce a systematic treatise on law, but many observations pertaining to law are scattered through their work (Beirne and Quinney 1982; Cain and Hunt 1979; Cowling 2008). Marx (and Engels) characterized law as "epiphenomenal," meaning that law reflects the society in which it developed. In Western European states, then, law is simply a reflection of the capitalist economy, and as an element of capitalism, law is complicit in the oppression, exploitation, and alienation of ordinary people, or workers. Law is an aspect of class domination, or the domination of the working class (proletariat) by the ownership class (the bourgeoisie). In a truly communist society, there would be no need for law, and law (along with the state) would "wither away."

Because Marx's observations about law are simply scattered through work produced over many years, and because the pronouncements are not always consistent, interpretations of Marx's views on law beyond such general themes have varied. For example, in an **instrumental interpretation**, Marx is understood to hold the view that the capitalist ownership class directly controls the lawmaking and law-enforcing process. In a **structural interpretation**, the law (and the state) is seen as "relatively autonomous," which means that it is not directly controlled by the capitalist ownership class but nevertheless is oriented toward the long-term survival of the capitalist system. This second interpretation appears to be more sophisticated and credible because it allows one to understand how laws (and prosecutions) can be directed against at least some capitalist practices (and capitalists) in capitalist societies, contributing to the long-term survival of these societies by fostering the notion that the law is neutral and fair.

Given the inconsistent observations on law found in the work of Marx, it is not surprising that students and followers of Marx have adopted different interpretations of the proper role of law in socialist, or communist, societies. Karl Renner (1870–1950), a native of the Austro-Hungarian empire (and for a time president of the Austrian Republic), produced an influential interpretation ([1904] 1949). For Renner, the uniformity of legal concepts across different economic systems suggests that Marx was wrong in characterizing law as "epiphenomenal." Rather, legal norms as such are neutral and are based on human relationships. Nevertheless, in capitalist societies these norms, and legal institutions generally, are manipulated to advance the interests of capitalism. It is this process of manipulation, not law itself, that should be abolished. In a similar vein, the British socialist historian E. P. Thompson (1978, pp. 258–269) argued that law was an inevitable feature of any complex society, that on balance the "rule of law" has historically been a force for good on behalf of ordinary people, and that accordingly law has a necessary role in any authentic socialist society. The early Soviet legal scholar E. B. Pashukanis is most closely associated with the view that law by its very nature is incompatible with a truly socialistic society (Beirne and Sharlet 1980; Milovanovic 2003). Although Pashukanis rejected the instrumentalist interpretation of law as a naked instrument of coercion controlled by the capitalist class, he replaced it with his **commodity exchange theory of law.** For Pashukanis, the very form of law reflects the commodity form of a capitalist society, and in law the "juridic subject" is the legal parallel to the exploited worker. In a fully developed socialistic society, then, policy and planning should replace law. Pashukanis was writing in the 1920s, when the newly established communist regime in the Soviet Union was still exploring how Russia might be transformed in a way consistent with Marx's vision. By the 1930s, the Soviet dictator Stalin had discovered that law and legal institutions could be used to consolidate his power and control; Pashukanis was attacked as a "legal nihilist" and disappeared in 1937, presumably murdered by Stalinist secret police.

The role of law in socialist and communist societies—and whether it has any proper role at all—was a historically contested terrain throughout the twentieth century. The typical pattern after a communist revolution has been an attempt to abolish law and legal institutions and to replace these institutions with **popular tribunals**, administering justice in accord with the goals of a true communism (Tay 1990). Over time, formal law and legal institutions have tended to re-emerge. By any criteria, horrendous injustices and genocidal campaigns have been carried out in the name of abolishing all remnants of a bourgeois, capitalist society and its "rule of law." This was conspicuously the case with the Chinese "cultural revolution" (1966–1976), when the fanatical Red Guard openly attacked all institutions and individuals deemed counterrevolutionary. It occurred as well during the genocidal campaign of the Khmer Rouge in Cambodia (1975–1979), when well over a million people were summarily executed on the grounds that they were a threat to, or did not fit in with, a projected radical agrarian communist society.

Whether these crimes can be blamed on a Marxist philosophy privileging "collective" justice over a concern for individual human rights or should be blamed principally on specific communist systems and leaders has been debated (Comaroff 1991). Of course, parallel horrors in the twentieth century occurred in many countries, from Hitler's Nazi Germany to Idi Amin's Uganda, which were totalitarian but hardly communist.

The Case of Russia/the Soviet Union

The Stalinist regime of the Soviet Union (from the 1920s to the 1950s) is widely regarded as one of the worst nightmares of the twentieth century and a prime case of law and legal institutions being used to achieve horrendous ends. Any consideration of the status of law in the Soviet Union, however, must begin with some attention to pre-revolutionary Russian law (Berman 1963; Hendley 2009). The Russian system of law was broadly rooted in the civil (Roman) law tradition but reflected as well the primitive and harsh customary law of the Mongols and other Russian ethnic tribes. The system of law that evolved under the Russian tsars was exceedingly autocratic. This law did not even pretend to embrace a principle of equality before the law; rather, separate courts and punishments were applied to serfs and to the nobility. Nor was there any allegiance to a rule of law, due process, or rational decision making. Secret police had almost limitless powers; judges were typically uneducated, immoral, and corrupt; trials were generally secret, taking the form of written presentations of evidence with no appeal possible. Lawyers were few and far between and were rarely involved in trials. Extremes of indulgence and severity were evident, with Draconian punishments possible, including exile, imprisonment, torture, and execution. Although some efforts were made under Tsar Peter the Great and Catherine the Great to Westernize the law, and some progressive reforms (including public trials, juries, the right to legal representation, and elected judges) were introduced in 1864 under Tsar Alexander II, these reforms were not widely understood nor adopted, and eventually the legal system reverted to autocratic rule by, or on behalf of, the tsar's successors. It is important to appreciate, then, that the Soviet legal system did not replace a progressive and fair-minded system of law; in fact, the Soviets adapted such traditional Russian institutions as the secret police for their own purposes.

Law in Soviet Russia after the Revolution was characterized by novelist Aleksandr Solzhenitsyn (1976, p. 522) as follows: "Our law is powerful, slippery, and unlike anything else on earth known as law."

The Russian Revolution in 1917 was one of the most dramatic events in twentieth-century history. Vladimir Lenin, the leader of the revolutionary Bolsheviks, basically adopted the interpretation of Marx, calling for a dictatorship of the proletariat and the withering away of law (Beirne and Hunt 1988). Although revolutionary tribunals were initially established and an effort was made to dismantle the existing system of law, a need for legal standards quickly became evident. Through much of the 1920s, in the era of "the New Economic Policy," much new law was passed, and a Soviet legal system was established on the rationale that it would contribute to paving the way for a truly communist society. The promotion of the revolutionary agenda—including a broad definition of counterrevolutionary activity and abolition of profit-making private enterprise—was one central objective of the law adopted during this period.

By the late 1920s, after the premature death of Lenin, there was a long period of growing domination by Joseph Stalin (until his own death in 1953), which began with forced collectivization of peasant farms and moved on to **show trials** of people perceived as threats to the regime; also, huge numbers of people deemed politically unreliable on some grounds or other were arrested and shipped off to the Gulag (Siberian prison camps). The "show trials" were staged in such a way as to educate the Soviet people at that time about the new social order to which they would have to adapt (Cassiday 2000). The jurist Andrei Vyshinsky played a key role in developing the **jurisprudence of terror** that transformed law during the Stalin era into a naked instrument operating on behalf of the regime (Sharlet and Beirne 1984). The powers of the police and courts were extended during this period. People were arrested and convicted without violating specific laws but on the basis that their actions (or words) were "analogous" to prohibited conduct.

In the Khrushchev Era (1953–1966), after Stalin's death, a rejection of the "excesses" of the Stalinist regime occurred, with some liberalization of laws. Reform took the form of attention to acts, not simply persons, and to circumstances, not simply ideological considerations. After Nikita Khrushchev was forced out of office in the mid-1960s, a second post-Stalinist era (1966–1990) took place, with a series of leaders (from Brezhnev to Gorbachev) who had survived and risen in the Byzantine world of Soviet politics. During this era renewed emphasis on law as a means for promoting social order, discipline, and morality occurred. Although efforts were made to eliminate some of the more arbitrary aspects of law and render it more orderly and predictable, it continued to face interference from and be subordinate to the needs of the communist state (which had clearly failed to wither away!). The size of the legal profession expanded considerably during this period, although it remained small relative to the American bar by a factor of at least 10. In the face of growing dissatisfaction with this legal system, especially its general indifference to individual human rights, Gorbachev, through his *glasnost* and *perestroika* program, initiated some liberalizing reforms to acknowledge such rights (Hazard 1990).

It is remarkable that the formal presumption of innocence—so central to Anglo-American criminal law—was only established in Russia in 1989, in a revision of the criminal law. But by this time any such reforms were too late to salvage the corrupt, disintegrating Soviet communist system itself, which collapsed in September 1991. With the collapse of communism, law in Russia (and in other postcommunist countries) faced formidable challenges (*see* Box 6.2).

BOX 6.2 LAW AFTER COMMUNISM IN
RUSSIA—AND ELSEWHERE

What was the fate of law in Russia (and former Soviet Republics and Eastern European countries) after communism was abandoned, in 1991 and earlier? Russia and the other former communist countries, with the exception of Czechoslovakia, had no democratic tradition (Czarnota 2003). The "transition" to a postcommunist society and legal order was certainly complex and difficult (Epstein, Knight, and Shvetsova 2001; Priban, Roberts, and Young 2003; Teitel 2000). Much law was systematically imported from the West (Dupre 2003). New legal institutions and orientations co-existed with the older institutions and attitudes. Some differences in legal patterns inevitably emerged in formerly communist countries—for example, with regard to the degree of judicial activism—as a consequence of different political circumstances (Smithey and Ishiyama 2002). In the formerly communist Eastern European countries, constitutional courts have assumed a central role in the legal system, although they have not been wholly successful in implementing a rule of law or asserting judicial independence (Schwartz 2000). The legal system can only play a limited role in legitimating emerging liberal democracies in these countries (Poibao 2002). Past wrongs have, as a rule, only been corrected selectively (Cartwright 2001). In the case of the Soviet Union, as indicated, law had gradually re-emerged largely as an instrument for achieving the purposes of the state. Accordingly, with the fall of a communist regime, a traditional attitude of cynicism or hostility toward law was common.

As is typically the case following a fundamental societal transformation, the crime rate for many conventional crimes rose dramatically in Russia following the collapse of the Soviet Union (Williams, Rodeheaver, and Huggins 2003). Three-person tribunals for trying those accused of crimes had survived. A new criminal code adopted in 2003 restored jury trials and extended more rights to those accused of serious crimes (Wines 2003). Juries participate in the most serious criminal cases in most parts of Russia today (Trochev 2008). Conviction rates have declined somewhat. Despite the extension of such formal rights, justice in practice remained arbitrary and corrupt in many respects (Myers 2003, 2004). Police powers to detain and coerce suspects, and politically or economically motivated prosecutions, continued to be common (Myers 2003). Hearings and trials are closed to public scrutiny, and options for appeal are more limited.

In a postcommunist Russia, a "negative" myth of law prevails, and people do not generally believe that anything can be achieved by law (Kurkchiyan 2009). Russia today ranks very low on "rule of law" indexes (Hendley 2009; Kahn 2006). It is characterized by pervasive corruption (Kahn 2006). Civil society in Russia is weak, and those who threaten the interests of the powerful are vulnerable. A prominent human rights activist was murdered with impunity (Hendley 2009). Russia has a dual legal system today. The courts handle routine cases, but powerful political officials tend to determine the outcomes in major cases (Hendley 2009; Trochev 2008). Today, however, the Constitutional Court is relatively independent (Trochev 2008). But ordinary Russians are often skeptical about the prospects for justice being realized.

It is striking to note that after wholly dominating Russia for more than 70 years, the Communist Party found itself on trial before a constitutional court following the new Russian president Boris Yeltsin's declaration banning it and seizing its assets (Kohan 1992). The Communist Party was accused of a long list of historical crimes, including the attempted destruction of the church, starvation of peasants, resettlement of ethnic groups, purging of political opponents, financing of terrorists, personal enrichment of party leaders, and the squandering of the country's economic resources in various ways.

The Case of China

In Oriental culture generally, and in the case of China specifically, law and formal legal proceedings—at least in their Western form—have been looked upon with disfavor. In part, this rejection reflects Confucianism, with its view of human nature as fundamentally good and capable of perfection. In this view, the elites of society should act in accord with unwritten ethical and moral codes. The nature of traditional Chinese law is nicely captured by the title of a book, *Law Without Lawyers, Justice Without Courts* (Goh 2002). Mediation has played a central role. To the extent that laws and courts are necessary, they should address only the activities of the common people, not the leadership class. In traditional Chinese culture, the patriarchal family, rather than the isolated individual, was the primary focus of concern (Tanner 1995), so social control was viewed primarily as a responsibility for the family and by extension the community. Furthermore, in a cultural value system emphasizing conformity to the group and self-control, conflicts, when they arise, are best handled by mediation and compromise rather than by litigation. Although a formal legal system with written codes, police, and prisons long existed in China, the country only adopted some Western-style legal codes and practices and allowed private practice lawyers in the first half of the twentieth century (Xu 2008). Despite the introduction of many modern reforms during the early part of the twentieth century, informal and corrupt dimensions of traditional Chinese justice endured (Xu 2008). The formal system of law co-existed with the informal system of law, and this form of co-existence has continued into the present era (Huang 2001; Sommer 2000). The informal legal system consists of the justice dispensed by relatives, friends, colleagues, and workplace or community leaders through informal proceedings; all people in China are subject to such justice.

Mao Tse-tung (or Zedong) led a successful communist revolution in China and established a new regime, the People's Republic of China, on the Chinese mainland in 1949. After the revolution, the Western-influenced legal system was largely abolished, along with the legal profession (Mühlhahn 2009; Xu 1995). As has been typically true in such circumstances, revolutionary tribunals administered a form of "popular justice," dedicated to advancing the aims of the revolution. To the extent that formal codes and procedures were adopted, they followed the Soviet model quite closely.

With disintegrating ties between China and the Soviet Union, and the emergence of the Cultural Revolution in 1966, much of the remaining formal legal system (including the written code of law) was swept away in the name of an anti-rightist, ongoing revolutionary struggle; an editorial in the *People's Daily* during this period was titled "In Praise of Lawlessness" (Leng 1977, p. 359). The revolutionary Red Guard ruled supreme, and mass trials of perceived enemies of the revolution were widely conducted, although by wholly political as opposed to traditional legal standards. Many Chinese, including some who would resurface later among the top leadership class, suffered greatly from the arbitrary form of justice administered (Ward 1997a). Following China's re-establishment of contacts with the West (including the United States) in the 1970s, and its efforts to stimulate greater economic development, re-establishment of a formal legal system began. This movement probably reflected the recognition that a reliable system of law was necessary if business relations with other nations were to be fostered.

From the early 1980s on, private enterprise was increasingly encouraged or permitted as a means of promoting economic development. A rising crime rate, including delinquency, gangs, drug trafficking, and conventional crime, was undoubtedly one consequence of this expansion of private enterprise, more freedom, and a growing gap between the well-off and the poor. The government responded with tough anti-crime programs and punishments (Smith 2001; Wong 2009; Zhang, Messner, and Liu 2008). An increase in corruption involving Chinese officials and their families was another consequence of these developments (Zhang 2001). In the face of understandable popular resentment of such corruption, the

Chinese government passed laws against official profiteering and attempted to crack down on such crime.

China not only faced formidable challenges in transforming its economy, it also contended with a long history of repression in a world increasingly concerned with human rights. In June 1989, state military forces suppressed and massacred some 5,000 unarmed students and workers participating in a pro-democracy protest demonstration in Tiananmen Square in Beijing; in the wake of this event, show trials were instituted in an attempt by the state to confront global criticism of the massacre and to affirm its commitment to resolving internal conflict by law and not simply by military might (Findlay 1989; Lubman 2000). By the early twenty-first century, many legal reforms had been instituted, with the introduction of numerous new laws, including a criminal procedure law (Eckholm 2003; Lin-Liu 2004; Ward 1997b). Civil liberties were extended, with the police now prohibited from detaining people indefinitely without formal charges; lawyers were made more readily accessible; and the presumption of innocence was affirmed. However, the government reserved the right to charge people with anti-state activity and to jail people on this charge. To Westerners, this power is viewed as a means of cracking down on dissidents. Although China has been much criticized for its human rights practices, it has become increasingly active within the international human rights community (China Rights Forum 2008). China itself has been under pressure to recognize independent trade unions, clarify prohibitions against discrimination, and support broader freedom of expression. Emerging Chinese corporations have also been under increasing pressure to adopt standards of corporate responsibility and respect for human rights (Bader 2008). Surprisingly, according to one source, state-owned Chinese companies have a better record in these areas than privately owned companies.

On the civil side, with international trade expanding steadily, many new law firms were opening in Beijing (Liu 2008; Potter 2004). Many global, international law firms have now established offices in China or have merged with local Chinese law firms (Liu 2008).

Through much of the history of the People's Republic of China, the criminal law has been administered in a way much at odds with procedures in the United States (Eckholm 2003; Rojek 1985; Zhang, Messner, and Liu 2008). Informal processes have dominated the control of crime, with self-criticism and answering to one's immediate group emphasized. Neighborhood associations and mediation units (known as **danwei**) were empowered to administer justice for a wide range of disputes and offenses and could issue warnings or impose fines. The far more limited formal court system was largely reserved for serious crimes or for criminal recidivists. Prosecutors (or procurators) had broad powers, and the matter of guilt or innocence would be determined largely by their investigation. A trial took the form of an inquisition as opposed to an adversarial contest. No exclusionary rule (exclusion of improperly seized evidence) existed, nor did a presumption of innocence (labeled by one commentator as "a worm-eaten dogma of bourgeois doctrine"). Defendants did not enjoy a right against self-incrimination; rather, a strong emphasis on a guilty plea and confession—regarded as therapeutic—governed.

Into the 1980s, the legal profession remained extraordinarily small (estimated to number between 3,000 and 15,000), and these few lawyers were state employees as opposed to private practitioners; legal education was essentially an undergraduate enterprise. Defendants in criminal cases often had to defend themselves or look to a relative or friend for assistance. When defense lawyers did become involved in criminal cases, it was only after the decision to prosecute had been made. The defense lawyer was not expected to contest the claims of the prosecutor but rather might make a plea for mercy or bring some mitigating circumstances on behalf of the defendant to the attention of the Court.

In the final decade of the twentieth century, China overhauled its legal system, expanding the rights of those accused of crimes (e.g., giving the right to legal representation) and training thousands of new lawyers (Potter 2004; Rosenthal 2000). Confessions on the part of criminal defendants became somewhat less common (He 2005; Lu and Miethe 2003). However, in this new environment, criminal defense lawyers confronted many challenges. The police could deny them access to clients, the court could deny them access to trial transcripts and other essential legal documents, and their witnesses could be intimidated by the authorities. A considerable gap still existed between formally granted rights and the actual implementation of those rights. The police in China view themselves as a social resource and tend to view crime as a personal affront (Wong 2009). "Confessions" were still sometimes beaten out of prisoners, despite the ban on such methods in the formal law. In some cases, criminal defense lawyers themselves, if they were especially pro-active in representing their clients, were prosecuted and jailed.

Two "People's Assessors" (lay judges without formal legal training) would determine the outcome of a criminal case in conjunction with the judge, and a majority vote governed. These People's Assessors were viewed as representing the conscience of the community. Contrary to what some might imagine, sentences could be mild, emphasizing ideological rehabilitation and prevention. Of course, those who committed heinous crimes or anti-state activities could expect harsh sentences, which might include lengthy confinement or summary execution.

Despite the dramatic changes in China during the recent era, both traditional and Maoist legal practices endure (Huang 2009). The Chinese Communist Party continues to overrule legal institutions to achieve its social control objectives (Diamant, Lubman, and O'Brien 2005). An analysis of responses that a newspaper legal advisor ("Dear Lawyer Bao") provided to inquiring readers found that the advice given reflected state interests rather than those of ordinary people seeking help (Michelson 2008). Although numerous new laws and regulations have been adopted in the recent era in China, noncompliance with these laws and regulations is still very common (He 2005). Chinese workers continue to prefer to resolve disputes informally, rather than turning to formal institutions of dispute resolution or informal mechanisms of social control resulting in both harsh and humane outcomes.

An American law professor who taught law students in China observed that the Chinese law students were more focused on learning the letter of the law ("black letter law") than in interpreting it, as is true of their American counterparts (Wald 2008). They are less inclined to consider the context within which law is implemented or the ideology underlying legal doctrine. Early in the twenty-first century, despite new attention to legal education, there were only 120,000 lawyers in a country of more than 1 billion people (Lin-Liu 2004, p. A43; Zhang, Messner, and Liu 2008). Whether China's growing interest in a rule of law reflects a real commitment to due process and human rights or is simply a strategic move to attract

BOX 6.3   LAW IN VIETNAM AND CAMBODIA

As is well-known, the United States fought an immensely costly and hugely controversial war in Vietnam, principally on the premise that this war was necessary to prevent Vietnam from becoming a communist country (with neighboring countries then following in its wake). Accordingly, it is historically ironic that despite the fact that the United States left Vietnam in 1975 in defeat, Vietnam has increasingly adopted (along with China) a free market economy and has been described as one of the most pro-American countries in the world (Kotkin 2008). Today, the United States is Vietnam's top trading partner.

As in the case of China, the communist party continues to dominate the political system despite promoting free market economic policies (Perlez 2006). Accordingly, a freeing up of many socialistic restraints on economic activity is counterbalanced by many ongoing restrictions on free speech and basic human rights. The official doctrine in Vietnam continues to claim that the law is rooted in "Marxism-Leninism and Ho Chi Minh thought" (Ho Chi Minh was the leader of Vietnam for several decades, through the war years), and the socialist dimension of law appears to be more pronounced under the present Vietnamese leadership than is the case with China (Uc 2005). Nevertheless, the adoption of laws in 1999 to 2000 that endorsed private enterprise for small- and medium-sized businesses contributed greatly to the growth of the Vietnamese economy and the reduction of poverty early in the twenty-first century (Kotkin 2008). A study of lawmaking in Vietnam finds that it favors the interests of business elites over small-scale entrepreneurs, and high levels of corruption remain

a problem (Gillespie 2008; Mirsky 2010). Vietnam's full-fledged integration into the global economy will depend on the elimination of the communist party and the development of a more democratic, transparent and effective political, legal, and regulatory system (Kotkin 2008). Legal professionals would play a central role in this process.

Cambodia was famously (and secretly) bombed by the United States during the Vietnam War and subsequently endured the mass killing of between 1 and 2 million people by the radical Khmer Rouge, which took over the government in 1975. The Khmer Rouge systematically tried to eliminate the entire professional classes, including judges and lawyers, to fulfill its mission of creating a classless agrarian utopia (Overland 2005). The cycle of killing only came to an end following an invasion by the Vietnamese army in 1978. Early in the twenty-first century, Cambodian law has been described as a hodgepodge of French colonial law, socialist law imposed by the Vietnamese, and indigenous Cambodian law. The police have virtually unchecked power and are widely feared. Becoming a lawyer depends on political connections rather than a legal education, and 80% of the judges have no legal training (in many cases, not even a high school diploma). Confessions are coerced, evidence is commonly ignored, and bribery is uniform in the Cambodian criminal justice system. By 2006 an initiative by Cambodia's secretary of state for justice was directed toward establishing a professional legal education as necessary to restore the people's trust in law. Only if this occurred, he believed, could Cambodia hope to break free of its vicious cycle of poverty.

more foreign investment remains to be seen. Other Asian countries are contending with law-related challenges as well (*see* Box 6.3).

SACRED LAW

Religion has been one important source of influence on law. The canon law of the Roman Catholic Church influenced civil law, and biblical principles have been incorporated into common law. The traditional legal systems of Asian countries reflect religious values as well, from Confucianism in China to Hinduism in India. For some systems of law, however, religious doctrine is the dominant—if not the exclusive—source of law, and there is no clear separation between the religious and the legal. As noted in Chapter 3, this was the case with the early American Pilgrim colony, where the law was derived directly from the Bible.

In a **sacred law tradition**, some sacred text—be it the Bible, the Talmud, or the Koran—is the basic source of law. No centuries-old sacred text, however, could anticipate the vast range of legal issues surfacing in the modern world. Accordingly, judges in such systems have creatively sought to find legal solutions for new problems by claiming they are being faithful to the wording of the sacred text, even when their rulings appear to be at odds with it. The term **legal fiction** has been applied to this type of legal creativity. As an example,

> In Jewish law, travel on the Sabbath was forbidden; people might walk 2,000 cubits from their towns, but no more. If a person needed to go a bit further, however, he or she could deposit some food at a place at the limit. The Rabbis treated this cache as a "temporary home," giving the person the right to go another 2,000 cubits. (Friedman 1977, p. 82)

Israel, founded as a Jewish state, has a legal system substantially dominated by religious doctrine, although there is some inevitable tension between religious and secular values.

In the Middle East generally the re-emergence of Islamic fundamentalism has inspired closer attention to its impact on law. Some 900 million people (or approximately one-fifth of the world's population, living in about 60 countries) subscribe to the Muslim faith. At least some countries with a dominantly Muslim population, including Saudi Arabia, Iran, and Libya, base their law on Islamic principles; in the case of the last two of these countries, recent fundamentalist counterrevolutions led to a synthesis of the religious and the legal. In some places (e.g., a province in Pakistan), **Islamic law (*Sharia'h*)** has been re-established, and this law is to take precedence over other sources of law (Gall 2003). The Sharia'h law in pre-modern Islamic societies, in one interpretation, mainly served to provide moral guidance to Muslims, but in the modern world it has become increasingly politicized and transformed (Hallaq 2009). For many Muslims, Sharia'h law was historically associated with respect for "the rule of law," but in the modern era was co-opted by rulers to serve their own purposes (Feldman 2008a). The call for a restoration of traditional Sharia'h law in Islamic states in the Mideast is at least in part a reaction against the autocratic rule of Arab monarchs.

Historically, Islamic or Sharia'h law was more liberal and humane than other past systems of law (Feldman 2008a). Such law traditionally prohibited unequal treatment of the rich and poor, protected property rights, and specifically prohibited bribery (Feldman 2008b). But there have always been repressive dimensions of Sharia'h law, including its harsh treatment of sodomy and of women who seek divorces. In Pakistan, as an Islamic republic, laws repugnant to Islam are regarded as invalid (Rohde 2005). Men can marry four wives; the testimony of women in court cases carries half the weight of that of men; women must produce four witnesses if they pursue a rape case; and the parents of a victim of honor killing can pardon the killer (Rohde 2005). Different interpretations of the Sharia'h lie at the heart of major conflicts (e.g., Shiites and Sunnis) in many Islamic countries today (Amanat and Griffel 2008). Islamic law generally relies on many non-coercive (e.g., emotional and cultural) means to induce compliance (Souiaiaia 2008). Many countries with a dominantly Muslim population (e.g., Syria, Egypt, Iraq, Lebanon, and Kuwait) have adopted much Western law, although they retain Islamic law on certain matters (e.g., family-related issues) (Freeland 1997; Ramadan 2009). The replacement of "God's law" by the law of "colonizers" in these Middle Eastern countries is seen as highly objectionable by Muslim fundamentalists (Hallaq 2003, p. 1718). This issue is a source of considerable conflict in many of these countries.

Because Islam is regarded by the faithful as a whole way of life—not something that can be compartmentalized as a religious practice—it follows that for true believers, a valid system of law must be wholly consistent with Islamic doctrine (Ezzati 2002; Kamali 2008). The Koran (the doctrine communicated by God through the prophet Muhammad in the seventh century A.D.) is the sacred text of Islam. The Koran, then, is one source of Islamic law (or "the path to follow"). There are other sources, including collections of teachings and sayings of Muhammad, judicial rulings on issues not specifically addressed by the sacred text, and reports of new principles established by jurists through analogy with established principles of Islamic law (Moore 1996). It must be emphasized that any ruling, whatever its source, cannot be inconsistent with the basic tenets of the Koran.

After 9/11, Islamic law (and the Muslim faith) were viewed by some people as an important source of inspiration for the attacks (Hallaq 2003). Fundamentalist terrorists profess an absolute commitment to the "law of Allah," as they interpret it (Sciolino 2008). In this interpretation, Islam is inherently inconsistent with democracy. The goal of Islamist terrorist groups is to restore a unified worldwide Muslim political community: the ummah, to be ruled by a centralized Islamic authority, the caliphate, governed by Sharia'h law, and organized to promote "jihad." Others, as defenders of the Islamic tradition, called attention to the many aspects of their law that promote peaceful, cooperative, and charitable behavior by people.

The criminal justice system under Islamic law operates differently from Western systems, with more focus on the person than on external facts (Haleem, Sharif, and Daniels 2003; Rosen 2000). Because there is no clear separation between public and private wrongs, accusers must initiate cases and must provide credible witnesses to support their accusations (Kusha 2002; Reichel 1999, p. 106). Ultimately, the parties involved may be required to take an oath to support their claims, with the prospect of a day of reckoning in the afterlife for lying—a powerful force toward inducing honesty. The concerns of victims tend to be taken seriously, and even in serious cases the court will allow the matter to be settled by restitution, if victims are agreeable. Proceedings tend to be conducted informally before a judge (there is no jury); defendants are generally expected to represent themselves, although counsel may assist them; trials on "moral" matters may be closed to the public; and judges are expected to apply the principles of sacred law to the evidence at hand (Moore 1996). The process of reviewing judicial decisions is somewhat informal; it may be undertaken by the trial judge himself, and only in limited circumstances does it go to a higher court (Powers 1992). Altogether, Islamic law proceedings tend to move along swiftly, although from a Western vantage point with somewhat inadequate attention to procedural safeguards.

Islamic law, at least as interpreted and applied in countries where fundamentalism is dominant, is viewed by many Westerners as reactionary, irrational, and barbaric (Collier 1994; Freeland 1997; Hallaq 2003). The notion of a "legal fiction" (mentioned earlier) arises here as well. Because of the traditional ban on paying interest found in the Koran, observant Muslims in the United States have had to develop creative new ways of arranging the financing of homes, so that these arrangements are in conformity with Islamic law (Maurer 2006). These arrangements include lease-to-own agreements, cost-plus contracts, and profit-loss sharing.

But other aspects of Islamic law concern Westerners more. Ritual religious practices are required, and such penalties as flogging for drinking alcoholic beverages, cutting off a hand for theft, death for blasphemy, and stoning people to death for adultery are sometimes implemented (Bearak 2001). Islamic (Sharia'h) law is widely viewed as severely limiting the rights of women, but there is some disagreement over whether this bias comes from the Koran (Qur'an) itself or from male interpreters of the Koran (Krivenko 2009; Souaiaia 2008). In one recent book the claim is made that the bias against women is embedded in Islamic law itself (Welchman 2007). Following Operation Iraqi Freedom, with the largely secular regime of Saddam Hussein replaced by a regime with a close association with Islam, there was a concern that the rights of women (and religious freedom) would decline (Filkins 2005). When British law was applied in Muslim countries, the women in those countries actually lost property rights they had enjoyed under Islamic law (Feldman 2008b). In some European countries, laws have been passed against the wearing of the veil (or hijab) by Muslim women in public, in part on the grounds that this is demeaning to women, but these laws have generated considerable controversy (Scott 2007). "Honor" killing of women for sexual conduct outside of marriage has been condoned in some countries, as has rape as a penalty for such conduct (*see* Box 6.1).

From within, and among at least some Western students, however, Islamic law is viewed as quite flexible and adaptable to modern conditions and at the same time as a means of maintaining the integrity of traditional Muslim values in the face of Western imperialism (Collier 1994; Miller 2003; Rosen 1989). Susan Hirsch (1998) argued, at odds with a commonly held view, that Muslim women employ the legal process quite effectively to address problems in their domestic lives. Whether the Islamic approach to law effectively deters crime is open to question; although Saudi Arabia has a low crime rate, Iran does not, which suggests that other factors (e.g., the economy) may play a critical role (Kusha 1998). In a world of increasing contacts between Westerners and Muslims, a correct understanding of Islamic law becomes all the more important. The preceding review of "Families of Law," however, should not be taken to encompass the legal systems of every country (*see* Box 6.4).

BOX 6.4   THE CASE OF JAPAN

Some legal systems do not fit neatly within one of the recognized families of law. For example, many former colonial nations in Africa and elsewhere are not easily categorized (Moore 1986). Also, some highly developed nations, such as Japan, are hybrids of different legal systems. The case of Japan is of particular interest to American students of the sociolegal because Japan's experience with law is so different from that of the United States (Feeley and Miyazawa 2002; West 2006). First, a traditional Oriental aversion to formal law is one important dimension of the Japanese experience. The earliest codes of law introduced into Japan, principally addressing rights of victims of crime and introducing harsh measures for offenders, were based on Chinese law of the period prior to the seventeenth century. During the so-called Tokugawa Period (1600–1868), social control was exercised largely by adherence to Confucian principles of conduct and communal family standards rather than by formal written law. The criminal law that did exist was exceptionally harsh, with torture as one element (Westermann and Burfeind 1991).

After 1868, Japan renewed contact with the West (after a long period of self-imposed isolation). During the latter part of the nineteenth century, a constitution reflecting Western influences (including many elements of French and, later, German law) was introduced into the Japanese legal system. These Western elements, however, came to be somewhat overshadowed by the country's growing militarism, which culminated with World War II. After the defeat of Japan in that war and the American occupation, a postwar era witnessed the adoption of a new constitution that reflected the American influence; it decreed diminished powers for the Emperor. Despite the borrowing of many elements of other legal systems (Chinese, French, German, and American), the Japanese legal system is not synonymous with any of these.

BOX 6.4 (cont'd.)

Japan apparently has the lowest crime rate of any developed nation. How can one explain this? For violent crime, the rate is close to 30 times lower than that in the United States; furthermore, both the crime rate and the imprisonment rate dropped dramatically through most of the post-World War II era (Reichel 1999, pp. 323–324; Sanders 1996, pp. 329–330). On the one hand, traditional cultural values emphasizing moral obligation to the community, compliance, and habits of order constrain criminal conduct; on the other hand, the broad network of police surveillance of citizens, strong neighborhood police programs, and extensive police powers in connection with arrest, detention, and interrogation also play a role in the low crime rate (Sanders 1996; Steinhoff 1993). In Japan, a strong emphasis on confession in criminal cases leads some 85% of those accused of crimes to "confess" (Sanders 1996, p. 335). Prosecutors in Japan enjoy some advantages over Western prosecutors (Dammer and Albanese 2011). The jury system—abolished in Japan in 1943—was reintroduced in 2009. Many Japanese people are leery of serving on juries and lack confidence in the fairness of jury verdicts. Also, many Japanese people who consult lawyers today are embarrassed to do so (Onishi 2008). The low crime rate, then, is perhaps best understood in terms of the interrelationship between cultural values and justice system practices.

Japan also has an extraordinarily low rate of civil litigation. By some measures, the rate of civil litigation in Japan is about one-twentieth of what it is in an American state (Sanders 1996, p. 329). Why? The traditional answer has stressed Japanese cultural aversion to invoking the formal processes of law. An alternative answer points to the institutional difficulties of engaging in litigation: cumbersome procedures, high fees, limited numbers of lawyers and judges, and the like (Feeley and Miyazawa 2002). Furthermore, a Civil Liberties Bureau provides extensive opportunities to mediate cases. Both the traditional and the alternative answers have a measure of truth. There can be little question that Japan has traditionally had an "informalist anti-law ideology of harmony and consensus," which has been deliberately promoted or encouraged by its leadership; its outlook has been likened to that of the Amish of Pennsylvania (Kidder and Hostetler 1990, p. 896). The significant differences between Japanese and Western perceptions of privacy, personal dignity, and honor are reflected in the different legal and social responses to scandal (West 2007). Private groups play a larger role than public law in addressing responses to scandal, but lawsuits in defense of one's honor are hardly unknown in Japan. A strong cultural emphasis on apology also minimizes civil litigation (Feeley and Miyazawa 2002; Westermann and Burfeind 1991). For example, when the President of Japan Airlines personally called on and apologized to the families of crash victims following a crash in 1982, in which the pilot was apparently liable, no lawsuits resulted (Wagatsuma and Rosett 1986, p. 488). The Japanese are also less focused on individual rights and more on a network of social relationships and on the importance of resolving differences within this network (Feldman 2000; Hamilton and Sanders 1992). Japan's high divorce rate is significantly attributed to a legal and regulatory circumstance that facilitated consensual divorce (Fuess 2004). Although divorce law in Japan has adapted in the recent era to take account of changing roles of men and women, not all of the changes have worked to the advantage of Japanese women, as one might have expected. The Japanese legal system has been found to be more responsive to some types of civil litigants (e.g., those infected by HIV-contaminated blood) and more efficient in returning lost property than the American legal system (Feldman 2000; West 2003). Japan's lower reliance on formal law can be seen in a positive and in a negative light. There may be less crime and civil litigation in Japan, but people in Japan have fewer rights and are less likely to realize personal justice than Americans.

THE HISTORICAL PERSPECTIVE ON LAW

American law is a product of our history and has also been a significant influence on our history. As the great associate justice of the U.S. Supreme Court, Oliver Wendell Holmes, Jr., once put it, "This abstraction called the Law is a magic mirror, [wherein] we see reflected, not only our own lives, but the lives of all men that have been" (Hall 1989, p. 3).

History is an ancient discipline and an enduring one. History has been used as a means of glorifying and celebrating the past; history meant to glorify is usually selective, disregarding events that might reflect poorly on that history's subject. History has also been used as a means of trying to learn from the past, and here history is far more likely to attend to the discreditable. History also serves as a rich source of entertainment, as many stories from our past are filled with drama and pathos. In the modern era, historians have been divided on the question of whether it is possible to provide a truly objective account of the past.

American law professors as a whole have not been all that interested in the history of law. Histories of law that were produced focused principally on the development of legal doctrine, on the English common law, and on the adoption of such law by the American system. James Willard Hurst, of the University of Wisconsin law school, is generally credited with having pioneered a new approach to legal history in the mid-twentieth century. In his *Growth of American Law* (1950), Hurst explored the social and economic factors that shaped American law over time; in this sense, Hurst applied the tenets of legal realism to legal history (Soifer 1992). Hurst shifted attention away from the great cases in appellate court decisions to the other institutions of law, such as the legislature. He saw an erosion of a sense of community in American life, which led to the development of law that basically ignored economic exploitation and conservation of the environment. His book expressed the faith that if law was to be reformed in a constructive way, such reform would have to be based on a deep understanding of the historical facts that shaped law. With this book and subsequent work, Hurst greatly influenced future generations of legal historians to immerse themselves in the realities of economic, political, and social life and the impact these forces have on law.

Lawrence M. Friedman of Stanford University Law School, writing in the Hurst tradition in *A History of American Law* ([1973; 1986] 2005) and elsewhere, has described American law as a mirror of society, constantly changing, adaptable, and functional, responding to real economic interests, concrete political groups, and various social forces. And Kermit Hall (1989), in *The Magic Mirror: Law in American History*, emphasizes that American law is pluralistic. In addition to law produced by courts and lawyers, legislatures, administrative agencies, and the executive branch produce law; so, too, in a sense, do such informal, nongovernmental institutions as the family, private associations, and trade groups. A history of American law must appreciate the complex interactions among these different sources of law.

The work of Hurst and Friedman has been criticized (fairly or not) as a form of functionalism, with too much stress on consensus and on law as responding to external economic and social forces (Soifer 1988, 1992). An alternative historical interpretation of American law views it as relatively autonomous (or independent), an instrument of power, and a force that lends legitimacy to the status quo. Such a view, for example, is advanced in Morton J. Horwitz's (1977) *Transformation of American Law, 1780–1860*. Horwitz attempts to reveal how American law in the nineteenth century was significantly shaped to advance and protect the interests of the rising business class. Law in the critical historical interpretation also has an ideological function: to help persuade the oppressed to accept the existing political and social system and to enable the oppressors to regard this system as just and fair (Tushnet 1977). Furthermore, the traditional accounts of legal history are viewed as tending to neglect or de-emphasize the situation of marginal members of society, which for most of this history includes women and people of color.

PRINCIPAL INFLUENCES ON AMERICAN LAW

What are the principal influences on American law? First, and obviously, American law reflects a Western European heritage, with the British (and Anglo-Saxon) heritage dominant.

It seems reasonable to suppose, then, that those Americans who are also part of this cultural heritage have adapted more easily to American law than would be true of those from non-Western cultures. A second general influence was surely the character and mission of the early colonists. Many of them—with the Pilgrims as the exemplary case—had suffered from some form of persecution in the Old World, and they were dedicated to creating a society based on new principles. The extent to which this was true varied among the different colonies, of course, and all of them, over time, would find themselves in conflict with the mother country on some matters (Nelson 2008).

The harsh living conditions prevailing in the early history of the colonies (and continuing in the American frontier through the later nineteenth century) required a system of law and justice that was often rough, informal, and practical. The American Revolution, which was all about legal rights (as opposed to the maldistribution of material wealth), obviously produced a whole new framework for a legal system based on democratic principles that were influenced by Enlightenment ideas of "unalienable human rights." The American legal system was also importantly shaped by the needs of an evolving capitalist economy, with its strong emphasis on individual enterprise and a free market. Of course, cultural values other than economic, such as patriarchy (male dominance) and racism, were also reflected in the law. Also, the "nation of immigrants" became increasingly heterogeneous, and the system of law was under some pressure to recognize such diversity—for example, with bilingual programs. Even in the earliest period, at least some colonists came from countries and cultures other than British and introduced into American law aspects their own heritage (*see* Box 6.5).

Some important influences on American law can be identified more specifically. First, the Bible has been influential in providing a moral foundation for American law; the law of the Pilgrim colony came quite directly out of the Bible. Second, from the outset, charters,

---

BOX 6.5 LAW ON THE WESTERN FRONTIER

The image of the Wild West is an enduring one in the American popular imagination. As a part of this image, lawlessness reigned, with disputes settled by six-shooters and gunfights (e.g., the showdown at the O.K. Corral). Certainly the history of law on the Western frontier is complex. Those who settled on the Western frontier brought with them much of their understanding of law from back East (Reid 2000). The frontier was a meeting place for English and French law, American and Spanish law, common and civil law. There was the law of the borderland, of the open range (and cattle drives), of the fur companies, and of the mining towns (Bakken 2000). In large parts of the West, the law of American Indian tribes prevailed, at least for a period of time. In Utah, a "theocracy" emerged under the rule of Mormon settlers, guided by their religious beliefs.

Recent historians of the West dispute the notion that Dodge City and other famous Western towns were as violent and lawless as they have been made out to be, and some argue that property rights were quite widely implemented and respected (Anderson and Hill 2004; Reid 2000, p. 8). But justice in the early era of the frontier was "rough," shoot-outs occurred, and vigilantism was not uncommon as well (Friedman 1986, 1993). Whether much of the violence that existed is best seen as enforcing law or defying it has been debated.

Judge Roy Bean of Langtry, Texas (a saloon-keeper and justice of the peace, without any legal education), declared himself "law West of the Pecos" and was arguably the most colorful jurist in American history (Trachtman 1974, p. 156). Bean simply ignored laws he didn't like and ruled in accordance with his personal predilections and interests. He dismissed a homicide case against an Irish railroad hand who had killed a Chinese worker, because he could find no specific law prohibiting the killing of a Chinese person. And he once fined a corpse the $40 found in the corpse's pocket, for carrying a concealed weapon.

codes, and constitutions have been important in American law, based on a strong inclination to produce a framework for a new type of society. American charters and the Constitution itself were influenced by earlier charters such as the English Magna Carta and the English Bill of Rights, both of which imposed constraints on centralized governmental authority (originally, the monarch). At the same time, the colonies were formed by private company charters and were subject to British control, at least until the Revolution. Third, the English common law was an important source, both in terms of its according judges the central role of interpreting law and in terms of specific legal principles and rules that came out of this tradition. Sir William Blackstone's ([1765–1769] 1979) *Commentaries on the Laws of England,* which fortuitously appeared shortly before the American Revolution, was a comprehensive summary of the core principles of the English common law, organized into four areas (rights of persons; rights of things, or property; private wrongs, or torts; public wrongs, or crimes), with rationales provided for the law. Although some Americans—notably Thomas Jefferson—criticized Blackstone for a conservative view of the legal system, his work provided a basic source for early American law and was a key text in early legal education (e.g., Abraham Lincoln learned law by reading Blackstone).

The common law was originally the law of the king's courts, however, and did not address all of the minor legal issues that might arise on a daily basis. Such issues were addressed by manorial (or local) law, and this aspect of law was especially familiar to colonists who came from small farming villages.

The civil law tradition of continental Europe, although less broadly influential than the English common law, also had some influence. First, from the outset, at least a certain proportion of colonists came from civil law countries, and over time this proportion increased dramatically. In certain colonies, such as that established in Louisiana by the French, the civil law tradition was dominant; in other colonies, in varying degrees, civil law elements were introduced. Second, the American Revolution was inevitably accompanied by strong anti-British sentiment, and this inspired lawmakers to look to the traditions of other European countries. And third, the civil law stress on the importance of the legislature was appealing to a new, democratic nation, as legislators are directly elected by the people whereas federal judges are not. American law reformers in the nineteenth and twentieth centuries who attempted to bring order to the maze of legislatively produced laws by producing codes of law were also influenced by this tradition; codes have had the most impact in certain branches of law, such as commercial law or tax law. Despite the legislative bias and the efforts at codification, however, the traditional common law norm according judges considerable power over the interpretation of both constitutional provisions and legislatively passed laws survived.

SLAVERY AND THE AFRICAN-AMERICAN EXPERIENCE OF LAW

Of the numerous threads that make up the tapestry of American legal history, it would be difficult to identify one more troublesome than the law's complicity in slavery and the overall African-American experience of law (Higginbotham 1978, 1996). From the outset, the American colonies contended with a shortage of labor. The use of indentured servants was one early response to this problem. The passage of these servants was paid for by a master, to whom the indentured servant owed between 4 and 7 years of service. Although such servants were not entirely without rights, as a practical matter they were little more than the personal property of the master for the period of indenture and could be easily abused. The first African-American slaves, brought to the American mainland in 1619 by John Rolfe of the Virginia colony, had a status equivalent in some respects to that of indentured servants; some who gained freedom became slave owners themselves (Berlin 1998). But from the outset, race cast African-Americans into a different situation from that of White servants (Morris 1996). Permanent slavery was unknown in the English common law, however, and only became formalized in the latter part of the seventeenth century. The basic law of slavery ("the peculiar institution") in America, then, was in existence for some 200 years (between 1660 and 1860). The nature of North American slavery varied considerably between different parts of the country and over time (Berlin 1998). In the Deep South, however, the law was shaped by the increasing economic dependence on slave labor; by owners' fear of the growing number of slaves and the need to control them for the safety of Whites; and by a racist ideology, which provided rationales for denying African-Americans full-fledged recognition as human beings.

Over time the slave codes became increasingly race-specific, with slave status inherited through the mother. In the interpretation of historian Frank Tannenbaum (1946), in *Slave and Citizen*, both the conditions of slavery itself and the intensity of racism ultimately took a more extreme form in North America than in Latin America. Tannenbaum attributed this difference to both the influence of the Catholic Church in Latin America (which accorded slaves recognition as souls, entitled to receive the sacraments) and the civil law tradition (which locked in some legal protections); in the predominantly Protestant United States, the humanity of slaves was less easily protected, and the more flexible common law tradition allowed for increasing control over slaves.

By the time of the American Revolution, then, all American colonies had legally sanctioned slavery, although beginning in 1780 with Pennsylvania, the Northern states moved toward its gradual abolition (Hall 1989). This period was also witness to one of the most profound contradictions in American legal history. Many of the same venerated Founding Fathers (notably Thomas Jefferson) who produced the Constitution and provided the framework for legal rights for future generations of Americans also owned other human beings. John Noonan ([1976] 1994), in addressing the paradox of the "Virginia liberators," invoked the metaphor of **"masks" of the law**. By seeing slavery in legal terms and imposing on slaves the "mask" of a legal concept, property, the Virginia liberators were able to avoid confronting the inherent inhumanity of the slave system. And as Noonan observed,

> Slavery's survival in Virginia after the Revolution...was assured by the cataloguing power, the rule-making capacity, the indifference to persons of—the law? That is to depersonalize those responsible: better say—the lawyers. Without their professional craftsmanship, without their management of metaphor, without their loyalty to the system, the enslavement by words more comprehensive than any shackles could not have been forged. ([1976] 1994, p. 529)

Although Jefferson, in his *Notes on the State of Virginia* ([1781] 1998), objected to a proposal calling for the emancipation of slaves born after a certain date, it would be a distortion to say that he (and other White Southerners) were wholly indifferent to the humanitarian issues surrounding slavery. Washington, for example, provided for the emancipation of his slaves following his death. The Constitution itself did not officially recognize slavery (in fact, the words "slave" and "slavery" do not appear in this document), but several clauses pertaining to rights over those in service and means of calculating the population for purposes of representation and taxation implicitly supported the rights of slaveholders (Hall 1989). Rather ironically, Jefferson's election to the presidency in 1801 only came about because slaves counted as three-fifths of a person for purposes of electoral college representation, giving Jefferson an edge over John Adams (Wills 2004).

On the one hand, the framers of the Constitution can be viewed as having missed a unique opportunity to renounce slavery (and racism), and accordingly they helped set the stage for the Civil War (Bell 1987). Waldstreicher (2009) argues that slavery is interwoven into the clauses of the Constitution. On the other hand, some say that the broad language and perspective of the Declaration of Independence and the Constitution made the dissolution of slavery inevitable (West 1998).

For several decades leading up to the Civil War, slavery was much debated and discussed in the American North (Baker 2006; DeLombard 2007). The erosion of support for slavery in this part of the country reflected, at least in part, far less economic dependence on slaves. Slave states all adopted slave codes reaffirming almost total control over slaves by the master; slaves' status as property shifted from real property to personal property (Morris 1996). With a growing anxiety on the part of White Southerners about the increasing size of the African-American population and the threat of free African-American people, the right to manumission (freeing slaves) was limited. But slaves had always been treated as persons, as opposed to property, when it came to misbehavior on their part and were subject to exceedingly harsh discipline and punishment. Of course, in the context of slavery, such acts as running away or attempting to poison the master could be interpreted as acts of rebellion against an unjust system (Schwarz 1988). Although over time some formal protections against physical abuse and being overworked and some limited procedural rights were extended to slaves, as a practical matter slave owners had substantial discretion in their handling of slaves (Finkelman 1997; Morris 1996). Slaves were severely constrained from testifying against White people in legal proceedings (Stroud 1956). An ironic historical footnote on this is the following story: George Wythe, a prominent legal authority in colonial Virginia who played a role in drafting laws pertaining to African-American people, was murdered by a grandnephew; the murderer could not be convicted for the crime, however, because the primary witness against him was an African-American woman, who was precluded by law from testifying (Bonsignore et al. 2002, p. 246). The principal form of protection for slaves from ultimate forms of abuse, including being murdered by their master, was this: they were valuable property (Hall 1989). Nevertheless, horrendous abuses were obviously perpetrated on slaves (*see* Box 6.6).

A landmark legal case in the 1850s brought into sharp relief the status of slaves in the eyes of American law. The case of ***Dred Scott v. Sandford* (1857)** involved a slave (Dred Scott)

BOX 6.6 SLAVERY TODAY

In the United States we learn about slavery first and foremost as a historical phenomenon, a shameful dimension of our distant past. Every school child learns that slavery was formally abolished in the United States during the Civil War, with the passage of the Thirteenth Amendment to the Constitution. But slavery, if defined as the coercive or violent control of one human being of another, is still widespread in the world today—by some estimates, there are some 27 million slaves globally, but in the United States, some 40,000 to 50,000 people could be described as enslaved. These phenomena are documented in Kevin Bales and Ron Soodalter's (2009) *The Slave Next Door*. The first author is a British sociologist who has written a series of books on contemporary slavery and is a leading activist to address this phenomenon, especially through his Free the

Slaves organization. Contemporary American slaves are found in domestic service, farm labor, factories, mines, and prisons—and of course in the sex work industry, where "human trafficking" has been long recognized and has sometimes been characterized as "White slavery." Enslaved people have even been found in prosaic American suburbs. Although of course no form of slavery is condoned by American law, U.S. government immigration policies are complicit in this phenomenon: first, by forcing desperate illegal immigrants into the hands of smugglers who then effectively enslave them, and second through the lack of enforcement of conditions under which legal "guest workers" are employed (Martinez 2009). The phenomenon of contemporary slavery in the United States has to be combated not only through raising awareness of it and encouraging active intervention but by addressing the complicity of existing laws as well.

who had traveled with his master to a free state territory (Minnesota) and then returned to a slave state (Missouri). Scott's claim was that he should be recognized as a citizen of Missouri and should be able to sue in federal court for his freedom. Chief Justice Roger Taney of the U.S. Supreme Court denied Scott's petition and held that an African-American person, whether free or slave, was not entitled to citizenship. This infamous decision reflected the judgment of a Supreme Court that had become increasingly pro-slavery and pro-business (Allen 2006). It was not necessarily inconsistent with the form of constitutional reasoning that prevailed at the time that it was handed down (Graber 2006). The *Dred Scott* decision, which might be read as the culmination of a long series of common law decisions that had reduced African-Americans to the status of property, is credited with having contributed to the contentious political environment that brought about the Civil War.

The Thirteenth Amendment to the Constitution declared the emancipation of slaves from their bondage. The Thirteenth Amendment was a foundation for civil rights and personal liberty case law during the course of American history after the Civil War (Tsesis 2004). If slavery was formally abolished in the United States as a consequence of the Thirteenth Amendment, it was hardly eliminated in all respects. Douglas Blackmon (2009) argues that hundreds of thousands of African-Americans in the American South were effectively re-enslaved by forced laborer practices (a consequence of being unable to pay substantial, unwarranted fines that were imposed on them). Whites were rarely, if ever, prosecuted for involuntary servitude during this period.

The history of the Fourteenth Amendment, however, is generally less familiar. The formal rationale for this amendment, which implements rights to "equal protection" and "due process" for all citizens, was to ensure that the Southern states would not pass laws stripping the newly emancipated former slaves of their basic rights (although behind-the-scenes concerns about the redistribution of political power were involved). Despite the Fourteenth Amendment, the Southern states in the latter part of the nineteenth century passed a series of laws, known as **Jim Crow laws** (or Black Codes), which effectively disenfranchised

African-Americans, reduced them to second-class citizenship, and imposed on them segregation from White people in many settings (e.g., in schools, hotels, and clubs, and on buses and trains) (Brandwein 2000; Epps 2006; Woodward 1957). In a series of decisions, the U.S. Supreme Court basically upheld these laws. *Plessy v. Ferguson* (1896) was the single most notorious of these decisions, setting forth a doctrine of "separate but equal." With this doctrine, the Supreme Court held that there was no constitutional barrier to segregated (or separate) facilities for African-Americans and Whites, although it also held that such facilities should be "equal." It is an interesting footnote to this case that Plessy himself was by appearance a White man who voluntarily identified himself to a railway conductor as a "colored" man and was accordingly excluded from riding in a rail car reserved for White people (Golub 2005). Through the middle of the twentieth century, then, African-Americans in the South—and to some extent in the North—endured many forms of discrimination and disadvantage.

The landmark U.S. Supreme Court decision in *Brown v. Board of Education* (1954) repudiated the separate but equal doctrine and called for the end of formal segregation with "all deliberate speed." The decision was not simply based on principles of legal reason; rather, social and behavioral science studies documenting the damaging effects of segregation on African-American schoolchildren were cited in the opinion. Many years of resistance and turmoil followed this decision, with the civil rights movement leading the ongoing challenge to segregation and discrimination, sometimes by specifically violating the segregationist laws and policies that continued to be enforced. (Walker 2009) The passage of the Civil Rights Act of 1964, declaring discrimination illegal as a matter of national policy, is taken to signal the final renunciation of formal segregation (Tsesis 2008). Unfortunately, no such law is able to resolve the deeply ingrained attitudes and patterns of behavior that had developed over a long period of time in the relations between African-Americans and White Americans.

At the onset of the twenty-first century, the tragic legacy of the slave laws and the laws upholding segregation in various forms endures in American society. If law has been able to abolish formal segregation, it has not been able to legislate racism out of existence (Bell 2004; Dorr 2008; Ogletree 2004). Indeed, law has been directly complicit in the construction of race and the resulting racism. Many African-Americans continue to suspect, with some justification, that elements of White racism influence a wide range of decisions and actions, including those of White officers of the law (e.g., the police, prosecutors, judges, and correctional personnel) (Alexander 2010; Mann 1993). African-Americans are disproportionately represented among those who are arrested, tried, convicted, and incarcerated (and executed) for conventional lawbreaking, and this indisputable fact can be interpreted in a number of different ways: as a reflection of African-Americans having less respect for law because of their historically negative experience with law; as a consequence of the enduring psychic and social damage brought about through slavery, segregation, and discrimination; and as a result of the racist decision making of a White-dominated system of criminal justice.

Legal measures intended to compensate on some level for past injustices to African-Americans and for their continuing underrepresentation in many privileged sectors of

American life (e.g., politics; elite schools; the professions) have recently been promoted and adopted. But affirmative action laws, busing laws, and voting rights laws (e.g., race-based districting designed to ensure the election of African-American candidates) have encountered resistance and, in some cases, a backlash from Whites on claims of reverse discrimination. At least some African-Americans have also questioned whether affirmative action policies are ultimately self-defeating if they continue to perpetuate the notion that African-Americans can only succeed when special accommodations are made for them (Lawrence 1998). Altogether, the movement toward any ultimate resolution of the legacy of slavery was sure to be reflected in developments within law as well as in attitudes and behavior responding to law.

THE CONTEXTUAL PERSPECTIVE ON LAW

Is law operational in every context, and what does law mean in extreme circumstances? In many aspects of our private lives, for example, we tend to think of ourselves as living independent of the law. Historically, heads of families were pretty much free to "govern" their family life as they pleased, with little prospect of outside interference. School principals and teachers in the classroom have also been accorded considerable leeway in making and administering their own rules and regulations. Private businesses, as well, have traditionally been left alone to determine procedures and practices governing the workplace. In the modern era, for better or worse, the law has become an increasingly obtrusive presence in the home, in the classroom, and in the workplace. For example, we expect the law to intervene if children or spouses are abused. Principals and teachers are more liable to legal action if their discipline of schoolchildren is deemed excessive. And laws pertaining to minimum wages, safety standards, and (more recently) sexual harassment are among the constraints on the freedom of employers.

The ongoing challenge in these contexts, then, is to determine what the proper balance should be between the rights of family members, teachers and students, and employers and employees in terms of self-determination and external law. When should the law intervene, and when should it leave people alone?

A second set of questions arises in the context of a new domain or one not clearly covered by existing legal jurisdiction. Human beings sometimes find themselves in circumstances in which they have no recourse to a formal system of law and must rely on some other means for resolving disputes. Although the lawlessness and violence of the mythic American Western frontier has been overstated, according to some historians, certainly there were circumstances where men (and it was largely men) resolved disputes by whatever means were available to them, and outside the boundaries of formal law (Friedman 1993, pp. 172–192). Increasingly in the modern world, disputes involving corporations occur in a transnational context—in "the space between the laws" (Michalowski and Kramer 1987)—where it is far from clear who has jurisdiction.

This type of issue long arose in connection with crimes and disputes occurring at sea. International maritime agreements spelled out some legal guidelines for such situations, however. And as humans increasingly find themselves engaged in space travel in the twenty-first century, these issues will also arise; indeed, we already have some international agreements on law in outer space.

A parallel set of questions arises in what can be called extreme situations and desperate circumstances. A famous nineteenth-century case in English law, *Queen v. Dudley and Stephens* (1882), addressed the situation of two seamen who killed a dying young sailor and consumed his flesh when they were all shipwrecked off the coast of Africa and found themselves floating in a small lifeboat for days on end (Simpson 1984). The survivors were eventually rescued and brought back to England to stand trial on homicide charges. Many sympathetic members of the British public felt that the ordinary law of homicide should not be applicable in such extreme circumstances, where survival was at stake. The Court disagreed, however, and found the accused guilty and liable to the death penalty (the sentence was commuted to 6 months in prison by the reigning queen, Victoria, who had followed the case with some interest, as did her subjects).

The circumstance of war provides a context that calls into question many conventional assumptions about law. War operates on principles diametrically at odds with the principles upon which legal institutions operate. War addresses disputes (or contending claims) with direct violence. War addresses disputes with direct violence, in forms typically prohibited by law. As Telford Taylor (1970, p. 19), a prominent student of law and warfare, has observed, "War consists largely of acts that would be criminal if performed in time of peace—killing, wounding, kidnapping, destroying, or carrying off other peoples' property." Of course, war over the ages has taken many different forms, and wars have been initiated or undertaken for very different reasons. At least some acts of war might be defended on the grounds that they are an extreme, if not absolutely necessary, form of social control exercised in response to the actions of criminal states. Certainly the Allied involvement in World War II against Adolf Hitler and Nazi Germany was justified in this way. At the end of the twentieth century and early in the twenty-first century, the interventions of NATO in the Bosnia and Libya crises were widely supported, although they were also criticized in some quarters (Hehir 2008; The Nation 2011). An ongoing debate addresses the extent to which American presidents are authorized by the U.S. Constitution to carry out war or whether this power resides with the U.S. Congress (Irons 2005; Wills 2010; Yoo 2010).

Although law and acts of war would seem to be directly at odds, a long history of attempts to impose some legal constraints on war-related activities exists (Chadwick 2003; Falk, Kolko, and Lifton 1971; McMahan 2009). The general guiding principle has been that the ravages of war should be mitigated as far as possible by prohibiting needless cruelties and other acts that spread death and destruction and are not reasonably related to the conduct of hostilities. In the medieval era, the laws of chivalry required the proper treatment of enemy soldiers taken into custody, as well as respectful treatment of civilians. International conferences in the nineteenth and twentieth centuries led to the adoption of rules of war (e.g., the Geneva Conventions) in response to the development of increasingly destructive weapons; to civilian populations made both more aware (e.g., through photography) of war's brutalities and more vulnerable to military action; and to the onset of the age of "total war." Obviously the rules of war have been widely violated. Furthermore,

It is one of the many darker ironies of twentieth-century history that, just as the codification of laws respecting noncombatants achieved further refinements, a whole surge of revolutionary struggles, civil wars, and insurgencies have made discriminate warfare more difficult than ever to implement. (Kennedy and Adreopoulos 1994, p. 215)

Global violence has expanded, especially since 9/11. Today we have ongoing discussion and debate on the ethical justifications for war, for terrorism, and for a "war on terrorism (Gerety 2005; Steinhoff 2007). Are terrorists most appropriately defined by law as "soldiers" or as "international criminals?"

Early in the twenty-first century, the single greatest threat was surely the possible use of nuclear weapons (Kauzlarich and Kramer 1998; Lichterman and Cabasso 2002; Scobliz 2010). Despite an International Court of Justice advisory opinion that the use or threat of nuclear weapons would be illegal, it was evident that the nuclear nations (including the United States) were not about to abandon these weapons.

It is well-understood that the effective operation of any military force requires a command structure, with subordinates obeying and carrying out the commands of superior officers. But how far should this principle be carried, especially when subordinates carry out atrocities either in response to a specific command or on the basis of their understanding of what is expected of them? The Nuremberg Trials of the surviving Nazi leadership and of those complicit in crimes of war or crimes against humanity established the principle that superiors' orders do not provide an uncontestable defense against charges of having committed acts at odds with international law and international accords on the laws of war (Douglas 2001; Landsman 2005). Although they have received far less attention historically, trials were also held in Tokyo after World War II for Japanese war criminals, some of whom were convicted and hung (Totani 2008). Whether these trials were simply a form of "victor's justice," or were an important application of and precedent for international law remains a matter of dispute. Soldiers have faced charges for deserting the battlefield or refusing to participate in acts of war. But they have also faced charges for acts carried out in the context of military operations. In his book, *A Rumor of War*, Philip Caputo (1977), who served as a lieutenant in Vietnam, provides us with a vivid sense of some contradictions involved in training soldiers to kill and then charging them with the crime of killing. In Caputo's case, he and his men killed two Vietnamese they took to be enemies and then found themselves facing charges by the legal office of the Army (*see* Box 6.7).

As is well-known, large numbers of Americans challenged the legality of American involvement in the Vietnam War, calling it an immoral imperialistic adventure. Because war was never specifically declared by Congress, its legality was challenged on constitutional grounds as well, but there were not enough votes on the U.S. Supreme Court in favor of hearing this case (Ely 1990). An international tribunal held in Sweden and chaired by the eminent philosopher Bertrand Russell found the United States guilty of war crimes under international law, but this tribunal had no means of implementing its finding against a powerful nation and its leadership (Falk, Kolko, and Lifton 1971, p. 73). Although at least one of the primary architects of the American involvement in the Vietnam War, Robert McNamara (1995), Secretary of Defense under Presidents Kennedy and Johnson, later conceded that

---

BOX 6.7 KILLING IN WAR: MORALITY AND LAW

There is a widespread understanding in our society that the deliberate killing of another person is not only a serious crime but is a
potent violation of morality as well. Yet many—but certainly not
all—members of society regard killing in the context of war as fundamentally different, often heroic and something to be celebrated
when it targets combatants on the other side (McMahan 2009).
Not only does the law sanction such killing (assuming that it is carried out within the parameters of the laws of war, and not—for
example—against unarmed civilians for purposes unrelated to the
war itself). But philosopher Jeff McMahan (2009), in *Killing in War*,
challenges the notion that killing in this context is moral, that when

political leaders command their armies to attack some enemy
army or population, the moral right of those attacked not to be
killed is negated. Furthermore, he challenges the notion that to
the extent that deliberate killing occurs in war, those who order
it but not those who carry it out are responsible for that killing,
whether or not one considers it morally acceptable. Altogether,
then, this author challenges the notion that the context of war puts
the killing that occurs in that context in a morally separate category. Needless to say, pacifists in particular have long advanced
some form of this argument, but the systematic attention of a contemporary philosopher to these questions can enrich our understanding of the moral status of killing in war.

---

decisions made by the American leadership were wrong, no member of this leadership was
ever formally tried before a legal tribunal.

Since the end of the Vietnam War, other military engagements have raised questions
from a legalistic perspective. For example, the International Court of Law found the United
States guilty of crimes against international law for its complicity in the mining of the
Nicaragua capital city's harbor during the civil war in that country (Simon 2002, p. 196).
Other American military initiatives (including invasions of Grenada and Panama), although
generally supported by the American people, were also challenged in relation to international law.

The 9/11 attacks on America gave rise to a declaration of "war on terror." But what kind
of "war" is this, and how do conventional laws of war apply to this circumstance? The
American response to 9/11 raised a range of law-related issues (*see* Box 6.8).

The pre-emptive attack of Iraq, designated Operation Iraqi Freedom, was viewed by
many as a violation of international law (Ackerman 2002; Donnelly-Cole 2007; Hoffmann
2003b). On the basis that President Bush led the United States into the war with false claims
about weapons of mass destruction and Iraqi involvement with the 9/11 attacks, calls for
his impeachment emerged (Holtzman 2006; Lueck 2004). Vincent Bugliosi (2008), the celebrated prosecutor of the notorious, homicidal Manson family, wrote a book calling for
the prosecution of President Bush on homicide charges. Some American military personnel
have been charged with murder in connection with the killing of civilians in Iraq (Shanker
and Tavernise 2006; von Zielbauer 2007).

Many other complex law-related issues arose as a consequence of this war, including
the following: Was the regime of Saddam Hussein a regime of law? Was international law
effective in containing Saddam Hussein? What was the nature and character of law in Iraq
following the fall of Saddam Hussein and the Baathist regime? Were interrogation tactics
utilized with those arrested by American forces in Iraq legitimate under international laws
of war (the Geneva Conventions)? What are the likely consequences for American military
forces disregard of the Geneva Conventions? Under what legal regime should those charged
with abuses in the Abu Ghraib case be charged and tried? Can civilians complicit in crimes

BOX 6.8 LAW AND THE WAR ON TERROR

In the new context of a post-9/11 world, what does law mean? The 9/11 attacks on the World Trade Center towers and the Pentagon were widely characterized as the single most brazen large-scale crimes carried out on American soil and were arguably a "watershed event" in American history (Dudziak 2003; Strawson 2002). A major new "war on terror" was declared (Crotty 2003; Heymann 2003). Do the ordinary laws of war apply in such a situation? In the observation of one commentator, "In some ways, September 11 has returned law to Ground Zero.... International law has been revealed as feeble, constitutional law as insecure, while human rights law has become negotiable" (Strawson 2002, p. xi).

International law was formulated principally to address the actions of states, not terrorist groups. Do constitutional protections apply when one is threatened by terrorist acts? Must human rights, civil liberties, and due process be privileged over security concerns? The Bush Administration undertook an invasion of Afghanistan on the premise that the Taliban leadership of that state was sheltering Osama bin Laden and Al Qaeda terrorists. Some of those captured in Afghanistan were then shipped to the United States military base at Guantanamo Bay and held without any access to ordinary due process. Domestically, the U.S. Patriot Act was adopted with many provisions compromising traditional civil liberties of Americans. The pre-emptive invasion of Iraq ("Operation Iraqi Freedom") was at least partially justified as a necessary initiative of the war on terror. In Afghanistan, at Guantanamo Bay, and in Iraq following the invasion, interrogation tactics were used in clear violation of the Geneva Conventions and incorporating torture and gross forms of abuse. Accordingly, many debates arose about the role of law, and the rule of law, in all of this (McGoldrick 2004).

The U.S. Patriot Act was widely criticized as having been adopted too hastily, infringing on a broad range of civil liberties, with little to show for it (Brown 2003). In the wake of 9/11, the effectiveness of an ever-widening web of surveillance, in addressing possible terrorist actions, was also questioned (Lyon 2003). In June 2004, the U.S. Supreme Court ruled that detainees at Guantanamo Bay, Cuba, being held as "enemy combatants" and suspected terrorists, were in fact entitled to some legal rights and access to courts (Greenhouse 2004c). Critics argued that the administration had exaggerated both the dangers posed by the detainees and the value of information obtained from them (Golden and Van Natta 2004). The ultimate resolution of competing views on these matters lies in the future.

In June 2004, a memorandum from high-level Bush Administration lawyers surfaced that justified the use of torture of detainees in Iraq, without conceding that extreme physical abuse and humiliation met the technical legal criteria for being defined as torture (Lewis and Schmitt 2004). In this interpretation, torture was only illegal if inflicting pain was its sole purpose and if it led to organ failure and death (Liptak 2004c). The Office of Legal Counsel lawyers, in their memorandum, claimed that President Bush was not bound by either federal anti-torture laws or international treaties prohibiting torture, because as the American Commander-in-Chief he had the authority to approve any tactics necessary to protect American security and American lives (Lewis and Schmitt 2004). Some prominent American law professors criticized this claim in harsh terms as wrongly advising that the president could authorize the use of torture methods, while defining torture itself in the narrowest possible terms (Liptak 2004c). If torture in some form were authorized, could it ever be legally supported, and might it actually "work" in the sense of obtaining vital information about planned insurgent or terrorist attacks?

The Bush Administration claimed that ordinary laws did not apply when contending with terrorists but also repudiated the extreme abuses undertaken by some American soldiers in these circumstances. What is legally permissible and what is not in a war against terrorism? If American forces failed to adhere to international laws of war, could Americans complain if other countries also failed to comply with those laws when holding American military personnel in captivity?

The challenge going forward would be to identify the optimal balance between adherence to the rule of law and effectiveness in addressing the ongoing threat of terrorism. Michael Ignatieff, an especially prolific and articulate proponent of a pragmatic response to these challenges, argued as follows:

> Sticking too firmly to the rule of law simply allows terrorists too much leeway to exploit our freedoms. Abandoning the rule of law altogether betrays our most valued institutions. To defeat evil, we may have to traffic in evils: indefinite detention of suspects, coercive interrogations, targeted assassinations, even pre-emptive war. These are evils because each strays from national and international law and because they kill people or deprive them of freedom without due process. They can be justified only because they prevent the greater evil. The question is not whether we should be trafficking in lesser evils but whether we can keep lesser evils under the control of free institutions. If we can't, any victories we gain in the war on terror will be Pyrrhic ones. (2004, p. 48)

Whether this "balanced" view will prevail in the war on terror, whether those who favor empowering the state to do whatever it deems necessary to defeat terrorists, or whether civil libertarians who oppose any measurable compromises with the rule of law will prevail remains to be determined. Law professor Philip B. Heymann (2003), a former deputy attorney general of the United States, argued that the "war" on terror calls for a broad strategy combining diplomacy, law enforcement, intelligence, targeted military interventions, and new international legal arrangements. Vigorous debates about the role of law are likely to be an ongoing aspect of the post-9/11 era.

of war in Iraq be tried under military law? Should Iraqi victims of abuse by American military personnel be able to sue in civil courts? What type of tribunal should have tried Saddam Hussein? Should Iraqis (military, governmental, civilians) be charged and tried for evil acts committed during the regime of Saddam Hussein? What is the legal basis of the sovereignty of the new Iraqi regime? How will a legitimate order of law be established in the new Iraq?

A few of the issues just raised can be explored a little further. First, almost immediately following the American invasion, Iraq descended into a chaotic situation of lawlessness (Andrews and Sachs 2003). Military invasions such as those undertaken by American forces in Afghanistan and Iraq after 9/11 inevitably have an immensely disruptive impact on the existing legal system in those countries (Moss 2006; Stromseth, Wippman, and Brooks 2007). The challenge in such "post-conflict" societies then arises: How does one best establish a viable legal system and "the rule of law"? Altogether, the situation in Iraq brought into especially sharp relief some of the questions that arise in relation to war and law. The relation among law, war, and violence is complex, then, and the circumstance of war offers us a singular context for thinking about law.

CONCLUSION

The anthropological, comparative, historical, and contextual perspectives on law considered in this chapter raise endlessly fascinating and persistently important questions about the nature of law in relation to social existence. These perspectives provide us with vantage points for studying and understanding law that differ from conventional, everyday ways of relating to law. Such perspectives should deepen and enrich our grasp of law in our lives.

KEY TERMS AND CONCEPTS

allotment
American Indian Movement (AIM)
Brown v. Board of Education (1954)
canon law
civil law tradition
codification
commodity exchange theory of law
common law tradition
danwei
double institutionalized

the dozens
Dred Scott v. Sandford (1857)
Eskimo Drum Song "Court"
ethnocentric tendencies
ethnographic approach
idealistic view of law
instrumental interpretation
Islamic law (*Sharia'h*)
Jim Crow laws
jurisprudence of terror
legal fiction
"masks" of the law
Plessy v. Ferguson (1896)

popular tribunals
pragmatic view of law
Queen v. Dudley and Stephens (1882)
sacred law tradition
show trials
social and cultural anthropology
socialist law tradition
structural interpretation
traditional view of law
tribal sovereignty
trouble cases

DISCUSSION QUESTIONS

1. Does law necessarily have to be an established set of rules with sanctions? Can customs such as the Eskimo Drum Song Court be law?
2. If American Indians are recognized as American citizens, why should minor crimes and some civil matters occurring on reservations be dealt with in tribal courts as opposed to state courts?

3. Discuss the principal, general influences on American law. Discuss specifically the role both the civil and common law traditions played in influencing the law. As we enter the twenty-first century, what do you think will become the major influences on law?

4. Explain John Noonan's metaphor of "masks" of law. Discuss how Thomas Jefferson played a role in the slavery issue. Does Noonan's metaphor offer any possible explanation as to why slavery was able to endure for more than 200 years?

5. Should soldiers in the military be prosecuted for the killing or torturing of enemies captured in war? Include comments on the William Calley and Abu Ghraib cases in your response.

CHAPTER 7

THE LEGAL PROFESSION

Lawyers are all over; lawyers are everywhere. At least in the United States, lawyers seem to be everywhere. The highest political officials in the American political system are disproportionately lawyers. Lawyers are not only at the center of political life but are also conspicuously present in social, cultural, and economic arenas of American life. Lawyers are frequently called on by the media to comment on the major issues of the day.

Because matters involving law (from sensational murder cases to major civil lawsuits) dominate the news generally, the public is also exposed to the actions of still more lawyers. Inevitably, then, newsmagazines and newspapers devote much space to law-related matters, with the role of lawyers highlighted. Judges and prosecutors are among the public officials most frequently in the news. Television has also increasingly featured real trials. Court TV is a cable channel exclusively devoted to such trials, and some trials (e.g., the O. J. Simpson trial in the 1990s and the Scott Peterson trial in the 2000s) become something akin to a national obsession. Nonfiction accounts of legal cases featuring lawyers have been staples of the bestseller lists.

The fascination with legal matters is reflected in the entertainment side of the media as well. Shows featuring lawyers are staples of prime time television. They have included *Perry Mason*, *The Defenders*, and *Owen Marshall* in an earlier era and *L.A. Law*, *The Practice*, and *Law & Order* more recently. On daytime TV, such shows as *The People's Court*, *Judge Judy*, and *Divorce Court* have been popular fare, featuring judges resolving actual or dramatized cases. Countless films feature lawyers, often portrayed in heroic terms in earlier films but more negatively in recent films (Chase 2002; McCann and Haltom 2008; Papke 2001). In high-profile feature films over the past two decades—for example, *Class Action* (1991), *A Civil Action* (1998), and *Erin Brockovich* (2000)—lawyers have been portrayed in contradictory ways, taking on the establishment or furthering corruption and dishonesty, sometimes in a stereotypical fashion (McCann and Haltom 2008). But lawyers clearly entertain us.

Reflecting traditional patterns and values, the lawyers portrayed have been principally male and white. Historically, when female lawyers appeared in films, they were often portrayed in stereotypical or negative terms; only some more recent films have featured female lawyers as relatively independent professionals (Bailey and Hale 1998, pp. 185–191; Caplow

1999). Many bestselling novels (e.g., those of John Grisham and Scott Turow) focus on lawyers as well. As David Ray Papke (1995, p. 3) has observed, "No other culture so frequently and prominently features lawyers in its plays, novels, and movies." Stewart Macaulay (1987, p. 197) claimed that "more Americans learn about their legal system from television and film than from firsthand experience." Nicole Rafter (2001, p. 24) argued that "[t]he influence of movies' representations of criminal law is now international in scope." Although such observers note that media representations of lawyers and the legal process are often distorted, they agree that these representations are very influential in how people think about lawyers. They may not only inspire some to apply for law school, they may even affect the courtroom behavior of lawyers themselves (Margolick 1990). Any serious understanding of lawyers, then, must attend to how lawyers are portrayed in the popular culture.

Many members of society may harbor the hope that they will not personally have to retain a lawyer; in the long haul, however, some contact is inevitable: a real estate closing occurs; an accident happens, followed by a lawsuit; a will must be implemented; a divorce is sought, and child custody is in question; personal bankruptcy arises; an investment loss raises questions of fraud; and so on. In all such circumstances, and not simply the obvious but generally unanticipated circumstance in which one is charged with a criminal act, a lawyer is likely to be retained. Lawyers, then, are all over; lawyers are everywhere. This chapter attempts to provide a general understanding of the nature and character of the legal profession and legal education.

A BRIEF HISTORY OF THE LEGAL PROFESSION

Americans today generally assume that if they find themselves charged with a significant violation of law or become parties to a major lawsuit, they will be represented by a lawyer. Through most of history, however, those in trouble with the law or parties to litigation were not represented by lawyers (Friedman 1977; Vago 2009). In preliterate societies, nothing that we might recognize as a legal profession ever existed. Even if lawyers in some rudimentary form can be traced far back in the tradition of Western developed nations, it does not follow that those who found themselves in a court of law also had lawyers. Rather, through most of history, people generally were expected to make their own case; this remains true in many countries today.

The origins of the legal profession in the Western tradition are traced principally back to ancient Rome, where certain individuals were allowed to argue cases on behalf of others (Brundage 2008; Friedman 1977, p. 21). Those who were especially knowledgeable about law, and were consulted on legal issues, were known as *Juris Prudentes* (Vago 2009). It is certainly ironic from the modern perspective that the orators who represented people before courts or tribunals were not permitted to collect a fee for this service. Over time, as the Roman Empire expanded during the Imperial Period, a legal profession emerged in response to the increasing complexity of the law itself. With the fall of Rome and the coming of the Dark Ages, the role of lawyers shrank. Such lawyers as could be found in premodern Europe were often affiliated with the Church and addressed issues arising in canon law (Berman 1983; Brundage 2008). The re-emergence of the legal profession as an important force in continental European countries is linked with the emergence of a capitalist economy, as such an economic system creates a substantial demand for legal services.

The American legal profession is primarily descended from the English tradition. In one reading, the origins of the contemporary legal profession are traced to medieval times. In early England, litigants represented themselves, but the role of "lawyer" emerged by the late thirteenth century, and the call for legal services became more common (Harding 1973). For "legal services," in medieval times people relied on notaries, advocates, proctors, and counselors. But even in medieval times we find expressions of suspicion of and disdain toward those who acted as lawyers in some capacity (Brundage 2008). Political revolutions, from the seventeenth century on, have had as one of their prime objectives getting rid of lawyers. Lawyers, the legal profession, and the courts have been prime targets of political revolutions—in America, France, and elsewhere. In one interpretation, the legal profession in different countries has been shaped by the revolutions that occurred in those countries (Burrage 2006). The legal profession has played and continues to play a central role in political struggles in countries all over the world (Halliday, Karpik, and Feeley 2007). Early legal practitioners received their training through apprenticeship and in some cases at the **Inns of Court**, where judges and other parties with court-related business resided (and socialized) during the trial term (Prest 1986). In the Middle Ages, English lawyers had several different functions: as agents, appearing in court on behalf of someone else; as advocates, trained in oratory to make arguments before court on behalf of clients; and as jurisconsults, or advisers on legal matters (Jeffery 1962, pp. 314–315). Into the eighteenth century, no conception of lawyer in the modern sense existed, as many different parties provided various legal services. These parties included scriveners, or writers of legal documents; pleaders, or those who filed pleas; and conveyancers, or those who prepared instruments for transfer of property. Only by the end of the eighteenth century did the legal profession emerge as a full-time occupation, with licensing for practice, a professional association, an emerging monopoly over legal services, a code of ethics, and growing emphasis on formal education in law (Lemmings 2000). In England a basic division emerged between **barristers**, or trial lawyers, and **solicitors**, or office lawyers.

LAWYERS IN AMERICA

In America, none of the first settlers in the seventeenth century was a lawyer (Hall 1989). Certainly, life in the early colonies had little to attract lawyers. Furthermore, many of the original settlers were antagonistic toward lawyers, who were associated with the upper classes and with the religious persecution many of these settlers had endured in England. Indeed, laws were passed in the seventeenth century in a number of colonies to prohibit the collection of fees for legal services, and an early visitor to Pennsylvania reported:

> they have no lawyers. Everyone is to tell his own case, or some friend for him....'Tis a happy country. (Roth and Roth 1989, p. 49)

Only gradually did some individuals begin to practice law on a part-time basis; the law they practiced was less technical than that in England. Typically these lawyers were educated in law by apprenticeship, although some traveled to England to learn law at the Inns of Court. With the evolution of colonies into rapidly growing centers of commerce and trade throughout the eighteenth century, greater reliance on lawyers became inevitable, and hostility toward them declined (Burrage 2006). Accordingly, by the time of the American Revolution, lawyers were conspicuously present. Some of the most famous leaders in the revolutionary cause—including John Adams, Thomas Jefferson, and John Marshall—were lawyers, and lawyers were especially well-represented among the signers of the Declaration of Independence, members of the Constitutional Convention, and representatives to the first Congress (Schwartz 1974, p. 17). For the most part, however, members of the legal profession tended to be conservatives who sided with the King, and many left the Colonies.

When the Frenchman Alexis de Tocqueville ([1835–1840] 1945) visited the relatively young republic of the United States in the 1820s, he made the astute observation that lawyers had become the "new aristocracy," having moved into the power vacuum created by a society that repudiated the notion of a ruling class of the nobility. It has continued to be the case in the subsequent history of the United States that lawyers have been vastly over-represented in the government and political system. As of the beginning of the twentieth-first century, well over half (or 27 of 44) of American presidents had been lawyers (*see* Box 7.1). During the last years of the twentieth century, both the president (Bill Clinton) and, for the first time, the First Lady (Hillary Rodham Clinton) were lawyers. Early in the twenty-first century, President Barack Obama and First Lady Michelle Obama also were both lawyers.

At times, as much as two-thirds of the U.S. Senate and one-half of the House have been lawyers (Gordon 2002, p. 306). Among state governors and legislators, as well as among local elected officials, lawyers have been over-represented (Meinhold and Hadley 1995, p. 366). By the end of the twentieth century, the representation of the legal profession among state legislators in particular had declined quite significantly (e.g., in New York State, from 61% in 1969 to 34% in 1999) (Perez-Pena 1999). Legislative duties had expanded to the point that it was increasingly difficult to maintain a legal practice on the side, state legislative salaries were no longer competitive with private practice income, and financial disclosure requirements for legislators compelled lawyers to reveal more than they wished about their legal practice and clients.

Despite some proportional decline, lawyers remain a dominant force in American political life. Although this situation is not unique to the United States, as lawyers are

---

BOX 7.1 LAWYER PRESIDENTS

American presidents who were lawyers, had a legal education, or taught law were Adams (John and John Quincy), Jefferson, Madison, Jackson, Van Buren, Tyler, Polk, Fillmore, Pierce, Buchanan, Lincoln, Hayes, Garfield, Arthur, Cleveland, Benjamin Harrison, McKinley, Taft, Wilson, Coolidge, Franklin D. Roosevelt, Nixon, Ford, Clinton, and Obama. In 2008 American voters for the first time elected former constitutional law professors to both the presidency and the vice presidency: Barack Obama and Joseph Biden (Larsen 2009). William Howard Taft, Woodrow Wilson, and William Jefferson Clinton are three other American presidents who were professors of law or jurisprudence, and Taft became Chief Justice of the United States after serving as president (Gross 2004). Other presidents (George Washington and Harry Truman) held law-related posts, such as justice of the peace or county judge, without any formal legal education.

over-represented in the governments of at least some other countries, the American case is especially striking. Even when lawyers do not hold elective or appointive office here, they wield extraordinary political influence as power brokers and lobbyists.

Tocqueville ([1835–1840] 1945) recognized that lawyers as a whole tend to be conservative, because their own interests are aligned with a stable order governed by formal rules. Of course, numerous exceptions to this tendency can be identified. Jerome Auerbach (1976) has argued that elite lawyers from the nineteenth century on have been directly complicit in perpetuating many forms of injustice and inequality in America. Throughout much of the nineteenth century, however, most lawyers were unaffiliated solo practitioners who rode the circuit to appear before courts in session in their general area (Friedman 2004, pp. 231–232). Also, at that time neither a law degree nor a college education was required to practice law, and admission to practice was open. Most lawyers acquired their legal knowledge principally through self-education and apprenticeship (Abel 1986). In the first half of the nineteenth century, in particular, there was relatively little regulation of legal practice (Burrage 1988). Great oratorical skills—famously represented by Daniel Webster—were much emphasized in an era when argument before the court was at the heart of legal practice. Abraham Lincoln was in some respects a representative lawyer of his time in the United States (Steiner 2006). Although Lincoln took on the whole range of legal matters, debt collection played an important part in his practice (Dirck 2007).

By the latter part of the nineteenth century, in response to the exploding growth of industrial capitalism and expanding cities teeming with new immigrants, the legal profession also grew and changed (Hall 1989). During this period, for example, large law firms closely affiliated with major corporations and big businesses began to appear, and "office lawyering" skills involving drafting of legal documents and negotiation with adversaries became increasingly important.

LAWYERS IN THE TWENTIETH CENTURY—AND THE TWENTY-FIRST

Throughout the twentieth century, the legal profession in the United States experienced periods of little growth, followed by periods of formidable growth and diversification (Abel 1989; Gordon 2002). At the beginning of this century, a tightening of requirements for entrance into the legal profession took place (Vest 2000). The apprenticeship system was almost entirely replaced as a mode of entry into the profession by college education and law school, with a 3-year curriculum ultimately becoming the standard (although as late as 1917 no American state required law school attendance as a condition for engaging in legal practice; Abel 1986, p. 382). Law schools affiliated with elite universities had the most prestige and provided the most probable route to a successful career with a prominent law firm or eventual service in a high position within the government.

Passing the bar exam became a universal condition for admittance to legal practice (Vest 2000). Bar exams became more rigorous from 1876 on (Abel 1986, p. 380). By 1940, passing a state bar exam was a condition for admittance to legal practice in every state (Hall 1989, p. 258). The American Bar Association (ABA) and state bar associations, through the course of the twentieth century, adopted various requirements and rules that would enhance their

BOX 7.2 LAW LICENSES AND GOOD CHARACTER

To win admission to the bar, it is not sufficient that prospective lawyers have acquired a law degree and passed the bar exam; they must also be found to be "of good character." The standards for good character have varied historically and among states and have been applied somewhat inconsistently (e.g., rejecting a candidate with parking offenses but approving a convicted child molester) (Allen 1999). Most states allow felons with proper credentials to practice law (Janofsky 2001). But applicants have been turned down if they were in arrears on child support payments, had neglected to settle overdue debts, or had been convicted of substance abuse and had not sought treatment. Altogether, denial of admission to the bar on the character issue is rare.

Some cases have raised exceptional or provocative issues for the character test. In a New York case, a lawyer who had bludgeoned his wife and three children to death and had been found not guilty by reason of insanity sought restoration of his license to practice law after having completed many years of psychiatric treatment (Margolick 1993a). In 2001 a man who served 17.5 years for killing two men in connection with a drug deal sought a license to practice law in Arizona (Janofsky 2001). His wife, a former judge, supported his case. In a 2009 decision, a panel of five New York judges denied admission to the bar to a man carrying a debt of close to a half-million dollars (Glater 2009c). A significant percentage of this debt was acquired by taking out student loans. The unsuccessful applicant in this case argued, quite plausibly, that without being able to practice law he would be unable to repay the debt—with fees, interest, and penalties growing by some $10,000 a month. With large numbers of law students having acquired high debt, this case was a significant possible precedent. Is the fact that one has taken on high debt and has no income indicative in some reliable way of "poor character" and future poor judgment in a professional capacity? Speculatively, would such individuals—contending with huge financial pressures—be significantly more likely to defraud clients and become parties to other forms of fraudulent activity?

control over who would be allowed to practice law and would protect the economic interests of private lawyers. Accordingly, those without formal credentials were largely excluded from practicing law, and minimum fee schedules were adopted to deter lawyers from engaging in costly price cutting (*see* Box 7.2).

Although the dominance of White Anglo-Saxon Protestant males declined somewhat in the first half of the twentieth century, with the entry into legal practice of second-generation offspring of the immigrants who had poured into the country, women and African-Americans were systematically (and formally) excluded for much of this period (Gordon 2002). Only in the last several decades of the twentieth century was there a significant movement of women into the legal profession. (The influx of women and their experience is discussed later in this chapter.) People of color also entered the legal profession in larger numbers during this period. Despite the rapidly changing makeup of the legal profession, it is still clearly the case early in the twenty-first century that White males disproportionately occupy the most prestigious judgeships and law firm partnerships and continue to dominate the ABA, as well as the legal profession itself (Glater 2001b; Glater 2006b; Kelly 2007). But this dominance was certain to erode during the course of the twenty-first century.

THE ABA

The **American Bar Association** (ABA; founded in 1878) and state bar associations came to play especially important roles in the development of the legal profession in the twentieth century (Gordon 2002; Vest 2000). For most of this history, the ABA has been dominated by White males, only declaring in 1943 that members would not be excluded on the basis of race, creed, or color. By the end of the century, the ABA had become the largest professional association in the world. The bar association has taken an active role in promoting reform in legal education, establishing standards for admission to the bar and drafting uniform laws for adoption by the states. It engages in many other activities, including the sponsorship of research and the publication of various journals and reports. The ABA's American Bar Foundation (ABF; founded in 1952) has been a major promoter of interdisciplinary law and society research, with both in-house researchers and grants to outside researchers (Garth 2007). In 1908 it adopted Canons of Professional Ethics (replaced in 1969 with the Code of Professional Responsibility). Despite its adoption of such codes and initiatives to promote more equal access to justice, the primary objective of the ABA, in one standard interpretation, has been the protection and advancement of the professional and economic interests of lawyers (*see* Box 7.3).

WHAT CONTEMPORARY LAWYERS DO

Through the mid-twentieth century, the vast majority of American lawyers (some 90%) were in private practice, and of these, the majority (some 60%) were solo practitioners. In the second half of the twentieth century, the American legal profession underwent changes (Abel 2003; Gordon 2002). It began to grow rapidly in response to an expanding economy. Law school applications multiplied dramatically, enabling law schools to be more selective. Also, from the early 1970s on, they began to admit growing numbers of women and minorities. The law profession became increasingly competitive, especially during periods of economic stagnancy and downsizing. In the 1970s, the U.S. Supreme Court struck down bar association minimum-fee schedules and bans on lawyers' advertising, which allowed lawyers to compete more aggressively for clients.

During the economic downturn at the end of the first decade of the twenty-first century, a growing number of people chose to represent themselves in legal proceedings (Broderick and George 2010; Glater 2009b) (*see* Box 7.3). People seeking to represent themselves are not necessarily poor people, but may be middle class individuals and small business owners under severe financial pressure. Most of those who appear in New York family courts represent themselves; up to 95% of those appearing in paternity and child support cases do so. Judges and law clerks inevitably find this trend burdensome, as they must provide much guidance to such lay people as plaintiffs and defendants. Judges may also find themselves in a bind when private parties are clearly making errors while representing themselves, when the judge is supposed to be a neutral party and not an advocate for one side or the other. These lay people also request waivers of court fees that they

---

BOX 7.3 LEGAL SELF-HELP

Early in the twenty-first century, do-it-yourself legal assistance was a fast-growing business (Hines 2001). Franchises such as We the People claim to offer people only "information," but some state bar officials claimed that such centers were engaged in unauthorized practice of law. Do such franchises fill a need for people who cannot afford lawyers, as they claim, or are they overcharging for purely clerical work, as some critics contend? Many people (up to 90% in some jurisdictions) cannot afford legal assistance in domestic disputes, as well as in matters involving bankruptcy, landlord–tenant disputes, and wills. Those who represent themselves in civil cases are designated *pro se* (for oneself) litigants.

cannot afford. Some legal self-help clinics and bar association programs offer at least limited forms of assistance to those seeking to represent themselves in legal proceedings. Forty-one states have rules that allow lawyers to "unbundle" their services and provide "limited scope" representation. This is at odds with the traditional notion that lawyers stay with a case from beginning to end.

In a series of decisions in the 1960s and 1970s, the Court also struck down state rules prohibiting (as unlawful solicitation) labor union lawyers from voluntarily advising injured union members and dependents (Seron 1993, p. 400; Kelly 2007). With the expansion of rights to representation for poor people accused of crimes (with the government supplying or at least paying for the lawyers), as well as the growth of governmental regulatory agencies, the percentage of lawyers in private practice declined, whereas the numbers working for the government on some level increased.

In the private sector, lawyers increasingly joined law firms, and some law firms became huge, with thousands of lawyers working in branches spread across the country (Galanter and Palay 1991; Gordon 2002). The partners in such law firms may well draw seven-figure annual incomes, depending on the size of profits. Most of the lawyers working in these firms are salaried associates, who may hope to make partner after 7 years of service; the majority in a large firm will not be invited to be partners and will have to move on. **Rainmakers** (partners who are able to attract a significant number of high-paying clients to the law firm) are inevitably prized as partners; some high-profile politicians are offered partnerships in major law firms less for their skills as lawyers than for their rainmaking potential.

Corporations and businesses also hired lawyers as full-time employees (in-house lawyers) in increasing numbers (Nelson and Nielsen 2000). At the same time, legal clinics began to open, providing ordinary citizens with convenient, economical legal services. Jacoby and Meyer pioneered this approach in the late 1970s and by the 1990s had some 150 branch offices nationwide. Franchise law firms provided mass production of standardized legal services, although this also meant that lawyers in these firms were less autonomous, less well-compensated, and less satisfied (Kelly 2007; Van Hoy 1997a). Prepaid legal service plans also became more common. With these plans, individuals or associations pay a preset monthly fee that gives them access to a lawyer's services for such matters as house closings or reviews of contracts. In the mid-twentieth century, the great majority of American lawyers (perhaps 85%) were self-employed, but in the early twenty-first century fewer than half are, and most of those coming out of law school secure their first jobs as employees (Abel 2003; Kelly 2007). The increasing percentage of lawyers who find themselves working for an organization of some kind must adjust to the needs of the organization. The traditional status of lawyers as independent and autonomous is obviously eroding.

Lawyers are being called upon to address an expanding repertoire of matters, beyond such traditional legal issues as wills, contracts, personal injury lawsuits, and the like. Corporate lawyers are becoming increasingly involved in a range of business-related issues on behalf of clients, and the lines of demarcation between legal and financial matters are eroding. Some multinational partnerships are taking advantage of an increasingly globalized world to pair up foreign lawyers—who cannot practice domestically—with American lawyers who can (Abel 2003, p. 805). Lawyers for ordinary private citizens face increasing competition from banks, real estate agents, and other providers of services and have to be creative in offering new services to their clients. In many areas of legal practice, lawyers have to find the right balance between aggressive pursuit of their client's case and flexibility toward negotiating a resolution of conflict; the emotional minefield of divorce law exemplifies this issue (Mather, McEwen, and Maiman 2001). They also have to persuade clients who may be determined to achieve vengeance to focus on a legally realistic settlement of their case. The work of lawyers has been described as involving the "management of uncertainty" in a constant process of interaction with clients and other lawyers, among other parties (Flood 1991; Shamir 1995). Changes in the justice system in the United States—and in the legal profession itself—have pushed lawyers to focus increasingly on conflict resolution and to use strategies involving negotiation, mediation, and collaboration to achieve results (Macfarlane 2008). With the emergence of a variety of social movements, lawyers have been called on to represent new constituencies and new types of claims, such as women's rights, gay rights, environmental protection, and consumer protection.

In the context of a struggling economy from 2008 on, legal billing practices were undergoing change (Glater 2009a; Slater 2010). There has been a movement away from hourly billing to flat fees for legal services, as businesses attempt to save money on their legal costs. Businesses have discovered that legal "scut work" (e.g., page-by-page review of documents) can be done less expensively by contract lawyers or even non-lawyers, rather than highly paid young associates in law firms (Slater 2010). The system of elite law firms paying graduates of elite law schools high salaries just out of law school is increasingly viewed as legal apprenticeship training at the expense of clients.

In recent years, the law as a profession has gone through another cycle of diminished appeal. Law school applications dropped quite significantly after 2004. It has become more difficult to become a partner in a law firm today, in part because of increasing merging of law firms (Williams 2008). By 2007 the market for lawyers was declining, although at that point some graduates of elite law schools were commanding as much as $160,000 as starting salaries (Efrati 2007). But with growing numbers of law school graduates, and some new constraints on law suits (e.g., for personal injury and medical malpractice), the marketplace for lawyers was eroding, and graduates from lower tier law schools who worked as solo practitioners were, in many cases, struggling. According to some sources, there is much career and job dissatisfaction among lawyers, with some 20% experiencing depression at some point during their professional lives (Williams 2008). Rather strikingly, almost 50% of lawyers in an ABA survey (in 2007) said they would not recommend to a young person that he or she pursue a career as a lawyer.

LAWYERS' IDEOLOGICAL ORIENTATIONS AND PRO BONO WORK

As noted earlier, lawyers as a whole have tended to be conservative, and they have disproportionately represented the privileged and the powerful. It is also a long-standing tradition for many law firms to do a certain amount of **pro bono** (free) legal work for clients who cannot afford to pay legal fees. The ABA encourages but does not require law firms to do a certain amount of such work. One law firm, Hale and Dorr, describes its pro bono work as including:

> criminal defense for the indigent, drug treatment programs, death row cases, representation of handicapped advocacy groups, public policy cases, and cases involving freedom of speech…real estate work for community development corporations and other organizations dedicated to providing shelter to low-income and homeless individuals, battered women, the elderly, and people with HIV/AIDS. (quoted in Nader and Smith 1996, p. 341)

On the whole, however, pro bono work tends to be carried out on a modest scale, if at all, and rarely draws on the skill, knowledge, and connections of powerful law firms to challenge fundamental inequities, as opposed to commonplace injustices (Nader and Smith 1996, pp. 339–347). Support for doing pro bono work is not uniform across the legal profession. Lawyers in different kinds of practices may be more or less supportive of doing such work, with lawyers in large law firms generally more supportive and receiving more incentives to engage in pro bono work than lawyers in other circumstances (Granfield 2007). Support for doing pro bono work is hardly driven in all cases by idealism; some solo practitioners may engage in such work in the hope that it will eventually produce paying clients. Some high-profile law firms have hired or assigned lawyers to exclusively oversee their pro bono work (Donovan 2008). One such firm reported 100,000 hours of pro bono work in a recent year. With declining support for legal assistance to poor people, reliance on pro bono work has increased (Sandefur 2007). But the availability of such pro bono work is vulnerable to market pressures, with less such work undertaken in states where lawyers collectively are not doing well financially or feel threatened by unauthorized practice of law.

Some lawyers have been liberal in orientation. Since its foundation in 1917, the American Civil Liberties Union, for example, has ardently championed the defense of the Bill of Rights, broadly interpreted (Walker 1990). The National Lawyers Guild, founded in 1936, has promoted a leftist agenda. It has been active in advocating progressive legislation on such matters as rent control, in defense of union workers, on behalf of international justice and human rights, in opposition to repressive legislation directed at political dissidents, and on behalf of women, gays, and other beleaguered or discriminated-against constituencies (Black 1971; Brown 1938). A list of prominent progressive American lawyers, from the late nineteenth century on, would include Belva Lockwood, Louis D. Brandeis, Clarence Darrow, Samuel Leibowitz, Charles H. Houston, Ralph Nader, and Morris Dees (Klebanow and Jonas 2003). In the 1960s era in particular, some lawyers came to be identified with radical causes; William Kunstler, a key lawyer in the Chicago 7 case involving leading radicals of the time, was arguably the most famous of these (Black 1971; Langum 1999). More recently, the term **cause lawyering** has been adopted for lawyers whose highest priority is their ideological commitment and dedication to bringing about social change in the form of reducing social, economic, and political inequality (Sarat and Scheingold 1998, 2001; Scheingold and Sarat 2004). The term is principally associated with leftists promoting progressive reforms, although, of course, some lawyers are dedicated to promoting right-wing and fundamentalist causes (e.g., putting prayer back in the schools and criminalizing abortion). Cause lawyers have now been the focus of considerable scholarly attention, addressing, among other things, the constraints on them, the strategic decisions they make, their impact on social movements and their place in the larger culture (Sarat and Scheingold 2005, 2006, 2008). Cause lawyers who represent specific causes—and may move on following a significant victory—have been distinguished in some discussions from political lawyers, who have long-term commitments to a particular political ideology (Halliday, Karpik, and Feeley 2007). Conservative cause lawyers, for the most part, focus on a specific cause (such as the pro-life movement) (Paik, Southworth, and Heinz 2007). But at least some such lawyers attempt to merge morality, market freedom, and individual liberty concerns and to facilitate cooperation among different conservative constituencies. In the recent era some lawyers have become prominent in conservative organizations, although they sometimes find themselves at odds with populist conservative elements that are part of these organizations (Southworth 2008). Conservative lawyers who represent business interests are less likely to be ideologically committed than conservative lawyers who represent religious or libertarian groups.

In authoritarian third-world countries, cause lawyering has been primarily associated with defensive tactics in challenging repression of dissidents and other "enemies of the state"; in liberal, developed countries, cause lawyers have typically had more freedom to affirmatively promote basic reforms (Sarat and Scheingold 1998). Cause lawyers are centrally involved in human rights issues, such as the Israel/Palestinian situation (Hajjar 1997; Sarat and Scheingold 2001). Lawyers affiliated with the Center for Constitutional Rights successfully argued before the U.S. Supreme Court to allow detainees at Guantanamo Bay to challenge their detentions in court (Liptak and Janofsky 2004). In the current generally conservative political environment in the United States, however, cause lawyers have often been fighting losing battles and must settle for occasional minor victories (e.g., keeping death row clients alive a little longer as opposed to bringing about the abolition of the death penalty) (White 2005). In this context, expanding the grounds for exceptions to harsh penalties (e.g., relating to mental competency) is also regarded as a victory.

By the beginning of the twenty-first century, the American legal profession was extraordinarily large, heterogeneous, and divided; it was less autonomous, more specialized, and more competitive than in previous times (Abel 2003; Gordon 2002). The legal profession in an emerging postmodern world has been interpreted as playing a critically important role in determining the distribution of power and wealth in society, all too often on behalf of the powerful and privileged (Cain and Harrington 1994).

A COMPARATIVE PERSPECTIVE ON THE LEGAL PROFESSION

The legal profession in civil law, Islamic, and socialist countries differs significantly from the form it takes in the United States (Abel and Lewis 1995; Neelakantan 2005; Pue and Sugarman 2003). To begin with, no unified legal profession represented by a common association such as the ABA exists. Judges and practicing lawyers are educated with different curricula and do not share a common identity. Law is studied as part of an undergraduate curriculum, and both the content and the pedagogical style of legal education are different from that in common law countries. The largest percentage of those who study law go into the civil service, serve as judges or prosecutors, or work for a commercial enterprise rather than becoming private practitioners. Although many forces in the recent era have led to an expansion of the numbers going into some form of legal practice in civil law countries, as has been true in common law countries, numerous differences in terms of self-identification, mode of entry into the field, and form of practice persist between the two systems.

The case of Japan, which was substantially influenced by the civil law tradition, is especially striking. Recognition of a distinctive legal profession did not exist prior to the 1860s (Rokumoto 1988). A legal system, roughly modeled on that of Germany, was introduced only at about this time, and the special standing of judges and prosecutors was recognized. Because of the traditional Japanese aversion to formal litigation, the legal profession grew very slowly. Japan has only 20,000 lawyers, or 1 lawyer for every 6,300 people, compared with 1 lawyer for every 471 people in the United States (Brender 2002, p. A48). In Japan, one finds districts with as many as 50,000 people, without a single lawyer among them (Onishi 2008). Almost half of Japan's lawyers are concentrated in the capital, Tokyo; elsewhere, one finds approximately 1 lawyer for every 30,000 people! Many "legal" functions in Japan are carried out by parties other than lawyers, including the equivalent of paralegals (Sanders 1996, p. 321). Lawyers, for the most part, are part of the civil service, they are not likely to specialize, and much of their work is quite routine. The handling of debt is the principal source of work for Japanese lawyers today (Onishi 2008). Japanese people are much less likely than Americans to seek out lawyers.

With expanded pressure to adhere to the rule of law, in 2004 Japan created a new system of law schools organized to produce more and better lawyers (Saegusa 2009). This new type of law school is more closely modeled on American law schools, but it has not yet transformed the traditional legal system of Japan. Some 74 law schools have opened since 2004 (Onishi 2008). The exceedingly difficult bar exam, passed by only 3% of those who have taken it, is currently being reformed. Of those who do pass, many do not go on to the formal practice of law but go into business or some other pursuit. Despite the poor odds of being admitted to legal practice, for those who do succeed, it is not an especially prestigious or necessarily lucrative career. Although a more adversarial legal culture was developing in Japan, lawyers continued to play a more limited role than in the United States.

THE STRATIFICATION OF THE BAR AND THE ORGANIZATION OF LEGAL PRACTICE

All American lawyers have some things in common. In our era they have almost certainly completed 3 years of law school, have passed a bar exam, and are subject to a professional code of ethics. All lawyers have acquired some familiarity with basic principles of law, the language of law, and standard legal practices. And in a very general sense, all lawyers share a professional status with a mix of positive and negative connotations. But beyond this, the legal profession is highly stratified, with vast differences in the nature of lawyers' practices, incomes, lifestyles, and identities (Gordon 2002; Heinz et al. 2005). Indeed, some scholars say that lawyers reflect class divisions within the larger society, with some lawyers part of a capitalist class and others part of a worker class.

STRATA

On the high end in terms of income and social prestige, we find **corporate lawyers**, or "Wall Street" lawyers. They are most likely to be White males from privileged backgrounds, are graduates of elite universities and law schools (e.g., Harvard, Yale, and Stanford), enjoy six- and seven-figure annual incomes, and represent wealthy and powerful corporations, financial enterprises, and individuals (Smigel 1964; Dinovitzer and Garth 2007; Nader and Smith 1996). They spend most of their time not in courtrooms but in meetings with clients (whom they advise) and other parties and drafting letters, reviewing complex legal documents, negotiating settlements, and the like (Flood 1991). Early in the twenty-first century, corporate law firms were still offering recent law school graduates very high salaries (Mansnerus 2001). For the most part, corporate lawyers were thriving.

On the other end of the scale, we find struggling **solo practitioners** working out of small offices in inner-city neighborhoods (Carlin 1994). They are more likely to be members of ethnic, racial, or religious minorities who have attended public colleges and night law schools. Most earn a modest income by providing moderate- or low-income individual clients with a variety of services, including representation against criminal charges, drawing up of wills, representation in landlord–tenant disputes, and the like. The substantial majority of moderate- and low-income individuals with civil troubles end up without legal representation, however (Winter 2002). Some law schools urge their graduates to pursue practices on behalf of such underserved clients, but this is not an easy sell.

At odds with what one might expect, lawyers with elite law school degrees are more likely to express dissatisfaction with their career choices and to seek new job opportunities as lawyers than lawyers with degrees from the lower tier law schools (Dinovitzer and Garth 2007). This is perhaps best explained by different expectations (i.e., graduates of lower tier law schools are more likely to come from modest social circumstances and to be glad that they have achieved a professional status).

Of course, between the extremes, there are lawyers practicing in a great diversity of settings and circumstances. According to one major study of the Chicago bar, lawyers are likely to have far more in common with their clients than with each other (Heinz and Laumann 1982). The legal profession is very heterogeneous.

ORGANIZATION

The legal profession has undergone complex changes in the recent era that do not lend themselves readily to generalization. The legal profession has greatly expanded, and lawyers are more likely to be involved in highly complex matters (Kelly 2007). Today lawyers are more often parts of organizations, and their autonomy and independence has been increasingly constrained by these organizations.

Early in the twenty-first century, about two-thirds of Chicago lawyers are working in corporate law, and more than one-third of lawyers are working in large firms (greater than

30 lawyers) (Heinz et al. 2005). The divide in terms of income between well-compensated and modestly compensated lawyers is growing. Legal practice is increasingly specialized, with the number of solo practitioners continuing to decline (Heinz et al. 1998; Van Hoy 2001). But if large corporate law firms have become more common, small firms and solo practitioners are hardly extinct. Of the approximately 75% of American lawyers today who are in private practice, about half of these work alone, with another 15% in very small law firms (Morrissey 2006, p. 270). Altogether, however, solo law practice is likely to decline.

Among lawyers who continued to work solo or in small firms, some adhere to a **traditional style of lawyering** (emphasizing independence, autonomy, client service, and community networks) and some adopt a **commercial** or **entrepreneurial style of lawyering** (emphasizing business and market concerns) (Gordon 2002; Seron 1996). In the emerging economy, those with a commercial orientation may be better positioned to survive in a competitive environment. For some areas of legal practice (e.g., example, negligence, divorce, and criminal defense), there appears to be an oversupply of lawyers early in the twenty-first century (Mansnerus 2001). Lawyers in other areas of practice contend with special challenges. Immigration lawyers serve an especially vulnerable clientele and today find themselves in the middle of an especially contentious social issue (Levin 2009). They are sustained by a strong community of fellow immigration lawyers. Although most solo or small-firm lawyers are generalists, some concentrate in one of the following areas: business-corporate, real estate, tax, personal injury, divorce, will-probate-estate, criminal, or collections (Carlin 1994). Much of the work performed in these areas is routine and requires little in the way of professional skills.

Prominent lawyers are increasingly accepting positions as **in-house counsel** for private companies or organizations (Donovan 2006). In-house counsel are full-time employees of a company. It is especially attractive to companies that have important business with the government to hire lawyers who had successful, high-level positions within the government.

The characteristics described in the preceding paragraphs pertain to the great majority of American lawyers (more than 85%) who are concentrated in metropolitan areas. A study of country lawyers found that they operate differently from their big-city counterparts (Landon 1990). **Country lawyers** have to be especially sensitive to the perceptions and values of their community, which makes it difficult for them to take on controversial cases (e.g., defending an alleged sexual abuser, filing a civil suit against the local school board, or suing a popular local doctor for malpractice). These lawyers are especially likely to become deeply involved in the lives of their clients, who may well be relatives, neighbors, or friends. Although such lawyers are typically conservative in their outlook, they also tend to embrace a small-town sympathy for the underdog or the beleaguered individual up against an impersonal bureaucratic institution.

A special type of "legal practitioner" is also worthy of mention here: the **jailhouse lawyer** (Liptak 2010c). Some prison inmates spend much time in the prison law library, largely self-educating themselves about law, and then they not only prepare briefs and appeals relating to their own case but may offer such services and advice to other inmates. Shon Hopwood, a convicted bank robber, managed to transform himself into an accomplished Supreme Court practitioner while in prison. Following his release from prison in 2008, he hoped to go to law school.

LAWYER–CLIENT RELATIONSHIPS

Whose interest is the lawyer truly representing? Ralph Nader and Wesley J. Smith (1996, p. xvi) differentiate between the role of attorney, who represents a client's interests, and lawyer, who is a professional with duties to the justice system and the public interest. Although the more familiar term *lawyer* is adopted in the discussion that follows, the majority surely function more as attorneys in the sense just suggested. Any lawyer typically contends with conflicting pressures and obligations. Obviously a lawyer is supposed to represent the best interests of the client. But lawyers are also sworn officers of the court, as well as members of a larger public. The lawyer is formally obligated not to be a party to a sworn falsehood in court. Also, the lawyer may be oriented toward cooperating with other court figures (the **courtroom workgroup**, including the judge and opposing lawyer) with whom the lawyer must maintain an ongoing relationship. The lawyer cannot easily be indifferent to the views and well-being of the larger public, as both professional and personal relationships can be jeopardized if the lawyer takes steps seen as harmful to the public interest. Lawyers in a more direct sense naturally are concerned with their own self-interest, including maximizing their income.

The richer and more powerful the client, the more likely that the client will dominate the lawyer and the lawyer will have to do the client's bidding. But corporate lawyers, and those representing the rich, are not necessarily simply hired guns. First, they often come from a background similar to that of corporate executives and share the same values and outlook. Second, wherever possible, they may put their own interests before those of the client. In a study of elite lawyers during the New Deal era, for example, Ronen Shamir (1995) found that these lawyers' crusade against the New Deal was driven more by its perceived threats to their own interests as lawyers than threats to the interests of their corporate clients. At the same time, corporate lawyers have been accused of zealously protecting and advancing the interests of powerful corporations in ways that compromise the rights, interests, and physical well-being of ordinary citizens, consumers, and workers. Ralph Nader and Wesley J. Smith (1996) set forth a potent and thorough indictment of the ways in which corporate lawyers lobby, negotiate, obfuscate, manipulate, and even break laws on behalf of their clients, resulting in multiple forms of harm to the rest of society. More specifically, power lawyering leads to:

> the radical concealment of vital health and safety information, the chronic delay, obstructionism, corporate destruction of documents, make-work, over-billing, the stifling of competition against investors and small business, the hamstringing of proper law enforcement, the merger deals driven by the enrichment of a few at the expense of workers and investors. (Nader and Smith 1996, p. 346)

When corporate lawyers find it necessary to settle with plaintiffs, they negotiate a confidential settlement, which results in monetary compensation for the plaintiffs but the absence of information and warnings to the general public. The silicone breast implant case was one example of this practice.

Lawyers whose clients are ordinary citizens are supposed to represent the best interests of their clients, ideally in a manner that is socially constructive. Unfortunately, many empirical studies suggest that lawyers all too often put their own interests before those of their clients, with the practice of **overlawyering** (providing unnecessary services) and overbilling especially egregious examples of such self-interest (Felstiner 1998). If corporate lawyers are at least sometimes dominated by their clients, then lawyers for ordinary citizens are more likely to dominate their clients (Abel 1989, p. 204). Of course, this is a somewhat broad generalization, and many factors can come into play in determining whether lawyer or client assumes the upper hand or they work together on strategy in the particular case. What clients want and what lawyers believe is ethically permissible for them may be at odds (Bernstein 2003). Much evidence suggests that clients often experience their lawyers as arrogant, paternalistic, lacking in empathy, uncommunicative, inattentive, and the like (Felstiner 1998, p. 63). In part, such responses might be attributed to the professional socialization of lawyers, who learn to focus on the legal logic in a case as opposed to the emotional dimensions often experienced by clients. Because people often seek a client when they find themselves in stressful circumstances, they may well seek emotional comfort from their lawyers. *Therapeutic jurisprudence* refers to an approach to lawyering wherein the lawyer does not limit herself to offering legal advice but actively contributes to a process of "healing" for clients (Wexler 2008). But paradoxically, according to one study, clients perceived lawyers who offered much emotional comfort as less competent as attorneys than those who did not (Henningsen and Cionea 2007). The main thing clients want from lawyers is a successful resolution of their case. In divorce cases, in particular, lawyers are likely to face special challenges in keeping emotionally overwrought clients focused on legal realities (Sarat and Felstiner 1995). If lawyers fail to return calls and to move forward on cases, however, this is mainly a consequence of the fact that lawyers, typically insecure about sources of future income, take on more cases than they can comfortably handle (Felstiner 1998). Clients, then, are not infrequently frustrated (and are sometimes angered) in their dealings with lawyers, and lawyers seem to be disproportionately stressed, overwhelmed, and alienated. Of course, there are numerous exceptions to such generalizations (i.e., satisfied clients and fulfilled lawyers).

In an increasingly complex legal environment, it has become more common for lawyers themselves to have other lawyers advise them or represent them on matters relating to their legal practices (Glater 2004). More major law firms have been appointing general counsels to assume this type of responsibility within the law firm. This trend has been at least partially viewed as a response to high-profile cases (e.g., the Andersen accounting firm case) in which lawyers face criminal charges for obstruction of justice as a consequence of their actions as well as an environment of greater regulation and aggressive plaintiff lawyers.

PUBLIC DEFENDERS AND APPOINTED COUNSEL FOR INDIGENTS

Historically, lawyers have disproportionately worked for the rich and the middle class. The poor, for the most part, had to represent themselves, and they were obviously at a great disadvantage in doing so. In the late nineteenth century, legal services for the poor were funded by private sources, primarily to represent the working poor who were owed money or who had suffered uncompensated injury or some other injustice (Katz 1982). In the last several decades of the twentieth century, legal services for the poor came to be primarily funded by the state, and (perhaps ironically) the legal matters often targeted discriminatory state policies against the poor. By the latter part of the twentieth century, these services had become quasi private (while funded by states) and had shifted from focusing on reforming the law to providing direct services to the poor (Kessler 1987). Legal services and aid to the poor expanded substantially during this period. Nevertheless, "the American Bar Association estimates that 80 percent of the legal problems faced by poor citizens go unassisted" (Nader and Smith 1996, p. 339). These problems include the most basic issues of adequate food, decent shelter, and protection from abuse.

Public defenders who represent indigents charged with crimes occupy a somewhat paradoxical position in the U.S. legal system (McIntyre 1987). We have a tradition, affirmed by the highest courts, that those charged with serious crimes are entitled to a defense. The landmark case of *Gideon v. Wainwright* (1963) established the constitutional right to representation for indigents facing felony charges; in 1972, this right was extended in *Argersinger v. Hamlin* to misdemeanor cases involving jail time. Although many states had already provided indigent defendants with attorneys, it now became necessary to provide all such defendants who could not afford lawyers with legal counsel. Roughly one-third of all American states have statewide public defender systems (Hoffman 2007). Many of the criminally accused are social pariahs whom the public wants to see incarcerated. The paradox lies in the state supporting public defenders who represent people the state is vigorously attempting to prosecute. Some commentators say that the principal purpose of the public defenders office is to legitimate the system of law and its claims of due process and fairness. Whether public defenders are truly committed to their clients' interests or to the interest of the court system has been debated. Public defenders may not experience the same anxieties about generating enough clients to pay the bills as private practice lawyers do, but they often contend with severe pressures, including excessively large caseloads. And when lawyers for the poor take on cases and go into court, they are often at a disadvantage because of the typical judge and juror biases against the lifestyle and life choices of their clients (Emmelman 2003). Despite evidence that many appointed lawyers are quite dedicated, the hurdles facing them are formidable.

In an oft-cited study, Abraham Blumberg (1967) found that the person who most frequently suggested that a defendant in a criminal case plead guilty was the defense lawyer. In Blumberg's interpretation, these lawyers "con" their clients into waiving their constitutional rights because *(1)* a guilty plea is the most efficient means of settling cases and *(2)* the defense lawyer's primary commitment is to cooperate with the agenda of the courtroom workgroup (including the prosecutor and the judge) rather than to act in the client's interest. Of course, in an alternative interpretation, it is often in the client's interest to plead guilty in return for some form of leniency, and the defense lawyer's advice may indeed serve the client's interest. Almost certainly, public defenders fall somewhere along a continuum, with those on one end zealously committed to giving clients the best possible defense and those on the other end cynically focused on disposing of cases efficiently.

THE DECLINING SUPPORT FOR LEGAL SERVICES FOR THE POOR

Legal services for the poor first received federal funding in the 1960s, as part of President Johnson's War on Poverty (Edelman 2009). But since the Reagan Administration of the 1980s, conservative forces have engaged in an ongoing, ultimately successful effort to cut funding for these legal services (Kilborn 1995). Conservatives were especially angry about lawyers for the poor filing class action lawsuits on behalf of their clients against the government or private businesses. Congressional financial support for civil legal assistance to poor people has continued to decline during the recent era, most dramatically when conservative political leaders have been in power (Edelman 2009; Sandefur 2007; Shepard 2007). Other sources of funding for legal services programs—state or local, private, or derived from attorney fees—have also often been declining. Congressional action has resulted in restrictions on class action lawsuits on behalf of poor people and litigation relating to access to welfare benefits, as well as reimbursement of attorneys' fees in certain kinds of cases.

Lawyers who serve poor clients may be drawn to such work by their ideals, but then often find themselves contending with harsh realities (Shdaimah 2009). Legal service attorneys in the Deep South mainly represent clients in such everyday circumstances as evictions, consumer issues, problems relating to government benefits programs, and marital or custody disputes (Edelman 2009; Shepard 2007). But in all parts of the country it has become increasingly difficult to find lawyers willing to represent the poor (Fritsch and Rohde 2001; Lueck 2004; Saulny 2003c). They have been demoralized by relentless attacks on them when they challenge government or private business practices, by the decline of financial support for their services, and by the exceptionally modest compensation they receive. When such lawyers challenge the government in fundamental ways, their efforts encounter considerable resistance.

In recent years, public defenders in at least seven states have complained of overwhelming workloads that severely compromise their capacity to fulfill the constitutional mandate to provide counsel to indigent defendants (Eckholm 2008). These public defenders have simply refused to take on new cases. Public defenders often find they have difficulty supporting a family on the modest income they earn, and experienced public defenders are increasingly bailing out of the system. Indigent criminal defendants increasingly must spend long periods of time in jail waiting for a lawyer to become available to represent them. Inevitably, in these circumstances, indigent defendants are more likely to be either directly or indirectly pressured to waive rights to trial and plead guilty to charges against them. In 2010, New York's highest court allowed a lawsuit challenging that state's public defender system to go forward (Glaberson 2010). The principal plaintiff in the case claimed that the public defender in her case did nothing to defend her but rather pressured her to plead guilty to the felony charges (trying to sneak marijuana to her imprisoned husband) lodged against her. One study found that the average sentence for clients of public defenders was almost three times longer than that of clients who had private lawyers (Hoffman 2007). The more serious the case, the more likely that private counsel will be retained. Some clients in legal cases are "marginally indigent": They might be able to draw on some resources available to them to hire private lawyers but may opt not to, especially if the charge against them is fairly minor and their guilt is fairly obvious.

Poor people seeking representation in civil matters are even less able to get any legal representation at all than those involved in criminal cases. Altogether, a crisis has developed with regard to meeting legal needs of the poor.

WOMEN IN THE LEGAL PROFESSION

The legal profession, through most of its history, has been an overwhelmingly male profession. As Richard Abel has noted:

> No women were admitted to practice until the 1870s, and about a dozen of the forty-five jurisdictions continued to exclude them as late as 1900. Some professional associations barred women until 1937, and some law schools continued to do so until 1972. (1988, p. 202)

The first women who entered the legal profession in the late nineteenth and early twentieth centuries were relatively few and far between and had to overcome some formidable barriers and biases against them (Mossman 2006). According to one study, these women tended to adopt different legal arguments than their male counterparts, when they found themselves involved in contested cases.

As late as 1963, only 3% of American lawyers were women. Beginning in the late 1960s, however, this began to change (Drachman 1998). In the 16-year period between 1967 and 1983, for example, enrollment of women in ABA-accredited law schools increased from 4.5% to 37.5% of the total (Abel 1989). By the end of the twentieth century, almost half of law school graduates were women, and at the outset of the new millennium, women constituted roughly 33% of the American legal profession (in Canada, the numbers are even more striking: from a ratio of 1 woman to 38 men in 1961 to 1 to 2.4 by 1991) (Hagan and Kay 1995). Early in the new century, the number of women entering law school in the United States began to slightly exceed the number of men (Glater 2001a). Women have now become lawyers in many countries around the world, not just in the United States (Schultz and Shaw 2003). By any measure, then, there has been a dramatic transformation in the gender composition of the profession (Kay 1997). What difference has it made? Despite the dramatic influx of women in the legal profession and the erosion of many barriers, the legal profession is still dominated by men and remains a fundamentally masculine institution (Leiper 2006). But the increasing presence of women in the legal profession is surely transforming the nature of this profession in some ways.

JOBS AND MONEY

Although the formal barriers against admission of women to the bar have been swept away, much discrimination has persisted. Originally, many law firms resisted taking on women lawyers because they believed that their principal clients would not accept women as lawyers; for the most part, however, this did not become a problem (Epstein 1993).

Empirical studies provide some evidence that stereotypes about women still play some role in the hiring process of female lawyers (Gorman 2005). Law firms that cater to companies with high-level female executives are more likely to promote female lawyers in their own firm (Beckman and Phillips 2005). Although women now make up about 50% of law students and 44% of associate lawyers and have slightly better law school grades on average than men, they still constitute less than 20% of law firm partners; in recent years, they have been promoted to partner at a somewhat higher rate than previously (Glater 2006a). Female lawyers are more likely than male lawyers to seek public interest law jobs and are more likely to work part-time than male lawyers (Firm Report 2009; Hagan and Kay 2007). And women are more likely than men to leave legal practice for family-related reasons. For various reasons, women are less likely than men to make choices that might maximize their opportunities and are less likely to be in positions to make professionally advantageous contacts. But the extent to which the disadvantaged position of women (relative to men) in the legal profession can be attributed to discrimination against them or to choices they make because they tend to have different priorities than men continues to be debated.

CULTURAL VALUES AND STYLES

The legal profession has been dominated by males historically, and so it has also reflected strongly male cultural values and styles (Menkel-Meadow 1985). Even after women began to be admitted to law schools (in the case of Harvard Law School, only from 1950 on), they continued to face resentment and harassment and a form of education strongly biased to favor males (A. Bernstein 1996; Rhode 2003). In a study titled *Becoming Gentlemen: Women, Law School, and Institutional Change*, Lani Guinier, Michelle Fine, and Jane Balin (1997) have found that female law students are substantially more likely to enter law school committed to public interest law and to fighting for social justice than their male counterparts, but by the time they graduate, their outlook and aspirations are much more like those of male students. In addition, female students are more likely than males to experience alienation and to feel excluded in law school. They generally do not do as well academically as males and are more likely to regard themselves as psychologically damaged by the law school experience. The authors of this study conclude that the law school environment and pedagogical approach must be transformed in ways that are more encouraging to female students.

The very nature of the adversary system is based on aggressive confrontation, conflict, and domination—values traditionally associated with males. When growing numbers of women enter the legal profession, do they adapt to this masculine, even "macho," culture, or do they transform it? Apparently there is no simple answer to this question (Bogoch 1997; Pierce 1995; Thornton 1996). Some female criminal defense lawyers feel that they are betraying their gender when they adopt the male adversarial style (Siemsen 2004). At least some women adopt the aggressive, competitive, and combative male role and may even exceed most male lawyers on these attributes; many others adopt a style that puts more emphasis on a humane, caring, and mediation-oriented approach to legal matters and to client relations. One study of male and female divorce lawyers found that both sexes tended to be reluctant to get involved with the emotional issues clients typically raise, but female lawyers were at least more likely to be willing to put aside purely legal questions and address such issues (Bogoch 1997). At the same time, according to this study, female clients (as well as male clients) in divorce cases tend to be more deferential toward male lawyers than toward female lawyers.

WORK AND FAMILY

Many women have clearly found great satisfaction in their careers as lawyers, but women also encounter special pressures and conditions somewhat less likely to affect men (Epstein 1993; Flaherty 1999). They tend to experience more emotional stress than their male counterparts, especially early in their careers (Siemsen 2004). Although both male and female lawyers can experience some measure of depression and dissatisfaction with their legal career, one study finds that female lawyers are more likely than their male counterparts to internalize these feelings and to experience despondency (internal) rather than express job dissatisfaction (external) (Hagan and Kay 2007). Many female lawyers continue to experience sexual harassment. Women collectively experience their legal careers differently than their male counterparts. The time pressures involved in the early stages of a legal career (to qualify for partnership or build up a clientele) sometimes call for 80-hour work weeks and coincide with a stage of life (their 20s and 30s) when many women hope to marry and have children. The traditional assumption of the male-dominated legal profession was that young (male) lawyers had wives at home to attend to all domestic and childcare responsibilities; obviously, young female lawyers typically don't have wives, and they are somewhat less likely than young male lawyers to have spouses or partners willing to fully share such responsibilities. Female lawyers tend to face more intense conflicts between their professional and personal lives and pay a heavier toll in their personal lives if they put their careers first. A female lawyer found that the demands of her job put in jeopardy the case for obtaining custody of her children (Petersen 1998). Successful female lawyers are less likely than their male counterparts to be married and have children (Abramson 1988; Epstein 1993). All six male members of the U.S. Supreme Court in 2010 were married; the three female members of the Court were a widow, a divorced woman, and a never-married woman.

Even when women in major law firms receive essentially the same pay as men, they are likely to perceive themselves as disadvantaged when it comes to job assignments, promotions, and opportunities to litigate cases (Lewin 1989; Reichman and Sterling 2002). They find themselves with fewer opportunities to cultivate the after-hours networking that is so crucial for advancement in legal careers. Furthermore, in one survey, some 60% of female lawyers reported that they had experienced unwanted sexual attention on the job (Lewin 1989). Altogether, it is not surprising that a higher percentage of women than men become disenchanted with the legal profession, and women leave legal practice 60% more quickly than men (Bach 1995; Kay 1997). They become disillusioned with long hours and large workloads, inadequate pay for what they do, the perception that they will not be made partner, boring or distasteful work, and a general discomfort with the adversarial nature of their work. Although such problems are also experienced by some male lawyers, the evidence suggests that the problems are more widespread or intense for female lawyers. Although some law firms have taken steps to improve the conditions for women to retain their services (e.g., by installing on-site child care), it seems clear that both the culture and the institutional practices of the legal profession will have to change significantly before women are fully integrated into the profession.

LEGAL ETHICS

There is a long history of low regard for the ethics of lawyers, stretching back to the ancient Greeks (Luban 1994). The American public today often associates lawyers with dishonesty and betrayal (Glaberson 2006). A legal ethics professor notes that lawyers always seem to be thinking of new ways to get into trouble (Wendel 2006). The need for lawyers to commit to professional ethics is quite clear (Krieger 2009). The subtitle of a book by a law professor pinpoints a fundamental dilemma in the world of law: *The Importance of Being Honest: How Lying, Secrecy and Hypocrisy Collide with Truth in Law* (Lubet 2008). A lack of honesty by lawyers and judges generates a broad range of problems.

LAW SCHOOL OFFERINGS

Formal attention to professional ethics has been widely incorporated into the law school curriculum only in the recent era, essentially after the high-profile exposure of unethical conduct by lawyers in the Watergate affair in the early 1970s. Indeed, at that time the ABA began requiring an ethics course in all accredited law school programs (Mangan 1998). Although some law schools have adopted reasonably creative approaches to education in ethics, many have simply taken the narrow approach of familiarizing students with ABA rules and informing them how to avoid being disciplined by the bar (Metzloff and Wilkins 1995). Some commentators argue that law students should be taught to actively pursue moral issues with their clients, whatever the outcome (Bennett 2001). In the view of James Elkins (1985c), the problem of teaching ethics cannot be separated from contemplation of the nature of legal education itself, which tends to promote ethical insensitivity.

Law students seem to dislike being required to take a **professional responsibility course**, on the grounds that such courses tend to be preachy, patronizing, and unnecessary (Niehoff 2006). Also, it is difficult to demonstrate that exposure to such a course will produce ethical behavior when law school graduates are faced with the ambiguities and formidable pressures encountered in real-life legal practices (Mangan 1998; Mello 1996). At least some law professors believe that existing professional responsibility courses are largely useless when they teach law students how to comply with bar codes of ethics but fail to address the broader ethical dilemmas intertwined with the daily work of lawyers (Chemerinsky 1985; Del Mar 2009). They would like to see education in ethical matters integrated into all courses rather than being "ghettoized" in a single course.

CONFLICTS OF INTEREST

Conflicts of interest arise virtually daily in the lives of all lawyers and generate some complex challenges for them (Shapiro 2002). In one view, globalization of commerce, growth in the size of corporations, and the growing mobility of lawyers have produced conflicts of interest that are increasingly difficult to resolve (Griffiths-Baker 2002). The ABA has historically done a poor job of addressing conflicts of interest, which law professor Deborah Rhode (2000) believes require an independent oversight structure that would put public interests first. Some appellate court justices have suggested that a conflict of interest alone would not guarantee a new trial for a criminal defendant.

ADVERSARIAL ISSUES

In the course of their legal education, lawyers become conscious of and are expected to adopt an **adversarial ethic**, holding that the lawyer has a primary responsibility to the welfare of his or her client and that this responsibility must take precedence over most (but not necessarily all) other obligations. Furthermore, as part of the adversarial ethic, a lawyer is expected to make the best possible case on behalf of the client, or on behalf of the state if the lawyer is a prosecutor, rather than to attempt getting at the truth by laying out all available evidence on both sides of a case in an even-handed and dispassionate way. At least on the defense side, it is not the obligation of lawyers to discriminate right from wrong and ensure just outcomes. Tim Dare (2009) defends the dishonesty and deviousness and other acts committed by lawyers that might in other circumstances be regarded as immoral, when they are performed on behalf of clients. But David Luban (2007), a leading legal ethicist, questions the notion that lawyers as "hired guns" are largely absolved from ethical constraints on the actions they undertake within the adversary system. In a case that went before the U.S. Supreme Court, the question arose on whether a federal law imposing some restrictions on the kind of advice that bankruptcy lawyers could provide to clients was a good idea (Liptak 2009h). In part, the case hinged on whether such a law improperly infringed on the free speech rights of lawyers.

The **lawyer–client confidentiality principle** is involved here as well. This principle holds that lawyers should not disclose possibly incriminating revelations made to them by clients in the course of consultations. The rationale for this principle is that a client can only obtain full-fledged representation and an effective defense if the client does not have to be concerned that the lawyer will report incriminating or otherwise harmful disclosures made during lawyer–client conferences. However, by the standards of the ABA, if a client discloses the intent to take actions that might cause death or do bodily harm to another person, then the lawyer is permitted (but not required) to report this despite the confidentiality principle (Nader and Smith 1996, p. 350). Aside from such extreme circumstances, the ABA Code effectively prohibits lawyers from taking any direct action when they are aware of ongoing criminality by their client, although they may attempt to talk the client out of such action or they may withdraw from representing the client. Confidentiality rules have kept lawyers who know their own client is guilty of a serious crime from revealing that the wrong man was convicted for the crime or from exposing prosecutorial misconduct if their own client benefited (Liptak 2008a). In one case, a lawyer's silence kept a man he knew to be innocent in prison for 26 years (Liptak 2008b). Although legal ethics rules vary among states, lawyers typically may violate confidentiality with clients to prevent bodily injury or death—including the implementation of the death penalty. Even if a client dies, however, confidentiality standards may still be in effect. Early in the twenty-first century, in the wake of post-9/11 terrorism fears, corporate scandals, and other such concerns, the legal profession was under growing pressure to limit some aspects of the traditional lawyer–client confidentiality principle (Glater 2003b). The ABA at this time approved a new standard permitting lawyers to disclose confidences about the crimes of employees if it was deemed necessary to protect the company. The ABA also approved rules that would allow, but not require, lawyers to disclose client confidences if the lawyer's own actions had been used in connection with furthering the client's crime, and if substantial financial harm to others was involved.

Of course, it should also be emphasized that ethical issues are not entirely restricted to the defense. Prosecutors may engage in various forms of unethical conduct, especially when they are so eager to obtain convictions that they deliberately conceal evidence favorable to the defense (exculpatory evidence) or even knowingly present false evidence unfavorable to the defense in court. For example, in one case that was the subject of two books, a 17-year-old boy was convicted of murdering his mother in a trial where a key witness known to the prosecutor was not called, although that witness would have raised fundamental questions about the prosecution's case (Barthel 1977; Connery 1977). The boy was acquitted in a subsequent trial. Many other such cases could be cited.

The adversarial ethic has been endorsed on the claim that the truth in any particular case is most likely to emerge at the end of the adjudicative process if the two sides are allowed to make the strongest possible cases for their version of the facts. In criminal cases in particular, the adversarial ethic allows the defense to counter more effectively the great power of the state, minimizes the chances of harsh punishments being imposed unjustly, and helps protect constitutional rights and civil liberties (Luban 1994). Some lawyers fully internalize this ethic and claim to be entirely comfortable with it; others report that they experience discomfort or chagrin when they find themselves expected to engage in advocacy on behalf of a client who is not believable to them and who they may believe is guilty of heinous wrongdoing (Mills 1971; Wishman 1981). More generally, lawyers have been somewhat divided on whether this duty to serve clients zealously should indeed take precedence over all other duties (e.g., to religious faith or to society) and whether it is acceptable for a lawyer to knowingly present a false case (Allegretti 1996; Glenn 2008b; Lubet 2001). A prosecutor (who formerly served as a public defender) argued that in some cases zealous advocacy of those accused of crimes has destructive consequences (Shutt 2002). For example, in a California case, the lawyer defending the alleged abductor and murderer of a 7-year-old girl attacked in court the sexual practices of the girl's parents, severely traumatizing them and outraging onlookers. Accordingly, in this commentator's view, defense lawyers should consult with an ethics tribunal when such issues arise. The commitment to the adversarial ethic can clash dramatically with the value system of the lay culture. The title of a book by one defense lawyer quite concisely captures a common public attitude: *How Can You Defend Those People?* (Kunen 1983). More broadly, should the legal profession be re-organized to incorporate community concerns (Parker 2000)? Such debates will surely continue.

REPRESENTING SOCIAL PARIAHS

Representing social pariahs, such as Oklahoma City bomber Timothy McVeigh or accused Al Qaeda terrorists, is regarded as ethically appropriate (and even commendable) within the internal legal culture (*see* Box 7.4). The general public, however, may be both perplexed and angry when lawyers vigorously defend people who are believed to have committed heinous crimes (Precht 2003). Motivations for taking on social pariahs as clients vary and may include the belief that our system of justice works best when even those accused of the most heinous crimes receive the best possible defense. A lawyer may also be motivated to take on such cases because they represent a special opportunity to demonstrate outstanding legal skills and because such cases are likely to enhance the lawyer's fame and may lead to various opportunities to earn large fees or royalties.

The confidentiality principle has sometimes produced a harsh clash between the lay value system and the internal ethic of the legal profession. In one well-known case in 1973, in upstate New York, a man named Robert Garrow was suspected of being guilty of a string of rapes/murders of several young co-eds (Alibrandt and Armani 1991). He informed his lawyer, Frank Armani, of the location of the corpses of two of these co-eds. The lawyer then visited this location, a cave in the woods, and took photographs of the corpses. But when the prosecutor in this high-profile case refused to consider negotiating for a lighter sentence in return for information on the crimes, Armani refrained from sharing with the prosecutor, or the anguished father of one of the missing girls, what he had learned from his client. When all of this came out many months later, during Garrow's trial, many people were outraged over the lawyer's actions. But when the prosecutor brought the matter before the state bar association, it supported the lawyer's claim that he had only acted in the best interest of his client as his professional role required of him. As a somewhat ironic sequel to this case, the lawyer assisted the police with information when Garrow escaped from prison some 5 years later, and Garrow was tracked down and killed. Because the lawyer no longer represented Garrow, he had no special reservations about cooperating in the hunt for the fugitive.

COUNSELOR OR CO-OFFENDER?

The line between being a lawyer and being an offender is sometimes blurred. In the extreme case, lawyers become criminals or part of criminal mobs (as in the case of the *consigliere* for a Mafia family). Lawyers who represent major criminals, such as illicit drug smugglers, may be suspected of complicity with their clients. One government response to such a concern has taken the form of seizing fees to lawyers that can be shown to come from illegal enterprises.

An ethical gray zone may also arise when a lawyer (or law firm) becomes aware of ongoing illegal conduct by a client. In one case, for example, a prominent New York City law firm became aware that its major client was engaged in an ongoing computer leasing fraud and did not blow the whistle on the client (Taylor 1983). Was this in line with the firm's obligation to honor confidentiality between itself and the client, as the firm later claimed, or was it an unethical effort by the law firm to continue receiving a lucrative retainer fee from its major client? The ABA has generally held that lawyers should not blow the whistle on clients in such cases. Lawyers may, however, attempt to dissuade a client from behaving illegally or unethically and may choose to withdraw from representing a client who disregards such advice.

When a lawyer or law firm offers advice to a client on how to commit illegal acts while minimizing chances of being caught, a line has been crossed, and the lawyer becomes liable to criminal charges. Lawyers have issued false and, in some cases, willfully incorrect opinions that have been linked with securities fraud but have typically only been pursued in those cases where they could be shown to have directly profited from the fraud (Norris 2007). More than one prestigious law firm was accused of complicity in the savings and loan frauds of the 1980s, which resulted in billions of dollars of losses to the federal banking insurance system and the American taxpayers; the ABA was more critical of the federal agency initiating the charges against the lawyers than of the lawyers involved (Simon 1998). A law professor who teaches legal ethics argues that lawyers failed to live up to their ethical and professional obligations in cases such as Enron, where they were parties to massive corporate deceptions, and the torture memos, where they advanced rationales on behalf of the government to justify the use of torture (Wendel 2006). Parallel concerns arose in the wake of the financial meltdown of 2008.

LYING AND PERJURY

Because a lawyer is a sworn officer of the court as well as an advocate for clients, the lawyer is not supposed to persuade a client to lie under oath or knowingly elicit false testimony

---

BOX 7.4 EFFECTIVE LAWYER OR TERRORIST CO-CONSPIRATOR?

Lawyers defending accused terrorists face especially daunting ethical challenges, especially in the political environment after 9/11. In 2004, Lynne Stewart, a lawyer long involved with radical causes, was tried on charges that she violated a law making it a crime to support foreign terrorist organizations (Preston 2004). More specifically, she was accused of funneling messages to the supporters of her client, Sheik Omar Abdul Rahman, that he had withdrawn his support for a ceasefire against enemies in Egypt. In addition, she was accused of violating an agreement she signed with prison authorities explicitly prohibiting communications with the press from her client. The Sheik was convicted in 1995 on conspiracy charges relating to the original bombing attempt on the World Trade Center and other terrorist plots (Preston 2004). Stewart did not deny passing along the message but contended that effective advocacy of her client's interests meant that she had to keep him visible to his supporters, and passing along such messages was part of that. She believed that these actions would enhance her chances of obtaining better prison conditions

for her client. The prosecutors in the case argued that she had stepped over the line from representing her client to becoming an active participant in terrorist activity. Although some lawyers supported the government's prosecution in this case, others expressed concern that it could place lawyers representing accused terrorists (and other social pariahs) in an untenable situation, which would seriously compromise the right to counsel of such accused terrorists.

Stewart was convicted on all charges in February 2005 (Preston 2005). In November, 2009, Stewart surrendered to begin serving a 28-month sentence (Moynihan 2009). Although the sentencing judge acknowledged the seriousness of her offense, he also acknowledged "her long record of representing the disadvantaged, the destitute, and the despised." In July, 2010, a federal judge increased Stewart's original sentence to 10 years, almost five times as long (Eligon 2010). The rationale for this increase was the conclusion that the original sentence was insufficient for the offense, as prosecutors claimed in their appeal, and that Stewart's statements to the press following her conviction suggested a lack of remorse on her part.

(or knowingly introduce fraudulent documents and evidence) in sworn statements in court, and the lawyer who is found to have violated this rule can be prosecuted (Lubet 2008).

In the famous Watergate case of the 1970s, for example, the Counsel to President Nixon, John Dean, went to prison because he was found to have coached other parties in the case to lie before the grand jury. The lawyer is supposed to attempt to persuade clients not to perjure themselves, and here the ABA has held that the lawyer does have an obligation to blow the whistle on a client who cannot be persuaded to refrain from lying under oath. Alternatively, a lawyer might drop a client or stand mute while a client testifies in such circumstances.

Obviously, a significant tension exists between the rules of legal ethics prohibiting a lawyer from putting a witness on the stand whom he or she knows will lie and a lawyer's obligation to protect the confidentiality of a client's conversations. Of course, there is much reason to believe that lawyers all too often either know or strongly suspect that the client is lying under oath, but lawyers may typically protect themselves by not attempting to independently establish the veracity of the client's account. In strategic terms, the lawyer may simply choose to focus on what facts can and cannot be established by the prosecutor (or the opposing side) and what challenges can be directed at this case. A lawyer may adopt the stance of being morally neutral.

OTHER ETHICAL ISSUES

In addition to the ethical issues surrounding perjury and lawyer–client confidentiality, there are many other ethical issues bearing on the legal profession. The establishment of the legal profession has historically regarded solicitation of legal clients as unethical. Lawyers who approached accident victims and survivors, for example, and offered their services were historically stigmatized as **ambulance chasers**. In recent times, the Supreme Court has upheld state bans on approaching accident victims for business.

Although the U.S. Supreme Court in 1977 struck down the ban on advertising by lawyers, some specific forms of advertising (e.g., a female lawyer in a seductive pose; a male lawyer in a boxing outfit, prepared to do battle for clients) have been viewed as undignified and arguably unethical (Glendon 1994, p. 54). In an increasingly competitive environment in the early twenty-first century, more law firms are using advertising to attempt to establish broad images that set them apart from the competition (Hines 2001). Some law firms even advertise on subways (Mansnerus 2000). But only false or misleading ads are illegal.

With the **power of attorney** that may be granted lawyers (which gives them unusual control over clients' financial affairs), lawyers have special opportunities to take advantage of and steal from clients, and some do. Lawyers who are appointed guardians for incapacitated people, and lawyers who are appointed arbiters in custody battles, have sometimes been accused of unethical, corrupt, and illegal activities (Eaton 2004; Glaberson 2004). Some classes of people, then, are especially vulnerable to exploitation by unethical lawyers.

Contingency fees, which provide lawyers with a percentage share of any recovery made in civil cases (with no money to the lawyers if they lose the case), have been defended as a device enabling clients who are not wealthy to sue richer and more powerful entities that have done some harm to them (Kritzer 2004a; Mackinnon 2008). Contingency fees as high as 40% have been upheld, when challenged, when the court has accepted the argument that the complexity of the case and the benefit to the client of the successful outcome warranted such a high fee (Hartocollis 2007). But at least in some cases the size of the contingency fee seems obscenely large, and in certain class action suits the lawyers may seem to be the primary beneficiaries (Liptak 2003a; Meier and Abramson 1998). Lawyers representing three states (Florida, Mississippi, and Texas) in cases against tobacco companies were awarded a staggering $8.2 billion in contingency fees; a single law firm claimed some $25 billion and collected more than $3 billion; a law firm that invested $10 million in time and expenses was awarded $178 million in fees; one lawyer, who seems to have been only marginally involved in the litigation, demanded more than $200 million in fees; another lawyer recovered the equivalent of $200,000 an hour for his work (Beam 2004; Meier and Oppel 1999). Does a contingency fee system facilitate much-needed litigation on behalf of ordinary people against powerful corporate entities engaged in harmful actions, or does it promote a form of legalized extortion principally benefiting greedy lawyers?

Lawyers have also been regarded as unethical when they initiate meritless suits (e.g., against hospitals and doctors) on the chance that they will be able to persuade a jury to favor a sympathetic client. On the other hand, lawyers can face an ethical dilemma when they are committed to representing a client who, for various reasons, they may no longer wish to represent, because when lawyers drop their clients they may put them in legal jeopardy. The ultimate form of unethical conduct by lawyers, as was suggested before, arises when lawyers themselves become party to, or even initiate and direct, illegal and harmful activity.

DISCIPLINING WRONGDOERS

Historically, the ethical codes and actions of the ABA have been driven more by the objective of advancing and protecting the economic interests of the profession than by the objective of ensuring that lawyers act ethically. The ABA Code of Ethics has always been full of contradictions. For example, it has been permissible for lawyers to get what amounts to kickbacks on title insurance sold to their home-buying clients (without necessarily revealing this arrangement to clients), but it has been deemed unethical for attorneys to proffer advice to people about their rights and then accept a fee to help vindicate those rights (Lieberman 1978). Historically, according to the ABA Code, it was unethical to charge too low a fee, but the code did not recognize a fee that was unethical because it was too high; in a 1975 decision, however, the U.S. Supreme Court declared the minimum fee rule of the code illegal. If a lawyer is sued by a client or if a lawyer attempts to collect an unpaid fee, the ABA Code allows for violation of the confidentiality rule. The ABA rejected proposals that would make it easier for lawyers to partner with and share fees with non-lawyers (Perlman 2003).

Traditionally the ABA assumed the primary responsibility for disciplining lawyers, although in the more recent era, judicially appointed commissions have taken over this responsibility in most American states (Arnold and Kay 1995, p. 323). The **disbarment** of unethical lawyers (taking away from them their license to practice) has been applied rarely, and then mainly against lawyers whose behavior is so egregious that it threatens the reputation of the legal profession itself (Schneyer 1991). More specifically, solo practitioners with a modest practice have been far more vulnerable as targets of ethical complaints and disciplinary action than have lawyers affiliated with large, prosperous law firms (Abel 2008). Richard Abel is a UCLA law professor and a long-standing, prominent figure in law and society scholarship. In *Lawyers in the Dock: Learning from Attorney Disciplinary Proceedings*, Abel (2008) explores in great depth some cases of disciplinary proceedings against lawyers. The "betrayal of trust" is a central theme of his study. Lawyers can be disciplined for such matters as misappropriating funds from clients' accounts, solicitation of personal injury clients ("ambulance chasing"), sexual harassment, and conviction of criminal charges. Abel focused on three types of lawyer malfeasance: client neglect, overreaching on fees, and excessive zeal in pursuing cases. The seven contested disciplinary cases involved solo practitioners, and Abel believes such practitioners are the most likely to engage in ethical misconduct; these lawyers are especially likely to be overworked and underpaid. The inability of the lawyers charged to admit that they had done anything wrong and the roles of both need and greed in leading lawyers to ethical lapses were among other themes of this study. Critics raised questions about how representative these cases are and whether they are best explained by individual moral lapses as opposed to institutional and systemic factors (Kritzer 2009; Wald 2009). There is certainly much evidence that corporate lawyers who are members of large law firms can engage in egregiously unethical activities, although they may be less likely to be formally disciplined for these activities. With a strong trend toward globalization at the start of the twenty-first century and the proliferation of international tribunals, the need for an international code of ethics has been recognized (Vagts 1996). However, the challenge of policing legal practice across borders is formidable.

LEGAL EDUCATION

Through most of history, education to be a lawyer principally took the form of apprenticeship with a lawyer and the reading of legal treatises, such as Blackstone's Commentaries. In the English tradition this process became somewhat formalized at the Inns of Court, where lawyers resided while court was in session, socialized with each other, and acquired a fuller knowledge of the law (Goodrich 2008). However, law was regarded as a largely practical skill and was not deemed a suitable topic for higher education. Sir William Blackstone, in the mid-eighteenth century, occupied the first university chair in law at Oxford. In the American colonies, at this time, George Wythe in Virginia offered a short course of study (lasting weeks, not years) on law, ultimately situated at William and Mary College. It is a truly remarkable fact that for some of the giants in American legal history, including Thomas Jefferson and the great U.S. Supreme Court Chief Justice John Marshall, this course was the sum total of their formal legal education. Some Americans during the pre-Revolutionary period traveled to England for their legal education.

The first full-fledged American law school was established in Litchfield, Connecticut, in 1784 by Judge Tapping Reeve (Friedman 2005, p. 239). This independent school educated many leading legal figures of the nineteenth century and helped firmly establish the notion of formal legal education. In the nineteenth century, major universities (e.g., Harvard, Yale, and Columbia) established law schools, although through much of that century most lawyers continued to get their education through apprenticeship and self-study. In the university law schools, lectures by legal practitioners on such topics as evidence, equity, contracts, and wills were the standard pedagogical style until the last part of the century.

In 1870, Christopher Columbus Langdell was appointed dean of the Harvard Law School (Kimball 2009; Sutherland 1967). Langdell had been somewhat unsuccessful as a practitioner but was highly regarded as a legal analyst. He viewed law as a science, best learned by having students read appellate case opinions and then analyze the principles that governed, or should have governed, the outcome. Despite some initial resistance, this **case method** of legal education approach to law became dominant over the next century or so. Texts increasingly took the form of collections of case opinions, with commentary. The case method is still widely used and both defended and criticized (Jakab 2007).

The so-called **Socratic method** was Langdell's other influential—although controversial—contribution to legal education (Kimball 2009; LaPiana 1995; Rhode 2001). The essence of this method involves a dialogue between professor and student, with the professor directing probing questions about case opinions at students; the process is intended to sharpen the students' ability to identify core principles and refine their understanding of legal reasoning. It continues to be debated whether this method succeeds in teaching students to "think like a lawyer" and be fast on their feet in legal contests or is a means of terrorizing and humiliating students with reasoning skills irrelevant to much of the work they will be doing.

Harvard Law Professor Lloyd Weinreb (2005) claims that the use of analogy is fundamental to—and in certain respects distinctive to—legal reasoning. Richard Schauer (2009) questions whether there really is such as thing as legal reasoning and, if so, whether it is something good.

Throughout the twentieth century, the completion of law school, with a course of study of more than 3 years, has been the conventional means of acquiring a legal education and becoming a lawyer. A small number of states allow individuals who have not attended or have dropped out of law school to take the bar examination if they have apprenticed in a law office (Associated Press 2005). The state of New Hampshire now allows law students to obtain admission to the bar by demonstrating court skills in lieu of passing a traditional bar exam (Mangan 2008). The elite law schools (e.g., Harvard) and the organized ABA cooperated in developing standards for admissions, curriculum, and entry into practice (Stevens 1983). The 3-year curriculum became standard in law schools in the twentieth century. There is an old adage that "first year they scare you to death, second year they work you to death, and third year they bore you to death" (Kahlenberg 1992, p. 159) (*see* Box 7.5). The standard of 3 years for law school has been questioned, with some law schools (e.g., Northwestern University School of Law) making possible the acquisition of a law degree in 2 years.

Most law schools publish a law review, and some law schools publish several reviews. Law reviews are journals originally established at law schools to provide students with training in legal writing; today they publish law-related scholarship varying greatly in style and focus. Altogether, some 425 law reviews are published in America (Glendon 1994, p. 205).

BOX 7.5   HARVARD LAW SCHOOL'S NEW
CURRICULUM

In 2006, Harvard Law School undertook a major overhaul of its curriculum—remarkably enough, the first such transformation in more than a hundred years—to better prepare its students for legal practice in the twenty-first century (McArdle 2008; Saenz 2006). Going back to the late nineteenth century, Harvard has played a central role in shaping legal education. The current curriculum revision was spearheaded by the law school's dean, Elena Kagan, now an associate justice of the U.S. Supreme Court. From the fall of 2008 on, Harvard Law students have been required to take a course on legislation and regulation and one on international or comparative law. After the first year, students can opt to organize their program of study in these areas: Law & Government; Law & Business; International and Comparative Law; Law, Science & Technology; and Law & Social Reform. Both the interdisciplinary and the clinical dimension of the law school experience are emphasized in this new curriculum, with students being allowed to cross-register for courses taught outside the law school. Problem-solving skills get more attention in this curriculum, with less emphasis on such traditional courses as Contracts and Torts (Harvard Law Bulletin 2010b). The new international law requirement recognizes the increasingly transnational character of law (Zeder 2008). "International law" now transcends relations between nations and encompasses international business; cross-border crime; environmental, labor, and immigration issues; and human rights.

Historically, law students with the best grades received prestigious appointments as law review editors, although in the more recent era writing samples and affirmative action criteria have also played a role in these appointments.

RECENT CHANGES

From the 1960s on, some significant changes have occurred in legal education (McKay 1985; Morrissey 2006). As the applicant pool increased dramatically, existing law schools expanded and new law schools opened; law schools became more selective in accepting applicants; women (and to a lesser degree, people of color), who had been historically excluded or admitted in small numbers, flocked to law schools; and school accreditation standards were tightened.

Despite considerable initiatives in the recent era to increase minority enrollments at American law schools, by the end of the first decade of the twenty-first century, they were declining (Lewin 2010; The National Jurist 2008). Historically, African-American and Hispanic students did less well than White students on standardized tests such as the Law School Admission Test (L.S.A.T.); these scores had been improving, but minority students were still far more likely to be denied law school admission than White students. In one controversial interpretation, affirmative action programs have actually harmed African-American law students because it resulted in their being admitted to law schools where the program was too difficult for them, and they ended up dropping out in large numbers (Liptak 2005). Altogether, minorities are under-represented among new lawyers.

Law schools in the recent era have in some respects improved with new buildings, cutting edge technology, smaller teacher–student ratios, and more scholarly, productive faculty members (Morrissey 2006). But on the other side of these positive developments, they have contributed to the escalating cost of a law school education. Law school applications have periodically experienced upsurges of applications. An upsurge in the early 1990s, for example, was attributed at least in part to the influence of a popular television show, L.A. Law, which offered a glamorous and exciting image of legal practice (Flood 1994; Margolick 1990). Law school applications declined in the 1990s, then began to rise again early in the twenty-first century, but declined toward the end of the first decade (Glater 2001a; Williams 2010). Law schools become more attractive in a declining economy, as business degrees become somewhat less appealing. But the cycles of law school applications are also affected by perceptions of demands for lawyers and perhaps by the evolving image of the legal profession in the popular culture.

CRITIQUES OF LEGAL EDUCATION

Legal education has been criticized on many grounds (Kissam 2003; Shaffer and Redmount 1977). Derek Bok (1983), a former president of Harvard University and previously a professor and dean of the Harvard Law School, complained, in a widely cited speech, that too many of the best and brightest students were going to law school to prepare themselves for careers engaging in expensive litigation on behalf of privileged clients instead of pursuing careers in such fields as science and engineering, focusing on curing diseases, and designing better products. Law Professor Roger Cramton (1978) has written of the "ordinary religion of the law school classroom" as including the following dogma: "a moral relativism tending toward nihilism, a pragmatism tending toward an amoral instrumentalism, a realism tending toward cynicism, an individualism tending toward atomism, and a faith in reason and democratic processes tending toward mere credulity and idolatry."

The Socratic approach, as suggested earlier, has been criticized as autocratic, demeaning, male-dominated, and irrelevant to much of legal practice. A best-selling account of the first year at Harvard Law, Scott Turow's (1977) *One L* documents how law school education seems to transform people, displacing appropriate emotional responses and ethical concerns with logical reasoning and strategic thinking. James Elkins (1979, p. 143), who has written extensively on legal education and legal ethics, calls attention to "the tragedy of a legal education which successfully indoctrinates students into 'thinking like a lawyer' but stifles idealism, social consciousness and creativity." For Philip Kissam (2003), law school emphasizes simplistic and superficial interpretive and writing skills and promotes a conservative outlook. For Peter d'Errico (1975), law school fosters the pathology of legalism and teaches students to seek and use power as opposed to truth and justice. For Duncan Kennedy (1983/2001), law school reinforces the hierarchies that divide society into unequal strata, and the elite law schools direct students to careers representing the rich and the powerful. For Susan Sturm and Lani Guinier (2003), legal education is complicit in reinforcing racist images. For Deborah Rhode (2003), the law school curriculum suffers from a gender bias. For Douglas Litowitz (2006), law school is traumatic, not inspiring, and tends to subvert the social conscience of law students (*see* Box 7.6).

Quite a number of studies have documented a turning away from idealism among law students (Erlanger et al. 1996; Granfield 1992; Stover 1989). Most of the students who enter law school expressing an interest in pursuing a career in public interest law (here defined as representation of the poor and powerless or the protection of consumers and citizens) have abandoned that interest by the end of their law school years. For graduates of elite law schools, the line of least resistance is to pursue elite private sector jobs, and they adopt various rationalizations for doing so, as opposed to, for example, pursuing public interest jobs (Schleef 2006).

BOX 7.6 PRESIDENT BARACK OBAMA AS LAW STUDENT AND LAW PROFESSOR

President Barack Obama has a degree from Harvard Law School, where he was the elected the first African-American president of its law review, and he taught constitutional law at the University of Chicago Law School (Larsen 2009; Stern 2008). As a law student, President Obama was remembered more as a mediator and conciliator rather than someone who took sides in ideological disputes. He impressed his professors for his mastery of details and insistence on working through all aspects of a decision before arriving at a conclusion (Stern 2008). Obama could certainly have obtained a lucrative position as a corporate lawyer but chose instead to move to Chicago, where he worked as a community organizer, joined a small law firm, and quite soon ran for office as a state legislator. He also taught law part-time. President Obama's law teaching focused on issues of rights, race, and gender (Kantor 2008, 2009). Specific topics of courses he taught included due process and equal protection, voting rights, and election law. As a law professor, he was remembered for focusing on the complicated dimensions of laws and unintended consequences of laws. He was skeptical of court-led efforts at social change and was in that sense a minimalist; he was interested in real-world consequences of laws and was in that sense a pragmatist; he was interested in how society distributes power and was in that sense a structuralist. Questions he asked students focused on consequences: "What would happen if a mother's welfare grant did not increase with the birth of additional children? As a state legislator, how much could he be influenced by a donor's contribution?" President Obama as a law professor seemed disdainful of formalism, or the idea that law is decided independent of the social and political context. Although as a politician and president Obama must sometimes take stances and approaches different from those he adopted as a law professor, clearly his professional experience with law influenced him profoundly.

Some new laws as well as loan repayment programs have facilitated opportunities for law school graduates to pursue public interest jobs (Weyenberg 2008). Quite a large number of law schools have adopted programs to encourage pursuit of public interest law careers. But according to one recent study, law school debt is not a major factor in why more law students do not pursue public service jobs (McGill 2006). Rather, the prestige of private sector corporate positions and the relatively limited number of public service law jobs are more important factors. In 2005, in the interest of encouraging a higher percentage of its law students to consider pursuing public service careers, Harvard Law School offered tuition breaks to students willing to make a commitment to such careers (Glater 2005). At least some law graduates will pursue public service careers when lucrative private sector law jobs are less available. Early in the twenty-first century, in response to this situation, the Harvard Law School was requiring students to donate 40 hours of legal work in addition to its other incentives for students to go into public service and related work (Glater 2001a). The best students disproportionately go to work for elite law firms that represent large corporations and wealthy individuals. Although it is not entirely clear how much of the shift away from public interest work can be attributed to the law school experience—pressure to pay off law school loans surely plays a role in determining career choices—there is at a minimum little reason to believe that this experience vigorously promotes idealism and public interest concerns.

Law schools have somewhat different missions, adapting their curricula to the types of legal practices their students are likely to undertake (McGill 2003). But legal education overall continues to contend with the basic tension between promoting an intellectual understanding of and critical thinking toward legal issues and the practical objective of preparing students to obtain jobs and function as working lawyers. Much of daily legal practice involves negotiation as opposed to analysis of legal opinions, but the former skill was little emphasized in the traditional law school curriculum. However, in the recent era, many alternatives to doctrinal analysis and the Socratic method have been introduced.

Clinical (hands-on) practice, role-playing, moot court, negotiating skills, computer-aided instruction, and the like receive more emphasis. Lawrence Friedman has called for replacing the present curriculum with one that is half clinical training and half training in such disciplines as history, sociology, economics, philosophy, and comparative law (Margolick 1983, p. 30). In other words, law students would spend half their time learning to be lawyers and half their time being educated. In the recent era, clinical law programs have become increasingly common in law schools (Willis and Barlyn 2007). These programs attempt to provide students with hands-on experience with legal practice and were in part established in response to the perception that legal education placed too much emphasis on teaching students to think analytically about law or some area of legal doctrine. The Harvard School of Law now has at least 15 clinical law programs, including The Negotiation and Mediation Clinic, The Cyberlaw Clinic, the Child Advocacy Program, the Criminal Prosecution Clinic, the Environmental Law and Policy Clinic, the Immigration and Refugee Clinic, the Sports Clinic, and the War Crimes Prosecution Clinic (Harvard Law Bulletin 2008). The University of San Francisco School of Law has an Investor Justice Clinic where students attempt to assist investors who have lost money as a consequence of unauthorized or imprudent trades by their stockbrokers (Mangan 2009). Clinical law program experiences should be both educational and intrinsically rewarding for law students who participate in them. A *Clinical Law Review* out of the NYU School of Law focuses on clinical law issues.

Law schools have traditionally been resistant to curricular reform. A Vanderbilt University law dean complains that law schools teach students to think like lawyers: "1870s lawyers" (Mangan 2008b). A Carnegie Foundation report in 2007 identified many limitations of the existing law school curriculum, including too little training to practice law (Schmidt 2009). At least some law schools have adopted major curriculum reforms (*see* Box 7.5).

Stanford University's law school has adopted a more interdisciplinary focus, along with more clinical law courses. Mock court experiences and the use of games and simulations have been promoted (Mangan 2008c; Maharg 2007). Such curriculum changes can be found at other law schools as well. Some law schools have promoted specialized concentrations— for example, on environmental law or intellectual property law (Schmidt 2009). But some commentators question whether these programs detract from a broad legal education and really provide an advantage in the legal job market.

One commentator argues that in an increasingly globalized world, and one where foreign clients are a significant part of the clientele of American law firms, the teaching of foreign law needs to be more fully incorporated into the American law school curriculum (Fontana 2006). Law students have to be educated to be able to function in different systems of law (Lebel-Grenier 2006; Strauss 2006). American legal education has for some time been "exported" to other countries around the world, when natives of those countries either study in American law schools and return home or American law schools influence law schools in other countries (Moliterno 2008).

In the wake of the economic recession at the end of the first decade of the twenty-first century, a law student argued that law schools were obliged to provide more information about career prospects for their graduates and take more steps to assist law students with their debt, in addition to adopting a greater focus on teaching practical skills and hiring more legal practitioners as adjunct faculty (Thies 2010). By 2009, even graduates of elite law schools were contending with uncertain job prospects, along with high debt (as high as $200,000) incurred to acquire their law school education (Shih 2009). Elite law school graduates were now more likely to consider government and public interest law jobs, although even these were less available than formerly. Harvard University Law Professor David Wilkins, while acknowledging the challenging current circumstances confronting law school graduates, anticipates new opportunities from experimentation and innovation in the organization of law firms, from broader adoption of government regulations, and from expanding globalization (Harvard Law Bulletin 2010). Law school students would have to be adaptable and creative to contend with new challenges.

Early in the twenty-first century, leading law schools such as New York University (NYU) and Yale were adopting an increasingly globalized and international approach (Bollag 2001; Johns and Freeland 2007). In 2003 the new dean of the Yale Law School, Harold Hongju Koh, noted that just as law schools late in the nineteenth century shifted attention from state to national law, now law schools must shift more attention from national to international law (Santora 2003b). "Global law teaching" has become fashionable in law schools (Valcke 2004). Law students must be prepared to function in a globalized world.

THE CRITIQUE OF THE LEGAL PROFESSION

The image of the legal profession in American life is remarkably contradictory. On the one hand, some of the most venerated heroes in American history have been lawyers, including Thomas Jefferson and Abraham Lincoln among presidents, John Marshall and Oliver Wendell Holmes, Jr. among Supreme Court justices, Daniel Webster and Sam Ervin, Jr. among statesmen, and Clarence Darrow and Ralph Nader among lawyers for the people. The legal profession in many respects is viewed as a prestigious occupation; many parents have encouraged their children to pursue legal careers, and large numbers apply annually for admission to law school. Lawyers have not infrequently been portrayed heroically in the media, whether as crusading reformers or courageous advocates on behalf of the wrongfully accused. That lawyers are so often elected to high office cannot be reconciled with the notion of a uniformly negative image of lawyers.

On the other hand, an enduring tradition that reviles lawyers and is critical of them is also part of the American cultural heritage (*see* Box 7.7). Relatively high levels of hostility are directed toward lawyers in America, and confidence in their integrity has been relatively low. Lawyers are commonly accused of dishonesty, amorality, greed, and incompetence; the claim is made that there are too many of them and that they are responsible for an excess of litigation (Black and Rothman 1998; Crier 2003; Re 1994). In the recent era, a number of presidents (e.g., Carter, Reagan, and both Presidents Bush) have considered it politically advantageous to attack lawyers on various grounds (for promoting unequal justice; for stifling economic growth; for initiating frivolous lawsuits) (Oppel and Justice 2004). A Chief Justice of the Supreme Court during the modern era, Warren Burger, claimed that about half of all lawyers were fundamentally incompetent (Footlick 1978, p. 98). A judge on the U.S. Court of Appeals, Laurence Silberman (1998), expressed concern that excessive lawyering harms both politics and the economy. A retired justice of the California Court of Appeals,

BOX 7.7 LOWERING THE BAR: LAWYER JOKES

Did you hear about the post office having to cancel its commemorative issue honoring lawyers? It seems that it was too confusing—people didn't know which side of the stamp to spit on. (p. 198)

A doctor and a lawyer in two cars collided on a country road. The lawyer, seeing that the doctor was shaken up, helped him from the car and offered him a drink from his hip flask. The doctor accepted and handed the flask back to the lawyer, who closed it and put it away. "Aren't you going to have a drink yourself?" asked the doctor. "Sure, after the police leave," replied the attorney. (p. 160)

[A lawyer explaining his fees to his client] "If you want justice, it's two hundred dollars an hour. Obstruction of justice runs a bit more." (p. 238)

A businessman was involved in a lawsuit that dragged on for years. One afternoon he told his attorney, "Frankly, I'm getting tired of all this litigation." The lawyer replied, "Nonsense. I propose to fight this case down to your last nickel." (p. 133)

A man went to see a lawyer and asked what his least expensive fee was. The lawyer replied, "$50 for three questions." Stunned, the man asked, "Isn't that a lot of money for three questions?" "Yes," the lawyer said. "What is your final question?" (pp. 85–86)

Did you hear the good news and the bad news? The good news is that a bus load of lawyers just ran off the cliff. The bad news is that there were three empty seats on the bus. (p. 213)

Lawyers—but especially American lawyers—have long been a special target of jokes, perhaps reflecting the profoundly conflicting perceptions of and feelings about lawyers, a strong dependence on them mixed with formidable resentment. Marc Galanter (2005), a University of Wisconsin emeritus law professor and leading student of the legal profession, has produced the most comprehensive study of lawyer jokes: *Lowering the Bar: Lawyer Jokes and Legal Culture* (Abel 2006; Tamanaha 2005). Lawyers also seem to be an easy—and not politically incorrect—target of many forms of citizen anger. Although there is a long tradition of lawyer jokes, Galanter found that both the quantity and nastiness of such jokes had increased since the early 1980s, perhaps as a reflection of growing public anxiety about and hostility toward civil litigation and many other law-related developments. Galanter suggests that we can learn much about cultural attitudes toward law and lawyers by studying jokes about lawyers.

Macklin Fleming (1997), claimed that contemporary legal practice was too much driven, with pernicious consequences, by an obsession with money. A dean of the Yale Law School, Anthony Kronman (1993), claimed that the profession has lost sight of an earlier ideal of a lawyer-statesman. A law professor and leading student of the legal profession, Richard Abel (1986) has argued that the American legal profession's practices are shaped by, and reflect, capitalist inequality. A distinguished lawyer (and corporate CEO), Sol Linowitz (1994) claimed that lawyers have lost their independence and are too beholden to the marketplace. A former district attorney and judge, Catherine Crier (2003), has blamed lawyers for a wave of frivolous lawsuits causing great harm to our society. In *The Destruction of Young Lawyers*, Douglas Litowitz (2006), himself a lawyer and law professor, set forth a fairly comprehensive critique of the legal profession, including the claims that young lawyers are often unhappy; the bar exam is a pointless ritual; law firm associates are alienated and exploited; law firms engage in much unproductive activity, often promoting injustice, not justice; and technology in the law office creates more burdens for lawyers and the legal system than it resolves. Young people contemplating applying to law school and becoming lawyers could usefully expose themselves to Litowitz's "brief" against law school and a legal career, as a means of testing the depths of their own commitment and to minimize the chances of having illusions about what they are facing. Clearly, an internal critique of the legal profession is quite pervasive.

With the great growth in the size of the legal profession, it has become fiercely competitive, and the suspicion of overlawyering (lawyers generating unnecessary work and

BOX 7.8   YOUNG LAWYERS SUE BAR EXAM PREP COMPANY

A law degree from an accredited law school is not sufficient to qualify someone to become a lawyer. A bar exam must also be passed. It is somewhat paradoxical that 3 years of law school education does not specifically prepare someone to pass the bar exam. Many law students, accordingly, enroll in a bar prep course, paying a private company a significant fee to do so. The bar prep course typically involves an intensive program of 2 months of 5-day-a-week (3- to 4-hour) classes. In 2005, law students filed a class action lawsuit against a company, BAR/BRI, which is the largest bar exam prep enterprise (Glater 2007a). The basic claim against this company was that it had achieved an illegal monopoly in providing preparation for the bar exam and was overcharging its customers by some $1,000. In 2007, a settlement of the case included a payment of $49 million by the company, with a payout of approximately $125 to each of the plaintiffs in the class action lawsuits. Many of these plaintiffs were angry about this settlement.

unsupported billing) frequently arises. Legal costs in the contemporary era rose more rapidly than the rate of inflation, and tens of billions of dollars are annually expended on legal bills. Furthermore, tens of thousands of complaints against lawyers are filed annually on a national level, and legal malpractice cases have increased. Calls for reforms are commonplace. Recommended reforms would make legal representation available to the poor and more affordable to other members of society, take various measures to discourage needless litigation, create more alternatives to resolving disputes not dependent on lawyers, and would impose more oversight on unethical or exploitative practices of lawyers. Some commentators express concern over the continuing under-representation of minorities among lawyers, and they contend that steps supposedly taken to enhance the "quality" of lawyers end up discriminating against minority law students.

THE LEGAL PROFESSION IN THE TWENTY-FIRST CENTURY

It seems unavoidable that the legal profession will continue to play a central role in American life in the twenty-first century. However, some questions concerning the future of the profession are unsettled. Will it continue to grow and expand exponentially, as it did in the final decades of the twentieth century? Will the massive movement of women into the legal profession—and, to a lesser extent, the movement of minorities—fundamentally transform the character of the profession, or is it women and minorities who will be transformed? Will the changes in the market for legal services that occurred during the latter part of the twentieth century continue to transform the profession, with the virtual disappearance of solo practitioners and the continuing growth of law mega firms, legal clinics, and public sector lawyers? The massive expansion of information technology, in conjunction with forces promoting rational, economically efficient use of resources, is sure to influence legal practice in many ways. In part because of unsustainable economic pressures on law students, it is very possible that the far less costly option of an online law education will become increasingly attractive (Morrissey 2006). An explosion of online law-related blogs was transforming the way lawyers were communicating about issues and concerns in their field (Glater 2005). Richard Susskind (2009) argues that new communication technologies are transforming the nature of legal services, although the legal profession has been slow to adapt to these new technologies. Many forms of traditional legal work today are being standardized and computerized. Susskind predicts that as the expectations of legal clients change, lawyers will have to offer a broader range of new kinds of services to clients if they are to survive. The "outsourcing" of legal work to "offshore" legal service centers (e.g., based in India) was one growing trend of the current period (Barlyn 2008; Daly and Silver 2007). Law firm clients and law firms themselves could save large sums of money by having routine legal research and "scut work" performed by offshore lawyers (e.g., paying $60 an hour as opposed to $400 an hour). But such outsourcing also generates a range of ethical concerns, especially because offshore lawyers are not necessarily bound by U.S. restrictions relating to confidentiality and conflicts of interest. In one scenario, those who need legal services will increasingly turn to the Internet and will seek fast, expert, inexpensive legal advice from **electronic lawyers**, which could potentially decimate traditional legal practice (Gordon 2002, p. 329; Wall and Johnstone 1997). Perhaps the most fundamental question about the future of the legal profession is this: Will lawyers continue to be aligned principally with the forces of power and privilege, or will they become associated increasingly with challenges to inequality and injustice?

KEY TERMS AND CONCEPTS

adversarial ethic	corporate lawyers	power of attorney
ambulance chasers	country lawyers	pro bono
American Bar Association (ABA)	courtroom workgroup	professional responsibility course
barristers	disbarment	public defenders
case method of legal education	electronic lawyers	rainmakers
cause lawyering	Inns of Court	Socratic method
commercial/entrepreneurial style of lawyering	*Juris Prudentes*	solicitors
contingency fees	lawyer-client confidentiality principle	solo practitioners
	overlawyering	traditional style of lawyering

DISCUSSION QUESTIONS

1. Should pro bono work be required of all lawyers, whether they are in a firm or solo practitioners? What effect might such work have on society if all lawyers did even a small amount?
2. Discuss the dangers involved when corporate lawyers attempt to protect the interests of their corporate clients. How do they lose sight of what it means to be a lawyer when they settle cases confidentially that the public should know about?
3. Why are some people apprehensive about hiring a female lawyer? What can women contribute to the legal world that men cannot? Do you think women tend to adapt to the "macho" culture or transform it?
4. How important is it to have "professional responsibility" courses in law school? Are they effective? Do you agree with the decision made by the New York State Bar Association in the *Garrow* case that his lawyer, Frank Armani, was acting in the best interest of his client? Is it your impression that Lynne Stewart (*see* Box 7.4) was appropriately convicted for actions impermissible for a lawyer?
5. Will it ever be realistic to have a world of "electronic lawyers"? How do you see the legal profession in the twenty-first century? What is it that motivates most lawyers who practice law today? Will this change?

CHAPTER 8

LEGAL INSTITUTIONS AND PROCESSES: AN OVERVIEW

Over the course of time, human beings have developed legal institutions to formally administer the law. A legal institution is a system with a patterned set of procedures and practices addressing matters of law. As societies become increasingly complex, different types of legal institutions evolve to address specific types of disputes or particular classes of people. This chapter identifies some key elements of major systems of justice within our society, with special emphasis on their social dimensions. The review that follows is a highly selective discussion, and only passing reference is made to some of the countless specific features of these systems. Its aim is to provide some sense of the basic nature of these co-existing systems of justice and some of the principal issues confronting them. The chapter looks at the following legal systems: criminal justice, juvenile justice, civil justice, regulatory justice, military justice, and informal justice. Each of the different systems of justice claims to address a particular class of offenses or disputes effectively and fairly.

LAW AND THE CRIMINAL JUSTICE SYSTEM

The branch of law and justice most visible to the general public is that pertaining to crime. The criminal justice system is widely featured in the media, although many aspects of its operation are represented in a distorted manner (Carrabine 2008; Lenz 2003; Rapping 2003). The decisions made by the criminal justice system are especially dramatic, sometimes involving questions literally of life and death.

In the recent era, many Americans have been frustrated and disappointed with the perceived failure of the criminal justice system to respond effectively to the crime problem (Gest 2001; Ismaili 2011). At the same time, some Americans—typically holding liberal or progressive ideas—have been concerned with ensuring that full-fledged due process is accorded all those accused of lawbreaking (*see* Box 8.1). A basic tension exists, then, between crime control as the primary objective of the criminal justice system and respect for due process as the primary obligation of the criminal justice system (Zalman 2011). In addition, some

BOX 8.1   THE CRIME DECLINE AND THE
CRIMINAL JUSTICE SYSTEM

The quite dramatic decline in conventional crime in the United States since the mid-1990s has been much analyzed and discussed; a confluence of factors seems to have contributed to this decline, including factors relating to demographics (population patterns), the state of the economy, policing practices, and mass imprisonment—but it has proven difficult to demonstrate the relative impact of the different factors (Barker 2010). Broader

changes in the American culture and social fabric may well have played a role. Although crime in New York City has declined dramatically (overall, by some 40%) since 2001, by 2010 some forms of violent crime (including homicide) were on the rise (Rivera and Baker 2010). Jonathan Simon (2007) argues that over a period of decades since the late 1960s, political leaders have exploited American fear of crime, which has led to broader state power and a more punitive criminal justice system without necessarily making Americans safer.

tension exists between other objectives of the criminal justice system, including avenging wrongdoing and reaffirming society's basic moral commitments; being fair and imposing just deserts on lawbreakers; not doing more harm than good by intervening in the lives of minor offenders; rehabilitating criminals and restoring them to society as constructive citizens; and fostering reconciliation between offenders and victims. Western criminal justice systems have become increasingly oriented toward extending control and regulation and privileging retribution and incapacitation over rehabilitation and reconciliations (Currie 2010; McSherry, North, and Bronitt 2008). There are many active controversies in criminal justice, including the broad issue of whether the criminal justice system should emphasize aggressive policing and punishment or employ preventive and reconciliative strategies, which are more effective and more just (Frost et al. 2010; McLaughlin et al. 2003). Such controversies are enduring.

The origins of a criminal justice system go far back in history, to a time when a certain class of harmful acts came to be defined as violations of the king's peace, and the state began to process such offenses on behalf of the king (Gatrell, Lenham, and Parker 1980). Over time, a system evolved with an enforcement component (policing), an adjudicative component (the courts), and a correctional component (prisons), with the prosecutorial office sometimes regarded as a fourth branch of criminal justice (Friedman 1993). One of the distinctive features of the American criminal justice "system" is its fragmented character and absence of centralized control, which means it is not a coordinated, integrated system (Jacob 1996, p. 33). Criminal justice agencies and courts may be federal, state, or local; in a parallel vein, criminal law is formulated by Congress, state legislatures, and (regarding offenses) local councils. Accordingly, policy, practices, and political pressures vary considerably across all these lines.

DEFINING CRIME

The basic elements of a legal conception of crime include the commission of a forbidden act (or, in certain circumstances, the failure to act) within a particular jurisdiction and criminal intent (i.e., evil intent, criminal purpose, or knowledge of the wrongfulness of the conduct).

Crimes vary greatly in terms of their seriousness and identifiable consequences. The most basic distinction has been between felonies and misdemeanors (although treason [aiding and abetting the enemy] and offenses [minor forms of lawbreaking such as jay-walking] are also separate categories). **Felonies** are serious crimes, punishable by up to life in prison or, in some cases, by death; conviction of a felony may entail loss of certain basic rights as a citizen. **Misdemeanors** are less serious offenses, typically punishable by a fine or no more than a year in jail; conviction of a misdemeanor does not result in a loss of citizenship rights.

THE POLICE

For many people, the police are "the law." The police are regarded as standing between a society based on law and order and a society based on crime and chaos. The police themselves, confronting the difficult—if not impossible—challenge of effectively controlling crime, often define their own mission in moral terms, as a battle of good versus evil (Brown 2011; Herbert 1996). Conversely, a long tradition of suspicion of or outright hostility toward the police is also part of the American experience: on the frontier, in the early ethnic neighborhoods of new immigrants settled in big cities, among racial minorities generally, and among radicals and dissidents. Some see the police as agents of the people, primarily serving the needs of the community; others say that the police emerged in complex, modern societies as instruments of social control, created by and acting principally on behalf of the dominant classes (Robinson 2002; Schmalleger and Worrall 2010). A number of different conceptions of the proper primary role of the police can be identified (Wilson 1968). The media generally have emphasized the **crime-fighter** role, with the police aggressively pursuing major offenders. A second role conception is **law enforcer**, with police enforcing all laws—not just those pertaining to major crimes—in an even-handed manner. A third role model is **watchman**, with the police basically maintaining a presence in the community in the interest of preserving order and deterring crime. Finally, a fourth conception stresses the notion of the police as **providers of social services**. Of course, in real life the police tend to play a mixture of roles, but the perceived primacy of one or the other of these role conceptions varies, with individual police officers themselves holding different views.

Discretionary Decision Making

The police have considerable discretion, or choice, in their job-related decision making (Riksheim and Chermak 1993; Scaramella, Cox and McCamey 2011). Many factors—situational, attitudinal, and administrative (relating to department policy and structure)—affect their decision making. Research suggests that situational factors are especially influential in the arrest decision but that administrative factors are determinate for other kinds of decisions (Worden 1989). The police often use their discretion in positive ways, to enforce law more efficiently (disregarding minor, inconsequential violations of the law) and to mitigate the effects of harsh or unreasonable laws (by refusing to enforce them). The police, in many cases, provide useful services to citizens beyond what is required of them by their formal duties.

The worst abuses of police discretionary decision making might be summarized this way: **bribery, bigotry**, and **brutality**. First, throughout their history the police have too often been bribed (or corrupted), especially in relation to victimless crime laws (e.g., gambling, prostitution, drugs) (Kleinig 1996). This persistent corruption seems to reflect unusual opportunities for police to generate bribes, the existence of ineffective or unpopular laws, and the discrepancy between the police officer's considerable situational power and his or her income. Second, throughout their history many police officers have been bigoted and have enforced the law in a biased manner. In the American experience, there is a long (and ugly) history of predominantly White police officers treating African-Americans differently from White people (e.g., arresting them more readily) (Jones-Brown and King-Toler 2011). Among other consequences, such bigotry has promoted distrust of the police and has sometimes precipitated major race riots. Third, throughout their history the police have too often engaged in brutality (or the excessive use of force, beyond what was called for in the situation). Persons suspected of crimes have been beaten, sometimes as a means of extracting confessions from them. Police brutality, especially in conjunction with bigotry, has also contributed to hostility toward the police. Various types of reforms, guidelines, and internal or external investigations have attempted to address these extreme forms of abuse of police discretion.

TRENDS

The modern police force was established in the early part of the nineteenth century, but through much of that century and into the twentieth, police were often poorly educated, amoral, and unprofessional in their conduct (Schmalleger 2011; Walker 1980). Throughout the twentieth century a recurrent theme has been the need for more professional policing, and the push in this direction escalated in 1967 following the release of an influential presidential commission report calling for more educated police. A greater emphasis on higher education for the police followed, along with more sophisticated means of screening those unsuited for policing. During the 1960s the police also had to learn to live with the constraints imposed on them by a series of decisions by the U.S. Supreme Court under Chief Justice Warren; the most famous and controversial of these was the *Miranda* decision (1966), requiring the police to warn those accused of crimes of their rights. Although the U.S. Supreme Court has upheld the *Miranda* decision, it has compromised its reach, and police interrogation practices have often found ways around its constraints (Corsianos 2009; McInnis 2009).

In still another basic shift, beginning in the early 1970s, minorities and women were actively recruited for policing. The expanded representation of minorities and women on police forces has enhanced the confidence of minorities and women in the police, as both groups have in the past experienced abuses or mistreatment at the hands of White male police officers. Although minority and female police officers have continued to experience some forms of discrimination and disadvantages in terms of promotions, they clearly enhance the effectiveness of the police in many aspects of policing.

In the recent era some special emphasis has been placed on **community policing** (Clear and Dammer 2003; Weisburd and Braga 2006). The concept of community policing does

---

BOX 8.2 COMMUNITY NOTIFICATION LAWS

Community notification laws have now been adopted in some form in all 50 states and within federal law (Ayoub 2009). Contrary to a common impression, such laws are not entirely new and have seminal roots in registration laws going back to the nineteenth century or earlier. In the 1930s, Los Angeles, in response to a perceived influx of gangsters, adopted the first American registration laws. Wayne Logan (2009), in *Knowledge as Power: Criminal Registration and Community Notification Laws in America*, examines these laws and some of their unintended consequences quite comprehensively. In the recent era, registration laws applied to convicted sex offenders have received the most attention. In the highest profile case leading to the adoption of such laws, in 1994 a 7-year-old in New Jersey was lured to the home of a neighbor who was a convicted (but paroled) sex offender and was raped and murdered. "Megan's Law" was adopted in the wake of this horrendous crime, mandating that communities in New Jersey be notified when sex offenders were released into their midst. An earlier case in 1989 in Washington state, involving the abduction, rape, and mutilation of a 7-year-old boy, led to the adoption of an offender notification law in that state. The U. S. Supreme Court has upheld the constitutionality of such laws and denied that they are an impermissible form of punishment or a violation of due process rights. And the American public has been strongly supportive of these laws, perhaps understandably so in light of

what happened in the cases that gave rise to them. Today, then, some 600,000 people are on these registration lists. But the community notification laws have critics, especially focused on the unintended negative consequences of these laws. First, they may provide communities with a false sense of security, because in the overwhelming majority of cases (perhaps 95%) children are molested not by strangers but by people familiar to them: family members, friends, acquaintances, coaches or teachers, and other trusted parties. Obviously the lists don't include first-time offenders, and they do include some individuals who don't represent a significant threat, such as those charged with public urination. Contrary to a widespread perception, not all forms of sexual molestation are incurable conditions, and recidivism rates vary considerably between different classes of sexual offenders. Then the registration process persuades some offenders to go underground, where they cannot be monitored at all. As a practical matter, given the huge numbers, even those properly registered on the lists cannot generally be monitored. In some cases vigilantes have harassed, attacked, and, in a handful of cases, murdered registrants; families of registrants as well as individuals mistakenly placed on lists or confused with registrants have also been stigmatized and victimized. Although the sexual offender registration laws are highly unlikely to be repealed, for political reasons, it is important to be aware of their limitations and their possible dysfunctional dimensions.

---

not have a single meaning but generally refers to a de-emphasis on legalistic policing and arrest and more emphasis on building rapport with community members, crime prevention, and victim assistance, with greater deference to the will of the community itself (*see* Box 8.2). Some commentators say that the movement to community policing was driven by the need of the police to enhance their legitimacy, or the need to increase community support of the police (Crank 1994). However, community policing calls for new controls on police discretion, in the view of other commentators (Livingston 1997; Websdale 2001). Because community police tend to have fewer constraints imposed on them, some commentators expressed concern that these police would make more decisions reflecting personal predilections and racial biases rather than basing decisions on legalistic grounds. Following 9/11, the community policing model faced new challenges, with the shift of priorities to combating terrorism (Brown 2011; Oliver 2007). It was far from clear that the agenda of a newly established Homeland Security model was compatible with the community policing model.

Some emerging trends in policing have been identified (Schmalleger 2011; Wakefield 2003). First, a dramatic expansion of private policing has occurred, to the point where private police now outnumber public police in the United States and many other countries; also, there are more civilian support personnel for policing. Second, in addition to the wider adoption of community policing, the police have attempted to develop more efficient strategies for traditional crime fighting and order-maintenance functions. Third, police have been subjected to more oversight and supervision from various government and civilian entities, which many police officers resent. The basic challenge faced by policing in the future is to respond effectively to the public's ongoing fear of crime without at the same time compromising human rights or intensifying the existing inequalities between the circumstances of the rich and the poor. Following 9/11, police sought broad powers to engage in surveillance and monitor political activity (Flynn 2002; Lyon 2003). It remains to be seen whether policing practices over the long term have been fundamentally transformed.

THE COURTS

The adjudicative branch of government, or the courts, is the symbolic centerpiece of the American system of justice. A study of many different courts demonstrated that processing of cases and decision making is at least partly guided by the particular subculture (value system) of the court (Ostrom et al. 2007). The courts in the criminal justice system are formally organized to operate according to an adversary model, with a "contest" between the prosecution and the defense, but in fact the vast majority of cases are disposed of (in most large jurisdictions) with some form of negotiation, or **plea bargaining** (Fisher 2003; Schmalleger 2011). The image of a full-scale criminal trial is deeply embedded in Americans' collective consciousness because such trials—both real and dramatized—are featured in the media. But relative to the number of criminal cases in which a trial could occur, only a small percentage (10%, in most jurisdictions) actually go to trial (Jacob 1996, p. 42). When constraints are placed on plea bargaining, either the justice system must find a way to hold more trials or prosecute fewer cases.

The prosecutor and the defense attorney are typically portrayed as adversaries, but as some commentators point out, they are typically part of a **courtroom workgroup**, more often committed to the smooth, efficient functioning of the court than to the public or the defendant (Neubauer and Meinhold 2004; Eisenstein, Flemming, and Nardulli 1999). In the lower courts in particular, a form of **rough justice** is said to prevail, with mainly poor defendants hustled through the system with little real concern for their due process rights (Robertson 1974; Robinson 2002). The metaphor of the assembly line, then, has been applied to the operation of the courts. At every stage, the poor and minorities are at a disadvantage. As one classic example, middle-class and wealthy people accused of crimes—even serious crimes—rarely sit in jail awaiting trial for any significant period of time. Rather, they are able to get out on bail, even if the bail amount is high. Historically, however, accused individuals who are poor have often been unable to make even modest bail and have sat in jail for many months awaiting disposition of their case or trial. DNA and other forms of evidence have established that a not insignificant number of these defendants are wrongfully convicted (Westervelt and Humphrey 2001). Justice is far from equal (*see* Box 8.3).

BOX 8.3   PROBLEM-SOLVING COURTS

Problem-solving courts are a significant new development in our criminal justice system. These courts were first established as recently as 1989, but have now been established in all 50 states as well as many foreign countries (Eaton and Kaufman 2005; Marble and Worrall 2009; Nolan 2009). In traditional courts, judges preside over legal proceedings, may make determinations of who has won and who has lost, and impose sentences or damages. But in problem-solving courts, judges go beyond these functions to address chronic social problems and attempt to address ways to modify the future behavior of those appearing before them. In doing so, they typically work with a range of other agencies and entities. Such problem-solving courts have been established to address drug-related issues as well as domestic violence and mental health issues, with a potential to expand to other social problem areas—for example, DUI issues—in the future. The basic purpose of these courts is to recognize that many individuals charged with violations of the criminal law are in trouble because of substance abuse issues, mental health issues, or domestic discord issues, and if one hopes to minimize the chances of further violations of the law, then one must address these broader issues. Accordingly, these courts are especially focused on gathering as much information as possible, involving the community where appropriate, and applying a form of individualized justice that is oriented toward outcomes, including the needs of any victims in the case. Judges get special training for problem-solving court duty, often refer to those who appear before them as clients (not defendants), and may monitor the progress of these individuals for months or years after their appearance in court. Some critics of these courts, however, express concern over the broad discretion of the judges; they believe that principally White, middle class judges impose their values on people from different social circumstances and often end up imposing onerous and harsh conditions on them. If traditional legal rights are compromised by these courts, a critic wonders if they represent a return to an earlier inquisitorial form of justice.

Many defendants who go to trial opt for a **bench trial** before a judge, at least partly on the premise that they will face harsher consequences if convicted in a jury trial. This choice is always a gamble, as some research suggests that juries are more likely to acquit than are judges. Jury trials are not an option in most countries.

Trials are a high-profile dimension of our culture and both reflect and can also influence the larger culture within which they occur (Ferguson 2008; Umphrey 2008). Although Americans regard trial-by-jury as essential to a true democracy, and it is guaranteed by the Bill of Rights, trial by jury has also been criticized as unnecessary, wasteful, and incompetent. Some critics have remarked that juries are not even typically composed of peers of the defendant.

A substantial body of sociolegal research has explored many aspects of the jury as an institution, including the dynamics of its decision making (Vidmar and Hans 2007). Many factors—including attributes of both defendants and jurors themselves—have been found to bias jury decisions (*see* Box 8.4). The pervasive availability of Google and Twitter, accessible via iPhones and BlackBerrys, has now complicated the jury trial process, with jurors able to both access and send out information pertaining to a trial (Schwartz 2009a). A juror may undertake a Google search on a criminal defendant or access evidence excluded from the trial. Calls for a mistrial have occurred in some of these cases. But one recent survey of research on American juries concludes that on the whole they make sound decisions, almost always in agreement with that of the judge in the case (Vidmar and Hans 2007).

BOX 8.4   JURY NULLIFICATION

Juries sometimes vote their conscience (especially in political cases), even when that judgment is at odds with the evidence and the law. Such **jury nullification** is celebrated by some and criticized by others (Neubauer and Meinhold 2004, p. 417). Jury nullification has specifically been defended as a crucial instrument in protecting basic liberties (Lehman 1997); it has been criticized as the wrong answer to biases in the criminal justice system (Estrich 1998). Early in the twenty-first century, some states were moving toward extending a constitutional right to juries to engage in nullification, on the grounds that it empowers juries to arrive at just outcomes when some laws themselves may be unjust (Liptak 2002a). Both conservatives and liberals may support jury nullification, although on different grounds. Butler (1995) has made a provocative argument in favor of African-American jurors exercising jury nullification powers to counter the demonstrable bias against African-Americans built into the existing criminal justice system. For example, African-American jurors could refuse to vote for conviction in crack cocaine cases involving African-American defendants, on the grounds that the crime is victimless and a disproportionately high percentage of African-American defendants (relative to Whites in parallel cases) are imprisoned on such charges. In this view, if the likely harm from conviction outweighs any likely harm from acquittal, then the jury should acquit despite highly incriminating evidence.

Sentencing

If either a judge or jury finds a defendant guilty, a sentence must be imposed, typically by the judge. Here, too, a substantial body of sociolegal research has investigated the bases for this important decision (Mears 1998; Tata and Hutton 2002; von Hirsch and Ashworth 1992). Judges in the past had considerable discretion in sentencing, and, as one consequence, significant disparities in sentences were given offenders with similar records and attributes. Since the late 1970s, the federal system and many state systems have adopted **sentencing guidelines** as one controversial constraint on judicial discretion (Behre and Ifrah 2003; Uelmen 1992). Sentencing guidelines use a number of criteria, such as the seriousness of the offense itself, mitigating circumstances (e.g., not using a weapon), the degree of injury, and the past record of the offender, to specify a presumptive sentence for a particular offender. If judges choose to impose a sentence that departs from the guidelines, they are required to provide some written justification for doing so.

The introduction of sentencing guidelines in the United States has led to longer average prison sentences and has contributed to prison overcrowding (Tonry and Hatlestad 1997). Early in the twenty-first century, many state legislatures had concluded that uniformly harsh sentences for those convicted of serious crimes were not effective as a response to the crime problem and had created massively overcrowded prisons (von Zielbauer 2003). As a consequence, many states eliminated some mandatory sentences, facilitated treatment options, and in other ways attempted to reduce the size of prison populations. Sentencing guidelines have been criticized on many grounds, including the claim that they create new sentencing disparities and interfere with the judge's application of common sense to cases (Stith and Cabranes 1998). More specifically, some criminologists have criticized the harsh sentences of the recent guidelines era as out of proportion to the harm of the criminal conduct they address (McCoy 1997). Judges have typically resented and been frustrated by constraints placed on their decision making by sentencing guidelines (Clemetson 2007). Many judges argue that the best justice results if judges are entrusted with considerable leeway in imposing the most appropriate sentence in the case before them. In June 2004, the U.S. Supreme Court struck down sentencing guidelines used in Washington State (Greenhouse 2004e; Stith and Stuntz 2004). The proper balance between the judge and the jury in determining facts applied to sentences was at stake. Because many other states had similar guidelines, the future of the sentencing guidelines was also at stake.

Those who have been convicted of crimes in the American system have the option of appealing the decision to a higher court; if they are able to raise a significant constitutional issue, then the case may be appealed right up to the U.S. Supreme Court. Most appeals are based on an alleged violation of procedural due process rights. Although criminal conviction appeals have increased in the recent era and impose a considerable burden on appellate courts, they rarely result in calls for outright reversal of a conviction or a call for a retrial. Criminal case appellants who are able to secure the services of topflight attorneys willing to invest a significant amount of time in their cases are more likely to be successful on appeal.

Victims' Rights

In the earliest systems of justice, the victim of a crime was often at the center of the legal proceedings (Karmen 2010). In the Western system of criminal justice, however, the victim, over time, came to be pushed aside and had no real voice in the proceedings. Victims were called only as a witness to be questioned on certain particulars of the crime. Since the early 1970s, victims' rights advocacy groups have had some success in promoting legislation that extends to victims more rights (e.g., providing a victim's impact statement) and greater sensitivity (e.g., prohibiting defense attorneys in rape cases from questioning the victim of a rape on her past sexual history) (Doak 2008; Dubber 2002). Although support for crime victims might seem uncontroversial, some critics claim that these new rights end up seriously compromising the rights of those accused of crimes. For example, well-educated, articulate victims may be especially successful in persuading jurors to focus on emotional dimensions of their cases, and this can work against the interests of inarticulate, unsympathetic defendants being tried on circumstantial evidence.

THE CORRECTIONAL SYSTEM

The correctional system is the final basic component of the criminal justice system. Although prisons are the most conspicuous feature of the correctional system, a substantial majority of those declared guilty of criminal charges are not sent to prison but are fined, put on probation (under court supervision), or briefly jailed. Those sent to prison are disproportionately from disadvantaged classes and, in the United States, are disproportionately African-American (Clear, Cole, and Reisig 2011). The prison system has long been criticized as harming rather than rehabilitating most incarcerated offenders; nevertheless, in the recent era the prison population grew exponentially, in response to both increasing public and political demands to get tough with criminals and the requirements of the sentencing guidelines (Garland 2001). This punitive response toward crime was much more pronounced in the United States than in Europe (Gottschalk 2009; Melosi 2008). As a practical matter, the high rates of imprisonment were very costly and are being reconsidered for that reason alone (Butterfield 2003). Public attitudes toward punishment were evolving (Roberts and Hough 2002). And for different reasons, increasing numbers of both conservatives and liberals were challenging the "tough on crime" punitive approach (Liptak 2009h). These concerns ranged from excessive government power and the high costs of mass incarceration to the demonstrable injustices to the socially disadvantaged..

CONCLUSION

In a democratic society with a high crime rate, the criminal justice system inevitably confronts many challenges. The appropriate and inappropriate use of discretion at all stages of the criminal justice system is one major issue (Walker 1993). Ongoing evidence of various forms of racial and ethnic bias in the operation of this system is especially disturbing (Sampson and Lauritsen 1997). Social science theory and research can and should play an important role in shaping anticrime policies (Frost et al. 2010). In the course of the twenty-first century, this system is sure to face ongoing pressures to improve its effectiveness and efficiency without becoming intrusive in the lives of ordinary citizens and without compromising basic rights of these citizens.

LAW AND THE JUVENILE JUSTICE SYSTEM

The juvenile justice system, by specific design, tends to receive substantially less attention than the criminal justice system. Juvenile proceedings are supposed to take place behind closed doors, and to protect young offenders from the stigma of being labeled criminals, the names of juveniles accused of crimes are not supposed to appear in the news media. Nevertheless, juvenile justice itself has been an important societal preoccupation, and the juvenile justice system has been a target for criticism on various grounds.

Juveniles pose various challenges for a system of law. Traditionally, children were especially vulnerable before the law. On the one hand, they had no standing as plaintiffs in civil proceedings. Fathers, in particular, had almost unlimited control over other family members, including their children, whose legal status combined elements of noncitizen, slave, pet, and property. In the Massachusetts Bay Colony (in the mid-seventeenth century), a father could bring a "stubborn or rebellious son" of at least 16 years of age before a magistrate to be put to death (Beales 1985). Although this is certainly an extreme example, it shows how extraordinary parental control was over children's lives. Until the recent era the law extended little protection to children abused by their parents, and children have not generally had rights regarding the basic conditions of their lives. On the other hand, juveniles who committed violations of the law, if they were past the age of infancy (in the common law tradition, age 7 years), were not formally defined as different from adult offenders. Children could be burned alive, drowned, or hanged, although it was not the norm to subject them to such harsh sanctions. Nevertheless, as late as the early part of the nineteenth century, there are cases on record of children as young as age 8 or 9 years being hanged for petty crimes.

CHILDREN'S CHARACTER

Philosophical views of children have varied over the ages. One historian says that prior to the fifteenth century, children were seen principally as miniature adults (Aries 1962). Another historian, however, says that among Puritans, children and youths were clearly differentiated from adults (Beales 1985). In some eras and societies, children have been regarded as inherently sinful, in need of vigilance and stern discipline from the earliest ages. In others, they have been seen as innocents in need of protection from the corrupting influences of the world.

When children have come to the attention of the law, it has not always been obvious how they should be classified. Some children are clearly victims of neglect and abuse and need the protection of the law. Other children (especially those well into their teens) are clearly predators from whom society requires protection by law. Still other children (so-called **status offenders**) are viewed as engaged in behavior signaling that the law must take steps to protect them from themselves (e.g., running away from home; truancy; sexual promiscuity). In any number of cases, however, it is far from clear which of these categories is most appropriate for a particular child. Accordingly, considerable overlap may exist among the categories of neglected child, juvenile delinquent, and status offender.

Even when a child has clearly committed an offense that, if committed by an adult, would be regarded as a serious crime, the complicated metaphysical question of responsibility arises. In other words, at what age does a child become truly capable of understanding the consequences of his or her actions to the point that the child should be held responsible for committing actions in violation of the law? Such questions continue to be debated vigorously. Different states have adopted different ages for protecting juveniles from adult sanctions or processing them as adults. In a case where two high school buddies committed a heinous crime (e.g., the rape and murder of two young girls), one has faced life imprisonment and the other incarceration for no more than a few years, with release by age 21 years, because one was just over and the other just under the cutoff age for juvenile disposition. No easy solution to the ultimate arbitrariness of these kinds of distinctions exists.

ESTABLISHMENT OF JUVENILE COURTS

Throughout the course of the nineteenth century, various social reform movements (notably, the **child-saving movement**) called for recognizing that children were different from adults and so required different protections and procedures (Whitehead and Lab 2009). Although some initiatives for separate hearings and separate reformatories were adopted by the mid-nineteenth century, it was only in 1899 that a truly autonomous juvenile court was established in Chicago, Illinois. In the first quarter of the twentieth century, virtually all other American states established juvenile courts and a separate juvenile justice system.

The official rationale of the reformers who promoted a separate juvenile justice system was that children were fundamentally different from adults, and it was in their interest as well as that of society to help them—through close supervision and rehabilitative programs—rather than to make punishment the priority. Although some scholars largely accept this standard account and view the establishment of the juvenile court as a "child-saving" progressive reform, others have argued that it was actually motivated by growing fear of hordes of immigrant children flooding into American cities and the desire to exercise greater control over them (as well as other problem children) (Platt 1977). In still another interpretation, the juvenile court was established principally as a formalization of the general trend toward greater discretionary control over children (Rosenheim et al. 2002; Sutton 1985). In all likelihood, then, some mixture of motives and objectives was involved (Regoli, Hewitt, and DeLisi 2010; Willison, Mears, and Butts 2011).

In line with its paternalistic philosophy of the court acting in place of parents and for the best interest of the child, the juvenile justice system afforded juveniles brought before it few, if any, due process rights. Although the relative informality of the juvenile court proceedings may have benefited some of the juveniles brought before the court, it also resulted in other juveniles being remanded to juvenile correctional facilities on the basis of slender or nonexistent evidence. Furthermore, despite the claim that juvenile correctional facilities were supposed to rehabilitate juvenile offenders, these facilities typically had many punitive and stigmatizing attributes and were likely to be experienced as punishment by the juvenile inmates.

EXTENSION OF DUE PROCESS RIGHTS

During the Warren Court era of the 1960s, a series of U.S. Supreme Court decisions extended more formal rights to juveniles brought before the juvenile courts: *Kent v. U.S.* (1966) prohibited these courts from making procedurally arbitrary decisions; the landmark *In re Gault* (1967) established that juveniles were entitled to certain basic due process rights, such as notification of charges, protection against self-incrimination, the right to confront witnesses, and the right to have a written transcript of the proceedings; a third case, *In re Winship* (1970), established that the standard of proof beyond a reasonable doubt must be applied in cases where a juvenile faces incarceration in a locked facility.

Although broader due process rights have been extended to juveniles accused of violating the law, it does not follow that these rights are uniformly implemented in practice, and the overall operation of the juvenile courts continues to be considerably more informal than that of the adult criminal courts. Questions have been raised on whether juveniles have the maturity to participate in their own defense (Scott and Steinberg 2008). Although juveniles accused of crimes are expected to display remorse, a law professor questions the ability of courts to interpret such emotional states and the validity of remorse as a predictor of future behavior (Duncan 2002). Much evidence of bias in the operation of juvenile justice can certainly be identified (Rosenheim et al. 2002). A far higher percentage of male juveniles than females have always gotten into trouble with the law, but historically female juveniles were more likely than males to be processed by the juvenile justice system for sex-related behavior. In one view, then, the juvenile justice system has been a manifestation of male dominance and has been used against female juveniles to reinforce traditional role expectations for females (Alder 1984; Chesney-Lind 1978; Shelden 1998). Lower-class inner-city youths, especially African-Americans and other minorities, have also been disproportionately brought into the juvenile justice system; the misdeeds of middle-class suburban White youths have traditionally been more likely to be overlooked or disposed of with informal discretion (Chambliss 1973b; Sampson and Laub 1993). It appears, then, that juvenile justice processing has been applied most vigorously to those segments of the juvenile population viewed as most threatening to the influential White middle class. It may be, however, that lower class single-parent mothers may be more likely than middle class parents to turn to the juvenile courts when they find themselves unable to control their children.

CYCLES OF HARSHNESS AND LENIENCE

The juvenile justice system continues to endure conflicting demands: to protect and nurture wayward (and abused) children; to grant juveniles, as young citizens, due process rights; to protect society from harmful predators; and so on. The juvenile justice system appears to have undergone alternating cycles emphasizing either harshness or lenience (Bernard 1992). In the **punitive cycle** (associated with a more conservative political environment), the general public has become fearful over youth crime, especially when it takes the form of extreme violence, and has called for tough measures to incapacitate and punish juvenile offenders. Protection from juvenile predators is the priority here. But in a decision handed down in 2010, the U.S. Supreme Court (6/3) declared that juveniles who commit crimes that do not result in a death may not be sentenced to life in prison without parole (Liptak 2009g). In the **lenience cycle** (associated with a more liberal political environment), the general public has become disenchanted with punitive measures (which are viewed as largely ineffective) and disturbed by revelations of severe abuse of juveniles in correctional facilities. The long-term needs of juveniles themselves—and, by extension, society—is the priority here. Both the perceived ineffectiveness and the harmfulness of subjecting juveniles to juvenile justice system processing during this cycle call for "radical nonintervention," which means that many minor forms of juvenile deviance and misbehavior are tolerated and that justice system processing is reserved for serious juvenile predators (Schur 1973). Early in the twenty-first century, the juvenile justice system continued to have a strongly punitive dimension, and the most appropriate focus for these courts continued to be debated (Scott and Steinberg 2008). These developments can be attributed both to the more conservative political environment of this period and the public perception (fostered by the media) of an increase in especially gruesome and violent crimes by juveniles (*see* Box 8.5).

A century after the establishment of the first juvenile court in Chicago, controversy over the future of the juvenile justice system was vigorous (Springer and Roberts 2011; Rosenheim et al. 2002; Tanenhaus 2004). Those involved with juvenile justice were divided not only on the question of how far juveniles should be held morally and criminally responsible for their offenses but also on whether the juvenile courts should be abolished because they were both ineffective and unfair or should be retained because they were more responsive to the special circumstances of children (Scott and Steinberg 2008). The twentieth century witnessed the establishment of a full-fledged juvenile justice system, but the twenty-first century has to contend with the troubled and somewhat unsatisfactory legacy of this history.

BOX 8.5 JUVENILE WAIVERS

In the late 1970s, many states began to adopt procedures to facilitate the processing and punishing of serious juvenile offenders as adults. These waivers (or transfers) of juvenile cases to adult criminal courts reflect the action of state legislative bodies, responding to public pressure (Feiler and Sheley 1999; Secret 2011). According to polls, the American public overwhelmingly (90%) supports such waivers for violent juvenile offenders, with at least two-thirds supporting waivers for juveniles who commit property and drug-related offenses (Wu 2000). Unsurprisingly, such support declines in the case of younger juvenile offenders; disturbingly, it increases if the juvenile is African-American (Feiler and Sheley 1999). In Florida, early in the twenty-first century, a number of high-profile cases involving juveniles as young as age 13 years were waived to adult jurisdiction (Canedy 2002). Florida,

1 of 15 states allowing prosecutors rather than judges to make the waiver decision, had almost 400 prisoners under age 18 years in adult prisons.

Proponents of juvenile waivers to criminal court argue that they are a necessary measure against tough, dangerous juvenile offenders; contribute to the deterrence of juvenile offenses; and reflect the public will. Critics contend that waivers are ineffective and inappropriate, are applied inconsistently and in a discriminatory manner, and in the long-term damage and make more threatening juveniles who will eventually be released into society (O'Connor and Treat 1996). By 2011, most states were prosecuting fewer teenagers in adult courts, having recognized the dysfunctional consequences of doing so (Secret 2011). The increasing reliance on and support for waivers of juveniles to adult criminal courts is a major challenge to the original rationale for the establishment of a separate juvenile justice system.

LAW AND THE CIVIL JUSTICE SYSTEM

On the whole, less public and political attention has focused on the civil justice system than on the criminal justice system, although in the recent era the civil justice system has begun to attract more attention than in the past (McIntosh and Cates 2009; White 2003). Major criminal trials are a staple of the media, and some become a national obsession. The civil justice system has, for the most part, a lower profile than the criminal justice system, although some civil proceedings do receive considerable publicity: for example, when a celebrity divorce is contested, a major corporation is sued, or a patently absurd claim is pursued. The civil justice system has an impact on the lives of large numbers of ordinary people, sometimes in profound ways.

The civil justice system is arguably the oldest of the different justice systems, because the earliest courts in ancient times were organized to provide remedies to those who could establish that they had been harmed by some other party. From this early time, a primary objective for the civil justice system has been for the state to provide an orderly (nonviolent) mechanism for the resolution of interpersonal disputes. Increasingly in the modern era, disputes between individuals and organizations, or between different organizations, are involved. The civil law is concerned with private, not public, wrongs as well as disputes between private parties (although the government is sometimes a party in these suits) (Abraham 2008). Some civil justice issues (such as tort law reform and the challenge to no-fault divorce) have an increasingly public profile. In one definition, "any court proceeding in which the objective is not the infliction by the state of punishment for unlawful acts is termed a civil proceeding" (Mayers 1973, p. 12). The civil trial in the United States has evolved over time (Sward 2003). The most basic elements of such trials are relatively unchanging.

The range of possible civil harms and disputes is exceptionally broad. Of course, the vast majority of disputes—between husbands and wives, landlords and tenants, consumers and retailers, and so on—are resolved without resorting to law. Disputes are social constructs, not "things." They may be transformed into civil lawsuits by evolving through several stages: first, the recognition that a particular experience has been injurious (naming); second, attributing the injury to another (blaming); and third, asking for a remedy (claiming) (Felstiner, Abel, and Sarat 1989). Even when people do turn to the law, some form of settlement as opposed to a court trial is the norm. These settlements—for example, in the case of divorce—may occur in the **shadow of the law** (Mnookin and Kornhauser 1979). This notion means that the formal law greatly influences how people define their troubles and formulate their claims. Whether such an influence exists has been disputed (Jacob 1992).

IS THERE A LITIGATION EXPLOSION?

The claim that Americans have for some time been too inclined to sue each other and that we have been experiencing a "litigation explosion" was recounted earlier in this text. It is difficult to reliably measure litigation across time and place, however, so this claim has been challenged (Abraham 2008; Burke 2002). If the likelihood of formal litigation increases when people have proportionally more dealings with others with whom they are not on intimate terms, then we should expect more civil lawsuits in America as such patterns of contact increase; on the other hand, if formal litigation is viewed as economically inefficient by businesses, then we should expect less litigation in a highly developed capitalist society. Although civil filings in the United States increased at a rate several times the rate of increase in the population in the recent era, most of these cases involve petty disputes (often in small claims courts), domestic matters (mainly uncontested divorces), and estate matters (also typically uncontested) (Friedman 1996b, p. 56). Of some 20 million civil cases filed in a given year, then, only a very small proportion involve major litigation on substantial matters.

There has been an increase in certain types of civil litigation (e.g., rights-related; product liability; medical malpractice) as well as in the number of class action suits and multimillion-dollar civil judgments. And some evidence suggests that civil litigation filings increase in the face of tort law reform, as prospective plaintiffs fear the new laws will limit their options (Abraham 2008). Tort lawsuits have multiple objectives, including retribution for harm, the extraction of compensation, and deterrence of harmful conduct (Baker 2001). It has generally been more difficult to extract compensatory payments from individuals than to get settlements from insurance companies.

The inclination to sue is linked with such factors as class membership. Neither the very rich nor the very poor are likely to settle their disputes by turning to law; the upper middle class, however, has both the resources and the peer support to encourage a higher level of litigation (Silberman 1985). Obviously, the more serious a dispute is, the more likely it will lead to litigation. Also, if a lawyer is contacted, litigation is more likely (*see* Box 8.6).

BOX 8.6 SOME MAJOR TYPES OF CIVIL LAW

The term *tort* is used for a private injury caused by one party to another (in the form of injury *either* to a person or to property) (Shapo 2003; White 2003). In classical legal terms, a **tort** involves a breach of duty (broadly defined) by one party toward another, with some form of injury resulting. A tort may be intentional—for example, in a case of defamation of character—although no violation of the criminal code is involved. A large percentage of tort actions, however, arise out of unintentional actions (or failures to act), such as negligence. Automobile accidents, for example, typically involve negligence and are the most common basis for litigation in the United States (Jacob 1996, p. 59). If an injury of some kind is claimed, then it must be shown that an act (or inaction) on the part of the party being sued is the proximate (direct and necessary) cause of the injury.

Issues of contributory negligence on the part of the injured party may arise. In some cases, the doctrine of strict liability is in effect. This means that the party being sued may be held liable if harm can be shown, even in the absence of any deliberate action on the part of this party. For example, this standard is applied if a consumer suffers some identifiable harm after using a defective product.

In addition to torts, the civil justice system covers a vast range of disputes arising out of all manner of business and personal dealings. Contracts are a central element of a complex, modern society, especially where many of one's dealings are with relative strangers (Campbell, Collins, and Wighman 2003). A contract has been defined, quite concisely, as "an enforceable promise about what is owed to and by people who have entered into some sort of exchange relationship with one another" (McIntyre 1994, p. 13). Many issues arise in connection with claims that the terms of a contract have not been properly fulfilled; the contract was signed in ignorance or under some form of duress; or the contract is fraudulent or unconscionable on some grounds.

Another class of civil cases concerns issues pertaining to property. Property in complex, modern societies takes many forms, from real property (such as land) to intellectual property (such as a patent, copyrighted creative work, or trademark). In an immensely influential law review article in 1964, Charles Reich, then a professor at Yale Law School, identified new forms of government-created property (including welfare benefits, government employment, occupational licenses, franchises, government contracts, subsidies, and services), which in turn have become a basis of civil litigation (Minda 1995). Civil suits can arise over conflicting claims of possession of property or unauthorized use of someone's property. Cases contesting the validity of wills and trusts would also fit into this category.

Family law, of course, encompasses matters pertaining to separation, annulment, and divorce as well as to custody issues. This may be the single-most emotionally vulnerable realm of civil litigation, and it is one requiring arbitrators and judges to make painfully difficult decisions (Maccoby and Mnookin 1992).

Beyond these basic categories of civil litigation, one finds an almost endless range of other matters, including cases involving every imaginable form of commercial transaction and business arrangement, labor and management cases (including such matters as working conditions and job loss), and cases alleging violation of civil rights or other rights.

Civil litigation in the contemporary era is more likely than in the past to involve class action suits, in which large numbers of plaintiffs (e.g., consumers injured by a particular product; workers jeopardized by dangerous working conditions) join together in a lawsuit (McIntosh and Cates 2009; Stolberg 2003). Corporations are the most common targets of these class action suits, and altogether some of the most significant and highest-stake civil litigation involves corporations. Early in the twenty-first century, they were in the forefront of the effort to impose tighter limitations on tort lawsuits (Redish 2009). Koenig and Rustad (2001) have challenged the perception that frivolous lawsuits against large corporations are common, and they contend that tort lawsuits are necessary for the protection of American consumers.

JUDGMENTS OF DAMAGES

The single most common remedy sought in a civil proceeding is monetary damages. Strictly speaking, a judicial finding of a monetary judgment is a declaration of the right of the winning party to such payment, although if it is not made voluntarily, then a sheriff might seize and sell property belonging to the losing party to satisfy the judgment. These monetary damages are divided between compensation for direct losses and punitive damages for the wrong done to the plaintiff. As a rule, it is easier to establish a figure for compensatory damage (e.g., through hospital bills or lost wages) than an appropriate dollar figure for punitive damages. In the recent era, in particular, figure amounts in the millions—occasionally, even in the billions—are sometimes awarded in civil cases. Civil litigation directed at major tobacco companies in the final years of the twentieth century was one high-profile instance of multibillion-dollar judgments. Such outcomes are especially likely to be reported in the media, of course, but they are rare. Even in these cases, an appeals court often reduces, sometimes drastically, the size of the original award. The monetary damages in typical cases amount to several thousand dollars, not several million (Jacob 1996, p. 49). Some people who have been victims of terrorism have pursued civil lawsuits against various parties (*see* Box 8.7).

Many civil suits seek some form of remedy other than monetary damages: a divorce or custody of children, a job restored or an unfairly denied promotion granted, a contract

---

BOX 8.7 CIVIL LAWSUITS, HUMAN RIGHTS ABUSES, AND TERRORISM

Can those who claim to have been victims of human rights abuses by states or corporations based in foreign countries sue? In June 2004, the U.S. Supreme Court upheld the right of foreigners who believe they have been victims of human rights abuses to sue in federal courts (Greenhouse 2004f). This ruling was rooted in an interpretation of the Alien Tort Claims Act, enacted by the first American Congress in 1789, to authorize federal court jurisdiction "of any civil action by an alien for a tort only committed in violation of the law of nations, or a treaty of the United States." This act, originally intended to combat piracy, was little invoked until the 1980s, when some federal courts began applying it in international human rights cases. The George W. Bush Administration and international business interests opposed this application of civil law, which has been used, for example, by citizens of Myanmar to allege that an international conglomerate, Unocal, knew of and profited from forced labor in their country. It has also been invoked on behalf of Guatemalan victims of torture, Haitian dissidents, and survivors of the Bosnian genocide. Although the majority of the Supreme Court upheld the right to sue under the Alien Tort Claims Act, the Court stated that the law should be applied with "judicial caution," whereas dissenters objected that it was a form of illegitimate judicial lawmaking that could interfere with American foreign policy efforts.

Terrorist attacks are conventionally viewed as among the most heinous of crimes, calling for a potent military and criminal justice system response. But what role, if any, does civil law play in the "war" on terrorism? In the wake of 9/11, some lawsuits were initiated against airlines, terrorist groups, and some foreign governments, including Iraq, Iran, Libya, and Saudi Arabia (Glaberson 2003). An American lawyer, Ron Motley, filed a civil lawsuit against Saudi charities, financial institutions, prominent individuals, and members of the royal family on the claim that they directly or indirectly sponsored the 9/11 attacks by financially supporting institutions and entities they knew to be fostering terrorism (Senior 2004). This action was certainly controversial, with some viewing it as an appropriate response to financing of terrorism and others viewing it as a dangerous form of interference in international diplomacy by a self-interested lawyer. In other words, was this a new form of wartime jurisprudence; a glorified, globalized tort suit; or simply worldwide ambulance chasing? The lawsuit was at least partially based on Congressional antiterrorism laws, enacted in the 1990s, that criminalized providing "material support" for terrorist activities and authorized civil lawsuits by terror victims. Some Saudis were combating claims that they funded terrorists by using Britain's tough libel laws to go after those making any such claims (Lyall 2004). And in Arab countries, people might well regard the American civil lawsuits as outrageous acts by the world's richest nation against prominent Muslim charitable entities dedicated to assisting the needy people in Arab countries.

Furthermore, the possibility of civil lawsuits for terrorism is a two-way street. Iraqi civilians have invoked Belgium's "universal jurisdiction" law in their efforts to sue American officials for civilian injuries during the Gulf War in 1991, and Saudi Arabian lawyers were supposedly recruiting Iraqi clients to sue members of the George W. Bush Administration for actions taken in Operation Iraqi Freedom.

enforced or voided. In some cases, plaintiffs seek an **injunction**, or an order that the other party either perform some act or cease engaging in some activity. An injunction is generally regarded as more extreme than the awarding of monetary damages and is not often granted by the courts.

CIVIL COURT PROCEEDINGS

Just as is the case with the criminal justice system, civil cases may be pursued in state courts or federal court. Although the vast majority of civil lawsuits are heard in state courts, some increase in federal cases has occurred. A very small class of cases (e.g., disputes on water rights between two states) might go directly to the U.S. Supreme Court. Most federal cases are heard in lower federal courts (district courts). Cases involving a federally granted right (e.g., the right to be free of discrimination) as well as maritime cases arising at sea are civil matters heard in federal court. Cases involving citizens (or, increasingly, corporations) in different states (diversity cases) where an excess of $10,000 in monetary damages is sought may also be taken to federal courts. The balance of civil disputes are directed to a state court; minor matters are assigned to informal small claims courts, and those involving major issues and substantial financial claims are assigned to the formal civil court.

Although claimants in small claims courts make their own case without the assistance of a lawyer, formal civil court proceedings are difficult, if not impossible, for laypeople to navigate. Although major corporations and businesses have in-house counsel or pay major law firms retainers and large hourly fees to represent them, small businesses and ordinary citizens must typically pay their own lawyers. For some kinds of cases (e.g., divorce), a fixed fee rather than an hourly fee may be involved. Poor people who cannot afford such fees must turn to some form of legal aid, but such aid is not always readily available. The contingency fee system (in which the attorney receives a percentage of the monetary damages recovered, if any, but nothing if the case is lost) has been justified as a means of enabling ordinary citizens to sue for harm incurred without having to pay legal fees they cannot afford, especially if the case is unsuccessful. On the other hand, the contingency fee system has also been criticized for encouraging greedy plaintiffs and lawyers to go after defendants with "deep pockets."

Specific procedures in the civil court systems of the various states vary somewhat, although the most basic elements are fairly uniform. Many civil complaints are filed without any serious expectation of taking the case to trial but rather as a tactic for securing a favorable judgment or settlement (Liptak 2007). In fact, the vast majority of civil cases are resolved by a default judgment (i.e., a judgment on behalf of the plaintiff when the defendant fails to respond) or a negotiated settlement. If cases do go to trial, they may be heard by a judge or a jury. The use of juries in civil cases is rare outside of the United States and is also controversial on some grounds; some say that lay juries are not competent to understand issues in complex civil cases and are too prone to manipulation by lawyers playing on their sympathy. Juries in civil cases do not, as a rule, find against doctors and corporations that are sued, despite a common claim to that effect (Vidmar and Hans

2007). The percentage of civil cases resolved by jury trials has been declining (Glaberson 2001a). Many potential jurors fear the financial consequences of serving on a jury (e.g., lost business, no paycheck), but in a recession at least some unemployed people welcome the modest stipend paid to jurors (typically $15–$30 a day) (Schwartz 2009b). Juries are far more likely to be used in personal injury cases than in cases involving sophisticated business dealings.

The civil justice system differs from the criminal justice system in that it does not have large enforcement and vast correctional components. The civil justice system is mainly concentrated in the court. But the civil justice system is not wholly without enforcement and correctional dimensions. Sheriffs, for example, are empowered to make seizures of property to satisfy claims. Some civil cases—for example, failure to make child support payments—may result in jail time. (Fig. 8.1 summarizes the way cases move through the criminal, juvenile, and civil justice systems.)

Millions of Americans in any given year will find themselves parties to a civil proceeding, from divorce to a major tort claim against a corporation. In the contemporary era, major corporations and prestigious professionals such as doctors have sometimes bitterly complained that they are victims of a civil litigation system that is out of control. On balance, however, the evidence strongly suggests that the poor and powerless are more likely to be at a disadvantage through inadequate or nonexistent representation and through judgments against them that they can ill afford.

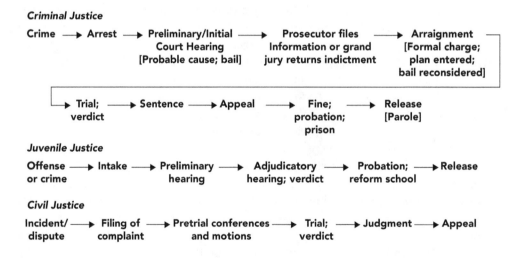

FIGURE 8.1 How Cases Move Through the Criminal Justice System, the Juvenile Justice System, and the Civil Justice System*

LAW AND THE ADMINISTRATIVE/REGULATORY JUSTICE SYSTEM

Administrative law and the regulatory system of justice are generally far less visible than either the criminal justice system or the civil justice system. Yet throughout much of the twentieth century, and especially in the final decades of the century, administrative law and regulatory justice became increasingly important and pervasive (Adler 2007; Parker and Braithwaite 2003). In one sense of the term, administrative justice is nothing new, as administrative and judicial functions were often combined in an earlier time (e.g., governors in the American colonies also served as judges) (Mayers 1973, p. 74). Here, the term **administrative law** refers to the body of law that both creates and governs administrative and regulatory agencies. The term *administrative* or *regulatory justice* refers to the various boards, commissions, and agencies that enforce rules and hold administrative hearings on, or adjudicate, cases in their particular jurisdiction. "Regulatory law/justice" specifically refers to the rules made and enforced by the regulatory agencies, although the terms *administrative* and *regulatory law* are sometimes used interchangeably (Carter 1983; Stewart 2003). Examples of administrative agencies hearing cases could include the Immigration Service deportation hearings, a Workers' Compensation Board hearing relating to an on-the-job injury and disability payments, Equal Employment Opportunity Commission (EEOC) hearings on a claim of job discrimination, and National Labor Relations Board hearings on union complaints against management. Although any of these matters can be appealed to a court in the formal civil justice system, the vast majority of such matters are resolved on the administrative level; many factors (including costs) discourage appeals to the courts. Within administrative agencies, those who perform judicial functions ideally are not also involved in administrative functions (to avoid conflicts of interest), but in many state agencies such functions are not really separated. One important form of administrative justice is carried out on both the federal and state levels by various regulatory agencies, and such regulatory justice will be the focus of this section.

ECONOMIC REGULATION VERSUS SOCIAL REGULATION

Some form of marketplace regulation was characteristic of even ancient civilizations. Throughout the feudal period in Europe, the market was heavily regulated on behalf of the Crown. The American experience with regulation has been one of ongoing tension between calls for more and calls for less regulation of a wide range of activities. So-called economic regulation (addressing market relations such as securities transactions) has generally been less resisted by the business community than so-called social regulation (addressing harmful consequences of productive activity such as environmental pollution) (Croley 2008; Ogus 2001). Although most businesses benefit from the market stability promoted by economic regulation, social regulation tends to cut into profits. Although the commerce clause of the U.S. Constitution provided a foundation for regulation, the nineteenth century was dominated by a "laissez-faire" economic philosophy and involved relatively little regulation in the modern sense. The first federal regulatory agency, the Interstate Commerce Commission (ICC), was created in 1887 by Congress to protect various parties from unfair rates and practices of railroads. During the twentieth century, there were three major waves of regulatory activity: the Progressive Era (1900–1914), when such acts as the Pure Food and Drug Act (1906) were passed, addressing unsafe production practices; the New Deal (1930s), when agencies such as the Securities and Exchange Commission (SEC) were created, addressing unscrupulous market activities; and the Great Society (late 1960s to early 1970s), when various agencies were created, such as the Environmental Protection Agency (EPA) and the Occupational Safety and Health Administration (OSHA), addressing a range of unsafe business practices. Some other significant regulatory agencies, in addition to those named, include the Food and Drug Administration (FDA), the Federal Trade Commission (FTC), the Federal Aviation Agency (FAA), the Federal Communications Commission (FCC), and the Consumer Product Safety Commission.

The regulatory agencies are somewhat unusual entities within the American system of government because they have legislative, executive (enforcement), and judicial functions.

Legislative Functions

First, the regulatory agencies have been authorized by Congress to create specific rules within their area of responsibility (e.g., the EPA produces rules pertaining to environmental practices, and the OSHA produces rules pertaining to workplace conditions). This authorization might seem to be in violation of a Constitutional prohibition against Congress delegating lawmaking powers to any other entity. But the Supreme Court has held that the rule-making of regulatory agencies is essentially filling in details of laws, not lawmaking itself. As a practical matter, Congress (and state legislative bodies) cannot produce the countless specific standards and rules in the many different areas of activity overseen by the various regulatory agencies. Congress (or the state legislature) officially has oversight powers over this regulatory agency rule-making, but it typically defers to the agencies' expertise. The courts too have traditionally deferred to the judgments of these agencies (May 2007; Watry 2002), although this deference has declined somewhat.

Enforcement Functions

The regulatory agencies are empowered to enforce the rules they have created, but they are still bound by Constitutional standards in this process. Regulatory enforcement styles vary greatly, and an ongoing debate divides those who favor agencies emphasizing compliance and those who favor agencies stressing deterrence, or the choice between persuasion and punishment (Kagan, Cunningham, and Thornton 2003; Parker and Braithwaite 2003). Sociolegal scholars have attempted to identify the specific types of regulatory strategies (e.g., relating to consumer financial protection or relating to pollution) that are most likely to be effective (Abbott 2009; Faure, Oyus, and Philipsen 2009). Regulatory enforcement all too often fails to deter the harmful practices of corporations and businesses. "Responsive regulation" attempts to build moral commitment into compliance with regulations (Parker 2007). Both practical considerations (i.e., the vast number of businesses to be regulated and the huge resources of at least some of these businesses) as well as political philosophy (e.g., progressive or conservative) influence choices that regulators make in this respect. Different approaches to regulation have been characterized as management-based, technology-based, and performance-based, with each approach effective in some circumstances and less so in others (Coglianese and Lazer 2003). Regulatory enforcement differs from conventional policing enforcement because it relies heavily on self-policing by those within its jurisdiction. When violations of regulatory rules are brought to the attention of regulatory agencies, the notifications can come from many sources, including consumer complaints, government investigations, congressional committee investigations, business competitors, the media, and employees (Clinard and Yeager 1980, pp. 81–83). Although regulatory agencies may actively initiate investigations, such investigation involves a complex, costly commitment, so more often than not an agency investigation is a reaction to complaints from others.

Judicial Functions

When it is determined that further action or hearings are appropriate, regulatory agencies can act informally in many circumstances, without observing due process guidelines (Kagan, Cunningham, and Thornton 2003; Mashaw 2007). If the investigation uncovers a serious violation of criminal law, then the regulatory agency can refer the matter to the Department of Justice for possible criminal prosecution. Regulatory agencies often prefer not to do this, for a variety of reasons (e.g., it is a concession of their failure to prevent such wrongdoing; they lose control of the case; it may be counterproductive in terms of long-term relations with the industry being regulated). More often, the regulatory agency holds its own hearings on violations. A fairly large body of law, codified by the Administrative Procedure Act (APA) in 1946, governs formal agency proceedings (Moore, Magaldi, and Gray 1987, p. 120). Agency hearings most typically take the form of quasi-criminal proceedings but are less formal than regular court hearings and trials (Metzger et al. 1986, p. 36). Such hearings are presided over by an administrative judge or hearing examiner, who is independent of agency personnel. Defendants can have attorneys, but they are not entitled to a jury trial. Administrative judges and hearing examiners are empowered to impose various orders or sanctions on defendants, including cease-and-desist orders (equivalent to injunctions), special orders (e.g., directives intended to correct past conduct or to call for product recalls), consent orders (negotiations regarding certain actions), summary orders (e.g., prevention of the sale of food), and license suspension or revocation (Clinard and Yeager 1980, p. 94; Frank and Lombness 1988). Also, they can impose fines. Regulatory agency cases may be referred for criminal action or may lead to civil suits. Appeals from hearing decisions must first go through an internal agency appeal process and only then are eligible for appellate court review, although appellate courts have typically been reluctant to overturn agency decisions (Adler 2007). When agency decisions are overturned, the basis for such reversals is likely to be a determination that the decision was fundamentally arbitrary, capricious, or discriminatory; was not based on substantial evidence; violated applicable constitutional safeguards; or exceeded the statutory authority of the agency.

FOCUS OF CONTROVERSY

As suggested before, the administrative justice of regulatory agencies has been a focus of ongoing controversy. At the end of the first decade of the twenty-first century, the question of whether more regulatory law—and more regulation generally—could help avoid future financial meltdowns was much debated and hugely consequential (Johnson and Kwak 2010; Samuel 2009). Many business interests and political conservatives have regarded the regulatory agencies as inefficient, ineffective governmental bureaucracies that interfere—with unfortunate economic consequences—in the operation of the free market. Regulators themselves are viewed as unelected, faceless bureaucrats rendering incompetent decisions. These interests favor abolishing most of the regulatory agencies or, at a minimum, stripping them of the means to interfere with and penalize businesses. The other side of the controversy comes from citizen/consumer/worker activists and political progressives, who are more likely to express concern over **agency capture**, which here means that agencies are too influenced by or even dominated by the industries they are supposed to regulate (in part, because the regulators often come out of those industries and expect to return to them). These interests typically favor adopting policies strengthening the autonomy or independence of regulatory agencies and arming them with powerful means to oversee (and, if necessary, punish) the various industries. Regulatory agencies often contend with many competing political pressures and may try to protect themselves by adopting a stance of political neutrality (Huber 2007). The debate over regulatory agencies, and administrative justice generally, is sure to continue.

LAW AND THE MILITARY JUSTICE SYSTEM

The military has traditionally had laws of its own and has administered its own justice system, going back at least to the time of the ancient Romans (Richards 2007; Lurie 2001; Morris 2010). During warfare, and occasionally as a consequence of an especially sensational case, military justice comes to the attention of the larger public. For the most part, however, military justice receives little public attention and interest. Throughout history, the military has been the dominant political force in at least some countries and has sometimes imposed its own autocratic and harsh form of justice on a whole society. Also, *de facto* military governments have sometimes been imposed on defeated enemies by the victorious side, as was the case after World War II, when a temporary government was imposed on the defeated Japan, and on Iraq following "Operation Iraqi Freedom" in 2003.

Americans, however, have been traditionally leery of direct military involvement in affairs of state (as have citizens of other democratic nations), and for the most part some lines of separation between military and civil government affairs have been maintained. High-level military commanders have often been influential in state affairs, however, and some prominent generals (from Washington to Eisenhower) have become presidents. In some circumstances, military commanders and military laws dominated the existing law.

Military justice typically refers to the ongoing administration of justice by military commanders to those under their command (Morris 2010). This system of justice has its roots in the Articles of War implemented by the Continental Congress in 1775, as well as in the Constitution, executive orders, and statutes. The Uniform Code of Military Justice, which has been revised periodically over the years, spells out the specific provisions of the relevant law. Although the civilian justice system has traditionally avoided interfering with military justice, the decisions of military courts are subject to review by federal courts; in 1950, a Court of Military Appeals, made up of civilian appointees, was established to provide some oversight on decisions made within a purely military environment.

Military justice has jurisdiction over all those who are serving in one of the branches of the military, whether as draftees, enlisted members, or commissioned officers; it also has some jurisdiction over civilians serving with or accompanying military forces and may be used in cases involving foreign spies. The principal rationale for military justice is to maintain the order and discipline necessary for the successful fulfillment of the military's mission. Obviously, any form of aid to the enemy is regarded as an especially serious offense, but fundamental violations of military discipline are also treated seriously. The improper treatment of enemy captives or disposition of captured property, as well as misconduct as a prisoner of war, are also significant violations within the context of war.

Existing military law has been criticized as imposing a strong obligation of obedience to the commands of superior officers; this obligation can obviously conflict with principles proscribing blatantly illegal conduct. Osiel (1999) calls for a transformation of military law that would stress tactical imagination, self-discipline, and loyalty to immediate comrades rather than blind obedience to superior orders.

The Judge's Advocate General's Corp (JAG Corp) has as its purpose ensuring proper discipline in military situations. In a study of the JAG Corps during the Vietnam War, a military historian concluded that it failed to achieve its objective, in part because of the military being involved in the complex mission of nation building (Allison 2006). Some parallel challenges have arisen in Iraq and Afghanistan during more recent American military initiatives. As the United States is not at war most of the time, military justice cases principally address violations of military discipline. Although some such violations are specifically spelled out—for example, failure to obey an order—a court martial is also possible for "conduct unbecoming an officer and a gentleman" (or gentlewoman), which is sufficiently vague to allow for fairly broad application (Myren 1988, p. 96; Schlueter 2007). For example, in a military increasingly made up of both men and women, charges of sexual harassment and rape have become more common. Some commentators argue that such charges, and criminal charges generally, should be addressed by civilian courts or military courts independent of commanders (Myers 2004). Although serious criminal charges can be referred to civilian courts, they may also be addressed by military courts. The alleged severe abuse of Iraqi prisoners in Abu Ghraib prison by American soldiers was addressed by a military court (Wong 2004a). There have also been calls for enlarging the current size of the jury (five) for military capital cases (Bonner 2001). Much military justice is carried out behind closed doors, with considerable discretion accorded to the military commanders and judges involved (*see* Box 8.8).

The military tribunals that hear court martial cases are composed of superior officers, who are not typically the peers of those being tried (Myers 2004). Because these officers are chosen by the commanding officer within the particular jurisdiction, it is a legitimate concern that they may be controlled by this superior and may be more concerned with fulfilling military objectives than with doing justice. An unresolved question, then, is whether the somewhat authoritarian character of much military justice can be comfortably reconciled with expectations of full respect for individual rights and due process.

BOX 8.8 MILITARY VERSUS CIVILIAN JUSTICE IN
THE WAKE OF 9/11

There is a long U.S. history of restrictions on civil liberties and constitutional rights during times of war, but there has been no uniform extension of "military law and justice" during these periods (Richards 2007; Stone 2007). Typically wartime restrictions have been challenged as unconstitutional and eventually are repealed. The restrictions imposed following 9/11 are in some respects less expansive than those adopted in earlier "wars" but are especially open-ended in terms of the timeframe for the restrictions. The levels of secrecy on government actions during this period, however, were unprecedented.

Since 9/11, ongoing issues have surfaced on whether accused terrorists, on the one hand, and American soldiers in Iraq and Afghanistan accused of crimes, on the other hand, are most appropriately dealt with by military or civilian justice. The methods used to seize, hold, and interrogate suspected terrorists clearly clashed with basic constitutional rights but were justified as necessary in a "war" against terrorism (Dickey 2007). Some of the tactics used also appeared to violate international laws of war encompassed by the Geneva conventions. Military lawyers assigned to defend suspected terrorists have frequently challenged the procedures applied to their clients, and especially the use of torture (Lewis 2008). The Bush Administration claimed that any torture that occurred was the work of a few bad apples, but much evidence surfaced that it was deliberate policy from the top command. Secret memoranda by government lawyers claimed that the president had the legal authority to order of

the torture of terrorism suspects. Some American military guards prosecuted for beating prisoners to death were defended on the basis that the parameters for what was and was not permitted in dealing with such prisoners were not clear. In 2006 three American soldiers suspected of killing three detainees in Iraq and threatening to kill another soldier if he reported the shootings were charged with premeditated murder and obstruction of justice by U.S. military officials (Shanker and Tavernise 2006). American marines were also charged with killing Iraqi civilians (von Zielbauer 2007). In cases such as these, conflicts typically arise over whether the accused should be tried by the American military justice system or by the Iraqi criminal justice system.

Some 100 lawyers who have represented detainees at Guantanamo Prison, as well as those who have been held at CIA jails and other special detention facilities for accused terrorists, have provided revealing personal accounts of their experiences (Denbeaux and Hafetz 2009). Military commissions have had little success in convicting suspected terrorists (Ephron 2007). The U.S. Supreme Court ruled against the Bush Administration in several key cases involving the appropriate venue for holding and trying suspected terrorists (Lewis 2008). There was much opposition to the Obama Administration proposal to try a major 9/11 terrorist suspect in the civilian justice system instead of in a military proceeding (Lithwick 2009c). The attempt to prosecute suspected terrorists for their intentions and not simply their actions is one of the more controversial legal initiatives of the post 9/11 era (Waldman 2006). Altogether, many complex legal disputes arise in the wake of a "war on terrorism," broadly defined.

INFORMAL JUSTICE: ALTERNATIVE DISPUTE RESOLUTION AND MEDIATION

Law and the formal systems of justice inspire much frustration, huge economic costs, and endless conflict. The formal system of justice is experienced by many as intimidating or inaccessible. It is widely believed, with some justification, that the powerful and privileged tend to have the advantage in this system of justice. In a now classic article titled "Why the Haves Come Out Ahead: Speculations on the Limits of Legal Change," Galanter (1974) argued that financially and organizationally stronger parties tend to prevail in litigation over weaker parties, especially to the extent that they are "repeat players" in the court system. Subsequent research has generally confirmed this thesis (e.g., Kritzer and Silbey 2003; Wheeler et al. 1987).

Of course, it has always been true, and continues to be true, that countless disputes between different parties are resolved informally, without turning to law. Even when cases or disputes do go before the formal system of law, they are most likely to be resolved informally.

The great majority of criminal cases are settled by plea bargaining; the vast majority of civil cases are settled by negotiation (Emmelman 1996; Raiffa 2003). As a general proposition, the more complex and developed a society is, the more it will rely on formal law and legal institutions to resolve disputes. Preliterate and less developed societies are more likely to resolve disputes informally.

AMERICAN TRADITION

Within the American tradition, a commitment to informal justice on the part of some has always been a factor. As was noted elsewhere, the earliest American settlers were often hostile toward lawyers and formal legal institutions, especially if they had suffered from persecution in the Old World. Among the Puritans and the Quakers, for example, a strong bias in favor of informal justice prevailed (indeed, some contemporary students of nonconflictive forms of dispute resolution look to the Quakers as a model; Cownie and Bradney 2000). On the Western frontier, disputes were often settled outside the boundaries of formal law, and small Western ranchers in the modern era continue to seek justice outside the formal law in many cases (Bakken 2000; Ellickson 1991). As Auerbach (1983) recounted, not only these early communities but many later American communities as well—including utopian nineteenth-century communities (e.g., Oneida and the Mormon settlements), ethnic immigrant communities (e.g., Scandinavian and Chinese immigrants), and workforce/commercial communities (e.g., the labor movement and chambers of commerce)—rejected formal litigation and sought to resolve disputes by informal means. Over time, according to Auerbach, alternatives to formal law came to be manipulated by the state as a means of limiting the rights of the disadvantaged. Whether informal justice resulted in less authoritarian, fairer, and generally superior justice for the parties involved is a matter of interpretation and debate (Hartley 2002; Henry 2007; Pavlich 1996). Religious and other community leaders who oversee these informal procedures obviously may administer capricious, biased, and even cruel outcomes; in the ideal circumstance, of course, they resolve disputes fairly, harmoniously, and efficiently.

The contemporary call for greater reliance on informal justice—or **alternative dispute resolution (ADR)**—can be interpreted in different ways (Palmer and Roberts 2007; Hartley 2002). On the one hand, ADR, typically some form of mediation, can be endorsed as a more humane, open, equitable, conciliatory, understandable, and efficient means of settling cases. The parties avoid the alienating, power-influenced, class-biased, conflict-oriented, argot-ridden, and often costly and time-consuming dimensions of the formal legal system. On the other hand, ADR, and informal justice generally, has been criticized on the grounds that it leads to a more arbitrary form of justice governed more by biases than by due process; that it saves the state money at the expense of other parties; that it creates a lower tier of justice to resolve disputes of the underprivileged; that it puts the powerless at an even greater disadvantage than they face in the formal system of justice; and that it expands the scope of the state's involvement in people's lives (Fiss 1984; Henry 1985; Palmer and Roberts 2007). In this view, informal justice distracts people from the fundamental problems in society and transforms their troubles into interpersonal disputes.

Accordingly, informal justice in a capitalist system may simply serve to mask inherent inequalities and help preserve the system rather than making it more equitable and fair.

POPULAR JUSTICE

The term *informal justice* is sometimes used interchangeably with, or parallel to, *popular justice, vigilante justice, community justice, neighborhood justice,* and *private justice.* These related terms, however, tend to have distinctive connotations. **Popular justice** is most closely associated with the form of justice administered within postrevolutionary societies, such as Russia, China, and Cuba after their communist revolutions. The essence of such justice is that it rejects the formal system of law and courts (viewed as instruments of capitalist class interests) and replaces it with popular tribunals made up of political leaders and representatives of the people, and these tribunals apply the principles of revolutionary doctrine and future objectives to dispose of cases. Although in the early stages of postrevolutionary societies, popular justice has often been embraced enthusiastically and has substantial participation and interest from ordinary citizens, the trend has been toward gradual reintroduction of increasingly formal systems of law. Although such popular justice may have advanced some revolutionary objectives and, in at least some individual cases, resulted in correcting past injustices, much injustice also clearly has resulted. Arbitrary, and sometimes cruel, judgments have been imposed on many people not protected by due process, and whole lives, families, and communities have been effectively destroyed.

The term *popular justice* is not unique to communist societies, however, and in the American context it has been applied to justice influenced or determined by popular (public) opinion, which is sometimes at odds with the formal rule of law (Walker 1980). In the more extreme cases, such popular justice has taken the form of **vigilante justice** (or mob justice) and lynch law (Feenan 2002). In the frontier West and in the traditional South, for example, a very rough form of vigilante or mob justice was sometimes administered, with vulnerable parties (e.g., African-American people in the South) subjected to flogging, expulsion, or lynching on the mere rumor or suspicion of some wrongdoing, without any attention to due process (Brown 1979; Friedman 1993). Vigilante justice was justified by frontier communities as necessary to maintain a civilized way of life in the absence of formal legal institutions and among traditional Southerners as necessary to preserve their way of life in the face of interference by outside forces.

COMMUNITY JUSTICE

Community justice is a somewhat more neutral term for the administration of justice by a particular community, although the membership of a "community" is not always obvious (Schneider 2007; Miller 2001). Such justice is administered by lay people who are members of a community in some sense of the term (e.g., live in a common area, belong to a professional association, are part of a university) (Henry 1981, pp. 186–188). Although there are many factors that obstruct the capacity of disadvantaged communities to address crime and disorder within their communities, some strategies have been identified that have the potential to overcome these obstacles (Schneider 2007). The related term **neighborhood**

justice refers to justice administered with federal funding at neighborhood justice centers, established in many American communities in the 1970s. Trained mediators, who may or may not be lawyers, attempt to resolve disputes between parties who may have been referred to the center by the formal court and have agreed to such a resolution of their case. The several hundred such centers tend to serve large metropolitan areas, however, and so do not typically involve neighbors—in the conventional sense of the term—administering justice for each other. Accordingly, the centers have been criticized as another means of expanding state control (Hofrichter 1987). Ideal objectives of these courts, such as lower costs and more informal, efficient resolution of cases, have not always been met (Tomasic and Feeley 1982). And the closely related term **private justice** refers to the resolution of disputes from within a private institution, typically a business (Henry 1981). Again, all these terms may be used interchangeably.

Although community justice institutions are supposed to implement the values of a particular community in a democratic fashion, the makeup of the community tribunal is not necessarily the outcome of a democratic means of selection. Community courts typically have procedural guidelines but also have considerable discretion in how they interpret and carry out the guidelines. Professional associations, as noted elsewhere, have proceedings to discipline their members and in extreme cases to strip them of their license to practice. Such disciplinary bodies often have been viewed as more concerned with protecting the image and financial well-being of the profession than with administering justice to individuals and protecting the general public. Internal disciplinary hearings held by colleges are also examples of such community, or private, justice. For example, a co-ed who has been raped by a date may choose to take the matter to a college disciplinary tribunal rather than report it to the police, so she can avoid the stress of publicity and criminal justice proceedings. In some cases, however, the complainant may feel that the college is more concerned with protecting its reputation and avoiding publicity than with taking appropriate action against the accused; also, the accused may feel he has been subjected to accusations and stigmatization on the basis of a false case that could not hold up in a court of law. Restorative justice (addressed in Chapter 3) is especially appropriate for community-based informal justice programs, because it highlights a cooperative venture on the part of the offender, the victim, and the community to repair harm rather than to focus on punishing crime (Woolford and Ratner 2008). Reparations and restitution on the part of the wrongdoer are one constructive part of this.

A system of justice is not necessarily either formal or informal (*see* Box 8.9). Rather, a continuum between the highly formal and the thoroughly informal may be said to exist (Menkel-Meadow 2004; Norrie 1996). Formal law and informal law are often interdependent (Feenan 2002; Harrington 1985; Henry 1983). Civil courts sometimes require that parties attempt to resolve differences first through mediation (Clarke and Gordon 1997; Hartley 2002). The juvenile justice courts, as discussed above, are a classic example of a system of justice combining informal and formal elements. Although the informality of the juvenile courts traditionally has been justified as being in the best interest of juveniles appearing before the court, recently more formalism has been re-introduced to protect the rights of these juveniles.

BOX 8.9 SMALL TOWN JUSTICE AS
INFORMAL JUSTICE

A significant amount of justice is administered in very low-profile town or village courts that dispense what is largely informal justice—that is, justice little governed by formal law and legal procedures (Glaberson 2006). These courts have their roots in colonial courts established when lawyers were few and far between and can be found today in some 30 states. Although they principally address traffic violations, they also deal with a broad range of other matters such as evictions, disputes between neighbors, and misdemeanors. In New York State, more than 1,200 such courts (sometimes called "justice courts") exist, with three-quarters of them presided over by local justices who are not lawyers. These justices are often former police officers, truck drivers, laborers, or retirees, among other backgrounds, without a formal legal education and, in some cases, not even a high

school diploma. Some of these justices—who receive only a few days of training following their appointment—are clearly ignorant of basic legal principles or indifferent to them. One of these justices, with 13 years of service, stated, "I just follow my own common sense. And the hell with the law." Such an approach inevitably leads to a very uneven dispensation of justice. Actual evidence and fundamental legal rights are often disregarded, and at least some of those who appear in these courts end up being jailed illegally. Overt biases, including racial and gender-related biases, arise in this context. A justice who was a former state trooper with a high school diploma, after denying an order of protection to a woman whose husband had beaten her, was heard to comment: "Every woman needs a good pounding every now and then." Although there is a long history of criticism of these courts and attempts to reform them, they have somehow survived into the twenty-first century.

SMALL CLAIMS COURT

Small claims courts are an example of a legal institution with both formal and informal dimensions (Conley and O'Barr 1990; Vidmar 1984). On the one hand, a judge presides over small claims court cases and imposes a decision on the parties involved. On the other hand, the proceedings are far more informal than those in conventional court hearings. Each party states his or her own case, and the judge directs questions to each of the parties. Cases that might go into small claims courts include disputes between neighbors (e.g., regarding boundaries or nuisances), personal loans, shoddy goods, inadequately performed services, landlord/tenant matters (e.g., on securities), minor accidents involving cars, dog bites or pet-related damages, and the like. Millions of Americans have been exposed to small claims court proceedings through TV shows such as *The People's Court*, although research suggests that small claims court litigants often come to the court with unrealistic expectations of what the court will do for them and are then disappointed (O'Barr and Conley 1988).

Although ideally the small claims court allows ordinary individuals seeking nominal damages to obtain justice without incurring the formidable expenses involved in hiring a lawyer and suing in a formal civil court proceeding, in fact a disproportionate percentage of those who initiate small claims court proceedings are businesspeople trying to collect debts or landlords trying to collect rents, often from poor people (Conley and O'Barr 1990). When small claims court cases are mediated, some evidence indicates that minority females do less well than others (LaFree and Rack 1996).

MEDIATION AND ARBITRATION

Any discussion of informal justice must also distinguish between some crucial terms. The term **adjudication** is most commonly applied to a formal system for resolving disputes that is presided over by a judge, and accordingly this process is not typically associated with informal justice. **Arbitration** also involves a judge or third party that imposes a resolution on a dispute, but typically it is more informal than adjudication. A key feature of arbitration is that the two parties to a dispute have mutually agreed to subject themselves to it. Arbitration can be used in the whole range of disputes, from local school board/teacher disputes to those between nations. In the recent era, sentiment opposed to the use of arbitration in international disputes appears to have hardened in the U.S. Congress (Carbonneau 2007). Binding arbitration involves parties who have agreed to abide by the ruling of the arbitrator (Bockstiegel 2009). Labor/management disputes, for example, are not infrequently resolved by bringing in an arbitrator who resolves the dispute. **Mediation** gets to the essence of informal justice. A mediator is called in to attempt to clarify issues for the parties to a dispute and possibly to suggest some forms of resolution. But the mediator is a facilitator only and does not impose a solution (Relis 2009).

Mediation has been increasingly used, for example, in domestic violence, divorce, and custody cases. Indeed, in many states, couples seeking divorce are first required to subject themselves to mediation. Most reasonable people would agree that, other things being equal, it is preferable to have mediation rather than a judge-imposed solution in a case in which a father and mother of minor children, for example, are disputing the custody of the children as a consequence of their divorce. Surely it would be better if the parents could be helped in working out a mutually acceptable custody arrangement between themselves rather than to battle out the custody issues in court, with the children sometimes called on to testify against one or the other of their parents. In domestic violence cases, however, at least some feminists have raised the question of whether it is really fair and humane to subject the abused spouse (typically the wife) to an attempt to "mediate" over issues arising from the abuse, or whether mediation in these cases principally serves to allow a violent and abusive spouse (typically the husband) to avoid criminal prosecution (Crowe and Field 2007/2008). When parties to mediation have a long-standing relationship, they generally must choose among abandoning the relationship, negotiating a compromised and provisional settlement of their differences, and achieving a reconciliation oriented toward the restoration of their original relationship. The question of whether formal litigation or informal mediation produces more just outcomes for the parties involved does not have a simple or single answer (Crowe and Field 2008; Relis 2009; Tackaberry 2009). Many factors enter into the perceptions of these processes by the participants in them.

The call for informal justice has been based on both idealistic and practical grounds. Idealistically, informal justice has been justified as a fairer, more humane, and more democratic means of achieving justice as well as a repudiation of the bureaucratized, debasing, and inequitable formal legal system. In practical terms, informal justice has been promoted as a means of avoiding the costs and delays associated with the formal legal system. No sweeping generalizations about informal justice are likely to be accurate. One can find many circumstances in which those involved fervently believe that it has produced a better and more just outcome and many other circumstances in which gross injustices have resulted. Informal justice must be evaluated cautiously, with attention to the specific form and context.

CONCLUSION

Our society has developed a range of institutions and procedures to address the many different kinds of harm that people do to one another and the disputes in which they engage (*see* Table 8.1 for a brief comparison of the justice systems discussed here). Although many disputes are settled between people on their own, in a complex society, various kinds of formal institutions and procedures are needed to attend to disputes that cannot (or should not) be so resolved. The formal procedures of these institutions are generally invoked in a small minority of cases; most are resolved by some form of informal procedure. But in view of the frustrations and costs associated with the formal procedures of justice, there are those who support alternative dispute resolution, ideally as independent of the formal systems of justice as possible. Nevertheless, all too often alternative dispute resolution has been co-opted by the legal establishment. Formal and informal procedures for dispute resolution (and the disposition of cases involving harmful conduct) will always co-exist. One of the questions for the future is whether the momentum promoting informal justice procedures will continue to grow; another is whether costly, frustrating, and inequitable aspects of the formal justice systems can be more successfully addressed and reformed.

TABLE 8.1 A COMPARISON OF JUSTICE SYSTEMS*

Justice system	Objective or focus	Basic procedure	Adjudicator	Standard of proof
Criminal justice	Controlling, preventing, and punishing crime	Adversarial trial; plea negotiation	Judge; jury	Beyond a reasonable doubt
Juvenile justice	Controlling and rehabilitating juvenile offenders	More inquisitorial and informal	Judge; probation officer	Beyond a reasonable doubt; often discretionary
Civil Justice	Resolving disputes formally	Adversarial; negotiated	Judge; jury	Clear and convincing evidence; preponderance of evidence
Administrative justice	Regulating important or dangerous activities	Administrative hearing	Administrative judge; hearing officer	Substantial evidence; often discretionary
Military justice	Maintain order and discipline within military	Military court; hearing	Military tribunal; unit commander	From equivalent to criminal justice to discretionary
Informal justice	Alternative to formal justice system for dispute resolution	Informal hearing	Arbitrator; mediator; community	Merits of case; mutual consent; often discretionary

* The different justice systems may use different procedures and standards, depending on the nature of the case being addressed; accordingly, this table should only be taken as an approximation of some key differences between them.

KEY TERMS AND CONCEPTS

adjudication	felony	popular justice
administrative law	injunction	private justice
agency capture	jury nullification	punitive cycle
alternative dispute resolution (ADR)	lenience cycle	racial profiling
arbitration	martial law	rough justice
bench trial	mediation	sentencing guidelines
child-saving movement	military justice	shadow of the law
community justice	misdemeanor	status offenders
community policing	neighborhood justice	tort
courtroom workgroup	plea bargaining	vigilante justice

DISCUSSION QUESTIONS

1. Discuss the concept of discretion in the criminal justice system, especially as it pertains to police officers and judges. How much discretion should these professionals be awarded? When offered too much, do you think police officers have a tendency to abuse such discretion? Can judges impose sentences that are more fair if they can use their discretion instead of relying on sentencing guidelines?

2. Should a juvenile who commits a serious crime, such as premeditated murder, still be treated as a juvenile and subjected to the separate juvenile justice system? Explain.

3. Is the American civil litigation system really "out of control"? How does the system seem to be taken advantage of at times?

4. Discuss the positive and negative aspects of the administrative justice system. How can the power that certain agencies have to function legislatively, executively, and judicially both be beneficial and possibly result in negative consequences?

5. What benefits does alternative dispute resolution bring to the American justice system? Should ADR be relied on more often than it is? How could it possibly help such a highly litigious society?

CHAPTER 9

LEGAL CULTURE AND LEGAL BEHAVIOR

Law in our lives does not exist in a vacuum. Rather, people have varying degrees of knowledge about the law, they form attitudes toward law and legal institutions, and they develop patterns of behavior in relation to law (Friedman 1975, p. 193; Friedman and Perez-Perdomo 2003). The term **legal culture** has been adopted to describe public knowledge and attitudes toward law, although patterns of behavior are typically not included as a part of legal culture (Friedman and Scheiber 1996; Nelken 2009). Lawrence Friedman (1997, p. 34), the leading proponent of the concept, has written that legal culture "refers to ideas, values, expectations and attitudes towards law and legal institutions, which some public or some part of the public holds." People's ideas about law, in turn, are assumed to influence their behavior. David Nelken calls for differentiating more clearly between *legal culture* (collective [shared] meanings of the law) and *legal consciousness* (attitudes toward the law) (Bruinsma and Nelken 2007).

LEGAL CULTURE

Legal culture refers both to the ideas of elites and other special interests within society and to ideas held by "ordinary people," or the general public. Legal culture is significant because it has an impact on the legal system; changes in cultural attitudes can lead to changes in law. It is also true that changes in law can influence cultural attitudes. For example, the American movement toward desegregation reflected the discomfort of growing numbers of Americans with a segregated society, and this attitude influenced lawmakers. At the same time, the legal rulings and legal reforms—for example, *Brown v. Board of Education* (1954) and the Civil Rights Act (1964)—also made legal discrimination less culturally acceptable over time. Furthermore, as Friedman (1997, p. 34) observed, changes in the social environment generate new demands on the legal system: "Somebody invents the motor car and later we see modifications in tort law, and a massive pile of new regulations: on drivers' licenses, rules of the road, drunk driving, air bags, and so on."

Culture shapes different understandings of facts and personhood in different societies (Rosen 2006; Sarat, Douglas, and Umphrey 2007b). Law can only be properly understood within a particular cultural context. The cultural context influences the choices legislators and judges must make between matters that are properly regulated by law and matters that are best left to private parties to work out among themselves (Zelizer 2005). The cultural context of different countries profoundly influences the patterns relating to civil (tort) litigation (Engel and McCann 2009). So some countries experience dramatic rises in tort litigation and others do not. Some types of mass litigation (e.g., against tobacco countries) are supported and successful in one country but not another. Some forms of behavior (e.g., sexual harassment) are defined as grounds for civil litigation in one country but not another. Friedman (2009) has written about the changing practices relating to wills and the transfer of property following death as a mirror for evolving cultural and social values in relation to American families. American legal culture differs in varying degrees from the legal cultures of other countries; for example, it differs somewhat from the legal culture of England and still more so from that of Japan. A study of American and Japanese responses to corporate lawbreaking found that Americans were more likely to favor punishments imposed on individual corporate executives, whereas Japanese respondents tended to focus more on extracting apologies from these corporate offenders (Sanders, Hamilton, and Yuasa 1998). These different responses reflect different cultural values in the United States and Japan. However, contacts between different cultures have expanded, and legal systems in these different cultures adapt to these contacts. Legal culture must be understood in global and national terms and on other levels as well. With an increasingly globalized world, is it the case that there is now a global legal culture (Gessner 2007; Nelken 2006)? Globalization in the legal realm appears to have complex and sometimes contradictory effects in different countries, rendering broad generalizations about any such effects questionable. But democratization and the entry of women in growing numbers into the legal profession are developments shared by the legal cultures of many countries (Friedman and Perez-Perdomo 2003) (*see* Fig. 9.1). The growing number of transnational legal

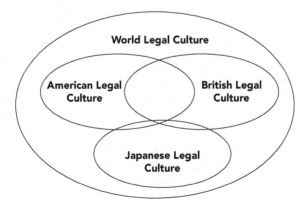

FIGURE 9.1 American Legal Culture in Relation to Some Other Legal Cultures

transactions promotes the adoption of a common legal framework and culture, but the extent to which true harmonization between different legal cultures will occur remains unsettled.

AMERICAN LEGAL CULTURE

What are the elements of American legal culture? Certainly, Americans have been greatly interested in law and legal issues relative to other cultures, despite the fact that they hold contradictory attitudes toward law. Americans tend to venerate the rule of law and at the same time are often hostile to lawyers, burdensome legal proceedings, and state interventions in private lives. American cultural attitudes toward legal issues evolve over time; they are hardly homogeneous at any point in time (Burt 2002; Karsten 2002; Mann 2002). In the recent era, "political correctness" has been an especially controversial element of the legal culture. Some commentators claim that Americans are obsessed with legal rights and entitlements, and other commentators describe Americans as "law avoiders" (Engel and Munger 1996). Of course, in such a large country it is not surprising to find evidence of contradictory tendencies.

David Engel and Frank Munger (1996) have suggested that although Americans talk easily about legal rights and entitlements, it does not necessarily mean that they will follow through by initiating legal action. Specifically, in their study of disabled individuals, they found that these Americans are often conflicted in their own minds about asserting legal rights extended to them by the Americans With Disabilities Act. Nevertheless, even if they do not choose to formally pursue these rights, they are influenced by the knowledge that they have such legal rights.

Despite the qualifications stated above, it is common to attribute litigiousness—or a willingness, even eagerness, to sue—to American legal culture (Kagan 2001). Does American culture really stress such conflict, or does it stress harmony? In a study of residents of a New York City suburb, M. P. Baumgartner (1988) found that people go to considerable lengths to resolve grievances without confrontation and without resorting to formal legal action. According to Baumgartner, "Moral minimalism dominates the suburbs. On a day-by-day basis, life is filled with efforts to deny, minimize, contain, and avoid conflict" (1988, p. 127). Whether such moral minimalism signifies strong or weak social control within a particular community is a matter of some dispute (Schneider 1990). However, the findings of Baumgartner's study do challenge an image of Americans as relentlessly litigious. It is indisputable that there is a great deal of litigation in American society—proportionately far more than in many other developed nations. The sources of this "adversarial legalism" include, on the one hand, the nature of the political system and, on the other hand, the self-interested promotion of litigation by the large core of American lawyers.

The claim that Americans *(1)* have become more litigious than in the past; *(2)* are more litigious than people in other countries; and *(3)* are clearly in the midst of a "litigation explosion" has been challenged (Friedman 1996b; Nelken 2003). In one reading, those who campaign for restrictions on lawsuits often subscribe to conservative values emphasizing individual responsibility and strong support for the promotion of private enterprise (McCann and Haltom 2006). As suggested earlier in this text, litigation is not so easily—or obviously—defined. If litigation is thought of as active, contested lawsuits, some types of lawsuits are more common today and others are less common.

If Americans are not necessarily more likely to sue today than in the past, they are more likely to expect the law to address injustice and loss. Friedman (1985, p. 5) identified a demand for what he calls **total justice,** or "a general expectation of recompense for injuries and loss" as an important emerging dimension of American legal culture. This expectation leads to demands for new legal rules or to the use of informal dispute resolution and only sometimes to formal litigation.

The promotion of a fear of crime is one of the defining features of contemporary American culture, as well as other Western cultures (Lee 2007). In one interpretation, the punitive character of American criminal justice in the recent era is a response to growing uneasiness about social and economic status in a rapidly changing society, on the part of the historically dominant group (Wacquant 2009). The tough drug laws of the recent era have been specifically characterized as driven in important ways by fear of minorities, and accordingly as inherently racist (Provine 2007). In the final decades of the twentieth century, then, relatively strong support for a "get tough on crime" approach emerged as an attribute of American legal culture (Gest 2001; Scheingold 1997). A move toward favoring harsher criminal sentencing also reflected a reaction against more liberal social policies in other areas (Gaubatz 1995). Public support for harsh penalties is often based on perceptions that have been influenced by the media but are based on mistaken and distorted information about the reality of crime (Roberts and Stalans 1997; Robinson 2002). Over time, an enduring leveling off or decline in the conventional crime rate could lead to significant changes in public attitudes toward punishing criminals, but this has yet to happen in America.

A basic tension exists, then, between American frustration with costly, inefficient lawsuits and American commitment to individual and social justice and between a demand for both due process and respect for privacy and for efficient, tough crime control. Friedman (1990) has also argued that Americans have come to live in a **republic of choice,** or a cultural environment in which they at least believe that they have many rights and many different choices. Modern technology and the increasing expectation of change have contributed to this situation.

Friedman's interpretation has been criticized on a number of grounds, including its overly optimistic assessment of American legal culture, its relative neglect of power, conflict, and inequality, and its overly generalized character (e.g., Herzog 1992). In response, Friedman (1992) argued that it is valid and necessary to formulate broad generalizations, even when one can find many exceptions to these generalizations and that beliefs within a legal culture are not always consistent with objective evidence of actual conditions. He has conceded that he likes many of the achievements of American legal culture, including a spread of due process, the welfare state, laws against discrimination, no-fault divorce laws, and the expansion of liability (for harms they cause) for corporations and professionals (Friedman 1985, p. 151; 1992, p. 165). Of course, American legal culture can also be accused of complicity in the ongoing oppression of or discrimination against disadvantaged groups, social inequality, the tolerance of various forms of violence, and so on. Law, supported by cultural values, is an instrument that can both legitimate existing inequalities and provide means of resisting and challenging domination (Edelman 2001; Lazarus-Black and Hirsch 1994). Legal culture incorporates some contradictory tendencies, then.

AMERICAN LEGAL SUBCULTURES

Law must increasingly take into account cultural pluralism—that is, the fact that people with very different cultural values live within a single legal system (Cotterrell 2006b; Shah 2005). All contemporary legal systems that are multicultural experience some pressure to make special legal accommodations for the cultural practices of minorities within their midst (Shabani 2007). There are enduring tensions between requiring assimilation into the dominant culture and accommodating diverse cultural practices, between promoting formal legal equality for all and according some members of society a special status because of their specific cultural belief system.

Throughout its history, America has become increasingly multicultural, with a large influx of immigrants from all parts of the world. Although American law in principle is supposed to protect minorities, much evidence suggests that the law has been biased toward promoting the cultural values of the dominant (i.e., White Anglo-Saxon Protestant) group and promoting the assimilation of minorities into the American cultural mainstream (Norgren and Nanda 1996). One central question for law today is whether the state can respect cultural differences between groups, while also protecting the rights of vulnerable constituencies (e.g., Muslim women) (Shachar 2001). According to Friedman (1984, p. 28), the idea of a single standard for all has, in recent decades, been on decline in American legal culture. What he calls **plural equality** refers to the acceptance of different standards or languages for different groups. For example, in a Wisconsin case, the U.S. Supreme Court upheld the right of the Amish to keep their children out of high school. Hispanic Americans, or Latinos, constitute an increasing percentage of the American population. For many Latinos, Spanish is their primary or exclusive language, which has sometimes led to legal conflicts in a society in which English is the dominant language (Norgren and Nanda 1996). The "English-only" norm has been challenged as discriminatory.

It is clear that not only individual Americans but also subcultures and different socio-economic classes within American society have different attitudes toward law and legal institutions, ranging from uncritical support for them to a dedication to destroy them. Middle-class suburban Americans, for example, are regarded as highly supportive of law; improvident anarchists and survivalists have been antagonistic toward important dimensions of the legal system. The Mormons in America early in their history found themselves at odds with American law. For example, their practice of polygamy led to legal persecution by the American national government (Norgren and Nanda 1996). Most Mormons abandoned polygamy and adapted to the demands of the national legal norms, however, and became conservative supporters of the formal legal order.

The experience of African-Americans with American law has been more complex. Slavery and its aftermath were discussed in Chapter 6. With good reason, inner-city African-Americans have been less trusting of law and legal institutions than middle class suburban White Americans. This issue is explored more fully later in this chapter.

Legal cultural values can also vary locally—that is, somewhat different norms, attitudes, and practices relating to law may prevail in different local communities (Kritzer and Zemans 1993). Accordingly, in some communities legal cases are more likely to be filed and formally addressed than in other communities (*see* Box 9.1).

BOX 9.1 LEGAL CULTURE OF AMERICAN
COMMUNITIES

In the recent era, several anthropologists and sociologists have explored the legal culture of ordinary Americans living in particular communities. In a study of several small New England county courts, Barbara Yngvesson (1993) found much concern with having rights vindicated by the law, as well as a certain measure of resistance to authority. People in these communities often bring complaints to the courts when they believe they have been abused or exploited by another person with whom they have some type of relationship; the court clerks must, in many cases, explain to these people that their complaint does not meet the appropriate legal criteria. Women, in particular, turn to the court in the hope that it will use its power to discipline a male partner who is abusing them. Sometimes the court clerk will offer some informal advice or will attempt to mediate the dispute involved.

In a study of legal consciousness in two small New England towns, Sally Engle Merry (1990) found that the townspeople turned to courts only reluctantly, when all else had failed in resolving some dispute or situation where they needed help. The plaintiffs who go to court do not think of their problems in terms of specific legal doctrines or rules but more in terms of basic rights involving their parental authority, their property, or some other matter of personal concern. Those who go to court as plaintiffs are disproportionately White, middle-aged homeowners, and women of average means, with 1 or 2 years of college education. For Merry, the turn to courts does not reflect the collapse of community so much as it reflects American cultural values of individualism and egalitarianism, as well as policies adopted by the state in the recent era that encourage or at least facilitate initiating legal actions. People go to court to reaffirm their privacy rights as well as other rights. When poor people turn to the courts to pursue entitlements (e.g., disability payments), they are empowered in one sense, but paradoxically, in another sense they increase their dependence on the state. Altogether, Merry regards the

turn to courts as a form of searching for a new community and moral authority that will uphold and affirm such American cultural values as autonomy, self-reliance, and tolerance.

In a study conducted in a middle-Atlantic state, Ewick and Silbey (1998, p. 28) found that their respondents did not spend much time thinking about law, but when they did, they experienced it in quite different ways:

- An objective, disinterested realm
- A game, or terrain for tactical encounters
- A product of power

Here, too, people tended to turn to the law only reluctantly, resolving disputes informally whenever they could. When people did turn to law it was typically when the alternatives didn't seem to work and to assert values, rights, or some conception of justice. People were often frustrated by the law's inability to take their special, personal circumstances into account and to address their troubles effectively. Law, then, was not experienced as a uniformly positive force in people's lives or one always deserving of deference and respect.

All of these studies have focused on the legal consciousness of those who are part of the broad mainstream of American life. Levine and Mellema (2001), using the Ewick and Silbey study as a point of departure and a framework, have explored the meaning of law in the lives of women involved in the street-level drug economy, who constitute a loose "community" of sorts. For these very marginalized women, the experience of law is complex. They typically ignore it when they can. Although law does not deter them from law-breaking, their behavior is influenced by efforts to avoid the attention of law; when they are swept into legal proceedings, they seek loopholes that work to their advantage. These women typically attempt to settle disputes with others outside the framework of the formal law, although they may invoke the language (e.g., "rights") of formal law. For these extremely marginalized individuals, then, law is both "everywhere and nowhere."

INTERNAL LEGAL CULTURE

The aspects of legal culture discussed so far pertain to the lay legal culture of the general public. In addition to the legal culture of the general public, there is also an **internal legal culture** (Friedman 1975, pp. 223–224). This term refers to the values and attitudes of those within the legal profession toward law and the legal system. Although considerable overlap exists between the internal legal culture and the popular, or lay, legal culture differences can also be identified. For example, on the whole, the internal legal culture is more committed to the **adversarial ethic** (which calls on criminal defense lawyers to make the best possible case, within the rules, for the client, regardless of how heinous the crime the client may have committed) than is the general public (which often cannot comprehend how lawyers can defend "those people"). Those within the legal profession tend to be more oriented toward formal, logical legal reasoning than the general public, which may be more oriented toward the human or emotional dimensions of cases.

Those within the legal profession are well-positioned to translate their attitudes and values into social policy, especially if they are over-represented among lawmakers, as they typically are. Cotterrell (1997), in his critique of the concept of legal culture, made a case for **legal ideology** instead, with this term specifically referring to the ideas about law coming from the state and from within the profession, whose power to impose these ideas on the general public is accordingly highlighted. Perhaps it is best to think of legal culture as having various different dimensions, with the legal ideology of the dominant group especially influential on (but not wholly determining) the law-related beliefs of the general public (*see* Box 9.2).

Finally, in a world moving toward "globalization," is American legal culture becoming more influential in the world at large? Friedman (2002, p. 572) characterized law as "an American export." Yves Dezalay and Bryant Garth (1996) have argued that as international trade involving China has increased exponentially and as American-based multinationals are key players in this process, the role of Western formal law has become ever more dominant and lawyers have assumed an increasingly central role in business conduct. In contrast, Appelbaum (1998) argued that the Eastern preference for informal, extralegal forms of business will successfully resist the Western, or American, influence. Appelbaum wrote that *guanxi* (the traditional Chinese reliance on gift-giving and bestowing of favors as a basis for business dealings) will continue to play a central role in the Eastern world and will not be displaced by formal legal practices. *Guanxi* was not successfully repressed by the communist regime and is evident in the new Asian economies.

BOX 9.2 CULTURAL DEFENSES

In increasingly heterogeneous societies made up of people from widely different cultural backgrounds and heritages, it is quite inevitable that clashes between the requirements of the state's official law and cultural beliefs and practices of some groups will arise (Foblets and Dundee-Renteln 2009; Renteln 2005, 2007). When a cultural defense is offered in a legal proceeding, the defendant is asking the court to recognize that although the act they performed may violate the state's law, it should be viewed within the context of their cultural heritage and community, which may have promoted or at least accepted this act. A cultural defense may also involve a plea for exemption from certain laws because of a cultural heritage at odds with these laws. For example, in the United States it has been invoked by Navajo defendants in relation to the use of the hallucinogen peyote and

by Cambodian natives charged with eating a dog. The defense has, in some form, now arisen in countries all over the world. Inevitably, the use of this defense is controversial, especially when it is invoked to excuse, for example, killing another person as a matter of "honor" within a particular cultural value system.

A critic raises the concern that the discussion of a cultural defense has focused too much on minority and immigrant groups and has neglected how a cultural defense might be invoked by the powerful and privileged (Rowen 2010). For example, could an executive defendant in a corporate crime case claim that his actions were oriented to be consistent with the corporate culture, and accordingly individual blameworthiness be mitigated? Cultural defenses could also be raised in war crimes cases. Altogether, a range of complex issues can arise in relation to a cultural defense.

LAW, COMMUNITY, AND IDENTITY

The preceding discussion has suggested that the concept of legal culture is very broad. In a complex, heterogeneous society such as the United States, then, one can expect to find numerous co-existing (and sometimes overlapping) subcultures of attitudes and values pertaining to law. Much about these legal subcultures remains to be learned. But some studies have been made of the attitudes toward and understandings of law within particular communities.

The notion of community is central to the social existence of human beings. Almost all of us, unless we are hermits or living in very isolating circumstances, belong to one or more communities. Most of us find it necessary to orient ourselves toward the laws, rules, or norms of these several different communities to which we belong. This circumstance was described as one of **legal pluralism**. Obviously, then, people may experience conflicting demands—for example, from their religious community and from the political community of which they are a part. Also, communities can provide a means of resisting or confronting law, and sometimes communities actively organize to resist or challenge law (*see* Box 9.3).

The idea of community is often associated with a past when people are seen as having lived in close, caring communities; much concern in the present is expressed over the dissolution of such communities (Greenhouse 1988). Of course, communities in the past often imposed severe limitations on the freedom (and privacy) of their members, persecuted community members who deviated in any measurable way from community norms, and deliberately excluded from community membership those who were seen as different. The "stranger"—the refugee, immigrant, or non-citizen—is often marginalized or discriminated against by law (Sarat, Douglas, and Umphrety 2010). Communities have specifically been in conflict with, and have engaged in the persecution of, other communities. The "White" community passed laws promoting racial inequality and prohibiting interracial marriages (and "miscegenation") in some form throughout the United States following the Civil War, in part in response to the fear of economic competition from racial minorities (Edwards 2009; Pascoe 2008). Community rights may clash with democratic principles (Sistare, May, and Francis 2001). Communities as a whole, then, have a mixed history of positive and negative contributions to the human experience.

In the present era, there has been a celebration of certain forms of community ties, and claims have been put forth on behalf of communities (e.g., of minority group members, the disabled, or gay people). The term **identity politics** is sometimes used to describe the highlighting of ties to communities, especially communities that have historically been the targets of discrimination or persecution (Haney-Lopez 2003; Minow 1997). Cultural pluralism and an era of identity politics pose complex questions for law (Gutmann 2003; Sarat, Garth and Kagan 1999). The paradox and challenge here is to determine when community membership should matter and when it should be irrelevant. On the one hand, the U.S. Supreme Court has prohibited the use of challenges in jury selection to specifically exclude members of a particular community from serving on the jury; on the other hand, the U.S. Census Bureau has attempted to classify and identify people by group (community) memberships, in part to provide data for addressing problems of discrimination. Growing numbers of Americans do not fit easily into traditional identity categories. For example, Mexican-Americans are both White and non-White, American and Hispanic or Latino (Gomez 2007). Issues of ethnic identity arise in other countries in North and South America as well (French 2009). Demeaning stereotypes of Latinos contributed to discriminatory legal treatment of them (Bender 2005). In the case of *Hernandez v. Texas,* the U. S. Supreme Court legitimated unequal treatment of Mexican-Americans (Garcia 2008). This case influenced the development of a Latino identity.

Engagement with law, whether as a legal professional or as a layperson, helps shape the identity of members of society (Dan-Cohen 2002; Goldberg, Musheno, and Bower 2001; Sarat, Douglas, and Umphrey 2002). According to Engel and Munger (2003), the Americans With Disabilities Act has in important ways enhanced the self-image of Americans with disabilities, as well as their aspirations and perceptions of them by others. The role of law in the formation of the identities of children in transracial adoptions is less clear (Fogg-Davis 2002; Hearst 2002). But within both national and international law in the recent era, individuals have been accorded more freedom of choice in relation to constituting their identity (Franck 2000). In an increasingly globalized world, identity becomes less fixed on nationality but may relate increasingly to bonds linked with race, ethnicity, gender, religion, age, and sexual orientation that cut across national borders (Moran 2006; Spiro 2008). If this trend continues, it should have a profound influence on the nature of law. We have calls for universal, egalitarian citizenship, joining people around the world in democratic solidarity (Brunkhorst 2005). It remains to be seen how successful such calls will be. Law and identity are intertwined on many different levels.

BOX 9.3 COMMUNITY VALUES AND THE CASE OF PORNOGRAPHY

In certain kinds of cases, the law makes assumptions or claims about communities, and such assumptions or claims may or may not be correct. For example, one criterion for identifying pornographic material prohibited by law is that the material is "offensive to community standards" (Linz et al. 1995). This standard raises a number of problems. First, and obviously, much pornographic material is broadly distributed, especially with the explosion of Internet pornography, but different communities across the nation are unlikely to embrace a single standard for what they find offensive (Paul 2004). Within cities of any size, one can surely find smaller communities with quite different standards for what is offensive. In a conservative county in Utah, it was found that videos deemed pornographic and offensive to community standards were consumed at a disproportionately high rate by members of that community (Egan 2000). Also, in pornography cases, the application of "community standards" has often relied on inferences and intuitions as opposed to scientifically valid surveys of community standards, if only for practical reasons. Ironically, a study by Linz and colleagues

(1995) found that sexually explicit material not generally offensive to a particular community was subjected to vigorous prosecution in the name of the law, whereas violent materials clearly offensive to the same community were not subject to legal prosecution. Accordingly, important discrepancies between the legal code and community standards for sex and violence can be established. When the law claims to be acting on behalf of the community—in the case of pornography, as well as in other situations—it does not necessarily follow that its actions are truly in accord with the values and preferences of the community. Inevitably, then, at least some part of the community is likely to be deeply offended by the law and may actively protest against it. Some commentators claim that a "porn culture" has now become pervasive within American society as a whole, with a range of harmful consequences (Hall and Bishop 2007; Sarracino and Scott 2008). Pornographic films have been shown on some college campuses—sometimes with administrative approval and sometimes scheduled by student programming committees—although this has generated some controversy (Moltz 2009). Inevitably some communities both on campus and off take offense at these screenings.

LAW AS PRODUCT: THE MAKING OF LAWS

Written records of lawmaking have been left from some of the earliest human societies, and the inclination to make new laws has been an enduring feature of human history. Why do laws get made? This basic question has elicited different answers from different sources. The most conventional answer in elementary American civics lessons has been that law reflects the will of the people, implemented by their elected representatives. This notion can be regarded as a somewhat extreme example of a consensus, or functionalist, perspective on lawmaking. On the other end of the spectrum, radical (or leftist) adherents of conflict theory see the rich and powerful (elites) controlling and manipulating the lawmaking process for their own benefit and self-interest. Another view (pluralist), standing somewhere between these two extremes, sees lawmaking as a process involving competing interest groups who mobilize forces, with varying degrees of success, to pressure lawmakers to adopt laws they favor. In an attempt to find an alternative to the radical elitist and the pluralist perspectives on lawmaking, William Chambliss (Chambliss and Zatz 1993) has advanced a dialectical theory of lawmaking, which says laws are adopted to resolve various contradictions, conflicts, and dilemmas confronting society in a particular historical context.

PUBLIC DEMAND AND MORAL ENTREPRENEURS

Altogether, legislative lawmaking reflects a complex mixture of interests and pressures, with a different mixture of factors involved in the introduction of particular laws (Loewenberg 2007; Vago 2009). Legislative law-making is driven far too much by what plays well politically in the short-term—including tax cuts, "pork barrel" projects, and generous contracts for powerful corporations and unions—rather than what is in the long-term public interest. Legislators have also been criticized for being too focused on extending the perks and privileges of public office, including overly generous benefits, travel allowances, and pensions. In a study of the introduction of the Illinois seat belt law, for example, Maguire, Hinderliter, and Faulkner (1990) found that moral entrepreneurs (auto safety activists) and special interests (the auto industry) were most responsible for how the law developed; the law was not a response to general public demand and objective facts. The "general public," although hardly a unified entity, may share some broad values or may sometimes be aroused about a particular concern, creating pressure for legislative action. Laws proscribing homicide obviously reflect a broad consensus that the willful taking of another person's life is intolerable in a civilized society. Recent laws enacted in response to general public demand include the Three-Strikes-and-You're-Out law (requiring mandatory life in prison following conviction for a third felony) and Megan's law (requiring notification of a community if a released sex offender is living in its midst). Each of these laws was adopted largely in response to an especially heinous abduction, rape, and murder of a young girl in separate and highly publicized cases (Shichor and Sechrest 1997). However, lawmakers sometimes pass deliberately ambiguous laws, compelling the judicial branch to interpret these laws (Lovell 2003). Legislative lawmaking thus has various objectives.

Moral entrepreneurs take it upon themselves to crusade actively for new laws (Monrone 2003). The temperance movement early in the twentieth century crusaded on behalf of the adoption of the Volstead Act, prohibiting the sale and distribution of liquor; Mothers

Against Drunk Driving (MADD) mobilized to campaign for tougher penalties for those convicted on charges of driving under the influence (DUI).

Law professors, through their law review articles, books, and public testimony, also aspire to contribute to the making of law (Tushnet 2010). The extent to which legal scholars significantly influence the shape of law has been a matter of some debate.

LOBBIES

Those who lobby for new laws, modifications in existing laws, or the repeal of existing laws are not necessarily motivated by moralistic or public interest concerns. By the end of the twentieth century, interest groups were playing an increasingly important role in the lawmaking process in the United States (Koshner 1998; Samuels 2006). Much effective lobbying is carried out on behalf of various business or professional interests who are motivated primarily by self-interest or to protect the economic well-being of their constituency (Abramson 1998). Lobbying by a wide range of private interest groups increased exponentially in the recent era. Because no single private interest group can stay at the heart of, or dominate, the lawmaking process, one influential study claimed that a "hollow core" is at the center of this process (Heinz et al. 1993). These lobbying interests may be more successful in blocking unwanted legislation than in initiating new legislation. Powerful economic interests often have considerable advantages in the legislative and administrative arena because politicians depend on their financial support for campaign expenses. In addition, various government agencies or entities may actively lobby on behalf of laws either because their expertise has led them to realize a need for the laws or because their own agency or operation can benefit with a bigger budget and increases in personnel (Luchansky and Gerber 1993). Legislative lawmakers themselves may take the initiative in proposing new laws, either on the basis of a perceived political advantage to themselves or perhaps because, as dedicated public servants, they perceive a need for the new law. Figure 9.2 outlines the stages in the making of statutory law.

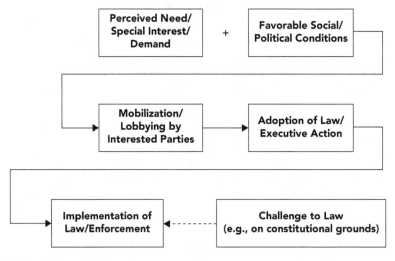

FIGURE 9.2   The Making of Statutory Law

JUDGES AND THE EXECUTIVE BRANCH

Judges, at least those in common law countries, also make law. Specifically, the opinions of appellate court justices take the form of law; when the U.S. Supreme Court declares legalized segregation to be unconstitutional or requires that those accused of crimes be informed of their rights, it is making law (Ball 2002; Klein 2002; Teninbaum 2007). In the United States, the justices of the U.S. Supreme Court, and other federal judges, are appointed for life, which is supposed to free them from the influence of political pressures or the public passions of the moment. However, their ideological commitments and past record of decisions are important factors in justices or judges being appointed in the first place. More often than not, judges remain reasonably faithful to these earlier commitments and make rulings of law consistent with these commitments.

Where judges are elected and face re-election, it stands to reason that they may be influenced in their rulings by political considerations. Judge-made law is supposed to be based on principled legal reasoning, although, as was noted earlier, there are basic disagreements over such matters as whether judges should largely defer to the intentions of legislators (and, in constitutional law, the Founding Fathers) or should take the law in new directions consistent with a perception of society's present needs.

Law in a real sense is also made by those in the executive branch of the government and by those in the administrative agencies. The executive branch often provides much of the expertise and initial drafting of laws adopted by legislative bodies and then uses its discretion in determining how (if at all) legislative law is enforced. Administrative or regulatory agencies (as discussed in Chapter 8) are empowered to adopt, enforce, and administer a broad range of administrative laws. Prosecutors become "crime creators" (i.e., create new categories of crime) through their discretionary power to interpret the law; for example, by extending the statutory prohibition against delivering drugs to a minor to a circumstance in which pregnant women were using drugs, prosecutors effectively created the law of prenatal drug use (Maschke 1995). In general, prosecutors tend to be especially political in orientation and may be somewhat biased in their lawmaking function toward making law consistent with the perceived public will. Of course, other factors, including the prosecutor's own beliefs and convictions, will influence prosecutorial lawmaking.

LAW AS COMMUNICATION

Much of law is inevitably expressed in words, and language is central to legal proceedings (Pether 2010; Robinson 2003; Stacy 2008). As O'Barr and Conley put it,

> language is the essential mechanism through which the power of law is realized, exercised, reproduced, and occasionally challenged and subverted. Most of the time, law is talk; the talk between disputants; the talk between lawyers and clients; the courtroom talk among lawyers, parties, judges, and witnesses; the legal talk that gets reduced to writing as statutes and judicial opinions.... (1998, p. 129)

The words and language of law (e.g., *due process, equal protection, criminal responsibility, beyond a reasonable doubt,* etc.) may be subjected to endless interpretation and

---

BOX 9.4 THE LANGUAGE OF LAW SCHOOL:
LEARNING TO THINK LIKE A LAWYER

While attending law school, law students are educated about many aspects of law, but they also have to acquire the special language of law. Anthropologist Elizabeth Mertz (2007), in *The Language of Law School: Learning to 'Think like a Lawyer'*, engaged in systematic observation of and transcription of the process of acquiring the language of law as it occurred in eight contract courses in eight different U.S. law schools. A traditional claim on behalf of this language is that it is "objective" and "neutral" and allows law students to address legal issues independent of ideology and emotion. But Mertz's analysis exposes some of the ways in which this supposedly neutral language of law is skewed to support the interests of the powerful over the powerless and to undermine the capacity of law students to make sound moral judgments about legal matters. The blood-less language of law works against the tendency of empathy for fellow human beings, or as a commentator on Mertz's book puts it, "Can you talk like a lawyer and still think like a human being?" (Conley 2009). More specifically, in her observations of the dialogue between law professors and their students in contracts classes, Mertz contends that the language of law tends to distort the understanding of the conflicts that arise in contract disputes, obscuring, for example, the significance of gender and race in such cases. The language of law that students learn turns legal "parties" into abstract entities or types—"buyers" and "sellers"—but too often strips away the social realities of the actual experiences of these parties. The language of law, accordingly, deflects critical social and moral analysis.

---

debate about their meaning, expressed in still more words (Fleury-Steiner 2002; Levi and Walker 1990). Lawyers and judges must learn to choose their words in legal proceedings with great care, and ideally with technical precision, as the choice of one word over another can have immense consequences. At the same time, lawyers may in some cases choose words that will obscure things they do not want to concede. In rape cases, the specific use of language can play a key role in determining the outcome (Ehrlich 2001; Matoesian 2001). Language in rape cases is importantly influenced by cultural images and values and in turn may influence cultural conceptions of rape victims and alleged rapists.

Altogether, words are the principal tools of the legal profession. Law has a language and terminology of its own. Students of law must learn to master the language of law itself if they are to perform effectively as lawyers (*see* Box 9.4). A disproportionately high percentage of legal terms are Latin words. Lawyers are sometimes accused of invoking unfamiliar legal jargon to score technical points in a case rather than to communicate something clearly. Judges are sometimes accused of using language in their opinions that is ambiguous, subject to different interpretations, or deliberately manipulated. Linguistic analysis has been applied to an understanding of the "selective literalism" of judges (Tiersma and Solan 2004). For example, what criminal suspects interpret as a police officer's indirect command may be interpreted by the court as simply a request; when suspects tentatively raise the question of seeing counsel, the court may decide they did not actually "request" counsel. And the language of ordinary litigants and witnesses is often at odds with the technical legal language lawyers and judges may insist upon, and these litigants are frustrated when their attempts to tell their stories in their own terms are interrupted by judges and lawyers insisting that they limit themselves to "legally relevant" answers (Conley and O'Barr 1990) (*see* Box 9.5).

In an increasingly globalized world, with more and more transnational dealings, the need to understand the meaning of foreign legal concepts intensifies (Bhatia, Candlin, and Allori 2008). A misunderstanding of foreign legal concepts can have significant negative consequences.

LANGUAGE AND IDEOLOGY

Judges today are sometimes monitored by advocacy groups and can get themselves into trouble by expressing "politically incorrect" or fundamentally insensitive sentiments and viewpoints. For example, some judges have been severely criticized and even removed from their position when they appeared to disparage the experiences of rape victims (Soothill, Walby, and Bagguley 1990). In a case that caused an uproar in Italy, that country's Supreme Court overturned a rape conviction on the grounds that the woman involved was wearing blue jeans at the time, and according to the Court, blue jeans cannot be removed "without the active cooperation of the person who is wearing them"; accordingly, consensual sex rather than rape must have occurred (Calavita 2001, p. 89).

Lawyers have been accused of manipulating language as a means of tricking or confusing hostile witnesses. Victims of such crimes as rape may be led by a shrewd defense lawyer into using, or agreeing to the use of, terminology that reframes the rape in terms of a consensual encounter. The language of predominantly male judges and police when they speak to women making complaints in domestic dispute cases has all too often suggested a gender-based bias. The language of some law, then, is said to be biased and to covertly express a male outlook and male interests (O'Barr and Conley 1998, pp. 3, 60–77; Beaman-Hall 1996). Taslitz (1999, p. 9) argued that men are taught to view language as a tool, or weapon, to achieve particular goals, whereas women learn to view language as a means of strengthening relationships and mediating disputes.

BOX 9.5 FORENSIC LINGUISTICS

Roger Shuy (1993, 1998) is a linguist who has testified as an expert witness, or has been a consultant, in a large number of legal cases, as a result of a chance encounter with an attorney on an airplane in 1979. Linguists are trained to analyze and interpret the complex structure and patterns of verbal communications between human beings. Tape recordings of conversations or other forms of verbal communication are sometimes key pieces of evidence in legal cases. Accordingly, a linguist may analyze "speech acts" involving "offering, agreeing, threatening, admitting, lying, promising, and requesting" (Shuy 1993, p. xix). Has someone clearly solicited or agreed to accept a bribe, or not? Has someone attempted to extort money from another person

or threatened that individual, or not? Has someone really conspired to commit murder or simply listened while another party spoke of committing murder? Has a suspect in a criminal case truly confessed, or not?

It is not the task of the linguist to determine guilt or innocence, but the linguist can analyze the use of language and can offer an expert opinion on whether particular verbal acts and exchanges support what is being alleged. A linguist can offer some basic principles for conducting effective and fair-minded interrogations and evaluating the use of deceptive language. A linguist can offer some guidelines for determining whether a confession is valid.

The law, Taslitz suggested, promotes the invocation of patriarchal stories adopting a male-centered point of view, and the law is directly complicit in the silencing of women. He believed that legal procedures should be changed to prohibit the exploitation of race- and gender-based stereotypes in court proceedings, to restrict or eliminate male biases, and to promote forms of reasoning consistent with the experiences and outlook of women. The voices of women are too often silenced by the language and method of law. In American courtroom cases involving non-English-speaking defendants, the accuracy and clarity with which courtroom interpreters render legal terms has significant consequences (Mason 2008). Defendants' legal rights can be significantly compromised by deficient translations.

The language of law, intertwined with ideology, played a key role in both the United States and South Africa in re-interpreting the history of indigenous peoples, stripping them of rights, and relegating them to "reservations" and "homelands" (Mertz 1988). The language of law, then, has been yet another device used to maintain or extend power.

SEMIOTICS

Semiotics is the study of signs, or linguistic codes. Semiotics has been applied to representations of law that foster both tolerance and intolerance toward diverse, religious, ethnic, and cultural groups (Wagner and Bhatia 2009). Milovanovic (2003) has applied a critical semiotic perspective to law and the legal process as a means of exposing the uses of language and various signs by some powerful interests, at a cost to others with less power. His perspective included the following assumptions:

- Language is value-laden, not neutral.

- Language structures thought.

- A political economy leads some forms of "discourse," or understandings of the world and ways of communicating, to be dominant over others.

- Politicians, judges, psychiatrists, and the like are in a position to impose their form of discourse on others—citizens, defendants, patients—with less power.

- Lawyers are manipulators of the dominant form of discourse or language.

- Open and fair communication is possible only in a society in which structural forms of inequality and exploitation have been eliminated.

Although virtually any form of legal communication has been interpreted in terms of signs, signs in the conventional sense play an important role in law. The term **official graffiti** has been applied to countless signs—such as the familiar "Stop" sign and "No Smoking" sign—that convey prohibitions, warnings, instructions, and the like (Hermer and Hunt 1996). In one interpretation, such signs, which are differentiated from conventional graffiti by being legitimated by the state, reflect an overload of law in our environment and become an efficient means of announcing rules and extending control over people's lives.

THE MEDIA

Law is communicated. When legislative bodies adopt new laws and judges issue new opinions, these new laws and opinions have to be communicated to the larger public. For the most part, this communication takes place through the media, which are quite selective about what they communicate. Accordingly, public knowledge of new law and legal rulings is incomplete and is biased in favor of the newsworthy. Images and representations of law and justice are importantly shaped by the mass media, which influences the form and character of the law itself (Masson and O'Connor 2007; McCann and Haltom 2006; Sarat, Douglas, and Umphrey 2005b). Law and news have actually been compared with each other; the coverage of law in the news has a profound political and social impact (Ericson 1996; Rapping 2003). Both law and news are oriented toward an event, which is dramatized, and toward individualizing problems; both are based in an institutional setting, claim to follow rules stressing objectivity and fairness, and dramatize what they produce. Overall, the news may have somewhat less credibility and legitimacy because of the large size of its audience and the immediacy of its communications. But the news plays an important role in shaping the way people make sense of the social order and of the law itself (Ericson 1996; Gies 2008). The media's coverage of a trial may play an important role in determining its historical significance (Chiasson 1997). There has been much discussion of regulatory failure in relation to, for example, the Wall Street financial meltdown of 2008 and the Gulf of Mexico oil spill catastrophe of 2010. The media may well have played a role in promoting the adoption of deregulation or weakened regulation in the recent era by highlighting stories of regulatory unreasonableness (Almond 2009). The news communicates much about law and legal institutions.

The meaning of law and legal issues can be uncovered from exploration of the popular culture—that is, from books, films, and so on (O'Neill 2009). Films have often represented legal proceedings and addressed law-related matters, and both influence our understanding of law and can provide points of departure for a critique of law (Burgess 2008; Chase 2002; Silbey 2001). Television, in particular, has played a central role in shaping the way people think about legal issues in America, including such issues as abortion, euthanasia, homelessness, sexual abuse, divorce, and parental responsibility (Jarvis and Joseph 1998; Rapping 2003). Television dramatizations of crime and criminal justice influence public opinion on these crucial topics (Lenz 2003). Televised trials today expose a broad segment of the general public to the realities of legal proceedings, although the cases featured tend to be atypical; also, the public may actually be exposed to evidence not presented to the jury, which leads to different conclusions on the part of the public (Giles and Snyder 1999; Goldfarb 1998). Media representations of trials may promote different value systems. In one analysis, the popular American daytime courtroom program *Judge Judy* promotes a stronger emphasis on free market values and individual responsibility than was true of another such courtroom program, *The People's Court* (Kohm 2006).

BOX 9.6 LEX POPULI: THE JURISPRUDENCE OF HARRY POTTER

Many of the readers of this text are surely well-versed in the world of Harry Potter (unlike the author of the text, who has never read a line of the Harry Potter books). Law professor William McNeil (2007), in *Lex Populi: The Jurisprudence of Popular Culture*, argues that public engagement with important law-related issues can be fostered if law professors themselves engage with popular culture and explore how it enriches our understanding of legal issues. In one chapter, he offers up a jurisprudential interpretation of the world of Harry Potter. MacNeil notes that conventional trials (e.g., of the "Death-Eaters") are featured in the Harry Potter books, as are "trials by ordeal" meted out by Lord Voldemort. Overall, in these books, a tension exists between fair resolution and outright revenge, between the rule of law versus the rule of man. Some (e.g., Bagman) are treated too leniently, some (e.g., Barty, Jr.) too harshly, contrasting the principle of equality before the law with the reality of judicial bias. A "police state" is suggested by the use of grudge informers and forced confessions. The world of Hogwarts reproduces the common status inequities of actual societies. In MacNeil's reading, author J. K. Rowling implicitly questions whether extension of emancipation and legal rights to subordinate groups is ultimately beneficial or potentially creates even more problems. He interprets Rowling as questioning whether law can bring about desirable social change, which reflects the skepticism of critical legal scholars on the role of law. Rights and law itself, in this reading, are ambiguously represented in the Harry Potter novels. MacNeil suggests that this ambivalence about law could also reflect author Rowling's experiences with efforts to ban her books and intellectual property rights lawsuits directed at her. Ultimately, a legal system that cannot easily differentiate between good and evil, Death-Eaters and White Wizards, is set forth in the world of Harry Potter.

Another law professor, Gary Pulsinelli (2008), raises the question: Are we Goblins or Muggles? In his interpretation, Goblins in *Harry Potter and the Deadly Hallows* believe that creators of artistic works maintain ownership rights in their work if it is sold, whereas in the Muggle (non-magical human) world property rights are typically negated upon the sale of tangible objects. But evolving legal views of intellectual property rights suggest that the Muggle world is moving toward wider adoption of the Goblin view of property rights.

People also learn about law from other sources: observations and instructions from family and peers, the school curriculum, lessons in church, books, and direct experiences (*see* Box 9.6). Both the messages about law and the specific content of what one learns about law from these different sources may be contradictory and not easily reconciled, which contributes to some of the confusion about law.

LEGAL NARRATIVES

In the recent era, a growing number of students of law have developed an interest in law as story, or narrative (Ball 2000; Hanafin, Geary, and Brooker 2004; Heinzelman 2010). One theme, explored earlier, looks at literature as a source of stories that often have much to teach about the nature of law. Another viewpoint focuses on law itself and legal cases as stories that have to be understood in narrative terms. In trials, for example, the lawyers involved typically tell stories with the objective of persuading the jury (or judge) to accept their story as the more persuasive one in the case. Ethnographic research has established, however, that laypeople who appear in court—as plaintiffs, defendants, witnesses, or jurors—tend to tell stories in a somewhat different form than do legal professionals (Conley and O'Barr 1990; Dingwall 2000; Fleury-Steiner 2002). Laypeople tell stories that include much legally irrelevant detail but seem to the person telling the story appropriate for understanding the sequence of events involved and how this provides an account of blameworthiness, or its absence. Stories, then, are central to the legal process, although stories in law take many different forms.

LEGAL SOCIALIZATION

Newborn infants know nothing about law. The infant is an anarchist by default—that is, the infant is utterly indifferent to rules and order and simply does what he or she can to satisfy needs and curiosity (e.g., howling in the middle of the night for food or pushing a plate off a highchair tray). But over time, if human beings are to become social beings, they must be socialized to conform to the rules and expectations of society and to acquire the values and attitudes of their primary group. **Legal socialization** eventually becomes a part of this process. It has been defined as "the process through which members of a society acquire [their] legal values, such as fairness, equality, and justice, and [their] norms of rule-governed behavior" (Cohn and White 1997, p. 152).

Legal socialization typically follows more urgent stages of socialization (e.g., toilet training, eating with a fork and spoon, learning to speak, asking for something instead of taking it). As Torney (1977, p. 134) has observed, "The socialization of children into the legal system includes diverse objectives: children must come to recognize laws, perceive their functions, accurately view their sources, develop appropriate attitudes toward those who enforce them, and guide their own behavior to conform to morality and legality." A study of a sample of 10,000 Mexican youths concluded that a promotion of understanding of law and legal reasoning can somewhat offset influences promoting delinquency and criminality in this population (Grant 2006). How, then, are people socialized about law? In part, we are taught specific lessons about the content and purpose of law, in school and at home; in part, we acquire understandings about and attitudes toward law through our exposure to law-related stories and accounts on television, in films, and in the print media; and in part we are socialized about law through our direct experiences as litigants, as victims, as defendants, or as jurors (*see* Table 9.1).

In its earliest stages, the legal socialization of young children can hardly be separated from their instruction in matters of morality. According to the Swiss psychologist Jean Piaget (1932) and the American psychologist Lawrence Kohlberg (1969), in the earliest stages of life children are "premoral"—that is, what feels good is good and what feels bad is bad (however, some recent research suggests that babies may have a capacity for altruism and empathy; Bloom 2010). Children typically move on to the next stage of moral socialization—the conventional stage—in which goodness is equated with what is approved of by peers and by other important figures in a child's life. A minority of children eventually move on to a principled stage of moral reasoning, in which the morality of a particular action or circumstance is evaluated in terms of its relation to a coherent set of defensible moral principles.

The cognitive developmental model can be contrasted with other models for learning about or becoming oriented toward morality and law: in the *accumulation model*, children are simply the passive recipients of law-related information passed on by their parents and other sources within their environment; in the *identification model*, the child imitates the adults in his or her environment; in the *role transfer model*, the child takes on the role of a subordinate and generalizes from the role in the home to that in the political system (Torney 1977). And on another dimension, the psychologist Carol Gilligan (1982) has claimed that female

TABLE 9.1 AGENTS OF LEGAL SOCIALIZATION

General	Specific	Specialized
Family/Peers/Professionals	Personal encounters/ experiences with law	Internship/Apprenticeship in law-related occupation
School/Church	Courses addressing law; books addressing law	Law school; grad study in law-related areas; police academy
Media	TV shows; films; songs about law	Documentaries about law

children are more oriented toward an "ethic of care" and male children are more oriented toward an "ethic of justice." Whichever of these models, or combinations of models, is correct, an understanding of and images of law are acquired in the course of the socialization process.

Attitudes and orientations toward law are not likely to be wholly formed by early experiences but may evolve over time. The term **legal consciousness** has been used to characterize this ongoing experience, awareness, and perception of law (Marshall and Barclay 2003; Nielsen 2000). This is a dynamic process, with people bringing to many everyday circumstances their understanding of law and in turn being influenced in their attitudes by their experiences with law. Studies of legal consciousness suggest that the power of the law is more a function of people's beliefs and values than what is on the books; people experience law both positively and negatively; law may define and constrain choices, but it does not determine them. In one concise formulation, "individuals are often strategic in their mobilization of law, invoking it when it helps them, ignoring it when it might hurt, and generating more suitable practices and institutions when law is inadequate" (Marshall and Barclay 2003, p. 624). In a study of radical environmental activists, a sociologist advanced the notion of "under the law" as a form of legal consciousness that views the law as a protector and defender of a fundamentally illegitimate social order—that is, one that promotes the destruction of the environment (Fritsvold 2009). Legal socialization and experiences of law are intimately related to behavior in relation to law.

LEGAL BEHAVIOR: COMPLIANCE AND DISCRETION

Why do people obey, or disobey, the law, and should people always obey the law? This question was answered in part in the preceding section: They obey the law because they have learned to do so (or disobey because they have failed to learn to do so). Furthermore, they have learned and internalized values that persuade them that they should obey the law. Philosophers through the ages have grappled with the question of whether it is natural for human beings to conform or natural for them to behave in an antisocial way, and they have come up with different answers to this question. Philosophers have also contended with the question of whether human beings have the capacity to make freely willed, voluntary choices of how to behave or whether human behavior is simply determined by various forces acting upon individuals. Such questions remain, and there are competing conceptions of human nature and human will, as well as the position that no fundamental human nature exists. Is law the natural expression of the human tendency to conform and cooperate, or is law an alien set of restrictions imposed by the powerful on the weak? Such questions, alluded to earlier, arise here as well. However one answers the question of human nature and the nature of law, no serious observer would deny that human beings learn about law and acquire specific attitudes and values pertaining to law in the course of becoming socialized and educated.

CONFORMITY

For the most part, we human beings become habituated to behaving in ways that conform with the law. In many respects, conformity is the line of least resistance, or the easiest and most natural thing to do. Of course, another aspect of the legal socialization process is the acquisition of values and beliefs that are in conformity with the demands of the law. In addition to internalization (of values promoting conformity with law), people may also be influenced by **identification**, or a social bond with those who create and enforce the law. The term **compliance** has been applied to circumstances where people obey law or orders because they hope for reward or fear punishment (Kelman and Hamilton 1989; May 2004). Compliance can be a function of good intentions and a sense of obligation, as well as a desire to avoid the negative consequences of failure to comply. A sociolegal study traces a long history within American law of assuming a lesser capacity to comply with law on the part of some minorities, which is characterized as "juridical racialism" (Weiner 2006). The concept of **legal behavior** can also be introduced here. Legal behavior has been defined as "any piece of voluntary conduct, influenced in any way by a norm, rule, decision, [or] order..." (Friedman 1977, p. 115) (*see* Box 9.7).

BOX 9.7 EVERYBODY BREAKS THE LAW SOME OF THE TIME

Most of us like to think of ourselves as law-abiding, but most of us also violate certain laws. Among the more common violations of law, one could include parking illegally, speeding, failing to recycle, evading taxes, lying to customs agents, gambling illegally, smoking where prohibited, copying software illegally, and stealing TV signals (Adler and Lambert 1993). Such violations occur because people regard the laws involved as trivial, unnecessary, unfair, or unreasonable. Sometimes people violate laws simply because they can get away with it and sometimes because they enjoy a small thrill by defying authority. Running red lights is certainly common; a psychologist in New York City observed one in four cars running a red light (Freedman 1975). When the mayor of New York City called for a crackdown on jaywalking—an exceptionally common offense—many of those receiving summonses expressed disgust (Rohde 1998). If a society enforces too many laws that people are inclined to disregard, it may encourage a lack of respect for law. Are there laws that should be violated more often than they are? One's right to dissent is a frequently celebrated dimension of the American political system but, in Jarret Lovell's interpretation, less exercised by ordinary citizens today than it should be (Lovell 2009). In his view, the many forms of injustice perpetrated by the state and by corporations should inspire higher levels of disobedience and dissent. Activists who do engage in civil disobedience often (but not uniformly) experience harsh treatment at the hands of the police and judges but also experience a sense of common purpose and solidarity with fellow activists. Americans celebrate Martin Luther King, Jr., Day, but many may not know that he was arrested for challenging segregation laws in the South (Zick 2008). Many other examples of historical figures who knowingly violated laws but are today venerated for their actions could be given.

In real life, then, a complex mixture of factors may influence people's behavior in relation to law. The law's basic appeal is normative, trying to persuade people to comply with law because they have a moral obligation to do so and because the values promoted by the law are consistent with their own. The law here also has an educational purpose—that is, it attempts to teach people the difference between right and wrong. Another strategy adopted by the law is utilitarian, or practical. For example, if you follow certain procedures, you will be granted a license to practice some professional calling, for which practice you may be well paid. Ultimately, however, law relies on coercion—force or the threat of force. Those who fail to comply with law face the prospect of a fine or prison or, in the extreme case, the death penalty.

Tom Tyler (1990), a psychologist, has produced a book titled *Why People Obey the Law*. Tyler basically finds that normative (or moral) as opposed to instrumental (or practical) considerations are central to obedience of law. In particular, people are found to obey a law if it emanates from a source they regard as legitimate (**legitimacy of law** is discussed in the following section). More specifically, when people view the legal order as using fair procedures, they tend to view it as legitimate. In addition, people's personal morality—and the desire most people have to view themselves as moral beings—plays a central role in obedience to law, more so than fear of the consequences of being caught breaking laws. Although such findings may be helpful in understanding why middle class White women are less likely to engage in conventional forms of lawbreaking than lower-class minority males, they are less helpful in understanding much white collar crime. Nor does this approach to understanding why people obey law probe the question of how the legitimation of law is generated and promoted in the first place.

Tyler and associates (Tyler and Huo 2002; Tyler and Rasinski 1991) contended that people are more likely to comply with the police and decisions of a court if they believe that the police have acted fairly and the court has arrived at its ruling in a procedurally fair manner. A critic of this view has suggested that compliance is more likely to be linked with institutional legitimacy or fear of negative consequences than with perceptions of fairness (Gibson 1989, 1991). A more narrowly focused study found that when the police acted in a procedurally fair manner in the course of making an arrest in domestic violence cases, repeat incidents of domestic violence were less likely to occur (Paternoster et al. 1997). Some experimental research supports the claim that people will obey laws not only when they regard them as legitimate, or fear being punished if they don't obey the law, but also because they expect others to obey—so obedience of the law can become a self-fulfilling prophecy (McAdams and Nadler 2008). This claim has been illustrated in relation to stop lights: Most drivers comply because they expect other drivers to do so and recognize that harmful consequences (e.g., traffic accidents) can occur if drivers fail to do so. Although the findings of studies of this type should be interpreted with some caution, they do strongly suggest a significant influence on the part of normative evaluations of law and legal proceedings.

OBEYING EVIL ORDERS

A related question arises: Why do people obey orders they should not obey, when the orders are intrinsically evil or immoral? In a famous social psychology experiment, Stanley

Milgram (1974) set up a situation in which subjects were instructed by the experimenter to administer an electrical shock to people (actually, the experimenter's stooges) who appeared to be failing in the performance of an assigned task. Most of the subjects obeyed the experimenter's instruction to administer shocks. This finding was interpreted to mean that most people would perform harmful (or evil) acts if the order to do so came from a legitimate authority figure. Although aspects of this experiment have been controversial, it remains immensely influential in the study of obedience to evil orders (Blass 2000). It was invoked, along with the Stanford mock prison study that demonstrated that student subjects would engage in cruel behavior if assigned as prison guards, to explain the behavior of American soldiers at Abu Ghraib prison in Iraq in 2004 (Zimbardo 2007). These soldiers, who subjected detainees to severe abuse and degradation, may also have come to accept torture as appropriate in a post-9/11 world.

Kelman and Hamilton (1989), in *Crimes of Obedience*, are among those who have addressed this question. The participation of a large number of Germans (and other nationals) in the Nazi Holocaust of World War II, the slaughter of several hundred Vietnamese villagers by Lt. William Calley and his troops during the Vietnam War, and the Watergate break-in (and cover-up) during the Nixon Administration are three familiar examples of such **crimes of obedience**. Of course, there is no single answer to the question of why people obey evil orders, and many of the different forms of explanation for legal behavior outlined above come into play. Specific factors involved in crimes of obedience may range from personality to culture. Overall, however, those who engage in crimes of obedience tend to be people who feel obliged to obey orders, even if it requires them to suspend their own moral views. At least some of those who engage in such crimes—in all the cases referred to above—went beyond specific orders and undertook illegal or evil activities that seemed to them to advance the objectives of the organization. As for attributions of responsibility for such crimes of obedience, a survey found that Americans tend to be divided between those who blame the superiors who gave the orders and those who blame the people who obeyed the orders.

DETERRENCE

The coercive response of the law has several purposes: to avenge wrongdoing and to make a strong moral statement that certain behavior is wholly unacceptable in a civilized society, to incapacitate those who represent a danger to other members of society, and to deter. The concept of **deterrence** is important in criminal law (Paternoster 1987; Schubert 2004). The law basically attempts to deter on two different levels: general and specific. On the one hand, it hopes to deter members of the general public from breaking laws by making an example of lawbreakers who are caught, processed by the criminal justice system, and appropriately punished. On the other hand, it also seeks to deter the specific offender who is being punished from repeating the offense, or any other criminal offense. Deterrence differs from incapacitation in that it addresses the psychological level, whereas incapacitation addresses the physical aspect of misbehavior. Obviously, deterrence fails in a fairly high percentage of cases, as people continue to break laws despite being aware of the possibility of being subjected to penal sanctions, and lawbreakers who have been punished get out and commit new offenses in a significant percentage of cases.

The effectiveness of deterrence is linked with the particular character of the law-breaking. In this sense, so-called **expressive crimes**—committed for emotional reasons or in the heat of passion—should be less affected by the threat of punitive sanctions than **instrumental crimes**, which are planned and carried out for gain (Chambliss 1967). But, again, many factors can enter into choices to comply with or ignore law, so there are many exceptions to any such proposition.

The effectiveness of deterrence has been linked principally with the *certainty,*, *severity*, *uniformity*, and *celerity* of punishment. Perhaps the principal reason behind the law's frequent failure to deter behavior is the broad absence of certainty that any particular act of lawbreaking will result in identification, apprehension, and the imposition of some form of punishment. Indeed, for many offenses, the odds heavily favor the lawbreaker. Severity is less important, but if the punishment is excessively mild, the lawbreaking behavior is unlikely to be deterred. Uniformity refers to the notion that like offenders are accorded like sentences; with the adoption of the U.S. Sentencing Guidelines, greater uniformity has been achieved, although the deterrent value of this uniformity is still somewhat unclear. If one offender is sharing a cell with another offender, and the two offenders have generally identical records and have committed the same types of crime but are doing sentences that vary greatly in length, then uniformity is obviously absent. In these circumstances, the convicted person with the harsher sentence is likely to see the legal system as being as arbitrary as a lottery and to deeply resent that sentence.

Finally, celerity refers to the speed with which the punishment is imposed. Punishment or its threat is likely to be more effective as a deterrent the sooner after the law-breaking episode it is applied. In our system of law, those accused of crimes are accorded due process; as a consequence, the punishment is often applied only long after the event, which by that time may seem like ancient history to the offender. In sum, then, a number of factors, or combinations of factors, influence the effectiveness of deterrence. Even if deterrence often fails, it is an overstatement to suggest that law can have no deterrent effect. After all, if no threat of punishment existed for tax evasion, much evidence suggests that fudging on taxes would be even more extensive than it is today.

LEGITIMATION OF THE LEGAL SYSTEM

If people do not believe in some fundamental way that they are obliged to comply with law—that the legal system and the legal authorities are deserving of compliance—then law as an instrument of social control is bound to fail. The idea of the **legitimation of a legal system** captures some of the principal concerns of this chapter. Every legal culture explicitly or implicitly adopts a view of what makes a legal system valid and deserving of support and obedience.

The German sociologist Max Weber ([1954] 1967, 1964, 1978) made some fundamental contributions to the concept of *legitimacy*. His use of the term in various places included notions of belief, claim, justification, promise, and self-justification. For present purposes, "legitimacy" is broadly construed in Weberian terms as that which is justified (i.e., "right") and demanding of support (i.e., "binding"). Compliance with a legal system as such should not be confused with legitimation; some degree of legitimation is required for the very emergence of, or continued endurance of, the legal system. Legitimation of a system implies, at a minimum, acceptance but need not necessarily mean absolute commitment. In contemporary society, legal-rational grounds for legitimation have achieved increasing significance, whereas in the past traditional authority and charismatic appeal were relatively more important bases for legitimation.

The concept of legitimation has been criticized. Hyde (1983) has argued that the concept cannot be adequately operationalized (i.e., put into a measurable form) and cannot be easily disentangled from other motives for obedience to law. Hyde asserted that habituation and rational, calculated self-interest explain obedience to law. While conceding some of the problems with the concept of legitimation, the author of this text (Friedrichs 1986b) has argued in response that the concept of legitimation is worth retaining with reference to the capacity of human beings to make autonomous moral assessments of the legal order (whether or not such assessments coincide with self-interest).

More broadly, legitimacy may describe both a state of affairs and a process, and is generally considered to be at least a desirable and at most a necessary element of a stable and effective political (or legal) order (Friedrichs 1979). Ultimately, legitimacy involves explicit or implicit justifications for the authority of an order, on the one hand, and the development of a sense of obligation on the part of subjects of that order, on the other. When a significant percentage of the population no longer regards the legal system as legitimate, or worthy of their respect and obedience, then there is a **legitimacy crisis** (Friedrichs 1980). Such a crisis should not be confused with the related crisis in confidence, when a sizable proportion of the population experiences diminishing faith in the system's leadership, although the two types of crises may well affect each other (*see* Box 9.8).

BOX 9.8 AFRICAN-AMERICANS AND LEGITI-
MATION OF THE AMERICAN LEGAL
ORDER

It is well-known that African-Americans are disproportionately processed by the criminal justice system and make up a vastly disproportionate part of the American prison population. In the recent era, a staggering 1 of 3 young African-American men, at any given point in time, was involved with the criminal justice system (Elikann 1996; Free 2003). Various explanations have been offered for this disparity (Wilbanks and Mann 1996). Some commentators have claimed that it principally reflects the higher levels of involvement in lawbreaking by young African-American men. Others have viewed it as a function of the similarly disproportionate representation of African-Americans among the disadvantaged. A third form of explanation has viewed these outcomes as a consequence of racism and discriminatory decision making by predominantly White criminal justice personnel.

Although no one explanation may fully explain the disproportionate representation of African-Americans in prison, a long and enduring history of discriminatory treatment surely plays a significant role. A response to this history is the relative absence of legitimacy of the legal system for many African-Americans. Slavery, after all, was constructed and supported by this legal order, as was the systematic segregation of and discrimination against African-Americans (especially in the South) in the century following the Civil War. African-Americans have a historical legacy of a legal system, then, that did not extend basic rights to them, did not protect the rights they enjoyed, and was directly complicit in a denial of rights.

BOX 9.8 (cont'd.)

Despite *Brown v. Board of Education* (1954), the Civil Rights Act of 1964, affirmative action laws of the more recent era, and other such legal efforts to correct or make amends for past injustices, many African-Americans have continued to experience various types of disadvantages. In the 1960s, and sporadically since then, a series of explosive riots occurred in African-American inner-city neighborhoods, clearly an expression of anger about enduring forms of racism and discrimination (especially on the part of the police) and frustration with the gap between the promise of equality and the reality of so many disadvantaged African-American lives. On some level, however, African-American patterns of lawbreaking can surely be linked with reservations about or the direct repudiation of the legitimation of the American legal system and of the corresponding obligation to comply with law (Davis 1974). This repudiation was most starkly articulated by African-American militants such as the Black Panthers in the late 1960s and early 1970s but seems to be broadly diffused, even when it is not specifically expressed.

The introduction of a "Black rage" defense for criminal conduct also reflects the position that the experience of racial oppression generates an understandable sense of rage that may manifest itself in illegal behavior that can be linked with the idea of delegitimation of the legal order (Harris 1997).

Two high-profile cases in the 1990s highlighted the distrust by African-Americans of a White-dominated justice system: the beating of Rodney King by White police officers and the officers' subsequent acquittal in their first trial (with major protests and rioting in African-American neighborhoods in Los Angeles) and the not-guilty verdict by a predominantly African-American jury in the O. J. Simpson trial, a verdict based partly on evidence of racism by White police officer Mark Furhman, a key investigator of the crime (Gibbs 1996).

Various recent studies have found dramatic differences between White Americans and African-Americans on confidence in law enforcement (Johnson 1997, p. 12; Wiley 2004). In one of these surveys, some 63% of Whites expressed great confidence, as opposed to only 26% of African-Americans. Only 8% of White Americans expressed little or no confidence, whereas more than one-third (35%) of African-Americans expressed this view. In a Canadian study of responses to a widely reported interracial homicide, it was found that well-educated African-Americans who had had recent contact with the police were especially likely to perceive injustice in the response of the criminal justice system to this incident. Perhaps only if the residual effects of the dismal history of White oppression of and exploitation of African-Americans is resolved can we expect to witness a broader legitimation of the American legal order in the African-American community.

LEGITIMATING LAW: THE CASE OF SOUTH AFRICA

The case of law in South Africa is discussed here because it illustrates in an especially striking way some of the themes pertaining to legal culture and legal behavior—specifically the legitimation of law. The case of South Africa is a fascinating one for students of the sociolegal and comparative legal systems on more general terms. First, South Africa's official legal system cannot be easily classified in one of the principal families of law. Second, through much of its history over the past several hundred years, law was clearly one major means used by Whites to dominate and oppress Blacks. Third, South Africa represents a striking case of legal pluralism, insofar as a number of different systems of popular justice long co-existed with the official legal system. And fourth, South Africa's transformation into a democracy raises various important questions about the role of law in this process and about the appropriate legal response to the injustices of the past.

The democratization of South Africa in the early 1990s is surely one of the more dramatic occurrences of the recent era (Klug 2000). More specifically, a country that had denied the great majority of its inhabitants (Black South Africans) a vote held a democratic election in 1994, and Nelson Mandela became the first Black South African president of the nation. It is all the more remarkable that only several years earlier, on February 11, 1990, Mandela had been released from prison after serving 27 years of a life sentence on a treason charge.

Obviously the earliest form of law in the South African region was the tribal law of the indigenous peoples of South Africa. When Europeans, primarily Dutch, settled in South Africa from the seventeenth century on, they imposed a form of civil law. The British began settling in South Africa in the nineteenth century, and their political dominance for a time, following the Boer War early in the twentieth century, led to the increasing introduction of common law elements into the legal system, with trials basically modeled on the British pattern (Chanock 2001; Milton 1987, p. 36). From the beginning of the twentieth century, a series of laws was adopted that stripped Black South Africans of rights to land ownership in most of South Africa and relocated most Blacks to segregated areas, ultimately designated as "homelands"; the process of denying American Indians their dominance over the land and relocating them to reservations had parallels with the South African situation, although in South Africa Blacks always far outnumbered Whites (Mertz 1988).

When the Afrikaner Nationalist Party came to power in 1948, some of the British influences in the legal system diminished; for example, the jury system was abolished in the 1950s. The Afrikaners who dominated this party were Whites descended from the early Dutch settlers. Gibson and Gouws (1997, p. 173) observed, "[T]o a degree uncharacteristic of dictatorial regimes, South Africa relied heavily on law as an instrument of political repression during the dark days of apartheid." Largely through the institutions of law, then, the Nationalist Party created the notorious **apartheid** system, which imposed multiple forms of segregation, discrimination, and control on the black majority of the population (Davis 1986; Steytler 1987). More specifically, apartheid included denial of South African citizenship and the vote to Blacks; establishment of governmental control of land and of freedom of movement, especially with "pass laws" and "influx control"; segregation of facilities; and repression of dissent.

The White South African government, identifying with developed Western nations, claimed that it was in accord with "the rule of law," although its constitutional system and various legislative enactments and "extralegal" actions (e.g., death squads assassinating anti-apartheid activists) largely seemed to negate the claim (Foster, Sandler, and Davis 1987; Jacobs 2004; Thompson 1986). The official system of law, claiming to adhere to the principles of legal positivism, was also used as a means of maintaining control over Black South Africans; no bill of rights was in existence. Some 17 million Blacks, from the beginning of the twentieth century on, were believed to have been arrested and prosecuted under influx control and pass laws (Steytler 1987, p. 70). Blacks who ended up in one of the official courts typically found themselves in a thoroughly alien environment, facing a White judge, speaking a language they did not understand, and applying rules unfamiliar to them (Dlamini 1988).

Although in the final period of the apartheid regime many forms of "petty" apartheid were eliminated, a variety of measures, culminating with a "state of emergency" declaration in 1985, broadly extended the state's powers of social control (Milton 1987). Large numbers of Blacks were shot down in protests, detained, tortured, and killed while in custody (Webster 1987). The principal thrust of the system of law surely seemed to many to be the maintenance of White power and privilege.

As noted earlier, however, a vast system of informal law, operating on various different levels, was also part of the Black experience in South Africa (McCall 1995; Nina 1993; Pavlich 1992). These alternative systems of justice have been variously labeled popular justice, community justice, and private justice. A study of justice in a large Black township, for example, found that it was "administered" by gangs, cultural movements, *ad hoc* neighborhood vigilante groups, community councils, and *Makgotla*, which are unofficial people's courts operating under tribal authority, administering indigenous native law (Hund and Kotu-Rammopo 1983). If certain conduct (especially anti-state activity) defined as criminal by the official code of law was not so regarded by Black South Africans, at least some conduct considered criminal (e.g., mundane street crime) in the townships was of no concern to the official legal system (Hund 1988). The White South African government, however, viewed emerging forms of popular justice (e.g., vigilante courts) as increasingly threatening toward the end of its regime and tried to outlaw them (Nina 1993).

The great majority of Black township residents turned to one of the informal mechanisms of social control with their grievances and accusations rather than to the formal system of justice established by Whites, although at least a minority continued to rely on the formal courts (McCall 1995). Mediation, rather than a judge-imposed ruling, was featured in the popular, or private, system of justice (Nina 1993). The popular justice of the *Makgotla* focuses more on issues of character than on the facts or the rules emphasized by the official system. However, such popular justice at least sometimes degenerates into a form of mob rule or vigilante justice. The "necklace"—placing a burning tire around the head of an accused person, leading to an especially tortured death—was the most notorious manifestation of this form of justice (Scheper-Hughes 1995). Furthermore, these courts typically reflected the patriarchal (or sexist) biases of the culture (Pavlich 1992). Such factors, as well as the fact that they all too often were both politically divisive and ineffective in addressing larger political issues, led to some deterioration of support for popular justice courts among Black South Africans.

Although law was heavily implicated in the establishment and maintenance of apartheid, it also became a weapon—both as a sword and as a shield—in the struggle against apartheid, in part because there were few other weapons readily available and in part because elements of a historical commitment to "the rule of law" prevented its use solely and exclusively as an instrument for the protection of White political purposes (Abel 1995b). Those who challenged the apartheid system on some issue certainly lost many cases in the courts, but they also won some cases. The government's professed allegiance to the rule of law and its claim that the courts operated fairly were important bases for its further claim to be legitimate and deserving of compliance (Davis 1986; Ellmann 1995; Gibson and Gouws 1997). Commitment to the rule of law at the end of the White regime could also be seen as a reflection of Whites' concern about their own vulnerability in a post-apartheid society in which no strong commitment to the rule of law had been established (Haysom and Kahanovitz 1987, p. 198). However, during the final period of White rule, it was said that Black South Africans accorded government laws less legitimacy than virtually any other governed group, and large majorities expressed negative attitudes toward law and legal institutions (Human Sciences Research Council 1985; McCall 1995, pp. 64–65; Steytler 1987, p. 68).

Although Black South Africans certainly experienced many negative aspects of law during the apartheid era, various polls conducted during the post-apartheid era suggested that they held more favorable views of the legal system than one would expect (Ellmann 1995; Gibson and Gouws 1997). According to a poll conducted in 1996, well after democratization, Black South Africans were generally distrustful of all social institutions (only Nelson Mandela, the first South African President, was widely trusted), but the legal system came off less poorly than many other social institutions (Gibson and Gouws 1997). If at least some Black South Africans had developed some confidence in the legal system (but not the police), it may be attributed to the fact that many other institutions of White South Africa were experienced as even less trustworthy and fair. Perhaps unsurprisingly, although White South Africans remained strongly committed to the rule of law following democratization, their trust in the legal system declined significantly (Gibson and Gouws 1997). Black South Africans, on the other hand, were far less committed to the rule of law and were more concerned with substantive justice than with procedural formality.

Ultimately, White minority dominance of South Africa could not be sustained because such a system was too widely regarded as not legitimate or not deserving of respect and compliance. As one commentator observed near the end of the apartheid regime, "Perhaps more than any other state and social order, South Africa stands illegitimate and repressive before its own people" (Greenberg 1987, p. 1). Traditionally, the White minority in South Africa relied heavily on Western racism intermixed with special elements of Afrikaner culture (including the theological rationales emanating from the Dutch Reformed Church) to promote its legitimacy claims. The pervasive level of control over the media and other sources of information was also a central element in promoting legitimating claims. In the final years of rule, the White government attempted to maintain legitimacy and power by a mixture of reforms (e.g., eliminating petty forms of apartheid) and coercion (e.g., the Emergency Act, giving the police broad powers). Ultimately, a recognition developed in the last White government, under F. W. De Klerk, that democratization (with protections built in for the white minority) was the only viable means of resolving the ongoing legitimacy crisis.

In the years leading up to and those following the transition to democracy, South Africa was plagued with increasing crime and much violence in the Black townships, with anxiety over this wave of crime overtaking earlier concerns about political violence (Hutton 1997). The township violence was widely, and understandably, condemned as "senseless" in light of the fall of the apartheid regime; an anthropologist responded by asking, "Did 'senseless violence' imply that the police were 'sensible' in their attacks and raids on Black townships? Was 'senseless violence' a racist code for irrational Black violence, as opposed to rational, sensible white violence?" (Scheper-Hughes 1995, p. 147). Despite the high level of concern about crime and violence, the policies of the criminal justice system—at odds with trends in many Western nations, including those of the United States—became more liberal. The death penalty (commonly imposed in apartheid South Africa) was abolished; magistrates received training in race and gender sensitivity; and rehabilitation was stressed in sentencing, on the premise that many offenders were victims of apartheid (Hutton 1997). Whether such practices would endure in the long run, especially if rates of crime and violence continued to increase, was an open question.

In view of the historical role of law in the repression of Black South Africans, it would have been understandable if the new government, elected following democratization with African National Congress leader Nelson Mandela as President, moved to abolish existing legal institutions. Mandela had been tried and convicted of treason and had been sentenced to life in prison (and served some 27 years in harsh conditions) by this legal system. Although a new constitution was adopted and reforms were instituted, much of the existing legal system was retained. Mandela's commitment to the rule of law was not necessarily embraced by all his associates, who for many years had operated outside the tradition of formal law. Retention of the legal system reflected the government's concern with potential chaos as a result of a wholesale abandonment of law and legal institutions, a need to retain a good measure of confidence from both South African Whites and outside investors in the economy, and perhaps, in some respect, on the part of Mandela and others for what had finally been accomplished through legal means.

The new government faced a large and sensitive challenge: What should it do about the many crimes, injustices, and human rights abuses perpetrated by or on behalf of the apartheid regime as well as the opposition forces? More specifically, could it reconcile the potentially conflicting objectives of exposing the truth about past atrocities and penalizing the offenders (Berat and Shain 1995, p. 166)? In other words, was it only by offering amnesty to past offenders that one could hope to obtain true accounts of past crimes? If the government were to satisfy the understandable desire of past victims of these crimes (and their survivors) for avenging the wrongdoing, it could jeopardize support for the newly established democratic institutions (especially among anxious White South Africans). In one of its first acts, the new democratic government established a remarkable Truth and Reconciliation Commission, empowered to grant amnesty to those who confessed truthfully about past political crimes. Needless to say, the work of this Commission was controversial, with demands for justice sometimes conflicting with the pursuit of truth (*see* Box 9.9).

BOX 9.9 TRUTH COMMISSIONS AND PAST INJUSTICES

The endlessly complex question of how law and legal institutions should best address large-scale crimes of the past has been raised at a number of points in this book. With the establishment of a democratic South Africa early in the 1990s, that country adopted one approach to this question that has been both widely praised and criticized. Rather than attempting to identify, indict, and try those who had committed crimes under the South African apartheid regime, a Truth and Reconciliation Commission was established (Hayner 2002; Minow 1998; Rotberg and Thompson 2000). This approach was adopted, at least in part, because as a practical matter it was not possible to identify and bring to justice the huge number of individuals who were complicit in the crimes of apartheid, nor was it possible to compensate the even larger number of victims of this regime (Todorov 2001, p. 34). But the establishment of this Commission was also advocated on the claim that a reconciliative or restorative form of justice was preferable to a retributive or punitive form of justice. In addition, only through this approach would it be possible to recover the truth of what had really occurred during the apartheid regime, and it was argued that having a truthful record of what had occurred was of real value.

On the one hand, the South African Truth and Reconciliation Commission has been hailed as a model for a constructive, as opposed to a destructive, way of addressing large-scale crimes of the past (Boraine 2001; Minow 1998; Rotberg and Thompson 2000). On the other hand, perhaps inevitably, many South Africans

BOX 9.9 (cont'd.)

ultimately expressed disappointment or chagrin with the outcome of the Truth and Reconciliation Commission (Brody 2001; Gibson 2004). In various polls conducted in the late 1990s, some two-thirds of those surveyed thought that race relations in South Africa had deteriorated as a consequence of the Truth and Reconciliation Commission, and Whites in particular felt that it was unfair and biased (Rotberg and Thompson 2000, p. 19). It is far from clear that it succeeded in promoting more respect for the rule of law among Black South Africans. Certainly many of the victims felt that justice had not been realized, and resources to assist or compensate victims were inadequate. But many commentators note that South African democracy is still in its infancy, and a final historical verdict on the Truth and Reconciliation Commission is yet to come. It is also far from clear that any other form of addressing the crimes of the apartheid regime could have been more successful, and other responses could conceivably have had catastrophic consequences.

For South Africa, early in the twenty-first century, the challenges would remain formidable. Despite a relatively buoyant economy, the country was struggling with an epidemic of AIDS, a high crime rate, enduring unemployment and poverty, and rampant corruption (Jacobs 2004; Mda 2004). Could outbreaks of violence inspired by occult beliefs be effectively policed by a secular legal system with an orientation at odds with indigenous South African culture (Comaroff and Comaroff 2004)? Would the post-Mandela presidents be able to maintain a level of support comparable to that enjoyed by this historically unique figure? Could the commitment to the rule of law be maintained while addressing past injustices and present inequalities? The Constitutional Court of South Africa was much more successful in eradicating racist, sexist, and homophobic laws than in addressing basic social and economic rights (Davis 2010). Early in the second decade of the twenty-first century, a severe erosion of trust of politicians on all levels of government had occurred (Dugger 2011). The future well-being of South Africa and the legitimacy of its political system depended upon its leadership effectively addressing the pervasive corruption and the ongoing great disparities in wealth and in access to basic services.

CONCLUSION

Law intersects with culture at many points, and legal behavior has many different dimensions. The notion of community (and identity) is one key feature of the broader terrain of legal culture. That law has a language, and communicated law must also be understood as a critical aspect of legal culture. The process of lawmaking reflects some aspects of the legal culture but must also be seen in relation to specific institutional processes. And legal behavior cannot be separated from a consideration of legitimation as it relates to law. The case of South Africa illustrates some of the themes of the chapter and, as a fascinating case in its own right, can be linked with many issues explored in other chapters.

KEY TERMS AND CONCEPTS

adversarial ethic	identity politics	legitimacy of law/
apartheid	instrumental crimes	legitimation of a
communitarians	internal legal	legal system
compliance	culture	*makgotla*
crimes of obedience	legal behavior	official graffiti
deterrence	legal consciousness	plural equality
expressive crimes	legal culture	republic of choice
guanxi	legal ideology	semiotics
identification	legal socialization	total justice

DISCUSSION QUESTIONS

1. With issues such as whether sexual and violent materials are offensive, who should ultimately decide? Does it make sense to let the law decide such an issue for the community? Could any problems arise if each community made its own laws based on its values?

2. In what situations does the general public usually voice the greatest concern for new laws or for changes to be made to existing ones? Do most laws seem to be a reflection of elitist control over the powerless, or are they more of a general consensus of the population? Explain.

3. Discuss the power behind the language of the law. How do legal professionals have an advantage over laypeople, especially in the courtroom?

4. Discuss the process of legal socialization. Through what means, and when, are most people oriented toward the law? Explain how the news or media play a part in how we learn about the law. Why do you think most people who obey the law do so? Do moral reasons tend to play more of a role than rational reasons?

5. Compare the role of legitimation in the case of African-Americans and the law to the case of South Africans and the law. Are there any similarities to the cases?

CHAPTER 10

LAW IN FLUX:
LAW AND SOCIAL CHANGE

We want law to reflect basic values, to be a source of stability, to withstand the shift-ing winds of fashion and passions of the moment. At the same time, we want law to evolve with transformations in social attitudes and societal needs, to be flexible in new cir-cumstances, to lead society in the direction of emerging goals and aspirations.

Is law best thought of as responding to changes in the larger society or as an active instru-ment of those changes? Where is law heading as we move through the twenty-first century, and what will it look like in the future? Of course, law is endlessly complex and multifac-eted. Some aspects of law do endure with little, if any, real change over centuries; other parts of law undergo dramatic changes, sometimes within a relatively short space of time. Law is clearly both an object of social change and an instrument of social change. Some dimen-sions of law will change little, if at all, as we move through the twenty-first century, whereas other dimensions of law will change dramatically.

What is social change? Many of the changes in society are superficial, cosmetic, and insubstantial. Styles, fashions, and fads come and go. Yet, certain forms of social change are fundamental, structural, and consequential. Revolutions and major reforms can bring into being far-reaching and enduring changes. One of the ways in which the modern world is said to be different from the ancient and traditional world is that people have come to expect (and often insist upon) change in many aspects of their existence.

Many members of modern society welcome change, but others are resistant to at least some forms of change. Tensions and conflicts inevitably arise between those who are pro-moting social change (e.g., feminists) and those who are opposing it (e.g., traditionalists). Thus, law is used by some to promote social change that they want to see come into being; law is bitterly attacked by others for promoting social change they find distressing. Law is viewed by some as an instrument that should be used to lead the way in improving social conditions; law is viewed by others as an entity that should maintain the traditional values of society in defiance of passions of the moment. Some changes originate from without the legal system, others from within it (Friedman 1975, p. 270). Change may affect only the legal system itself, or it may have an impact within the larger society. Legal change, then, occurs on many different levels and takes many different forms.

Legal change may take a liberal, or progressive, direction, but it may also take a conservative, or reactionary, direction. In the liberal view, law should be reformed to promote more equality, broader opportunities, more protective rights, and so on. For conservatives, law should only be changed when it expands personal freedom, supports free enterprise, and reinforces traditional values. Conservatives typically view liberal legal initiatives as restricting individual rights, interfering with a capitalist economy, and reinforcing dependency or tolerating predatory crime. Liberals typically view conservative legal initiatives as protecting socially destructive rights (e.g., gun ownership), making the rich richer and the poor poorer, rendering those accused of crimes vulnerable to unjustly imposed punishment by the state, and depriving citizens of important privacy rights (e.g., the right to have an abortion). Legal change is a function of power, and all too often the powerful and privileged have used their influence on law to protect or extend their own interests. The historical path of legal change in America has been complex and contradictory. Americans have experienced cycles during which many progressive initiatives have been advanced, and other cycles during which reactionary measures have been dominant.

Should law be used as an instrument of social change and as a means of promoting good behavior? Those at the ideological extremes—anarchists and reactionaries—generally oppose such use of law. Radical anarchists regard legal reform within the existing system as an illusion (Amster et al. 2009). Law in its very form favors the advantaged, and the social system itself has to be radically transformed. As Peter Kropotkin ([1927] 1966, p. 295), a leading theorist of anarchism, put it, "No more laws! No more judges! Liberty, equality, and practical human sympathy are the only effectual barriers we can oppose to the antisocial instincts of certain among us." He has defined **anarchism** as "a principle or theory of life and conduct under which society is conceived without government—harmony in such a society being obtained, not by submission to law, or by obedience to any authority, but by free agreements..." (Kropotkin [1910] 1971, p. xi). On the other hand, the reactionary Nicholas Murray Butler (1923), a president of Columbia University, spoke out early in the twentieth century against the Fifteenth Amendment to the Constitution (extending the universal franchise) and the Eighteenth Amendment (prohibiting trade in liquor) as doing more harm than good and contributing to the general lawlessness in the country.

Law is both an object of social change and an instrument of social change, a dependent variable and an independent variable (E. Levine 1990; Vago 2009). These two dimensions of law and social change are intimately interrelated and cannot be easily separated. That is, when social conditions change, laws over time are likely to reflect such changes, but at the same time those welcoming social change or having some vested interest in it will often actively campaign for legal reforms that could speed up the pace of the desired social change. If, however, the civil rights laws of the 1960s reflected changing attitudes within society, they were also intended to promote racial integration and the demise of racial prejudice. If welfare law reforms of the 1990s reflected changing social attitudes about poverty and dependency, the reforms were also implemented with the claim that they could help bring about desirable changes in the behavior and attitudes of welfare recipients. Accordingly, any

---

BOX 10.1 FOUNDING FATHERS OF LAW AND
SOCIETY ON LEGAL REFORM

The pioneering students of law and society were intensely interested in the question of law and social change. Their views were
discussed in previous chapters on jurisprudence and on the sociology of law. But some of their key ideas can be briefly reviewed
here. For Sir Henry Maine ([1861] 2001), the primary law-related
transformation over time can be found in a shift in law from the
centrality of status (related to group membership) to contract
(related to voluntary individual agreements). Although it seems
indisputable that contracts have become more important in a
complex, modern society, it is worth noting that in the recent
era, status (e.g., gender, race, disability) has also been important
in a growing body of law. For Karl Marx (Cain and Hunt 1979),
law evolved into its modern form in conjunction with the rise of
capitalism; the transformation of society to communism should
lead to the obliteration of law. As we know, the attempt to eliminate law in post-revolutionary societies had largely devastating
consequences and could not be sustained in the long run. For
Herbert Spencer (1898), it was a mistake to use law as a means
of assisting the disadvantaged because this interfered with the
laws of nature and the principle of survival of the fittest. Although
Spencer's advice was largely disregarded in the twentieth century, conservatives have continued to embrace and promote
this position (with recent welfare law reforms at least partially
reflecting this). For Emile Durkheim ([1893] 1984), the principal
change over time was from a system of law with repressive (or
punitive) legal sanctions to one with restitutive (or compensatory)
sanctions. This claim has been challenged, because much law in
the modern world seems to be oriented toward controlling and
exploiting people. For Max Weber ([1954] 1967), law in contemporary bureaucratic, capitalist society takes on an increasingly
rational orientation, with an emphasis on objectivity, predictabil-
ity, and instrumentality. The rationalization of the law is far from
complete, however, and many irrational elements still survive.

---

separation of law as object of social change and law as instrument of social change, for purposes of discussion, is inevitably somewhat arbitrary (*see* Box 10.1).

Law and social change have been an ongoing preoccupation of contemporary students
of law and society. For some, especially those with a positivistic or functionalist orientation,
social scientists should dispassionately formulate law-like propositions about law and social
change that can be subjected to empirical testing. These themes were discussed in Chapter 5
but can be briefly reviewed here. Black (1976) formulated a series of propositions about the
relation between law and certain social variables, with the idea that these propositions can
be tested. For example, Black predicted that law varies inversely with other forms of social
control. This proposition inevitably suggests that as other forms of social control decline,
more law will have to be introduced in response. Lempert and Sanders (1986) attempted to
demonstrate how social science research can enable us to understand law and social change.
For example, such research provides some evidence of the impact of legal reforms (e.g., the
Civil Rights Act of 1964) on the enduring problem of racial inequality. Although these sociologists were committed to a scientific approach to understanding law and social change,
they also expressed the faith that this approach could provide a foundation for promoting
greater justice within society.

At the same time, some students of law and society have rejected the social science
approach to understanding law and social change in favor of critique and interpretation.
Quinney's ([1974] 2001) *Critique of Legal Order* sought to expose some of the many ways
in which contemporary American law is exploitative and oppressive, calling for a basic
societal transformation to overcome these conditions. Delgado and Stefanic (1994), in
Failed Revolutions: Social Reform and the Limits of Legal Imagination, suggested that only a

fundamental transformation in consciousness, not legal reform by itself, is likely to produce long-term change in a progressive direction. De Sousa Santos' (1995) *Toward a New Common Sense: Law, Science, and Politics in the Paradigmatic Transition* sought to expose the collapse of modernity and the emergence of a postmodern world, with a call for moving law in a whole new, emancipatory direction in the future. These students of law and society have called for their readers' active engagement in the process of legal and societal transformation.

LAW AS AN OBJECT OF SOCIAL CHANGE

Law changes over time. Law as an institution tends to become increasingly formal and complex as a society evolves and expands. Many factors contribute to the changes in law. First, the increasing size of the population alone tends to impose some pressures for change. The kind of law needed to govern a teeming city with millions of people is bound to be different from the kind of law called for in the case of a small, nomadic tribe. As a general rule, as people shift from small rural communities to urban centers, there is a need for new forms and types of law to respond to the special conditions of city life. Over time, for example, we need laws to allow people to live together in proximity without constant conflicts, and we need legal institutions that can process large numbers of defendants and litigants at the same time. In a parallel vein, with the emergence of a modern capitalist system, and of increasing numbers of large, complex organizations (such as industrial corporations), law must change to adapt to the realities of these new conditions. Over time, a vast complex of laws has developed in the realm of contracts—for example, because they are one key feature of this type of economy; a similar growth and expansion has occurred in the realm of corporate law, or the conditions governing corporations.

The introduction of ever more complex forms of technology inevitably produces a need for new laws. As one obvious example, the introduction of the automobile ultimately led to many new traffic laws. In the more recent era, the introduction of computers, and the very rapid spread of the Internet, has generated a demand for laws to respond to the whole new set of conditions created. The increasing capacity of sophisticated medical technology to keep people "alive" indefinitely is another example of an area where technology generates a need for new laws (e.g., on the proper role of physicians in allowing, or even facilitating, death).

Law changes, too, because groups of people perceive a discrepancy between what their values or their sense of rights call for and what the existing law permits or tolerates. Prohibition, early in the twentieth century, with its ban on the sale and distribution of liquor, came into being largely because supporters of the temperance movement campaigned for it over a long period of time. In the more recent era, Mothers Against Drunk Driving (MADD) has mobilized, with some success, for tougher laws against drunk drivers. Of course, the fact that some particular interest group in society mobilizes to bring new laws into existence or to repeal existing laws does not mean that such efforts are uniformly successful. The pro-life movement in America, for example, has not been able to bring about the outlawing of abortion, despite relentless campaigning on the issue over a period of decades.

Law changes for many reasons, only some of which have been suggested here. Law changes not only because of the actions of human beings, but also in response to natural

TABLE 10.1 FACTORS CONTRIBUTING TO LEGAL REFORM

- Growth of society (e.g., population growth)
- New economic system (e.g., capitalism)
- New technology (e.g., computers)
- New social conditions (e.g., urbanism)
- Moral entrepreneurs (e.g., MADD)
- Special interest groups (e.g., corporate lobbyists)
- Public interest considerations (e.g., communicated by idealistic legislators)

catastrophes, such as major hurricanes and earthquakes (Miller 2009). (Table 10.1 lists a number of factors contributing to legal reform.) (*See* Box 10.2.) Law changes because new sets of conditions may make such change necessary simply as a practical matter. For example, although the occasional dispute in a preliterate society can be handled by community leaders on an *ad hoc* basis, the processing of thousands of cases in a large contemporary urban justice system requires some form of a legal bureaucratic organization. Law changes because it is in the interest of parties who are in a position to determine or influence the nature of law to promote certain changes. The corporate business community, for example, has promoted changes in product liability law to minimize its exposure to consumer lawsuits. Somewhat idealistically, we like to believe that law changes because some people in a position to implement change (e.g., legislators or appellate court justices) arrive at the conclusion that the best interests of society as a whole are served by a change in law, the legal process, or legal institutions. But much evidence can be marshaled to demonstrate that politics, power, and special interests have played a larger role in bringing about legal change than have principled and altruistic objectives.

Efforts to reform law typically encounter many forms of resistance. Vago (2003, pp. 325–333) has efficiently identified many of these sources of resistance. They include social, economic, cultural, and psychological factors. In social terms, the upper class tends to resist legal reform that might compromise its advantages, and there are always specific parties who have a vested interest in maintaining the status quo (Handler 1978). If enough is at stake in a proposed legal reform, parties whose vested interests are threatened are likely to form an organized opposition to the proposed legal reform. The opposition to legal reform may be based on ideology, morality, or religious belief, as well as on economic or practical interests, or possibly some combination of both types of factors. The National Rifle Association (NRA), as one example, has had a long history of successfully organizing opposition to proposed gun control laws, although in the recent era it has been somewhat less successful in this regard; the NRA campaign against gun control reflects a combination of vested interests (of gun manufacturers and dealers) and ideology (the belief that citizens are constitutionally entitled to possess firearms without restrictions).

The source of resistance to legal reform may be specifically economic. This economic interest may reflect a desire to protect economic advantage or a perceived lack of economic resources

BOX 10.2 LAW AND CATASTROPHE:
HURRICANE KATRINA AND THE
DEEPWATER OIL SPILL

Law is strongly associated with order and stability. When catastrophes occur—ranging from revolutions and genocidal campaigns to earthquakes and hurricanes and oil spills—the orderly world of law is upended. But law can also be viewed as an institution that arises in part in response to catastrophes like war, is influenced by catastrophes, and attempts to restore order in the wake of catastrophes (Baum 2007; Sarat, Douglas, and Umphrey 2007c). However, the institutions of law can be overwhelmed by catastrophes.

Hurricane Katrina in September 2005, not only caused massive physical destruction in the Gulf Coast states but also left the legal system of Louisiana—which was especially hard hit by the hurricane—in a shambles (Applebome and Glater 2005). Legal paperwork and key evidence was washed away, judges and lawyers were dispersed and often unavailable for court proceedings, patrol cars and police headquarters were lost or damaged, detention centers were evacuated, and many courthouses were flooded. Revenue upon which the justice system was importantly dependent—from traffic and parking offenses—was obliterated in New Orleans because of the conditions in the city for a long period following the hurricane.

The hurricane also generated complex issues of legal liability for the losses sustained (Alford and Treaster 2005). Many homeowners had no flood insurance to begin with, but even those who did often had policies that distinguished between wind and water damage and flooding. The policies often exclude compensation for flooding, but it is hardly easy to differentiate between damage caused by wind or water and flooding.

Hurricane Katrina was especially noteworthy for bringing into sharp relief the immense disadvantage of poor people in catastrophic hurricanes, relative to better-off people, as well as the overall inadequacy of the federal response to the hurricane. In 2009, a federal court ruled that army engineers had some responsibility for the post-hurricane flooding, in relation to their work on the levees that were supposed to protect New Orleans. Further lawsuits in the wake of this catastrophe were anticipated.

The Gulf of Mexico states were again contending with a major catastrophe in 2010, with the explosion on British Petroleum's Deepwater Horizon oil rig, killing 11 workers and producing an oil spill labeled the worst environmental crisis in U.S. history (Lyall 2010; Urbina 2010). Huge economic damage was inflicted on the fishing, tourist, and energy industries, among other Gulf state enterprises. Where was law in all of this? The lack of adequate regulatory law, and the limited enforcement of existing law, played some role in the explosion occurring in the first place. That BP and its partners were civilly liable for the multibillion dollar damage caused by the explosion and oil spill was widely accepted, but questions remained on establishing the legitimate parameters of the claims made against the company. The possibility of criminal charges also arose. But for the student of law and society the paramount question was whether this monumental catastrophe would have a measurable impact on transforming the body of law that governs offshore oil drilling and related activities with potentially catastrophic consequences.

---

necessary to finance the reform. Corporations and businesses have long opposed legal reforms of all kinds that are perceived to cut into profit margins; such reforms include the imposition of new taxes and the setting of new liability, safety, or antipollution standards. As wealthy corporations and business associations typically have large economic resources available to them, for advertising campaigns or the like, these efforts have often been successful. Citizen and taxpayer advocacy groups have opposed legal reforms that are viewed as too costly, such as the extension of comprehensive, universal health-care coverage.

Cultural resistance to legal reform reflects concern with perceived threats to traditional customs and values. Indigenous peoples in colonial societies, for example, have often resisted legal reforms imposed on them by colonial governments when these reforms were at odds with their traditional way of life. When members of a particular group subscribe to the ethnocentric view that their way of life is superior to that of other people, they are likely to resist legal change that is viewed as influenced by external cultural values. Plain superstition may also play a role in resistance to legal change.

Finally, one can identify some psychological sources of resistance to legal reform. People are likely to resist legal reforms that are at odds with their personality, moral orientation, personal perceptions, or ingrained patterns of behavior. If someone has been accustomed to driving without a seatbelt for many years and does not regard such driving as especially risky, that individual may well oppose a law requiring people to wear seatbelts. Of course, an individual is not typically able to do much to stop a new law from being passed—unless the individual happens to occupy a crucial position within the political system—but individuals often express their unhappiness with new laws simply by refusing to comply with them.

LAW AS AN INSTRUMENT OF SOCIAL CHANGE

Does law also change the social and human world, or does it simply reflect changes in this world? New laws and legal reform efforts are uniformly introduced or initiated with the professed aim of improving society in some way and promoting better human behavior. It is widely believed that major U.S. Supreme Court decisions and major new legislative reforms lead to social change. The Warren Court of the 1950s and 1960s made many landmark decisions regarded as inspiring significant social and political reforms (Horwitz 1998). Although most scholarly attention has focused on the U.S. Supreme Court as a source of social change, the lower federal courts and the state courts can also play a key role in these changes (Schultz 1998).

Michael W. McCann (1994) argued that litigation and court decisions have made a significant difference in addressing pay equity issues. Women (and minorities) through much of the twentieth century were systematically paid less than White males for the same job. In the final decades of the century, these inequities began to be challenged in litigation at least partially inspired by the feminist movement. In the landmark decision *County of Washington, Oregon, v. Gunther* (1981), the U.S. Supreme Court supported claims of female prison guards for pay equity with male guards. Although subsequent court decisions in pay equity cases often interpreted claims in such cases somewhat narrowly, McCann claims that on balance the litigation and court actions did make a measurable difference in bringing about much broader pay equity for females and minorities. Even when the courts did not rule favorably on behalf of pay equity litigants, the legal activity itself proved useful in achieving pay equity objectives. It was not just prison guards but prisoners themselves who were affected by court rulings (Feeley and Rubin 1998). Until the mid-1960s the courts largely adopted a hands-off policy toward prison conditions, but subsequently they made a series of rulings requiring changes in prison conditions and an extension of rights of prisoners.

In contrast, Gerald N. Rosenberg (1991) concluded that the courts have little significant influence on social change. He reached this controversial conclusion about two of the most famous U.S. Supreme Court decisions—the *Brown v. Board of Education* (1954) decision on segregation and the *Roe v. Wade* (1973) decision on abortion—as well as about less famous decisions. These decisions are seen as largely reflecting change in society during the period in question; changes following the handing down of the decisions, then, reflect these other social forces. Because such change often occurs only years after the opinion is handed down, intervening social forces must be at work. Certainly, the hopes of legal reform activists have often been dashed, or severely compromised, in the years following a victory in the courts.

Despite the obliteration of legal segregation and discrimination following the *Brown* decision, by some measures de facto segregation (following White flight and other factors) actually increased in subsequent decades, and racial division and racism were not eliminated and were sometimes intensified. In a second edition of *The Hollow Hope*, Rosenberg (2008) focuses on the litigation in various states aimed at obtaining equal marital benefits for same-sex couples. He reiterates the overall lack of judicial independence and the limited enforcement powers of the judiciary. Critics contend that Rosenberg shifts to different criteria of success or failure of court decisions to support his thesis that court decisions do not lead to social change (Hall 2009; Moore 2008). Others also question the capacity of the judiciary to protect rights and foster social change.

Barnett (2010), in *Legal Concept, Social Concept*, argues that law and legal doctrine is shaped by society's needs and values, but law and legal doctrine have relatively little impact on social problems. He especially focuses on sex and age discrimination and the availability of contraceptives and abortion in this regard. He also raises the question of the likely adoption of legalized euthanasia in the future.

BOX 10.3 IMMIGRATION: THE OPTIMAL LEGAL
RESPONSE?

The United States has famously declared itself a "nation of immigrants," and of course, apart from descendants of Native Americans, virtually all Americans are descended from people who immigrated to America (and subsequently the United States) over the past 500 years or so. In the nineteenth century—despite a long history of ethnic and racist biases—immigrants to the United States were generally presumed to be future citizens, but during the course of the twentieth century immigrants came to be viewed in increasingly negative terms (Carens 2010; Motomura 2006). In the most recent era the large influx of illegal immigrants has generated considerable anxiety and hostility and much debate about the most appropriate legal response (Newton 2008; Swain 2007). The doctrine of offering political asylum for those fleeing oppressive circumstances and seeking safety and freedom is compromised by often harsh asylum policies (Bohmer and Shuman 2008). Although in many countries, including Western European countries, illegal immigrants provide cheap labor, they are socially excluded by law from sharing in a good life (Calavita 2005). Tens of millions of illegal immigrants in the United States lead precarious lives, largely devoid of rights, benefits, and standard protections, as a result of American deportation policies (Coutin 2007; Kanstroom 2007). Immigrant women and single mothers (e.g., from Asia) have been especially hard hit by the welfare law reforms in the United States (Fujiwara 2008). Effective law enforcement is compromised when illegal immigrants are fearful of cooperating with police in criminal investigations, because they may be deported (Coutin 2007; Gascon

2008). Carens (2010) argues that after five years in the country undocumented immigrants should be granted amnesty and some right. Johnson (2007) argues that we would be best off simply opening the borders (with only identifiable security risks barred) because illegal immigrant labor is both needed and unstoppable. However, obviously huge numbers of Americans are opposed to any such policy, imagining that "opening the floodgates" would lead to an unmanageable flow of immigrants from poor countries, with many harmful consequences. Johnson argues in response that this has not happened in Western Europe, with a widespread fear that Eastern Europeans would flood Western Europe when the establishment of the European Union led to abolishing existing border controls between European countries. Furthermore, employers who benefit from less costly immigrant labor could be required to contribute to a fund to compensate displaced American workers. Dauvergne (2008), in *Making People Illegal*, argues that immigration issues must be viewed and addressed on a global level, with current policies privileging national sovereignty leading to the imposition of terrible costs on weak and poor nations by powerful and rich nations. Today, as many as 50 million people do not have legal resident status where they live.

In 2010 there was considerable controversy in the United States when the governor of Arizona signed a new law that would give police in the state sweeping powers to interrogate and take into custody suspected illegal immigrants. One of the issues arising here was whether states were entitled to adopt such measures relating to illegal immigration or whether this should be a matter of federal policy.

New laws can have unintended consequences (Preston and Roots 2004). Conservatives in particular are associated with the position that laws introduced with the rationale that they will help the disadvantaged often work against their interest (although Karl Marx also took this position). For example, it is alleged that social security law leads to low-income people subsidizing the retirements of those better off than themselves, the minimum wage law leads to greater unemployment, laws providing incentives to produce more fuel-efficient vehicles lead to the production of lighter cars and more accident fatalities, and laws requiring landlords to renovate buildings actually persuade them to abandon buildings (Roots 2004). Medicaid laws, welfare laws, desegregation, busing, and affirmative action laws have all been criticized with special bitterness as having counterproductive effects. Two innovative economists, Stephen J. Dubner and Steven D. Levitt (2008), have identified unintended consequences of various laws from ancient times to the present. The Americans with Disabilities Act (ADA), intended to protect people with disabilities, in some cases has led health-care providers to avoid treating them and employers from hiring them in the first place, out of fear of mandated added expenses and possible lawsuits that could arise after doing so. For example, employers are concerned that they will be constrained from disciplining or firing disabled employees who turn out to be incompetent, so they avoid hiring such employees. Suk (2009) argues, in *At Home in the Law: How the Domestic Violence Revolution Is Transforming Privacy*, that over the past several decades the law has fostered a radical transformation of the meaning of "the home." The domestic violence legal initiatives define the home as a presumed site of violence and abuse, and the enforcement of these laws has many negative and harmful consequences, especially for lower income households. The traditional notion of the privacy and autonomy of the household, in this reading, has been greatly compromised. Families have been split apart on the basis of police interpretations of evidence of domestic violence, even when all the family members involved contest that interpretation. Of course this is a controversial thesis that many feminist legal scholars in particular would contest. Suk calls for a more open discussion directed toward achieving a better balance between privacy and safety. Proposed laws in relation to illegal immigrants have been much debated during the current era (*see* Box 10.3).

What are the conditions under which law is most likely to promote social change? Evan (1965), writing from a functionalist perspective, contended that the law is most likely to promote social change when it emanates from an authoritative source, it has an acceptable rationale, practical models for compliance have been identified, changes in patterns of enforcement are instituted over a reasonably brief period of time, enforcement agents are committed to change, positive as well as negative sanctions are used, and enforcement of the new law is reasonable. The emphasis in the conflict or critical perspective on the impact of legal change is very different, however (Chambliss 1973a; Kairys 1998). It says that to the extent that those in power have direct (or indirect) control over resources, they are in a position to impose their will on the powerless. If members of society adapt to legal reforms imposed on them by those in power, it is largely a matter of being coerced or manipulated into making such adaptations. The imposition of law is unlikely to be total, however, and various forms of resistance can arise to the extent that legal changes are experienced as inequitable or exploitative in some way.

A conflict approach can be applied to understanding how law itself changes. In a **dialectical perspective on lawmaking**, advanced by William Chambliss (e.g., Chambliss and Zatz 1993), the introduction of new laws is viewed as a process directed toward the resolution of various contradictions, conflicts, and dilemmas confronting society in a particular historical context. For example, the introduction of laws regulating the meatpacking industry in the early twentieth century and the more recent antipollution laws can be explained in terms of a resolution of conflicts between a public increasingly angry about unhealthy meat (or dangerous forms of pollution) and the short-term economic interests of meatpacking corporations (or corporate polluters); the new laws helped resolve conflicts by reassuring the public, on the one hand, while protecting long-term economic interests of major corporations, on the other.

Social activists who attempt to bring about social change through law may have different objectives in mind. Although much research has addressed how social movements (e.g., the gay/lesbian rights movement) have impacted on the law, some research also documents that such social movements can be influenced by legal change, so it is a two-way street (Kane 2010). In relation to developing countries in an increasingly globalized world, the role of law and legal institutions in bringing about progressive social changes has received significant attention (de Sousa Santos 2007; Gagarella, Domingo, and Roux 2006; Goodale 2008). It is in fact immensely challenging to measure accurately the impact of legal reform in developing countries because of the complex range of variables involved (Davis and Kruse 2007). De Sousa Santos (2007) calls for a transformation of legal education and the perspective of the judiciary (or courts) in developing countries, so that progressive social change is promoted and not impeded.

LEGAL REFORMS AND THEIR IMPACT

Specific legal reforms are best understood both in terms of the circumstances producing them and their impact on social conditions or patterns of behavior. Some legal reform movements come into being because a class of people (or advocates on their behalf) challenge their disadvantaged status. More law has been introduced and passed on behalf of the powerful and privileged, however. Does law succeed in diminishing inequality, or does it merely create the appearance of doing so? In the paragraphs that follow, a number of areas of law that address issues of inequality—especially economic inequality—are reviewed.

LAW AND THE ENVIRONMENT

Throughout much of history law has supported exploitation of the environment over its protection. Some forms of environmental protection can be traced back quite far in history, and in American history specifically some clean air and clear water laws go back to the nineteenth century (Burns and Lynch 2004; Friedman 2002). Individual lawsuits were sometimes pursued by property owners against factories that through pollution were harming them, but public initiatives on behalf of environmental concerns principally emerged in the latter part of the twentieth century. The period after World War II provided a foundation for contemporary environmental law (Brooks 2009). The environmental movement and environmental law gained greater visibility with the first Earth Day in 1970. During the decade from 1969 to 1979 over two dozen federal environmental laws were implemented, including the National Environmental Policy Act, the Federal Clean Air Act, the Federal Water Pollution Control Act, the Clean Water Act, the Federal Safe Drinking Water Act, and Superfund. There has also been considerable development of environmental law on the international level (Atapattu 2006). Environmental laws, and the establishment of the Environmental Protection Agency (in 1970), were inspired by some specific high-profile cases of citizens severely harmed (and sometimes killed) as a consequence of pollution, and the emergence of an environmentalist movement, especially from the late 1960s on. The notion of pollution as a form of corporate crime or violence emerged at this point (Burns and Lynch 2004). But the tensions between economic development and environmental protection are especially pronounced, and corporations and the business community generally have a long history of battling against environmental protection laws. In light of the high costs of compliance with environmental regulations, some commentators have called for a cost–benefit analysis approach, focusing on whether the benefits of proposed laws outweigh the measurable costs; some have favored technological solutions over those based on economic considerations (Driesen 2003; Sunstein 2002a). In the recent era, the challenge of environmental protection has come to be increasingly recognized as a global problem, which can be adequately addressed only by international law (Atapattu 2006). Are international environmental treaties truly effective, or merely symbolic, and what do they mean in the context of a free-market global economy? They appear to have been effective in some contexts and not in others. One of the challenges such law has to address is the vast disparity between developed and developing countries in relation to controls on environmentally harmful practices. The evolution of environmental law internationally has been erratic and uneven, but it seems evident that environmental challenges will grow exponentially through the twenty-first century, and pressure for effective legal responses is likely to grow as well.

LABOR LAW

Throughout most of history employers have had a tremendous advantage over employees, and this advantage was largely supported by law (Steinberg 2003). In the early part of the nineteenth century, most working people did not even have a right to vote; attempts at that time to form labor unions were treated by the courts as a form of criminal conspiracy and as an illegal attempt to interfere with free trade (Turkel 1996, p. 155). Although an 1841 case in Massachusetts established a precedent for the legal establishment of labor unions, the American courts (including the U.S. Supreme Court) were, more often than not, hostile toward labor interests throughout the nineteenth century and into the early part of the twentieth century. In an 1895 decision, *In re Debs*, the U.S. Supreme Court upheld a contempt citation against an important labor leader involved in a strike against the Pullman Railroad Car Company, and this decision reflected an enduring lack of support for a broad-based unionism (Papke 1999). The courts further ruled that the Sherman Antitrust Act was applicable to labor unions and that legislative bodies (including Congress) had limited authority to pass laws governing employer/employee relations.

Beginning in the latter part of the nineteenth century, labor/management conflict produced considerable disorder and sometimes erupted into violence. Following World War I, and especially as a consequence of the onset of the Great Depression in the 1930s, the U.S. Supreme Court (e.g., in *American Foundries v. Tri-City Council* [1921]) and the U.S. Congress (e.g., with the Norris-LaGuardia Act of 1932) made decisions or laws more favorable to labor, extending to workers the right to organize and to strike without outside interference. A landmark law, the **National Labor Relations Act (Wagner Act)**, was adopted in 1935, but its real meaning has been interpreted in conflicting ways. In the conventional interpretation, this act, by establishing a National Labor Relations Board and requiring management to engage in collective bargaining with unionized workers on all issues pertaining to the wages and conditions of work, effectively put workers (collectively) on an equal footing with management. In a dissenting interpretation, however, the Wagner Act was really intended to defeat union radicalism and through a series of appellate court opinions has been interpreted in a manner that continues to give management the upper hand in most disputes (Klare 1978).

In a backlash against the growing power of labor unions in the mid-twentieth century, the **Labor Management Relations Act (Taft-Hartley Act)** of 1948 declared certain union activities to be unfair labor practices. Although legal reforms between the end of the nineteenth century and the end of the twentieth century indisputably led to the improvement of some of the circumstances of employees, the notion that management and labor settle disputes as equals can certainly be challenged. Furthermore, changes in the American economy during the final decades of the twentieth century led to a decline in the proportion of American workers represented by unions, with a proportional decline in union power. Early in the twenty-first century, labor activists claimed that violations of workers' rights were still pervasive in the United States, with many constraints on the rights of workers to organize, strike, and bargain collectively (Pope, Kellman, and Bruno 2003). There is a long history of struggle to obtain equal employment opportunities for minorities, especially African-Americans, and that struggle is not over (Smith 2008).

With a workforce increasingly made up of non-unionized and immigrant workers, nongovernmental (civil society) organizations play a larger role in addressing and promoting the rights of vulnerable workers (Gleeson 2009). In one view, the National Labor Relations Act needs to be reformed because the statutory language of that act reflects the typical nature of the workplace in the 1930s, and workplace conditions in the early twenty-first century are dramatically different (Stone 2004; Warren and Liebman 2010). The Employee Free Choice Act (EFCA) introduced in Congress in 2010 was the first basic labor law reform in 30 years. Among other things, it would facilitate and protect union-organizing of workers. And in a globalized world, labor laws increasingly confront new conditions for workers (Conaghan, Fischl, and Klare 2002). In such a world, nation-states have less control on the conditions of labor.

WELFARE LAW

Throughout most of history, the poor and the disabled either have been ignored by the law or have been persecuted in the name of the law (Trattner 1999). Traditionally, poverty was regarded as a natural condition, and the poor were left to their own devices and private charity. The transient poor and the homeless poor, if they had no family to take them in, were often expelled from the community, sent to workhouses, put into stocks for public shaming, or thrown into debtors' prison. All of these practices within the English tradition, with the exception of debtors' prison, were widely adopted by the American colonies (Hall 1989, pp. 28–30; Katz 1986). The policy of extending some form of financial aid to dependent people evolved gradually throughout the nineteenth century. In the United States, pensions made available to Civil War veterans provided one model for government welfare, although this form of relief turned out to be costly and often corrupt (Skocpol 1992). Child support policies were more widely adopted in the late nineteenth century (Oldham and Melli 2000). Workmen's compensation for disabilities arising out of work was quite broadly supported. Over time, with the support of women's associations, government welfare was extended by law to a broader class of dependent people, especially women and children. In the 1930s, during the Depression, the Social Security system was introduced, and during the 1960s Medicaid and Medicare were implemented. These forms of welfare were clearly effective in reducing the poverty rate among the elderly. Although the Warren Court of the 1960s extended some constitutional protections to the poor, it never identified welfare benefits as a constitutional right (Bussiere 1997). Some of the Federal programs passed during the course of the twentieth century were structured in such a way as to be discriminatory toward African-Americans (Katznelson 2005). The primary beneficiaries of these laws were middle class White Americans.

Welfare as such came to be identified through much of the twentieth century with the extension of economic benefits to the dependent poor, especially single women and their children (Aid to Families With Dependent Children, or AFDC) (Teles 1996). Politically, it has always been more difficult to secure broad support for benefit programs for "targeted" populations (e.g., the poor) than for broad classes of people. Accordingly, there has been some debate over whether the poor are best helped by programs specifically focusing on their needs or by being incorporated into programs benefiting the middle class as well (Greenstein 1991; Skocpol 1992). Scholars have different interpretations of what welfare means for the poor and why welfare expanded through much of the twentieth century. Is welfare a form of charity, a practical inducement, or a right and, accordingly, a new form of property? To conservatives, bloated welfare programs represent a misguided, and counterproductive, liberal philosophy and do more harm than good. To moderates and liberals, welfare programs are an expression of compassion and a contemporary form of civic obligation; ideally, they enable individuals and families to rise out of poverty. In a well-known progressive or radical interpretation, welfare is a device used by those in power to control the poor, and welfare is extended more broadly in times of unrest to quell an uprising, whereas it is reduced (or withdrawn) in more stable times (Piven and Cloward 1971).

In 1964, in the face of considerable social unrest, President Johnson signed into law the "War on Poverty" called for by President Kennedy. But this war became somewhat neglected over time, in part because of the enormous distraction of another war—that in Vietnam. In the view of some, the principal beneficiaries of this war on poverty were government bureaucrats on different levels for whom it provided employment. Nevertheless, evidence has been marshaled to support the claim that the War on Poverty programs of the Johnson Administration did have some impact in reducing poverty (Jencks 1992). The long-term benefits of welfare in generally reducing poverty are far less clear.

Through much of its history, the contemporary American welfare system was attacked from many different vantage points—as counterproductive and riddled with corruption and, conversely, as administered in a mean and demeaning way (Zasloff 1998). There have been many myths about the attributes of those receiving welfare. For example, welfare was alleged to include a significant proportion of able-bodied but lazy men, women with many children, and people living well on their welfare income. Welfare was specifically blamed for promoting a dramatic increase in the breakup of families, the growing number of single mothers, and a rise in the rate of illegitimate births, although contrary evidence strongly suggested that these developments occurred independently of expanding welfare benefits and were linked more closely with shifting cultural values (Jencks 1992; Stoesz 1997). In the 1960s and early 1970s a coalition of forces (poor women, welfare advocates and lawyers) successfully challenged some of the most demeaning dimensions of welfare programs, which led to the expansion of welfare benefits and rights (Kornbluh 2007). In one important ruling (*Goldberg v. Kelly* [1970]), the U.S. Supreme Court ruled that pre-termination hearings had to be held before welfare benefits could be discontinued or reduced (Lens 2009). But these successes also helped fuel an anti-welfare backlash that led to the 1996 welfare reforms. But by the end of the twentieth century, the conservative viewpoint, with its central claim that the welfare system fosters a debilitating form of dependency and is wasteful and ineffective on many levels, came to prevail. In August 1996, President Clinton signed into law the **Personal Responsibility and Work Opportunity Act (PRWOA)**, ending the traditional system of welfare entitlements. In addition to imposing time limits and other restrictions on receipt of welfare, this law called for most welfare recipients to be integrated into the workforce. Various states and cities implemented parallel welfare reform policies of their own. The focus on welfare rights was increasingly replaced with a focus on individual responsibility. Gender, race, and class factors were all intertwined in these developments. The outcome of hearings challenging limitations on welfare benefits and rights today depend importantly on the philosophy of the hearing judge, with reformer judges sympathetic to welfare recipients and moralist judges more attuned to the individual responsibility theme (Lens 2009).

Although a majority of Americans apparently believed that legal reforms to welfare law had all too often done more harm than good and had certainly not reduced poverty in any significant way, many Americans were also uncomfortable with dumping large numbers of people into a situation where they would be desperately strapped for basic economic resources (and could be pressed into committing crimes to provide for themselves and their families) (Edelman 1997, p. 53). Various welfare-to-work programs in the past have failed because they were based on the false premise that the principal problem with the poor is that they lack a commitment to work; an alternative interpretation suggests that welfare dependency is much more a function of the deterioration of the low-wage labor market in many poor neighborhoods (Handler and Hasenfeld 1997). Furthermore, inequalities in the welfare programs of different states could be interpreted as negating the "equal protection" principle in our law (Whitaker and Time 2001). Some states are more generous with welfare benefits than others.

Did the welfare reform "work"? By 2006 (the tenth anniversary of the 1996 welfare reform law), welfare caseloads had dropped a remarkable 60%, although it wasn't always clear that the drop could be attributed to the new law as opposed to other factors, including a strong economy (Besharov 2006). In one interpretation, the welfare poor were transformed into the working poor, and some single mothers with especially troubled lives were cut adrift, having neither work nor welfare (Pear and Eckholm 2006). A study co-authored by a prominent law and society scholar, Joel Handler, concluded that the 1996 welfare reform in the United States failed, as the welfare bureaucracy continues to demonize poor single-mother families and to minimize the profound economic challenges faced by such families (Handler and Hasenfeld 2007). Minorities continue to be dramatically over-represented in the population served by the welfare system. African-American children constitute only 15% of the child population in the United States but account for some 45% of children in substitute care. Several studies have documented discriminatory treatment by child welfare agencies (Derezores, Poertner, and Testa 2005). Altogether, some important issues relating to welfare were unsettled. From 2010 on, with budget deficits a major concern on the federal state and local levels, all forms of welfare benefits were vulnerable to cuts.

There is little evidence that welfare law reform can effectively promote marriage or enforce child support in a constructive way. Many women on welfare are seeking refuge from domestic abuse and violence. Welfare reforms continue to punish true independence, attempting to force recipients to do "dirty" work or to depend on unreliable men. It seemed unlikely that past welfare policies would be revived in the twenty-first century, but some commentators were seeking a new vision of an affirmative welfare state of the future, based on political realities, emerging knowledge, and democratic initiatives (Munger 2003). With the beginning of a new century, it was still far from clear what the real impact of legal reform of welfare would be over time or whether the problem of poverty had to be addressed in other ways.

CIVIL RIGHTS LAW

No legal reform movement in America in the twentieth century had a higher social profile or was more fully documented than the civil rights movement. Although the origins of the civil rights movement can be traced far back, the major stages of the movement took place between the mid-1950s and the mid-1960s. The civil rights movement launched a basic challenge to legally sanctioned discrimination against African-American citizens, with segregated schools as the single-most visible symbol of this segregation. The celebrated *Brown v. Board of Education* (1954) decision, declaring official segregation unconstitutional, is typically credited with having played a significant role in bringing about an end to such segregation, despite substantial resistance from Southern courts (Sanders 1995). The adoption of a strategy of nonviolent protest, primarily under the inspirational leadership of the Reverend Martin Luther King, Jr., was a noteworthy attribute of the civil rights movement. This movement (with the help of television news broadcasts) drew the attention of the country to the Southern resistance to implementing *Brown v. Board of Education* and to the many demeaning and unjust dimensions of segregation. Accordingly, it contributed to a transformation of the political environment and passage of the Civil Rights Act of 1964 and the Voting Rights Act of 1965. Some further civil rights initiatives were promoted, paradoxically enough, during the Republican administration of Richard Nixon (Kotlowski 2002).

The Supreme Court decision in *Swann v. Charlotte-Mecklenburg Board of Education* (1971) authorized the controversial practice of busing children as a means of achieving integration. Although these laws were successful in sweeping away legal (or formal) discrimination and in promoting integration at least in certain circumstances, they have been far less successful in legislating racism and its consequences out of existence (*see* Box 10.4). The *Brown v. Board of Education* decision and the legal strategy leading up to this decision was focused on ending segregation but disregarded or marginalized many of the other—primarily economic—disadvantages endured by African-Americans (Goluboff 2007). The promise of the civil rights movement was accordingly only partially fulfilled.

WOMEN'S RIGHTS AND THE EQUAL RIGHTS AMENDMENT

Throughout most of recorded history, women have not enjoyed the same rights as men. Under traditional law, and in the English common law, women were treated as subordinate to or virtually the property of fathers or husbands (Grana 2010; VanBurkleo 2001). In general, women in the American colonies were somewhat better off under law than those in England—perhaps because there were fewer women and accordingly women were valued more—but they were still at a substantial disadvantage. Married women could not own property, sue, or enter into a contract independently of their husbands. They also could not vote. For all but the most serious crimes, women were regarded as acting on behalf of, or under the influence of, their husbands (Bartlett 1991). Although some women challenged the inferior legal status of women, little changed until the present era. From the early nineteenth century on, it is true, some rights of property ownership were granted to women as well as more equal standing in legal proceedings, but it is likely that such reforms served the interests of the larger society and of men who wanted to shield assets from creditors, not the interests of women.

BOX 10.4 HATE CRIMES

The concept of hate crime or bias crime was introduced in about 1980 as one more response to a long and ugly history of racism and intolerance. The "hate crime" doctrine was promoted by minorities' activists and had achieved significant legal recognition by the late 1990s (Jenness and Grattet 2001; Phillips and Grattet 2000). One study found that compliance with federal hate crime law is less likely to occur in places with larger African-American populations, at odds with what might be expected (King 2007). But even if race-based hate crime might occur in such places, these parts of the country are generally more conservative and have a stronger tradition of inter-racial conflict (in the American South), and hate crime laws are less widely promoted or reported in these places. **Hate (or bias) crime** laws imposed stronger punishments on offenders who committed crimes motivated by hate or bias. Lawrence (1999) argued in favor of these laws. He contended that crimes motivated by bias or hate injure the immediate victim, the target community, and society at large in ways exceeding the injury of parallel crimes not motivated by hate. Such crimes merit greater punishment because they represent an attack on racial harmony and equality, two of the highest values of Americans' society. Lawrence argued that hate crime laws do not necessarily conflict with Americans' commitment to free speech, as we can clearly distinguish between bias crime (a form of behavior) and racist speech (a form of expression).

Jacobs and Potter (1998) argued against the idea of a special category of hate crime or bias crime. They contended that (*1*) key terms in such laws, such as "prejudice," are ambiguous; (*2*) harsher punishments for minorities, who disproportionately commit inter-racial crimes, are the likely practical consequence of such laws; (*3*) existing law already has provisions for providing harsher punishment for more harmful crimes; and (*4*) the hate crime laws were adopted in response to an alleged but actually nonexistent new epidemic of hate crime.

The suffragist movement of the nineteenth century emerged, in part, out of the experience of women with the abolitionist movement (Dubois 1998). Although the women's rights movement of the nineteenth century is widely viewed as having led to the extension of voting rights and some employment-related rights for women, early in the twentieth century, this movement has also been interpreted as contributing to ongoing constraints on women's rights (Sullivan 2007). Again, the ultimate success of this movement early in the twentieth century in obtaining the vote for women has been viewed more as a reflection of the desire of White middle class males to retain political clout in the face of the growing hordes of European immigrants than as a full-fledged recognition of the inherent political rights of women.

Only with the emergence of the contemporary feminist movement (primarily from the early 1970s on) has there been a more fundamental extension of equal legal rights to women. Just as the suffragist movement emerged in part out of the abolitionist movement, the contemporary feminist movement was influenced by the involvement of women in the civil rights movement and the success of that movement in challenging unjust laws. Most states revised their laws to remove blatant forms of gender bias, and the U.S. Supreme Court, in a series of decisions, struck down formal biases against women in the operation of the justice system and in both criminal and civil law proceedings.

Throughout the 1970s, into the early 1980s, feminists campaigned for the adoption of an **Equal Rights Amendment (ERA)** to the U.S. Constitution, which would have prohibited as unconstitutional any form of discrimination against individuals for reasons of gender. However, this effort failed in 1982. Various reasons have been given for the failure of the ERA to pass (Hoff-Wilson 1986; Mansbridge 1986). Not only many men but a large number of women also opposed the ERA, on various grounds. Some argued that it was simply not necessary because state laws already prohibited significant forms of discrimination. Some feared that it would deprive women of certain privileges (from alimony to exclusion from the draft). Some stated an ideological objection to treating men and women alike. For at least some, the principal significance of the ERA was symbolic: It would assert, once and for all, that women were not subordinate to men and were entitled to the same rights as men. Whether an ERA, if reintroduced and ratified, will have a measurable positive impact on the lives of women is open to dispute. Early in the twenty-first century there were ongoing questions about the usefulness of focusing on equality as a basis for advancing the rights of women (Hunter 2008). Although many countries have now extended formal recognition of gender equality to women, a gap often exists between these commitments and the realities of the circumstances in which women find themselves (McClain and Grossman 2009). In the United States some ongoing forms of disadvantage for certain classes of women were still evident. The law and the criminal justice system continue to establish parameters to differentiate between good and bad mothers through a range of policies relating to reproductive rights of women (Flavin 2008). Battered women and incarcerated women who have children contend with discriminatory dimensions of the law. The law has also been shown to have failed pregnant minors, with the realities of mandated parental involvement in decisions relating to abortion being at odds with claims that they are consistent with protecting the best interest of these girls (Silverstein 2007).

Despite the removal of many specific forms of gender bias from law, the legal status of women by the end of the twentieth century was declared "still unequal," with many forms of discrimination still in effect (McColgan 2000). As long as significant economic and social differences divide the sexes, treating men and women alike under law will not produce true equality (Barker, Kirk, and Sah 1998). Traditional sexist attitudes have proved more enduring than formal laws. Corporate governance policies continue to perpetrate a gender gap in the executive suites of American corporations, with women still measurably under-represented (Branson 2007). Many unresolved issues remain, regarding pregnancy discrimination, custody, post-divorce property settlement, unequal compensation and pro-motion policies, comparable worth, taxation (especially as applied to benefits), and the overall treatment of physically and sexually abused women.

EQUAL OPPORTUNITY AND AFFIRMATIVE ACTION

Although America historically has been celebrated as the "land of opportunity," it has hardly been a land of equal opportunity. In response to the civil rights movement and the femi-nist movement, laws have been introduced to provide more equal opportunity for those belonging to categories or groups that have been victims of discrimination (e.g., minorities and women). Affirmative action has been an especially controversial legal response to the historical reality of unequal opportunity (Mosley and Capaldi 1996; Shuck 2003). Ideally, it is intended to correct for some of the consequences of past discrimination and to pro-duce much-needed diversity in influential occupations. The term *affirmative action* has been applied to programs calling for aggressive recruitment of and extension of special programs to minorities and under-represented groups as well as for specific quotas for such groups; the latter form of affirmative action has been far more controversial than the recruitment and special program form (Hall 1989, p. 330).

For groups victimized by discrimination (e.g., African-Americans and women), the origi-nal objective was to challenge laws and associated norms that specifically supported discrimi-nation. Prior to 1964, activist members of these groups and their leaders campaigned for race- and gender-blind policies. In the late 1960s and early 1970s, however, with most of the formal barriers gone, concern shifted to addressing the dramatic under-representation of peo-ple of color and women in elite educational institutions, prestigious professions, and busi-ness management. One scholar believes that the urban race riots of the late 1960s prompted government and business leaders to adopt policies that might promote higher levels of hiring of African-Americans, with the hope that this would reduce the level of anger and bitterness expressed by these riots (Skrentny 1996). The Republican Nixon Administration perceived a political benefit in supporting race-based affirmative action, because it would help pit two strong Democrat constituencies (union members and African-Americans) against each other. Once the affirmative action programs were in place, various managers and bureaucrats charged with hiring more people of color found it to be in their interest to implement affir-mative action programs.

The U.S. Supreme Court, beginning with the *Bakke* decision in 1978, handed down a series of decisions upholding some kinds of affirmative action programs (e.g., those involving preferences) while striking down others (e.g., those involving rigid quotas) (Hall 1989, p. 331). In one interpretation, the Supreme Court decision in *Bakke* is best understood as a choice by the Court to allow competing interest groups to work out the final resolution of this complex issue (Bybee 2000). In the latter half of the 1990s, affirmative action programs, which had come to include women along with more traditional disadvantaged groups, were the target of a significant backlash (Chavez 1998). In a number of states, voters supported an initiative to eliminate policies specifically assigning preference by race or gender; a significant decline in successful state university applications by traditional minorities was one consequence of these legal initiatives (Hacker 2003; Schmidt 2003). Some constituencies increasingly attacked affirmative action as a form of reverse discrimination, as promoting inter-racial resentment and conflict, as no longer justifiable (especially in the case of women), and as stigmatizing and counterproductive (by putting people in positions for which they were not qualified, and in which they would fail) (Pincus 2003). In particular, some challenged policies that might favor affluent women and people of color over economically disadvantaged others, including White males (Kahlenberg 1996). Accordingly, for some commentators, affirmative action programs should focus on class, not race (Zieharth 2003). Two 2003 U.S. Supreme Court decisions (*Gratz* and *Grutter*) upheld the constitutionality of affirmative action policies but were a source of ongoing controversy (Perry 2007). In 2006, Michigan voters approved a ban on affirmative action at public colleges in the state and for state government contracts (Jaschik 2006). In a 5/4 ruling in 2009, the U.S. Supreme Court ruled that White firefighters were subjected to impermissible race discrimination when a promotional exam on which they had done better than African-American candidates was discounted, on behalf of affirmative action objectives (Liptak 2009d). This decision was seen as imposing some new constraints on employers attempting to increase minority representation, especially among their higher ranked employees.

Affirmative action policies in higher education have been endorsed by the prominent jurisprudential scholar Ronald Dworkin (2000) as beneficial in promising a better educational environment for all and a less racially stratified society for everyone. Former presidents of two elite universities, Princeton and Harvard, produced a study late in this period documenting the success of affirmative action in bringing African-Americans into leading educational institutions and in contributing to their representation in influential and prestigious occupations (Bowen and Bok 1998). Some evidence suggested that for affirmative action programs to be successful, both the diversity and the integration rationales had to be combined (Jacobs 1998). But in a new century that would witness a great proportional growth in the size of the non-White population and a growing proportion of women in most fields, the long-term fate of affirmative action law remained unsettled. It seems likely, however, that affirmative action laws will be increasingly phased out. The ADA passed in 1990 was initially regarded as an important victory for people with disabilities. But the Courts have shifted away from strong support in cases arising out of this Act to a pro-defendant bias (Colker 2005). The U.S. Supreme Court in particular has chosen to read the ADA quite narrowly in relation to who qualifies to be protected and has resisted applying this Act to people without visible, traditional handicaps. The rights of obese or overweight people have also now become the focus of lawsuits alleging discrimination, although, historically, overweight people have not been recognized as a protected class in relation to prohibitions against discrimination, and obesity has not been classified as a disability (Kirkland 2008). There is ongoing controversy over the status of obesity as an involuntary condition or a consequence of voluntary overeating.

DOMESTIC VIOLENCE AND CHILD ABUSE

Another series of legal reforms has been inspired by the desire to protect vulnerable victims of directly harmful behavior who are regarded as not having been adequately protected by traditional law. Women (and children) have been victims of male violence through the ages, especially in the form of domestic violence (including child abuse) and rape. Historically, a patriarchal, male-dominated system of law largely refrained from intervening in cases of domestic violence and did not treat rape with the seriousness that it would have had if the victims had been men, not women. In the nineteenth century, the North Carolina court of appeals could still uphold, for a period of time, the right of husbands to physically chastise their wives, and even when the courts abandoned this position, they reaffirmed their reluctance to intervene in matters of "family government." The contemporary feminist movement, from the early 1970s on, played an important role in highlighting the many dimensions of violence toward women and in promoting changes in societal attitudes toward such violence and changes in law and the justice system response to such violence.

In the case of domestic violence, the evidence holds that women are far more likely than men to be seriously injured (or killed) by their spouses (or partners). Some 1,500 women in the United States are killed annually in domestic violence situations, and it has been estimated that close to 2 million are physically assaulted annually; it is somewhat encouraging, however, that homicides involving "intimate others" have steadily declined (Dugan, Nagin, and Rosenfeld 2003; Dusky 1996, p. 356; Tjaden and Thoennes 1998). Traditionally, local police have been reluctant to make arrests when responding to domestic violence situations. This reluctance has been rationalized, at least in part, by the claim that an arrest would make a bad situation even worse. Pioneering research undertaken in the 1980s indicated that less violence, rather than more, followed arrest, although one of the researchers involved cautioned about adopting policy based on this work (Sherman 1992). On the basis of such research, however, as well as in response to feminist demands for greater accountability in domestic violence cases, at least some states adopted mandatory arrest policies; only a small percentage of the arrested offenders are actually prosecuted and convicted, however (Martin 1994). Research has suggested that the adoption of domestic violence prevention resources can contribute to a decline in homicide by an intimate partner, but not always (Dugan, Nagin, and Rosenfeld 2003). For example, when prosecutors express a willingness to pursue violations of orders of protection, but then don't provide protection themselves, more homicides may occur.

Legal "orders of protection," or restraining orders, are granted more commonly today to individuals who live separately from a physically abusive partner. Women are more likely than men to seek such orders and tend to believe that such orders reflect support from and protection by the legal system (Ptacek 1999). Nevertheless, periodic reports of women (and children) who are killed by an estranged husband (or partner), despite having an order of protection, show that such orders can hardly guarantee safety.

The **Violence Against Women Act** was adopted in 1994 to extend increasing protection to women and children in abusive circumstances. It provided funding for shelters for battered women, a national hotline for victims, training on domestic violence for law enforcement officers, and support for state initiatives against domestic violence. It also facilitated bringing civil suits against abusers, especially in the absence of criminal prosecution. This expanded federal involvement with domestic violence was inevitably controversial. The U.S. Supreme Court has invalidated the provision of the Violence Against Women Act that allowed victims of gender-based violence to sue their attackers in federal court (Greenhouse 2000c). Women's rights advocates were disappointed with this narrow ruling.

The provision of shelters for abused women, as well as other services and forms of support, has benefited many victims, but no such initiatives can guarantee safety from enraged, violent men. Furthermore, over time, some states began to retreat from viewing battered women as victims of male domination in need of protection; instead, they took a "family conflict" view calling for therapeutic intervention for the whole family (Dixon 1995, p. 361). The single-most famous twentieth-century case of domestic violence was probably that of former professional football star O.J. Simpson, who was tried for the murder of his estranged wife, Nicole (and her visitor, Ron Goldman). Although Simpson was acquitted by a controversial jury verdict, evidence emerged in the trial (and a subsequent civil proceeding against him) that he had committed earlier acts of domestic abuse against his wife and had been treated with excessive lenience by law enforcement officers.

The "Battered Woman Syndrome" is another controversial outcome of the changing legal environment in response to domestic violence (Downs 1996; Maguigan 1998). A relatively small number of women charged with killing a husband (or male partner) have offered as a defense that they had been victims of a pattern of violent conduct over a significant period of time and that they had no realistic option to protect themselves (and their children) other than to kill their abuser. This defense, when offered, has not been uniformly successful, but at a minimum it has inspired more attention to the desperate circumstances in which some women find themselves. A movement to gain clemency for battered women convicted of killing their male partners gained some momentum in the final years of the twentieth century (Gagne 1998). The battered woman's defense itself is not formally recognized by law, incidentally; rather, **Battered Woman's Syndrome** refers to the introduction of expert testimony in certain criminal and civil proceedings (Maguigan 1998). Historically, the law has made it difficult for women to claim self-defense when they kill male partners; in part, this reflects a male-influenced interpretation of threat and reasonable behavior in response to threat (Gillespie 1989; Dixon 1995).

The physical and sexual abuse of children received rather limited attention from the legal system until the recent era (from the late 1960s on) (Bottoms, Kovera, and McAuliff 2002). Laws addressing the sexual abuse of children were adopted over a period of time and reflected evolving perceptions of childhood: from a single phase of innocence to a series of stages (Robertson 2005). Laws relating to child sexual abuse continue to be interpreted and applied in ways that reflect different views of judges of the basic dimensions and character of such abuse (Wright 2007). The corporal punishment of children was generally regarded as a parental prerogative, and even obligation, and only in the most extreme cases would the state intervene when children were abused or neglected. In the contemporary era, legal obligations were imposed on third parties (such as doctors and teachers) to report cases of abused children that came to their attention, and state agencies assumed greater responsibility in removing abused children from their homes (Ashford 1994). Social agencies and the courts have remained somewhat reluctant to take a child away from a natural parent permanently, however; consequently, one periodically reads about tragic cases of an abused child known to child services agencies who is beaten to death by a parent or a child returned by the court to an abusive parent and then killed. Many cases of severe child abuse never come to the attention of the courts, and altogether the law has failed to protect many children from severe abuse.

RAPE LAW

Rape, too, has been subject to significant legal reform in the recent era. According to Brownmiller's (1975) classic *Against Our Will*, the rape of a married woman in an earlier time was treated as adultery and that of an unmarried woman as a property crime against her father (because her bridal price declined in value). Indeed, the resolution of a rape case involving an unmarried woman sometimes took the form of marrying her off to the rapist. Furthermore, rape in a male-dominated society was openly accepted in some situations, such as war, where the women of the losing side were raped. Unfortunately, these practices are not extinct in the contemporary era. The courts in the Anglo-American tradition did not treat rape with the seriousness it might have been accorded if the victims had been men. The British justice Lord Hale declared that rape was the easiest charge to make and the hardest to prove. Corroboration (in the form of witness testimony or physical evidence) was required to obtain convictions in a rape case, which was not true for other types of physical assault. A larger culture that often blamed rape victims for their experience, as well as a justice system culture that treated their claims with skepticism or exposed them to demeaning forms of cross-examination, discouraged many victims from reporting the crime in the first place. Unsurprisingly, the rate of convictions in rape cases, or in the small percentage that resulted in arrest and trial, was typically low.

In the 1970s the feminist movement began mobilizing to change the perception of rape and the legal response to it (Toobin 2003). First, an ongoing enterprise involving such activities as "Take Back the Night" promoted attention to the devastating impact of rape on victims and its threat to women generally. Then feminists lobbied successfully for various reforms of existing rape laws. These reforms included *(1)* redefining rape to emphasize its violent nature; *(2)* removing the corroboration requirement; *(3)* adding a **rape shield** provision ordinarily prohibiting the introduction of evidence (or cross-examination) about the victim's past sexual conduct; *(4)* protecting children from sexual exploitation (while diminishing legal attention to consensual teenage sex); and *(5)* increasing the certainty of appropriate penalties (Berger, Searles, and Neuman 1988; Horney and Spohn 1991). Furthermore, laws in many states prohibiting the prosecution of husbands for raping their wives were eliminated (Gross 1991). Significant changes were introduced as well in the justice system handling of rape cases. For example, specially trained female officers were more likely to interview rape victims. Outside the formal justice system, various support services such as rape crisis centers were introduced. Although rape law reforms have occurred in many countries, the extent to which such reform has occurred is correlated with such factors as the strength of women's movements, the distribution of wealth, and the cultural emphasis on individualism (Frank, Hardinge, and Wosick-Correa 2009). In many developing countries in particular, women are little protected by law from being victims of rape.

It was the hope of those who promoted rape reform that reforms in the legal system's response to rape would transform public perceptions of rape, would diminish the trauma for victims in pursuing rape cases, and ideally would deter rape itself (Estrich 1987; Berger, Neuman, and Searles 1994). Scholarly studies of the impact of rape law reform, however, have found that entrenched attitudes and practices within the justice system tend to limit the practical effect of the reforms (Berger, Neuman, and Searles 1994; Horney and Spohn 1991; Temkin 2002). In a comprehensive survey of rape law reform, Caringella (2008) documents the discrepancies between what the laws ideally call for and what happens in the real world in relation to rape. Accordingly, a range of further reforms are still needed to diminish the enduring injustices associated with rape. Alexandre (2009) identifies two principal fears that arise in rape cases: *(1)* that innocent defendants will be victims of false accusations and *(2)* that the very real trauma of rape victims will be trivialized. She concludes that a revision of the treatment of consent in rape law and the unbiased application of "reasonable doubt" in such cases—especially when the victim is non-traditional (e.g., a prostitute)—is necessary to enhance justice in such cases. For the most part, then, the rape law reforms had somewhat limited effects on arrest policies and justice system processing of rape cases; such reform seems to have had limited impact on the rape rate or the conviction rate in rape cases, and it did not necessarily persuade a higher percentage of women to report rape cases to the authorities. To the extent that patterns of rape and victim reporting changed, other factors in the larger social environment are probably responsible. However, at a minimum, the rape law reforms have made an important symbolic statement about the seriousness of rape as a crime against women, and these reforms have somewhat reduced the trauma for many rape victims of pursuing their cases through the justice system. Another body of law has developed in recent years in response to unwelcome sexual attention experienced mainly by women (*see* Box 10.5).

HOMOSEXUALITY AND THE RIGHTS OF GAY PEOPLE

Homophobia has been interwoven into many dimensions of American law traditionally, with a long-standing negative impact on the lives of gay people (Ronner 2005). The perpetuation of negative stereotypes of gay people still influences law and legal decisions in ways that compromise basic rights. Nevertheless, dramatic changes have occurred in the realm of law and gay rights.

The issues surrounding the legal status of gay people are hardly new, and in one interpretation as early as the New Deal era of the 1930s, the U.S. government began to define

BOX 10.5 SEXUAL HARASSMENT AND THE LAW

Sexual harassment (overwhelmingly of women, by men) has been an age-old problem; however, only in the recent era (beginning about 1975), largely as a consequence of the efforts of committed feminists, did the law address it (Belknap and Erez 1997; MacKinnon and Siegel 2004). Originally sexual harassment laws focused on supervisor/employer demands for sex from subordinates, but by the mid-1980s they were broadened to incorporate a hostile environment (Tinker 2003). Sexual harassment laws and employer policies relating to sexual harassment differ considerably among Western nations (Zippel 2006). Public consciousness of sexual harassment emerged much later in Japan than it did in the United States (Uggen and Shinohara 2009). Although various factors play a role in such cross-cultural differences, the extent to which a mobilized feminist movement is present and has directed attention to this issue is one key factor (Baker 2008). Paradoxically, sexual harassment law has, in one interpretation, increased the sexual objectification of women in the larger culture.

With the adoption of sexual harassment laws, what had been a private trouble became a public issue as the boundaries between private and public sectors eroded (Roth 1999). Although sexual harassment remains a common occurrence, pursuit of legal action is relatively uncommon. Many complex and contentious issues continue to be debated in relation to sexual harassment, including these: How is it best defined? Should it be permissible to explore a plaintiff's sexual history? What about same-sex harassment? How can proscriptions on a hostile work environment be reconciled with free speech rights (Stein 1999)? Sexual harassment has been a problem in various work settings, including the military. High-profile cases in the recent era involved a prominent senator, Robert Packwood; a prospective U.S. Supreme Court Justice, Clarence Thomas, subsequently confirmed; and a president, Bill Clinton (LeMoncheck and Hajdin 1997). Despite the success of some sexual harassment lawsuits, some commentators suggest that there is still a wide schism between the law and women's experience of sexual harassment (Belknap and Erez 1997; Schulhofer 1998). This is likely to remain a contentious area of law for some time to come.

In *Davis v. Monroe County Board of Education* (1999), a divided (5-to-4) U.S. Supreme Court found against a school board in a district where school authorities had failed to respond to repeated complaints on behalf of a fifth-grade female student who was sexually harassed by a fellow student. Although dissenters on the Court expressed concern that a precedent would be established involving the Court in the inevitable squabbles of immature children, the majority asserted that the extreme circumstances in the case before them warranted a decision on behalf of the plaintiff.

Student-on-student sexual harassment has been a common occurrence on college campuses, but many colleges and universities have chosen to avoid responding in a substantial way (Williams 1999). Colleges have historically done little to protect students from sexual harassment (Franke 1998). In the wake of the *Davis* decision, colleges need to ensure that they have an effective sexual harassment policy in place, investigate complaints of harassment, and successfully resolve cases in which sexual harassment is found to have occurred.

homosexuality for various purposes (Canaday 2009). Over the past half-century, the gay community has adopted an approach in response to these government initiatives that focuses on legal rights for homosexuals and lesbians (Mezey 2007). Since about 1980, the gay rights movement moved from the margins of American politics to its center (Andersen 2005). The Lamda Legal Defense Fund, which is the principal gay rights law firm, has adopted shifting tactics over the years in its pursuit of legal rights for gay people, with a mixture of successes and failures. Altogether, the gay rights movement has had a measurable impact on society's understanding of such phenomena as sexuality, sex, gender, privacy, discrimination, and family (Barclay, Bernstein, and Marshall 2009). In one interpretation, family law has been flexible enough to adapt to changing perceptions of homosexuality, in cases involving parental, custody, and adoption rights of gay people (Richman 2008). Psychologists have assessed the evidence of the psychological impact on family relationships—including gay parents on their biological and adoptive children—and have not found clear evidence of harm (Cantor et al. 2006). Gay people who are parents have increasingly challenged the law's conventional understanding of the meaning of "family."

With regard to marriage, it is both a cultural and a legal institution, and there is some evidence that many gay couples have embraced the conventional cultural idea of marriage even when marriage has not been available to them legally (Hull 2006). Denmark, in 1989, became the first nation to recognize same-sex marriages, with other Scandinavian countries following in its wake (Eskridge and Spedale 2006). The "registration" of same-sex partners (not necessarily married partners) in these countries did not impact in any measurable way heterosexual marriage, divorce, and family-related patterns. In the United States, civil unions and domestic partnerships, with certain rights, were recognized in some states for same-sex couples. But the symbolic significance of marriage itself was clearly important to many homosexual couples. The case of *Goodridge v. Department of Public Health* in Massachusetts in 2003, upholding a right to marriage for same-sex couples, led to calls for that right in other states as well (Pinello 2006). This decision and what came in its wake could be said to contradict the thesis that court decisions do not promote measurable social change. But the issue of same-sex marriage remained a politically contentious issue nationally, as well as in many states, with various states passing constitutional amendments banning same-sex marriages. Same-sex marriage initiatives have been especially offensive to those adhering to conservative and traditional values (MacLeod 2008a; Peters 2009b). On the other hand, in the American "heartland" of Iowa, a unanimous court decision in *Varnum v. Brien* accorded civil marriage equality to same-sex couples. But California's Proposition 8 prohibiting same-sex marriages (passed by voters in that state in 2008) was vigorously challenged on constitutional grounds in 2010 (McKinley 2010). Lawyers challenging this proposition likened it to earlier laws prohibiting inter-racial marriage. During this period, initiatives proposing a ban on same-sex marriages had been put forth in more than half the American states (McVeigh and Diaz 2009). But polls also documented a significant drop in recent years in the percentage of Americans opposed to same-sex marriages, from about 75% in 1990 to not much more than 50% early in the twenty-first century. Although the campaign for same-sex marriage has as one central focus obtaining the same rights for homosexuals and lesbians that are enjoyed by heterosexuals, it has also importantly been about winning recognition in the larger culture for the legitimacy of gay relationships (Hull 2006). In turn, same-sex commitment ceremonies and same-sex wedding protests have the potential to influence the larger culture's understanding of marriage itself and have had some other measurable effects on social behavior and attitudes (Liptak 2011). The battle over same-sex marriage was sure to continue, with likely victories and losses on both sides, for some time to come.

Eskridge, Jr. (2008) has traced the long history of sodomy laws. Sodomy, by definition, does not refer specifically to sexual acts between males but rather to sex without the possibility of procreation, which includes oral/genital sex and anal sex. Law in the colonial era prohibited sodomy (or "buggery") and when enforced, which was rare, most typically involved cases of sex with animals. In the eighteenth and nineteenth centuries, the enforcement of such laws was exceptionally rare and then was applied principally to immigrants and African-American men. Through much of the twentieth century, these laws were enforced principally against male homosexuals, and in some jurisdictions public solicitation for sodomy was pursued quite aggressively by vice squad officers. Illinois, in the early 1960s, became the first state to decriminalize consensual sodomy. Gradually, other states took this step, but some states did not. At the outset of the twenty-first century, only 13 states still had laws on the books criminalizing consensual sodomy. In 1986, in *Bowers v. Hardwick*, the U.S. Supreme Court upheld the constitutionality of such laws—in this case, that of Georgia. But in the 2003 decision in *Lawrence v. Texas*, the Court reversed itself, holding such laws to be unconstitutional.

Early in the new century, it was difficult to say whether the significant progress made by gays toward achieving protection and some recognition of rights would continue to move forward until no formal legal differentiation between people on the basis of sexual preference existed or whether the existing legal reforms represented the basic limits of what a predominantly heterosexual population would tolerate.

VICTIMLESS CRIMES

Still another set of legal reforms has focused on so-called victimless crimes. The concept of **victimless crime** has been applied to activities that are by definition consensual and nonpredatory (Hardaway 2003; Meier and Geis 1997; Schur 1965). Among the activities included in this category are a range of other consensual sexual activities, from fornication to adultery. Many states have abolished adultery laws, and where they are still on the books they are rarely enforced, but they have not been specifically ruled as unconstitutional (Glater 2003a). Other activities designated victimless crimes are public drunkenness, illicit drugs, prostitution, pornography, and gambling. Responding to such activities has historically absorbed a significant percentage of the resources of criminal justice systems. The characterization of crimes as victimless has been challenged, however, with the claim that society as a whole, certain neighborhoods in particular, and many innocent parties (e.g., loved ones) suffer significant consequences from the existence of such crimes as illegal alcohol abuse, illicit drug use, illegal gambling, pornography, and prostitution. Laws proscribing such activities have been promoted on grounds of protecting people from themselves, as well as protecting in some sense the other entities or parties just identified. Even if the activities listed are not in themselves predatory, most of them are regarded as linked with predatory crime and certainly with organized crime activity. In varying degrees, these activities are in violation of religious values or proscriptions, and many people believe that societal tolerance of such activities fosters the erosion of the social and moral order.

Throughout much of the twentieth century, victimless crime laws were at the heart of vigorous controversy, and this has also been a dynamic area of law in the sense of much change in one direction or the other. Opponents of laws against victimless crime claim that they infringe on individual liberty and privacy rights; they make lawbreakers out of large numbers of conventional members of society; they stigmatize such conventional members of society and sometimes push them into further deviance or criminality; they promote disrespect for law and the criminal justice system (and consequently diminish cooperation); they deflect attention from underlying causes of deviant behavior; they impose an enormous burden on the criminal justice system and on taxpayers; the laws themselves, rather than the activities, promote predatory crime (e.g., when a drug addict commits a mugging to obtain money to pay the exorbitant price of illegal substances); the laws themselves, rather than the activities, provide opportunities for organized crime to exploit; they negate a large source of tax revenue; and they simply don't work.

Alcohol

The celebrated attempt early in the twentieth century to legally abolish alcohol from American life, Prohibition, was discussed earlier in this text (Okrent 2010; Smith 2010). It is often cited as the classic case to illustrate the proposition that one cannot legislate morality, because millions of Americans flagrantly violated the proscriptions on liquor during Prohibition; it was repealed in 1933. In one sense, the failure of law to sweep alcohol off the face of American life has been very costly, as alcoholism is highly correlated with a wide range of crimes, auto accidents (and accidents of all kinds), domestic violence, family discord, suicide, unemployment, and the like (Goode 2005, pp. 177–183). On the other hand, the majority of American adults cherish the right to drink alcohol in moderation and believe that neither they nor others suffer any significant negative consequences. A "new temperance movement" emerged in the more recent era (from the 1970s on), with the objective of limiting access to alcohol and attempting to persuade especially vulnerable parties (e.g., pregnant women) not to drink (Gusfield 1996). The success of this movement has been somewhat limited (*see* Box 10.6).

The reform of law in response to alcohol use that has directly harmful consequences, such as drunk driving, also moved in the direction of a tougher response, with harsher

---

BOX 10.6 CHANGING THE LEGAL DRINKING AGE

Despite a uniform legal drinking age of 21 years, it has been estimated that more than 10 million Americans under that age—including one-fourth of eighth graders and one-half of high school students—drink alcohol (Marshall 2007). So-called alcopops such as Bacardi Silver (flavored malt beverages with target audiences of the young) have been increasingly criticized as "training beer" that promotes underage drinking (Marshall 2007). Accordingly, calls for reclassifying these beverages legally and imposing new restrictions on them have emerged.

College drinking has received more recognition as a major public health problem in recent years, although it isn't clear that it has increased significantly over the past several decades (Dowdall 2009). Indeed, some commentators claim that since 2004 there has been a significant decline in the number of entering college students who drink alcohol (Busteed 2010). Whether or not that is accurate, drinking in college continues to have major negative consequences. Although drinking patterns vary considerably across different college campuses, altogether college drinking is deeply rooted in the American college culture (Dowdall 2009). Eight of

10 college students drink alcohol, and 4 of 10 are binge drinkers (Sack 2008). Some 1,700 college students (between ages 18 and 24 years) die every year in the United States resulting from alcohol-related injuries, almost 100,000 are victims of alcohol-fueled sexual assault or rape, and some 600,000 are injured in relation to alcohol consumption (Dowdall 2009; Gibraltar 2008; Sack 2008). Accordingly, college administrators continue to seek policies and practices in relation to alcohol on the campus that will minimize the harmful consequences. On some campuses, college presidents have pushed for tougher initiatives to curb alcohol abuse (Busteed 2010; Insider Higher Ed 2010). But college presidents are divided on whether their campuses would be better off if the legal drinking age was lowered. In the summer of 2008, 130 college presidents signed a statement calling for a reconsideration of the legal drinking age, with some other college presidents speaking out against this initiative (Gibraltar 2008; Sack 2008). The retired college president who spearheaded the call for reconsideration favors the licensing of drinkers as young as 18 years. The premise here is that if underage drinking on campus cannot be prevented—and clearly the minimum age law is widely violated—it would be better to have it out in the open and supervised.

sanctions. Such reforms importantly reflected lobbying efforts by Mothers Against Drunk Driving (MADD), an organization founded by a woman whose young daughter was killed by a drunk driver. Although the call for tougher penalties against drunk drivers was certainly understandable in terms of the human devastation caused by them, those who have studied the problem are not wholly in agreement about the most effective strategies for deterring drunken drivers (Jacobs 1989; Ross 1992a).

On public drunkenness and alcohol consumption more generally, there is ongoing social and cultural ambivalence and contradictions. The majority of American adults enjoy social drinking on some level and expect to have the right to engage in such drinking. Americans as a whole are also concerned about the harmful consequences of drinking to excess. Drinking problems continue to be characterized by some as a consequence of poor character and moral irresponsibility and by many others as a symptom of a sickness (alcoholism). It seems that the problems associated with alcohol consumption would have to be addressed principally as cultural and medical problems and that the legal response would have to play a more limited role.

Illicit Drugs

During the first half of the twentieth century, a series of laws were passed with the objective of criminalizing the sale and distribution of a range of drugs, such as heroin and marijuana. Some earlier efforts at prohibition or control of narcotics seemed to have been inspired by racism and fear of corrupt foreign influences, such as Chinese opium dens (Meier and Geis 1997, pp. 87–88). Although relatively few Chinese were involved in the opium business in the nineteenth century, they were targeted on the claim that they were, and accordingly this claim was used to justify discriminatory policies and exclusion laws directed at them (Ahmad 2007). The **Harrison Tax Act (1914)** established a basic framework for the illegal status of heroin and other so-called hard drugs. Although growing concern about narcotics addiction played some role, such legislation was not based on scientific evidence of the harmfulness of using narcotics. The **Marijuana Tax Act (1937)** provided a basis for declaring the sale, distribution, and possession of marijuana illegal in every state in the union (Musto 1973). Historically, marijuana had been quite easily available and little controlled in many parts of the country. In the 1930s, however, the Depression gave rise to considerable social unrest; by some accounts, the landholding classes out West were concerned about their poorly paid laborers getting high on readily available marijuana and making trouble. Also, the newly revived liquor industry, following repeal of Prohibition, was anxious about competition from marijuana. It is worth noting that in the 1920s marijuana was legal in many places, and alcohol was not; a decade or so later, the situation was reversed. An ambitious commissioner of the Federal Bureau of Narcotics, Harry Anslinger, testified before Congress that marijuana was a dangerous substance and had to be controlled; he claimed that it caused some users to go berserk and commit violent acts. Various forces, then, were involved in promoting laws criminalizing marijuana, but serious scientific or medical research into the actual effects of marijuana use was not a factor. Indeed, when commissions of scientists and physicians were eventually called on to provide some guidance on this question, they did not, for the most part, claim that hard evidence showed any significant harmful effect. The common claim of a significant link between drug use and criminal behavior has been challenged by research (Bennett and Holloway 2007; Moore 2007). Scientific evidence on the potential benefits and harms associated with marijuana use continued to be somewhat contradictory (McManis 2009).

Through most of the twentieth century, certain drugs (e.g., heroin, cocaine, and marijuana) were treated as illegal substances, and people dealing in or acquiring these drugs faced harsh penal sanctions. Millions have been arrested and hundreds of thousands have gone to prison or jail. The existence of these laws has obviously not deterred large numbers of people from involvement with these drugs. As is well-known, a great upsurge of usage generally occurred in the latter part of the 1960s and the early 1970s. Various reasons have been given for the dramatic increase in illicit drug usage, but the very fact of illegal status may well have played a role in promoting drug use as a specific act of defiance toward the established order and its leadership. On the one hand, an aggressively fought "War on Drugs," especially from the 1980s on, led to a huge volume of arrests and long prison sentences for drug offenders. The long-standing "War on Drugs" continues to be challenged as immensely costly with little, if any, demonstrable benefit (Benavie 2009; Decker 2010). In 2009 the newly appointed Obama Administration drug czar called for an end to this counterproductive war on drugs, and a shift to emphasizing treatment for those with substance abuse problems (Fields 2009).

Thirteen American states have legalized medicinal use of marijuana since 1996 (Goodnough 2009). But because federal laws remain in place prohibiting the sale and distribution of marijuana, access to marijuana is not uniformly easy (Chapkis and Webb 2008). Nevertheless, some commentators regard the legalization of medicinal use of marijuana in a growing number of states as a stepping stone to a possible end to the prohibition on marijuana sale and distribution generally (Parloff 2009). Canada and various European countries have moved toward much more liberal policies on drugs—marijuana in particular—than the United States (Schlosser 2004; Segre 2003). The American government's emphasis on a criminal justice system response to drugs, as opposed to an approach placing much more emphasis on education and treatment programs, has been widely criticized. In at least one interpretation, the War on Drugs has provided politicians with a symbolic opportunity to blame America's problems on a "dangerous class" disproportionately made up of young urban African-Americans and new immigrants, who are especially vulnerable to criminal justice processing (Gordon 1994). The War on Drugs is politically successful, we are told, because it sustains racial antagonism, plays into the media's need for theater, and serves the purposes of religiously oriented, conservative coalition politics (Baggins 1998).

A number of prominent scholars and social commentators have called for some form of legalization of drugs, on the premise that the costs of the War on Drugs have far outweighed any identifiable benefits, but a serious movement toward legalization seems politically untenable in the foreseeable future (Ryan 1998). Although the existing drug laws have obviously failed to deter millions of Americans from at least experimenting with one or more illicit drugs, the critics of legalization argue that drug use and addiction would become even more of a problem in the absence of legal controls. A truly effective reform of drug laws in a direction that would win broad public support remains a formidable challenge.

Sex Work and Pornography

The recent era has witnessed a dramatic rise in the whole range of sex-related commerce along with new forms of regulation for such commerce (Bernstein 2007; Scoular and Sanders 2010; Weitzer 2010b). Demand for pornography, lap-dancing, escorts, telephone sex, and sexual tourism appears to have expanded. Although some liberalization and legalization of sex work such as prostitution has occurred in various countries, punitive laws have also increased during the recent era. It is challenging to develop and adopt laws in relation to sex work that are realistic in terms of achieving objectives and do not unduly penalize vulnerable parties (e.g., female sex workers) (Thrupkaew 2009). The question of whether it is a good idea to legalize prostitution continues to be hotly debated (Lalasz 2008). But in the United States, the formal legalization of prostitution is not likely to be widely supported any time soon.

Overall levels of societal concern about pornography have waxed and waned during the course of the recent era, with extreme forms (e.g., images of bestiality) generating the most concern (McGlynn and Ward 2009). The Internet has greatly extended the scope of and engagement with child pornography (O'Donnell and Milner 2007). Consciousness of and stronger measures against this form of pornography have increased. The public screening of pornographic films on college campuses has become not uncommon but has generated some controversy and calls for action by legislators (Moltz 2009). Altogether, the dramatic growth of the porn industry in recent years has occurred during a period when many political leaders claim to be proponents of "family values" and hostile to sexual liberalization, including pornography (Hall and Bishop 2007; Sarracino and Scott 2008). The extent to which pornography should be formally regulated or broadly tolerated continues to be debated.

Gambling

The American history of gambling is filled with contradictory legal policies (Bernard and Preston 2004; Skolnick 1978; Thompson 1994). Moral entrepreneurs were for a long time successful in having most forms of gambling outlawed in most parts of the United States (Nevada was a glaring exception). Of course, violation of antigambling laws was especially pervasive, and in many American neighborhoods bookmaking and numbers games were large-scale enterprises. Over the last several decades, however, one state after another not only legalized certain forms of gambling—especially off-track betting and lotteries—but actively promoted gambling that was run by and ideally benefited state programs (e.g., programs for education or for the elderly). The movement toward legalization was partly driven by recognition of the futility of many existing antigambling laws but also by the irresistible temptation to raise state revenue without imposing or raising taxes directly (typically unpopular with voters). The primary movers behind legalized gambling, then, were gaming industry interests and political officials or legislators seeking profits or a relatively painless source of state revenue, not citizens (Goodman 1996). In an environment of economic recession from 2009 on there was growing pressure to legalize but tax a range of victimless crimes (Gillespie 2009; Klein 2009; McKinley 2010). Legalized gambling has now generated billions of dollars of tax revenue, and legalizing currently prohibited forms (e.g., cyberspace betting) could generate billions more.

Americans spend more than $400 billion a year on legalized gambling, and this gambling produces some $40 billion in revenue. But it is far from clear that legalized gambling enhances the overall economy of states that adopt and aggressively promote it (Dao 2004; Goodman 1996). Furthermore, legalized gambling incurs many costs, ranging from deflecting discretionary income from other legitimate businesses (e.g., restaurants and theaters), promoting crime and criminal justice system expenditures, and producing personal tragedies for addictive gamblers, their families, and those with whom they had personal and business relationships. Although regulations to aid problem gamblers have been adopted in many jurisdictions, critics have suggested that these regulations may be counterproductive (Bernard and Preston 2004).

Legalized gambling has been characterized as a **regressive tax,** in the sense that those with modest or low incomes contribute disproportionately to this revenue. Gambling entrepreneurs who seek licensing for casino operations typically encounter a certain amount of resistance. Many citizens continue to regard gambling as inherently immoral, as addictive and personally destructive to some individuals, and as corrupting or damaging to neighborhoods, governments, and society generally. Although the momentum early in the twenty-first century was toward broader legalization of gambling, much ambivalence or active opposition to this trend survives.

CONCLUSION

It should be evident from this review of legal reform that law is indeed both a dependent and an independent variable. Citizens, organizations, and government functionaries have conflicting agendas about legal reform (*see* Table 10.2). Law both reflects changing social conditions and plays a role in transforming social conditions. Law is attacked for not playing a more dynamic role in promoting social change on some of these issues and also attacked for doing more social harm than good in relation to these issues. The calls for more (or tougher) law versus less (or milder) law on victimless crime issues is especially intense and divisive. The laws on victimless crime inevitably engage people's most fundamental beliefs about morality and human nature. It seems likely that victimless crime law in the twenty-first century will continue to be contested terrain and subject to significant change and reform.

BASIC TRENDS IN LAW AND SOCIAL CHANGE IN AMERICA

American law and the American legal system undergo constant change, but it is difficult to make broad generalizations about the nature of such change because for almost every

TABLE 10.2 CONFLICTING AGENDAS IN RELATION TO LEGAL REFORM

More formal law	vs.	Less formal law
More regulation	vs.	Less regulation
Crime control	vs.	Due process
Expanded individual rights	vs.	Greater community responsibility

trend, one can find a countertrend. It is indisputable that over time Americans have become reliant on more law—or at least more secular, formal law—as an inevitable response to the increasing size, heterogeneity, and complexity of American society. A countertrend of turning to alternative forms of dispute resolution has also been a characteristic of the recent era in American law, in part as a response to the frustrations and costs associated with reliance on formal law. Two basic questions arise about this countertrend: Just how far can it go in an increasingly large, complex, and heterogeneous society? And to what extent does the turn to informal law in some form really represent a fundamental break with formal law, as opposed to a means to extend the scope and discretion involved in law?

Historically, the formal legal system has all too often worked to the advantage of the powerful and the privileged. A movement toward greater reliance on informal law, then, could in at least some circumstances be helpful to powerless and poorer people; in many other circumstances, however, it could provide broader opportunities to take advantage of them.

In the course of the twentieth century, there was an increasing shift from an optimistic view that law could play a constructive role in the "social engineering" of society to a growing concern that a "hyperlegalistic" society was having a paralyzing impact on American society (Sarat, Garth, and Kagan 2002). There was also a shift to increasing reliance on the federal (as opposed to state) law (Friedman 2002). Many new demands were imposed on law during the course of the twentieth century.

REGULATORY LAW

Self-regulation has always played a key role in the world of business, but in an increasingly complex transnational business environment produces new challenges for law, which must establish favorable conditions for self-governance (Dilling, Herberg, and Winter 2008). Issues relating to regulation intersect in various complex ways with issues relating to rights, because regulations may be seen as compromising rights (Darian-Smith and Scott 2009). The problem of global warming and climate change has generated large new challenges for international regulation of the environment (Haines, Reichman and Scott, 2008). So have new developments in biogenetic technology (Brownsword 2008). The worst financial crisis since the Great Depression, in 2008, and the worst environmental catastrophe in U.S. history (the Gulf of Mexico BP oil spill), in 2010, were two major events that forcefully reminded Americans of the need for strong regulatory oversight. The corporate and business world continues to be generally resistant to regulation as a counterproductive, inefficient, and unnecessary force in a free-market economy.

DUE PROCESS

Due process rights have in many ways expanded in American law; some say that the expansion is a function of a more inclusive and more confident society. The Warren Court of the 1960s handed down a series of decisions significantly expanding the due process rights of defendants in criminal cases. This trend has sought to make amends for the inequities and injustices typically encountered by criminal defendants through most of history. When people perceive that crime is rising, however, a countertrend emerges, calling for the curtailment of rights of those accused of crimes (and even more so of those convicted of having committed crimes). Over the long term, alternating cycles of crime control and due process have occurred, although the crime-control cycle has seemed to be entrenched in the more recent era. On the one hand, the U.S. Supreme Court in various cases has tended to narrow the scope of the due process rulings, without specifically overruling them. On the other hand, the U.S. Congress and various state legislative bodies have passed numerous "tough on crime" laws. This tension between realizing crime control and due process objectives is sure to endure as well. It remains to be seen whether measures adopted in the post-9/11 environment to combat terrorism will permanently compromise commitments to due process rights of all those accused of crimes.

ENTITLEMENTS AND RIGHTS

The general movement toward an expansion of individual rights and group entitlements is also a significant trend within American law. Again, this trend could be interpreted as belated acknowledgment within American law of the many disadvantages experienced by individuals (and groups) such as women, African-Americans, gay people, the disabled, the elderly, and so forth. But here, too, there is a countertrend in calls for more responsibility toward the welfare of the community itself and the imposition of a higher degree of personal responsibility on individuals, including those coming from substantially disadvantaged homes. The welfare reform movement could be viewed, at least in part, as a demand for greater individual accountability and diminished individual entitlement. The backlash against affirmative action, at the end of the twentieth century, was a symptom of the countertrend on behalf of individual rights and against group-based entitlements. The search for an optimal balance between individual rights and responsibility, group entitlements, and the needs of the larger community or society is also sure to continue in the twenty-first century.

TECHNOLOGY

Throughout the twentieth century, the law had to contend with new forms of technology that required new laws (*see* Box 10.7). In the early part of the century, the automobile and the telephone generated new law; at the end of the century, cyberspace and biogenetic engineering were generating the need for new law. Whether the law should facilitate the use of new forms of technology or should impose constraints on it is an enduring source of controversy.

LAW IN THE TWENTY-FIRST CENTURY

The idea of a society without law has been the dream of various social philosophers, with Karl Marx probably the most famous of these. In a utopian society, there would be no need for law because human beings would live together in a state of perpetual harmony and in a spirit of cooperation and sharing. In a certain sense, preliterate human societies and, in the context of modern societies, some families and small communities (such as communes) live without law, unless one stretches the meaning of the term *law* so broadly that it encompasses

---

BOX 10.7 WHO OWNS THE SKY?

The ownership of land has been a core focus of law since time immemorial, but "who owns the sky"? This is the topic of Stuart Banner's (2008) book of that title. An ancient doctrine of *cujus maxim* extended to property owners some rights to usable air space immediately above their property, but the twentieth century development of flight confronted the law with a whole new set of challenges. Although the right of planes to fly through the sky was generally accepted, as late as the 1940s it was unclear whether low-flying planes were trespassing on property over which they flew, and it was unsettled in some respects whether state or federal law governed flight. In *United States v. Cassidy* (1946), the U. S. Supreme Court upheld a uniform nationwide rule about the right to flight sought by the aviation industry. Of course a whole range of legal issues relating to flight have arisen and continue to lead to litigation, such as the noise and dangers associated with low-flying planes. But the obvious usefulness of planes led to law adapting to facilitate flight. On the other hand, legal doctrine also influenced the aviation industry—for example, leading to the development of airports quite distant from cities to minimize infringements on rights of property owners and city residents. Flight changed the law and the law shaped patterns of flight. Going forward in the twenty-first century, it is quite certain that issues relating to the law of outer space will become increasingly important and complex. Since 1957 and the launching of the satellite Sputnik by the Soviet Union, a series of space law treaties and accords have been drafted and implemented.

---

any and all norms governing human conduct. Earlier in this book, however, some space was devoted to the disastrous consequences in a recent era—for example, in Russia and in China—of efforts to establish large-scale societies without law. If the hope for a society without laws has not become entirely extinct (there are, after all, still anarchists in our midst), it has few believers.

Most serious thinkers would concede that law in some form is an absolutely necessary and wholly unavoidable feature of any complex modern society. And many commentators celebrate the general expansion of law during the twentieth century as one of the great achievements of that century. However, even among the many who concede the inevitability and accomplishments of law, some insist that there is altogether too much law, that the excessive growth of law has to be combated vigorously, and that we can and should find ways to reduce the scope of law's presence in our lives and to rid legal institutions of cumbersome forms of red tape, confusion, and delay. Some argue that we presently have laws that we do not need or that do more harm than good (e.g., laws prohibiting the distribution and use of marijuana and other illicit drugs). Others believe that we are presently lacking some laws we need to prevent egregious harm to other beings (e.g., laws prohibiting abortion). If history provides any lesson, we can expect battles over such issues to continue. On another front, it seems likely that vigorous debate will continue for some time on whether we have too much regulatory law or too little in such areas as environmental protection, worker safety, and consumer product liability.

The ultimate crisis for a legal system comes when a significant proportion of its constituency loses fundamental faith in it and no longer believes that it has an obligation to comply. The collapse of the Soviet Union in the final years of the twentieth century was one famous case attesting to the potential for a **legitimacy crisis** in a large-scale society to contribute to the transformation of that society and its legal system. The transformation of South Africa, early in the last decade of the century, from an undemocratic system wholly dominated by a White minority to an electoral democracy, was also importantly linked to a legitimacy crisis. Across North Africa and the Middle East, at the outset of the second decade of the new century, major challenges to the legitimacy of autocratic and corrupt regimes broke out. In the twenty-first century, if there are increasing expectations of the legal system that the system cannot effectively address, then that could contribute to a loss of belief in, and support for, the system.

Friedman (1985) has written of the increasing expectation through the twentieth century that the legal system will provide a just resolution to every wrong and denial of a right. If such a trend continues during the twenty-first century, disenchantment and disappointment with the legal system are likely to increase. If the view that the law systematically favors some segments of society over others expands, then this could also contribute to the emergence of a legitimacy crisis. Although the perceived legitimation of the political (and economic) system is not necessarily synonymous with the perceived legitimation of the legal system, they are closely related. Accordingly, the fate of law is in important ways tied to the fate of the larger political economy; however, law and the legal system might continue to enjoy support even when the political system loses it if law is viewed as autonomous (or independent) and a critically important instrument for addressing the limitations or injustices of the political economy.

POLITICS

Law and politics are intertwined in numerous ways. Law is a product of political institutions and processes. Law also plays a role in the governance of the political process. Some tension arises when law and political agendas are at odds in some way, when law is regarded as intervening inappropriately in political processes, or when the political is regarded as intervening inappropriately with the law or legal institutions. In the recent era a legal institution, the U.S. Supreme Court, was widely criticized for handing down a decision resolving the 2000 presidential election controversy (MacKenzie 2002). In the eyes of some, this resolution of the election was at odds with democratic principles. Also, during this period, the question arose over whether it was a good idea to have a law that allows voters to "recall" a duly elected governor and vote that governor out of office prematurely. This question arose in connection with the successful recall in 2003 of California Governor Gray Davis and the election of actor Arnold Schwarzenegger to succeed him (Bowler and Cain 2004; Purdum 2003). Would this establish a precedent for political chaos in many states, and would it inhibit sitting governors from adopting unpopular but necessary policies out of fear of inspiring a recall movement?

The role of money in corrupting the political process has been a matter of considerable concern for some time. A **Bipartisan Campaign Reform Act** (the **McCain-Feingold Act**), passed by the U.S. Congress in 2002, seeks to close loopholes allowing corporations, unions, and other big money players to donate large amounts of unregulated "soft" money for political candidates (Waxman 2002). This law was challenged as a violation of First Amendment free-speech rights of would-be donors, but in 2003 the U.S. Supreme Court, in a 5-to-4 decision, upheld the law (L. Greenhouse 2003g). A more conservative U.S. Supreme

Court, in the controversial 5-to-4 *Citizen's Union* decision, upheld the right of corporations to fully fund political campaigns (Dworkin 2010). Moneyed special interests have always been imaginative in finding ways to circumvent such efforts by law to limit their influence, and it was far from clear that this new law would really accomplish its stated objective.

When high-level government officials are suspected of some form of law breaking, how should the legal system respond? Should these officials be investigated by the ordinary processes of law, or by special processes (i.e., the appointment of independent counsel)? Altogether, the law intersects with political questions in numerous complex ways.

SCIENCE

Early in the twentieth century, the German sociologist Max Weber advanced the thesis that rationalization was becoming increasingly critical to the operation of the legal system. That is, law was becoming increasingly oriented toward rational, logical procedures and moving away from a focus on divine right and superstition. Not everyone is convinced that all our problems have rational solutions, and Campos (1998, p. viii) referred to our "irrational worship of rationality."

In the twentieth century, indisputably, reliance on science (and scientific evidence) became more important generally within law. One projection for the future of law in the twenty-first century envisions a continued and growing emphasis on science and a scientific approach. Some say that the courts in the last part of the twentieth century increasingly administered a form of **technocratic justice,** moving away from traditional legal values and practices. Technocratic justice, in this context, refers to reliance on scientific and technical knowledge and the realization of practical objectives as the basis for legal decision making (Heydebrand 1979, p. 33; Stryker 1989, p. 342). It is not evident, however, that legal institutions rely increasingly on technocratic (scientific/technical) expertise in a uniform way, and in at least some instances such reliance has apparently been reduced (Feldman 2009; Goodman 2008; Stryker 1989). Tensions and conflicts over the proper place and scope of science in the legal process are likely to continue.

In general, however, scientific evidence has been introduced into legal cases more often than in the past, despite the fact that law and science are rooted in different cultural systems and have somewhat different approaches to establishing "truth" (Feldman 2009; Jasanoff 1995, 2001; Moreno 2003). In the twentieth century, science sometimes clashed with religious values within a legal setting. Early in the century, the famous *Scopes* trial (featuring a confrontation between evolutionary theory and religion) highlighted this clash. Although the religious perspective was at least formally triumphant in that particular trial, which took place in the Southern U.S. Bible Belt, science generally became an increasingly dominant force within law during the course of the century. Because different forms of expertise and criteria for truth claims can be found within science, the handling of scientific evidence and testimony within the legal system is often complicated or troublesome.

For most of the twentieth century, the **Frye Test** dominated judicial thinking about the admissibility of scientific evidence (Jasanoff 1995). In this test, the criteria for accepting expert opinion into evidence depended on whether a viewpoint had gained general acceptance in its particular field (or among the expert's peers) (Jasanoff 2001). In a 1993 case, *Daubert v. Merrill Dow Pharmaceuticals, Inc.*, the U.S. Supreme Court rejected sole reliance on peer review and instead called on courts to assess the validity of scientific testimony or evidence on the basis of *(1)* whether the reasoning or methodology underlying the testimony or evidence is scientifically valid and *(2)* whether that reasoning or methodology can be properly applied to the facts in the case. Expert witnesses play an important role in American legal proceedings. In most of the world, judges select the expert witnesses, but in the American system each side hires and pays its experts (Liptak 2008c). This approach has been criticized on the basis that it leads to "bought" testimony—that is, experts will be partisan, testifying to support whichever side is paying them. Another question that arises in relation to expert witnesses is whether jurors can effectively evaluate conflicting scientific testimony by experts on opposite sides of a case. On the other hand, some commentators question the very notion of a truly neutral expert witness. To the extent that expert witnesses attempt to restrict themselves solely to scientific criteria, they may find themselves under pressure in court to conform to the law's demand for clear-cut answers even if the science doesn't support such answers. In one view, jurors will believe experts whose demeanor or credentials impress them—not their testimony itself. Many legal proceedings rely heavily on the testimony of expert witnesses, especially those with scientific credentials. The validity of relying on such scientific expertise has been challenged.

Lie detector (or polygraph) tests have been used in the American legal system as one means of discriminating between truth and untruth in both criminal and civil law cases. Lykken (1998) asserted that no scientifically acceptable estimate of the accuracy of lie detector tests exists. However, Dery (1999) argued that polygraph evidence has been estimated to be up to 90% reliable and, in any case, is more reliable than many other forms of evidence (e.g., psychiatric testimony, fingerprint evidence, eyewitness testimony, and handwriting identification) that have been found admissible in American courts of law. Since 1988, it has been illegal for most private sector employers to require that employees take a lie detector test. In about half the American states, lie detector evidence can be introduced under some circumstances, and federal courts have historically considered such evidence on a case-by-case basis.

With DNA evidence increasingly important in criminal cases (in some dramatic instances, freeing men from death row), inevitable questions arise about variations in DNA testing results and alleged false claims relating to DNA (Clarke 2007; Lynch et al. 2008). Jurors were found to have followed and evaluated evidence in a trial study involving a fairly complex DNA test (Vidmar and Hans 2007). Although DNA evidence can still be contested, then, it is likely to play an increasingly important role in criminal cases.

In a world of complex (and sometimes disturbing) new scientific developments (e.g., in the realms of nuclear fission and fusion, human genetics, and artificial intelligence), it is inevitable that we need scientific expertise to contend with the legal (and moral) issues arising out of these developments (Goldberg 1994; Lemmons and Waring 2006) (*see* Box 10.8). Although it seems likely that scientific innovations and breakthroughs will become incorporated into the operation of the system of law, two basic questions arise: Just how

---

BOX 10.8 NEUROSCIENCE AND THE TRANS-
FORMATION OF LAW

Neuroscience—a branch of science that studies the way the brain operates and how it impacts human behavior—has made significant strides in the recent era. Increasingly, scientific evidence has been introduced into criminal proceedings to try to persuade a jury or judge that the accused did not have meaningful control over his behavior, especially if the accused has been accused of murder (Rosen 2007). Proponents of neuroscience believe that its application to criminal cases will impact questions of guilt and punishment and will help disclose biases and lies of participants in the legal process. Some commentators are concerned that the use of brain scanning technology will further erode privacy and mental freedom. Could advances in neuroscience ever reach a level where they could decisively repudiate the traditional moral and legal assumption that people must be held responsible for their conduct (barring a narrow set of exceptions, such as insanity)? If that ever occurs, then it goes without saying that it would have huge implications for the whole legal system.

---

far will the scientific approach to justice go, and is scientific justice superior to traditional human justice? On the first point, will there eventually be a point where sophisticated computers discriminate between true and false testimony and render verdicts? Even if such a movement toward a scientific justice is possible, is it desirable? Or will it produce a wholly dehumanized form of justice? The nature of scientific criteria for truth and legal criteria for truth may be fundamentally incompatible (Jasanoff 2001; Timmermans 2006). Certainly, scientific evidence is often misunderstood or distorted in court proceedings to achieve some legal end. In a 2009 decision, the U. S. Supreme Court ruled that crime laboratory reports may not be used against criminal defendants at trial unless the analysts who produced the reports are available to testify in court (Liptak 2009c). As scientific evidence and testimony becomes progressively more important in both criminal and civil law cases, many challenges continue to arise (Caudill and LaRue 2006; Cranor 2006; Goodman 2008). These include the ongoing gaps in scientific knowledge, and the difficulties in many cases in discriminating between general and specific causation or establishing direct causal effects.

Finally, one of the big questions for law, going forward, is how it will address complex questions arising in a "posthuman" era (Amestoy 2003). The term *posthuman* has been applied to a range of issues such as genetic manipulation, stem cell research, artificial intelligence, and cloning. If scientific breakthroughs lead to an extension of what it means to be human, then the law must respond appropriately to this situation.

GLOBALIZATION

Globalization has been one of the dominant themes of the recent era, and there are many reasons to believe that pressures for globalization will intensify (Dicken 2003). The emergence of a "global legal order" is part of this (Halpin and Roeben 2009). The term **globalization** has many different meanings but in its most basic form refers to the increasing economic, political, and cultural interconnectedness of the world. Globalization is sometimes regarded as a force promoting the spread of Western standards of living to other parts of the world; alternatively, some warn that globalization can contribute to greater concentrations of power and a greater divide between the rich and the poor (Silbey 1997). It is far from clear that the Western legal model—as opposed to an Eastern, or Chinese, legal model—will prevail as the world becomes globalized (Appelbaum 1998). In the realm of law, it seems safely predictable that international law and transnational law will assume increasing importance in the years ahead. But globalization also confronts a countertrend of revived ethnic nationalism and localism. Some aspects of law, then, will reflect a shift to the global and the transnational; other aspects of law will reflect intensified local and ethnic concerns. These tensions and conflicts are sure to be an important story in the twenty-first century.

In an increasingly globalized world, traditional claims of sovereignty tend to erode, and it becomes increasingly necessary to focus on transnational concerns. International policing goes back at least to the World War I period and was intensified after World War II (Deflem 2002; Sheptycki 2002). Interpol is the principal international policing agency, although it is more of a centralized clearinghouse for cross-border crime information than a full-fledged international policing entity. Altogether, it has become increasingly necessary for policing agencies to operate transnationally (*see* Box 10.9).

The role of states as "police" with regard to violations of international law is a tremendously complex matter. Under what circumstances should nations undertake humanitarian interventions in other parts of the world? This issue has arisen in the recent era, and it will surely arise again and again in the twenty-first century (Lepard 2002). Difficult ethical, legal, and practical considerations are involved in the decision to intervene or not. The United States intervened in Somalia in the 1990s but not in the Rwanda genocide during the same decade. In the view of critics, U.S. foreign interventions have been carried out over the years principally to advance special interests or to extend U.S. domination over the world (Chomsky 2003).

BOX 10.9 GLOBALIZATION, INTERNATIONAL LAW AND REGULATION

The global dimensions of law have some roots in developments that occurred hundreds of years ago, including the Papal Revolution and the Protestant Reformation (Goldman 2007). More recently, the United Nations and the European Union have had some measurable effects on global legal development. Over a long period of time, Western nations have been exporting the rule of law to developing nations around the world (Carothers 2006). Transnational law is being appropriated by many individual nations, with an endlessly complex process of legal change and development resulting (Von Benda-Beckmann, von Benda-Beckmann, and Griffiths 2005). And global policing has become more common in the recent era, with attempts to provide policing assistance to developing countries that have gone through recent strife and instability (e.g., a civil war) (Goldsmith and Sheptycki 2007). Global policing is resisted and resented in many developing countries as an effort by developed Western nations to impose their own values and agendas on other countries (Andreas and Nadelmann 2006). The establishment of the permanent International Criminal Court (ICC) at the outset of the new century was still another significant development in the evolving globalization of law. To date, this court has focused principally on cases emanating out of Africa (Clarke 2009). It continues to face many challenges in realizing its objectives and is viewed by some as afflicted with contradictory dimensions. International tribunals of accused war criminals clash with traditional notions of national sovereignty and accordingly are widely challenged (Moghalu 2008). It remains to be seen how the tensions between applying international standards of justice and respecting national sovereignty will play out. And there are others areas of challenge in the globalization of law. It has proven difficult, for example, to achieve international agreement on the optimal ways of regulating genetically modified foods (Pollack and Shaffer 2009). In a globalized world, cooperation between nations in the regulation of taxes becomes more imperative, as does the need to address tax havens which the wealthy use to avoid paying taxes (Sharman 2006). Although the globalization of law is certain to expand, its specific parameters are sure to be contested.

For some, it would be best to strengthen the United Nations' capacity to prevent violent conflict and to intervene in cases of genocide (Sriram and Wermester 2003). It remains to be seen whether effective, universally supported standards and procedures for humanitarian intervention will emerge under international law.

Early in the twenty-first century, the United States is widely regarded as the world's only superpower, inevitably inspiring much resentment and fear. The United States continues to "export" its philosophy of law and specific elements of its legal system (Dezalay and Garth 2002; Snyder 2004). Its efforts to export democracy could backfire in the developing world, however, promoting ethnic hatred and political instability (Eakin 2004; Chua 2003). The United States faces an especially large challenge toward getting its policy initiatives recognized as legitimate (or valid) by the rest of the world (Kagan 2004). This country has been deemed profoundly hypocritical for demanding that other nations implement internationally recognized human rights standards but not permitting its own human rights practices to be judged in any international legal forum.

For many centuries, philosophers, jurists, and political scientists have speculated on the necessary conditions for achieving enduring peace between nations (Murphy 2003). The notion of global or world governance in some form has been viewed as a utopian dream by some. Others consider this potential a dangerous idea, as it would involve an immense concentration of power. A movement toward a global system of law would require a cultural transformation of the traditional outlook of citizens of states, who would integrate the notion of responsibilities toward citizens of all nations into this new outlook. Slaughter (2004) has argued that a form of global governance is already in place, with a complex web of "governmental networks" linking government officials in different nations, who cooperatively oversee and enforce international agreements. It seems likely that a movement toward enhancing and formalizing these networks will occur in the twenty-first century in an ever more interdependent world.

THE FUTURE OF LAW

The perpetual gaps between the haves and the have-nots on all levels (i.e., between countries, between social groups, between individuals) will likely endure as one of the major challenges for law in the twenty-first century. By at least some measures, the gaps actually widened toward the end of the twentieth century. This piece of data provides some support for Marx's celebrated prediction that under capitalism, the rich would get richer and the poor would get poorer; of course, Marx was wrong about many things. To the extent that law is viewed as complicit in maintaining or perpetuating social inequality, it will be the target of ongoing hostility and challenge from the disadvantaged and their allies. Conversely, law may continue to be viewed as a potentially powerful instrument for promoting greater social equality and the fairer distribution of scarce resources (*see* Box 10.9).

On the future of law, then, the only thing one can assert with some degree of confidence is that law will change, in ways large and small, as we move through the twenty-first century. It is far from clear, however, exactly what form the changes will take. By understanding as fully as possible the character and nature of law in our lives, we should be better prepared to understand the legal changes we are sure to encounter and, ideally, to contribute to these changes in a constructive way.

BOX 10.10 HUMAN RIGHTS AND THE LAW

The promotion and protection of universal human rights has been a core theme of international politics since the end of World War II in particular, although with earlier roots (e.g., the nineteenth century campaign against slavery) (Stacy 2009). Practices relating to the granting of amnesty to those who have been found guilty of human rights offenses varies considerably among different countries, with some resistant to forgiveness and others quite forgiving (Mallinder 2008). But the international attention to human rights has also influenced the development of human rights within particular states, although such initiatives can be significantly contested within these states. There is no universal agreement on the meaning and parameters of human rights, and for many people in developing nations human rights all-too-often seem to involve the imposition of Western norms and interests on their way of life (Goodale 2009; Goodale and Merry 2006; Stacy 2009). On the other hand, the promotion of human rights is viewed by some as a means of addressing the increasing interdependence of people of different nationalities, such as those who belong to the European Union (Porsdam 2009). Issues of global human rights in the twenty-first century intersect with issues of sovereignty, cultural and regional differences, and civil society (Stacy 2009). Issues of global human rights also intersect with issues of health, hunger, refugee status, avoidance of torture, and environmental safety (Gibney and Skogly 2010). Transnational corporations are parties to international trade agreements that call for some respect for global human rights, but such corporations are often complicit in violations of rights—including basic rights to food and shelter—in the relentless pursuit of profit (Aaronson and Zimmerman 2008; Dine 2005; Hernandez-Truyal, Esperanza, and Powell 2009). Some of the more specific issues that arise in this connection include: conscripted child labor, sustainable development, promotion of health, equality of women, human trafficking, indigenous peoples, poverty, citizenship, and economic sanctions.

The question has been raised: Are claims on behalf of universal human rights overstated, and should rights be linked to an individual's contributions to the well-being of society (Osiatynski 2009)? Attention to rights, in one view, should be counterbalanced with attention to other important social values. Thousands of cases relating to social rights specifically have been adjudicated in countries around the world (Langford 2008). Altogether, issues relating to human and social rights are quite certain to be major sources of concern and controversy in the years ahead.

KEY TERMS AND CONCEPTS

anarchism
battered women syndrome
Bipartisan Campaign Reform Act (McCain-Feingold Act)
cultural orientation
Equal Rights Amendment (ERA)
Frye Test
globalization
Harrison Tax Act (1914)
hate (or bias) crime
instrumental orientation

International Criminal Court (ICC)
Labor Management Relations Act (Taft-Hartley Act)
legitimacy crisis
Marijuana Tax Act (1937)
National Labor Relations Act (Wagner Act)
Personal Responsibility and Work Opportunity Act (PRWOA)

political orientation
rape shield
regressive tax
technocratic justice
Universal Declaration of Human Rights
universal jurisdiction
victimless crime
Violence Against Women Act

DISCUSSION QUESTIONS

1. Explain how law is both an independent and a dependent variable in relation to social change. Review the conditions under which law is most likely to promote social change as well as the sources of resistance to legal reform. Which views do you tend to agree with the most? Why?

2. What message did President Clinton send to America when he signed the Personal Responsibility and Work Opportunity Act (PRWOA) in 1996? How would such an action substantiate the claim cited on numerous occasions throughout the text that laws and the legal system make the rich richer and the poor poorer?

3. Why does it seem that domestic violence and rape, two of the most violent acts known to exist (usually against women), are among the hardest for our legal system to control? Would the laws be any different, or the reforms of greater significance, if men were the primary targets of violence?

4. Why don't laws seem to deter drug users? Would legalization of at least marijuana be a step in the right direction in our "War on Drugs"? Would an emphasis on education and treatment programs, rather than an emphasis on a criminal justice system response, make more of a difference?

5. Does the administration of "technocratic justice" have the potential to create a more "exact" system of legal decision making? What are the pros and cons of the movement toward more reliance upon science within our legal system?

APPENDIX A
CASE BRIEFING: A RUDIMENTARY
SKILL IN LEGAL ANALYSIS

Even students new to the study of law can acquire a basic practical understanding of legal analysis (and reasoning) in the form of case briefing. In reading appellate court opinions, what should one look for? Here, in outline form, are some of the elements of case briefing.

I. Preliminary Questions:

    A. *Type of Case*: Is it a criminal case or a civil case? In American case opinions, a case titled *U.S. v.* or *Commonwealth of PA. v.* indicates a criminal case, prosecuted in the state's name, whereas a case titled *Smith v. Jones*, involving private parties, indicates a civil proceeding (the *v.*, of course, stands for *versus*). But as the state may be a party to a civil proceeding, the appearance of the state in the case title does not guarantee that the case is a criminal proceeding. Ultimately, of course, the answer to this question must be found in the nature of the case (i.e., is it about burglary or divorce?).

    B. *Parties to the Case*: Who is being charged, by whom, or who is suing who else? Who is the defendant, and who is the prosecutor or plaintiff?

    C. *Court Hearing Case*: Which court has produced the opinion? One should be able to determine the answer to this (e.g., is it the U.S. Supreme Court or the Supreme Court of some state) from the captioning of the case.

    D. *Time/Place*: When did the case occur, and where? Importantly, on this point, one should not confuse the year given in the captioning of the case with the year when the incident giving rise to the case occurred. The first-mentioned year refers to the year when the appellate court opinion was handed down. In many cases the appellate court opinion is handed down a few years after the original incident in the case. The date of the original incident should be found in the court's summary of the facts of the case.

E.   Where Can the Opinion Be Found? If one finds the following: State v. Tages, Court of Appeals of Arizona (1969) 10 Ariz. App. 127, 457 P.2d 289, this indicates that the opinion can be found in two different reporters of cases; the number preceding the abbreviated reporter title is the volume, the number following it is the first page of the published opinion (if a second page number is given, it is calling attention to a part of the opinion that is being discussed). Both sources are provided mainly because some law libraries or lawyers may subscribe to only one of these reporters.

F.   *How Did the Case Get to the Present Court?* The published opinion will not typically provide an answer to this question, but one should understand the difference between cases that reach state supreme courts on the basis of a mandatory right of appeal and cases that reach the U.S. Supreme Court on a writ of certiorari, which means that the Court has exercised its discretion (on the basis of the votes of at least four justices) to hear the case.

II.   *Basic Facts in the Case:* At or near the outset of the appellate court opinion, one should find a summary of the principal facts in the case. Of course, it is the trial court and its jury (or, if it is a bench trial, the judge) that determines the facts in a legal case. Appellate courts generally accept the trial courts' findings on the facts, although the appellate court may determine that some legal error occurred in the process of arriving at the facts or attempting to apply law to them. However, in any given case an almost endless string of facts could be produced. The student of law must learn to discriminate between facts that are deemed legally relevant and those that are legally irrelevant. In a case involving a contractual dispute, the defendant's height may well be legally irrelevant; on the other hand, in a criminal case involving an eyewitness description or forensic evidence indicating a perpetrator of a certain size, the defendant's height may be highly relevant.

III.   *Legal Provisions:* What rules of law are cited in the opinion as applicable to the case? For example, a particular statutory law on homicide, or on grounds for divorce, might be cited. In addition, are any constitutional provisions cited? For example, in a case involving search and seizure, the Fourth Amendment of the Constitution will arise and will be cited.

IV.   *Issue:* If a case is appealed to a higher court, it cannot be appealed solely on the basis that the appellant was unhappy with the decision in the case. The court of appeals must be presented with one or more issues upon which the case is appealed. A *substantive issue* pertains to the law invoked in the case in the first place and claims that it was misapplied. For example, someone convicted of selling pornographic books may claim that the statute criminalizing pornography does not apply to the books in question, which are claimed to be a legitimate form of artistic expression. In a case of this nature a constitutional issue may also be invoked, on the claim that the prosecution and conviction violated a First Amendment right to free speech. A *procedural issue,* on the other hand, addresses alleged error in the justice system procedure. For example, someone convicted of a crime may claim that he was not given the *Miranda* warning (on the right to remain silent) at the point of arrest, or that the incriminating evidence was improperly seized, or that the judge allowed inadmissible testimony to be given at the trial, or that the jury was improperly charged. A specific appeal may raise both substantive and procedural issues—more than one in each case—in the hope that on at least one of these issues the court of appeals will agree with the appellant and reverse the judgment.

V. *Decisions (Holding):* Judges (unlike some professors) cannot equivocate; at the end of the trial they must make a decision (or administer the jury's decision) and declare who has won and who has lost. The holding in the case should be clearly stated at the end of the opinion. The holding in the case, however, may only represent a partial victory for one side: for example, a defendant in a criminal case may be found guilty of one charge but not another; a plaintiff in a civil case may be granted only part of what the original lawsuit demanded.

VI. *Reasoning:* In the American legal system the court of appeals is generally expected to provide reasons for its holdings. A court of appeals may refuse to consider an appeal without providing a reason for doing so. In important and novel cases, however, the court of appeals is likely to provide some chain of reasoning for its decision, or holding. One or more legal principles may be enunciated as well as keys to the holding. And in the American common law tradition one or more precedents (or earlier, similar cases) may be cited in support of the holding in the present case. (The important issues surrounding the citation of precedents, and the principle of *stare decisis,* are discussed in Chapter 2.) In addition to precedents, other sources may be cited in support of a holding. In the past, in particular, it was not uncommon to cite traditional authority (e.g., the Bible; a prominent legal sage, such as Lord Coke); in the modern era appellate court judges have been more likely to cite the findings of empirical research.

VII. *Separate Opinions:* A court of appeals always issues an opinion on behalf of the court (based on the vote of the majority of the justices on the court), but appellate court justices may also opt to deliver separate opinions of their own. In a concurring opinion the justice agrees with the holding of the court but adopts a different line of reasoning or may want to express reservations on some implications of the holding. In a dissenting opinion the justice disagrees with the holding and expresses reasons for this disagreement. Although only the court's opinion has any binding legal force, both concurring and dissenting justices take the trouble to formulate their opinions at least in part because they hope their line of reasoning will be adopted in future cases on the issue at hand.

VIII. *Policy Analysis/Sociohistorical Analysis:* In the context of a law and society focus one wants to go beyond the internal legal elements of an appellate court opinion. Although one will not necessarily or even probably find the answers to questions posed by the analysis in the opinion, ideally one finds ways to answer them. First, what is the sociohistorical context of the case? For example, one can clearly understand opinions in nineteenth-century cases involving divorce or the abuse of wives if one knows something about norms and values pertaining to marital relations and rights in that time (and place). Second, what are the extralegal influences on the opinion? In other words, what considerations other than strictly legal considerations contributed to the reasoning and holding of the court? Again, one may not be able to identify these factors, but hypothetically they might include political or religious beliefs of the justices; bigotry, racism, and sexism; personality factors or personal connections to parties to the case; and so on. Third, what is the historical significance of the case? At least some cases have an immense impact on subsequent historical developments. For example, the *Dred Scott* (1857) decision of the U.S. Supreme Court, upholding the notion of slaves as property, was one of the precipitants of the Civil War. Fourth, what are the policy implications of the case? For example, the *Miranda* (1966) decision requiring the provision of a warning to remain silent to people being arrested changed police policy. Finally, what does a normative evaluation of the case produce? In other words, do you think the court's ruling was good or bad, ethically and morally justifiable, or not? Of course on this level personal, subjective evaluation enters. For example, Americans are sharply divided on whether the *Roe* v. *Wade* (1973) decision, striking down laws prohibiting abortion, was a good or bad decision.

IX. *Legal Terminology:* Law has a language, or a long list of terms, that are invoked in legal opinions. Students of law must learn this language. In the American legal system Latin terms in particular are quite common. *Mens rea,* "the thing in the mind," or criminal intent, and *bona fide,* "in good faith," are just two of the more familiar of these terms.

APPENDIX B
LAW IN OUR LIVES: FILMS

Countless films and documentaries have been produced that feature lawyers or legal proceedings or address legal issues. The listing below is quite selective. For example, it does not include documentaries on purely technical legal matters (e.g., "How to Commence a Civil Litigation," "Power Cross-Examination," "Practical Evidence," and "Client Interviewing"). Law and the legal profession have been exceptionally popular topics for feature films, so the listing here, too, is quite selective, weighted toward more recent films. Cinemania (a Microsoft CD-ROM software product) can be used to search for feature films with law-related themes. First Search is especially useful in searching for documentary films on law-related themes. This listing was compiled with some assistance from Karen Heckman of the University of Scranton Media Research Center, and Sarah Buckley, for the first edition of the book; from Lynne Modzelesky for the second edition; and from Sharon Finnerty of the University of Scranton Media Research Center and Elizabeth Barna and Anthony Policastro for this edition.

Principal distributors of documentaries listed here are:

Insight Media, 2162 Broadway, New York, NY 10024–6620; Tel: (212) 721–6316; Fax: (212) 799–5309; www.insight.media.com

Films for the Humanities & Sciences (FHS), PO Box 2053, Princeton, NJ 08543–2053; Tel: (800) 257–5126; Fax: (609) 275–3767; http://www.films.com

Chapter 1: Introduction

Documentaries:
  The Bill of Rights: A Living Document 30 min., 1997, BQK8097 [FHS]
  Taking Liberties, 60 min., 2007, ETS Pictures
  The People vs. Larry Flynt, 1996

Michigan v. Kevorkian: The Trial of Dr. Death 50 min., 1994, #3S370 [Insight]

Pleading Insane 50 min., 1994, #3S385 [Insight]

The Second Amendment: The Right to Bear Arms, 26 min., 2002

The New Seven Deadly Sins: Common Mistakes That Lead to Litigation, 2007

Eighth Amendment: The Death Penalty 52 min., 2002, #3AG829 [Insight]

In the Shadow of Watergate: Campaign Finance Reform 26 min., #CGJ8832 [Insight]

The Patriot Act Under Fire, 23 min, 2003, #JWY33191 [FHS]

Is Compromising Civil Rights Justified in the War on Terrorism?, 25 min, 2002 #3AG845 [Insight]

Liberty and Security in the Age of Terrorism, 58 min, 2003 #JWY32699 [FHS]

Chapter 2: Law: Its Meaning and Logic

Documentaries:

Our Legal System 1993, #GR518 [Insight]

Our Constitution: A Conversation, 2005

Intent: Searching for Meaning in the Constitution, 60 min., ETS Pictures, 2007

Key Constitutional Concepts, 2006

The Judicial Branch of Government 1996, #GR456 [Insight]

Legal Precedent 30 min., 2002, #3AH754 [Insight]

Strictly Speaking [On Original Intent] 60 min., BQK4912 [FHS]

Mr. Justice Douglas 52 min., 1972 [Carousel Films]

Justice Harry A. Blackmun, Man in the Middle 60 min., BQK4907 [FHS]

Mr. Justice Brennan 60 min., BQKa4909 [FHS]

Justice Sandra Day O'Connor 60 min., BQK4913 [FHS]

Justice Lewis F. Powell 60 min., BQK4916 [FHS]

Chapter 3: Law, Justice, and the Moral Order

Documentaries:

Legislating Morality: There Oughta Be a Law! 28 min., 1996, BQK6387 [FHS]

Sex for Sale: Should Prostitution Be Legal? 15 min., BQK7634 [FHS]

Me and the Mosque (2005)

Chapter 4: Jurisprudence and the Study of Law

Documentaries:

Natural Law: What It Is & Why We Need It 1997 [International Catholic Univ.]

Ronald Dworkin: The Meaning of the Constitution 60 min., BQK4910 [FHS]

Blind Justice: Women and the Law 30 min., BQK1608 [FHS]

Chapter 5: The Law and Society Movement

Chapter 6: Comparative and Historical Perspectives on Law and Society

Documentaries:
The Criminal Justice System: U.S. vs. England 48 min., 1995, #GR523 [Insight]
China's Legal System 30 min., 1991, #3S194 [Insight]
The People's Court, 2007
Incident at Oglala 90 min., 1992 [Live Home Video]
The Road to Brown 58 min., 1990 [California Newsreel]
Brown v. Board of Education Mac/Windows CD-ROM, 1996, #3S297 [Insight]
The Nuremberg War Crimes Trial 60 min., 1996, #GR532 [Insight]
The Legacy of Nuremberg, 50 min., 1995, FHS

Chapter 7: The Legal Profession

Feature Films:
The Accused (1988)
Anatomy of a Murder (1958)
The Big Easy (1987)
Cape Fear (1961) (1991)
A Civil Action (1998)
Class Action (1991)
The Client (1994)
Defenseless (1990)
Erin Brockovich (2000)
Fair Game (1995)
A Few Good Men (1991)
The Firm (1993)
Guilty As Sin (1993)
Inherit the Wind (1960)
Jagged Edge (1985)
Judicial Consent (1994)
Judgment at Nuremberg (1961)
And Justice for All (1979)
To Kill a Mockingbird (1962)
Legal Eagles (1986)
Love Crimes (1991)
Michael Clayton (2007)
Music Box (1989)
My Cousin Vinny (1990)
Other People's Money (1991)
The Pelican Brief (1993)
Philadelphia (1993)
Physical Evidence (1988)
Primal Fear (1996)
Reversal of Fortune (1990)
Suspect (1987)
The Verdict (1982)

Witness for the Prosecution (1957)
Young Mr. Lincoln (1939)
Runaway Jury (2003)
I Am Sam (2001)

Documentaries:

A Lawyer Walks into a Bar – http://www.alawyerwalksintoabar.com/trailer.htm1#
Alan Dershowitz: A Portrait in the First Person 24 min., 1991, BQK5220 [FHS]
Attorneys for the Unpopular 28 min., 1994, BQK5402 [FHS]
The Defenders 50 min., 1996, #3S341 [Insight]
Justice Is a Constant Struggle 28 min., 1987 [Univ. of Calif. Media]
Lawyers on Trial 29 min., 1996 BQK6385 [FHS]
The Good That Lawyers Do 56 min., 1999 [Washington Univ. School of Law]
Conflicts of Interest and Other Ethical Issues for Attorneys 64 min., 1992 [Bar Association of San Francisco]
Imagining a new way to practice; first women in the law, 2004 [I.B.E.B. Video Productions-OCLC: 55872160]

Chapter 8: Legal Institutions and Processes: An Overview

Documentaries:

Understanding the Criminal Justice System 3 volumes, 20 min. each, 1996, #3S299 [Insight]
The Judicial Branch (2006)
In the Eyes of the Law 25 min., 1995, #GR500 [Insight]
The Rodney King Case: What the Jury Saw in California v. Powell 120 min., 1992, #3544 [Insight]
And Justice for All? 60 min., 1992, BQK5033 [FHS]
Plea Bargains: Dealing for Justice 26 min., BQK4593 [FHS]
Judgment Day: Should the Guilty Go Free, 65 min., 2002, #JWY31681[FHS]
Crime and Punishment in America 120 min., 1997 [PBS Home Video]
Understanding the Juvenile Justice System 3 volumes, 20 min. each, 1996, #GRS19 [Insight]
Family Mediation: We Can Work It Out 29 min., #CGJ8904 [Insight]
Restorative Justice: For Victims, Communities and Offenders 25 min. [U. of Minn.]
Restorative Justice: Victim Empowerment Through Mediation and Dialogue 20 min. [U. of Minn.]
Quest for Justice: Legal Services and the Poor, 52 min, 2002 #JWY32633 [FHS]

Chapter 9: Legal Culture and Legal Behavior

Documentaries:

American Law: How It Works (2005)
Democracy in a Different Voice: Lani Guinier 54 min., 1995, #GR508 [Insight]
The American Civil Liberties Union: A History 57 min., 1997, BQK7613 [FHS]
The Executive Branch of Government 30 min., 1994, BQK8093 [FHS]
The Judicial Branch of Government 35 min., 1996, BQK8277 [FHS]
Lawmakers, Lawmaking, and the Law 60 min, BQK6185–87 [FHS]
How a Bill Becomes a Law 30 min., 1993, BQK8094 [FHS]

Chapter 10: Law in Flux: Law and Social Change

Documentaries:

Gender Justice: Women's Rights Are Human Rights 41 min., 1996 [Unitarian Universalist]

Sexual Harassment in the 21st Century, 22 min., 2000 #3AH720 [Insight]

All in a Day's Work [Sexual Harassment] 25 min., 1993 [Institute for Labor]

Affirmative Action: The History of an Idea 56 min., 1996, BQK6552 [FHS]

Legitimating Morality: Affirmative Action and the Burden of History 29 min., #CGJ6388 [Insight]

Understanding the Requirements of the Law (Individuals with Disabilities) (2005)

Hate on Trial: Challenging the First Amendment 3 Parts: 49, 70, 23 min., CGJ6853 [Insight]

Pot Shops – 60 Minutes (2007)

War on Drugs: Winners and Losers, 93 min., 2001 [HV5801.W37 2001- U of S Media Collection – FFH]

Gay Marriage and the Constitution, 22 min., 2004, #JWY33377 [FHS]

Golden Venture (Borders) (2006)

Lives for Sale (Illegal immigration) (2007)

DNA: A Question of Reliability 48 min., 1995, #GR496 [Insight]

Technology and Legal Issues: Ownership and Copyright on the Web 60 min., 1997, #3S381 [Insight]

The Constitution in Cyberspace Law 68 min., 1996 [Sweet Pea Productions]

Cyberspace: Freedom or Regulation? 29 min., 1996, BQK6392 [FHS]

In Search of International Justice, 2006

APPENDIX C
LAW IN OUR LIVES ON THE INTERNET

The Internet is expanding and evolving daily and has become a vast storehouse of information and communication. The listing below is provisional and highly selective. It includes a number of Web sites and net-related resources that are deemed especially relevant to the focus of this book. Because Web sites often have links with other, related sites, this listing merely provides certain points of departure for searches for information pertaining to law in our lives. In light of the exceptionally dynamic character of the net, no claim is made here that all the sites listed are still being maintained as you read this note. This listing was compiled with assistance from Kara Kosiorowski, Ann Marie Lutz, and Martyna Sleszynska, for the original edition. Jacqueline Maquine assumed responsibility for revising the listing for the second edition. Elizabeth Barna and Anthony Policastro made some additions for this edition. The following book provided basic information for the original compilation: James Evans, *Law on the Net* (Berkeley, CA: Nolo Press, 1996) (updated on a CD-ROM version). Some additional books or sources that were consulted include:

Biehl, Kathy. 2000. *The Lawyer's Guide to Internet Legal Research.* Lanham, MD: Scarecrow Press.
Halvorson, R. R., and Reva Basch. 2000. *Law of the Super Searchers: The Online Secrets of Top Legal Researchers.* Medford, NJ: Cyberage Books.
Long, Judy A. 2000. *Legal Research Using the Internet.* Albany, NY: West Legal Studies.

Web Sites of Selected Law-Related Organizations
    The American Association for Justice
        www.justice.org
    American Bar Association
        http://www.abanet.org/home.cfm
    American Civil Liberties Union
        http://www.aclu.org

Academy of Criminal Justice Sciences
   http://www.acjs.org
American Health Lawyers Association
   http://www.healthlawyers.org/Pages/Default.aspx
American Judicature Society
   http://www.ajs.org
Bureau of Justice Statistics
   http://www.ojp.usdoj.gov/bjs/
Center on Crime, Communities, and Culture
   http://www.soros.org/initiatives/justice
Community Policing Information
   http://www.communitypolicing.org
COPS (Community Oriented Policing Services)
   http://www.cops.usdoj.gov/
Federal Judicial Center
   http://www.fjc.gov
Graduate School Information
   http://www.clas.ufl.edu/CLAS/american-universities.html
Handgun Control, Inc.
   http://www.handguncontrol.org
Interlaw, Org.
   http://www.interlaw.org/AboutInterlaw.asp
International Court of Justice
   http://www.icj-cij.org
Juvenile Justice Clearinghouse
   http://www.criminology.fsu.edu/jjclearinghouse/main_jjrmdp_web_page.htm
Law School Directory
   http://law.gradschools.com
Law and Society Association
   http://www.lawandsociety.org
Legislative Activity of the U.S. Congress
   http://thomas.loc.gov/
Lesbian & Gay Law Association
   http://www.le-gal.org/site/
Lindesmith Center Library (Drug Issues)
   http://www.lindesmith.org/homepage.cfm
Mothers Against Drunk Driving (MADD)
   http://www.madd.org
National Association of Criminal Defense Lawyers
   http://www.criminaljustice.org
National Bar Association
   http://www.nationalbar.org/news/conferences/wileybranton2004.shtml
National Center for State Courts
   http://www.ncsconline.org
National Criminal Justice Reference Service
   http://www.ncjrs.org

346 LAW IN OUR LIVES

National District Attorneys Association
http://www.ndaa-apri.org
National Drugs and Crime Clearinghouse
http://www.ncjrs.org/drgswww.html
National Institute of Justice (NIJ)
http://www.ojp.usdoj.gov/nij/
National Lawyers' Association
http://www.nla.org
National Lawyers' Guild
http://www.nlg.org
National Rifle Association
http://www.nra.org/
Penal Reform International (PRI)
http://www.penalreform.org/english/frset_pre_en.htm
Southern Poverty Law Center
http://www.splcenter.org
U.S. Dept. of Justice
http://www.usdoj.gov
U.S. Federal Courts
http://www.uscourts.gov
U.S. Supreme Court
http://www.supremecourtus.gov
http://www.law.cornell.edu/supct/

General Information on Law and Law-Related Topics

Court TV Glossary of Legal Terms (legal dictionary)
http://www.wwlia.org/diction.htm
Find Law
http://www.findlaw.com
International Association of Independent Law Firms
http://www.interlaw.org/interlaw/index.asp
Judicial Watch
http://www.judicialwatch.org
Nolo Press: Self-Help Law and Access to Law
http://www.nolopress.com
Quicklaw American Internet Law Library
htp://www.currentlegal.com/lawlibrary/
Yahoo Law
http://dir.yahoo.com/government/law/

List Servers and Newsgroups
Numerous list servers address law-related issues. These lists include Abortion and Reproductive Rights; Americans With Disabilities Act; Animal Rights Alert; Child Abuse; Civil Rights Law; Criminal Justice; Dispute Resolution; Environmental Law; Family Law; Feminism and the Law; Free Speech Law; Future Law; History of Law; International Law; Juvenile Justice; Law Schools; Legal

Ethics; Miscarriages of Justice; Gay Law; National Organization for the Reform of Marijuana Laws; Poverty Law; Violence; Youth Rights.

Especially relevant list servers include:

Law and Politics Book Reviews: Reviews of books on law and politics, broadly defined
To Subscribe by e-mail: listser@listserver.acns.nwu.edu
Subject: anything
Message: subscribe LPBR-L our name

Law and Society: Discussion about law and society issues
To subscribe by e-mail: listserv@polecat.law.indiana.edu
Subject: anything
Message: subscribe Law And our name

Legal Studies: Discussion about law-related teaching at the undergraduate level
To subscribe by e-mail: listserv@listserv.law.cornell.edu
Subject: anything
Message: subscribe Legal Studies our name

New Law Books: Information on newly published legal texts
To subscribe by e-mail: listserve@lawlib.wuacc.edu
Subject: anything
Message: subscribe new law books

Psychology and Law: Discussion of issues involving the interaction of psychology and law
To subscribe by e-mail: listserv@utepvm.ep.utexas.edu
Subject: anything
Message: PsyLaw

Numerous newsgroups also address legal issues, including many of the same listed above for list servers. Newsgroups include Alt. Censorship, Misc. Legal, and Talk. Abortion.

Web Sites on Some Selected Law and Society Issues
Annotated Guide to Some Broadly Focused Web Sites:
Law and Justice
  http://www.ilj.org
This Web site provides information about an Institute for Law and Justice.

Law and Morality
  http://www.unquietmind.com/mislaid_v.html
This Web site provides a brief view of how law interacts with moral views. It also has a table
  of contents that can link you to other web sites on aggression, crime, social injustice, and
  related topics.

Law and Philosophy
Yale Center for Law and Philosophy
  http://www.law.yale.edu/yclp/
Stanford Encyclopedia of Philosophy: Theories of Criminal Law
  http://plato.stanford.edu/entries/criminal-law/

Legal Ethics
   http://www.nobc.org
This Web site provides basic information about legal ethics issues, and links to related sites.
   http://www.legalethics.com/
A legal Web site focusing on issues associated with the use of technology by legal
   professionals

Sociolegal Studies
   http://www.osu.edu/units/law/socio.htm
This Web site provides some information about a Center for Sociolegal Studies.

Web Sites on Legal Issues:
Abortion
Abortion Laws of the World (7 Countries)
   http://cyber.law.harvard.edu/population/abortion/abortionlaws.htm
National Abortion Right Action League (pro-choice)
   http://www.naral.org
National Right to Life Committee (pro-life)
   http://www.nrlc.org

Aging
National Senior Citizens Law Center
   http://www.nsclc.org

Animal Rights
Animal Legal Defense Fund
   http://www.aldf.org
Animal Rights Resource Site
   http://www.animalconcerns.org

Copyright
The Copyright Web site
http://www.benedict.com/

Cyber-Crime
Computer Crime & Intellectual Property Section: United States Department of Justice
   http://www.cybercrime.gov/
CyberLaws
   http://cyberlaws.us/
Computer Security Act of 1987
   http://csrc.nist.gov/groups/SMA/ispab/documents/csa_87.txt

Death Penalty
Death Penalty Information Center
   http://www.deathpenaltyinfo.org

Disabilities
American Association of People with Disabilities
   http://www.aapd.com

Cornell University Law School: International Law Overview
    http://topics.law.cornell.edu/wex/International_law

Globalization
United Nations on International Law
    http://www.un.org/en/law/index.shtml

Human Rights
The Human Rights Campaign
    http://www.hrc.org/

Marriage/Divorce
Cornell Legal Informational Institute (Marriage)
    http://www.law.cornell.edu/topics/marriage.html
Cornell Legal Informational Institute (Divorce)
    http://www.law.cornell.edu/topics/divorce.html
Divorce Home Page
    http://www.primenet.com/~dean/
Gay & Lesbian Politics
    http://www.indiana.edu/~glbtpol/
Lambda Legal Defense and Education Fund
    http://www.lambdalegal.org/cgi-bin/iowa/index.html

Peacenet
Peacenet at the Institute for Global Communications
    http://www.igc.apc.org/peacenet/

Poverty
National Law Center on Homelessness & Poverty
    http://www.nlchp.org

Privacy Rights
Privacy Rights Clearinghouse
    http://www.privacyrights.org

Women's Rights and Resources
Commission on Women in the Profession
    http://sunsite.unc.edu/cheryb/women/wresources.html</APX-List>

REFERENCES

Aaronson, Susan A., and Jamie M. Zimmerman. 2008. *Trade Imbalance: The Struggle to Weigh Human Rights Concerns in Trade Policymaking.* New York: Cambridge University Press.

Abbott, Carolyn. 2009. *Enforcing Pollution Control Regulation: Strengthening Sanctions and Improving Deterrence.* Oxford: Hart Publishing.

Abel, Richard L. 1986. "Lawyers." Pp. 369–444, in Leon Lipson and Stanton Wheeler, eds. *Law and the Social Sciences.* New York: Russell Sage Foundation.

_____. 1988. "United States: The Contradictions of Professionalism." Pp. 186–243, in

Richard L. Abel and Philip S. C. Lewis, eds. *Lawyers in Society.* Berkeley: University of California Press.

_____. 1995a. *The Law and Society Reader.* New York: New York University Press.

_____. 1995b. *Politics by Other Means: Law in the Struggle Against Apartheid, 1980–1994.* New York: Routledge.

_____. 2003. "Lawyers and Legal Services." Pp. 796–816, in Peter Cane and Mark Tushnet, eds. *The Oxford Handbook of Legal Studies.* New York: Oxford University Press.

_____. 2008. *Lawyers in the Dock: Learning from Attorney Disciplinary Proceedings.* New York: Oxford University Press.

_____. 2010. "Law and Society: Project and Practice." Pp. 1–23, in John Hagan, Kim Lane Scheppele, and Tom R. Tyler, eds. *Annual Review of Law and Social Science.* Palo Alto, CA: Annual Reviews.

Abel, Richard, and Philip S. C. Lewis, eds. 1989. *American Lawyers.* New York: Oxford University Press.

_____. 1995. *Lawyers in Society: An Overview.* Berkeley: University of California Press.

Abraham, Kenneth S. 2008. *The Liability Century: Insurance and Tort Law from the Progressive Era to 9/11.* Cambridge: Harvard University Press.

Abramson, Jill. 1988. "For Women Lawyers, an Uphill Struggle." *New York Times Magazine* (March 6): 36–37, 73–75.

_____. 1998. "The Business of Persuasion Thrives in Nation's Capital." *New York Times* (September 29): A1.

Ackerman, Bruce. 2002. "The Legality of the Use of Force." *New York Times* (September 21): A15.

Adams, David M. 2000. *Philosophical Problems in Law,* 3rd ed. Belmont, CA: Wadsworth/Thomson Learning.

Adler, M. 2007. "Administrative Law and Agencies, Politics of." Pp. 25–30, in David S. Clark, ed. *Encyclopedia of Law and Society.* Los Angeles: Sage.

Adler, Matthew D., and Eric A. Posner, eds. 2001. *Cost-Benefit Analysis: Legal, Economic, and Philosophical Perspectives.* Chicago: University of Chicago Press.

Adler, Mortimer J., and Charles Van Doren. 1977. *Great Treasury of Western Thought.* New York: R. R. Bowker.

Adler, Stephen J., and Wade Lambert. 1993. "Just About Everyone Violates Some Laws, Even Model Citizens." *Wall Street Journal* (March 17): 1.

Agger, Ben, and Timothy W. Luke. 2008. *There is a Gunman on Campus: Tragedy and Terror at Virginia Tech.* Lanham, MD: Rowman & Littlefield.

Ahdar, Rex J., ed. 2000. *Law and Religion.* Burlington, VT: Ashgate Publishing.

Ahmad, Diana L. 2007. *The Opium Debate and Chinese Exclusion Laws in the Nineteenth-Century American West.* Reno: University of Nevada Press.

Alder, Christine. 1984. "Gender Bias in Juvenile Diversion." *Crime & Delinquency* 30: 400–414.

Aleinikoff, T. Alexander. 2002. *Semblances of Sovereignty: The Constitution, the State, and American Citizenship.* Cambridge, MA: Harvard University Press.

Alexander, Larry, and Emily Sherwin. 2001. *The Rule of Rules: Morality, Rules, and the Dilemma of Law.* Durham, NC: Duke University Press.

Alexander, Michelle. 2010. *The New Jim Crow.* New York: The New Press.

Alexandre, Michele. 2009. "'Girls Gone Wild' and Rape Law: Revising the Contractual Concept of Consent & Ensuring an Unbiased Application of 'Reasonable Doubt' When the Victim Is Non-Traditional." *American University Journal of Gender, Social Policy & The Law* 17: 41–79.

Alford, Jeremy, and Joseph B. Treaster. 2005. "Was It Wind or Water? Gulf Coast Lawyer Is Taking on Insurers." *New York Times* (September 21): C1.

Ali, Mohammad Hasan. 2009. "*Capitol Records v. Thomas* and the Future of Peer-to-Peer File-Sharing Litigation." *Boston University Journal of Science and Technology Law* 15: 161–180.

Ali, Shahreen, Savriti Goonesekere, Emilio Garcia Mendez, and Rebecca Rois-Kohn. 2007. *Protecting the World's Children: Impact of the U.N. Convention on the Rights of the Child in Diverse Legal Systems.* New York: Cambridge University Press.

Alibrandt, Tom, and Frank H. Armani. 1991. *Privileged Information.* New York: HarperCollins.

Allegretti, Joseph G. 1996. *The Lawyer's Calling: Christian Faith and Legal Practice.* New York: Paulist Press.

Allen, Austin. 2006. *Origins of the Dred Scott Case: Jacksonian Jurisprudence and the Supreme Court, 1837–1857.* Athens, GA: University of Georgia Press.

Allen, Mike. 1999. "Beyond the Bar Exam." *New York Times* (July 11): 4/3.

Allison, William Thomas. 2006. *Military Justice in Vietnam: The Rule of Law in an American War.* Lawrence, KS: University Press of Kansas.

Almond, Paul. 2009. "The Dangers of Hanging Baskets: 'Regulatory Myths' and Media Representations of Health and Safety Regulations." *Journal of Law and Society* 36: 352–375.

Alschuler, Albert W. 2000. *Law Without Values: The Life, Work, and Legacy of Justice Holmes.* Chicago: University of Chicago Press.

Althouse, Ann. 2005. "Innocence Abroad." *New York Times* (September 19): A25.

Amanat, Abbas, and Frank Griffei. 2008. *Shari'a: Islamic Law in the Contemporary Context.* Stanford, CA: Stanford University Press.

Amestoy, Jeffrey L. 2003. "Uncommon Humanity: Reflections on Judging in a Post-Human Era." *New York University Law Review* 78: 1581–1596.

Amster, Randall, Abraham DeLeon, Luis A. Fernandez, Anthony J. Nocella, II, and Deric Shannon. 2009. *Contemporary Anarchist Studies: An Introductory Anthology of Anarchy in the Academy.* New York: Routledge.

Amsterdam, Anthony G., and Jerome Bruner. 2000. *Minding the Law.* Cambridge, MA: Harvard University Press.

Anastaplo, George. 2009. *Reflections on Life, Death, and the Constitution.* Lexington: The University of Kentucky Press.

Andersen, Ellen Ann. 2005. *Out of the Closets and into the Courts: Legal Opportunity Structure and Gay Rights Litigation.* Ann Arbor: University of Michigan Press.

Anderson, Jane E. 2009. *Law, Knowledge, Culture: The Production of Indigenous Knowledge in Intellectual Property Law.* Northhampton, MA: Edward Elgar Publishing.

Anderson, Jerry L. 2004. "Law School Enters the Matrix: Teaching Critical Legal Studies." *Journal of Legal Education* 54: 201–205.

Anderson, Terry L., and Peter J. Hill. 2004. *The Not So Wild, Wild West: Property Rights on the Frontier.* Stanford, CA: Stanford University Press.

Anderson, Terry L., Bruce Benson, and Thomas Flanagan, eds. 2006. *Self-Determination: The Other Path for Native Americans.* Stanford, CA: Stanford University Press.

Andreas, Peter, and Ethan Nadelmann. 2006. *Policing the Globe: Criminalization and Crime Control in International Relations.* New York: Oxford University Press.

Andrews, Edmund L., and Susan Sachs. 2003. "Iraq's Slide Into Lawlessness Squanders Good Will for U.S." *New York Times (May* 18): A1.

Anleu, Sharon L. Roach. 1992. "Critiquing the Law: Themes and Dilemmas in Anglo-American Feminist Legal Theory." *Journal of Law and Society* 19: 423–440.

Appelbaum, Richard P. 1998. "The Future of Law in a Global Economy." *Social & Legal Studies* 7: 172–192.

Applebome, Peter, and Jonathan D. Glater. 2005. "Storm Leaves Legal System A Shambles." *New York Times* (September 9): A1.

Aquinas, Thomas. [1266–1272] 1993. *The Treatise on Law* (R. J. Henleu, ed.). Notre Dame, IN: University of Notre Dame Press.

Arend, Anthony C. 2003. "A Methodology for Determining an International Legal Rule." Pp. 23–50, in Charlotte Ku and Paul F. Diehl, eds. *International Law: Classic and Contemporary Readings.* Boulder, CO: Lynne Rienner Publishers.

Aries, Phillipe. 1962. *Centuries of Childhood.* New York: Vintage.

Aristodemou, Maria. 2000. *Law and Literature: Journeys From Here to Eternity.* New York: Oxford University Press.

Armstrong, Troy L., Michael H. Guilfoyle, and Ada Pecos Melton. 1996. "Traditional Approaches to Tribal Justice: History and Current Practice." Pp. 46–53, in Marianne A. Nielsen and Robert Silverman, eds. *Native Americans, Crime, and Justice.* Boulder, CO: Westview Press.

Arnold, Bruce L., and Fiona M. Kay. 1995. "Social Capital, Violations of Trust, and the Vulnerability of Isolates: The Social Organization of Law Practice and Professional Self-Regulation." *International Journal of the Sociology of Law* 23: 321–346.

Arrigo, Bruce A., Dragan Milovanovic, and Robert Carl Schehr. 2005. *The French Connection in Criminology: Rediscovering Crime, Law, and Social Change.* Albany: State University of New York Press.

Ashford, Jose B. 1994. "Child Maltreatment Interventions: Developments in Law, Prevention, and Treatment." *Criminal Justice Review* 19: 271–285.

Associated Press. 2005. "Skipping Law School. Lincoln Did It. Why Not the Valoises?" *New York Times* (September 21): A23.

Atapattu, Sumudu A. 2006. *Emerging Principles of International Environmental Law.* Ardsley, NY: Transnational Publishers, Inc.

Auerbach, Jerold. 1976. *Unequal Justice: Lawyers and Social Change in Modern America.* London: Oxford University Press.

_____. 1983. *Justice Without Law? Resolving Disputes Without Lawyers.* New York: Oxford University Press.

Austin, John. [1832] 1954. *The Province of Jurisprudence Determined* (H. L. A. Hart, ed.). London: Weidenfeld & Nicolson.

Aviv, Rachel. 2007. "File-Sharing Students Fight Copyright Constraints." *New York Times* (October 10): B7.

Ayoub, Nina. 2009. "A Community's Right to Know." *Chronicle of Higher Education Review* (October 30): B17.

Bach, Amy. 1995. "Nolo Contendere." *New York* (December 11): 49–55.

Backus, Mary Sue. 2008. "The Adversary System Is Dead; Long Live the Adversary System: The Trial Judge as the Great Equalizer in Criminal Trials." *Michigan State Law Review* 2008: 945–993.

Bader, Christine. 2008. "Business & Human Rights: Corporate Recognition and Responsibility." *China Rights Forum* 1: 7–12.

Baer, Judith A. 1999. *Our Lives Before the Law: Constructing a Feminist Jurisprudence.* Princeton, NJ: Princeton University Press.

Baggins, David. 1998. *Drug Hate and the Corruption of American Justice.* Westport, CT: Greenwood Publishing.

Bailey, Frankie Y., and Donna C. Hale. 1998. *Popular Culture, Crime, and Justice.* Belmont, CA: West/ Wadsworth.

Baker, Carrie N. 2008. *The Women's Movement Against Sexual Harassment.* New York: Cambridge University Press.

Baker, Nancy V. 2006. *General Ashcroft: Attorney at War.* Lawrence: University Press of Kansas.

Baker, Tom. 2001. "Blood Money, New Money, and the Moral Economy of Tort Law in Action." *Law & Society Review* 35: 275–319.

_____. 2005. *The Medical Malpractice Myth.* Chicago and London: University of Chicago Press.

Bakken, Gordon M. 2000. *Law in the Western United States.* Norman: University of Oklahoma Press.

Bales, Kevin, and Ron Soodalter. 2009. *The Slave Next Door: Human Trafficking and Slavery in America Today.* Los Angeles: University of California Press.

Ball, Howard. 2002. *The Supreme Court in the Intimate Lives of Americans: Birth, Sex, Marriage, Childbearing, and Death.* New York: New York University Press.

_____. 2007. *Bush, the Detainees, and the Constitution: The Battle Over Presidential Power in the War on Terror.* Lawrence: University Press of Kansas.

Ball, Milner S. 2000. *Called by Stories: Biblical Sagas and Their Challenge for Law.* Durham, NC: Duke University Press.

Banakar, Reza. 2007. "Sociological Jurisprudence." Pp. 1409–1410, in David S. Clark, ed. *Encyclopedia of Law & Society.* Los Angeles: Sage.

Banakar, Reza, and Max Travers, eds. 2002. An *Introduction to Law and Social Theory.* Portland, OR: Hart.

Bandes, Susan. 1999. *The Passions of Law.* New York: New York University Press.

Banner, Stuart. 2002. *The Death Penalty—An American History.* Cambridge, MA: Harvard University Press.

———. 2005. *How the Indians Lost Their Land, Law and Power on the Frontier.* Cambridge, MA: Belknap and Harvard University Press.

———. 2007. *Possessing the Pacific: Land, Settlers, and the Indigenous People from Australia to Alaska.* Cambridge, MA: Harvard University Press.

———. 2008. *Who Owns the Sky? The Struggle to Control Airspace from the Wright Brothers On.* Cambridge, MA: Harvard University Press.

Barak, Aharon. 2005. *Purposive Interpretation in Law.* Princeton, NJ: Princeton University Press.

Barak-Erez, Daphen, and Aeyal M. Gross, eds. 2007. *Exploring Social Rights: Between Theory and Practice.* Portland, OR: Hart Publishing.

Barclay, Scott, Mary Bernstein, and Anna-Maria Marshall, eds. 2009. *Queer Mobilizations: LGBT Activists Confront the Law.* New York: New York University Press.

Barkan, Elazar, and Alexander Karn, eds. 2006. *Taking Wrongs Seriously: Apologies and Reconciliation.* Stanford: Stanford University Press.

Barkan, Steven E. 1983. "Jury Nullification in Political Trials." *Social Problems* 31: 28–44.

———. 2009. *Law and Society: An Introduction.* Upper Saddle River, NJ: Pearson.

———. 2011. "U.S. Corrections Policy Since the 1970s." Pp. 135–158, in Karim Ismaili, ed. *Criminal Justice Policy: A Contemporary Reader.* Sudbury, MA: Jones & Bartlett Learning.

Barker, Christine R., Elizabeth A. Kirk, and Monica Sah, eds. 1998. *Gender Perceptions and the Law.* Brookfield, VT: Ashgate Publishing.

Barker, Vanessa. 2010. "Explaining the Great American Crime Decline: A Review of Blumstein and Wallman, Goldberger and Rosenfeld, and Zimring." *Law & Social Inquiry* 35: 489–516.

Barlyn, Suzanne. 2008. "Call My Lawyer … in India." *Time* (April 14): *Global* 1–2.

Barnett, Larry D. 2010. *Legal Construct, Social Concept: A Macrosociological Perspective on Law.* New Brunswick, NJ: Transaction.

Barrett, Kimberly, and William H. George, eds. 2004. *Race, Culture, Psychology, and Law.* Thousand Oaks, CA: Sage.

Barthel, Joan. 1977. *A Death in Canaan.* New York: Dell.

Bartlett, Katharine T. 1991. *Gender and Law: Theory, Doctrine, Commentary.* New York: New York University Press.

Bartol, Curt, and Anne M. Bartol. 2004. *Introduction to Forensic Psychology.* Thousand Oaks, CA: Sage.

Barzilai, Gad. 2003. *Communities and Law: Politics and Cultures of Legal Identities.* Ann Arbor: University of Michigan Press.

———, ed. 2007. *Law and Religion.* Burlington, VT: Ashgate Publishing Co.

Bass, Gary J. 2000. *Stay the Hand of Vengeance.* Princeton, NJ: Princeton University Press.

Basson, Lauren L. 2008. *White Enough to Be an American? Race Mixing, Indigenous People, and the Boundaries of State and Nation.* Chapel Hill: The University of North Carolina Press.

Baum, Marsha L. 2007. *When Nature Strikes: Weather Disasters and the Law.* Westport, CT: Praeger.

Bauman, Richard W. 2002. *Ideology and Community in the First Wave of Critical Studies.* Toronto: University of Toronto Press.

Baumgartner, Frank R., Suzanna L. De Boef, and Amber E. Boydstun. 2008. *The Decline of the Death Penalty and the Discovery of Innocence.* New York: Cambridge University Press.

Baumgartner, M. P. 1988. *The Moral Order of a Suburb.* New York: Oxford University Press.

———, ed. 1999. *The Social Organization of Law.* 2nd ed. San Diego, CA: Academic Press.

———. 2001. "The Sociology of Law in the United States." *American Sociologist* 32: 99–113.

Baxter, Hugh. 2002. "System and Lifeworld in Habermas's Theory of Law." *Cardozo Law Review* 23: 473–615.

Baylis, Elena. 2009. "Reassessing the Role of International Criminal Law: Rebuilding National Courts through Transnational Networks." *Boston College Law Review* 50: 1–85.

Bazar, Emily. 2006. "Native American? The Tribe Says No." *USA Today* (November 29): 1A.

Bazelon, Emily. 2005. "What Would Zimbabwe Do?" *Atlantic Monthly* (November): 48–52.

Beales, Ross W. 1985. "In Search of the Historical Child: Miniature Adulthood and Youth in Colonial New England." Pp. 7–26, in N. Ray Hiner and Joseph M. Hawes, eds. *Growing Up in America: Children in Historical Perspective.* Urbana: University of Illinois Press.

Beam, Alex. 2004. "Greed on Trial." *Atlantic Monthly* (June): 96–108.

Beaman-Hall, Lori. 1996. "Legal Ethnography: Exploring the Gendered Nature of Legal Method." *Critical Criminology 7:* 53–74.

Bearak, Barry. 2001. "Death to Blasphemers: Islam's Grip on Pakistan." *New York Times* (May 12): A3.

Beccaria, C. [1764] 1988. *On Crimes and Punishments.* New York: MacMillan.

Becker, Christine M., and Damon J. Phillips. 2005. "Interorganizational Determinants of Promotion: Client Leadership and the Attainment of Women Attorneys." *American Sociological Review* 70: 678–701.

Becker, Howard S. 1963. *Outsiders.* New York: Free Press.

Beckett, Katherine. 1997. *Making Crime Pay: Law and Order in Contemporary American Politics.* New York: Oxford University Press.

Behre, Kirby D., and A. Jeff Ifrah. 2003. "Perspectives on the Federal Sentencing Guidelines and Mandatory Sentencing." *American Criminal Law Review* 40: 5–18.

Beirne, Piers, and Alan Hunt. 1988. "Law and the Constitution of Soviet Society: The Case of Comrade Lenin." *Law & Society Review* 22: 575–614.

Beirne, Piers, and Richard Quinney, eds. 1982. *Marxism and Law.* New York: John Wiley.

Beirne, Piers, and Robert Sharlet. 1980. *Pashukanis: Selected Writings on Marxism and Law.* London: Academic Press.

Belknap, Joanne, and Edna Erez. 1997. "Redefining Sexual Harassment: Confronting Sexism in the 21st Century." *The Justice Professional* 10: 143–159.

Bell, Catherine, and Val Napoleon, eds. 2008. *First Nations Cultural Heritage and Law: Case Studies, Voices, and Perspectives.* Vancouver: UBC Press.

Bell, Derrick A., Jr. 1980. *Race, Racism, and American Law.* 2nd ed. Boston: Little, Brown.

_____. 1987. *And We Are Not Saved: The Elusive Quest for Racial Justice.* New York: Basic Books.

_____. 1992. *Faces at the Bottom of the Well.* New York: Basic Books.

_____. 2004. *Silent Covenants:* Brown v. Board of Education *and the Unfulfilled Hopes for Racial Reform.* New York: Oxford University Press.

Bell, Jeannine. 2002. *Policing Hatred: Law Enforcement, Civil Rights, and Hate Crime.* New York: New York University Press.

Belluck, Pam. 2003. "States Moving to End Tribes' Tax-Free Sales." *New York Times* (September 28): A24.

_____. 2004a. "Massachusetts Gives New Push to Gay Marriage." *New York Times* (February 5): A1.

_____. 2004b. "Hundreds of Same-Sex Couples Wed in Massachusetts." *New York Times* (May 18): A1

Belsky, Martin H., ed. 2002. *The Rehnquist Court: A Retrospective.* New York: Oxford University Press.

Benavie, Arthur. 2009. *Drugs: America's Holy War.* New York: Routledge.

Bender, Leslie. 1990. "Feminist (Re)torts: Thoughts on the Liability Crisis, Mass Torts, Power, and Responsibility." *Duke Law Journal* (September): 848–912.

Bender, Steven W. 2005. *Greasers and Gringos: Latinos, Law, and the American Imagination.* New York: New York University Press.

Benesh, Sara C., and Malia Reddick. 2002. "Overruled: An Event History Analysis of Lower Court Reaction to Supreme Court Alteration of Precedent." *Journal of Politics* 64: 534–550.

Bennett, Jessica, and Mary Chapman. 2008 "An Equal-Opportunity Crackdown." *Newsweek* (July 28): 9.

Bennett, Trevor, and Katy Holloway. 2007. *Drug Crime Connections.* New York: Cambridge University Press.

Bennett, Walter. 2001. *The Lawyer's Myth: Reviving Ideals in the Legal Profession.* Chicago: University of Chicago Press.

Bentham, Jeremy. [1776] 1960. A *Fragment on Government* (W. Harrison, ed.). Oxford, UK: Basil Blackwell.

_____. [1789] 1970. *An Introduction to the Principles of Morals and Legislation* (J. H. Burns and H. L. A. Hart, eds.). London: Athlone Press.

Benton, Lauren. 2002. *Law and Colonial Cultures: Legal Regimes in World History, 1400–1900.* New York: Cambridge University Press.

Ben-Yehuda, Nachman. 1997. "Political Assassination Events as a Cross-Cultural Form of Alternative Justice." *International Journal of Comparative Sociology* 38: 25–47.

Berat, Lynn, and Yossi Shain. 1995. "Retribution or Truth-Telling in South Africa? Legacies of the Transitional Phase." *Law & Social Inquiry* 20: 163–189.

Berger, Ronald J., W. Lawrence Neuman, and Patricia Searles. 1994. "The Impact of Rape Law Reform: An Aggregate Analysis of Police Reports and Arrests." *Criminal Justice Review* 19: 1–22.

Berger, Ronald J., Patricia Searles, and W. Lawrence Neuman. 1988. "The Dimensions of Rape Reform Legislation." *Law & Society Review* 22: 329–357.

Berkin, Carol. 2002. *A Brilliant Solution: Inventing the American Constitution.* New York: Harcourt.

Berlin, Ira. 1998. *Many Thousands Gone: The First Two Centuries of Slavery in North America.* Cambridge, MA: Belknap Press.

Berman, Harold J. 1963. *Justice in the U.S.S.R.: An Interpretation of Soviet Law.* New York: Vintage.

———. 1966. *Soviet Criminal Law and Procedure: The RSFSR Codes.* Cambridge, MA: Harvard University Press.

———. 1974. *The Interaction of Law and Religion.* Nashville, TN: Abingdon Press.

———. 1983. *Law and Revolution: The Formation of the Western Legal Tradition.* Cambridge, MA: Harvard University Press.

———. 1993. *Faith and Order: The Reconciliation of Law and Religion.* Atlanta, GA: Scholars Press.

———. 2004. *Law and Revolution, II—The Impact of the Protestant Reformations on the Western Legal Tradition.* Cambridge, MA: Harvard University Press.

Berman, Jesse. 1969. "The Cuban Popular Tribunals." *Columbia Law Review* 69: 1317–1354.

Bernard, B. J., and Frederick W. Preston. 2004. "On the Shoulders of Merton—Potentially Sobering Consequences of Problem Gambling Policy." *American Behavioral Scientist* 47: 1395–1405.

Bernard, Thomas J. 1992. *The Cycle of Juvenile Justice.* New York: Oxford University Press.

Bernat, Frances P. 2007. "Gender." Pp. 630–634, in David S. Clark, ed. *Encyclopedia of Law & Society.* Los Angeles: Sage.

Bernstein, Anita. 1996. "A Feminist Revisit to the First-Year Curriculum." *Journal of Legal Education* 46: 217–232.

———. 2003. "Foreword: What Clients Want, What Lawyers Need." *Emory Law Journal* 52: 1053–1064.

Bernstein, Elizabeth. 2007. *Temporarily Yours: Intimacy, Authenticity, and the Commerce of Sex.* Chicago: University of Chicago Press.

Berrigan, Daniel. 1970. *The Trial of the Catonsville Nine.* Boston: Beacon Press.

Besharov, Douglas J. 2006. "End Welfare Lite As We Know It." *New York Times* (August 15): A19.

Bessen James, and Michael J. Meurer. 2008. *Patent Failure: How Judges, Bureaucrats, and Lawyers Put Innovators at Risk.* Princeton, NJ: Princeton University Press.

Bhatia, Vijay, Christopher N. Candlin, and Paola Evangelisti Allori, eds. 2008. *Language, Culture and the Law: The Formulation of Legal Concepts across Systems and Cultures.* New York: Peter Lang Publishers.

Bindreiter, Uta. 2002. *Why Grundnorm? A Treatise on the Implications of Kelsen's Doctrine.* The Hague: Kluwer.

Birke, Richard. 2007. "Mediation." Pp. 1007–1010, in David S. Clark, ed. *Encyclopedia of Law and Society.* Los Angeles: Sage.

Birla, Ritu. 2009. *Stages of Capital: Law, Culture, and Market Governance in Late Colonial India.* Durham, NC: Duke University Press.

Bishop, Joseph, Jr. 1974. *Justice Under Fire: A Study of Military Law.* New York: Charterhouse.

Bix, Brian. 1996. "Natural Law Theory" Pp. 223–240, in Dennis Patterson, ed. *A Companion to Philosophy of Law and Legal Theory.* Cambridge, MA: Blackwell Publishers.

———. 2009. *Jurisprudence: Theory and Context.* Durham, NC: Carolina Academic Press.

Black, Amy E., and Stanley Rothman. 1998. "Shall We Kill All the Lawyers First? Insider and Outsider Views of the Legal Profession." *Harvard Journal of Law and Public Policy* 21: 835–860.

Black, Donald. 1976. *The Behavior of Law.* New York: Academic Press.

———. 1983. "Crime as Social Control." *American Sociological Review* 48: 34–45.

———. 1989. *Sociological Justice.* New York: Oxford University Press.

———. 1993. *The Social Structure of Right and Wrong.* San Diego, CA: Academic Press.

———. 1995. "The Epistemology of Pure Sociology." *Law and Social Inquiry* 20: 829–870.

———. 2000. "Dreams of Pure Sociology." *Sociological Theory* 18: 343–367.

———. 2007. "Relativity, Legal." Pp. 1292–1294, in David S. Clark, ed. *Encyclopedia of Law & Society.* Los Angeles: Sage.

Black, Jonathan, ed. 1971. *Radical Lawyers.* New York: Avon.

Blackmon, Douglas A. 2009. *Slavery by Another Name: The Re-Enslavement of Black Americans from the Civil War to World War II.* New York: Anchor Books.

Blackstone, William. [1765–1769] 1979. *Commentaries on the Laws of England*. Chicago: University of Chicago Press.

Blank, Robert H., and Janna C. Merrick, eds. 2005. *End-of-Life Decision-Making: A Cross-National Study*. Cambridge, MA: MIT Press.

Blass, Thomas, ed. 2000. *Obedience to Authority: Current Perspectives on the Milgram Paradigm*. Mahwah, NJ: Lawrence Erlbaum.

Bloom, Anne. 2001. "The 'Post-Attitudinal Moment': Judicial Policy-Making Through the Lens of the New Institutionalism." *Law & Society Review* 35: 219–230.

Bloom, Paul. 2010. "The Moral Life of Babies." *New York Times Magazine* (May 9): 45–49, 56.

Blum, John Morton. 1991. *Years of Discord: American Politics and Society, 1961–1974*. New York: W. W. Norton.

Blumberg, Abraham. 1967. "The Practice of Law as a Confidence Game: Organizational Cooptation of a Profession." *Law & Society Review* 1: 15–39.

Blumenthal, Ralph. 2008. "Court Says Texas Illegally Seized Sect's Children." *New York Times* (May 23): A1.

Bockstiegel, Karll-Heinz. 2009. "Past, Present, and Future Perspectives on Arbitration." *Arbitration* 75: 181–187.

Bogart, W. A. 2002. *Consequences: The Impact of Law and Its Complexity*. Toronto: University of Toronto Press.

Bogle, Rick. 2003. "Animal Experimentation and Human Rights." *Human Rights Review* 4: 53–61.

Bogoch, Bryna. 1997. "Gendered Lawyering: Difference and Dominance in Lawyer-Client Interaction." *Law & Society Review* 31: 677–712.

Bogus, Carl T. 2001. *Why Lawsuits Are Good for America: Disciplined Democracy, Big Business, and the Common Law*. New York: New York University Press.

Bohannon, Paul. 1967a. "The Differing Realms of Law." Pp. 45–58, in Paul Bohannon, ed. *Law and Warfare*. Garden City, NY: Natural History Press.

———, ed. 1967b. *Law and Warfare*. Garden City, NY: Natural History Press.

Bohmer, Carol, and Amy Shuman. 2008. *Rejecting Refugees: Political Asylum in the 21st Century*. London and New York: Routledge.

Bok, Derek. 1983. "A Flawed System of Law Practice and Training." *Journal of Legal Education* 33: 570–585.

Bollag, Button. 2001. "A Law School on the Move Takes a Global Approach." *Chronicle of Higher Education* (January 12): A43–A44.

Bollinger, Lee C., and Geoffrey R. Stone, eds. 2002. *Eternally Vigilant: Free Speech in the Modern Era*. Chicago: University of Chicago Press.

Bonsignore, John, Ethan Katsh, Peter d'Errico, Ronald M. Pipkin, Stephen Arons, and Janet Rifkin, eds. 2002. *Before the Law,*. 7th ed. Boston: Houghton Mifflin.

Boon, Andrew, and Julian Webb. 2008. "Transnational Legal Education." *Journal of Legal Education* 58: 79–121.

Boraine, Alex. 2001. *A Country Unmasked*. New York: Oxford University Press.

Bordewich, Fergus M. 1996. "Revolution in Indian Country." *American Heritage* (July/August): 34–46.

Borg, Marian J., and Karen F. Parker. 2001. "Mobilizing Law in Urban Areas: The Social Structure of Homicide Clearance Rates." *Law & Society Review* 35: 435–466.

Bork, Robert. 1990. *The Tempting of America*. New York: Free Press.

Bosniak, Linda. 2006. *The Citizen and the Alien: Dilemmas of Contemporary Membership*. Princeton, NJ: Princeton University Press.

Bottoms, Bette L., Margaret B. Kovera, and Bradley D. McAuliff. 2002. *Children, Social Science, and the Law*. New York: Cambridge University Press.

Bottoms, Bette L., Cynthia J. Najdowski, and Gail S. Goodman, eds. 2009. *Children as Victims, Witnesses, and Offenders: Psychological Science and the Law*. New York: Guilford Publications.

Boucock, Cary. 2000. *In the Grip of Freedom: Law and Modernity in Max Weber*. Toronto: University of Toronto Press.

Bowen, William G., and Derek Bok. 1998. *The Shape of the River: Long-Term Consequences of Considering Race in College and University Admissions*. Princeton, NJ: Princeton University Press.

Bowler, Shaun, and Bruce Cain. 2004. "Introduction—Recalling the Recall: Reflections on California's Recent Political Adventure." *PS: Political Science and Politics* 37: 7–10.

Boyle, Elizabeth Heger. 2005. "Introduction: Forum on the Work of Laura Nader." *Law & Society Review* 39: 943–944.

Boyle, James. 2008. *The Public Domain: Enclosing the Commons of the Mind*. New Haven, CT: Yale University Press.

Bracey, Dorothy H. 2006. *Exploring Law and Culture*. Longrove, IL: Waveland Press.

Braithwaite, John. 2002a. *Restorative Justice and Responsive Regulation.* New York: Oxford University Press.

———. 2002b. "Rules and Principles: A Theory of Legal Certainty." *Australian Journal of Legal Philosophy* 27: 47–82.

Branch, Taylor. 1988. *Parting the Waters: America in the King Years, 1954–1963.* New York: Simon & Schuster.

———. 1998. *Pillar of Fire: America in the King Years, 1963–1968.* New York: Simon & Schuster.

Brandwein, Pamela. 2000. "Slavery as an Interpretive Issue in the Reconstruction Congresses." *Law & Society Review* 34: 315–366.

Branson, Douglas M. 2007. *No Seat at the Table: How Corporate Governance Keeps Women Out of America's Boardrooms.* New York: New York University Press.

Brender, Alan. 2002. "Japan Tries to Reform How It Trains Lawyers." *Chronicle of Higher Education* (February 15): A47–A48.

Brenner, Saul, and Joseph M. Whitneyer. 2009. *Strategy on the United States Supreme Court.* New York: Cambridge University Press.

Brigham, John. 2009. "Seeing Jurisprudential Issues from Law Being '…All Over." *Law & Policy* 31: 381–404.

Brinig, Margaret F. 2000. *From Contract to Covenant: Beyond the Law and Economics of the Family.* Cambridge, MA: Harvard University Press.

Broder, John M. 2003a. "Firefighters File Suit Over Chaplains in Rank." *New York Times* (May 28): A10.

———. 2003b. "Victims Angered and Upset by Ruling Freeing Molesters." *New York Times* (July 13): A12.

———. 2004. "Schwarzenegger Files Suit Against Bobblehead Maker." *New York Times* (May 18): A16.

Broderick, John T., Jr., and Ronald M. George. 2010. "A Nation of Do-It-Yourself Lawyers." *New York Times* (January 2): A21.

Brody, Reed. 2001. *Justice: The First Casualty of Truth.* Princeton, NJ: Princeton University Press.

Brook, Heather. 2007. *Conjugal Rites: Marriage and Marriage-like Relationships Before the Law.* New York: Palgrave MacMillan.

Brooks, Karl Boyd. 2009. *Before Earth Day: The Origins of American Environmental Law, 1945–1970.* Lawrence: University Press of Kansas.

Brown, Ben. 2011. "Combative and Cooperative Law Enforcement in Post-September 11th America." Pp. 49–76, in Karim Ismaili, ed. *U.S. Criminal Justice Policy: A Contemporary Reader.* Sudbury, MA: Jones & Bartlett Learning.

Brown, Dee. 1971. *Bury My Heart at Wounded Knee.* New York: Holt, Rinehart & Winston.

Brown, Esther L. 1938. *Lawyers and the Promotion of Justice.* New York: Russell Sage.

Brown, Michael F. 2003. *Who Owns Native Culture?* Cambridge, MA: Harvard University Press.

Brown, Richard M. 1979. "Historical Patterns of American Violence." Pp. 19–48, in H. D. Graham and Ted Robert Gum, eds. *Violence in America.* Beverly Hills, CA: Sage.

Brownmiller, Susan. 1975. *Against Our Will: Men, Women, and Rape.* New York: Simon & Schuster.

Brownsword, Roger. 2008. *Rights, Regulation, and the Technological Revolution.* New York: Oxford University Press.

Bruff, Harold H. 2009. *Bad Advice: Bush's Lawyers in the War on Terror.* Lawrence: University Press of Kansas.

Bruinsma, Fred, and David Nelken, eds. 2007. *Explorations in Legal Cultures.* The Hague: Elsevier.

Brundage, James A. 2008. *The Medieval Origins of the Legal Profession: Canonists, Civilians and Courts.* Chicago: University of Chicago Press.

Bruni, Frank. 2010. "At the Vatican, Up Against the World." *New York Times* (March 28): Week 1.

Brunkhorst, Hauke. 2005. *Solidarity: From Civic Friendship to a Global Legal Community.* Cambridge, MA: Massachusetts Institute of Technology Press.

Brutsch, Christian, and Dirk Lehmkuhl, eds. 2007. *Law and Legalization in Transnational Relations.* New York: Routledge.

Buchanan, Allen E. 1982. *Marx and Justice: The Radical Critique of Liberalism.* Totowa, NJ: Rowman & Littlefield.

Buck, A. R., John McLaren, and Nancy E. Wright, eds. 2001. *Land and Freedom: Law, Property Rights and the British Diaspora.* Burlington, VT: Ashgate.

Budzieszewski, J. 2008. "Natural Law Revealed." *First Things* (September): 29–33.

Bugliosi, Vincent. 2008. *The Prosecution of George W. Bush for Murder.* New York: Perseus Books.

Burgess, Susan. 2001. "A Fine Romance: Keith Whittington's Originalism and the Drama of U.S. Constitutional Theory." *Law & Society Review* 35: 931–942.

Burgess, Susan. 2008. *The Founding Fathers, Pop Culture, and Constitutional Law: Who's Your Daddy?* Burlington, VT: Ashgate.

Burke, Thomas F. 2002. *Lawyers, Lawsuits, and Legal Rights: The Battle Over Litigation in American Society.* Berkeley and Los Angeles: University of California Press.

Burley Justine, ed. 2004. *Dworkin and His Critics: With Replies by Dworkin.* Oxford, UK: Blackwell.

Burman, Sandra B., and Barbara E. Harrell-Bond, eds. 1979. *The Imposition of Law.* New York: Academic Press.

Burns, Robert P. 2009. *The Death of the American Trial.* Chicago: University of Chicago Press.

Burns, Ronald G., and Michael Lynch. 2004. *Environmental Crime: A Sourcebook.* New York: LFB Scholarly Publishing.

Burrage, Michael. 1988. "Revolution and the Collective Action of French, American, and English Legal Professionals." *Law & Social Inquiry* 13: 225–277.

_____. 2006. *Revolution and the Making of the Contemporary Legal Profession: England, France, and the United States.* Oxford: Oxford University Press.

Burt, Robert A. 2002. *Death Is That Man Taking Names: Intersections of American Medicine, Law, and Culture.* Berkeley and Los Angeles: University of California Press.

Burton, Steven J. 1985. *An Introduction to Law and Legal Reasoning.* Boston: Little, Brown.

Bush, Sharon L. 2002–2003. "Beware the Associations: How Homeowner's Associations Control You and Infringe Upon Your Inalienable Rights." *Western State University Law Review* 30: 1–30.

Bussiere, Elizabeth. 1997. *(Dis)Entitling the Poor: The Warren Court, Welfare Rights, and the American Political Tradition.* University Park: Pennsylvania State University Press.

Busteed, Brandon. 2010. "Is High-Risk Drinking at College on the Way Out?" *Chronicle of Higher Education* (March 19): A76.

Butler, Nicholas Murray. [1923] 1970. "Law and Lawlessness." Pp. 158–175, in Laurence Veysey, ed. 1970. *Law and Resistance: American Attitudes Toward Authority.* New York: Harper & Row.

Butler, Paul. 1995. "Racially Based Jury Nullification: Black Power in the Original Justice System." *The Yale Law Journal* 105: 677–726.

Butterfield, Fox. 2003. "With Cash Tight, States Reassess Long Jail. Terms." *New York Times* (November 10): A1.

Bybee, Keith J. 2000. "The Political Significance of Legal Ambiguity: The Case of Affirmative Action." *Law & Society Review* 34: 263–290.

_____, ed. 2007. *Bench Press: The Collision of Courts, Politics and the Media.* Stanford, CA: Stanford University Press.

Cadiz, Laura. 2008. "Fifteen Volumes of Animal Law." *Animal Law* 15: 1–6.

Caenegem, R. C. van. 1988. *The Birth of the English Common Law,* 2nd ed. Cambridge, UK: Cambridge University Press.

_____. 1992. *An Historical Introduction to Private Law.* Cambridge, UK: Cambridge University Press.

_____. 2002. *European Law in the Past and the Future: Unity and Diversity Over Two Millennia.* New York: Cambridge University Press.

Cahill, Mia L., and Debra Horowitz. 2007. "Sexual Harassment." Pp. 1367–1369, in David S. Clark, ed. *Encyclopedia of Law & Society.* Los Angeles: Sage.

Cahn, Edmund. 1949. *The Sense of Injustice.* Bloomington: Indiana University Press.

Cahn, Naomi R. 2009. *Test Tube Families: Why the Fertility Market Needs Legal Regulation.* New York: New York University Press.

Cain, Maureen, and Christine Harrington. 1994. *Lawyers in a Postmodern World: Translation and Transgression.* Buckingham, UK: Open University Press.

Cain, Maureen, and Man Hunt, eds. 1979. *Marx and Engels on Law.* London: Academic Press.

Calabresi, Guido. 1970. *The Cost of Accidents.* New Haven, CT: Yale University Press.

Calabresi, Guido, and Phillip Bobbitt. 1978. *Tragic Choices.* New York: W. W. Norton.

Calavita, Kitty. 2001. "Blue Jeans, Rape, and the 'De-Constitutive' Power of Law." *Law & Society Review* 35: 89–115.

_____. 2002. "Engaged Research, 'Goose Bumps,' and the Role of the Public Intellectual." *Law & Society Review* 36: 5–27.

_____. 2005. *Immigrants at the Margins: Law, Race, and Exclusion in Southern Europe.* Cambridge, UK: Cambridge University Press.

_____. 2010. *Invitation to Law & Society: An Introduction to the Study of Real Law.* Chicago: The University of Chicago Press.

Calhoun, Craig, Paul Price, and Ashley Timmer, eds. 2002. *Understanding September 11.* New York: New Press.

Campbell, David, Hugh Collins, and John Wighman, eds. 2003. *Implicit Dimensions of Contract: Discrete, Relational and Network Contracts.* Portland, OR: Hart.

Campos, Paul F. 1998. *Jurismania: The Madness of American Law.* New York: Oxford University Press.

Canaday, Margot. 2009. *The Straight State: Sexuality and Citizenship in Twentieth Century America.* Princeton, NJ: Princeton University Press.

Cane, Peter. 2002. *Responsibility in Law and Morality.* Portland, OR: Hart Publishing.

Canedy, Dana. 2002. "Boys' Case Is Used in Bid to Limit Trials of Minors as Adults." *New York Times* (October 6): 26.

———. 2003. "Advocates of Equal Rights Amendment Resume Their Fight." *New York Times* (May 4): A41

Canter, David, and Rita Zukauskiene, ed. 2008. *Psychology and Law: Bridging the Gap.* Burlington, VT: Ashgate Publishing Co.

Cantor, Elizabeth, James C. Black, Campbell D. Barrett, and Donald J. Cantor. 2006. *Same-Sex Marriage: The Legal and Psychological Evolution in America.* Middletown, CT: Wesleyan University Press.

Caplow, Stacy 1999. "Still in the Dark: Disappointing Images of Women Lawyers in the Movies." *Women's Rights Law Reporter* 20: 55–71.

Caputo, Philip. 1977. A *Rumor of War.* New York: Henry Holt.

Caravita di Toritto, Beniamino, Jutta Kramer, and Hans-Peter Schneider, eds. 2009. *Judge Made Federalism: The Role of Courts in Federal Systems.* Baden Baden, Germany: Nomos Verlagsgesellschaft.

Carbonneau, Thomas E. 2007. "'Arbitracide': The Story of Anti-Arbitration Sentiment in the U.S. Congress." *The American Review of International Arbitration* 18: 233–278.

Carens, Joseph H. 2010. *Immigrants and the Right to Stay.* Cambridge, MA: MIT Press.

Caringella, Susan. 2008. *Addressing Rape Reform in Law and Practice.* New York: Columbia University Press.

Carlin, Jerome E. 1962. *Lawyers on Their Own: A Study of Individual Practitioners in Chicago.* New Brunswick. NJ: Rutgers University Press.

———. 1994. *Lawyers on Their Own: The Solo Practitioner in an Urban Setting.* San Francisco: Austin & Winfield.

Carothers, Thomas, ed. 2006. *Promoting the Rule of Law Abroad: In Search of Knowledge.* Washington, D.C.: Carnegie Endowment for International Peace.

Carrabine, Eamonn. 2008. *Crime, Culture and the Media.* Cambridge, UK: Polity Press.

Carrese, Paul O. 2003. *The Cloaking of Power: Montesquieu, Blackstone, and the Rise of Judicial Activism.* Chicago: University of Chicago Press.

Carrington, Paul. 1984. "Of Law and the River." *Journal of Legal Education* 34: 222–238.

Carrington, Paul D., and Trina Jones, eds. 2006. *Law and Class in America: Trends Since the Cold War.* New York: NYU Press.

Carter, Lief H. 1983. *Administrative Law and Politics: Cases and Comments.* Boston: Little, Brown.

Carter, Lief, and Thomas F. Burke. 2001. *Reason in Law,* 6th ed. New York: Longman.

Carter, Stephen L. 1993. *The Culture of Disbelief: How American Law and Politics Trivialize Religious Devotion.* New York: Basic Books.

———. 1998. *The Dissent of the Governed: A Meditation on Law, Religion, and Loyalty.* Cambridge, MA: Harvard University Press.

———. 2001. *God's Name in Vain: The Wrongs and Rights of Religion in Politics.* New York: Basic Books.

Cartwright, A. L. 2001. *The Return of the Peasant: Land Reform in Post-Communist Romania.* Burlington, VT: Ashgate Publishing.

Cass, Ronald A. 2001. *The Rule of Law in America.* Baltimore, MD: Johns Hopkins University Press.

Cassiday, Julie A. 2000. *The Enemy on Trial: Early Soviet Courts on Stage and Screen.* DeKalb: Northern Illinois University Press.

Castanzo, Mark. 2004. *Psychology Applied to Law.* Belmont, CA: Wadsworth.

Castile, George Pierre. 2006. *Taking Charge: Native American Self-Determination and Federal Indian Policy, 1975–1993.* Tucson: University of Arizona Press.

Caudill, David S., and Lewis H. LaRue. 2006. *No Magic Wand: The Idealization of Science in Law.* Lanham, MD: Rowman and Littlefield.

Chadwick, Elizabeth. 2003. "It's War, Jim, But Not as We Know It: A 'Reality-Check' for International Laws of War?" *Crime, Law & Social Change* 39: 233–262.

Chamallas, Martha. 1999. *Introduction to Feminist Legal Thought.* New York: Aspen Law & Business.

Chambliss, William J. 1967. "Types of Deviance and the Effectiveness of Legal Sanctions." *Wisconsin Law Review* (Summer): 703–714.

———. 1973a. *Sociological Readings in the Conflict Perspective.* Reading, MA: Addison-Wesley.

———. 1973b. "The Saints and the Roughnecks." *Society* 11: 24–31.

Chambliss, William J., and Robert Seidman. 1982. *Law, Order, and Power.* 2nd ed. Reading, MA: Addison-Wesley.

Chambliss, William J., and Marjorie Zatz. 1993. *Making Law: The State, the Law, and Structural Contradictions.* Bloomington: Indiana University Press.

Chander, Anupam, Lauren Gelman, and Margaret Jane Radin, eds. 2008. *Securing Privacy in the Internet Age.* Stanford, CA: Stanford University Press.

Chanock, Martin. 2001. *The Making of South African Legal Culture, 1902–4936: Fear, Favour, and Prejudice.* New York: Cambridge University Press.

Chapkis, Wendy, and Richard J. Webb. 2008. *Dying to Get High: Marijuana as Medicine.* New York: NYU Press.

Charles, J. Daryl. 2008. *Retrieving the Natural Law – A Return to Moral First Things.* Grand Rapids, MI: William B. Eerdmans Publishing Company.

Chase, Anthony. 1997. 2002. *Movies on Trial: The Legal System on the Silver Screen.* New York: New Press.

Chavez, Lydia. 1998. *The Color Blind: The Battle to End Affirmative Action.* Berkeley: University of California Press.

Chemerinsky, Erwin. 1985. "Pedagogy Without Purpose: An Essay on Professional Responsibility Courses and Casebooks." *AB F Research Journal* 189–199.

————. 2008. *Enhancing Government: Federalism for the 21st Century.* Stanford, CA: Stanford University Press.

Chesney-Lind, Meda. 1978. "Judicial Paternalism and the Female Status Offender: Training Women to Know Their Place." Pp. 376–391, in Barry Krisberg and James Austin, eds. *The Children of Ishmael.* Palo Alto, CA: Mayfield.

Chew, Pat K., ed. 2001. *The Conflict and Culture Reader.* New York: New York University Press.

Chiasson, Lloyd. Jr., ed. 1997. *The Press on Trial: Crimes and Trials as Media Events.* Westport, CT: Greenwood.

China Rights Forum 2. 2008. "Take Action: Tiananmen: 2008 and Beyond." *China Rights Forum* 2: 41–46.

Chomsky, Noam. 2003. *Hegemony or Survival: America's Quest for Global Dominance.* New York: Metropolitan Books.

Chriss, James J. 2008. *Social Control: An Introduction.* London: Polity Press.

Christodoulidis, Emilios, and Scott Veitch, eds. 2001. *Lethe's Law: Justice, Law and Ethics in Reconciliation.* Portland, OR: Hart Publishing.

Chronicle of Higher Education. 2007. "Robert Bork's Trip-and-Fall Lawsuit." *The Chronicle of Higher Education* (June 29): B4.

Chua, Amy. 2003. *World on Fire: How Exporting Free Market Democracy Breeds Ethnic Hatred and Global Instability.* New York: Doubleday.

Cigar, Norman, and Paul Williams. 2002. *Indictment at the Hague: The Milosevic Regime and Crimes of the Balkan Wars.* New York: New York University Press.

Clark, David S., ed. 2007. *Encyclopedia of Law & Society.* Los Angeles: Sage.

Clarke, George. 2007. *Justice and Science: Trials and Triumphs of DNA Evidence.* New Brunswick, NJ: Rutgers University Press.

Clarke, Kamari Maxine. 2009. *Fictions of Justice: The International Criminal Court and the Challenge of Legal Pluralism in Sub-Saharan Africa.* Cambridge: Cambridge University Press.

Clarke, Stevens H., and Elizabeth Ellen Gordon. 1997. "Public Sponsorship of Private Settling: Court-Ordered Civil Case Mediation." *Justice System Journal* 19: 311–339.

Clear, Todd R., George F. Cole, and Michael D. Reisig. 2011. *American Corrections.* 9th edition. Belmont, CA: Wadsworth/Cengage Learning.

Clear, Todd R., and Harry R. Dammer. 2003. *The Offender in the Community.* Belmont, CA: Thomson/Wadsworth.

Clemetson, Lynette. 2007. "Judges Look to New Congress for Changes in Mandatory Sentencing Laws." *New York Times* (January 9): A12.

Clinard, Marshall B., and Peter C. Yeager. 1980. *Corporate Crime.* New York: Free Press.

Clinton, Robert L. 1997. *God and Man in the Law: The Foundations of Anglo-American Constitutionalism.* Lawrence: University Press of Kansas.

Clinton, Robert N. 2002. "There Is No Federal Supremacy Clause for Indian Tribes." *Arizona State Law Journal* 34: 113–260.

Cloud, John. 1999. "Law on Bended Knee." *Time* (September 13): 32–33.

————. 2004. "How Oregon Eloped." *Tune* (May 17): 56–62.

Coase, Ronald. 1960. "The Problem of Social Cost." *Journal of Law and Economics* 3: 1–44.

Coblentz, Stanton A. 1970. *The Militant Dissenters.* New York: A. S. Barnes.

Cochran, Robert F., Jr. 1997. "Christian Perspectives on Law and Legal Scholarship." *Journal of Legal Education* 47: 1–18.

Cochran, Robert F., Jr., ed. 2008. *Faith and Law: How Religious Traditions from Calvinism to Islam View American Law.* New York: New York University Press.

Cockburn, Alexander. 2010. "Marijuana, Boom and Bust." *The Nation* (April 19): 9.

Coglianese, Cary, and David Lazer. 2003. "Management-Based Regulation: Prescribing Private Management to Achieve Public Goals." *Law & Society Review* 37: 691–730.

Cohen, Adam. 2006. "Looking Back on Louis Brandeis on His 150th Birthday." *New York Times* (November 4): A26.

Cohen, Esther. 1986. "Law, Folklore, and Animal Lore." *Past and Present* 110: 6–37.

Cohen, Felix. 1935. "Transcendental Nonsense and the Functional Approach." *Columbia Law Review* 35: 809–849.

Cohen, Jonathan M. 2002. *Inside Appellate Courts: The Impact of Court Organization on Judicial Decision Making in the United States Courts of Appeals.* Ann Arbor: University of Michigan Press.

Cohen-Almagor, Raphael. 2001. *Speech, Media, and Ethics: The Limits of Free Expression.* New York: Palgrave.

Cohn, Ellen S., and Susan O. White. 1997. "Legal Socialization Effects on Democratization." *International Social Science Journal* 152: 151–172.

Coleman, Jules L., Scott Shapiro, and Kenneth Einar Hinma, eds. 2004. *The Oxford Handbook of Jurisprudence and Philosophy of Law.* New York: Oxford University Press.

Coleman, Jules L., and Ori Simchen. 2003. "Law." *Legal Theory* 9: 1–41.

Colker, Ruth. 2005. *The Disability Pendulum: The First Decade of the Americans with Disabilities Act.* New York: New York University Press.

Collier, Charles W. 2000. *Basic Themes in Law and Jurisprudence.* Cincinnati, OH: Anderson.

Collier, Jane F. 1994. "Intertwined Histories: Islamic Law and Western. Imperialism." *Law & Society Review* 28: 395–408.

Collier, Richard, and Sally Sheldon. 2008. *Fragmenting Fatherhood: A Socio-Legal Study.* Portland, OR: Hart Publishing Co.

Collins, Paul M., Jr. 2008. *Friends of the Supreme Court: Interest Groups and Judicial Decision-Making.* New York: Oxford University Press.

Comaroff, Jeane, and John L. Comaroff, eds. 2006. *Law and Disorder in the Postcolony.* Chicago: University of Chicago Press.

Comaroff, John. 1991. "Re-Marx on Repression and the Rule of Law." *Law & Social Inquiry* 15: 671–678.

Comaroff, John, and Jean Comaroff. 2004. "Policing Culture, Cultural Policing: Law and Social Order in Postcolonial South Africa." *Law & Social Inquiry* 29: 513–547.

Combs, Nancy Amoury. 2007. *Guilty Pleas in International Criminal Law: Constructing a Restorative Justice Approach.* Palo Alto, CA: Stanford University Press.

Conaghan, Joanne, Richard M. Fischl, and Karl Klare, eds. 2002. *Labor Law in an Era of Globalization: Transformative Practices and Possibilities.* New York: Oxford University Press.

Conley, John M. 2009. "Can You Talk Like a Lawyer and Still Think Like a Human Being? Mertz's *The Language of Law School.*" *Law & Social Inquiry* 34: 985–1015.

Conley, John, and William M. O'Barr. 1990. *Rules Versus Relationships: The Ethnography of Legal Discourse.* Chicago: University of Chicago Press.

———. 2004. "A Classic in Spite of Itself: The Cheyenne Way and the Case Method in Legal Anthropology." *Law & Social Inquiry* 29: 179–218.

Connery, Donald S. 1977. *Guilty Until Proven Innocent.* New York: Putnam.

Conot, Robert. 1983. *Justice at Nuremberg.* New York: Harper & Row.

Cook, Kimberly J. 1998. *Divided Passions: Public Opinion on Abortion and the Death Penalty.* Boston: Northeastern University Press.

Cookson, Catherine. 2001. *Regulating Religion: The Courts and the Free Exercise Clause.* New York: Oxford University Press.

Cooter, Robert D. 2000. *The Strategic Constitution.* Princeton, NJ: Princeton University Press.

Cooter, Robert, and Thomas Ulen. 2008. *Law & Economics. Fifth edition.* Boston: Pearson.

Corsianos, Marilyn. 2009. *Policing and Gendered Justice: Examining the Possibilities.* Toronto, ON: University of Toronto Press.

Costanzo, Mark, Daniel Krauss, and Kathy Pezdek, eds. 2007. *Expert Psychological Testimony for the Courts.* Mahwah, NJ: Lawrence Erlbaum Associates.

Cotterrell, Roger. 1986. *The Sociology of Law: An Introduction.* London: Butterworths.

———. 1989. *The Politics of Jurisprudence: A Critical Introduction to Legal Philosophy.* Philadelphia: University of Pennsylvania Press.

_____. 1991. "The Durkheimian Tradition in the Sociology of Law." *Law & Society Review* 25: 923–945.

_____. 1997. "The Concept of Legal Culture." Pp. 13–32, in David Nelken, ed. *Comparing Legal Cultures.* Aldershot, UK: Dartmouth.

_____. 1998. "Why Must Legal Ideas Be Interpreted Sociologically?" *Journal of Law and Society* 25: 171–192.

_____. 2004. "Selznick Interviewed: Philip Selznick in Conversation With Roger Cotterrell." *Journal of Law & Society* 31: 291–317.

_____. 2006a. *Law in Social Theory.* Burlington, VT: Ashgate.

_____. 2006b. *Law, Culture and Society: Legal Ideas in the Mirror of Social Theory.* Aldershot, UK: Ashgate.

_____. 2007a. "Emile Durkheim." Pp. 443–445, in David S. Clark, ed. *Encyclopedia of Law & Society.* Los Angeles: Sage.

_____. 2007b. "Sociology of Law." Pp. 1413–1420, in David S. Clark, ed. *Encyclopedia of Law & Society.* Los Angeles: Sage.

Coutin, Susan Bibler. 2007. *Nations of Emigrants: Shifting Boundaries of Citizenship in El Salvador and the United States.* Ithaca, NY: Cornell University Press.

Cover, Robert M. 1986. "Violence and the Word." *Yale Law Review* 95: 1601–1629.

Cowan, Alison Leigh. 2004. "Man Accepts a Plea Deal in Case of Wife's Suicide." *New York Times* (May 12): B5.

Cowling, Mark. 2008. *Marxism and Criminological Theory.* London: Palgrave/MacMillan.

Cownie, Fiona, and Anthony Bradney. 2000. *Living Without Law: An Ethnography of Quaker Decision Making, Dispute Avoidance, and Dispute Resolution.* Brookfield, VT: Ashgate.

Coy, Jason P. 2008. *Strangers and Misfits: Banishment, Social Control, and Authority in Early Modern Germany.* Leiden: Brill.

Cramton, Roger. 1978. "The Ordinary Religion of the Law School Classroom." *Journal of Legal Education* 34: 155–167.

Crane, Gregg D. 2002. *Race, Citizenship, and Law in American Literature.* New York: Cambridge University Press.

Crank, John P. 1994. "Watchman and Community: Myth and Institutionalization in Policing." *Law & Society Review* 28: 325–351.

Cranor, Carl F. 2006. *Toxic Torts: Science, Law, and the Possibility of Justice.* New York: Cambridge University Press.

Crary, David. 2001. "Should States Have a Role in Boosting Marriage, Combatting Divorce?" *Scranton Times* (February 4): Cl.

Crenshaw, Kimberle. 1989. "Demarginalizing the Intersection of Race and Sex: A Black Feminist Critique of Antidiscrimination Doctrine, Feminist Theory and Antiracist Doctrine." *University of Chicago Legal Forum* 189: 139–142.

Crier, Catherine. 2003. *The Case Against Lawyers.* New York: Broadway Books.

Croley, S. P. 2008. *Regulation and Public Interest: The Possibility of Good Regulatory Governance.* Princeton, NJ: Princeton University Press.

Cross, Frank B. 2007. *Decision Making in the U. S. Court of Appeals.* Stanford, CA: Stanford University Press.

_____. 2009. *The Theory and Practice of Statutory Interpretation.* Stanford, CA: Stanford University Press.

Crotty, William J., ed. 2003. *The Politics of Terror: The U.S. Response to 9/11.* Boston: Northeastern University Press.

Crowe, Jonathan, and Rachael Field. 2007–2008. "The Problem of Legitimacy in Mediation." *Contemporary Issues in Law* (2007–2008): 48+.

Crowley, Jocelyn Elise. 2008. *Defiant Dads: Fathers' Rights Activists in America.* Ithaca, NY: Cornell University Press.

Current Biography. 1993. "Richard Posner." Pp. 471–474, in J. Graham, ed. *Current Biography.* New York: H. W. Wilson.

_____. 1994. "Catharine MacKinnon." Pp. 364–367, in J. Graham, ed. *Current Biography.* New York: H. W. Wilson.

_____. 2008. "Cass R. Sunstein." *Current Biography* (October): 85–89.

Currie, David P. 2005. *The Constitution in Congress: Democrats and Whigs, 1892–1861.* Chicago: University of Chicago Press.

Currie, Elliott. 2010. "On Being Right, but Unhappy." *Criminology & Public Policy* 9: 1–10.

Custer, Lawrence B. 1986. "Ordeal by Touch." *American Heritage* (April/May): 93–97.

Czarnota, Adam. 2003. "Globalization, Legal Transplants, and Unhappiness: Post-Communist Experiences." Pp. 213–229, in Catherine Dauvergne, ed. *Jurisprudence for an Interconnected Globe.* Aldershot, UK: Ashgate.

d'Errico, Peter. 1975. "The Law Is Terror Put Into Words." *Learning and the Law.* Chicago: American Bar Association.

Daly, Gail M. 2008. "There's No Law Library on the Starship 'Enterprise'." *Journal of Legal Education* 58: 455–462.

Daly, Mary C., and Carole Silver. 2007. "Flattening the World of Legal Services? The Ethical and Liability Minefields of Offshoring Legal and Law-Related Services." *Georgetown Journal of International Law* 38: 401–448.

Dammer, Harry R., and Jay S. Albanese. 2011. *Comparative Criminal Justice Systems.* Fourth edition. Belmont, CA: Wadsworth Cengage Learning.

Dan-Cohen, Mein 2002. *Harmful Thoughts: Essays on Law, Self and Morality.* Princeton, NJ: Princeton University Press,

Daniels, Cynthia R. 1993. *At Women's Expense: State Power and the Politics of Fetal Rights.* Cambridge, MA: Harvard University Press.

Dao, James. 2004. "Bill to Allow Slot Machines Is Passed in Pennsylvania." *New York Times* (July 5): A 10.

Dare, Tim. 2009. *The Counsel of Rogues? A Defence of the Standard Conception of the Lawyer's Role.* Burlington, VT: Ashgate.

Darian-Smith, Eve. 2004. "Ethnographies of Law." Pp. 545–568, in Austin Sarat, ed. *The Blackwell Companion to Law and Society.* Malden, MA: Blackwell.

Darian-Smith, Eve, ed. 2007. Ethnography and Law. Burlington, VT: Ashgate Publishing Co.

Darian-Smith, Eve, and Colin Scott. 2009. "Regulation and Human Rights in Socio-Legal Scholarship." *Law & Policy* 31: 271–281.

Darnton, Robert. 2009. "Google and the New Digital Future." *The New York Review of Books* (December 17): 82–84.

Dauvergne, Catherine, ed. 2003. *Jurisiprudence for an Interconnected Globe.* Aldershot, UK: Ashgate.

_____. 2008. *Making People Illegal: What Globalization Means for Migration and Law.* New York: Cambridge University Press.

Davey, Monica. 2004. "In Court, AIM Members Are Depicted as Killers." *New York Times* (February 5): A18.

Davies, Margaret. 2008. "Theory in Legal Research." pp. 1165–1167, in Peter Cane and Joanne Conaghan, eds. *The New Oxford Companion to Law.* New York: Oxford University Press.

Davies, Wade, and Richmond L. Clow, eds. 2009. *American Indian Sovereignty and Law: An Annotated Bibliography.* Lanham, MD: The Scarecrow Press.

Davis, D. M. 1986. "Political Trials and Civil Liberties in South Africa." *Natal University Law and Society Review* 1: 87–98.

_____. 2010. "South African Constitutional Jurisprudence: The First Fifteen Years." Pp. 285–300, in J. Hagan, ed. *Annual Review of Law and Social Science.* Palo Alto: Annual Reviews.

Davis, F. James. 1962. "Law as a Type of Social Control." Pp. 39–61, in F. James Davis, Henry H. Foster Jr., C. Ray Jeffery, and E. Eugene Davis. *Society and the Law: New Meanings for an Old Profession.* New York: Free Press.

Davis, Jeffrey. 2008. *Justice Across Borders: The Struggle for Human Rights in U.S. Courts.* New York: Cambridge University Press.

Davis, John. 1974. "Justification for No Obligation: Views of Black Males Toward Crime and the Criminal Law." *Issues in Criminology* 9: 69–87.

Davis, Kevin E., and Michael B. Kruse. 2007. "Taking the Measure of Law: The Case of the *Doing Business* Project." *Law & Social Inquiry* 32: 1095–1119.

Daynes, Kathryn M. 2001. *More Wives Than One: Transformation of the Mormon Marriage System, 1840–1910.* Urbana: University of Illinois Press.

Dear, John. 1997. *Apostle of Peace: Essays in Honor of Daniel Berrigan.* Maryknoll, NY: Orbis Books.

de Been, Wouter. 2008. *Legal Realism Regained: Saving Realism from Critical Acclaim.* Stanford, CA: Stanford University Press.

Decker, Scott H. 2010. "Shifts in Drug Policy: The More Things Change, the More They Stay The Same." *Crime, Law & Social Change* 53: 515–517.

Deflem, Mathieu. 2002. *Policing World Society. Historical Foundations of International Police Cooperation.* New York: Oxford University Press.

_____. 2002. *Sociology of Law: Visions of a Scholarly Tradition.* West Nyack, NY: Cambridge University Press.

deGrazia, Edward. 1992. *Girls Lean Back Everywhere: The Law of Obscenity and the Assault on Genius.* New York: Random House.

Deigh, John. 2008. *Emotions, Values, and the Law.* Oxford: Oxford University Press.

Delgado, Richard. 2003. *Justice at War: Civil Liberties and Civil Rights During Times of Crisis.* New York: New York University Press.

Delgado, Richard, and Jean Stefanie. 1994. *Failed Revolutions: Social Reform and the Limits of Legal Imagination.* Boulder, CO: Westview Press.

Del Mar, Maksymilian. 2009. "At the Lectern: Moral Education in Law School and Law Firms." *Journal of Legal Education* 59: 298–304.

DeLombard, Jeannine Marie. 2007. *Slavery on Trial: Law, Abolitionism, and Print Culture.* Chapel Hill: University of North Carolina Press.

Denbeaux, Mark, and Jonathan Hafetz, eds. 2009. *The Guantanamo Lawyers: Inside a Prison Outside the Law.* New York: New York University Press.

Derezores, Dennette M., John Poertner, and Mark F. Testa, eds. 2005. *Race Matters in Child Welfare: The Overrepresentation of African American Children in the System.* Washington, D.C.: CWLA Press.

Dershowitz, Alan M. 2008. *Is There a Right to Remain Silent? Coercive Interrogation and the Fifth Amendment After 9/11.* New York: Oxford University Press.

Dery, George M., III. 1999. "Mouse Hunting with an Elephant Gun: The Supreme Court's Overkill in Upholding a Categorical Rejection to Polygraph Evidence in *United States v. Scheirer.*" *American Journal of Criminal Law* 26: 227–256.

Dezalay, Yves, and Bryant Garth. 1996. *Dealing in Virtue: International Commercial Arbitration and the Construction of a Transnational Legal Order.* Chicago: University of Chicago Press.

———, eds. 2002. *Global Prescriptions: The Production, Exportation, and Importation of a New Orthodoxy.* Ann Arbor: University of Michigan Press.

Diamant, Neil J., Stanley B. Lubman, and Kevin J. O'Brien, eds. 2005. *Engaging the Law in China: State, Society, and Possibilities of Justice.* Stanford, CA: Stanford University Press.

Diamond, Stanley. 1973. "The Rule of Law Versus the Order of Custom." Pp. 318–343, in Donald Black and Maureen Mileski, eds. *The Social Organization of Law.* New York: Seminar Press.

Dicken, Peter. 2003. *Global Shift: Reshaping the Global Economic Map in the 21st Century.* New York: Guilford.

Dickey, Christopher. 2007. "The Constitution in Peril." *Newsweek* (October 8): 60–63.

Dickinson, Laura A., ed. 2007. *International Law and Society: Empirical Approaches to Human Rights.* Burlington, VT: Ashgate.

Dickstein, Morris, ed. 1999. *The Revival of Pragmatism: New Essays on Social Thought, Law, and Culture.* Durham, NC: Duke University Press.

Dilling, Olaf, Martin Herberg, and Gerd Winter, eds. 2008. *Responsible Business: Self-Governance and Law in Transnational Economic Transactions.* Portland, OR: Hart Publishing.

DiMento, Joseph F. C. 2003. *The Global Environment and International Law.* Austin: University of Texas Press.

Dine, Janet. 2005. *International Trade and Human Rights.* New York: Cambridge University Press.

Dingwall, Robert. 2000. "Language, Law, and Power: Ethnomethodology, Conversation Analysis, and the Politics of Law and Society Studies." *Law and Social Inquiry* 25: 885–911.

Dinovitzer, Ronit, and Bryant G. Garth. 2007. "Lawyer Satisfaction in the Process of Structuring Legal Careers." *Law & Society Review* 41: 1–50.

Dirck, Brian. 2007. *Lincoln the Lawyer.* Urbana: University of Illinois Press.

Dixon, Jo. 1995. "The Nexus of Sex, Spousal Violence, and the State." *Law and Society Review* 29: 359–376.

Dlamini, C. R. M. 1988. "The Influence of Race on the Administration of Justice." *South African Journal of Human Rights* 4: 37–54.

Dnes, Antony W., and Robert Rowthorn, eds. 2002. *The Law and Economics of Marriage and Divorce.* New York: Cambridge University Press.

Doak, Jonathan. 2008. *Victims' Rights, Human Rights, and Criminal Justice: Reconceiving the Role of Third Parties.* Portland, OR: Hart Publishing.

Doan, Alesha E. 2007. *Opposition & Intimidation: The Abortion Wars and Strategies of Political Harassment.* Ann Arbor: University of Michigan Press.

Dolgin, Janet L. 1997. *Defining the Family: Law, Technology, and Reproduction in an Uneasy Age.* New York: New York University Press.

Dombrink, John, and Daniel Hillyard. 2007. *Sin No More: From Abortion to Stem Cells, Understanding Crime, Law, and Morality in America.* New York: New York University Press.

Donnelly-Cole, Damien S. 2007. "Not Just a Few Bad Apples: The Prosecution of Collective Violence" *Washington University Global Studies Law Review* 5: 159–186.

Donovan, James M. 2008. *Legal Anthropology: An Introduction.* Lanham, MD: AltaMira Press/Rowman & Littlefield Publishers, Inc.

Donovan, Karen. 2006. "The Lure of the In-House Job." *New York Times* (June 16): C6.

Donovan, Karen. 2007. "New York Law Firms Struggle with New Restrictions on Advertising." *New York Times* (July 3): Bus. 3.

Dorsen, Norma, ed. 2002. *The Unpredictable Constitution.* New York: New York University Press.

Douglas, Davison M. 2001. "The Jeffersonian Vision of Legal Education." *Journal of Legal Education* 51: 185–211.

Douglas, William O. 1980. *The Court Years: 1939–1975.* New York: Random House.

Dowd, Nancy E., and Michelle S. Jacobs. 2003. *Feminist Legal Theory: An Anti-Essentialist Reader.* New York: New York University Press.

Dowdall, George W. 2009. *College Drinking: Reframing a Social Problem.* Westport, CT: Praeger.

Downs, Donald Alexander. 1996. *More Than Victims: Battered Women, the Syndrome Society, and the Law.* Chicago: University of Chicago Press.

Drachman, Virginia G. 1998. *Sisters in Law: Women Lawyers in Modern American History.* Cambridge, MA: Harvard University Press.

Dreisbach, Christopher. 2009. *Ethics in Criminal Justice.* Boston: McGraw Hill.

Dreisbach, Daniel L. 2002. *Thomas Jefferson and the Wall of Separation Between Church and State.* New York: New York University Press.

Driesen, David M. 2003. *The Economic Dynamics of Environmental Law.* Cambridge, MA: MIT Press.

Driver, Justin. 2010. "Why Law Should Lead." *The New Republic* (April 8): 28–32.

Dubber, Markus Dirk. 2002. *Victims in the War on Crime: The Use and Abuse of Victims' Rights.* New York: New York University Press.

———. 2006a. *The Sense of Justice: Empathy in Law and Punishment.* New York: New York University Press.

———. 2006b. "Criminal Law in Comparative Context." *Journal of Legal Education* 56: 433–443.

Dubner, Stephen J., and Steven D. Levitt. 2008. "Unintended Consequences: Why do Well-Meaning Laws Backfire?" *New York Times Magazine* (January 20): 18–19.

Dubois, Ellen Carol. 1998. *Women's Suffrage and Women's Rights.* New York: New York University Press.

Dudas, Jeffrey R. 2008. *The Cultivation of Resentment: Treaty Rights and the New Right.* Stanford, CA: Stanford University Press.

Dudziak, Mary L., ed. 2003. *September 11 in History: A Watershed Moment.* Durham, NC: Duke University Press.

Dugan, Laura, Daniel S. Nagin, and Richard Rosenfeld. 2003. "Exposure Reduction or Retaliation: The Effects of Domestic Violence Resources on Intimate-Partner Homicide." *Law & Society Review* 37: 169–198.

Dugger, Celia W. 1996, "Tug of Taboos: African Genital Rite vs. U.S. Law." *New York Times* (December 28): A 1.

———. 2011. "South Africa Exults Abroad but Frets at Home." *New York Times* (April 20): A4.

Duncan, Martha Grace. 2002. "So Young and So Untender: Remorseless Children and the Expectations of the Law." *Columbia Law Review* 102: 1469–1526.

Dupre, Anne Proffitt. 2008. *Speaking Up: The Unintended Costs of Free Speech in Public Schools.* Cambridge, MA: Harvard University Press.

Dupre, Catherine. 2003. *Importing the Law in Post-Communist Transitions: The Hungarian Constitutional Court and the Right to Human Dignity.* Portland, OR: Hart Publishing.

Durkheim, Emile. [1893] 1984. *The Division of Labor in Society.* New York: Free Press.

———. [1897] 1951. *Suicide.* New York: Free Press.

Dusky, Lorraine. 1996. *Still Unequal: The Shameful Truth About Women and Justice in America.* New York: Crown.

Duthu, N. Bruce. 2008a. *American Indians and the Law.* New York: Penguin.

———. 2008b. "Broken Justice in Indian Country." *New York Times* (August 11): Op-Ed Page.

Duxbury, Neil. 1995. *Patterns of American Jurisprudence.* Oxford: Oxford University Press.

———. 2001. *Jurists and Judges: An Essay on Influence.* Portland, OR: Hart.

———. 2003. "A Century of Legal Studies." Pp. 950–987, in Peter Cane and Mark Tushnet, eds. *The Oxford Handbook of Legal Studies.* New York: Oxford University Press.

———. 2008. *The Nature and Authority of Precedent.* New York: Cambridge University Press.

———. 2009. "Golden Rule Reasoning, Moral Judgment, and Law." *Notre Dame Law Review* 84: 1529–1605.

Dworkin, Ronald. 1977. *Taking Rights Seriously.* Cambridge, MA: Harvard University Press.

———. 1985. A *Matter of Principle.* Cambridge, MA: Harvard University Press.

———. 1986. *Law's Empire.* Cambridge, MA: Harvard University Press.

_____. 1993. *Life's Dominion*. New York: Alfred A. Knopf.

_____. 1996. *Freedom's Law*. Cambridge, MA: Harvard University Press.

_____. 2000; 2002. *Sovereign Virtue: The Theory and Practice of Equality*. Cambridge, MA: Harvard University Press.

_____. 2006. *Justice in Robes*. Cambridge, MA: Harvard University Press.

_____. 2010. "The 'Devastating' Decision." *The New York Review of Books* (February 25): 39.

Eakin, Hugh. 2001. 2004. "When U.S. Aided Insurgents, Did It Breed Future Terrorists?" *New York Times* (April 10): B7.

Eaton, Leslie. 2004. "For Arbiters in Custody Battles, Wide Powers and Little Scrutiny" *New York* Times (July 10): Metro 1.

Eaton, Leslie and Leslie Kaufman. 2005. "Judges Turn Therapist in Problem-Solving Court." *New York Times* (April 26): A1.

Eckholm, Erik. 2003. "Petitioners Urge China to Enforce Legal Rights." *New York Times* (June 2): A9.

_____. 2008. "Citing Workload, Public Lawyers Reject New Cases." *New York Times* (November 9): A1.

Edelman, Lauren B. 2004. "Rivers of Law and Contested Terrain: A Law and Society Approach to Economic Rationality." *Law & Society Review* 38: 181–197.

Edelman, Lauren B., and Mark C. Suchman, eds. 2007. *The Legal Lives of Private Organizations*. Burlington, VT: Ashgate Publishing Co.

Edelman, Murray. 2001. *The Politics of Misinformation*. New York: Cambridge University Press.

Edelman, Peter. 1997. "The Worst Thing Bill Clinton Has Done." *Atlantic Monthly* (March): 43–58.

_____. 2009. "… And a Law for Poor People." *The Nation* (August 3/10): 23–26.

Edwards, Laura P. 2009. *The People and Their Peace: Legal Culture and the Transformation of Inequality in the Post-Revolutionary South*. Chapel Hill: University of North Carolina Press.

Edwards, Mark A. 2006. "Law and the Parameters of Acceptable Deviance." *Journal of Criminal Law & Criminology* 97: 49–81.

Efrati, Amir. 2007. "A Stingier Job Market Awaits New Attorneys." *Wall Street Journal* (September 24): A1.

Egan, Timothy. 1998a. "New Prosperity Brings New Conflict in Indian Country" *New York Times* (March 8): A1.

_____. 1998b. "Backlash Growing as Indians Make a Stand for Sovereignty." *New York Times* (March 9): A1.

_____. 1999. "Technology Sent Wall Street Into Market for Pornography." *New York Times* (October 23): A1.

_____. 2000. "Erotica, Inc." *New York Times* (October 23): A1.

Ehrlich, Eugen. [1913] 1936. *Fundamental Principles of the Sociology of Law*. New York: Russel & Russel.

_____. 1922. "The Sociology of Law." *Harvard Law Review* 36: 130–145.

Ehrlich, J. W. 1959. *Ehrlich's Blackstone*. New York: Capricorn.

Ehrlich, Susan, 2001. *Representing Rape: Language and Sexual Consent*. New York: Routledge.

Eichenwald, Kurt. 2006. "With Child Sex Sites on the Run, Nearly Nude Pictures Test Laws." *New York Times* (August 20): A1.

Eisenstein, James, Roy B. Flemming, and Peter F. Nardulli. 1999. *The Contours of Justice: Communities and Their Courts*. Lanham, MD: University Press of America.

Eisgruber, Christopher L. 2001, *Constitutional Self-Government*. Cambridge, MA: Harvard University Press.

Eisgruber, Christopher L., and Lawrence G. Sager. 2006. *Religious Freedom and the Constitution*. Cambridge, MA: Harvard University Press.

Eligon, John. 2008. "Judge Rules Restaurateur's Suit Over an Expensive Umbrella Not Worthy of the Court." *New York Times* (September 13): B3.

Eligon, John. 2010. "Sentence Is Sharply Increased for Lawyer Convicted of Aiding Terror." *New York Times* (July 16): A22.

Elikann, Peter T. 1996. *The Tough-on-Crime Myth*. New York: Plenum.

Elkins, James R. 1979. "The Paradox of a Life in Law." *University of Pittsburgh Law Review 40:* 129–168.

_____. 1985a. "On the Emergence of Narrative Jurisprudence: The Humanistic Perspective Finds a New Path." *Legal Studies Forum* 9: 123–156.

_____. 1985b. "Ethics: Professionalism, Craft, and Failure." *Kentucky Law Journal* 73: 937–965.

_____. 1985c. "The Pedagogy of Ethics." *Journal of the Legal Profession* 10: 37–83.

Elkins, James, ed. 1990. "Pedagogy of Narrative: A Symposium." *Journal of Legal Education* 40: 1–250.

Ellickson, Robert C. 1991. *Order Without Law: How Neighbors Settle Disputes.* Cambridge, MA: Harvard University Press.

———. 2008. *The Household: Informal Order Around the Hearth.* Princeton, NJ: Princeton University Press.

Ellis, Kate, Nan D. Hunter, Beth Jaker, Barbara O'Dair, and Abby Tallmer, eds. 1986. *Caught Looking: Feminism, Pornography, and Censorship.* New York: Real Comet Press.

Ellis, Mark R. 2007. *Law and Order in Buffalo Bill's Country.* Lincoln: University of Nebraska Press.

Ellis, Richard E. 2007. *Aggressive Nationalism: McCulloch v. Maryland and the Foundation of Federal Authority in the Young Republic.* New York: Oxford University Press.

Ellmann, Stephen. 1995. "Law and Legitimacy in South Africa." *Law & Social Inquiry* 20: 407–479.

Elshtain, Jean Bethke. 1995. *Democracies on Trial.* New York: Basic Books.

Ely, John Hart. 1990. "The American War in Indochina, Part I: The (Troubled) Constitutionality of the War They Told Us About." *Stanford Law Review* 42: 877–926.

Emmelman, Debra S. 1996. "Trial by Plea Bargain: Case Settlement as a Product of Recursive Decision Making." *Law & Society Review* 30: 335–360.

———. 2003. *Justice for the Poor: A Study of Criminal Defense Work.* Aldershot, UK: Ashgate.

Engel, David M., and Frank W. Munger. 1996. "Rights, Remembrance, and the Reconciliation of Difference." *Law & Society Review* 30: 7–53.

———. 2003. *Rights of Inclusion: Law and Identity in the Life Stories of Americans With Disabilities.* Chicago: University of Chicago Press.

Engel, David M., and Michael McCann, eds. 2009. *Fault Lines: Tort Law as Cultural Practice.* Stanford, CA: Stanford University Press.

English, Peter W., and Bruce D. Sales. 2005. *More Than the Law: Behavioral and Social Facts in Legal Decision Making.* Washington, DC: American Psychological Association.

Ephron, Dan. 2007. "Disorder in the Court." *Newsweek* (October 15): 31.

Epps, Garrett. 2006. *Democracy Reborn: The Fourteenth Amendment and the Fight for Equal Rights in Post-Civil War America.* New York: Henry Holt and Company.

———. 2009. *Peyote vs. the State: Religious Freedom on Trial.* Norman: University of Oklahoma Press.

Epstein, Cynthia. 1993. *Women in Law,* 2nd ed. Urbana: University of Illinois Press.

Epstein, Lee, Jack Knight, and Olga Shvetsova. 2001. "The Role of Constitutional Courts in the Establishment and Maintenance of Democratic Systems of Government." *Law & Society Review* 35: 117–164.

Epstein, Richard A. 2009. "How Other Countries Judge Malpractice." *Wall Street Journal* (June 30): A15.

Ericson, Richard V. 1996. "Why Law Is Like News." Pp. 195–230, in David Nelken, ed. *Law as Communication.* Aldershot, UK: Dartmouth.

Erikson, Kai T. 1966. *Wayward Puritans: A Study in the Sociology of Deviance.* New York: John Wiley.

Erlanger, Howard S., Mia Cahill, Charles R. Epp, and Kathleen M. Haines. 1996. "Law Student Idealism and Job Choice: Some New Data on an Old Question." *Law & Society Review* 30: 851–864.

Eskridge, William N., Jr. 2008. *Dishonorable Passions: Sodomy Laws in America, 1861–2003.* New York: Viking Press.

Eskridge, William N., Jr. and Darren R. Spedale. 2006. *Gay Marriage: For Better or for Worse? What We've Learned from the Evidence.* New York: Oxford University Press.

Essig, Mark. 2003. "Continuing the Search for Kinder Executions." *New York Times* (October 21): A27.

Estrich, Susan. 1986. "Rape." *Yale Law Journal* 95: 1087–1184.

———. 1987. *Real Rape.* Cambridge, MA: Harvard University Press.

———. 1998. *Getting Away With Murder: How Politics Is Destroying the Criminal Justice System.* Cambridge, MA: Harvard University Press.

Etzioni, Amitai. 1968. *The Active Society.* New York: Free Press.

———. 1996a. "The Responsive Community: A Communitarian Perspective." *American Sociological Review* 61: 1–11.

———. 1996b. "The Attack on Community: The Grooved Debate." *Society* 32: 12–17.

———. 2000. "Social Norms: Internalization, Persuasion, and History." *Law & Society Review* 34: 157–178.

Ewald, William B. 2007a. "Aristotle." Pp. 92–93, in David S. Clark, ed. *Encyclopedia of Law & Society.* Los Angeles: Sage.

———. 2007b. "Plato." Pp. 1109–1110, in David S. Clark, ed. *Encyclopedia of Law & Society.* Los Angeles: Sage.

Ewick, Patricia, and Susan S. Silbey. 1995 "Subversive Stories and Hegemonic Tales: Toward a Sociology of Narrative." *Law & Society Review* 29: 197–226.

_____. 1998. *The Common Place of Law: Stories From Everyday Life.* Chicago: University of Chicago Press.

Ewing, Sally. 1987. "Formal Justice and the Spirit of Capitalism: Max Weber's Sociology of Law." *Law & Society Review* 21: 487–512.

Ezzati, Abu A. 2002. *Islam and Natural Law.* London: ICAS Press.

Fagelson, David. 2006. *Justice as Integrity: Tolerance and the Moral Momentum of Law.* Albany: State University of New York Press.

Falk, Richard A., Gabriel Kolko, and Robert J. Lifton, eds. 1971. *Crimes of War.* New York: Vintage.

Fanon, Frantz. 1968. *The Wretched of the Earth.* New York: Grove Press.

Farahany, Nita A. 2009. *The Impact of Behavioral Sciences on Criminal Law.* New York: Oxford University Press.

Farber, Daniel A., and Suzanna Sherry. 1997. *Beyond All Reason: The Radical Assault on Truth in American Law.* New York: Oxford University Press.

Faure, Michael, Anthony Ogus, and Niels Philipsen. 2009. "Curbing Consumer Financial Losses: The Economics of Regulatory Enforcement." *Law & Policy* 31: 161–191.

Feeley, Malcolm M., and Edward L. Rubin. 1998. *Judicial Policy Making and the Modern State: How the Courts Reformed America's Prisons.* New York: Cambridge University Press.

_____. 2008. *Federalism: Political Identity and Tragic Compromise.* Ann Arbor: University of Michigan Press.

Feeley, Malcolm M., and Setsuo Miyazawa. 2002. *The Japanese Adversary System in Context.* New York: Palgrave.

Feenan, Dermot, ed. 2002. *Informal Criminal Justice.* Burlington, VT: Ashgate.

Feest, Johannes. 2007. "International Institute for the Sociology of Law." Pp. 806–807, in David S. Clark, ed. *Encyclopedia of Law and Society.* Thousand Oaks, CA: Sage.

Feiler, Stephen M., and Joseph F. Sheley. 1999. "Legal and Racial Elements of Public Willingness to Transfer Juvenile Offenders to Adult Court." *Journal of Criminal Justice* 27: 55–64.

Feinberg, Joel, and Hyman Gross. 1977. *Justice: Selected Readings.* Princeton, NJ: Princeton University Press.

Feldman, Eric A. 2000. "Blood Justice: Courts, Conflict, and Compensation in Japan, France, and the United States." *Law & Society Review* 34: 651–701.

Feldman, Noah. 2005. *Divided by God: America's Church-State Problem – and What We Should Do About It.* New York: Farrar, Straus & Giroux.

_____. 2008a. *The Fall and Rise of the Islamic State.* Princeton, NJ: Princeton University Press.

_____. 2008b. "Why Shariah" *New York Times Magazine* (March 16): 47–51.

_____. 2008c. "When Judges Make Foreign Policy." *New York Times Magazine* (September 28): 50+.

Feldman, Robin. 2009. *The Role of Science in Law.* New York: Oxford University Press.

Feldman, Stephen M. 2008. *Free Expression and Democracy in America: A History.* Chicago: University of Chicago Press.

Felstiner, William. 1998. "Justice, Power, and Lawyers." Pp. 55–79, in Bryant G. Garth and Austin Sarat, eds. *Justice and Power in Sociolegal Studies.* Chicago: Northwestern University Press.

Felstiner, William, Richard L. Abel, and Austin Sarat. 1989. "The Emergence and Transformation of Disputes: Naming, Blaming, and Claiming." Pp. 468–470, in J. Bonsignore et al., *Before the Law*, 4th ed. Dallas, TX: Houghton Mifflin.

Ferguson, Robert A. 1984. *Law and Letters in American Culture.* Cambridge, MA: Harvard University Press.

_____. 2008. *The Trial in American Life.* Chicago: University of Chicago Press.

Ferrari, Vincenzo. 2007. "Functions of Law." Pp. 610–616, in David D. Clark, ed. *Encyclopedia of Law and Society.* Thousand Oaks, CA: Sage.

Feuer, Alan. 2001. "Lawyering by Laymen." *New York Times* (January 22): Bl.

Fields, Gary. 2009. "White House Czar Calls for End to 'War on Drugs'." *The Wall Street Journal* (May 14): A3.

Filkins, Dexter. 2003. "Honor Killings Defy Turkish Efforts to End Them." *New York Times* (July 13): A3.

_____. 2005. "Secular Iraqis Say New Charter May Curb Rights." *New York Times* (August 24): A1.

Findlay, Mark. 1989. "Show Trials in China: After Tiananmen Square." *Journal of Law and Society* 16: 352–359.

Finkel, Norman J. 2001, *Not Fair! The Typology of Commonsense Unfairness.* Washington, DC: American Psychological Association.

Finkelman, Paul. 1997. *Slavery and the Law* Madison, WI: Madison House.

_____. 2007. "Foreign Law and American Constitutional Interpretation: A Long and Venerable Tradition." *NYU Annual Survey of Law* 63: 29–62.

Finnis, John. 1980. *Natural Law and Natural Rights.* Oxford, UK: Clarendon Press.

_____. 2003. "Law and What I Truly Should Decide." *American Journal of Jurisprudence* 48: 107–130.

Firm Report, The. 2009. "Women Outnumber Men among Part-Time Lawyers." *The National Jurist* (February): 8.

Fish, Stanley. 1997. "Mission Impossible: Settling the Just Bounds Between Church and State." *Columbia Law Review* 97: 2255–2333.

_____. 2005. "Intentional Neglect." *New York Times* (July 19): A21.

Fisher, George. 2003. *Plea Bargaining's Triumph: A History of Plea Bargaining in America.* Palo Alto, CA: Stanford University Press.

Fiss, Owen. 1984. "Against Settlement." *Yale Law Review* 93: 1073–1090.

_____. 2003. *The Law as It Could Be.* New York: New York University Press.

_____. 2007. "The Fragility of Law." *Yale Law Review* (Summer): 39–42.

Fitzpatrick, Peter. 2008. *Law as Resistance: Modernism, Imperialism, Legalism.* Burlington, VT: Ashgate.

Fixico, Donald L. 2008. *American Indians in the Modern World.* Lanham, MD: AltaMira Press.

Flaherty, Julie. 1999. "14-Hour Days? Some Lawyers Say 'No.' " *New York Times* (October 6): G1.

Flavin, Jeanne. 2008. *Our Bodies, Our Crimes: The Policing of Women's Reproduction in America.* New York: New York University Press.

Fleming, Macklin. 1997. *Lawyers, Money, and Success: The Consequences of Dollar Obsession.* Westport, CT: Greenwood.

Fleury-Steiner, Benjamin. 2002. "Narratives of the Death Sentence: Toward a Theory of Legal Narrativity." *Law & Society Review* 36: 549–576.

Flood, John. 1991. "Doing Business: The Management of Uncertainty in Lawyers' Work." *Law & Society Review* 25: 41–71.

_____. 1994. "Shark Tanks, Sweatshops, and the Lawyer as Hero? Fact as Fiction." *Journal of Law and Society* 21: 396–405.

Flynn, Kevin. 2002. "Police Ask to Change the Rules and Ease Restrictions on Political Investigations." *New York Times* (September 26): A18.

Foblets, Marie-Claire, and Alison Dundee-Renteln, eds. 2009. *Multicultural Jurisprudence: Comparative Perspectives on the Cultural Defense.* Portland, OR: Hart Publishing Co.

Foderaro, Lisa W. 2009. "Naming Children for Nazis Puts Spotlight on the Father." *New York Times* (January 20): A27.

Fogg-Davis, Hawley. 2002. *The Ethics of Transracial Adoption.* Ithaca, NY: Cornell University Press.

Fontana, David. 2006. "American Law School Meets the World." *Chronicle of Higher Education* (May 26): B10–B11.

Footlick, Jerrold. 1977. "Too Much Law?" *Newsweek* (January 10): 42–47.

_____. 1978. "Lawyers on Trial." *Newsweek* (December 11): 98–100.

Forsyth, Miranda. 2007. "A Typology of Relationships Between State and Non-State Justice Systems." *Journal of Legal Pluralism* 56: 67–108.

Foster, D. H., D. Sandler, and D. M. Davis. 1987. "Detention, Torture, and the Criminal Justice Process in South Africa." *International Journal of the Sociology of Law* 15: 105–120.

Foster, Hamar, Benjamin L. Berger, and A. R. Buck, eds. 2008. *The Grand Experiment: Law & Legal Culture in British Settler Societies.* Vancouver and Toronto: UBC Press.

Foucault, Michel. 1977. *Discipline and Punish: The Birth of the Prison.* New York: Vintage.

Fox, Renee C., and Judith P. Swazey. 2008. *Observing Bioethics.* New York: Oxford University Press.

Francioni, Francesco, ed. 2001. *Environment, Human Rights, and International Trade.* Portland, OR: Hart.

Franck, Thomas M. 2000. *The Empowered Self Law and Society in the Age of Individualism.* New York: Oxford University Press.

Frank, David John, Tara Hardinge, and Kassia Wosick-Correa. 2009. "The Global Dimensions of Rape-Law Reform: A Cross-National Study of Policy Outcomes." *American Sociological Review* 74: 272–290.

Frank, Jerome. 1930. *Law and the Modern Mind.* Garden City, NY: Anchor.

_____. 1949. *Courts on Trial.* Princeton, NJ: Princeton University Press.

Frank, Nancy, and Michael Lombness. 1988. *Controlling Corporate Illegality.* Cincinnati, OH: Anderson.

Franke, Ann H. 1998. "The Message From the Supreme Court: Clarify Sexual-Harassment Policies." *Chronicle of Higher Education* (July 17): B6–B7.

Frankford, David M. 1995. "Social Structure of Right and Wrong: Normativity Without Agents." *Law and Social Inquiry* 20: 787–828.

Free, Marvin D., Jr. 2003. *Racial Issues in Criminal Justice: The Case of African Americans.* Westport, CT: Praeger.

Freedman, Jonathan. 1975. "Running the Red." *New York* (November 17): 117–119.

Freeland, Richard. 1997. "Islamic Law: An Introduction." *New Law Journal* (June 13): 893–896.

French, Jan Hoffman. 2009. *Legalizing Identities: Becoming Black or Indian in Brazil's Northeast.* Chapel Hill: University of North Carolina Press.

Fried, Charles. 2004. *Saying What the Law Is.* Cambridge, MA: Harvard University Press.

Fried, Joseph P. 1999. "Gun Marketing Is Issue in Trial Against Makers." *New York Times* (January 6): A1.

Friedman, Barry. 2009. "Benched." *The New Republic* (September 23): 7–9.

_____. 2010. *The Will of the People: How Public Opinion Has Influenced the Supreme Court and Shaped the Meaning of the Constitution.* New York: Farrar, Straus and Giroux.

Friedman, David D. 2000. *Law's Order: What Economics Has to Do With Law and Why It Matters.* Princeton, NJ: Princeton University Press.

Friedman, Lawrence M. [1973; 1986] 2005. *A History of American Law.* New York: Simon & Schuster.

_____. 1975. *The Legal System.* New York: Russell Sage.

_____. 1977. *Law and Society: An Introduction.* Englewood Cliffs, NJ: Prentice Hall.

_____. 1984. "Two Faces of Law." *Wisconsin Law Review* 1984: 13–34.

_____. 1985. *Total Justice.* New York: Russell Sage.

_____. 1986. "The Law and Society Movement." *Stanford Law Review* 38: 763–780.

_____. 1990. *The Republic of Choice: Law, Authority, and Culture.* Cambridge, MA: Harvard University Press.

_____. 1992. "I Hear a Cacophony: Herzog and *The Republic of Choice.*" *Law & Social Inquiry* 17: 159–166.

_____. 1993. *Crime and Punishment in American History.* New York: Basic Books.

_____. 1996a. "Borders: On the Emerging Sociology of Transnational Law." *Stanford Journal of International Law* 32: 65–90.

_____. 1996b. "Are We a Litigious People?" Pp. 53–78, in L. M. Friedman and H. N. Scheiber, eds. *Legal Culture and the Legal Profession.* Boulder, CO: Westview Press.

_____. 1997. "The Concept of Legal Culture: A Reply." Pp. 33–40, in David Nelken, ed. *Comparing Legal Cultures.* Aldershot, UK: Dartmouth.

_____. 1998a. *American Law: An Introduction,* 2nd ed. New York: W. W. Norton.

_____. 1998b. "Law Reviews and Legal Scholarship: Some Comments." *Denver University Law Review* 75: 661–668.

_____. 2002. *American Law in the 20th Century.* New Haven, CT: Yale University Press.

_____. 2004. *Private Lives: Families, Individuals, and the Law.* Cambridge, MA: Harvard University Press.

_____. 2007a. *Guarding Life's Dark Secrets: Legal and Social Controls over Reputation, Propriety, and Privacy.* Stanford, CA: Stanford University Press.

_____. 2007b. "Law and Society Association, The." Pp. 922–924, in David S. Clark, ed. *Encyclopedia of Law & Society.* Los Angeles: Sage.

_____. 2009. *Dead Hands: A Social History of Wills, Trusts, and Inheritance Law.* Stanford, CA: Stanford University Press.

Friedman, Lawrence M., and Rogelio Perez-Perdomo, eds. 2003. *Legal Cultures in the Age of Globalization: Latin America and Latin Europe.* Palo Alto, CA: Stanford University Press.

Friedman, Lawrence M., Rogelio Perez-Perdomo, and Manuel A. Gomez, eds. 2011. *Law in Many Societies: A Reader.* Stanford, CA: Stanford University Press.

Friedman, Lawrence M., and Harry Scheiber. 1996. *Legal Culture and the Legal Profession.* Boulder, CO: Westview Press.

Friedrich, Carl J. 1963. *The Philosophy of Law in Historical Perspective.* 2nd ed. Chicago: University of Chicago Press.

Friedrichs, David O. 1979. "The Law and the Legitimacy Crisis: A Critical Issue for Criminal Justice." Pp. 290–311, in R. G. Iacovetta and Dae H. Chang, eds. *Critical Issues in Criminal Justice.* Durham, NC: Carolina Academic Press.

_____. 1980. "The Legitimacy Crisis in the United States: A Conceptual Analysis." *Social Problems* 27: 540–555.

_____. 1981. "The Problem of Reconciling Divergent Perspectives on Urban Crime: Personal Experience, Social Ideology, and Scholarly Research." *Qualitative Sociology* 4: 217–228.

_____. 1986a. "Critical Legal Studies and the Critique of Criminal Justice." *Criminal Justice Review* 11: 15–22.

_____. 1986b. "The Concept of Legitimation and the Legal Order: A Response to Hyde's Critique." *Justice Quarterly* 3: 33–50.

_____. 1990a. "Narrative Jurisprudence and Other Heresies: Legal Education at the Margin." *Journal of Legal Education* 40: 3–18.

_____. 1990b. "Law in South Africa and the Legitimacy Crisis." *International Journal of Comparative and Applied Criminal Justice* 14: 189–199.

_____. 2004. *Trusted Criminals: White Collar Crime in Contemporary Society*, 2nd ed. Belmont, CA: ITP/ Wadsworth.

Friedrichs, Natasha I. 2002. "Abortion Protesting." *Georgetown Journal of Gender and the Law* 2: 291–306.

Fritsch, Jane, and David Rohde. 2001. "Legal Help Often Fails New York's Poor." *New York Times* (April 8): A1.

Fritsvold, Erik D. 2009. "Under the Law: Legal Consciousness and Radical Environmental Activism." *Law & Social Inquiry* 34: 799–824.

Frost, Natasha, Joshua D. Freilich, and Todd R. Clear. 2010. *Contemporary Issues in Criminal Justice Policy.* Belmont, CA: Wadsworth.

Fuess, Harald. 2004. *Divorce in Japan: Family, Gender, and the State, 1600–2000.* Stanford, CA: Stanford University Press.

Fujiwara, Lynn. 2008. *Mothers Without Citizenship: Asian Immigrant Families and the Consequences of Welfare Reform.* Minneapolis: University of Minnesota Press.

Fuller, Lon L. 1940. *The Law in Quest of Itself.* Boston: Beacon Press.

_____. 1969. *The Morality of Law.* New Haven, CT: Yale University Press.

_____. 1981. *The Principles of Social Order.* Durham, NC: Duke University Press.

Fusaro, Peter C., and Ross Miller. 2002. *What Went Wrong at Enron.* New York: John Wiley & Sons.

Gagarella, Roberto, Pilar Domingo, and Theunis Roux. 2006. *Courts and Social Transformation in New Democracies: An International Voice for the Poor.* Burlington, VT: Ashgate.

Gagne, Patricia. 1998. *Battered Women's Justice: The Movement for Clemency and the Politics of Self-Defense.* New York: Twayne Publishers.

Gajda, Amy. 2009. *The Trials of Academe: The New Era of Campus Litigation.* Cambridge, MA: Harvard University Press.

Galanter, Marc. 1974. "Why the Haves Come Out Ahead: Speculations on the Limits of Legal Change." *Law & Society Review* 9: 95–160.

_____. 2005. *Lowering the Bar: Lawyer Jokes and Legal Culture.* Madison, WI: University of Wisconsin Press.

_____. 2006. "In the Winter of Our Discontent: Law, Anti-Law, and Social Science." Pp. 1–15, in John Hagan, ed. *Annual Review of Law and Social Science.* Palo Alto, CA: Annual Reviews.

Galanter, Marc, and Thomas M. Palay. 1991. *Tournament of Lawyers: The Transformation of the Big Law Firms.* Chicago: University of Chicago Press.

Gall, Carlotta. 2003. "Pakistani Legislators Approve Islamic Law for Province." *New York Times* (June 3): A3.

Garcia, Ignacio M. 2008. *White but Not Equal: Mexican Americans, Jury Discrimination and the Supreme Court.* Tucson: University of Arizona Press.

Garland, David, ed. 2001. *Mass Imprisonment: Social Causes and Consequences.* Thousand Oaks, CA: Sage.

Garrow, Carrie E., and Sarah Deer. 2004. *Tribal Criminal Law and Procedure.* Blue Ridge Summit, PA: Altamira.

Garth, Bryant. 2007. "American Bar Foundation." Pp. 58–59, in David S. Clark, ed. *Encyclopedia of Law & Society.* Los Angeles: Sage.

Garth, Bryant, and Austin Sarat, eds. 1998a. *Justice and Power in Sociolegal Studies.* Chicago: Northwestern University Press,

_____. 1998b. *How Does Law Matter?* Chicago: Northwestern University Press.

Garth, Bryant, and Joyce Sterling. 1998. "From Legal Realism to Law & Society: Reshaping Law for the Last Stages of the Social Activist Stage." *Law & Society Review* 32: 409–472.

Gascon, George. 2008. "The Laws Cops Can't Enforce." *New York Times* (July 31): Op-Ed.

Gates, Henry Louis, Jr. 2010. "Ending the Slavery Blame-Game." *New York Times* (April 23): Op-Ed Page.

Gatrell, V.A.C., Bruce Lenham, and Geoffrey Parker. 1980. *Crime and the Law: The Social History of Crime in Western Europe Since 1500.* London: Europa.

Gaubatz, Kathlyn Taylor. 1995. *Crime in the Public Mind.* Ann Arbor: University of Michigan Press.

Gawande, Atul. 2009. "Testing, Testing." *The New Yorker* (December 14): 34–41.

Gaylin, Willard. 1974. *Partial Justice: A Study of Bias in Sentencing.* New York: Vintage.

Gentithes, Michael. 2009. "In Defense of Stare Decisis." *Willamette Law Review* 45: 799–822.

Geoghegan, Thomas. 2007. *See You in Court: How the Right Made America a Lawsuit Nation.* New York: The New Press.

George, Robert P. 1999. *In Defense of Natural Law.* New York: Oxford University Press.

Gerety, Tom. 2005. "The War Difference: Law and Morality – Counter-Terrorism." *University of Cincinnati Law Review* 74: 147–165.

Gerhardt, M. J. 2008. *The Power of Precedent.* New York: Oxford University Press.

Gerstenfeld, Phyllis B. 2011. *Hate Crimes.* Los Angeles: Sage.

Gessner, Volkmar. 2007. "Culture, Global legal." Pp. 367–369, in David S. Clark, ed. *Encyclopedia of Law and Society.* Los Angeles: Sage.

Gest, Ted. 2001. *Crime and Politics: Big Government's Erratic Campaign for Law and Order.* New York: Oxford University Press.

Gewirtz, Paul, and Chad Golder. 2005. "So Who Are the Activists?" *New York Times* (July 6): Op-Ed.

Gibbs, Jack P. 1989. *Control: Sociology's Central Notion.* Champaign: University of Illinois Press.

Gibbs, Jewelle Taylor. 1996. *Race and Justice: Rodney King and O. J. Simpson in a House Divided.* San Francisco: Jossey-Bass.

Gibbs, Nancy. 2007. "The Polygamy Paradox." *Time* (October 1): 48–50.

Gibney, Mark, and Sigrun Skogly, ed. 2010. *Universal Human Rights and Extraterritorial Obligations.* Philadelphia: University of Pennsylvania Press.

Gibraltar, Jonathan. 2008. "The Wrong Idea on the Drinking Problem." *Inside Higher Ed* (September 11).

Gibson, James L. 1989. "Understandings of Justice: Institutional Legitimacy, Procedural Justice, and Political Tolerance." *Law & Society Review* 25: 469–496.

———. 1991. "Institutional Legitimacy, Procedural Justice, and Compliance With Supreme Court Decisions: A Question of Causality." *Law & Society Review* 25: 631–635.

———. 2004. "Truth, Reconciliation, and the Creation of a Human Rights Culture in South Africa." *Law & Society Review* 38: 5–40.

Gibson, James L., and Amanda Gouws. 1997. "Support for the Rule of Law in the Emerging South African Democracy." *International Social Science Journal* 152: 173–193.

Gies, Lieve. 2008. *Law and the Media: The Future of an Uneasy Relationship.* New York: Routledge-Cavendish.

Giles, Robert, and Robert W. Snyder, eds. 1999. *Governing the Courts: Free Press, Fair Trials, and Journalistic Performance.* New Brunswick, NJ: Transaction.

Gillespie, Cynthia K. 1989. *Justifiable Homicide: Battered Women, Self-Defense, and the Law.* Columbus: Ohio State University Press.

Gillespie, John. 2008. "Localizing Global Rules: Public Participation in Lawmaking in Vietnam." *Law & Social Inquiry* 33: 673–707.

Gillespie, Nick. 2009. "Paying With Our Sins." *New York Times* (May 17): Week 14.

Gillespie, Tarleton. 2007. *Wired Shut: Copyright and the Shape of Digital Culture.* Cambridge and London: MIT Press.

Gilligan, Carol. 1982. *In a Different Voice.* Cambridge, MA: Harvard University Press.

Gitlin, Todd. 1987. *The Sixties.' Years of Hope, Days of Rage.* New York: Bantam.

Glaberson, William. 1998a. "A Law School Where Jesus Is the Ultimate Case Study." *New York Times* (November 25): A1.

———. 1998b. "In a Judicial 'What If,' Indians Revisit a Case." *New York Times* (October 26): A12.

———. 2000a. "Legal Shortcuts Run Into Some Dead Ends." *New York Times* (October 8): 4/4.

———. 2000b. "The Legal Profession Smells a Rat." *New York Times* (October 22): 4/5.

———. 2001a. "Juries, Their Powers Under Siege, Find Their Role Is Being Eroded." *New York Times* (March 2): A1.

———. 2001 b. "Dispute Over Faxed Ads Draws Wide Scrutiny After $12 Million Award." *New York Times* (July 22): A18,

———. 2003. "Using the Gavel to Strike at Terror." *New York Times* (September 14): A35.

———. 2004. "Grand Jury Urges Overhaul of Legal Guardianship System." *New York Times* (March 3): B1.

———. 2006. "In Tiny Courts of New York, Abuses of Law and Power." *New York Times* (September 25): A1.

———. 2008. "Blow to Bush, Judges Orders Guantanamo Detainees Freed." *New York Times* (October 8): A1.

———. 2010. "Court Rules That Suit on Public Defender System Can Proceed." *New York Times* (May 7): A20.

Glater, Jonathan D. 2001a. "Harvard Law Tries to Increase Appeal." *New York Times* (April 16): A12.

———. 2001b. "Law Firms Are Slow in Promoting Minority Lawyers to Partner Roles." *New York Times* (August 7): A1.

———. 2003a. "Adultery May Be a Sin, But It's a Crime No More." *New York Times* (April 17): A16.

———. 2003b. "Pressure Increases for Tighter Limits on Injury Lawsuits." *New York Times* (May 28): A1.

———. 2003c. "Bar Association in a Shift on Disclosure." *New York Times* (August 13): C4.

———. 2004. "Study Disputes View of Costly Surge in Class-Action Suits." *New York Times* (January 14): C1.

———. 2005. "Harvard Law, Hoping Students Will Consider Public Services, Offers Tuition Break." *New York Times* (March 18): A14.

———. 2006a. "Opening Arguments, Endlessly." *New York Times* (October 7): C6.

———. 2006b. "Straight 'A' Student: Good Luck Making Partner." *New York Times* (December 3): Week 3.

———. 2007. "Young Lawyers Sue, and Little Changes." *New York Times* (February 25): Business 1.

———. 2009a. "Billable Hours Giving Ground at Law Firms." *New York Times* (January 30): A1.

———. 2009b. "Amateur Hour in Court." *New York Times* (April 10): B1.

———. 2009c. "Aspiring Lawyer Finds Debt Is Bigger Hurdle Than Bar Exam." *New York Times* (July 2): A1.

———. 2009d. "Again, Deb Disqualifies Applicant from the Bar." *New York Times* (November 27): B3.

Gleeson, Shannon. 2009. "From Rights to Claims: The Role of Civil Society in Making Rights Real for Vulnerable Workers." *Law & Society Review* 43: 669–700.

Glendon, Mary Ann. 1991. *Rights Talk: The Impoverishment of Political Discourse.* New York: Free Press.

———. 1994. A *Nation Under Lawyers: How the Crisis in the Legal Profession Is Transforming American Society.* New York: Farrar, Straus and Giroux.

Glenn, David. 2008a. "Our Hidden Prejudices, on Trial." *Chronicle of Higher Education Review* (April 25): B12–B14.

———. 2008b. "An Appeal for Transparency Muddies the Legal Waters." *Chronicle of Higher Education Review* (September 19): B14–B16.

———. 2009. "'Torture Memos' vs. Academic Freedom." *Chronicle of Higher Education* (March 20): B11–12.

Glenn, H. Patrick. 2003. "A Transnational Concept of Law." Pp. 839–862, in Peter Cane and Mark Tushnet, eds. *The Oxford Handbook of Legal Studies.* Oxford, UK: Oxford University Press.

———. 2005. *On Common Laws.* Oxford: Oxford University Press.

Goddard, Michael. 2009. *Substantial Justice: An Anthropology of Village Courts in Papua New Guinea.* Herndon, VA: Berghahn Books.

Goh, Bee Chen. 2002. *Law Without Lawyers, Justice Without Courts.* Surrey, UK: Ashgate.

Goldberg, David Theo, Michael Musheno, and Lisa C. Bower, eds. 2001. *Between Law and Culture: Relocating Legal Studies.* Minneapolis: University of Minnesota Press.

Goldberg, Stephanie. 1992, "The Law, a New Theory Holds, Has a White Voice." *New York Times* (July 17): A23.

Goldberg, Steven. 1994. *Culture Clash: Law and Science in America.* New York: New York University Press.

———. 2000. "Bringing the Practice to the Classroom: An Approach to the Professionalism Problem." *Journal of Legal Education* 50: 414–430.

Goldberg, Victor. 2006. *Framing Contract Law: An Economic Perspective.* Cambridge, MA: Harvard University Press.

Goldberg-Ambrose, Carole. 1994. "Of Native Americans and Tribal Members: The Impact of Law on Indian Group Life." *Law & Society Review* 28: 1123–1143.

Golden, Tim, and Don Van Natta, Jr. 2004. "U.S. Said to Overstate Value of Guantanamo Detainees." *New York Times* (June 21): A1.

Golder, Ben and Peter Fitzpatrick. 2009. *Foucault's Law.* New York: Routledge.

Goldfarb, Ronald. 1998. *TV or Not TV: Television, Justice, and the Courts.* New York: New York University Press.

Golding, Martin P., ed. 1966. *The Nature of Law: Readings in Legal Philosophy.* New York: Random House.

———. 1975. *Philosophy of Law.* Englewood Cliffs, NJ: Prentice Hall.

———. 1986. "Jurisprudence and Legal Philosophy in Twentieth Century America: Major Trends and Developments." *Journal of Legal Education* 36: 441–4180.

Goldman, David B. 2007. *Globalisation and the Western Legal Tradition: Recurring Patterns of Law and Authority.* New York: Cambridge University Press.

Goldsmith, Andrew, and James Sheptycki, eds. 2007. *Crafting Transnational Policing: Police Capacity Building and Global Policing Reform.* Oxford, UK: Hart Publishing.

Goldsmith, Jack L. 2007. *The Terror Presidency: Law and Judgment Inside the Bush Administration.* New York: W. W. Norton.

Goldstein, Evan R. 2008. "The New Paternalism." *Chronicle of Higher Education Review* (May 9): B8–B11.

Golub, Mark. 2005. "*Plessy* as 'Passing': Judicial Responses to Ambiguously Raced Bodies in *Plessy v. Ferguson.*" *Law & Society Review* 39: 563–600.

Goluboff, Risa L. 2007. *The Lost Promise of Civil Rights.* Cambridge, MA: Harvard University Press.

Gomez, Laura E. 2007. *Manifest Destinies: The Making of the Mexican-American Race.* New York: New York University Press.

Goodale, Mark. 2008. *Dilemmas of Modernity: Bolivian Encounters with Law and Liberalism.* Stanford, CA: Stanford University Press.

Goodale, Mark, ed. 2009. *Human Rights: An Anthropological Reader.* Malden, MA: Wiley-Blackwell.

Goodale, Mark, and Sally Engle Merry, eds. 2007. *The Practice of Human Rights: Tracking Law Between the Global and the Local.* New York: Cambridge University Press.

Goodale, Mark, and Elizabeth Mertz. 2007. "Anthropology of Law." Pp. 68–75, in David S. Clark, ed. *Encyclopedia of Law & Society.* Los Angeles: Sage.

Goode, Erich. 2005. *Deviant Behavior;* 7th ed. Upper Saddle River, NJ: Prentice Hall.

———. 2008. *Deviant Behavior;* 8th ed. Upper Saddle River, NJ: Pearson/Prentice Hall.

Goodman, Maxine D. 2008. "Slipping Through the Gate: Trusting *Daubert* and Trial Procedures to Reveal the 'Pseudo-Historian' Expert Witness and to Enable the Reliable Historian Expert Witness – Troubling Lessons from Holocaust-Related Trials." *Baylor Law Review* 60: 824–879.

Goodman, Robert. 1996. *The Luck Business: The Devastating Consequences and Broken Promises of America's Gambling Explosion.* New York: Free Press.

Goodnough, Abby. 2009. "Marijuana Licensing Fails to Chase the Shadows." *New York Times* (October 10): A12.

Goodrich, Peter. 2008. "Inns of Court." Pp. 588–589, in Peter Cane and J. Conaghan, eds. *The New Oxford Companion to Law.* Oxford, UK: Oxford University Press.

———. 2009. "Intellection and Indiscipline." *Journal of Law and Society* 36: 460–480.

Goold, Benjamin J. 2004. *CCTV and Policing: Public Area Surveillance and Police Practices in Britain.* New York: Oxford University Press.

Gordon, Diane. 1994. *The Return of the Dangerous Classes: Drug Prohibition and Policy Politics.* New York: W. W. Norton.

Gordon, Robert W. 1985. "Letter." *Journal of Legal Education* 35: 1–9, 13–16.

———. 2002. "The Legal Profession." Pp. 287–336, in Austin Sarat, Bryant Garth, and Robert A. Kagan, eds. *Looking Back at Law's Century.* Ithaca, NY: Cornell University Press.

Gorman, Elizabeth H. 2005. "Gender Stereotypes, Same-Gender Preferences, and Organizational Variation in the Hiring of Women: Evidence from Law Firms." *American Sociological Review* 70: 702–728.

Gorman, Elizabeth H., and Fiona Kay. 2010. "Racial Minority Representation in Large U.S. Law Firms." *Studies in Law, Politics, and Sociology* 52: 211–238.

Gottfredson, Michael, and Michael Hindelang. 1979. "A Study of *The Behavior of Law.*" *American. Sociological Review* 44: 3–18.

Gottschalk, Marie. 2009. "The Long Reach of the Carceral State: The Politics of Crime, Mass Imprisonment, and Penal Reform in the United States and Abroad." *Law & Social Inquiry* 34: 439–472.

Gould, Jon B. 2001. "The Precedent That Wasn't: College Hate Speech Codes and the Two Faces of Legal Compliance." *Law & Society Review* 25: 345–392.

Gouldner, Alvin W. 1966. *Enter Plato.* Part II. New York: Harper Torchbooks.

Graber, Mark. 2006. *Dred Scott and the Problem of Constitutional Evil.* Cambridge: Cambridge University Press.

Graham, Hugh David, and Ted Robert Gurr-. 1969. *Violence in America: Historical and Comparative Perspectives.* New York: New American Library.

Grana, Sheryl J. 2010. *Women and Justice;* 2nd ed. Lanham, MD: Rowman and Littlefield.

Granfield, Robert. 1992. *Making Elite Lawyers: Visions of Law at Harvard and Beyond.* New York: Routledge, Chapman & Hall.

Granfield, Robert. 2007. "The Meaning of Pro Bono: Institutional Variations in Professional Obligations among Lawyers." *Law & Society Review* 41: 113–146.

Grant, Heath B. 2006. *Building a Culture of Lawfulness: Law Enforcement, Legal Reasoning and Delinquency among Mexican Youth.* New York: LFB Scholarly Publishing.

Greenawalt, K. 2008. *Religion and the Constitution: Volume 2: Establishment and Fairness*. Princeton, NJ: Princeton University Press.

Greenberg, David F. 1983. "Donald Black's Sociology of Law: A Critique." *Law & Society Review* 17: 337–368.

Greenberg, S. 1987. *Legitimating the Illegitimate*. Berkeley: University of California Press.

Greene, Elizabeth. 2000. "David Post: Freeing Cyberspace From the Rule of Law." *Chronicle of Higher Education* (October 20): A14.

Greenhouse, Carol J. 1988. "Courting Difference: Issues of Interpretation and Comparison in the Study of Legal Ideologies." *Law & Society Review* 22: 687–707.

Greenhouse, Linda. 1999a. "47% in Poll View Legal System as Unfair to Poor and Minorities." *New York Times* (February 24): A12.

———. 1999b. "States Are Given New Legal Shield by Supreme Court." *New York Times* (June 24): A1.

———. 1999c. "Cases Give Court Chances to Define Church and State." *New York Times* (September 19): A1.

———. 2000a. "Supreme Court Shields States From Lawsuits on Age Bias." *New York Times* (January 12): A1.

———. 2000b. "Weighing Restrictions on Legal Aid for Poor." *New York Times* (April 4): A20.

———. 2000c. "Women Lose Right to Sue Attackers in Federal Court." *New York limes* (May 16): A1.

———. 2000d. "Justices Reaffirm Miranda Rule, 7–2; A Part of Culture." *New York Times* (June 27): A1.

———. 2001a. "Divided Justices Back Full Arrests on Minor Charges." *New York Times* (April 25): A1.

———. 200lb. "Justices Set Aside Ruling Against Prayer Organizers." *New York Times* (October 10): A13.

———. 2001c. "Justices Weigh Lawyers' Ethical Obligations." *New York Times* (November 6): A14.

———. 2002a. "'Virtual' Child Pornography Ban Overturned." *New York Times* (April 17): A1.

———. 2002b. "Citing 'National Consensus,' Justices Bar Death Penalty for Retarded Defendants." *New York Times* (June 21): A1.

———. 2002c. "Justices Say Death Penalty Is Up to Juries, Not Judges." *New York Times* (June 25): A1.

———. 2002d. "States' Listings of Sex Offenders Raise a Tangle of Legal Issues." *New York Times* (November 4): A12.

———. 2003a. "Justices, 6–3, Rule Workers Can Sue States Over Leave." *New York Times* (May 28): A1.

———. 2003b. "Will the Court Move Right? It Already Has." *New York Times* (June 22): Week 3.

———. 2003c. "Justices Back Affirmative Action by 5 to 4, but Wider Vote Bans a Racial Point System." *New York Times* (June 24): A1.

———. 2003d. "Justices, 6–3, Legalize Gay Sexual Conduct in Sweeping Reversal of Court's '86 Ruling." *New York Times* (June 27): A1.

———. 2003e. "Supreme Court to Consider Case on 'Under God' in Pledge to Flag." *New York Times* (October 15): A1.

———. 2003f. "Post 9/11 Detainee Cases on Supreme Court Docket." *New York Times* (November 3): A7.

———. 2003g. "Justices Resist Religious Study Using Subsidies." *New York Times* (December 3): A1.

———. 2003h. "Justices, in a 5-to-4 Decision, Back Campaign Finance Law That Curbs Contributions." *New York Times* (December 11): A11.

———. 2004a. "Court Says States Need Not Finance Divinity Studies." *New York Times* (February 26): A1.

———. 2004b. "Court Hears Case on U.S. Detainees." *New York Times* (April 29): A1.

———. 2004c. "Justices Affirm Legal Rights of 'Enemy Combatants.'" *New York Times* (June 29): A1.

———. 2004d. "8 Justices Block Effort to Excise Phrase in Pledge." *New York Times* (June 15): A1.

———. 2004e. "Justices, in Bitter 5–4 Split, Raise Doubts on Sentencing Guidelines." *New York Times* (June 25): A1.

———. 2004f, "Human Rights Abuses Worldwide Are Held to Fall Under U.S. Courts." *New York Times* (June 30): A21.

———. 2004g. "The Year Rehnquist May Have Lost His Court." *New York Times* (July 5): A1.

———. 2005. "The Supreme Court, 5–4, Forbids Execution in Juvenile Crime." *New York Times* (March 2): A1.

———. 2007. "Precedents Begin Falling for Roberts Court." *New York Times* (June 21): A21.

Greenhouse, Steven. 2003a. "Going for the Look, But Risking Discrimination." *New York Times* (July 13): A12,

———. 2003b. "Overweight, but Ready to Fight." *New York Times* (August 4): B1.

———. 2003c. "Foes of Idle Hands, Amish Seek an Exemption From a Child Labor Law." *New York Times* (October 18): A9.

Greenstein, Robert. 1991. "Relieving Poverty: An Alternative View." *Brookings Review* (Summer): 34–35.

Grey, Thomas C. 1996. "Modern American Legal Thought." *Yale Law Journal* 106: 493–517.

Griffin, James. 2008. *On Human Rights*. New York: Oxford University Press.

Griffiths, Anne. 2009. "Law, Space, and Place: Reframing Comparative Law and Legal Anthropology." *Law & Social Inquiry* 34: 495–507.

Griffiths, John. 1986. "What Is Legal Pluralism?" *Journal of Legal Pluralism* 24: 1–55.

Griffiths, John, Heleen Wyers, and Maurice Adams. 2008. *Euthanasia and Law in Europe*. Portland, OR: Hart Publishing Co.

Griffiths-Baker, Janine. 2002. *Serving Two Masters: Conflicts of Interest in the Modern Law Firm*. Portland, OR: Hart Publishing.

Gromet, Dena M., and John M. Darley. 2009. "Punishment and Beyond: Achieving Justice Through the Satisfaction of Multiple Goals." *Law and Society Review* 43: 1–37.

Gross, Emanuel. 2006. *The Struggle of Democracy Against Terrorism: Lessons from the United States, the United Kingdom, and Israel*. Charlottesville University of Virginia Press.

Gross, Hyman. 1979. *A Theory of Criminal Justice*. New York: Oxford University Press.

Gross, Joseph J. 1991. "Marital Rape: A Crime? A Comparative Law Study of the Laws of the United States and the State of Israel." *International Journal of Comparative and Applied Criminal Justice* 15: 207–216.

Gross, Norman, ed. 2004. *America's Lawyer Presidents: From Law Office to Oval Office*. Evanston, IL: Northwestern University Press.

Gross, Oren, and Fionnuala Ni Aolain. 2006. *Law in Times of Crisis: Emergency Powers in Theory and Practice*. Cambridge: Cambridge University Press.

Guinier, Lani, Michelle Fine, and Jane Balin. 1997. *Becoming Gentlemen: Women, Law School, and Institutional Change*. Boston: Beacon Press.

Gunther, Vanessa Ann. 2006. *Ambiguous Justice: Native Americans and the Law in Southern California, 1848–1890*. East Lansing: Michigan State University Press.

Gurnham, David. 2009. *Memory, Imagination, Justice: Intersections of Law and Literature*. Burlington, VT: Ashgate/Lund Humphries Publishing Co.

Gusfield, Joseph R. 1963. *Symbolic Crusade: Status Politics and the American Temperance Movement*. Urbana: University of Illinois Press.

———. 1996. *Contested Meanings: The Construction of Alcohol Problems*. Madison: University of Wisconsin Press.

Gutmann, Amy. 2003. *Identity in Democracy*. Princeton, NJ: Princeton University Press.

Haack, Susan. 2004. "Truth and Justice, Inquiry and Advocacy, Science and Law." *Ratio Juris* 17: 15–26.

Habermas, Jurgen. 1996. *Between Facts and Norms: Contributions to a Discourse Theory of Law and Democracy*. Cambridge, MA: MIT Press.

Hacker, Andrew. 2003. "Saved?" *New York Review of Books* (August 14): 22–24.

Hackney, James R., Jr. 2007. *Under Cover of Science: American Legal-Economic Theory and the Quest for Objectivity*. Durham, NC: Duke University Press.

Hafner-Burton, E., K. Tsutsui, and J. W. Meyer. 2008. "International Human Rights Law and the Politics of Legitimation: Repressive States and Human Rights Treaties." *International Sociology* 23: 115–141.

Hagan, John. 2010. *Who Are the Criminals?* Princeton, NJ: Princeton University Press.

Hagan, John, and Fiona Kay. 1995. *Gender in Practice: A Study of Lawyers' Lives*. New York: Oxford University Press.

———. 2007. "Even Lawyers Get the Blues: Gender, Depression, and Job Satisfaction in Legal Practice." *Law & Society Review* 41: 51–78.

Haines, Fiona, Nancy Reichman, and Colin Scott. 2008. "Problematizing Legitimacy and Authority in *Law & Policy*." *Law & Policy Review* 30: 1–11.

Haire, Susan B., Donald R. Songer, and Stefanie A. Lindquist. 2003. "Appellate Court Supervision in the Federal Judiciary: A Hierarchical Perspective." *Law & Society Review* 37: 143–168.

Hajjar, Lisa. 1997. "Cause Lawyering in Transnational Perspective: National Conflict and Human Rights in Israel/Palestine." *Law & Society Review* 31: 473–504.

———. 2004. "Religion, State Power, and Domestic Violence in Muslim Societies: A Framework for Comparative Analysis." *Law & Social Inquiry* 29: 1–38.

Hale, Dame Brenda. 2003. "A Pretty Pass: When Is There a Right to Die?" *Common Law World Review* 32: 1–14.

Haleem, Muhammad Abdel, Adel Omar Sharif, and Kate Daniels. 2003. *Criminal Justice in Islam: Judicial Procedure in the Sharia*. London: St. Martin's Press.

Hall, Ann C., and Mardia J. Bishop, eds. 2007. *Pop-Porn: Pornography in American Culture*. Westport, CT: Praeger.

Hall, Kermit L. 1989. *The Magic Mirror: Law in American History*. New York: Oxford University Press.

Hallaq, Wael B. 2009. *Sharii'a: Theory, Practice, Transformations*. New York: Cambridge University Press.

Halliday, Simon, and Patrick Schmidt, eds. 2009. *Conducting Law and Society Research: Reflections on Methods and Practices*. New York: Cambridge University Press.

Halliday, Terence C., Lucien Karpik, and Malcolm M. Feeley, eds. 2007. *Fighting for Political Freedom: Comparative Studies of the Legal Complex and Political Liberalism*. Portland, OR: Hart Publishing.

Halliday, Terence C., Joachim Savelsberg, Kim Lane Scheppele, and Robert Kidder. 2002. "The ASA Sociology of Law Section: Reflections on the First Decade." *Amici* 9: 1–10,

Halpin, Andrew, and Volker Roeben, eds. 2009. *Theorising the Global Legal Order*. Oxford: Hart Publishers.

Haltom, William, and Michael McCann. 2004. *Distorting the Law: Politics, Media, and the Litigation Crisis*. Chicago: University of Chicago Press.

Hamburger, Philip. 2002. *Separation of Church and State*. Cambridge, MA: Harvard University Press.

———. 2008. *Law and Judicial Duty*. Cambridge, MA: Harvard University Press.

Hamill, Sean D. 2009. "Students Sue Prosecutor in Cellphone Photos Case." *New York Times* (March 26): A21.

Hamilton, V. Lee, and Joseph Sanders. 1992. *Everyday Justice: Responsibility and the Individual in Japan and the United States*. New Haven, CT: Yale University Press.

Hanafin, Patrick, Adam Geary, and Joe Brooker, eds. 2004. *Law and Literature*. Oxford, UK: Blackwell.

Handler, Joel F. 1978. *Social Movements and the Legal System: A Theory of Law Reform and Social Change*. New York: Academic Press.

———. 1992. "Postmodernism, Protest, and the New Social Movements." *Law & Society Review* 26: 697–732.

Handler, Joel, and Yeheskel Hasenfeld. 1997. *We the Poor People: Work, Poverty, and Welfare*. New Haven, CT: Yale University Press.

———. 2007. *Blame Welfare, Ignore Poverty and Inequality*. Cambridge: Cambridge University Press.

Haney-Lopez, Ian F. 2003. *Racism on Trial: The Chicano Fight for Justice*. Cambridge, MA: Harvard University Press.

Hans, Valerie P. 2000. *Business on Trial: The Civil Jury and Corporate Responsibility*. New Haven, CT: Yale University Press.

———. "Science on Trial." *Cornell Law Forum* 34: 4–10.

Hans, Valerie P., and Neil Vidmar. 2008. "The Verdict on Juries." *Judicature* (March-April): 226–230.

Hansen, Mark. 2009. "A Reluctant Rebellion." *ABA Journal* (June): 54–59.

Hansford, Thomas G., and James F. Spriggs II. 2006. *The Politics of Precedent on the U. S. Supreme Court*. Princeton, NJ: Princeton University Press.

Hardaway, Robert M. 2003. *No Price Too High: Victimless Crimes and the Ninth Amendment*. Westport, CT: Praeger.

Harding, Alan. 1973. *A Social History of English Law*. Gloucester, MA: Peter Smith.

Harivandri, Zsuleh E. 2010. "Invisible and Involuntary: Female Genital Mutilation as a Basis for Asylum." *Cornell Law Review* 95: 599–626.

Harmon, Amy. 2004. "A Real-Life Debate on Free Expression in a Cyberspace City." *New York Times* (January 15): A1.

Harpwood, Vivienne H. 2007. *Medicine, Malpractice, and Misapprehensions*. New York: Routledge-Cavendish.

Harrington, Christine. 1985. *Shadow Justice: The Ideology and Institutionalization of Alternatives to Courts*. Westport, CT: Greenwood Press.

Harrington, Michael. 1973. *Socialism*. New York: Bantam.

Harris, Brian. 2006. *Injustice, UK: State Trials from Socrates to Nuremberg*. Gloucestershire: Sutton Publishing.

Harris, Douglas C. 2008. *Landing Native Fisheries: Indian Reserves and Fishing Rights in British Columbia, 1849–1925*. Vancouver, BC: UBC Press.

Harris, Paul. 1997. *Black Rage Confronts the Law*. New York: New York University Press.

Harrison, James. 2007. *The Human Rights Impact of the World Trade Organization*. Portland: Hart Publishing.

Hart, H. L. A. 1961. *The Concept of Law*. Oxford, UK: Clarendon Press.

Hartley, Roger. 2002. *Alternative Dispute Resolution in Civil Justice Systems*. New York: LFB Scholarly Publishing.

Hartocollis, Anemona. 2007. "Court Calls a 40% Fee to Lawyers Defensible." *New York Times* (November 19): B3.

Harvard Law Bulletin. 2010a. "Lawyers Without Borders." *Harvard Law Bulletin* (Winter): 8–10.

———. 2010b. "A Conversation with the New Dean." *Harvard Law Bulletin* (Winter): 14–19.

———. 2010c. "The Clinics at a Glance." *Harvard Law Bulletin* (Winter): 31.

Hasnas, John. 1995. "The Myth of the Rule of Law." *Wisconsin Law Review* (1995): 199–234.

Hayden, Cara J. 2009. "Supreme Decisions." *Pitt Magazine* (Spring): 12–15.

Hayner, Priscilla B. 2002. *Unspeakable Truths: Facing the Challenge of Truth Commissions.* New York: Routledge.

Haysom, N., and S. Kahanovitz. 1987. "Courts and the State Emergency." Pp. 187–198, in G. Moss and I. Obery, eds. *South Africa Review 4.* Johannesburg, RSA: Ravan Press.

Hazard, John N. 1990. "Where Are the Peril Points?" *Law and Social Inquiry* 15: 521–534.

He, Baogang, and Hannah Murphy. 2007. "Global Social Justice at the WTO? The Role of NGOs in Constructing Global Social Contracts." *International Affairs* 83: 707–727.

He, Xin. 2005. "Why Do They Not Comply with the Law? Illegality and Semi-Legality among Rural-Urban Migrant Entrepreneurs in Beijing." *Law & Society Review* 39: 527–562.

Heald, Paul J., ed. 1998. *Literature and Legal Problem Solving: Law and Literature as Ethical Discourse.* Durham, NC: Carolina Academic Press.

Hearst, Alice. 2002. "Multiculturalism, Group Rights, and the Adoption Conundrum." *Law & Society Review* 36: 489–505.

Hehir, Aidan. 2008. *Humanitarian Intervention after Kosovo: Iraq, Darfur, and the Record of a Global Civil Society.* London: Palgrave.

Heinz, John P., and Edward O. Laumann. 1982. *Chicago Lawyers: The Social Structure of the Bar.* New York: Russell Sage.

Heinz, John P., Edward O. Laumann, Robert L. Nelson, and Ethan Michelson. 1998. "The Changing Character of Lawyers' Work: Chicago in 1975 and 1995." *Law & Society Review* 32: 751–775.

Heinz, John P., Edward O. Laumann, Robert L. Nelson, and Robert H. Salisbury. 1993. *The Hollow Core: Private Interests in National Policy Making.* Cambridge, MA: Harvard University Press.

Heinzelman, Susan Sage. 2010. "Imaging the Law: The Novel." Pp. 213–240, in A. Sarat, M. Anderson, and C. O. Frank, eds. *Law and the Humanities: An Introduction.* Cambridge: Cambridge University Press.

Hellerstein, William E. 2002. "No Rights of Prisoners." Pp. 71–82, in Herman Schwartz, ed. *The Rehnquist Court.* New York: Hill & Wang.

Hendley, Kathryn. 2009. "Rule of Law, Russian-Style." *Current History* (October): 339–340.

Hendricks, Steve. 2006. *The Unquiet Grave: The FBI and the Struggle for the Soul of Indian Country.* New York: Thunder's Mouth Press.

Henningsen, David Dryden, and Ioana Cionea. 2007. "The Role of Comforting Skill and Professional Competence in the Attorney-Client Relationship." *Journal of Legal Education* 57: 530–538.

Henry, Stuart. 1981. "Decentralized Justice: Private v. Democratic Informality." Pp. 179–191, in S. Henry, ed. *Informal Institutions: Alternative Networks in the Corporate State.* New York: St. Martin's Press.

———. 1983. *Private Justice: Towards Integrated Theorizing in the Sociology of Law.* Boston: Routledge & Kegan Paul.

———. 1985. "Community Justice, Capitalist Society, and Human Agency: The Dialectics of Collective Law in the Cooperative," *Law & Society Review* 19: 303–327.

———. 2007. "Informal Law." Pp. 743–746, in David S. Clark, ed. *Encyclopedia of Law and Society.* Los Angeles: Sage.

Hensler, Deborah R., Nicholas M. Page, Bonita Demby-Moore, Beth Giddens, Jennifer Gross, and Erik K. Moller. 2000. *Class Action Dilemmas: Pursuing Public Goals for Private Gain.* Santa Monica, CA: Rand Institute.

Herbert, Steve. 1996. "Morality in Law Enforcement: Chasing 'Bad Guys' With the Los Angeles Police Department." *Law & Society Review* 30: 799–818.

Herget, James E. 2007. "Jurisprudence of Interest, American." Pp. 866–868, in David S. Clark, ed. *Encyclopedia of Law & Society.* Los Angeles: Sage.

———. 2007. "Realism, American Legal." Pp. 1270–1272, in David S. Clark, ed. *Encyclopedia of Law & Society.* Los Angeles: Sage.

Herman, Shael. 1993. *The Louisiana Civil Code: A European Legacy for the United States.* New Orleans: Louisiana Bar Foundation.

Hermer, Joe, and Alan Hunt. 1996. "Official Graffiti of the Everyday." *Law & Society Review* 30: 455–480.

Hernandez-Truyol, Berta Esperanza, and Stephen J. Powell. 2009. *Just Trade: A New Covenant Linking Trade and Human Rights.* New York: New York University Press.

Hershovitz, Scott, ed. 2006. *Exploring Law's Empire: The Jurisprudence of Ronald Dworkin.* Oxford: Oxford University Press.

Herzog, Don. 1992. "I Hear a Rhapsody: A Reading of *The Republic of Choice*." *Law & Social Inquiry* 17: 147–158.

Heumann, Milton, and Lance Cassak. 2003. *Good Cop, Bad Cop: Racial Profiling and Competing Views of Justice.* New York: Peter Lang.

Heydebrand, Wolf. 1979. "The Technocratic Administration of Justice." Pp. 29–64, in Steven Spitzer, ed. *Research in Law and Society* 2. Greenwich, CT: JAI.

Heyman, Steven J. 2008. *Free Speech & Human Dignity.* New Haven, CT: Yale University Press.

Heymann, Philip B. 2003. *Terrorism, Freedom, and Security: Winning Without War.* Cambridge, MA: MIT Press.

Higginbotham, Leon, Jr. 1978. *In the Matter of Color: Race and the American Legal Process: The Colonial Period.* New York: Oxford University Press.

———. 1996. *Shades of Freedom: Racial Politics and Presumptions of the American Legal Process.* New York: Oxford University Press.

Higgins, Michael. 1998. "Taking the Best Shot." *ABA Journal* 84: 79–81.

Hill, Claire A. 2004. "Law and Economics in the Personal Sphere." *Law and Social Inquiry* 29: 219–260.

Hines, Crystal Nix. 2001. "A Legal Eagle (His Ad Claims)." *New York Times* (November 15): C1.

Hirsch, Susan F. 1998. *Pronouncing and Persevering: Gender and the Discourses of Disputing in an African Islamic Court.* Chicago: University of Chicago Press.

Hirschl, Ran. 2004. *Toward Juristocracy: The Origins and Consequences of Constitutionalism.* Cambridge, MA: Harvard University Press.

Hitt, Jack. 2005. "The Newest Indians." *New York Times Magazine* (August 21): 36–41.

Hoebel, E. Adamson. [1954] 1967. *The Law of Primitive Man.* Cambridge, MA: Harvard University Press.

———. 1960. *The Cheyennes.* New York: Holt, Rinehart & Winston.

Hoff-Wilson, Joan. 1986. *Rights of Passage: The Past and Future of the ERA.* Bloomington: Indiana University Press.

Hoffman, Morris B. 2001. "Review of Life Without Values." *Stanford Law Review* 54: 597–625.

———. 2007. "Free-Market Justice." *New York Times* (January 8): A19.

Hoffman, Morris B., and Stephen J. Morse. 2006. "The Insanity Defense Goes Back on Trial." *New York Times* (July 30): Week 13.

Hoffmann, Stanley. 2003a. "World Governance: Beyond Utopia." *Daedalus* (Winter): 27–35.

———. 2003b. "America Goes Backward." *New York Review of Books* (June 12): 74–91.

Hofrichter, Richard. 1987. *Neighborhood Justice in Capitalist Society: An Expansion of the Informal State.* New York: Greenwood Press.

Holmes, Oliver Wendell, Jr. 1881. *The Common Law.* Boston: Little, Brown.

———. 1897. "The Path of the Law." *Harvard Law Review* 10: 457–478.

Holtzman, Elizabeth. 2006. "The Impeachment of George W. Bush." *The Nation* (January 30): 11–18.

Horney, Julie, and Cassia Spohn. 1991. "Rape Law Reform and Instrumental Change in Six Urban Jurisdictions." *Law & Society Review* 25: 117–153.

Horwitz, Morton J. 1977. *The Transformation of American Law, 1780–1860.* Cambridge, MA: Harvard University Press.

———. 1998. *The Warren Court and the Pursuit of Justice.* New York: Hill & Wang.

Houh, Emily M. S. 2006. "Still, at the Margins." *Law & Society Review* 40: 481–492.

Howard, Philip K. 2009. *Life Without Lawyers: Liberating Americans from Too Much Law.* New York: Norton.

Howard, Robert M., and Jeffrey A. Segal. 2002. "An Original Look at Originalism." *Law & Society Review* 36: 113–137.

Hu, Winnie. 2003. "The Smoking Ban: Clear Air, Murky Economics." *New York Times* (December 28): A1.

Huang, Philip C. C. 2001. *Code, Custom, and Legal Practice in China: The Qing and the Republic Compared.* Stanford, CA: Stanford University Press.

———. 2009. *Chinese Civil Justice, Past and Present.* Lanham, MD: Rowman & Littlefield.

Huber, Gregory A. 2007. *The Craft of Bureaucratic Neutrality: Interests and Influence in Governmental Regulation of Occupational Safety.* New York: Cambridge University Press.

Hull, Kathleen E. 2006. *Same-Sex Marriage: The Cultural Politics of Love and Law.* Cambridge, UK: Cambridge University Press.

Hull, N. E. H., and Peter Charles Hoffer. 2001. Roe v. Wade: *The Abortion Rights Controversy in American History.* Lawrence: University of Kansas Press.

Human Sciences Research Council. 1985. *The South African Society.* Pretoria, RSA: Human Sciences Research Council.

Hund, John. 1988. "Formal Justice and Township Justice." Pp. 203–216, in J. Hund, ed. *Law and Justice in South Africa.* Johannesburg, RSA: Centre for Intergroup Studies.

Hund, John, and M. Kotu-Rammopo. 1983. "Justice in a South African Township: The Sociology of Makgotla." *Comparative and International Law Journal of South Africa* 16: 179–208.

Hunt, Alan. 1993. *Explorations in Law and Society: Toward a Constitutive Theory of Law.* New York: Routledge.

Hunter, Rosemary, ed. 2008. *Rethinking Equality Projects in Law: Feminist Challenges.* Portland, OR: Hart Publishing.

Hurst, James Willard. 1950. *The Growth of American Law.* Boston: Little, Brown.

Huscroft, Grant, and Paul Rishworth, eds. 2002. *Litigating Rights: Perspectives from Domestic and International Law.* Portland, OR: Hart.

Hussain, Nasser. 2003. *The Jurisprudence of Emergency Colonialism and the Rule of Law.* Ann Arbor: University of Michigan Press.

Hutchinson, Allan C., ed. 2000. *It's All in the Game: A Non-Foundationalist Account of Law and Adjudication.* Durham, NC: Duke University Press.

Hutchinson, Allan C. 2009. *The Province of Jurisprudence Democratized.* New York: Oxford University Press.

Hutton, Neil. 1997. "Sentencing in the New South Africa: The Prospects for Reform." *International Journal of the Sociology of Law* 25: 313–335.

Hyde, Alan 1983. "The Concept of Legitimation in the Sociology of Law." *Wisconsin Law Review* 1983: 370–426.

Hyman, Dick. 1977. *It's Against the Law.* Pleasantville, NY: Reader's Digest.

Ignatieff, Michael. 2004. *The Lesser Evil.* Princeton, NJ: Princeton University Press.

Imperato, Andrew J. 2002. "The 'Miserly' Approach to Disability Rights." Pp. 195–212, in Herman Schwartz, ed. *The Rehnquist Court.* New York: Hill & Wang.

Inside Higher Ed. 2010. "The Anti-Amethyst Initiative." *Inside Higher Ed* (April 13).

Institute for Civil Justice. 1997. *Annual Report: 1996–1997.* Santa Monica, CA: Rand.

Irons, Peter. 2005. *War Powers: How the Imperial Presidency Hijacked the Constitution.* New York: Henry Holt & Company.

Ismaili, Karim. 2011. *U.S. Criminal Justice Policy: A Contemporary Reader.* Sudbury, MA: Jones & Bartlett Learning.

Israel, Jerold H., Yale Kamisar, and Wayne R. LaFave. 1993. *Criminal Procedure and the Constitution.* St. Paul, MN: West.

Ivison, Duncan, Paul Patton, and Will Sanders, eds. 2000. *Political Theory and the Rights of Indigenous Peoples.* New York: Cambridge University Press.

Jackson, Emily. 1992. "Catharine MacKinnon and Feminist Jurisprudence: A Critical Appraisal." *Journal of Law and Society* 19: 195–213.

Jackson. John P., Jr. 2001. *Social Scientists for Social Justice: Making the Case Against Segregation.* New York: New York University Press.

Jacob, Herbert. 1992. "The Elusive Shadow of Law." *Law & Society Review* 26: 565–590.

———. 1996. "Courts and Politics in the United States." Pp. 16–80, in H. Jacob, E. Blankenburg, H. M. Kritzer, D. M. Provine, and J. Sanders. *Courts, Law, and Politics in Comparative Perspective.* New Haven, CT: Yale University Press.

Jacobs, David, and Aubrey L. Jackson. 2010. "On the Politics of Imprisonments: A Review of Some Systematic Findings." Pp. 129–150, in J. Hagan, K. L. Scheppele, and T. R. Tyler, eds. *Annual Review of Law and Social Science.* Volume 6. Palo Alto, CA: Annual Reviews.

Jacobs, James B. 1989. *Drunk Driving: An American Dilemma.* Chicago: University of Chicago Press.

———. 2002. *Can Gun Control Work?* New York: Oxford University Press.

Jacobs, James B., and Kimberly Potter. 1998. *Hate Crimes: Criminal Law and Identity Politics.* New York: Oxford University Press.

Jacobs, Meg, William J. Novak, and Jullian E. Zelizer, eds. 2003. *The Democratic Experiment: New Directions in American Political History.* Princeton, NJ: Princeton University Press.

Jacobs, Sean. 2004. "The Unfinished Revolution."*The Nation* (May 17): 23–29.

Jacoby, Susan. 1983. *Wild Justice: The Evolution of Revenge.* New York: Harper & Row.

Jaffa, Harry V. 1994. *Original Intent and the Framers of the Constitution.* Washington, DC: Regnery Gateway.

Jaffer, Jameel, and Amrit Singh, eds. 2007. *Administration of Torture: A Documentary Record from Washington to Abu Ghraib and Beyond.* New York: Columbia University Press.

Jakab, Andras. 2007. "Dilemmas of Legal Education: A Comparative Overview." *Journal of Legal Education* 57: 253–265.

James, Stephen. 2007. *Universal Human Rights: Origins and Developments.* New York: LFB Scholarly Publishing.

Janofsky, Michael. 2001. "A Rare Legal Quest: From Murderer to Lawyer." *New York Times* (December 27): A14.

Jarvis, Robert M., and Paul R. Joseph. 1998. *Prime Time Law: Fictional Television as Legal Narrative.* Durham, NC: Carolina Academic Press.

Jasanoff, Sheila. 1995. *Science at the Bar: Law, Science, and Technology.* Cambridge, MA: Harvard University Press.

_____. 2001. "Judicial Fictions: The Supreme Court's Quest for Good Science." *Society* (May/June): 27–37.

Jaschik, Scott. 2006. "Michigan Votes Down Affirmative Action." *Insider Higher Ed* (November 8).

Jefferson, Thomas. [1781] 1998. *Notes on the State of Virginia.* New York. Viking Penguin.

Jeffery, C. Ray. 1962. "The Legal Profession." Pp, 313–356. in F. James Davis. Henry H. Foster Jr, C. Ray Jeffery, and E. Eugene Davis. *Society and the Law: New Meanings for an Old Profession.* New York: Free Press.

Jencks, Christopher. 1992. *Rethinking Social Policy: Race, Poverty and the Underclass.* Cambridge, MA: Harvard University Press.

Jenkins, Pamela J., and Steve Kroll-Smith. 1996. *Witnessing for Sociology: Sociologists in Court.* Westport, CT: Praeger.

Jenness, Valerie, and Ryken Grattet. 2001. *Making Hate a Crime: From Social Movement Concept to Law Enforcement Practice.* Russell Sage.

Johns, Fleur, and Steven Freeland. 2007. "Teaching International Law Across an Urban Divide: Reflections on an Improvisation." *Journal of Legal Education* 57: 339–361.

Johnson, David T. 2007. "Crime and Punishment in Contemporary Japan." Pp. 371–424, in Michael Tonry, ed. *Crime, Punishment, and Politics in Comparative Perspective.* Chicago: University of Chicago Press.

Johnson, David T., and Franklin E. Zimring. 2009. *The Next Frontier: National Development, Political Change, and the Death Penalty in Asia.* New York: Oxford University Press.

Johnson, Jean. 1997. "Americans' Views on Crime and Law Enforcement." *NIJ Journal* (September): 9–14.

Johnson, Kirk. 2007. "Case Against Polygamist Goes to the Jury in Utah." *New York Times* (September 22): A11.

_____. 2010. "Ruling by Montana Supreme Court Bolsters Physician-Assisted Suicide." *New York Times* (January 1): A17.

Johnson, Simon, and James Kwak. 2010. *13 Bankers: The Wall Street Takeover and the Next Financial Meltdown.* New York: Pantheon Books.

Jones-Brown, Delores, and Erica King-Toler. 2011. "The Significance of Race in Contemporary Urban Policing Policy." Pp. 21–48, in K. Ismaili, ed. *U. S. Criminal Justice Policy.* Pp. 21–48. Sudbury, MA: Jones & Bartlett Learning.

Kades, Eric. 2008. "The 'Middle Ground' Perspective on the Expropriation of Indian Lands." *Law & Social Inquiry* 33: 827–839.

Kagan, Robert. 2004. "A Tougher War for the U.S. Is One of Legitimacy." *New York Times* (January 24): B7.

Kagan, Robert A. 2001. *Adversarial Legalism: The American Way of Law.* Cambridge, MA: Harvard University Press.

_____. 2003. "On Surveying the Whole Legal Forest." *Law & Social Inquiry* 28: 833–872.

Kagan, Robert A., and Lee Axelrad, eds. 2000. *Regulatory Encounters: Multinational Corporations and American Adversarial Legalism.* Berkeley: University of California Press.

Kagan, Robert A., Neil Cunningham, and Dorothy Thornton. 2003. "Explaining Corporate Environmental Performance: How Does Regulation Matter?" *Law & Society Review* 37: 51–90.

Kagan, Robert A., Martin Krygier, and Kenneth Winston, eds. 2002. *Legality and Community: On the Intellectual Legacy of Philip Selznick.* Lanham, MD: Rowman & Littlefield.

Kahlenberg, Richard D. 1992. *Broken Contract: A Memoir of Harvard Law School.* Boston: Faber & Faber.

_____. 1996. *The Remedy: Class, Race, and Affirmative Action.* New York: Basic Books.

Kahn, Jeffrey. 2006. "The Search for the Rule of Law in Russia." *Georgetown Journal of International Law* 37: 353–410.

Kahn, Paul W. 1997. *The Reign of Law:* Marbury v. Madison *and the Construction of America.* New Haven, CT: Yale University Press.

Kairys, David. 1998. *The Politics of Law: A Progressive Critique.* New York: Basic Books.

Kalir, Doron M. 2001. "Taking Globalization Seriously: Towards General Jurisprudence." *Columbia Journal of Transnational Law* 39: 785–821.

Kalman, Laura. 1986. *Legal Realism at Yale: 1927–1960.* Chapel Hill: University of North Carolina Press.

———. 2002. "Professing Law: Elite Law School Professors in the Twentieth Century." Pp. 338–385, in A. Sarat, B. Garth, and R. A. Kagan, eds. *Looking Back at Law's Century.* Ithaca, NY: Cornell University Press.

Kalven, Harry. 1988. *A Worthy Tradition: Freedom of Speech in America.* New York: Harper & Row.

Kalven, Harry, and Hans Zeisel. 1966. *The American Jury.* Boston: Little, Brown.

Kamali, Mohammad Hashim. 2008. *Shari'ah Law: An Introduction.* Oxford: One World.

Kane, Melinda D. 2010. "You've Won, Now What? The Influence of Legal Change on Gay and Lesbian Mobilization, 1974–1999." *The Sociological Quarterly* 51: 255–277.

Kanstroom, Daniel. 2007. *Deportation Nation: Outsiders in American History.* Cambridge, MA: Harvard University Press.

Kant, Immanuel. [1785] 1998. *Groundwork of the Metaphysics of Morals* (Translated and edited by Mary Gregor). Cambridge, UK: Cambridge University Press.

———. [1788] 1998. *Critique of Practical Reason.* Milwaukee, WI: Marquette University Press.

Kantor, Jodi. 2008. "Teaching Law, Testing Ideas, Obama Stood Slightly Apart." *New York Times* (July 30): A1.

———. 2009. "As a Professor, a Pragmatist About the Supreme Court." *New York Times* (My 3): A1.

Kanyongolo, Fedelis. 2006. *Malawi: Justice Sector and the Rule of Law.* Johannesburg: Open Society Initiative for Southern Africa.

Kapai, Puja, and Anne S. Y. Cheung. 2009. "Hanging in a Balance: Freedom of Expression and Religion." *Buffalo Human Rights Law Review* 15: 41–79.

Kapardis, Andreas. 2004. *Psychology and Law: A Critical Introduction,* 2nd ed. New York: Cambridge University Press.

———. 2007. "Psychology and Law." Pp. 1227–1234, in David S. Clark, ed. *Encyclopedia of Law & Society.* Los Angeles: Sage.

Karmen, Andrew. 2010. *Crime Victims: An Introduction to Victimology.* 7th ed. Belmont, CA: Wadsworth/Cengage Learning

Karstedt, Susanne, ed. 2009. *Legal Institutions and Collective Memories.* Portland, OR: Hart Publishing.

Karsten, Peter. 2002. *Between Law and Custom: "High" and "Low" Legal Cultures in the Lands of the British Diaspora—The United States, Canada, Australia, and New Zealand, 1600–1900.* New York: Cambridge University Press.

Katsh, M. Ethan, and William Rose. 2007. *Taking Sides: Clashing Views on Legal Issues.* 13th ed. Guilford, CT: Dushkin Publishing Group.

Katz, Jack. 1982. *Poor People's Lawyers in Transition.* New Brunswick, NJ: Rutgers University Press.

Katz, Michael B. 1986. *In the Shadow of the Poorhouse: A Social History of Welfare in America.* New York: Basic Books.

Katznelson, Ira. 2005. *When Affirmative Action Was White: An Untold History of Racial Inequality in Twentieth-Century America.* New York: Norton.

Kauzlarich, David, and Ronald C. Kramer. 1998. *Crimes of the American Nuclear State: At Home and Abroad.* Boston: Northeastern University Press.

Kavanagh, Aileen, and John Oberdiek, eds. *Arguing About Law.* New York: Routledge.

Kay, Fiona. 1997. "Flight From Law: A Competing Risks Model of Departures From Law Firms." *Law & Society Review* 31: 301–335.

Keefe, Patrick R. 2005. *Chatter—Dispatches from the Secret World of Global Eavesdropping.* New York: Random House.

Kelly, Michael J. 2007. *Lives of Lawyers Revisited: Transformation and Resilience in the Organization of Practice.* Ann Arbor: University of Michigan Press.

Kelman, Herbert, and V. Lee Hamilton. 1989. *Crimes of Obedience: Toward a Social Psychology of Authority and Responsibility.* New Haven, CT: Yale University Press.

Kelman, Mark. 1987. *A Guide to Critical Legal Studies.* Cambridge, MA: Harvard University Press.

Kelsen, Hans. [1934] 1967. *Pure Theory of Law.* Berkeley: University of California Press.

Kempers, Margot. 1989. "There's Losing and Winning: Ironies of the Maine Indian Land Claim." *Legal Studies Forum* 13: 267–300.

Kennedy, David, and William W. Fisher, eds. 2007. *The Canon of American Legal Thought.* Princeton, NJ: Princeton University Press.

Kennedy, Duncan. 1983; 2001. *Legal Education and the Reproduction of Hierarchy: A Polemic Against the System.* New York: New York University Press.

———. 1997. *A Critique of Adjudication (fin de siècle).* Cambridge, MA: Harvard University Press.

Kennedy, Paul, and George J. Andreopoulos. 1994. "The Laws of War: Some Concluding Reflections."

Pp. 214–225, in Michael Howard, George J. Andreopoulos, and Mark R. Shulman, eds. *The Laws of War*. New Haven, CT: Yale University Press.

Kephart, William M., and William W. Zellner. 1991. *Extraordinary Groups*. 4th ed. New York: St. Martin's Press.

Kershaw, Sarah, and Monica Davey. 2004. "Plagued by Drugs, Tribes Revive Ancient Penalty." *New York Times* (June 18): A1.

Kessler, Mark. 1987. *Legal Services for the Poor: A Comparative and Contemporary Analysis of Inter-organizational Politics*. New York: Greenwood Press.

Kethineni, Sesha, ed. 2010. *Comparative and International Policing, Justice, and Transnational Crime*. Durham, NC: Carolina Academic Press.

Kidder, Robert L., and John A. Hostetler. 1990. "Managing Ideologies: Harmony as Ideology in Amish and Japanese Societies." *Law & Society Review* 24: 893–922.

Kilborn, Peter T. 1995. "Hard Times for Legal Aid, and Getting Harder." *New York Times* (October 7): 6.

Kimball, Bruce A. 2009. *The Inception of Modern Professional Education: C. C. Langdell, 1826–1906*. Chapel Hill: University of North Carolina Press.

King, Martin Luther, Jr. 1963. *Letter From Birmingham City Jail*. Philadelphia: American Friends Service Committee.

King, Ryan D. 2007. "The Context of Minority Group Threat: Race, Institutions, and Complying with Hate Crime Law." *Law & Society Review* 41: 189–224.

Kirby, Michael. 2004. *Judicial Activism: Authority, Principle and Policy in the Judicial Method*. London: Sweet & Maxwell.

Kirkland, Anna. 2008. *Fat Rights: Dilemmas of Difference and Personhood*. New York: New York University Press.

Kissam, Philip C. 2003. *The Discipline of Law Schools: The Making of Modern Lawyers*. Durham, NC: Carolina Academic Press.

Kitch, Edmund. 1986. "Law and the Economic Order." Pp. 109–150, in Leon Lipson and Stanton Wheeler, eds. *Law and the Social Sciences*. New York: Russell Sage.

Klare, Karl. 1978. "Judicial Deradicalization of the Wagner Act and the Origins of Modern Legal Consciousness, 1937–1941." Pp. 138–168, in Piers Beirne and Richard Quinney, eds. *Marxism and Law*. New York: John Wiley.

Klebanow, Diana, and Franklin L. Jonas. 2003. *People's Lawyers: Crusaders for Justice in American History*. Armonk, NY: M. E. Sharpe.

Klein, David E. 2002. *Making Law in the United States Courts of Appeals*. New York: Cambridge University Press.

Klein, David E., and Robert J. Hume. 2003. "Fear of Reversal as an Explanation of Lower Court Compliance." *Law & Society Review* 37: 579–606.

Klein, Joe. 2009. "It's High Time." *Time* (April 13): 19.

Kleinig, John. 1996. *The Ethics of Policing*. Cambridge, UK: Cambridge University Press.

_____. 2008. *Ethics and Criminal Justice: An Introduction*. New York: Cambridge University Press.

Klug, Heinz. 2000. *Constituting Democracy: Law, Globalism, and South Africa's Political Reconstruction*. New York: Cambridge University Press.

Kluger, Richard. 1975. *Simple Justice: The History of* Brown v. Board of Education *and Black America's Struggle for Equality*. New York: Knopf.

Koch, Wendy. 2008. "As Adoptees Seek Roots, States Unsealing Records." *USA Today* (February 13): 1.

Kocieniewski, David, and Robert Hanley. 2000. "An Inside Story of Racial Bias and Denial." *New York Times* (December 3): 53.

Koenig, Thomas H., and Michael L Rustad. 2001. *In Defense of Tort Law*. New York: New York University Press.

Kohan, John. 1992. "The Party on Trial." *Time* (July 20): 66–67.

Kohlberg, Lawrence. 1969. "The Cognitive-Developmental Approach to Socialization." Pp. 347–480, in David Goslin, ed. *Handbook of Socialization Theory and Research*. Chicago: Rand McNally.

_____. 1981. *The Philosophy of Moral Development: Moral Stages and the Idea of Justice*, Vol. I. San Francisco: Harper & Row.

Kohm, Steven A. 2006. "The People's Law versus Judge Judy Justice: Two Models of Law in American Reality-Based Courtroom TV." *Law & Society Review* 40: 603–727.

Kole, William J. 2008. "Experts Unveil Index to Check Nations' Rule of Law." *Associated Press On-Line* (July 7).

Koppel, Niko. 2007. "Are Your Jeans Sagging? Go Directly to Jail." *New York Times* (August 30): Styles 1.

Kornbluh, Felicia. 2007. *The Battle for Welfare Rights: Politics and Poverty in Modern America*. Philadelphia: University of Pennsylvania Press.

Korobkin, Russell, with Stephen R. Munzer. 2007. *Stem Cell Century: Law and Policy for a Breakthrough Technology.* New Haven, CT: Yale University Press.

Koshner, Andrew Jay. 1998. *Solving the Puzzle of Interest Group Litigation.* Westport, CT: Greenwood Press.

Kotkin, Stephen. 2008. "Let Saigons Be Saigons." *The New Republic* (January 30): 44–47.

Kotlowski, Dean J. 2002. *Nixon's Civil Rights: Politics, Principle, and Policy.* Cambridge, MA: Harvard University Press.

Krakauer, Jon. 2003. *Under the Banner of Heaven.* New York: Random House.

Kramnick, Isaac, and Lawrence Moore. 1996. *The Godless Constitution: The Case Against Religious Correctness.* New York: W. W. Norton.

Kress, Ken. 1987. "The Interpretive Turn." *Ethics* 97: 834–860.

Krieger, Marcia S. 2009. "A Twenty-First Century Ethos for the Legal Profession: Why Bother?" *Denver University Law Review* 86: 865–899.

Kries, Douglas. 2007. *The Problem of Natural Law.* Lanham, MD: Lexington Books.

Kritz, Neil J., ed. 1995. *Transitional Justice: How Emerging Democracies Reckon With Former Regimes.* Washington, DC: U.S. Institute of Peace Press.

Kritzer, Herbert M. 2004a. *Risks, Reputations, and Rewards: Contingency Fee Legal Practice in the United States.* Stanford, CA: Stanford University Press.

———. 2004b. "American Adversarialism." *Law & Society Review* 38: 349–383.

Kritzer, Herbert M. 2009. Review of: *Lawyers in the Dock,* by Richard L. Abel. *Law & Politics Book Review* 19 (June): 386–389.

Kritzer, Herbert M., and Susan S. Silbey, eds. 2003. *In Litigation: Do the 'Haves' Still Come Out Ahead?* Stanford, CA: Stanford University Press.

Kritzer, Herbert M., and Frances Kahn Zemans. 1993. "Local Legal Culture and the Control of Litigation." *Law & Society Review* 27: 535–557.

Krivenko, Ekaterina Yahyaoui. 2009. *Women, Islam and International Law.* Leiden: Martinus Nijhoff Publishers.

Kronman, Anthony. 1993. *The Lost Lawyer: Failing Ideals of the Legal Profession.* Cambridge, MA: Belknap Press of Harvard University Press.

Kropotkin, Peter. [1910] 1971. "Anarchism." Quoted in Marshall Shatz, ed. *The Essential Works of Anarchism.* New York: Bantam.

———. [1927] 1966. "Law, the Supporter of Crime." Pp. 289–295, in Leonard I. Krimerman and Lewis Perry, eds. *Patterns of Anarchy.* New York: Anchor.

Krumholz, Susan T. 2011. "Criminal Justice Policy and Problem-Solving Courts." Pp. 117–134, in K. Ismaili, ed. *U. S. Criminal Justice Policy: A Contemporary Reader.* Sudbury, MA: Jones & Bartlett Learning.

Kunen, James Simon. 1983. *"How Can You Defend Those People?"* New York: Random House.

Kurkchiyan, Marina. 2009. "Russian Legal Culture: An Analysis of Adaptive Response to an Institutional Transplant." *Law & Social Inquiry* 34: 337–364.

Kusha, Hamid R. 1998. "Revisiting the Islamic Shariah Law in Deterring Criminality: Is There a Lesson for Western Criminology?" *Crime and Justice International* 14: 9–10, 24–26.

———. 2002. *The Sacred Law of Islam: A Case Study of Women's Treatment in the Islamic Republic of Iran's Criminal Justice System.* Aldershot, UK: Ashgate.

Lacombe, Dany. 1994. *Blue Politics: Pornography and the Law in the Age of Feminism.* Toronto: University of Toronto Press.

LaFree, Gary, and Christine Rack. 1996. "The Effects of Participants' Ethnicity and Gender on Monetary Outcomes in Mediated and Adjudicated Civil Cases." *Law & Society Review* 30: 767–797.

Lake, Peter F. 2007. "Colleges and the Law After Virginia Tech." *Chronicle of Higher Education* (June 29): B6–B8.

Lalasz, Robert. 2008. "Should Prostitution Be Legalized?" *Chronicle of Higher Education Review* (March 28): B4.

LaMarche, Gara. 2009. "Repairing Our Broken Justice System." *The Nation* (October 5): 20–22.

Lammon, Bryan D. 2009. "What We Talk About When We Talk About Ideology: Judicial Politics Scholarship and Naive Legal Realism." *St. John's Law Review* 83: 231–305.

Landes, William M., and Richard A. Posner. 2003. *The Economic Structure of Intellectual Property Law.* Cambridge, MA: Harvard University Press.

Landler, Mark. 2008. "Assisted Suicide of Healthy 79-Year Old Renews German Debate on Right to Die." *New York Times* (April 3): A8.

Landon, Donald D. 1990. *Country Lawyers: The Impact of Context on Professional Practice.* New York: Praeger.

Landrine, Hope, and Elizabeth A. Klonoif. 1997. *Discrimination Against Women: Prevalence, Consequences, Remedies.* Thousand Oaks, CA: Sage.

Landro, Laura. 2009. "A Fight Against Fatal Error." *Wall Street Journal* (September 8): A19.

Landsman, Stephan. 2005. *Crimes of the Holocaust: The Law Confronts Hard Cases.* Philadelphia: University of Pennsylvania Press.

Langdell, Christopher Columbus. 1871. *Selection of Cases on the Law of Contracts.* Boston: Little, Brown.

Lange, David L., and H. Jefferson Powell. 2009. *No Law: Intellectual Property in the Image of an Absolute First Amendment.* Stanford, CA: Stanford University Press.

Langer, Laura. 2002. *Judicial Review in State Supreme Courts: A Comparative Study.* Albany: State University of New York Press.

Langford, Malcolm, ed. 2008. *Social Rights Jurisprudence: Emerging Trends in International and Comparative Law.* Cambridge, UK: Cambridge University Press.

Langum, David J. 1999. *William M. Kunstler: The Most Hated Lawyer in America.* New York: New York University Press.

Lanier, Charles S., William J. Bowers, and James R. Acker, eds. 2009. *The Future of America's Death Penalty: An Agenda for the Next Generation of Capital Punishment Research.* Durham, NC: Carolina Academic Press.

LaPiana, William P. 1995. "Honor Langdell!" *Law & Social Inquiry* 20: 761–764.

Larsen, Rebecca. 2009. "From the Classroom to the White House." *The National Jurist* (February): 23+.

Lauderdale, Pat. 1997. "Indigenous North American Jurisprudence." *International Journal of Comparative Sociology* 38: 131–148.

Laufer, William S., and Nien-he Hsieh. 2003. "Choosing Equal Injustice." *American Journal of Criminal Law* 30: 343–361.

Lavi, Shai J. 2005. *The Modern Art of Dying: A History of Euthanasia in the United States.* Princeton, NJ: Princeton University Press.

Law Commission of Canada. 2008. *Indigenous Legal Traditions.* Vancouver, BC: UBC Press.

Lawrence, Charles R. 1998. "Race and Affirmative Action: A Critical Race Perspective." Pp. 312–327, in David Kairys, ed. *The Politics of Law: A Progressive Critique,* 3rd ed. New York: Basic Books.

Lawrence, Charles R., and Mari J. Matsuda. 1997. *We Won't Go Back: Making the Case for Affirmative Action.* New York: Houghton Mifflin.

Lawrence, Frederick M. 1999. *Punishing Hate: Bias Crime Under American Law.* Cambridge, MA: Harvard University Press.

Lazar, Nomi Claire. 2007. "Three Gestures Toward Justice." *Political Theory* 35: 659–665.

Lazarus-Black, Mindie, and Susan F. Hirsch. 1994. *Contested States: Law, Hegemony, and Resistance.* New York: Routledge.

Lebel-Grenier, Sebastien. 2006. "What Is a Transnational Legal Education?" *Journal of Legal Education* 56: 190+.

Lee, Murray. 2007. *Inventing Fear of Crime: Criminology and the Politics of Anxiety.* Portland, OR: Willan Publishing.

Lehman, Godfrey D. 1997. *We the Jury: The Impact of Jurors on Our Basic Freedoms.* Amherst, NY: Prometheus Books.

Leiper, Jean McKenzie. 2006. *Bar Codes: Women in the Legal Profession.* Vancouver: UBC Press.

Lemmings, David. 2000. *Professors of the Law: Barristers and English Legal Culture in the Eighteenth Century.* New York: Oxford University Press.

Lemmons, Trudo, and Duff R. Waring, eds. 2006. *Law and Ethics in Biomedical Research: Regulation, Conflict of Interest, and Liability.* Toronto: University of Toronto Press.

LeMoncheck, Linda, and Mane Hajdin. 1997. *Sexual Harassment: A Debate.* Lanham, MD: Rowman & Littlefield.

Lempert, Richard, and Joseph Sanders. 1986. *An Invitation to Law and Social Science: Desert, Disputes, and Distribution.* New York: Longman.

Leng, Shao-chuan. 1977. "The Role of Law in the People's Republic of China as Reflecting Mao TseTung's Influence." *Journal of Criminal Law & Criminology* 68: 356–373.

Lens, Vicki. 2009. "Confronting Government After Welfare Reform: Moralists, Reformers, and Narratives of (Ir)responsibility at Administrative Fair Hearings." *Law & Society Review* 43: 563–592.

Lenz, Timothy O. 2003. *Changing Images of Law in Film and Television Crime Stories.* New York: Peter Lang.

Leo, John. 1983. "A New Furor Over Pedophilia." *Time* (January 17): 47.

Leonhardt, David. 2009. "A System Breeding More Waste." *New York Times* (September 23): B1.

Lepard, Brian D. 2002. *Rethinking Humanitarian Intervention.* University Park: Pennsylvania State University Press.

Lepore, Jill. 2009. "The Politics of Death." *The New Yorker* (November 30): 60–67.

Lerner, M. J., and S. C. Lerner. 1981. *The Justice Motive in Social Behavior.* New York: Plenum.

Lessan, Gloria, and Joseph F. Sheley. 1992. "Does Law Behave? A Macrolevel Test of Black's Propositions on Change in Law." *Social Forces* 70: 655–678.

Lessig, Lawrence. 2010. "For the Love of Culture: Google, Copyright, and Our Future." *The New Republic* (February 4): 24–30.

Levi, Edward H. 1949. *An Introduction to Legal Reasoning.* Chicago: The University of Chicago Press.

Levi, Judith N., and Anne G. Walker, eds. 1990. *Language in the Judicial Process.* London: Plenum.

Levin, Leslie C. 2009. "Guardians at the Gate: The Backgrounds, Career Paths, and Professional Development of Private US Immigration Lawyers." *Law & Social Inquiry* 34: 399–436.

Levine, Evyatar. 1990. *Legal Justice and Social Change: A Philosophy of Law.* Jerusalem: Rubin Mass.

Levine, Kay, and Virginia Mellema. 2001. "Strategizing the Street: How Law Matters in the Lives of Women in the Street-Level Drug Economy." *Law & Social Inquiry* 26: 169–207.

Levinson, Sanford. 2007. *Our Undemocratic Constitution: Where the Constitution Goes Wrong (And How We the People Can Correct It).* New York: Oxford University Press.

Levit, Nancy, and Robert R. M. Verchick. 2006. *Feminist Legal Theory: A Primer.* New York University: Press.

Lewin, Tamar. 1989. "Women Say They Face Obstacles as Lawyers." *New York Times* (December 4): A21.

———. 2010. "Law School Admissions Lag Among Minorities." *New York Times* (January 7): A22.

Lewis, Anthony. 2008. "Official American Sadism." *New York Review of Books* (September 25): 45–49.

Lewis, John A., and Philip E. Carlan. 2009. "The National Minimum Drinking Age Law: Perceptions of Its Effectiveness to Deter Juvenile Alcohol Use." *Criminal Justice Studies* 22: 167–179.

Lewis, Neil. 1998. "Switching Sides on Free Speech." *New York Times* (April 25): E1.

———. 2003. "Iraqis Just Recently Set Rules to Govern Tribunal." *New York Times* (December 15): A16.

———. 2007. "A Prosecution Tests the Definition of Obscenity." *New York Times* (September 28): A27.

Lewis, Neil A., and Eric Schmitt. 2004. "Lawyers Decided Ban on Torture Didn't Bind Bush." *New York Times* (June 8): A1.

Lichtblau, Eric. 2008. *Bush's Law: The Remaking of American Justice.* New York: Pantheon.

Lichter, Brian A., and David P. Baltmanis. 2009 "Foreword: Original Ideas on Originalism." *Northwestern University Law Review* 103: 491–494.

Lichterman, Andrew, and Jacqueline Cabasso. 2002. "The End of Disarmament and the Arms Race to Come." *Social Justice* 29: 73–93.

Lieberman, Jethro. 1978. *Crisis at the Bar: Lawyers' Unethical Ethics and What to Do About It.* New York: W. W. Norton.

Liebmann, George W. 2005. *The Common Law Tradition: A Collective Portrait of Five Legal Scholars.* New Brunswick, NJ: Transaction Books.

Light, Steven Andrew, and Kathryn R. L. Rand. 2007. *Indian Gaming and Tribal Sovereignty: The Casino Compromise.* Lawrence: University Press of Kansas.

Lin-Liu, Jen. 2004. "The Paper Chase Comes to China." *Chronicle of Higher Education* (May 14): A42–A44.

Lindquist, Stefanie, and Frank B. Cross. 2009. *Measuring Judicial Activism.* New York: Oxford University Press.

Linowitz, Sal. 1994. *The Betrayed Profession: Lawyering at the End of the Twentieth Century.* New York: Scribner.

Linz, Daniel, Edward Donnerstein, Bradley J. Shafer, Kenneth C. Land, Patricia L. McCall, and Arthur C. Graesser. 1995. "Discrepancies Between the Legal Code and Community Standards for Sex and Violence: An Empirical Challenge to Traditional Assumptions in Obscenity Laws." *Law & Society Review* 29: 127–168.

Lipka, Sara. 2005. "The Lawyer Is In." *Chronicle of Higher Education* (July 1): A19–22.

Lipkin, Robert J. 2000. *Constitutional Revolutions: Pragmatism and the Role of Judicial Review in American Constitutionalism.* Durham, NC: Duke University Press.

Liptak, Adam. 2002a. "A State Weighs Allowing Juries to Judge Laws." *New York Times* (September 22): A1.

———. 2002b. "Judging a Mother for Someone Else's Crime." *New York Times* (November 27): A7.

———. 2003a. "In 13 States, a United Push to Limit Fees of Lawyers." *New York Times* (May 26): A10.

———. 2003b. "Defending Those Who Defend Terrorists." *New York Times* (July 27): Week 4.

———. 2003c. "Leaks and the Courts: There's Law, But Little Order." *New York Times* (October 5): Week 3.

———. 2003d. "U.S. Suits Multiply, but Fewer Ever Get to Trial." *New York Times* (December 14): A1.

_____. 2003e. "Penalty for Young Sniper Could Spark Change in Law." *New York Times* (December 25): A12.

_____. 2004a. "Hate Speech and the American Way." *New York Times* (January 11): Week 3.

_____. 2004b. "NAFTA Tribunals Stir U.S. Worries." *New York Times* (April 18): A1.

_____. 2004c. "Legal Scholars Criticize Torture Memos." *New York Times* (June 25): A14.

_____. 2005. "For Blacks in Law School, Can Less Be More?" *New York Times* (February 13): Week 3.

_____. 2007. "Cases Keep Flowing In, but the Jury Pool Is Idle." *New York Times* (April 30): A10.

_____. 2008a. "Lawyer Reveals Secret, Toppling Death Sentence." *New York Times* (January 19): A1.

_____. 2008b. "When Law Prevents Righting a Wrong." *New York Times* (May 4): Week 4.

_____. 2008c. "Experts Hired to Shed Light Can Leave U.S. Courts in Dark." *New York Times* (August 12): A1.

_____. 2008d. "U.S. Court, a Longtime Beacon, Is Now Guiding Fewer Nations." *New York Times* (September 18): A1.

_____. 2009a. "Judging a Court with Ex-Judges Only." *New York Times* (February 17): A14.

_____. 2009b. "Images, the Law and War." *New York Times* (May 17): Week in Review 1.

_____. 2009c. "Justices Rule Crime Analysts Must Testify on Lab Results." *New York Times* (June 26): A1.

_____. 2009d. "Supreme Court Finds Bias Against White Firefighters." *New York Times* (June 30): A1.

_____. 2009e. "Religion Largely Absent in Argument About a Cross." *New York Times* (October 8): A16.

_____. 2009f. "Animal Cruelty Law Tests Free Speech." *New York Times* (November 6): A12.

_____. 2009g. "From 19th-Century View, Desegregation Is a Test." *New York Times* (November 10): A16.

_____. 2009h. "Right and Left Joint to Take on U.S. in Criminal Justice Cases." *New York Times* (November 24): A1.

_____. 2009i. "Federal Law Limiting Legal Advice Draws Particular Interest at the Supreme Court." *New York Times* (December 2): A26.

_____. 2010a. "Shapers of Death Penalty Give Up on Their Work." *New York Times* (January 5): A11.

_____. 2010b. "Justices, 5–4, Reject Corporate Campaign Spending Limit." *New York Times* (January 22): A1.

_____. 2010c. "As a Criminal, Mediocre; As a Jailhouse Lawyer, An Advocate Unmatched." *New York Times* (February 9): A12.

_____. 2010d. "Right to Free Speech Collides with Fight Against Terror." *New York Times* (February 11): A18.

_____. 2010e. "Justices Reject Ban on Depicting Animal Cruelty." *New York Times* (April 21): A1.

_____. 2010f. "Justices Tangle Over Cross in Desert." *New York Times* (April 29): A16.

_____. 2010g. "Justices Limit Life Sentences for Juveniles." *New York Times* (May 18): A1.

_____. 2010h. "Justices Uphold a Ban on Aiding Terror Groups." *New York Times* (June 22): A1.

_____. 2010i. "A Mailroom Mix-Up That Could Cost a Life." *New York Times* (August 3): A10.

_____. 2010j. "Justices Offer Receptive Ear to Business Interests." *New York Times* (December 19): A1.

_____. 2011. "A Tipping Point for Gay Marriage?" *New York Times* (May 1): Week 3.

Liptak, Adam, and Michael Janofsky. 2004. "Scrappy Group of Lawyers Shows Way for Big Firms." *New York Times* (June 30): A14.

Lithwick, Dahlia. 2002. "Personal Truths and Legal Fictions." *New York Times* (December 17): A35.

_____. "Imagining Life Without Lawyers." *Newsweek* (February 9): 20.

_____. 2009b. "Teens, Nude Photos and the Law." *Newsweek* (February 13): 18.

_____. 2009c. "Bring on the Show Trial." *Newsweek* (December 14): 28.

_____. 2010a. "Courtly Love." *Newsweek* (May 3): 21.

_____. 2010b. "Our Beauty Bias Is Unfair: But Should It Also be Illegal?" *Newsweek* (June 14): 20.

Litowitz, Douglas E. 1997. *Postmodern Philosophy and Law.* Lawrence: University Press of Kansas.

_____. 2006. *The Destruction of Young Lawyers.* Akron, OH: The University of Akron Press.

Liu, Sida. 2008. "Globalization as Boundary-Blurring: International and Local Law Firms in China's Corporate Law Market." *Law & Society Review* 42: 771–804.

Livingston, Debra. 1997. "Police Discretion and the Quality of Life in Public Places: Courts, Communities, and the New Policing." *Columbia Law Review* 97: 551–672.

Llewellyn, Karl. [1930] 1951. *The Bramble Bush.* Dobbs Ferry, NY: Oceana Publications.

_____. 1962. *Jurisprudence: Realism in Theory and Practice.* Chicago: University of Chicago Press.

Llewellyn, Karl N., and E. Adamson Hoebel. 1941. *The Cheyenne Way: Conflict and Case Law in Primitive Jurisprudence*. Norman: University of Oklahoma Press.

Lloyd, Dennis. 1970. *The Idea of Law*. Baltimore: Penguin.

Lloyd-Bostock, Sally. 1988. *Law in Practice: Applications of Psychology in Legal Decision Making and Legal Skills*. London: Routledge.

Locke, John. [1689] 1988. *Two Treatises on Government* (P. Laslett, ed.). New York: Cambridge University Press.

_____. [1690] 1965. *Treatise on Civil Government*. New York: Irvington.

Loeb, Elizabeth. 2008. Review of: *The Law and Society Canon*. *Law & Politics Book Review* 18: 267–271.

Loewenberg, Gerhard. 2007. "Legislatures and Lawmaking." Pp. 945–950, in David S. Clark, ed. *Encyclopedia of Law and Society*. Los Angeles: Sage.

Loewith, Karl. 1960. *Max Weber and Karl Marx*. London: Allen & Unwin.

Logan, Wayne A. 2009. *Knowledge as Power: Criminal Registration and Community Notification Laws in America*. Stanford, CA: Stanford University Press.

Lomonte, Frank D. 2010. "Ferpa Frustrations: It's Time for Reform." *Chronicle of Higher Education* (May 14): A33.

Loury, Glenn C. 2008. *Race, Incarceration, and American Values*. Cambridge, MA: MIT Press.

Lovell, George I. 2003. *Legislative Deferrals: Statutory Ambiguity, Judicial Power, and American Democracy*. Cambridge: Cambridge University Press.

Lovell, Jarret S. 2009. *Crimes of Dissent: Civil Disobedience, Criminal Justice, and the Politics of Conscience*. New York: New York University Press.

Lowell, Abbe David, and Kathryn C. Arnold. 2003. "Corporate Crime After 2000: A New Law Enforcement Challenge or Déjà Vu?" *American Criminal Law Review* 40: 219–240.

Lu, Hong, and Terance D. Miethe. 2003. "Confessions and Criminal Case Disposition in China." *Law & Society Review* 37: 549–578.

Luban, David. 1994. *Legal Modernism*. Ann Arbor: University of Michigan Press.

_____. 2007. *Legal Ethics and Human Dignity*. Cambridge: Cambridge University Press.

Lubet, Steven. 2001. *Nothing but the Truth*. New York: New York University Press.

_____. 2008. *The Importance of Being Honest: How Lying, Secrecy, and Hypocrisy Collide with Truth in Law*. New York: New York University Press.

Lubman, Stanley B. 2000. *Bird in a Cage: Legal Reform in China After Mao*. Stanford, CA: Stanford University Press.

Luchansky, Bill, and Jurg Gerber. 1993. "Constructing State Autonomy: The Federal Trade Commission and the Celler-Kefauver Act." *Sociological Perspectives* 36: 217–240.

Lueck, Thomas J. 2004. "Legal Aid Society President Resigns, Citing Shortage of Funds." *New York Times* (June 10): B4.

Luft, Sandra Rudnick. 2007. "Giambattista Vico." Pp. 1151–1152, in David S. Clark, ed. *Encyclopedia of Law & Society*. Los Angeles: Sage.

Lukes, Steven, and Andrew Scull, eds. 1983. *Durkheim and the Law*. Oxford, UK: Martin Robertson.

Lund, Nelson, and David B. Kopel. 2009. "Unraveling Judicial Restraint: Guns, Abortion, and the Faux Conservatism of J. Harvie Wilkinson III." *The Journal of Law & Politics* 25 (Winter): 1–18.

Lurie, Jonathan. 2001. *Military Justice in America*. Lawrence: University Press of Kansas.

Lutz, E. L., and Reiger, C., eds. 2009. *Prosecuting Heads of State*. New York: Cambridge University Press.

Lyall, Sarah. 2004. "Are Saudis Using British Libel Law to Deter Critics?" *New York Times* (May 22): B7.

_____. 2009. "Britain, Long a Libel Mecca, Reviews Laws." *New York Times* (December 11): A1.

_____. 2010. "In BP's Record, a History of Boldness and Blunders." *New York Times* (July 13): A1.

Lykken, David T. 1998. *A Tremor in the Blood: Uses and Abuses of the Lie Detector*. New York: Plenum.

Lynch, Michael, Simon A. Cole, Ruth McNally, and Kathleen Jordan. 2008. *Truth Machine: The Contentious History of DNA Fingerprinting*. Chicago: University of Chicago Press.

Lyon, David. 2003. *Surveillance After September 11*. New York: Polity.

Macaulay, Stewart. 1986. "Private Government." Pp. 445–518, in Leon Lipson and Stanton Wheeler, eds. *Law and the Social Sciences*. Beverly Hills, CA: Sage.

_____. 1987. "Images of Law in Everyday Life: The Lessons of School, Entertainment, and Spectator Sports." *Law & Society Review* 21: 185–218.

Macaulay, Stewart, Lawrence M. Friedman, and John Stookey, eds. 1995. *Law and Society: Readings on the Social Study of Law*. New York: W. W. Norton.

Maccoby, Eleanor E., and Robert Mnookin. 1992. *Dividing the Child: Social and Legal Dilemmas of Custody*. Cambridge, MA: Harvard University Press.

MacDonald, Gayle M., ed. *Social Context and Social Location in the Sociology of Law*. Petersborough, Ontario: Broadview Press.

Macfarlane, Julie. 2008. *The New Lawyer: How Settlement Is Transforming the Practice of Law*. Vancouver, BC: UBC Press.

MacFarquhar, Larissa. 2001. "The Bench Burner." *The New Yorker* (December 10): 78–89.

Machiavelli, Niccolo. [1513] 1976. *The Prince*. Paramus, NJ: Prentice Hall.

MacKay, Robert, Marko Bosnjak, Johan Deklerck, Christa Pelikan, Bas van Stokkom, and Martin Wright, eds. 2007. *Images of Restorative Justice Theory*. Frankfurt am Main: Verlag fur Polizeiwissenschaft.

MacKenzie, John P. 2002. "Equal Protection for One Lucky Guy." Pp. 23–38, in Herman Schwartz, ed. *The Rehnquist Court—Judicial Activism on the Right*. New York: Hill & Wang.

MacKinnon, Catharine A. 1987. *Feminism Unmodified: Discourses on Life and Law*. Cambridge, MA: Harvard University Press.

———. 1993. *Only Words*. Cambridge, MA: Harvard University Press.

———. 2005. *Women's Lives, Men's Lives*. Cambridge, MA. The Belknap Press of Harvard University Press.

———. 2006. *Are Women Human? And Other International Dialogues*. Cambridge, MA: The Belknap Press of Harvard University Press.

MacKinnon, Catharine A., and Reva B. Siegel, eds. 2004. *Directions in Sexual Harassment Law*. New Haven, CT: Yale University Press.

MacKinnon, F. B. 2008. *Contingent Fees for Legal Services*. New Brunswick, NJ: Transaction Books.

MacLeod, Adam J. 2008a. "The Search for Moral Neutrality in Same-Sex Marriage Decisions." *Brigham Young University Journal of Public Law* 23: 1–60.

———. 2008b. "All for One: A Review of Victim-Centric Justifications for Criminal Punishment." *Berkeley Journal of Criminal Law* 13: 31–64.

MacNeil, William P. 2007. *Lex Populi: The Jurisprudence of Popular Culture*. Stanford, CA: Stanford University Press.

Macpherson, Heidi Slettedahl. 2007. *Courting Failure: Women and the Law in Twentieth Century Literature*. Akron, OH: The University of Akron Press.

Magliocca, Gerard N. 2007. *Andrew Jackson and the Constitution: The Rise and Fall of Generational Regimes*. Lawrence: University Press of Kansas.

Maguigan, Holly. 1998. "It's Time to Move Beyond the Battered Woman Syndrome." *Criminal Justice Ethics* (Winter/Spring): 50–57.

Maguire, Brendan, Rebecca Hinderliter, and William Faulkner. 1990. "The Illinois Seat Belt Law: A Sociology of Law Analysis." *Humanity & Society* 14: 395–418.

Maienschein, Jane. 2003. *Whose View of Life? Embryos, Cloning, and Stem Cells*. Cambridge, MA: Harvard University Press.

Maine, Henry. [1861] 2001. *Ancient Law*. Piscataway, NJ: Transaction.

Malinowski, Bronislaw. 1926. *Crime and Custom in Savage Society*. London: Routledge & Kegan Paul.

Mallinder, Louise. 2008. *Amnesty, Human Rights and Political Transitions: Bridging the Peace and Justice Divide*. Portland, OR: Hart Publishing.

Maltz, Earl M., ed. 2003. *Rehnquist Justice: Understanding the Court Dynamic*. Lawrence: University Press of Kansas.

Mangan, Katharine. 2008a. "All Rise. Welcome to Law School." *Chronicle of Higher Education* (January 11): A10–A11.

———. 2008b. "Legal Educators Rethink How Lawyers Are Trained." *Chronicle of Higher Education* (January 11): A11.

———. 2008c. "N.H. Allows Law Students to Demonstrate Court Skills in Lieu of Bar Exam." *Chronicle of Higher Education* (July 4): A8–A9.

———. 2008d. "American Indian Law: A Surge of Interest on Campuses." *Chronicle of Higher Education* (September 26): B18–B20.

———. 2009. "Amid Downturn, Law Students Give Aggrieved Investors a Day in Court." *Chronicle of Higher Education* (April 3): A17.

Mangan, Mary. 1998. "Making Future Lawyers Squirm: Law Schools Focus on Ethical Dilemmas." *Chronicle of Higher Education* (March 20): A12–13.

Mann, Bruce H. 2002. *Republic of Debtors: Bankruptcy in the Age of American Independence*. Cambridge, MA: Harvard University Press.

Mann, Coramae Richey. 1993. *Unequal Justice: A Question of Color*. Bloomington: Indiana University Press.

Manning, Bayless. 1977. "Hyperlexis: Our National Disease." *Northwestern University Law Review* 71: 767–782.

Mansbridge, Jane J. 1986. *Why We Lost the ERA*. Chicago: University of Chicago Press.

Mansnerus, Laura. 2000. "From a Captive Audience, Clients." *New York Times* (November 16): B1.

_____. 2001. "As Law Firms Scramble for New Talent, the New Talent Reaps the Rewards." *New York Times* (January 30): C-4.

_____. 2003. "Questions Rise Over Imprisoning Sex Offenders Past Their Term." *New York Times* (November 17): A1.

Marble, David H., and John L. Worrall. 2009. "Problem-solving Courts." Pp. 771–779, in J. Mitchell Miller, ed. *21st Century Criminology: A Reference Handbook.* Los Angeles: Sage.

Marcuse, Herbert. 1966. "Ethics and Revolution." Pp. 133–148, in Richard T. DeGeorge, ed. *Ethics and Society.* Garden City, NY: Doubleday.

Margolick, David. 1983. "The Trouble With American Law School." *New York Times Magazine* (May 22): 20–38.

_____. 1990. "Ignorance of L.A. Law Is No Excuse for Lawyers." *New York Times* (May 6): 27.

_____. 1993a. "Horror's Stigma Still Clings to a Disbarred Lawyer." *New York Times* (May 15): 21.

Marietta, Jack D., and G. S. Rowe. 2006. *Troubled Experiment: Crime and Justice in Pennsylvania, 1682–1800.* Philadelphia: University of Pennsylvania Press.

Markovits, Richard S. 2008. *Truth or Economics: On the Definition, Prediction, and Relevance of Economic Efficiency.* New Haven, CT: Yale University Press.

Marks, Paula Mitchell. 1998. *In a Barren Land: American Indian Dispossession and Survival.* New York: William Morrow.

Marshall, Anna-Maria, and Scott Barclay. 2003. "In Their Own Words: How Ordinary People Construct the Legal World." *Law and Social Inquiry* 28: 617–628.

Marshall, Carolyn. 2007. "Drinks with Your Appeal Draw Growing Opposition." *New York Times* (April 13): A12.

Marshall, James. 1966. *Law and Psychology in Conflict.* Garden City, NY: Doubleday.

Marshall, Paul. 2005. *Radical Islam's Rules: The Worldwide Spread of Extreme Shari'a Law.* Lanham, MD: Rowman & Littlefield.

Marshall, Thomas R. 2008. *Public Opinion and the Rehnquist Court.* Albany: State University of New York Press.

Martin, Margaret. 1994. "Mandatory Arrest for Domestic Violence: The Courts' Response." *Criminal Justice Review* 19: 212–227.

Martinez, Samuel. 2009. "Book Review: The Slave Next Door." *Connecticut Journal of International Law* 25: 119–124.

Marx, Karl. [1867] 1962. *Capital* (F. Engels, ed.). Moscow: Foreign Language Publishing.

Maschke, Karen J. 1995. "Prosecutors as Crime Creators: The Case of Prenatal Drug Use." *Criminal Justice Review* 20: 21–33.

Mashaw, Jerry L. 2007. "Administrative Law and Agency Accountability." Pp. 30–34, in David S. Clark, ed. *Encyclopedia of Law and Society.* Los Angeles: Sage.

Mason, John Kenyon. 2007. *The Troubled Pregnancy: Legal Wrongs and Rights in Reproduction.* Port Chester, NY: Cambridge University Press.

Mason, Marianne. 2008. *Courtroom Interpreting.* Lanham, MD: University Press of America.

Masson, Antoine, and Kevin O'Connor, eds. 2007. *Representations of Justice.* Pieterlen, Switzerland: Peter Lang AG.

Masters, Roger D. 1990. "Law, Biology, and the Sense of Injustice: An Inquiry." *Gruyter Institute for Law and Behavioral Research* 3: 1, 4–6.

Mather, Lynn. 2003. "Reflections on the Reach of Law (and Society) Post-9/11: An American Superhero?" *Law & Society Review* 37: 263–281.

Mather, Lynn, Craig A. McEwen, and Richard J. Maiman. 2001. *Divorce Lawyers at Work.* New York: Oxford University Press.

Matoesian, Gregory M. 2001. *Law and the Language of Identity: Discourse in the William Kennedy Smith Rape Trial.* New York: Oxford University Press.

Matsuda, Mari J., Charles P. Lawrence III, Richard Delgado, and Kimberle Williams Crenshaw. 1993. *Words That Wound: Critical Race Theory, Assaultive Speech, and the First Amendment.* Boulder, CO: Westview Press.

Mattei, Ugo, and Laura Nader. 2008. *Plunder: When the Rule of Law Is Illegal.* Oxford: Wiley-Blackwell.

Matthiessen, Peter. 2009. "The Tragedy of Leonard Peltier vs. the US." *New York Review of Books* (November 19): A22.

Maurer, Bill. 2006. *Pious Property: Islamic Mortgages in the United States.* New York: Russell Sage Foundation.

Maxeiner, James R. 2008. "Some Realism about Legal Certainty in the Globalization of the Rule of Law." *Houston Journal of International Law* 31: 27–47.

May, Peter J. 2004. "Compliance Motivations: Affirmative and Negative Biases." *Law & Society Review* 38: 41–68.

_____. 2007. "Regulatory Regimes and Accountability." *Regulation and Governance* 1: 8–26.

Mayers, Lewis. 1973. *The Machinery of Justice.* Totowa, NJ: Littlefield, Adams.

Mayes, G. Randolph. 1989. "The Internal Aspect of Law: Rethinking Hart's Contribution to Legal Positivism." *Social Theory and Practice* 15: 231–255.

McAdams, A. James, ed. 1997. *Transitional Justice and the Rule of Law in New Democracies.* Notre Dame, IN: University of Notre Dame Press.

McAdams, Richard H., and Janice Nadler. 2008. "Coordinating in the Shadow of the Law: Two Contextualized Tests of the Focal Point Theory of Legal Compliance." *Law & Society Review* 42: 865–898.

McArdle, Elaine. 2008. "A Curriculum of New Realities." *Harvard Law Bulletin* (Winter): 17–23.

_____. 2010. "The Laws of Unintended Consequences." *Harvard Law Bulletin* (Winter): 31–34.

McCaffery, Edward J. 1997. "Ronald Dworkin, Inside-Out." *California Law Review* 85: 1043–1086.

McCall, George J. 1995. "Use of Law in a South African Black Township." *International Journal of the Sociology of Law* 23: 59–78.

McCann, Michael W. 1994. *Rights at Work: Pay Equity Reform and the Politics of Legal Mobilization.* Chicago: University of Chicago Press.

McCann, Michael, and William Haltom. 2006. "On Analyzing Legal Cultures: A Reply to Kagan." *Law & Social Inquiry* 31: 739–755.

_____. 2008. "Ordinary Heroes vs. Failed Lawyers—Public Interest Litigation in *Erin Brockovich* and Other Contemporary Films." *Law & Social Inquiry* 33: 1045–1070.

McClain, Linda C., and Joanna L. Grossman, eds. 2009. *Gender Equality: Dimensions of Women's Equal Citizenship.* New York: Cambridge University Press.

McColgan, Aileen. 2000. *Women Under the Law: The. False: Promise of Human Rights.* London: Longman.

McCoy, Candace. 1997. "Sentencing (and) the Underclass." *Law & Society Review* 31: 589–612.

McGill, Christa. 2003. "Different Agendas: Educational Hierarchy, Institutional Identities, and the Production of Lawyers." *Researching Law* 14: 2–7.

_____. 2006. "Educational Debt and Law Student Failure to Enter Public Service Careers: Bringing Empirical Data to Bear." *Law & Social Inquiry* 31: 677–708.

McGinty, Brian. 2008. *Lincoln & the Court.* Cambridge, MA: Harvard University Press.

McGlynn, Clare, and Ian Ward. 2009. "Pornography, Pragmatism, and Proscription." *Journal of Law and Society* 36: 327–351.

McGoldrick, Dominic. 2004. *From "9–11" to the "Iraq War 2003": International Law in an Age of Complexity.* Oxford, UK: Hart Publishing.

McInnis, Thomas N. 2009. *The Evolution of the Fourth Amendment.* New York: Lexington Books.

McIntosh, Wayne V., and Cynthia L. Cates. 2009. *Multi-Party Litigation: The Strategic Context.* Vancouver, BC: UBC Press.

McIntyre. Lisa J. 1987. *The Public Defender: The Practice of Law in the Shadows of Repute.* Chicago: University of Chicago Press.

_____. 1994. *Law in the Sociological Enterprise: A Reconstruction.* Boulder, CO: Westview Press.

McKay, Robert. 1985. "What Law Schools Can and Should Do (and Sometimes Do)." *New York Law School Law Review* 30: 491–516.

McKendall, Miriam J. 2010. "How to Navigate the Intersection of Student Disability and Discipline Issues." *Chronicle of Higher Education* (April 30): A23–A24.

McKinley, Jesse. 2010. "Latest Legal-Marijuana Push Is All About the Tax Revenue." *New York Times* (March 26): A1.

McLaughlin, Eugene, Ross Ferguson, Gordon Hughes and Louise Westmarland, eds. 2003. *Restorative Justice: Critical Issues.* London: Sage.

McMahan, Jeff. 2009. *Killing in War.* Oxford: Clarendon Press.

McManis, Sam. 2009. "It's OK; or Maybe Not." *Scranton Times-Tribune* (May 31): G8.

McNamara, M. Francis. 1960. *Ragbag of Legal Quotations.* Albany, NY: Matthew Bender.

McNamara, Robert. 1995. *In Retrospect: The Tragedy and Lessons of Vietnam.* New York: Times Books.

McSherry, Bernadette, Alan North and Simon Bronitt, eds. 2008. *Regulating Deviance: The Redirection of Criminalisation and the Futures of Criminal Law.* Portland, OR: Hart Publishing.

McVeigh, Rory, and Maria-Elena D. Diaz. 2009. "Voting to Ban Same-Sex Marriage: Interests, Values, and Communities." *American Sociological Review* 74: 891–915.

McVeigh, Shaun. 2007. "Postmodernism." Pp. 1158–1160, in David S. Clark, ed. *Encyclopedia of Law & Society.* Los Angeles: Sage.

McWhirter, Darien, and Jon Bible. 1992. *Privacy as a Constitutional Right.* New York: Quorum Books.

Mda, Zakes. 2004. "The Half-Revolution." *New York Times* (April 27): A25.

Mears, Daniel F. 1998. "The Sociology of Sentencing: Reconceptualizing Decision-Making Processes and Outcomes." *Law & Society Review* 32: 667–724.

Mehrotra, Ajay K. 2001. "Law and the Other Karl N. Llewellyn, Cultural Anthropology, and the Legacy of the Cheyenne Way." *Law & Social Inquiry* 26: 741–775.

Meier, Barry, and Jill Abramson. 1998. "Tobacco War's New Front: Lawyers Fight for Big Fees." *New York Times* (June 9): A1.

Meier, Barry, and Richard A. Oppel, Jr. 1999. "State's Big Suits Against Industry Bring Battle on Contingency Fees." *New York Times* (October 15): A1.

Meier, Robert F., and Gilbert Geis. 1997. *Victimless Crime? Prostitution, Drugs, Homosexuality, Abortion.* Los Angeles: Roxbury.

Meinhold, Stephen S., and Charles D. Hadley. 1995. "Lawyers as Political Party Activists." *Social Science Quarterly* 76: 364–380.

Melissaris, Emmanuel. 2009. *Ubiquitous Law: Legal Theory and the Space for Legal Pluralism.* Burlington, VT: Ashgate.

Mello, Michael. 1996. "The Centrality of Professional Ethics to the (Smart) Practice of Criminal Law, and the Confessions of a Professional Responsibility Professor." *Criminal Law Bulletin* 32: 168–171

Melone, Albert P., and Allan Karnes. 2003. *The American Legal System: Foundations, Processes, and Norms.* Los Angeles: Roxbury.

Melosi, Dario. 2008. *Controlling Crime, Controlling Society: Thinking about Crime in Europe and America.* Cambridge, UK: Polity Press.

Memon, Amina. 2003. *Psychology and Law: Truthfulness, Accuracy and Credibility.* Chicester, England: John Wiley.

Menkel-Meadow, Carrie. 1985. "Portia in a Different Voice: Speculations on the Women's Lawyering Process." *Berkeley Women's Law Journal* 1: 39–55.

———. 2004. "From Legal Disputes to Conflict Resolution and Human Problem-Solving: Legal Dispute Resolution in a Multi-disciplinary Context." *Journal of Legal Education* 54: 7–29.

Merrick, Amy. 2009. "Case Spurs Pharmacies' Fears of Lawsuits Over Drug Abuse." *Wall Street Journal* (October 28): 1.

Merry, Sally Engle. 1990. *Getting Justice and Getting Even: Legal Consciousness Among Working-Class Americans.* Chicago: University of Chicago Press.

———. 2004. "Colonial and Postcolonial Law." Pp. 569–588, in Austin Sarat, ed. *The Blackwell Companion to Law and Society.* Malden, MA: Blackwell.

———. 2006. *Human Rights & Gender Violence: Translating International Law into Local Justice.* Chicago: University of Chicago Press.

Merryman, John Henry. 1969. *The Civil Law Tradition.* Stanford, CA: Stanford University Press.

Mertha, Andrew C. 2005. *The Politics of Piracy: Intellectual Property in Contemporary China.* Ithaca, NY: Cornell University Press.

Mertz, Elizabeth. 1988. "The Uses of History: Language, Ideology, and Law in the United States and South Africa." *Law & Society Review* 22: 661–685.

———. 1994a. "Legal Loci and Places in the Heart: Community and Identity in Sociolegal Studies." *Law & Society Review* 28: 971–992.

———. 1994b. "A New Social Constructionism for Sociolegal Studies." *Law & Society Review* 28: 1243–1265.

———. 2007. *The Language of Law School: Learning to 'Think Like a Lawyer.'* New York: Oxford University Press.

———. 2008. *The Role of Social Science in Law.* Burlington, VT: Ashgate.

Metzger, M. B., J. P. Mallor, T. B. Barnes, and M. J. Phillips. 1986. *Business Law and the Regulatory Environment: Concepts and Cases, 6th ed.* Homewood, IL: Irwin.

Metzloff, Thomas B., and David B. Wilkins, eds. 1995. "Teaching Legal Ethics." *Law and Contemporary Problems* 58: 1–370.

Mezey, Susan Gluck. 2007. *Queers in Court: Gay Rights Law and Public Policy.* Lanham, MD: Rowman & Littlefield Publishers.

Michalowski, Raymond J., and Ronald C. Kramer. 1987. "The Space Between the Laws: The Problem of Corporate Crime in a Transnational Context." *Social Problems* 34: 34–53.

Michelson, Ethan. 2008. "Dear Lawyer Bao: Everyday Problems, Legal Advice, and State Power in China." *Social Problems* 55: 43–71.

Milgram, Stanley. 1974. *Obedience to Authority: An Experimental View.* New York: Harper & Row.

Mill, John Stuart. [1859] 1963. "On Liberty." Pp. 127–242, in *The Six Great Humanistic Essays of John Stuart Mill*. New York: Washington Square Press.

Miller, Judith. 2003. "Arms Control Racing Time and Technology." *New York Times* (December 6): B7.

Miller, Kenneth P. 2009. *Direct Democracy and the Courts*. New York: Cambridge University Press.

Miller, Lisa L. 2001. *The Politics of Community Crime Prevention*. Burlington, VT: Ashate.

————. 2008. *The Perils of Federalism: Race, Poverty, and the Politics of Crime Control*. New York: Oxford University Press.

Mills, C. Wright. 1959. *The Power Elite*. New York: Oxford University Press.

Mills, James. 1971. *On the Edge*. New York: Doubleday.

Mills, Jon L. 2008. *Privacy: The Lost Right*. New York: Oxford University Press.

Milovanovic, Dragan. 2003. *A Primer in the Sociology of Law, 3rd ed.* New York: Criminal Justice Press.

Milton, J. R. L. 1987. "Criminal Law in South Africa, 1976–1986." Pp. 34–54, in T. W. Bennett et al. *Alta Juridica*. Cape Town, RSA: Juta.

Minda, Gary. 1995. *Postmodern Legal Movements: Law and Jurisprudence at Century's End*. New York: New York University Press.

Minow, Martha. 1990. *Making All the Difference*. Ithaca, NY: Cornell University Press.

————. 1997. *Not Only for Myself: Identity, Politics, and Law*. New York: New Press.

————. 1998. *Between Vengeance and Forgiveness: Facing History After Genocide and Mass Violence*. Boston: Beacon Press.

————. 2005. "Hearsay." *Harvard Law Bulletin* (Fall): 6.

Mirsky, Jonathan. 2010. "Vietnam Now." *New York Review of Books* (June 24): 22–23.

Mitchell, Basil. 1970. *Law, Morality, and Religion in a Secular Society*. London: Oxford University Press.

Mitchell, Dalia Tsuk. 2007. *Architect of Justice: Felix S. Cohen and the Founding of American Legal Pluralism*. Ithaca, NY: Cornell University Press.

Mitchell, Lawrence E. 2001. *Corporate Irresponsibility: America's Newest Export*. New Haven, CT: Yale University Press.

Mnookin, Robert H., and Lewis Kornhauser. 1979. "Bargaining in the Shadow of Law." *Yale Law Journal* 88: 750–797.

Moghalu, Kingsley Chiedu. 2008. *Global Justice: The Politics of War Crime Trials*. Stanford, CA: Stanford University Press.

Moliterno, James E. 2008. "Exporting American Legal Education." *Journal of Legal Education* 58: 274–289.

Moltz, David. 2009. "Porn as Campus Attraction." *Inside Higher Ed* (April 3).

Monaghan, Peter. 2007. "The Growing Field of Animal Law Is Attracting Activists and Pragmatists Alike." *Chronicle of Higher Education* (June 29): A6.

Monrone, James A. 2003. *Hellfire Nation: The Politics of Sin in American History*. New Haven, CT: Yale University Press.

Montesquieu, Baron Charles de. [1748] 1886. *The Spirit of Laws*. Cincinnati, OH: Robert Clarke.

Moon, Richard, ed. 2008. *Law and Religious Pluralism in Canada*. Vancouver, BC: UBC Press.

Moore, Dawn. 2007. *Criminal Artifacts: Governing Drugs and Users*. Vancouver, BC: UBC Press.

Moore, Gary A., Arthur M. Magaldi, and John A. Gray. 1987. *The Legal Environment of Business: A Contextual Approach*. Cincinnati, OH: Southwestern Publishing.

Moore, Richter H., Jr. 1996. "Islamic Legal Systems: Traditional (Saudi Arabia), Contemporary (Bahrain), and Evolving (Pakistan)." Pp. 390–410, in Charles B. Fields and Richter H. Moore Jr. *Comparative Criminal Justice: Traditional and Nontraditional Systems of Law and Social Control*. Prospect Heights, IL: Waveland.

Moore, Sally Falk. 1986. "Legal Systems of the World: An Introductory Guide to Classifications, Typological Interpretations, and Bibliographical Resources." Pp. 11–62, in Leon Lipson and Stanton Wheeler, eds. *Law and the Social Sciences*. New York: Russell Sage.

Moore, Solomon. 2009. "Study Shows High Cost of Criminal Corrections." *New York Times* (March 3): A13.

Moore, Wayne D. 2008. Review of: *The Hollow Hope*, by Gerald Rosenberg. *Law & Politics Book Review* 18 (November): 1045–1054.

Mootz, Francis J, III. 2006. *Rhetorical Knowledge in Legal Practice and Critical Legal Theory*. Tuscaloosa: University of Alabama Press.

————. 2008. "Introduction to Recalling Vico's Lament: The Role of Prudence and Rhetoric in Law and Legal Education." *Chicago-Kent Law Review* 83: 1097–1107.

Moran, Leslie L. 2006. *Sexuality and Identity: International Library of Essays in Law and Society*. Burlington, VT: Ashgate.

Moreno, Joelle Anne. 2003. "Eyes Wide Shut: Hidden Problems and Future Consequences of the Fact-Based Validity Standard." *Seton Hall Law Review* 34: 89–104.

Morris, Lawrence J. 2010. *Military Justice: A Guide to the Issues.* Santa Barbara, CA: Praeger.

Morris, Lydia, ed. 2006. *Rights: Sociological Perspectives.* New York: Routledge.

Morris, Regan. 2006. "Picking the Wrong Mom and Pop to Sue." *New York Times* (June 1): B3.

Morris, Thomas D. 1996. *Southern Slavery and the Law, 1619–1860.* Chapel Hill: University of North Carolina Press.

Morrison, Wayne. 1997. *Jurisprudence: From the Greeks to Post-Modernism.* London: Cavendish.

Morrissey, Daniel J. 2006. "Saving Legal Education." *Journal of Legal Education* 56: 254–280.

Mosley, Albert G., and Nicholas Capaldi. 1996. *Affirmative Action: Social Justice or Unfair Preference?* Lanham, MD: Rowman & Littlefield.

Mosley, Walter. 2009. "Get Happy." *The Nation* (October 5): 23–24.

Moss, Debra Cassens. 1988. "Would This Happen to a Man?" *ABA Journal* (June 1): 50–55.

Moss, Michael. 2006. "Iraq's Legal System Staggers Beneath the Weight of War." *New York Times* (December 17): A1.

Mossman, Mary Jane. 2006. *The First Women Lawyers: A Comparative Study of Gender, Law and the Legal Professions.* Portland, OR: Hart Publishing.

Motomura, Hiroshi. 2006. *Americans in Waiting: The Lost Story of Immigration and Citizenship in the United States.* New York: Oxford University Press.

Moynihan, Colin. 2009. "Radical Lawyer Convicted of Aiding Terrorist Is Jailed." *New York Times* (November 20): A323.

Mueller, Ingo. 1991. *Hitler's Justice: The Courts of the Third Reich.* Cambridge, MA: Harvard University Press.

Mühlhahn, Klaus. 2009. *Criminal Justice in Chian: A History.* Cambridge, MA: Harvard University Press.

Munger, Frank. 1998. "Mapping Law and Society." Pp. 21–80, in A. Sarat et al., eds. *Crossing Boundaries: Traditions and Transformations in Law and Society Research.* Chicago: Northwestern University Press.

———. 2001. "Inquiry and Activism in Law and Society." *Law & Society Review* 35: 7–37.

———. 2003. "Poverty, Welfare, and the Affirmative State." *Law & Society Review* 37: 659–686.

Munoz, Vincent Phillip. 2010. *God and the Founders: Madison, Washington, and Jefferson.* New York: Cambridge University Press.

Murphy, Bruce Allen. 2003. *Wild Bill: The Legend and Life of William O. Douglas.* New York: Random House.

Musto, David F. 1973. *The American Disease: Origins of Narcotic Control.* New Haven, CT: Yale University Press.

Myers, Steven Lee. 2003. "What Chance Justice Is Done? Russia's System Is Questioned." *New York Times* (November 1): A1.

———. 2004. "Why Military Justice Can Seem Unjust." *New York Times* (June 6): Week 3.

Myers, Linda Brandt. 2008. "Finding the Facts that Challenge Our Assumptions about the World." Cornell University School of Law Forum: 10–14.

Myren, Richard A. 1988. *Law and Justice: An Introduction.* Pacific Grove, CA: Brooks/Cole.

Nader, Laura. 1997. *Law in Culture and Society.* Berkeley: University of California Press.

———. 2002. *The Life of the Law: Anthropological Projects.* Berkeley: University of California Press.

Nader, Laura, and Harry F. Todd Jr., eds. 1978. *The Disputing Process: Law in Ten Societies.* New York: Columbia University Press.

Nader, Ralph, and Wesley J. Smith. 1996. *No Contest: Corporate Lawyers and the Perversion of Justice in America.* New York: Random House.

Napier-Andrews, Nigel. 1976. *This Is the Law?* Garden City, NY: Doubleday.

The Nation. 2011. "The Libya Intervention." *The Nation* (April 11): 3–4.

Natoli, Marie. 2006. *Taking Sides: Clashing Views in Public Policy, Justice, and the Law.* Dubuque, Iowa: Contemporary Learning Systems.

Neelakantan, Shailaja. 2005. "Raising the Bar." *Chronicle of Higher Education* (December 2): A35–A36.

Nelken, David, ed. 2003. "Beyond Compare? Criticizing "The American Way of Law." *Law & Social Inquiry* 28: 799–831.

———. 2006. "Signaling Conformity: Changing Norms in Japan and China." *Michigan Journal of International Law* 27: 933–972.

———. 2009. *Beyond Law in Context: Developing a Sociological Understanding of Law.* Burlington, VT: Ashgate.

Nelson, Robert, and Laura Beth Nielsen. 2000. "Cops, Counsel, and Entrepreneurs: Constructing the Role of Inside Counsel in Large Corporations." *Law & Society Review* 34: 457–494.

Nelson, William E. 2008. *The Common Law in Colonial America, Volume 1: The Chesapeake and New England, 1607–1660.* New York: Oxford University Press.

Neubauer, David W., and Stephen S. Meinhold. 2004. *Judicial Process: Law, Courts, and Politics in the United States*. Belmont, CA: Thomson/Wadsworth.

Newman, Graeme. 1976. *Comparative Deviance*. New York: Elsevier.

Newman, Otto, and Richard De Zoysa. 1997. "Communitarianism: The New Panacea?" *Sociological Perspectives* 40: 623–638.

New York Times. 2007. "Bork v. Bork." *New York Times* (June 12): A30.

Newton, Lina. 2008. *Illegal, Alien or Immigrant: The Politics of Immigration Reform*. New York: New York University Press.

Niehoff, Leonard M. 2006. "The Lessons of Legal Ethics." *Chronicle of Higher Education* (May 12): B5.

Nielsen, Laura Beth. 2000. "Situating Legal. Consciousness: Experiences and Attitudes of Ordinary Citizens About Law and Sexual Harassment." *Law & Society Review* 34: 1055–1090.

Nielsen, Marianne O. 1996. "Contextualization for Native American Crime and Criminal Justice Involvement." Pp. 10–19, in M. O. Nielsen and R. A. Silverman, eds. *Native Americans, Crime, and Justice*. Boulder, CO: Westview Press.

Nina, Daniel. 1993. "Community Justice in a Volatile South Africa: Containing Community Conflict, Clermont, Natal." *Social Justice* 20 (3–4): 129–142.

Nobles, Richard, and David Schiff. 2006. *A Sociology of Jurisprudence*. Portland, OR: Hart Publishing.

Nolan, James L., Jr. 2009. *Legal Accents, Legal Borrowing: The International Problem-Solving Court Movement*. Princeton, NJ: Princeton University Press.

Nonet, Philippe, and Philip Selznick. [1978] 2001. *Law and Society in Transition*. New Brunswick, NJ: Transaction.

Noonan, John T., Jr. [1976] 1994. "Virginia Liberators." Pp. 524–529, in John Bonsignore et al., eds. *Before the Law, 5th ed*. Boston. Houghton Mifflin.

Norgren, Jill, and Serena Nanda. 1996. *American Cultural Pluralism and Law, 2nd ed*. Westport, CT: Praeger.

Norrie, Alan. 1996. "From Law to Popular Justice: Beyond Antinominalism." *Social & Legal Studies* 5: 383–404.

Norris, Floyd. 2007. "Should S.E.C. Act Against Lawyers?" *New York Times* (May 4): B1.

Nozick, Robert. 1974. *Amnesty, State, and Utopia*. New York: Basic Books.

Nuijten, Monique, and Gerhard Anders, ed. 2007. *Corruption and the Secret of Law: A Legal Anthropological Perspective*. Burlington, VT: Ashgate.

Nunn, Kenneth B. 1997. "Law as a Eurocentric Enterprise." *Law and Inequality* 15: 323–373.

Nussbaum, Martha C. 2004. "Danger to Human Dignity: The Revival of Disgust and Shame." *Chronicle of Higher Education* (August 6): B6–B9.

_____. 2006. "Reply to Amnon Reichman." *Journal of Legal Education* (June): 320–329.

O'Barr, William M., and John M. Conley. 1988. "Law Expectations of the Civil Justice System." *Law & Society Review* 22: 137–161.

_____. 1998. *Just Words: Law, Language, and Power*. Chicago: University of Chicago Press.

O'Connor, Jennifer M., and Lucinda K. Treat. 1996. "Getting Smart About Getting Tough: Juvenile Justice and the Possibility of Progressive Reform." *American Criminal Law Review* 33: 1299–1344.

O'Donnell, Ian, and Claire Milner. 2007. *Child Pornography: Crime, Computers, and Society*. Portland, OR: Willan.

O'Hagan, Timothy C. 1984. *The End of Law?* Oxford, UK: Basil Blackwell.

O'Hanlon, Stephen. 2009. "Towards a More Reasonable Approach to Free Will in Criminal Law." *Cardozo Public Law, Policy & Ethics Journal* 7: 395–428.

O'Manique, John. 2002. *The Origins of Justice: The Evolution of Morality, Human Rights, and Law*. Philadelphia: University of Pennsylvania Press.

O'Neil, Robert M. 2009. "A Fine Legal Mess: When Student Groups Collide With Anti-Bias Policy." *Chronicle of Higher Education* (November 22): A17–18.

O'Reilly, David. 2007. "Scalia Opines on Faith and Justice." *Philadelphia Inquirer* (October 17): A11.

Oakley, Francis. 2005. *Natural Law, Laws of Nature, Natural Rights: Continuity and Discontinuity in the History of Ideas*. London and New York: Continuum International Publishing Group.

Ogletree, Charles J., Jr. 2004. *All Deliberate Speed: Reflections on the First Half-Century of Brown v. Board of Education*. New York: W. W. Norton.

Ogletree, Chares J., Jr., and Austin Sarat, eds. 2009. *When Law Fails: Making Sense of Miscarriages of Justice*. New York: New York University Press.

Ogus, Anthony I., ed. 2001. *Regulation, Economics, and the Law*. Northampton, MA: Edward Elgar Publishing.

Okrent, Daniel. 2010. *Last Call*. New York: Scribner's.

Oldham, J. Thomas, and Marygold S. Melli, eds. 2000. *Child Support: The Next Frontier*. Ann Arbor: University of Michigan Press.

Oliver, Peter, Sionaidh Douglass Scott, and Victor Tadros, eds. 2000. *Faith in Law: Essays in Legal Theory.* Portland, OR: Hart.

Oliver, Willard M. 2007. *Homeland Security for Policing.* Upper Saddle River, NJ: Prentice Hall.

Oliverio, Annamarie. 1997. "The State of Injustice: The Politics of Terrorism and the Production of Order." *International Journal of Comparative Sociology* 38: 48–63.

Olsen, Frances E. 1995. *Feminist Legal Theory, Vols. I and II.* New York: Washington Square Press.

Olson, Marvin E., ed. 1970. *Power in Societies.* New York: Macmillan.

Olson, Susan M., and Albert W. Dzur. 2004. "Revisiting Informal Justice: Restorative Justice and Democratic Professionalism." *Law & Society Review* 38: 139–179.

Onishi, Norimitsu. 2008. "Lawyers in Rural Japan: Low Supply, Iffy Demand." *New York Times* (July 29): A10.

Oppel, Richard A., Jr. 2003. "House Expected to Pass Bill to Rewrite the Rules of Cross-Action Lawsuits." *New York Times* (June 12): A31.

Oppel, Richard A., Jr., and Glenn Justice. 2004. "Kerry Gains Campaign Ace, at Cost of Anti-Lawyer Anger." *New York Times* (July 7): A15.

Orrego, Cristobal. 2003. "H. L. A. Hart Arguments Against Classical Natural Law Theory." *American Journal of Jurisprudence* 48: 297–324.

Osiatynski, Wiktor. 2009. *Human Rights and Their Limits.* Cambridge, UK: Cambridge University Press.

Osiel, Mark J. 1999. *Obeying Orders: Atrocity, Military Discipline & the Law of War.* New Brunswick, NJ: Transaction.

Ostrom, Brian J., Charles W. Ostrom, Jr., Roger A. Hanson, and Matthew Kleiman. 2007. *Trial Courts as Organizations.* Philadelphia: Temple University Press.

Overland, Martha. 2005. "In Cambodia, Crafting Law Amid Chaos." *Chronicle of Higher Education* (April 15): A36–A38.

Overy, Richard. 2003. "The Nuremberg Trials: International Law in the Making." Pp. 1–29, in Philippe Sands, ed. *From Nuremberg to the Hague: The Future of International Criminal Justice.* Cambridge, UK: Cambridge University Press.

Packer, Herbert. 1968. *The Limits of the Criminal Sanction.* Palo Alto, CA: Stanford University Press.

Page, William H., and John E. Lopatka. 2007. *The Microsoft Case: Anti-Trust, High Technology and Consumer Welfare.* Chicago: University of Chicago Press.

Pagnattaro, Marisa Anne. 2001. *In Defiance of the Law: From Anne Hutchinson to Toni Morrison.* New York: Peter Lang.

Paik, Anthony, Ann Southworth, and John P. Heinz. 2007. "Lawyers of the Right: Networks and Organization." *Law & Social Inquiry* 32: 883–917.

Palmer, Larry I. 2000. *Endings and Beginnings: Law, Medicine, and Society in Assisted Life and Death.* Westport, CT: Greenwood.

Palmer, Michael, and Simon Roberts. 2007. "Dispute Resolution, Alternative." Pp. 421–426, in David S. Clark, ed. *Encyclopedia of Law and Society.* Los Angeles: Sage.

Palombella, Gianluigi, and Neil Walker, eds. 2009. *Relocating the Rule of Law.* Oxford, UK: Hart Publishing.

Papke, David Ray, ed. 1987. *Framing the Criminal: Crime, Cultural Work, and the Loss of Critical Perspective, 1830–1900.* Hamden, CT: Archon Books.

———. 1995. "Prime-Time Lawyers." *IU—Indianapolis Alumni Magazine* (Spring): 2–8.

———. 1998. *Heretics in the Temple: Americans Who Reject the Nation's Legal Faith.* New York: New York University Press.

———. 1999. *The Pullman Case: The Clash of Labor and Capital in Industrial America.* Lawrence: Kansas University Press.

———. 2001. "Law, Cinema, and Ideology: Hollywood Legal Films of the 1950s." *UCLA Law Review* 48: 1473–1493.

Parker, Christine. 2000. *Just Lawyers.* New York: Oxford University Press.

———. 2006. "The 'Compliance' Trap: The Moral Message in Response to Regulatory Enforcement." *Law & Society Review* 40: 591–622.

Parker, Christine, and John Braithwaite. 2003. "Regulation." Pp. 119–145, in Peter Cane and Mark Tushnet, eds. *The Oxford Handbook of Legal Studies.* New York: Oxford University Press.

Parks, Gregory S., Shayne Jones, and W. Jonathan Cardi, eds. 2008. *Critical Race Realism: Intersections of Psychology, Race, and Law.* New York: The New Press.

Parisi, Francesco. 2007. "Economics, Law and." Pp. 451–458, in David S. Clark, ed. *Encyclopedia of Law & Society.* Los Angeles: Sage.

Parloff, Roger. 2009. "How Pot Became Legal." *Fortune* (September 28): 141–161.

Parsons, Ronald A. 1998. "That Which Governs: An Essay on the Nature of Law and Its Relation to Justice." *South Dakota Law Review* 43: 172–187.

Partington, Martin. 2008. "Law's Reality: Case Studies in Empirical Research on Law: Introduction." *Journal of Law and Society* 35: 1–7.

Pascoe, Peggy. 2008. *What Comes Naturally: Miscegenation Law and the Making of Race in America.* New York: Oxford University Press.

Paternoster, Raymond. 1987. "The Deterrent Effect of the Perceived Certainty and Severity of Punishment: A Review of the Evidence." *Justice Quarterly* 4: 173–217.

Paternoster, Raymond, Robert Brame, Ronet Bachman, and Lawrence W. Sherman. 1997. "Do Fair Procedures Matter? The Effects of Procedural Justice on Spouse Assault." *Law & Society Review* 31: 163–204.

Patterson, Dennis. 1996a. *Law and Truth.* New York: Oxford University Press.

_____, ed. 1996b. *A Companion to Philosophy of Law and Legal Theory.* Cambridge, MA: Blackwell.

Paul, Pamela. 2004. "The Porn Factor." *Time* (January 19): 99–101.

Paulsen, Michael Stokes. 2009. "The Constitutional Power to Interpret International Law." *The Yale Law Journal* 118 (June): 1762–1843.

Pavlich, George. 1992. "People's Courts, Postmodern Difference, and Socialist Justice in South Africa." *Social Justice* 19: 29–45.

_____. 1996. *Justice Fragmented: Mediating Community Disputes Under Postmodern Conditions.* London: Routledge.

Peach, Lucinda. 2002. *Legislating Morality: Pluralism and Religious Identity in Law Making.* New York: Oxford University Press.

Pear, Robert, and Erik Eckholm. 2006. "A Decade After Welfare Overhaul, a Fundamental Shift in Policy and Perception." *New York Times* (August 21): A12.

Peck, Garrett. 2008. *The Prohibition Hangover: Alcohol in America from Demon Rum to Cult Cabernet.* New Brunswick, NJ: Rutgers University Press.

Pegram, Thomas R. 1998. *Battling Demon. Rum: The Struggle for a Dry America, 1800–1933.* Chicago: Ivan R. Dee.

Pence, Gregory. 2008–2009. "De-Regulating and De-Criminalizing Innovations in Human Reproduction." *Cumberland Law Review* 39: 1–14.

Perez-Pena, Richard. 1999. "Lawyers Abandon Legislatures for Greener Pastures." *New York Times* (February 21): Sect. 4. 3.

Perlez, Jane. 2006. "U.S. Competes With China for Vietnam's Allegiance." *New York Times* (June 19): A9.

Perlman, Andrew M. 2003. "Toward a Unified Theory of Professional Regulation." *Florida Law Review* 55: 977–1043.

Perry, Barbara. 2008. *Silent Victims: Hate Crimes Against Native Americans.* Phoenix: University of Arizona Press.

Perry, Barbara A. 2007. *The Michigan Affirmative Action Cases.* Lawrence: University of Kansas Press.

Peters, Jeremy W. 2009a. "Albany Reaches Deal to Repeal '70s Drug Laws." *New York Times* (March 26): A1.

_____. 2009b. "Advocates on Both Sides Seek Momentum on Same-Sex Marriage." *New York Times* (April 9): A22.

Peters, Shawn F. 2008. *When Prayer Fails: Faith Healing, Children, and the Law.* New York: Oxford University Press.

Petersen, Hanne, Rubya Mehdi, Gordon Woodman and Erik Sand, eds. 2008. *Law and Religion in Multicultural Societies.* Portland, OR: DJOF Publishing.

Petersen, Melody, 1998. "The Short End of Long Hours." *New York Times* (July 18): D1.

Pether, Penelope. 2010. "Language." Pp. 315–338, in A. Sarat, M. Anderson, and C. O. Frank, eds. *Law and the Humanities: An Introduction.* Cambridge, UK: Cambridge University Press.

Pfiffner, James P. 2008. *Power Play: The Bush Presidency and the Constitution.* Washington, DC: Brookings Institution Press.

Philippopoulos-Mihalopoulos, Andreas. 2010. *Niklas Luhmann: Law, Justice, Society.* Abingdon Oxon, UK: Routledge.

Phillips, Scott. 2003. "The Social Structure of Vengeance: A Test of Black's Model." *Criminology* 41: 673–708.

Phillips, Scott, and Ryken Grattet. 2000. "Judicial Rhetoric, Meaning-Making, and the Institutionalization of Hate Crime Law." *Law & Society Review* 34: 567–606.

Piaget, Jean. 1932. *The Moral Judgment of the Child.* New York: Keegan Paul Trench, Trubner.

Pierce, Jennifer L. 1995. *Gender Trials: Emotional Lives in Contemporary Law Firms.* Berkeley: University of California Press.

Pincus, Fred L. 2003. *Reverse Discrimination: Dismantling the Myth.* Boulder, CO: Lynne Rienner Publishing.

Pinello, Daniel R. 2006. *America's Struggle for Same-Sex Marriage.* New York: Cambridge University Press.

Piven, Francis Fox, and Richard Cloward. 1971. *Regulating the Poor.* New York: Vintage.

Platt, Anthony. 1977. *The Child Savers: The Invention of Delinquency, 2nd ed.* Chicago: University of Chicago Press.

Pocar, Valerio. 2007. "Animal Rights." Pp. 67–68, in David S. Clark, ed. *Encyclopedia of Law & Society*. Los Angeles: Sage.

Pohlman, H. L. 2007. *Terrorism and the Constitution: The Post-9/11 Cases*. Lanham, MD: Rowman & Littlefield Publishers, Inc.

Poibao, Jioi. 2002. *Dissidents of Law: On the 1989 Velvet Revolutions, Legitimations, Fictions of Legality, and Contemporary Versions of the Social Contract*. Burlington, VT: Ashgate.

Polgreen, Lydia. 2007. "Nigeria Turns from Harsher Side of Islamic Law." *New York Times* (December 1): A1.

Pollack, Mark A., and Gregory C. Shaffer. 2009. *When Cooperation Fails: The International Law and Politics of Genetically Modified Foods*. New York: Oxford University Press.

Polletta, Francesca. 2001. "The Laws of Passion." *Law & Society Review* 35: 467–493.

Ponte, Lucille M. 2009. "Preserving Creativity from Endless Digital Exploitation: Has the Time Come for the New Concept of Copyright Dilution?" *Boston University Journal of Science & Technology Law* 15 (Winter): 34–101.

Pope, James, Peter Kellman, and Ed Bruno. 2003. "Toward a New Labor Law." A Paper Presented at the Annual Meeting of the Law & Society Association, Pittsburgh (May).

Popkin, William D. 2007. *Evolution of Judicial Opinion: Institutional and Individual Styles*. New York: New York University Press.

Porsdam, Helle. 2009. *From Civil to Human Rights: Dialogues on Law and Humanities in the United States and Europe*. Northampton, MA: Edward Elgar Publishing.

Porto, Brian L, 2001. *May It Please the Court: Judicial Processes and Politics in America*. New York: Longman.

Posner, Eric. 2000. *Law and Social Norms*. Cambridge, MA: Harvard University Press.

_____. 2009. *The Perils of Global Legalism*. Chicago: University of Chicago Press.

Posner, Eric A., and Adrian Vermeule. 2007. *Terror in the Balance: Security, Liberty, and the Courts*. New York: Oxford University Press.

Posner, Richard A. 1988. *Law and Literature: A Misunderstood Relation*. Cambridge, MA: Harvard University Press.

_____. 1990. *The Problems of Jurisprudence*. Cambridge, MA: Harvard University Press.

_____ 1992. *Sex and Reason*. Cambridge, MA: Harvard University Press.

_____. 1995a. *Overcoming Law*. Cambridge, MA: Harvard University Press.

_____ 1995b. *Aging and Old Age*. Chicago: University of Chicago Press.

_____. 1998. *The Economic Analysis of Law*, 4th ed. Boston: Little, Brown.

_____. 1999a. *The Problematics of Moral and Legal Theory*. Cambridge, MA: Harvard University Press.

_____. 1999b. *An Affair of State: The Investigation, Impeachment, and Trial of President Clinton*. Cambridge, MA: Harvard University Press.

_____. 2003. *Law, Pragmatism, and Democracy*. Cambridge, MA: Harvard University Press.

_____. 2004. *Catastrophe: Risk and Response*. New York: Oxford University Press.

_____. 2006. *Not a Suicide Pact: The Constitution in a Time of National Emergency*. New York: Oxford University Press.

_____. 2008. *How Judges Think*. Cambridge, MA: Harvard University Press.

Potter, Pitman B. 2004. "Legal Reform in China: Institutions, Culture, and Selective Adaptation." *Law & Social Inquiry* 29: 465–495.

Pound, Roscoe. 1907. "The Need of a Sociological Jurisprudence." *The Green Bag* 19: 607–615.

_____. 1908. "Mechanical Jurisprudence." *Columbia Law Review* 8: 605–623.

_____. 1910. "Law in Books and Law in Action." *American Law Review* 44: 12–36.

_____. 1942. *Social Control Through Law*. New Haven, CT: Yale University Press.

_____. 1943. "A Survey of Social Interests." *Harvard Law Review* 57: 1–39.

_____. 1945. "A Survey of Public Interests." *Harvard Law Review* 58: 909–929.

Powell, H. Jefferson. 2008. *Constitutional Conscience: The Moral Dimension of Judicial Decision*. Chicago: University of Chicago Press.

Power, Lucas A., Jr. 2009. *The Supreme Court and the American Elite, 1789–2008*. Cambridge, MA: Harvard University Press.

Powers, David S. 1992. "On Judicial Review in Islamic Law." *Law Society Review* 26: 315–341.

Powers, Stephen P., and Stanley Rothman. 2002. *The Least Dangerous Branch? Consequences of Judicial Activism*. Westport, CT: Praeger.

Precht, Robert E. 2003. *Defending Mohammed: Justice on Trial*. Ithaca, NY: Cornell University Press.

_____. 2006. "Japan, the Jury." *New York Times* (December 1): A31.

Prest, Wilfrid R. 1986. *The Rise of the Barristers: A Social History of the English Bar, 1590–1640*. Oxford, UK: Clarendon Press.

Prest, Wilfrid, and Sharyn Roach Anleu, eds. 2004. *Litigation: Past and Present*. Sydney: University of New South Wales Press.

Preston, Frederick W., and Roger I. Roots. 2004. "Law and Its Unintended Consequences." *American Behavioral Scientist* 47: 1371–1375.

Preston, Julia. 2004. "U.S. Prosecutor Says Lawyer Aided Tenor." *New York Times* (June 23): B3.

_____. 2005. "Lawyer Is Guilty of Aiding Terror." *New York Times* (February 11): A1.

Pribin, Jiri, Pauline Roberts, and James Young, eds. 2003. *Systems of Justice in Transition: Central European Experiences Since 1989*. Aldershot, UK: Ashgate.

Probert, Rebecca, ed. 2007. *Family Life and the Law: Under One Roof*. Burlington, VT: Ashgate Publishing Co.

Provine, Doris Marie. 1996. "Courts in the Political Process in France." Pp. 177–248, in H. Jacob, E. Blankenburg, H. M. Kritzer, D. M. Provine, and J. Sanders, eds. *Courts, Law, and Politics in Comparative Perspective*. New Haven, CT: Yale University Press.

_____. 2007. *Unequal under Law: Race in the War on Drugs*. Chicago: University of Chicago Press.

Ptacek, James. 1999. *Battered Women in the Courtroom: The Power of Judicial Response*. Boston: Northeastern University Press.

Pue, W. Wesley, and David Sugarman, eds. 2003. *Lawyers and Vampires: Cultural Histories of the Legal Professions*. Portland, OR: Hart Publishing.

Pulsinelli, Gary. 2008. "Harry Potter and the (Re)Order of the Artists: Are We Muggles or Goblins." *Oregon Law Review* 87: 1101–1132.

Purcell, Edward A., Jr. 2008. *Originalism, Federalism, and the American Constitutional Enterprise: A Historical Inquiry*. New Haven: Yale University Press.

Purdum, Todd S. 2003. "As California Goes, So Goes the Country?" *New York Times* (September 21): Week 4.

Quinney, Richard. [1974] 2001. *Critique of Legal Order*. New Brunswick, NJ: Transaction.

_____. 1991. "The Way to Peace: On Crime, Suffering, and Service." Pp. 3–13, in H. E. Pepinsky and R. Quinney, eds. *Criminology as Peacemaking*. Bloomington: Indiana University Press.

Rabin, Robert L., and Stephen D. Sugarman, eds. 1993. *Smoking Policy: Law, Politics, and Culture*. New York: Oxford University Press.

_____, eds. 2001. *Regulating Tobacco*. New York: Oxford University Press.

Rackstraw, Jennifer H. 2003. "Reaching for Justice: An Analysis of Self-Help Prosecution for Animal Crimes." *Animal Law* 9: 243–266.

Radcliffe-Brown, A. 1922. *The Andaman Islanders*. Cambridge. UK: University Press.

Rafter, Nicole. 2001. "American Criminal Trial Films: An Overview of Their Development, 1930–2000." *Journal of Law & Society* 28: 9–24.

Raiffa, Howard. 2003. *Negotiation Analysis*. Cambridge, MA: Belknap.

Ramadan, Tariq. 2009. *Radical Reform: Islamic Ethics and Liberation*. New York: Oxford University Press.

Ramraj, Victor V., ed. 2008. *Emergencies and the Limits of Legality*. New York: Cambridge University Press.

Raphael, Steven, and Michael A. Stoll, eds. 2009. *Do Prisons Make Us Safer? The Benefits and Costs of the Prison Boom*. New York: Russell Sage Foundation.

Rapping, Elayne. 2003. *Law and Justice as Seen on TV*. New York: New York University Press.

Raskin, Jamin B. 2002. "The First Amendment: The High Ground and the Low Ground." Pp. 115–128, in Herman Schwartz, ed. *The Rehnquist Court—Judicial Activism on the Right*. New York: Hill & Wang.

Rasmusen, Eric B., ed. 2007. *Game Theory and the Law*. Cheltenham, UK: Edward Elgar Publishing.

Ravitch, Frank S. 2007. *Masters of Illusion: The Supreme Court and the Religion Clauses*. New York: New York University Press.

Rawls, John. 1971. *A Theory of Justice*. Cambridge, MA: Harvard University Press.

_____. 2001. *Justice as Fairness: A Restatement*. Cambridge, MA: Belknap Press of Harvard University Press.

Ray, Laura Krugman. 1999. "Autobiography and Opinion: The Romantic Jurisprudence of Justice William O. Douglas." *University of Pittsburgh Law Review* 60: 707–744.

Re, Edward D. 1994, "The Causes of Popular Dissatisfaction With the Legal Profession." *St. John's Law Review* 68: 85–136.

Redfield, Robert. 1967. "Primitive Law." Pp. 3–24, in Paul Bohannon, ed. *Law and Warfare: Studies in the Anthropology of Conflict*. Garden City, NY: Natural History Press.

Redish, Martin H. 2009. *Wholesale Justice: Constitutional Democracy and the Problem of the Class Action Lawsuit.* Stanford, CA: Stanford University Press.

Reece, Helen, ed. 1998. *Law and Science: Current Legal Issues, 1998 Vol. I.* New York: Oxford University Press.

Regoli, Robert M., John D. Hewitt, and Matt DeLisi. 2010. *Delinquency in Society. 8th edition.* Boston: Jones and Bartlett Publishers.

Reichel, Philip A. 1999. *Comparative Criminal Justice Systems: A Topical Approach. 2nd ed.* Upper Saddle River, NJ: Prentice Hall.

Reichel, Philip L. 2010. "Justice Systems in Selected Countries." Pp. 79–104, in Sesha Kethineni, ed. *Comparative and International Policing, Justice, and Transnational Crime.* Durham, NC: Carolina Academic Press.

Reichman, Amnon. 2008. "The 'Social', the 'Legal' and Law-and-Society Research: A Quest for a Canon amid Diverse Conversations." *International Sociology* 23: 181–193.

Reichman, Nancy, and Joyce Sterling. 2002. "Recasting the Brass Ring: Deconstructing and Reconstructing Workplace Opportunities for Women Lawyers." *Capital University Law Review* 29: 923–977.

Reichman, Ravit. 2009. *The Affective Life of Law: Legal Modernism and the Literary Imagination.* Stanford, CA: Stanford University Press.

Reid, John Phillip. 2000. "Introduction: The Layers of Western Legal History." Pp. 3–42, in Gordon M. Bakken, ed. *Law in the Western United States.* Norman: University of Oklahoma Press.

Reiman, Jeffrey. 1990. *Justice and Modern Moral Philosophy.* New Haven, CT: Yale University Press.

Reisman, W. Michael. 1999. *Law in Brief Encounters.* New Haven, CT: Yale University Press.

Relis, Tamara. 2009. *Perceptions in Litigation and Mediation: Lawyers, Defendants, Plaintiffs and Gendered Parties.* New York: Cambridge University Press.

Renner, Karl. [1904] 1949. *The Institutions of Private Law and Their Functions.* (O. Kahn-Freund, ed.) London: Routledge & Kegan Paul.

Renteln, Alison Dundes. 2005. *The Cultural Defense.* New York: Oxford University Press.

_____. 2007. "Political Science, Law and." Pp. 1137–1143, in David S. Clark, ed. *Encyclopedia of Law and Society.* Los Angeles: Sage.

Reuters. 2008. "Rape Victim Stoned to Death in Somalia Was 13, U.N. Says." *New York Times* (November 5): A12.

Revesz, Richard L., and Michael A. Livermore. 2008. *Retaking Rationality: How Cost-Benefit Analysis Can Better Protect the Environment and Our Health.* New York: Oxford University Press.

Rhea, Harry M. 2008. "The Nuremberg Effect on Contemporary International Criminal Justice." *Criminal Justice Studies* 21: 361–372.

Rhode, Deborah L. 2000. "Kicking the Socratic Method and Other Reforms for Law Schools." *Chronicle of Higher Education* (January 26): B15.

_____. 2001. "The Professional Responsibilities of Professors." *Journal of Legal Education* 51: 158–165.

_____. 2003. "Midcourse Corrections: Women in Legal Education." *Journal of Legal Education* 53: 475–488.

_____. 2010. *The Beauty Bias.* New York: Oxford University Press.

Rich, Motoko. 2003. "Homeowner Boards Are Blurring Line of Who Rules Roost." *New York Times* (July 27): A1.

Richards, Mark J., and Herbert M. Kritzer. 2002. "Jurisprudential Regimes in Supreme Court Decision Making." *American Political Science Review* 96: 305–320.

Richards, Peter Judson. 2007. *Extraordinary Justice: Military Tribunals in Historical and International Context.* New York: New York University Press.

Richards, Robert D., and Clay Calvert. 2009. "When Sex and Cell Phones Collide: Inside the Prosecution of a Teen Sexting Case." *Hastings Communications and Entertainment Law Journal* 32: 1–40.

Richland, Justin B. 2008. *Arguing with Tradition: The Language of Law in Hopi Tribal Court.* Chicago: University of Chicago Press.

Richland, Justin B., and Sarah Deer. 2009. *Introduction to Tribal Legal Studies. Second edition.* Lanham, MD: AltaMira Press.

Richman, Kimberly. 2008. *Courting Change: Queer Parents, Judges, and the Transformation of American Law.* New York: NYU Press.

Richtel, Matt. 2009. "Not Driving Drunk, but Texting? Utah Law Sees Little Difference." *New York Times* (August 29): A1.

Rickleen, Lauren Stiller. 2007. "Virginia Tech and the Challenge of Assuring Safety." *Chronicle of Higher Education* (May 11): B14.

Riksheim, Eric, and Steven Chermak. 1993. "Causes of Police Behavior Revisited." *Journal of Criminal Justice* 21: 353–382.

Ripstein, Arthur, ed. 2007. *Ronald Dworkin*. New York: Cambridge University Press.

Rivera, Ray, and Al Baker. 2010. "A Rise in Violent Crime Evokes City's Unruly Past." *New York Times* (April 12): A21.

Rivlin, Eliezer. 2009. "Thoughts on Referral to Foreign Law, Global Chain-Novel, and Novelty." *Florida Journal of International Law* 21: 1–28.

Roach, Kent. 2003. "Criminal Process." Pp. 773–795, in Peter Cane and Mark Tushnet, eds. *The Oxford Handbook of Legal Studies*. Oxford, UK: Oxford University Press.

Roberts, Julian V., and Mike Hough, eds. 2002. *Changing Attitudes Toward Punishment: Public Opinion, Crime and Justice*. Portland, OR: Willan.

Roberts, Julian V., and Loretta J. Stalans. 1997. *Public Opinion, Crime, and Criminal Justice*. Boulder, CO: Westview Press.

Roberts, Paul Craig, and Lawrence M. Stratton. 2000. *The Tyranny of Good Intentions: How Prosecutors and Bureaucrats Are Trampling the Constitution in the Name of Justice*. Roseville, CA: Prima Publishing.

Robertson, John A. 1974. *Rough Justice: Perspectives on Lower Criminal Courts*. Boston: Little, Brown.

Robertson, Stephen. 2005. *Crimes Against Children: Sexual Violence and Legal Culture in New York City, 1880–1960*. Chapel Hill: University of North Carolina Press.

Robinson, Marilyn. 2003. *Language and the Law: Proceedings From a Conference*. Buffalo, NY: William S. Hein.

Robinson, Matthew B. 2002. *Justice Blind? Ideals and Realities of American Criminal Justice*. Upper Saddle River, NJ: Prentice Hall.

Robinson, Paul A., and John M. Darley. 1995. *Justice, Liability, and Blame: Community Views and the Criminal Law*. Boulder, CO: Westview Press.

Robinson, Paul H. 1999. *Would You Convict?* New York: New York University Press.

Robson, Ruthann. 1998. *Sappho Goes to Law School: Fragments in Lesbian Legal Theory*. New York: Columbia University Press.

Rohde, David. 1998. "Officer Apprehends a Perpetrator. The Charge Is Jaywalking." *New York Times* (February 14): B1.

———. "A World of Ways to Say 'Islamic Law.'" *New York Times* (March 13): Week 4.

Rojek, Dean C. 1985. "The Criminal Process in the People's Republic of China." *Justice Quarterly* 2: 117–125.

Rokumoto, Kahel. 1988. "The Present State of Japanese Practicing Attorneys: On the Way to Full Professionalization." Pp. 160–199, in Richard L. Abel and Philip S. C. Lewis, eds. *Lawyers in Society: The Civil World, Vol. II*. Berkeley: University of California Press.

Rollins, Joe. 2002. "AIDS, Law, and the Rhetoric of Sexuality." *Law & Society Review* 36: 161–191.

Romano, Carlin. 2006. "The Last Judicial Idealist?" *Chronicle of Higher Education* (June 9): B13.

———. 2008. "Boss Nova." *Chronicle of Higher Education Review* (June 6): B6–B10.

Romero, Simon. 2007. "A Culture of Naming that Even a Law May Not Tame." *New York Times* (September 5): A4.

Ronner, Amy D. 2005. *Homophobia and the Law*. Washington, D.C.: American Psychological Association.

Roosevelt, Margot. 2006. "Psst, Your Car Is Watching You." *Time* (August 14): 58–59.

Roots, Roger I. 2004. "When Laws Backfire: Unintended Consequences of Public Policy." *American Behavioral Scientist* 47: 1376–1394.

Rosen, Deborah A. 2007. *American Indians and State Law: Sovereignty, Race, and Citizenship, 1790–1880*. Lincoln: University of Nebraska Press.

Rosen, Ellen. 2006. "Finding a Way Back to the Law." *New York Times* (May 26): Bus. 26.

Rosen, Jeffrey. 2000. *The Unwanted Gaze: The Destruction of Privacy in America*. New York: Random House.

———. 2008. "McJustice." *The New Republic* (November 5): 19–21.

———. 2010. "Nude Awakening." *The New Republic* (February 4): 8–10.

Rosen, Lawrence. 1989. *The Anthropology of Justice: Law as Culture in Islamic Society*. Cambridge, UK: Cambridge University Press.

———. 1992. "Law and Indigenous Peoples." *Law and Social Inquiry* 17: 363–371.

———. 2009. *Law as Culture: An Invitation*. Princeton, NJ: Princeton University Press.

Rosenau, Pauline Marie. 1992. *Post-Modernism and the Social Sciences: Insights, Inroads, and Intrusions*. Princeton, NJ: Princeton University Press.

Rosenbaum, Thane. 2004. *The Myth of Moral Justice: Why Our Legal System Fails to Do Right*. New York: HarperCollins.

Rosenberg, Gerald N. 1991. *The Hollow Hope: Can Courts Bring About Social Change?* Chicago: University of Chicago Press.

———. 2008. *The Hollow Hope: Can Courts Bring About Social Change? 2nd ed*. Chicago: University of Chicago Press.

Rosenblatt, Albert M. 2003. "The Law's Evolution: Long Night's Journey Into Day." *Cardozo Law Review* 24: 2119–2147.

Rosenfeld, Michel, and Andrew Arato. 1998. *Habermas on Law and Democracy*. Berkeley: University of California Press.

Rosenheim, Margaret K., Franklin E. Zimring, Davis S. Tanenhaus, and Bernardine Dohrn, eds. 2002. *A Century of Juvenile Justice*. Chicago: University of Chicago Press.

Rosenthal, Elisabeth. 2000. "In China's Legal Evolution, the Lawyers Are Handcuffed." *New York Times* (January 6): A1.

——— 2007. "Legal or Not, Abortion Rates Compare." *New York Times* (October 12): A12.

———. 2009. "When Texting Kills, Britain Offers Path to Prison." *New York Times* (November 2): A1.

Rosett, Arthur, and Donald R. Cressey. 1976. *Justice by Consent: Plea Bargains in the American Courthouse*. Philadelphia: J. B. Lippincott.

Ross, Hamish. 2001. *Law as a Social Institution*. Portland, OR: Hart.

Ross, H. Laurence. 1992a. *Confronting Drunk Driving: Social Policy for Saving Lives*. New Haven, CT: Yale University Press.

———. 1992b. "The Law and Drunk Driving." *Law & Society Review* 26: 219–230.

Ross, H. Laurence, and Robert B. Voas. 1989. *The New Philadelphia Story: The Effects of Severe Penalties for Drunk Driving*. Washington, DC: AAA Foundation for Traffic Safety.

Ross, Michael, and Dale Miller, eds. 2002. *The Justice Motive in Everyday Life*. Cambridge, UK: Cambridge University Press.

Rotberg, Robert I., and Dennis Thompson, eds. 2000. *Truth v. Justice: The Morality of Truth Commissions*. Princeton, NJ: Princeton University Press.

Roth, Andrew, and Jonathan Roth. 1989. *Devil's Advocates: The Unnatural History of Lawyers*. Berkeley, CA: Nolo Press.

Roth, Louise Marie. 1999. "The Right to Privacy Is Political: Power, the Boundary Between Public and Private, and Sexual Harassment." *Law & Social Inquiry* 24: 45–71.

Rothchild, Jonathan, Matthew Myer Boulton and Kevin Jung, eds. 2007. *Doing Justice to Mercy: Religion, Law and Criminal Justice*. Charlottesville: University of Virginia Press.

Rothe, Dawn L. 2009. *State Criminality: The Crime of All Crimes*. Lanham, MD: Rowman & Littlefield Publishers.

Rothstein, Edward. 2003. "Islam and the Unveiled Photograph." *New York Times* (June 14): B9.

Rotunda, Kyndra Miller. 2008. *Honor Bound: Inside the Guantanamo Trials*. Durham, NC: Carolina Academic Press.

Rousseau, Jean-Jacques. [1762] 1978. *On the Social Contract*. New York: St. Martin's Press.

Rowen, Jamie. 2010. "Review of: Multicultural Jurisprudence." *Law & Society Review* 44: 411–413.

Rutenberg, Jim. 2005. "Used Underwear? There Ought to Be a Law." *New York Times* (April 10): 33.

Ryan, Kevin F. 1998. "Clinging to Failure: The Rise and Continued Life of U.S. Drug Policy." *Law & Society Review* 32: 221–242.

Ryden, David K., and Jeffrey Polet, eds. 2005. *Sanctioning Religion? Politics, Law, and Faith-Based Public Services*. Boulder, CO: Lynne Rienner Publishers.

Sabar, Ariel, and Suevon Lee. 2007. "Judge Tries Suing Pants Off Dry Cleaner." *New York Times* (June 12): A13.

Sack, Kevin. 2008. "21: Should the Drinking Age Be Lowered?" *New York Times Education Life* (November 2): 20–23, 41.

Sack, Peter, and Jonathan Aleck, eds. 1992. *Law and Anthropology*. New York: New York University Press.

Sadurski, Wojciech. 1984. "Social Justice and Legal Justice." *Law and Philosophy* 3: 329–354.

Saegusa, Mayumi. 2009. "Why the Japanese Law School System Was Established: Co-optation as a Defensive Tactic in the Face of Global Pressures." *Law & Social Inquiry* 34: 365–398.

Saenz, Andrea. 2006. "Faculty Unanimously Overhauls First-Year Curriculum." *The Record* (October 12): 1–2.

Salter, Michael. 1997. "Habermas's New Contribution to Legal Scholarship." *Journal of Law and Society* 24: 285–305.

Salzman, Avi. 2006. "Court Ruling Clears Mother in Son's Suicide." *New York Times* (August 29): B1.

Sampson, Robert J., and John Laub. 1993. "Structural Variations in Juvenile Court Processing: Inequality, the Underclass, and Social Control." *Law & Society Review* 27: 285–311.

Sampson, Robert J., and Janet L. Lauritsen. 1997. "Racial and Ethnic Disparities in Crime and Criminal Justice in the United States." Pp. 311–374, in M. Tonry, ed. *Crime and Justice: A Review of the Research, Vol. 21*. Chicago: University of Chicago Press.

Samuel, Dorit. 2009. "The Subprime Mortgage Crisis: Will New Regulations Help Avoid Future Financial Debacles?" *Albany Government Law Review* 2: 217–258.

Samuel, Geoffrey. 2009. "Interdisciplinarity and the Authority Paradigm: Should Law Be Taken Seriously by Scientists and Social Scientists?" *Journal of Law and Society* 36: 431–459.

Samuels, Suzanne. 2006. *Law, Politics and Society*. Boston: Houghton Mifflin.

Sandefur, Rebecca L. 2007. "Lawyers' Pro Bono Service and American-Style Civil Legal Assistance." *Law & Society Review* 41: 79–112.

Sanders, Francine. 1995. "Brown v. Board of Education: An Empirical Examination of Its Effects on Federal District Courts." *Law & Society Review* 29: 731–755.

Sanders, Joseph. 1996. "Courts and Law in Japan." Pp. 315–388, in H. Jacob, E. Blankenburg, N. M. Kritzer, D. M. Provine, and J. Sanders. *Courts, Law, and Politics in Comparative Perspective*. New Haven, CT: Yale University Press.

Sanders, Joseph, and V. Lee Hamilton. 1992. *Everyday Justice: Responsibility for the Individual in Japan and the United States*. New Haven, CT: Yale University Press.

————, eds. 2001. *Handbook of Justice Research in the Law*. Norwell, MA: Kluwer/Plenum.

Sanders, Joseph, V. Lee Hamilton, and Toshiyuki Yuasa. 1998. "The Institutionalization of Sanctions for Wrongdoing Inside Organizations: Public Judgments in Japan, Russia, and the United States." *Law & Society Review* 32: 871–930.

Sanders, Mark. 2007. *Ambiguities of Witnessing: Law and Literature in the Time of a Truth Commission*. Stanford, CA: Stanford University Press.

Santora, Marc. 2003a. "After Son's Suicide, Mother Is Convicted Over Unsafe Home." *New York Times* (October 7): B1.

————. 2003b. "Battling the Darkness With the Law as His Lamp." *New York Times* (November 11): B2.

Santos, Boaventura de Sousa. 1995. *Toward a New Common Sense: Law, Science, and Politics in the Paradigmatic Transition*. London: Routledge.

————. 2007. *Towards a Democratic Revolution of Justice*. Sao Paulo, Brazil: Cortez.

Santos, Boaventura de Sousa, Joao Carlos Trindade, and Maria Paula Meneses, eds. 2006. *Law and Justice in a Multicultural Society: The Case of Mozambique*. Dakar, Senegal: Council for the Development of Social Science Research in Africa.

Sarat, Austin, ed. 2001. *Law, Violence, and the Possibilities of Justice*. Princeton, NJ: Princeton University Press.

————, ed. 2004. *The Social Organization of Law*. Los Angeles. CA: Roxbury.

————, ed. 2004. *Law in the Liberal Arts*. Ithaca, NY: Cornell University Press.

————, ed. 2007. "Death Penalty." Pp. 388–391, in David S. Clark, ed. *Encyclopedia of Law and Society*. Thousand Oaks, CA: Sage.

Sarat, Austin, Bryant Garth, and Robert A. Kagan, eds. 2002. *Looking Back at Law's Century*. Ithaca, NY: Cornell University Press.

Sarat, Austin, Lawrence Douglas, and Martha Umphrey, eds. 2002. *Lives in the Law*. Ann Arbor: University of Michigan Press.

————, eds. 2005a. *The Limits of Law*. Stanford, CA: Stanford University Press.

————, 2005b. *Law on the Screen*. Stanford, CA: Stanford University Press.

————, eds. 2007a. *Law and the Sacred*. Palo Alto, CA: Stanford University Press.

————, eds. 2007b. *How Law Knows*. Palo Alto, CA: Stanford University Press.

————, eds. 2007c. *Law and Catastrophe*. Stanford, CA: Stanford University Press.

————, 2010. *Law and the Stranger*. Stanford, CA: Stanford University Press.

Sarat, Austin, Marianne Constable, David Engel, Valerie Hans, and Susan Lawrence, eds. 1998a. *Everyday Practices and Trouble Cases*. Chicago: Northwestern University Press.

————. 1998b. *Crossing Boundaries: Traditions and Transformations in Law and Society Research*. Chicago: Northwestern University Press.

Sarat, Austin, and Thomas R. Kearns, eds. 1993. *The Fate of Law*. Ann Arbor: University of Michigan Press.

————, eds. 2001. *Human Rights: Concepts, Contests, and Contingencies*. Ann Arbor: University of Michigan Press.

Sarat, Austin, and William F. Felstiner. 1995. *Divorce Lawyers and Their Clients: Power and Meaning in the Legal Process*. New York: Oxford University Press.

Sarat, Austin, and Stuart Scheingold, eds. 1998. *Cause Lawyering*. New York: Oxford University Press.

_____. 2001. *Cause Lawyering and the State in a Global Era*. New York: Oxford University Press.

_____, eds. 2005. *The Worlds Cause Lawyers Make: Structure and Agency in Legal Practice*. Stanford, CA: Stanford University Press.

_____. Scheingold. 2006. *Cause Lawyers and Social Movements*. Stanford, CA: Stanford University Press.

_____, eds. 2008. *The Cultural Lives of Cause Lawyers*. New York: Cambridge University Press.

Sarracino, Carmine, and Kevin M. Scott. 2008. *The Porning of America*. Boston: Beacon Press.

Sartre, Jean-Paul. 1968. *"Preface" to Frantz Fanon, The Wretched of the Earth*. New York: Grove Press.

Sarwar, Beena. 2002. "Brutality Cloaked as Tradition." *New York Times* (August 6): Op Ed Page.

Sasso, Peggy. 2009. "Criminal Responsibility in the Age of 'Mind-Reading'." *American Criminal Law Review* 46: 1191–1244.

Saul, Stephanie. 2009. "Building a Baby, With Few Ground Rules." *New York Times* (December 13): A1.

Saulny, Susan. 2003a. "Volunteerism by Lawyers Is on the Rise." *New York Times* (February 19): B1.

_____. 2003b. "Lawyers' Ads Seeking Clients in Ferry Crash." *New York Times* (November 4): A1.

_____. 2003c. "Lawyers' Fees to Defend Poor Will Increase." *New York Times* (November 13): B1.

Saunders, David. 1997. *Anti-Lawyers: Religion and the Critics of Law and State*. New York: Routledge.

Savage, Charlie. 2009. "U.S. Will Settle Indian Lawsuit for $3.4 Billion." *New York Times* (December 9): A1.

Savage, Charlie, and Scott Shane. 2009. "Terror-War Fallout Lingers Over Bush Lawyers." *New York Times* (March 9): A1.

Scala, Dante J. 2007. "Henry Sumner Maine." Pp. 980–981, in David Clark, ed. *Encyclopedia of Law & Society*. Los Angeles: Sage.

Scaramella, Gene L., Steven M. Cox, and William P. McCamey. 2011. *Introduction to Policing*. Los Angeles: Sage.

Schauer, Frederick. 2009. *Thinking Like a Lawyer: A New Introduction to Legal Reasoning*. Cambridge, MA: Harvard University Press.

Schauer, Frederick, and Virginia J. Wise. 1997. "Legal Positivism as Legal Information." *Cornell Law Review* 82: 1080–1100.

Scheffer, Thomas. 2008. "Creating Comparability Differently: Disassembling Ethnographic Comparison in Law-in-Action." *Comparative Sociology* 7: 286–310.

Scheingold, Stuart A. 1997. *Politics, Crime Control, and Culture*. Brookfield, VT: Ashgate.

Scheingold, Stuart A., and Austin Sarat. 2004. *Something to Believe In: Politics, Professionalism, and Cause Lawyering*. Stanford, CA: Stanford University Press.

Scheper-Hughes, Nancy. 1995. "Who's the Killer? Popular Justice and Human Rights in a South African Squatter Camp." *Social Justice* 22: 143–164.

Scheppele, Kim Lane. 1994. "Legal Theory and Social Theory." Pp. 383–406, in John Hagan and Karen S. Cook, eds. *Annual Review of Sociology*, Vol. 20. Palo Alto, CA: Annual Reviews.

Schlag, Pierre. 1987. "The Brilliant, the Curious, and the Wrong." *Stanford Law Review* 39: 917–927.

Schleef, Debra. 2006. *Managing Elites: Professional Socialization in Law and Business Schools*. Lanham, MD: Rowman and Littlefield.

Schlosser, Eric. 2004. "Make Peace With Pot." *New York Times* (April 26): A19.

Schlueter, David. 2007. "Military Justice." Pp. 1021–1024, in David S. Clark, ed. *Encyclopedia of Law and Society*. Los Angeles: Sage.

Schmalleger, Frank. 2011. *Criminal Justice Today: An Introductory Text for the 21st Century*. Boston: Prentice Hall.

Schmalleger, Frank, and John L. Worrall. 2010. *Policing Today*. Upper Saddle River, NJ: Prentice Hall.

Schmidt, Peter. 2003. "Why Not a Remedy for Past Discrimination?" *Chronicle of Higher Education* (June 6): A20–A22.

_____. 2009. "Law Schools Customize Degrees to Students' Taste." *Chronicle of Higher Education* (January 9): A1, 7–8.

Schnayerson, Robert. 1986. *The Illustrated History of the Supreme Court of the United States*. New York: Harry Abrams.

Schneider, Carl E. 1990. "Social Structure and Social Control: On the Moral Order of a Suburb." *Law & Society Review* 24: 875–886.

Schneider, Elizabeth M. 2000. *Battered Women and Feminist Lawmaking*. New Haven, CT: Yale University Press.

Schneider, Stephen. 2007. *Refocusing Crime Prevention: Collective Action and the Quest for Community*. Toronto, ON: University of Toronto Press.

Schneyer, Ted. 1991. "Professional Discipline for Law Firms?" *Cornell Law Review* 77: 1–46.

Schofield, Philip. 2006. *Utility and Democracy: The Political Thought of Jeremy Bentham*. Oxford: Oxford University Press.

Schram, Sanford F., and Brian Caterino, eds. 2006. *Making Political Science Matter: Debating Knowledge, Research, and Method.* New York: New York University Press.

Schubert, Frank A. 2004. *Criminal Law: The Basics.* Los Angeles: Roxbury.

Schulhofer, Stephen J. 1998. *Unwanted Sex: The Culture of Intimidation and the Failure of Law.* Cambridge, MA: Harvard University Press.

Schultz, David A., ed. 1998. *Leveraging the Law: Using the Courts to Achieve Social Change.* New York: Peter Lang.

Schultz, Ulrike, and Gisela Shaw, eds. 2003. *Women in the World's Legal Professions.* New York: Oxford University Press.

Schuman, Howard. 2008. Method and Meaning in Polls and Surveys. Cambridge, MA: Harvard University Press.

Schur, Edwin M. 1965. *Crimes Without Victims.* Englewood Cliffs, NJ: Prentice Hall.

_____. 1968. *Law and Society: A Sociological View.* New York: Random House.

_____. 1973. *Radical Non-Intervention: Rethinking the Delinquency Problem.* Englewood Cliffs, NJ: Prentice Hall.

Schwartz, Bernard. 1974. *The Law in America.* New York: American Heritage Books.

Schwartz, Herman. 2000. *The Struggle for Constitutional Justice in Post-Communist Europe.* Chicago: University of Chicago Press.

Schwartz, John. 2002. "Court Blocks Law on Access to Web." *New York Times* (June 1): A1.

_____. 2003a. "Guarding Privacy vs. Enforcing Copyrights." *New York Times* (September 29): C1.

_____. 2003b. "File Sharing Pits Copyright Against Free Speech." *New York Times* (November 3): C1.

_____. 2009a. "As Jurors Turn to Google and Twitter, Mistrials Are Popping Up." *New York Times* (March 18): A1.

_____. 2009b. "Tilting at Internet Barrier, A Stalwart Is Upended." *New York Times* (August 11): A11.

Schwarz, Philip J. 1988. *Twice Condemned: Slaves and the Criminal Laws of Virginia, 1705–1865.* Baton Rouge: Louisiana University Press.

Schweik, Susan M. 2009. *The Ugly Laws: Disability in Public.* New York: New York University Press.

Sciolino, Elaine. 2008. "Britain Grapples with Role for Islamic Justice." *New York Times* (November 19): A1.

Sciulli, David. 2001. *Corporate Power in Civil Society: An Application of Societal Constitutionalism.* New York: New York University Press.

Sclater, Shelley Day, Fatemeh Ebtehaj, Emily Jackson, and Martin Richards, eds. 2009. *Regulating Autonomy: Sex, Reproduction and Family.* Portland, OR: Hart Publishing.

Scobliz, J. Peter. 2010. "What are Nukes Good For?" *The New Republic* (April 29): 22–27.

Scott, Elizabeth S., and Laurence Steinberg. 2008. *Rethinking Juvenile Justice.* Cambridge, MA: Harvard University Press.

Scott, Joan Wallach. 2007. *The Politics of the Veil.* Princeton: Princeton University Press.

Scott, Kyle. 2007. *Dismantling American Common Law: Liberty and Justice in Our Transformed Courts.* Lanham, MD: Lexington Books.

Scott, Rosamund. 2002. *Rights, Duties and the Body: Law and Ethics of the Maternal-Fetal Conflict.* Portland, OR: Hart.

Scoular, Jane, and Teela Sanders. 2010. "Introduction: The Changing Social and Legal Context of Sexual Commerce: Why Regulation." *Journal of Law and Society* (March): 1–11.

Scrivens, Louise. 2008. "Changing the Flaws in London's Laws." *BBC News* (August 28): 1.

Schauer, Frederick. 2009. *Thinking Like a Lawyer: A New Introduction to Legal Reasoning.* Cambridge, MA: Harvard University Press.

Seabury, Seth A., Nicholas M. Pace, and Robert T. Revile. 2004. "Forty Years of Civil Jury Verdicts." *Journal of Empirical Legal Studies* 1: 1–25.

Searcey, Dionne. 2009. "A Lawyer, Some Teens and a Fight Over 'Sexting.'" *Wall Street Journal* (April 21): A17.

Sebok, Anthony J. 1998. *Legal Positivism in American Jurisprudence.* New York: Cambridge University Press.

Secret, Mosi. 2011. "States Prosecute Fewer Teenagers in Adult Courts." *New York Times* (March 6): A1.

Segre, Sandro. 2003. *Controlling Illegal Drugs: A Comparative Study.* Hawthorne, NY: Aldine de Gruyter.

Seidenberg, Steven. 2009. "Copyright in the Age of YouTube." *ABA Journal* (February): 46–51.

Seidman, Louis Michael. 2001. *Our Unsettled Constitution: A New Defense of Constitutionalism and Judicial Review.* New Haven, CT: Yale University Press.

Selznick, Philip. 1992. *The Moral Commonwealth: Social Theory and the Promise of Community.* Berkeley: University of California Press.

Selznick, Philip. 2008. *A Humanist Science: Values and Ideals in Social Inquiry.* Stanford, CA: Stanford University Press.

Sen, Amartya. 2009. *The Idea of Justice.* Cambridge, MA: Belknap Press/Harvard University Press.

Senior, Jennifer. 2004. "A Nation Unto Himself." *New York Times Magazine* (March 14): 36–43, 52, 73, 77.

Seron, Carroll. 1993. "New Strategies for Getting Clients: Urban and Suburban Lawyers' Views." *Law & Society Review* 27: 399–418.

————. 1996. *The Business of Practicing Law: The Work Lives of Solo and Small Firm Lawyers.* Philadelphia: Temple University Press.

Seron, Carroll, ed. 2006. *The Law and Society Canon.* Burlington, VT: Ashgate.

Shabani, Omid A. Payrow, ed. 2007. *Multiculturalism and Law: A Critical Debate.* Cardiff: University of Wales Press.

Shachar, Ayelet. 2001. *Multicultural Jurisdictions: Cultural Differences and Women's Rights.* New York: Cambridge University Press.

Shaffer, Thomas L., and Robert S. Redmount. 1977. *Lawyers, Law Students, and People.* Colorado Springs, CO: Sheppard's.

Shaffern, Robert W. 2009. *Law and Justice from Antiquity to Enlightenment.* Lanham, MD: Rowman & Littlefield Publishers, Inc.

Shah, Prakash. 2005. *Legal Pluralism in Conflict: Coping with Cultural Diversity in Law.* London: Glasshouse Press.

Shain, Barry Alan, ed. 2007. *The Nature of Rights at the American Founding and Beyond.* Charlottesville: University of Virginia Press.

Shaman, Jeffrey M. 2001. *Constitutional Interpretation: Illusion and Reality.* Westport, CT: Greenwood.

Shamir, Ronen. 1995. *Managing Legal Uncertainty: Elite Lawyers in the New Deal.* Durham, NC: Duke University Press.

Shanker, Thom, and Sabrina Tavernise. 2006. "Murder Charges for 3 G.I.'s in Iraq." *New York Times* (June 20): A1.

Shanley, Mary Lyndon. 2001. *Making Babies, Making Families: What Matters Most in an Age of Reproductive Technologies, Surrogacy, Adoption, and Same-Sex and Unwed Parents.* Boston: Beacon.

Shapiro, Fred R. 1993. *The Oxford Dictionary of American Legal Quotations.* New York: Oxford University Press.

Shapiro, Susan. 2002. *Tangled Loyalties: Conflict of Interest in Legal Practice.* Ann Arbor: University of Michigan Press.

Shapo, Marshall S. 2003. *Tort Law and Culture.* Durham, NC: Carolina Academic Press.

Sharlet, Robert, and Piers Beirne. 1984. "In Search of Vyshinsky: The Paradox of Law and Terror." *International Journal of the Sociology of Law* 12: 153–177.

Sharman, J. C. 2006. *Havens in a Storm: The Struggle for Global Tax Regulation.* Ithaca, NY: Cornell University Press.

Shavell, Steven. 2004. *Foundation of Economic Analysis of Law.* Cambridge, MA: Belknap Press of Harvard University Press.

Shdaimah, Corey S. 2009. *Negotiating Justice: Progressive Lawyering, Low-Income Clients, and the Quest for Social Change.* New York: NYU Press.

Shea, Christopher. 1997. "Natural Law Theory Is at the Crux of a Nasty Intellectual Debate." *Chronicle of Higher Education* (February 7): A14–A15.

Shelden, Randall G. 1998. "Gender Bias in the Juvenile Justice System." *Juvenile and Family Court Journal* (Winter): 11–25.

Shelden, Randall G., and William B. Brown. 2003. *Criminal Justice in America: A Critical View.* Boston: Allyn & Bacon.

Sheleff, Leon S. 1997. *Social Cohesion and Legal Coercion: A Critique of Weber, Durkheim, and Marx.* Atlanta, GA: Rodopi.

Shepard, Kris. 2007. *Rationing Justice: Poverty Lawyers and Poor People in the Deep South.* Baton Rouge: Louisiana State University Press.

Sheptycki, J. W. E. 2002. *In Search of Transnational Policing: Towards a Sociology of Global Policing.* Aldershot, UK: Ashgate.

Sherman, Lawrence W. 1992. *Policing Domestic Violence: Experiments and Dilemmas.* New York: Free Press.

Shichor, David, and John W. Heeren. 1989. "Social Control in Socialist Societies: An Analysis of Five Major Characteristics." *Legal Studies Forum* 13: 215–238.

Shichor, David, and D. K. Sechrest, eds. 1997. *Three Strikes and You're Out.* Thousand Oaks, CA: Sage.

Shiell, Timothy C1998. *Campus Hate Speech on Trial.* Lawrence: University Press of Kansas.

Shih, Gerry. 2009. "Downturn Dims Prospects Even at Top Law Schools." *New York Times* (August 26): B1.

Shklar Judith N. [1964] 1986. *Legalism: Law, Morals, and Political Trials*. Cambridge, MA: Harvard University Press.

_____. 1990. *The Faces of Injustice*. New Haven, CT: Yale University Press.

Shook, Michael D., and Jeffrey D. Meyer. 1995. *Legal Briefs*. New York: Macmillan.

Shrage, Laurie. 2003. "Electoral Politics and Abortion." *Dissent* (Fall): 67–73.

Shrager, David S., and Elizabeth Frost. 1986. *The Quotable Lawyer*. New York: Facts on File.

Shuck, Peter H. 2003. *Diversity in America: Keeping Government at a Safe Distance*. Cambridge, MA: Belknap Press of Harvard University Press.

Shuck, Peter. 2007. "Affirmative Action Programs." Pp. 36–40, in David S. Clark, ed. *Encyclopedia of Law & Society*. Thousand Oaks, CA: Sage.

Shutt, J. Eagle. 2002. "On Criminal Defense, Zealous Advocacy, and Expanded Ethics Dialogue." *Journal of Crime and Justice* 25: 129–139.

Shuy, Roger W. 1993. *Language Crimes: The Use and Abuse of Language Evidence in the Courtroom*. Oxford, UK: Basil Blackwell.

_____. 1998. *The Language of Confession, Interrogation, and Deception*. Thousand Oaks, CA: Sage.

Siegel, Larry J. 2009. *Essentials of Criminal Justice. Sixth edition*. Belmont, CA: Sage.

Siemsen, Cynthia. 2004. *Emotional Trials: Moral Dilemmas of Women Criminal Defense Lawyers*. Boston: Northeastern University Press.

Sierra, Maria Teresa. 1995. "Indian Rights and Customary Law in Mexico: A Study of the Navahos in the Sierra de Puebla." *Law & Society Review* 29: 227–254.

Silberman, Laurence H. 1998. "Will Lawyering Strangle Democratic Capitalism? A Retrospective." *Harvard Journal of Law & Public Policy* 21: 607–621.

Silberman, Matthew. 1985. *The Civil Justice Process: A Sequential Model of the Mobilization of Law*. Orlando, FL: Academic Press.

Silbey, Jessica. 2001. "Patterns of Courtroom Justice." *Journal of Law and Society* 28: 97–116.

_____. 2002. "What We Do When We Do Law and Popular Culture." *Law and Social Inquiry* 27: 139–168.

Silbey, Susan S. 1997. "Let Them Eat Cake: Globalization, Postmodern Colonialism, and the Possibilities of Justice." *Law & Society Review* 31: 207–235.

Silverstein, Gordon. 2009. *Law's Allure: How Law Shapes, Constrains, Saves, and Kills Politics*. New York: Cambridge University Press.

Silverstein, Helena. 2007. *Girls on the Stand: How Courts Fail Pregnant Minors*. New York: NYU Press.

Simon, David. 2002. *Elite Deviance*, 7th ed. Boston: Allyn & Bacon.

Simon, James F. 1980. *Independent Journey: The Life of William O. Douglas*. New York: Harper & Row.

Simon, Jonathan. 2007. *Governing Through Crime: How the War on Crime Transformed American Democracy and Created a Culture of Fear*. New York: Oxford University Press.

Simon, Rita J. 2007. "Pornography." Pp. 1150–1152, in David S. Clark, ed. *Encyclopedia of Law & Society*. Los Angeles: Sage.

Simon, William H. 1998. "The Kaye Scholer Affair: The Lawyer's Duty of Candor and the Bar's Temptations of Evasion and Apology." *Law & Social Inquiry* 23: 243–296.

Simons, Marlise. 2000. "Dutch Become First Nation to Legalize Assisted Suicide." *New York Times* (November 29): A3.

Simpson, A. W. B. 1984. *Cannibalism and the Common Law: The Story of the Tragic Last Voyage of the Mignonette*. Chicago: University of Chicago Press.

Sistare, Christine, Larry May, and Leslie Francis, eds. 2001. *Groups and Group Rights*. Lawrence: University Press of Kansas.

Skedsvold, Paula R., and Tammy L. Mann. 1996. "The Affirmative Action Debate: What's Fair in Policy and Programs?" *Journal of Social Issues* 52: 1–160.

Skocpol, Theda. 1992. *Protecting Soldiers and Mothers: The Political Origins of Social Policy in the United States*. Cambridge, MA: Harvard University Press.

Skolnick, Jerome H. 1966. *Justice Without Trial*. New York: John Wiley.

_____. 1978. *House of Cards: Legalization and Control of Casino Gambling*. Boston: Little, Brown.

Skrentny, John David. 1996. *The Ironies of Affirmative Action: Politics, Culture, and Justice in America*. Chicago: University of Chicago Press.

Slater, Dan. 2010. "At Law Firms, Reconsidering the Model for Associates' Pay." *New York Times* (April 1): F10.

Slaughter, Anne-Marie. 2003. "An American Vision of International Law?" Pp. 125–132, in C. H. Brower and N. L. Perkins, eds. *Proceedings of the Ninety-Seventh*

Annual Meeting of the American Society of International Law. Washington, DC: American Society of International Law.

_____. 2004. *A New World Order.* Princeton, NJ: Princeton University Press.

Slobogin, Christopher. 2007. *Privacy at Risk: The New Government Surveillance and the Fourth Amendment.* Chicago, IL: University of Chicago Press.

Smigel, Erwin. 1964. *The Wall Street Lawyer.* Bloomington: Indiana University Press.

Smith, Craig S. 2001. "Chinese Fight Crime With Torture and Executions." *New York Times* (September 9): A1.

Smith, J. Donald. 2002. *Right-to-Die Policies in the American States: Judicial and Legislative Innovation.* New York: LFB Scholarly Publishing.

Smith, Kent W., and Karyl A. Kinsey. 1987. "Understanding Taxpayers' Behavior: A Conceptual Framework With Implications for Research." *Law & Society Review* 21: 639–663.

Smith, Philip. 2008. *Punishment and Culture.* Chicago: University of Chicago Press.

Smith, Robert Samuel. 2008. *Race, Labor, & Civil Rights: Griggs versus Duke Power and the Struggle for Equal Employment Opportunity.* Baton Rouge: Louisiana State University Press.

Smith, Russ. 2010. "Temperance Tantrum." *Wall Street Journal* (May 8–9): W8.

Smithey, Shannon Ishiyama, and John Ishiyama. 2002. "Judicial Activism in Post-Communist Politics." *Law & Society Review* 36: 719–742.

Smits, Jan M. 2008. *Elgar Encyclopedia of Comparative Law.* Northhampton, MA: Edward Elgar Publishing.

Snyder, Francis. 1996. "Law and Anthropology." Pp. 135–179, in Philip A. Thomas, ed. *Legal Frontiers.* Aldershot, UK: Dartmouth.

_____. 2004. "Economic Globalization and the Law in the Twenty-First Century." Pp. 624–640, in A. Sarat, ed. *The Blackwell Companion to Law and Society.* Malden, MA: Blackwell.

Sofsky, Wolfgang. 2008. *Privacy: A Manifesto.* Princeton, NJ: Princeton University Press.

Soifer, Avram. 1988. "Beyond Mirrors: Lawrence Friedman's Moving Pictures." *Law & Society Review* 22: 995–1016.

_____. 1992. "Reflections on the 40th Anniversary of Hurst's Growth of American Law." *Law and Social Inquiry* 17: 167–179.

Soley, Lawrence. 2002. *Censorship Inc.: The Corporate Threat to Free Speech in the United States.* New York: Monthly Review Press.

Solomon, Stephen D. 2007. *Ellery's Protest: How One Young Man Defied Tradition and Sparked the Battle Over School Prayer.* Ann Arbor: University of Michigan Press.

Solove, Daniel J. 2007. *The Future of Reputation: Gossip, Rumor, and Privacy on the Internet.* New Haven, CT: Yale University Press.

Solzhenitsyn, Alexandr. 1976. *The Gulag Archipelago: 1918–1956, Vols. V– II.* New York: Harper & Row.

Sommer, Matthew H. 2000. *Sex, Law, and Society in Late Imperial China.* Stanford, CA: Stanford University Press.

Soothill, Keith, Sylvia Walby, and Paul Bagguley. 1990. "Judges, the Media, and Rape." *Journal of Law and Society* 17: 211–233.

Souaiaia, Ahmed. 2008. *Contesting Justice: Women, Islam, Law, and Society.* Albany: SUNY Press.

Southworth, Ann. 2008. *Lawyers of the Right: Professionalizing the Conservative Condition.* Chicago: University of Chicago Press.

Spaeth, Harold J., and Jeffrey A. Segal. 1999. *Majority Rule or Minority Will: Adherence to Precedent on the U.S. Supreme Court.* New York: Cambridge University Press.

Speed, Shannon. 2008. *Rights in Rebellion: Indigenous Struggle and Human Rights in Chapas.* Stanford, CA: Stanford University Press.

Spencer, Herbert. 1898. *The Principles of Sociology, Vol. II.* New York: D. Appleton.

Spiermann, Ole. 2005. *International Legal Argument in the Permanent Court of International Justice: the Rise of the International Judiciary.* New York: Cambridge University Press.

Spiro, Peter J. 2008. *Beyond Citizenship: American Identity After Globalization.* New York: Oxford University Press.

Spitzer, Robert J. 2008. *Saving the Constitution from Lawyers: How Legal Training and Law Reviews Distort Constitutional Meaning.* New York: Cambridge University Press.

Spitzer, Steven. 1975. "Punishment and Social Organization: A Study of Durkheim's Theory of Penal Evolution." *Law & Society Review* 9: 613–635.

Spriggs, James F., and Thomas G. Hanford. 2002. "The U.S. Supreme Court's Incorporation and Interpretation of Precedent." *Law & Society Review* 36: 139–159.

Springer, David W., and Albert R. Roberts, eds. 2011. *Juvenile Justice and Delinquency*. Boston: Jones & Bartlett Publishers.

Sriram, Chandra Lekha, and Karin Wermester. 2003. *From Promise to Practice: Strengthening UN Capacities for the Prevention of Violent Conflict*. Boulder, CO: Lynne Rienner.

St. John, Warren. 2006. "New Breed of Lawyer Gives Every Dog His Day in Court." *New York Times* (September 3): 1.

Stacy, Helen M. 2001. *Postmodernism and Law: Jurisprudence in a Fragmenting World*. Burlington, VT: Ashgate.

Stacy, Helen M. 2009. *Human Rights for the 21st Century: Sovereignty, Civil Society, Culture*. Stanford, CA: Stanford University Press.

Stacy, Robin Chapman. 2008. *Dark Speech: The Performance of Law in Early Ireland*. Philadelphia: University of Pennsylvania Press.

Stefan, Susan. 2001. *Unequal Rights: Discrimination Against People With Mental Disabilities and the Americans With Disabilities Act*. Washington, DC: American Psychological Association.

Stein, Laura W. 1999. *Sexual Harassment in America: A Documentary History*. Westport, CT: Greenwood Press.

Steinberg, Marc W. 2003. "Capitalist Development, the Labor Process, and the Law." *American Journal of Sociology* 109: 445–495.

Steiner, Mark E. 2006. *An Honest Calling: The Law Practice of Abraham Lincoln*. DeKalb: Northern Illinois University Press.

Steinhoff, Patricia G. 1993. "Pursuing the Japanese Police." *Law & Society Review* 27: 827–850.

Steinhoff, Uwe. 2007. *On the Ethics of War and Terrorism*. Oxford: Oxford University Press.

Stelter, Brian. 2007. "'To Catch a Predator' is Falling Prey to Advertisers' Sensibilities." *New York Times* (August 27): E1.

Stern, Seth. 2008. "A Commander in Chief." *Harvard Law Bulletin* (Fall): 19–23.

Stevens, Robert B. 1983. *Law School: Legal Education in America From the 1850s to the 1980s*. Chapel Hill: University of North Carolina Press.

Stewart, Richard B. 2003. "Administrative Law in the Twenty-First Century." *New York University Law Review* 78: 437–460.

Steytler, Nico C. 1987. "Criminal Justice and the Apartheid State." Pp. 68–84, in A. J. Rycroft, L, S. Boule, M. K. Robertson, and F. R. Stiller, eds. *Race and the Law in South Africa*. Cape Town, RSA: Juta.

Stick, John. 1986. "Can Nihilism Be Pragmatic?" *Harvard Law Review* 100: 332–401.

Stinchcombe, Arthur L. 2001. *When Formality Works: Authority and Abstraction in Law and Organizations*. Chicago: University of Chicago Press.

Stith, Kate, and Jose A. Cabranes. 1998. *Fear of Judging: Sentencing Guidelines in the Federal Courts*. Chicago: University of Chicago Press.

Stith, Kate, and William Stuntz. 2004. "Sense and Sentencing." *New York Times* (June 29): A27.

Stoesz, David. 1997. "Welfare Behaviorism." *Society* (April/May): 68–77.

Stolberg, Sheryl Gay. 2003. "Class-Action Legislation Fails in Senate." *New York Times* (October 23): A23.

Stolberg, Sheryl Gay. 2009. "New Stem Cell Policy to Leave Thorniest Issues to Congress." *New York Times* (March 9): A1.

Stolberg, Sheryl Gay, and David E. Rosenbaum. 2005. "Court Nominee Prizes Modesty, He Tells Senate." *New York Times* (August 3): A1.

Stone, Geoffrey R. 2007. *War and Liberty: An American Dilemma: 1790 to the Present*. New York: W. W. Norton & Co.

Stone, Katherine V. W. 2004. *From Widgets to Digits: Employment Regulation for the Changing Workplace*. New York: Cambridge University Press.

Stover, Robert V. 1989. *Making It and Breaking It: The Fate of Public Interest Commitment During Law School* (H. Erlanger, ed.). Urbana: University of Illinois Press.

Strach, Patricia L. 2007. *All in the Family: The Private Roots of American Public Policy*. Stanford, CA: Stanford University Press.

Strauber, Ira L. 2002. *Neglected Policies: Constitutional Law and Legal Commentary as Civic Education*. Durham, NC: Duke University Press.

Strauss, Peter L. 2006. "Transsytemia – Are We Approaching a New Langdellian Moment? Is McGill Leading the Way?" *Journal of Legal Education* 56: 161–171.

Strawson, John, ed. 2002. *Law After Ground Zero*. Sydney, Australia: Glasshouse Press.

Streb, Matthew J. 2007. *Running for Judge: The Rising Political, Financial and Legal Stakes of Judicial Elections*. New York: New York University Press.

Strick, Ann. 1978. *Injustice for All*. New York: Penguin.

Stromseth, Jane, David Wippman, and Ross Brooks. 2007. *Can Might Make Rights? Building the Rule of Law After Military Interventions*. Cambridge: Cambridge University Press.

Stroud, George M. 1956. *A Sketch of the Laws Relating to Slavery in the Several States of the United States of America.* New York: Negro University Press.

Stryker, Robin. 1989. "Limits on Technocratization of the Law: The Elimination of the National Labor Relations Board's Division of Economic Research." *American Sociological Review* 54: 341–358.

Sturm, Susan, and Lard Guinier. 2003. "Learning From Conflict: Reflections on Teaching About Race and Gender" *Journal of Legal Education* 53: 515–547.

Suk, Jeannie. 2009. *At Home in the Law: How the Domestic Violence Revolution is Transforming Privacy.* New Haven: Yale University Press.

Sullivan, Dennis, and Larry Tifft. 2001. *Restorative Justice: Healing the Foundations of Our Everyday Lives.* Monsey, NY: Willow Tree Press.

Sullivan, Kathleen. 2007. *Constitutional Context: Women and Rights Discourse in Nineteenth Century America.* Baltimore, MD: The Johns Hopkins University Press.

Sullivan, Michael. 2008. "On Vico's *Universal Law* and Modern Law." *New Vico Studies* 26: 59–66.

Sullivan, Winnifred Fallers. 2009. *Prison Religion: Faith-Based Reform and the Constitution.* Princeton, NJ: Princeton University Press.

Sulzberger, A. G. 2010. "Defiant Judge Takes on Child Pornography Law." *New York Times* (May 22): A1.

Sumner, William Graham. [1906] 1960. *Folkways.* New York: Mentor.

Sunstein, Cass R. 1996. *Legal Reasoning and Political Conflict.* New York: Oxford University Press.

———. 2001. *Designing Democracy: What Constitutions Do.* New York: Oxford University.

——— 2002a. *Risk and Reason: Safety, Law, and the Environment.* New York: Cambridge University Press.

——— 2002b. "Taking Over the Courts." *New York Times* (November 9): A19.

Sunstein, Cass R. 2005. "The Philosopher-Justice." *The New Republic* (September 19): 29–34.

Sunstein, Cass R. 2009a. *A Constitution of Many Minds: Why the Founding Document Doesn't Mean What It Meant Before.* Princeton, NJ: Princeton University Press.

Sunstein, Cass R. 2009b. *On Rumors: How Falsehoods Spread, Why We Believe Them, What Can Be Done.* New York: Farrar, Straus & Giroux.

Sunstein, Cass R. 2009c. *Going to Extremes: How Like Minds Unite and Divide.* New York: Oxford University Press.

Susskind, Richard. 2009. *The End of Lawyers? Rethinking the Nature of Legal Services.* New York: Oxford University Press.

Sussman, Nadia. 2011. "After School in Brooklyn, West African Girls Share Memories of a Painful Ritual." *New York Times* (April 26): A22.

Sutherland, Arthur E. 1967. *The Law at Harvard.* Cambridge, MA: Harvard University Press.

Sutton, John P. 1985. "The Juvenile Court and Social Welfare: Dynamics of Progressive Reform." *Law & Society Review* 19: 107–145.

———. 2001. *Law/Society: Origins, Interactions, and Change.* Thousand Oaks, CA: Pine Forge Press.

Swain, Carol, ed. 2007. *Debating Immigration.* New York: Cambridge University Press.

Sward, Ellen E. 2003. "A History of the Civil Trial in the United States." *The University of Kansas Law Review* 51: 347–408.

Szablowski, David. 2007. *Transnational Law and Local Struggles: Mining, Communities and the World Bank.* Portland, OR: Hart Publishing.

Tackaberry, John. 2009. "Adjudication and Arbitration: The When and Why in Construction Disputes." *Arbitration* 75: 235–239.

Tamanaha, Brian Z. 2004. *On the Rule of Law: History, Politics, Theory.* New York: Cambridge University Press.

Tamanaha, Brian Z. 2005. Review of: *Lowering the Bar: Lawyer Jokes and Legal Culture. Law & Politics Book Review* 15: 929–932.

Tamanaha, Brian Z. 2006. *Law as a Means to an End: Threat to the Rule of Law.* New York: Cambridge University Press.

Tamanaha, Brian Z. 2009. "The Realism of Judges Past and Present." *Cleveland Law Review* 57: 77–91.

Tamanaha, Brian Z. 2010. *Beyond the Formalist-Realist Divide: The Role of Politics in Judging.* New York: Cambridge University Press.

Tanenhaus, David S. 2004. *Juvenile Justice in the Making.* New York: Oxford University Press.

Tannenbaum, Frank. 1946. *Slave and Citizen.* New York: Knopf.

Tanner, Harold. 1995. "Policing, Punishment, and the Individual: Criminal Justice in China." *Law and Social Inquiry* 20: 277–303.

Taslitz, Andrew E. 1999. *Rape and the Culture of the Courtroom.* New York: New York University Press.

Tata, Cyrus, and Neil Hutton, eds. 2002. *Sentencing and Society: International Perspectives.* Burlington, VT: Ashgate.

Tavernise, Sabrina. 2003. "In College and in Despair, With Parents in the Dark." *New York Times* (October 26): A31.

Tay, Alice Erh-Soon. 1990. "Communist Visions, Communist Realities, and the Role of Law." *Journal of Law & Society* 17: 155–169.

Taylor, Stuart, Jr. 1983. "Ethics and the Law: A Case History." *New York Times* (January 9): 31–33, 46–49.

Taylor, Telford. 1970. *Nuremberg and Vietnam: An American Tragedy.* New York: Bantam. Teitel, Ruth. 2000. *Transitional Justice.* New York: Oxford University Press.

Teles, Steven M. 1996. *Whose Welfare? AFDC and Elite Politics.* Lawrence: University of Kansas Press.

Teles, Steven M. 2008. *The Rise of the Conservative Legal Movement: The Battle for Control of the Law.* Princeton, NJ: Princeton University Press.

Temkin, Jennifer. 2002. *Rape and the Legal Process, 2nd ed.* Oxford, UK: Oxford University Press.

Temkin, Jennifer, and Barbara Krahe. 2008. *Sexual Assault and the Justice Gap: A Question of Attitude.* Oxford: Hart Publishing Co.

Teninbaum, Gabriel H. 2007. "Courts, Lawmaking by." Pp. 320–323, in David S. Clark, ed. *Encyclopedia of Law and Society.* Los Angeles: Sage.

Terry, Don. 1998. "Mother Rages Against Indifference." *New York Times* (August 24): A10.

Tewksbury, William J. 1967. "The Ordeal as a Vehicle for Divine Intervention in Medieval Europe." Pp. 267–270, in Paul Bohannon, ed. *Law and Warfare.* New York: Natural History Press.

Thaler, Richard H., and Cass Sunstein. 2008. *Nudge: Improving Decisions About Health, Wealth, and Happiness.* New Haven, CT: Yale University Press.

Thaman, Stephen C. 2007. "Legality and Discretion." Pp. 944–945, in David S. Clark, ed. *Encyclopedia of Law and Society.* Los Angeles: Sage.

Thierstein, Joel, and Yahya R. Kamalipour, eds. 2000. *Religion, Law, and Freedom: A Global Perspective.* Westport, CT: Praeger.

Thies, Daniel. 2010. "Rethinking Legal Education in Hard Times: The Recession, Practical Legal Education, and the New Job Market." *Journal of Legal Education* 59: 598–622.

Thompson, E. P. 1978. *Whigs and Hunters The Origin of the Black Act.* London: Penguin.

Thompson, H. 1986. "The Role of the Rule of Law in the Liberal State." *Natal University Law and Society Review* 1: 126–137.

Thompson, William N. 1994. *Legalized Gambling.* Santa Barbara, CA: ABC-Clio.

Thornton, Margaret. 1996. *Dissonance and Distrust: Women in the Legal Profession.* Melbourne, Australia: Oxford University Press.

Thrupkaew, Noy. 2009. "Beyond Rescue." *The Nation* (October 26): 21–24.

Tiersma, Peter M., and Lawrence M. Solan. 2004. "Cops and Robbers: Selective Literalism in American Criminal Law." *Law & Society Review* 38: 229–265.

Tigar, Michael E., and Madeleine R. Levy. 1977. *Law and the Rise of Capitalism.* New York: Monthly Review Press.

Timasheff, N. S. [1939] 1974. *An Introduction to the Sociology of Law.* Westport, CT: Greenwood Press.

Time. 1978. "TV Wins a Crucial Case." *Time* (August 21): 85.

Timmermans, Stefan. 2006. *Postmortem: How Medical Examiners Explain Suspicious Deaths.* Chicago: University of Chicago Press.

Tinker, Justine Eatenson. 2003. "Defining Sexual Harassment: Ambiguity, Perceived Threat, and Knowledge." *Amici* 10: 1, 3–5.

Tjaden, Patricia, and Nancy Thoennes. 1998. "Stalking in America: Findings From the National Violence Against Women Survey." *NIJ CDL Research in Brief* (April): 1–19.

Tocqueville, Alexis de. [1835–1840] 1945. *Democracy in America, Vols. I and II.* P. Bradley, ed. New York: Knopf.

Todorov, Tzvetan. 2001. "In Search of Lost Crime." *New Republic* (January 29): 29–36.

Tomasic, Roman. 1985. *The Sociology of Law.* London: Sage.

Tomasic, Roman, and Malcolm Feeley, eds. 1982. *Neighborhood Justice.* New York: Longman.

Tomlins, Christopher L. 2000. "Framing the Field of Law's Disciplinary Encounters: A Historical Narrative." *Law & Society Review* 34: 911–972.

Tomlins, Christopher L., and Bruce H. Mann, eds. 2001. *The Many Legalities of Early America.* Chapel Hill: University of North Carolina Press.

Toner, Robin. 2005. "In Complex Dance, Roberts Pays Tribute to Years of Precedent Behind Roe v. Wade." *New York Times* (September 14): A26.

Tonry, Michael, and Kathleen Hatlestad, eds. 1997. *Sentencing Reform in Overcrowded Times: A Comparative Perspective.* New York: Oxford University Press.

Toobin, Jeffrey. 2003. "The Consent Defense." *New Yorker* (September 1): 40–44, 87.

Toobin, Jeffrey. 2008. "Rich Bitch." *The New Yorker* (September 29): 38–47.

Torney, Judith. 1977. "Socialization and Attitudes Toward the Legal System." Pp. 134–144, in June Louin Tapp and Felice J. Levine, eds. *Law, Justice, and the Individual in Society: Psychological and Legal Issues.* New York: Holt, Rinehart & Winston.

Totani, Yuma. 2008. *The Tokyo War Crimes Trial: The Pursuit of Justice in the Wake of World War II.* Cambridge, MA: Harvard University Press.

Trachtman, Paul. 1974. *The Gunfighters.* Alexandria, VA: Time-Life Books.

Trattner, Walter I. 1999. *From Poor Law to Welfare State.* New York: Free Press.

Travers, Max. 2010. *Understanding Law and Society.* New York: Routledge.

Trevino, A. Javier. 1996. *The Sociology of Law: Classical and Contemporary Perspectives.* New York: St. Martin's Press.

———. 2001. "The Sociology of Law in Global Perspective." *American Sociologist* 32: 5–9.

Trevino, A. Javier, ed. 2006. *Classic Writings in Law and Society: Contemporary Comments and Criticisms.* New Brunswick, NJ: Transaction Publishing.

Tribe, Laurence H. 2008. *The Invisible Constitution.* New York: Oxford University Press.

Trochev, Alexei. 2008. *Judging Russia: Constitutional Court in Russian Politics 1990–2006.* Cambridge: Cambridge University Press.

Trosch, Louis Alfred, Sr. 2008. "Strengthening State Dog Fighting Laws in the Wake of the Michael Vick Case." *Business Law Review* 41: 104–133.

Trost, Christine, and Alison L. Gash, eds. 2008. *Conflict of Interest and Public Life: Cross-National Perspectives.* New York: Cambridge University Press.

Trubek, David M., and Alvaro Santos. 2006. *The New Law and Economic Development: A Critical Appraisal.* Cambridge: Cambridge University Press.

Tsesis, Alexander. 2004. *The Thirteenth Amendment and American Freedom: A Legal History.* New York: New York University Press.

Tsesis, Alexander. 2008. *We Shall Overcome: A History of Civil Rights and the Law.* New Haven, CT: Yale University Press.

Tsosie, Rebecca. 1997. "American Indians and the Politics of Recognition: Soifer on Law, Pluralism, and Group Identity." *Law and Social Inquiry* 22: 359–388.

Tullock, Gordon, Arthur Seldon, and Gordon L. Brady. 2002. *Government Failure: A Primer in Public Choice.* Washington, DC: Cato Institute.

Tuori, Kaarlo. 2002. *Critical Legal Positivism.* Aldershot, UK: Ashgate.

Turk, Austin T. 1969. *Criminality and Legal Order.* Chicago: Rand McNally.

Turkel, Gerald. 1990. "Michel Foucault: Law, Power, and Knowledge." *Journal of Law & Society* 17: 170–192.

———. 1996. *Law and Society: Critical Approaches.* Boston: Allyn & Bacon.

Turner, Stephen, and Regis A. Factor. 1994. *Max Weber: The Lawyer as Social Thinker.* London: Rout-ledge.

Turow, Scott. 1977. *One L.* New York: Putnam.

———. 1997. "The High Court's 20-Year-Old Mistake." *New York Times* (October 12): Op-Ed Page.

Tushnet, Mark. 1977. "Perspectives on the Development of American Law: A Critical Review of Fried-man's A History of American Law." *Wisconsin Law Review* 1977: 81–109.

——— 2003. *The New Constitutional Order.* Princeton, NJ: Princeton University Press.

———. 2010. "Academics as Law-Makers?" *University of Queensland Law Journal* 29: 19–28.

Twining, William E. 2000. *Globalization and Legal Theory.* London: Butterworths.

Twining, William. 2009. *General Jurisprudence: Understanding Law from a Global Perspective.* Cambridge: Cambridge University Press.

Twining, William, and Iain Hampsher-Monk, eds. 2003. *Evidence and Inference in History and Law: Interdisciplinary Dialogues.* Evanston, IL: Northwestern University Press.

Tyler, Tom R. 1990. *Why People Obey the Law.* New Haven, CT: Yale University Press.

———. 1998. "Justice and Power in Civil Dispute Processing." Pp. 309–346, in Bryant Garth and Austin Sarat, eds. *Justice and Power in Sociolegal Studies.* Chicago, IL: Northwestern University Press.

Tyler, Tom R., ed. 2007. *Legitimacy and Criminal Justice: International Perspectives.* New York: Russell Sage Foundation.

Tyler, Tom R. 2007. "Legitimation." Pp. 953–955, in David S. Clark, ed. *Encyclopedia of Law & Society*. Los Angeles: Sage.

Tyler, Tom R., and Yuen J. Huo. 2002. *Trust in the Law: Encouraging Public Cooperation With the Police and Courts*. New York: Russell Sage.

Tyler, Tom R., and Kenneth Rasinski. 1991. "Procedural Justice, Institutional Legitimacy, and the Acceptance of Unpopular U.S. Supreme Court Decisions: A Reply to Gibson." *Law & Society Review* 25: 621–635.

Uc, Dao Tri. 2005. "60 Years of Building a State Rule by Law." *Vietnam Law & Legal Forum* (September): 3–10.

Uelmen, Gerald F. 1992. "Federal Sentencing Guidelines: A Cure Worse Than the Disease." *American Criminal Law Review* 29: 899–905.

Uggen, Christopher, and Chika Shinohara. 2009. "Sexual Harassment Comes of Age: A Comparative Analysis of the United States and Japan." *The Sociological Quarterly* 50: 201–234.

Umphrey, Martha Merrill, ed. 2008. *Trials*. Burlington, VT: Ashgate Publishing Co.

Underwood, Barbara D. 1981. "Against Dichotomy." *Yale Law Journal* 90: 1004–1007.

Urbina, Ian. 2010. "Workers on Doomed Rig Voiced Concern on Safety." *New York Times* (July 22): A1.

Urofsky, Melvin I. 2010. *Louis D. Brandeis: A Life*. New York: Pantheon Books.

Uviller, H. Richard. 1999. *The Tilted Playing Field: Is Criminal Justice Unfair?* New Haven, CT: Yale University Press.

Vago, Steven. 2009. *Law & Society, 9th ed*. Englewood Cliffs, NJ: Prentice Hall.

Vagts, Detlev. 1996. "The International Legal Profession: A Need for More Governance?" *The American Journal of International Law* 90: 250–261.

Valcke, Catherine. 2004. "Global Law Teaching." *Journal of Legal Education* 54: 160–182.

Valencia-Weber, Gloria. 1994. "American Indian Law and History: Instructional Mirrors." *Journal of Legal Education* 44: 251–266.

Valls, Andrew. 2007. "Critical Race Theory." Pp. 353–355, in David S. Clark, ed. *Encyclopedia of Law & Society*. Los Angeles: Sage.

Valverde, Marianna. 2007. "Alcohol." Pp. 54–56. In David S. Clark, ed. *Encyclopedia of Law and Society*. Thousand Oaks, CA: Sage.

VanBurkleo, Sandra F. 2001. *"Belonging to the World": Women's Rights and American National Culture*. New York: Oxford University Press.

VanBurkleo, Sandra F., Kermit L. Hall, and Robert J. Kaczorowski, eds. 2002. *Constitutionalism and American Culture: Writing the New Constitutional History*. Lawrence, KS: University Press of America.

Van der Merwe, Hugo, Victoria Baxter, and Audrey R. Chapman, eds. 2009. *Assessing the Impact of Transitional Justice: Challenges for Empirical Research*. Washington, DC: United States Institute of Peace Press.

Vandevelde. Kenneth J. 1996. *Thinking Like a Lawyer: An Introduction to Legal Reasoning*. Boulder, CO: Westview Press.

Van Hoy, Jerry. 1997a. *Franchise Legal Firms and the Transformation of Personal Legal Services*. Westport, CT: Quorum Books.

———. 1997b. "The Practice Dynamics of Solo and Small Firm Lawyers." *Law & Society Review* 31: 377–387.

——— ed. 2001. *Legal Professions: Work, Structure, and Organization*. New York: Elsevier.

Van Seters, Paul, ed. 2007. *Communitarianism in Law and Society*. Lanham, MD: Rowman & Littlefield Publishers.

Vermeule, Adrian. 2009. *Law and the Limits of Reason*. New York: Oxford University Press.

Vest, Herb D. 2000. "Telling the Giant: Breaking the ABA's Stranglehold on Legal Education in America." *Journal of Legal Education* 50: 494–503.

Vidmar, Neil. 1984. "The Small Claims Court: A Reconceptualization of Disputes and an Empirical Investigation." *Law & Society Review* 18: 515–550.

Vidmar, Neil, and Valerie P. Hans. 2007. *American Juries: The Verdict*. Amherst, NY: Prometheus Books.

Vincent, Andrew. 1996. "Law and Politics." Pp. 106–134, in Philip A. Thomas, ed. *Legal Frontiers*. Aldershot, UK: Dartmouth.

Vinzant, John H. 2009. *The Supreme Court's Role in American Indian Policy*. El Paso: LFB Scholarly Publishing.

Vitello, Paul. 2009. "New Abuse Tack for Jewish Sects." *New York Times* (October 14): A1.

Vogler, Richard. 2005. *A World View of Criminal Justice*. Aldershot, UK: Ashgate.

Von Benda-Beckmann, Franz, Keebet von Benda-Beckmann, and Anne Griffiths, eds. 2005. *Mobile People, Mobile Law: Expanding Legal Relations in a Contracting World*. Aldershot, UK: Ashgate.

Von Benda-Beckmann, Franz, Keebet von Benda-Beckmann, and Julia Eckert, eds. 2009a. *Rules of Law and Laws of Ruling: On the Governance of Law*. Burlington, VT: Ashgate Publishing Co.

Von Benda-Beckmann, Franz, Keebet von Benda-Beck-mann, and Anne Griffiths, eds. 2009b. *Spatializing Law: An Anthropological Geography of Law in Society.* Burlington, VT: Ashgate.

Von Benda-Beckmann, Franz, Keebet von Benda-Beck-mann, and Anne Griffiths, eds. 2009c. *The Power of Law in a Transnational World: Anthropological Enquiries.* New York: Berghahn Books Inc.

Von Glahn, Gerhard. 1992. *Law Among Nations: An Intro-duction to Public International Law, 6th ed.* New York: Macmillan.

von Hirsch, Andrew, and Andrew Ashworth, eds. 1992. *Principled Sentencing.* Boston: Northeastern University Press.

von Savigny, Friedrich Karl. [1831] 1986. *On the Vocation of Our Age for Legislation and Jurisprudence.* Birming-ham, AL: Legal Classics Library.

von Zielbauer, Paul. 2003. "Rethinking the Key Thrown Away." New York Times (September 28): 41.

von Zielbauer, Paul. 2007. "Marines' Trials in Iraq Killings are Withering." *New York Times* (August 30): A1.

Voss, Frederick. 1989. *Portraits of American Law.* Washing-ton, DC: National Portrait Gallery.

Wacquant, Loic. 2009. *Punishing the Poor: The Neoliberal Government of Social Insecurity.* Durham, NC: Duke University Press.

Wagatsuma, Hiroshi, and Arthur Rosett. 1986. "The Implications of Apology: Law and Culture in Japan and the United States." *Law & Society Review* 20: 461–507.

Wagner, Anne, and Vijay K. Bhatia, eds. 2009. *Diversity and Tolerance in Socio-Legal Contexts: Explorations in the Semiotics of Law.* Burlington, VT: Ashgate.

Wakefield, Alison. 2003. *Selling Security: The Private Polic-ing of Public Space.* Portland, OR: Willan Publishing.

Wald, Eli. 2008. "Notes from Tsinghua: Law and Legal Ethics in Contemporary China." *Connecticut Journal of International Law* 23: 369–380.

Wald, Eli. 2009. Book Review of *Lawyers in the Dock.*" *Jour-nal of Legal Education* 59: 311+.

Waldman, Amy. 2006. "Prophetic Justice." *The Atlantic* (October): 82–93.

Waldstreicher, David. 2009. *Slavery's Constitution: From Revolution to Ratification.* New York: Hill and Wang.

Walker, Anders. 2009. *The Ghost of Jim Crow: How South-ern Moderates Used Brown v. Board of Education to Stall the Civil Rights Movement.* New York: Oxford Univer-sity Press.

Walker, Samuel. 1980. *Popular Justice: A History of Ameri-can Criminal Justice.* New York: Oxford University Press.

———. 1990. *In Defense of American Liberties: A History of the ACLU.* New York: Oxford University Press.

———. 1993. *Taming the System: The Control of Discre-tion in Criminal Justice, 1950–1990.* New York: Oxford University Press.

———. 1998. *The Rights Revolution: Rights and Commu-nity in Modern America.* New York: Oxford University Press.

Wall, David S., and Johnstone, Jennifer. 1997. "The Industrialization of Legal Practice and the Rise of the New Electronic Lawyer: The Impact of Technology on Legal Practice in the U.K." *International Journal of the Sociology of Law* 25: 95–116.

Ward, Richard. 1997a. "Public Security in Modern China." *Crime & Justice International* (April): 5–8.

———. 1997b. "China's Police: New Laws and Duties." *Crime & Justice International* (May): 12–17.

Warren, Cat, and Wilma B. Liebman. 2010. "'A Welcome Debate' over Labor Reform." *Academe* (January–Feb-ruary): 15–17.

Watry, Ruth Ann. 2002. *Administrative Statutory Interpre-tation: The Aftermath of Chevron v. Natural Resources Defense Council.* New York: LFB Scholarly Publishing.

Watson, Alan. 1995. *The Spirit of Roman Law.* Athens: The University of Georgia Press.

Waxman, Seth P. 2002. "Free Speech and Campaign Reform Don't Conflict." *New York Times* (July 10): Op Ed Page.

Webb, Jim. 2009. "Now is the Time to Reform Our Criminal Justice System." *Criminal Justice Ethics* 28: 163–167.

Weber, Bruce. 2009. "Umpires v. Judges." *New York Times* (July 12): Week 1.

Weber, Mark C. 2007. *Disability Harassment.* New York: New York University Press.

Weber, Max. 1949. *The Methodology of the Social Sciences.* New York: Free Press.

———. [1954] 1967. *On Law in Economy and Society* (Max Rheinstein, ed.). New York: Simon & Schuster.

———. 1964. *The Theory of Social and Economic Orga-nization* (A. M. Henderson and T. L. Parsons, trans.). New York: Free Press.

———. 1978. *Economy and Society, Vols. I and II* (Guen-ther Roth and Claus Wittich, eds.). Berkeley: Univer-sity of California Press.

Websdale, Neil. 2001. *Policing the Poor: From Slave Plantation to Public Housing.* Boston: Northeastern University Press.

Webster, David. 1987. "Repression and the State of Emergency." Pp. 141–172, in G. Moss and J. Obery, eds. *South Africa Review 4.* Johannesburg, RSA: Ravan Press.

Wegner, Judith Welch. 2010. "Response: More Complicated Than We Think." *Journal of Legal Education* 59: 623–656.

Weiner, Mark S. 2006. *Americans Without Law: The Racial Boundaries of Citizenship.* New York: NYU Press.

Weinreb, Lloyd L. 2005. *Legal Reason: The Use of Analogy in Legal Argument.* New York: Cambridge University Press.

Weisberg, Richard H. 1984. *The Failure of the Word.* New Haven, CT: Yale University Press.

———. 1992. *Poetics and Other Strategies of Law and Literature.* New York: Columbia University Press.

Weisbrod, Carol. 2002. *Emblems of Pluralism: Cultural Differences and the State.* Princeton, NJ: Princeton University Press.

Weisburd, David, and Anthony A. Braga. 2006. *Police Innovation: Contrasting Perspectives.* Cambridge, UK: Cambridge University Press.

Weitzer, Ronald. 2010a. "The Ethnography of Prostitution: New International Perspectives." *Contemporary Sociology* 39: 262–269.

Weitzer, Ronald. 2010b. "The Movement to Criminalize Sex Work in the United States." *Journal of Law and Society* 37: 61–84.

Welchman, Lynn. 2007. *Women and Muslim Family Laws in Arab States: A Comparative Overview of Textual Development and Advocacy.* Chicago: University of Chicago Press.

Welchman, Lynn, and Sara Hossain, eds. 2005. *"Honour": Crimes, Paradigms and Violence Against Women.* London: Zed Books.

Wellman, Carl. 1995. *Real Rights.* New York: Oxford University Press.

Wendel, W. Bradley. 2006. "What's Wrong with Being Creative and Aggressive?" *Cornell Law Forum* (Spring): 2–7.

West, Mark D. 2003. "Losers: Recovering Lost Property in Japan and the United States." *Law & Society Review* 37: 369–423.

West, Mark D. 2006. *Secrets, Sex, and Spectacle: The Rule of Scandal in Japan and the United States.* Chicago: University of Chicago Press.

West, Robin. 1988. "Jurisprudence and Gender." *University of Chicago Law Review* 55: 1–72.

———. 1997. *Caring for Justice.* New York: New York University Press.

———. 2003. "Reconsidering Legalism." *Minnesota Law Review* 88: 119–158.

West, Thomas G. 1998. *Vindicating the Founders: Race, Sex, Class, and Justice in the Origins of America.* Lanham, MD: Rowman & Littlefield.

Westermann, Ted D., and James W. Burfeind. 1991. *Crime and Justice in Two Societies: Japan and the United States.* Pacific Grove, CA: Brooks/Cole.

Westermarck, E. A. 1906. *The Origin and Development of Moral Ideas.* New York: Macmillan.

Westervelt, Saundra D., and John A. Humphrey, eds. 2001. *Wrongly Convicted: Perspectives on Failed Justice.* New Brunswick, NJ: Rutgers University Press.

Wexler, David B., ed. 2008. *Rehabilitating Lawyers: Principles of Therapeutic Jurisprudence for Criminal Law Practice.* Durham, NC: Carolina Academic Press.

Weyenberg, Michelle. 2008. "Debt Salvation." *The National Jurist* (March): 24–28.

Weyler, Rex. 1992. *Blood of the Land: The Government and Corporate War Against First Nations.* Philadelphia: New Society Publishers.

Wexler, David B., ed. 2008. *Rehabilitating Lawyers: Principles of Therapeutic Jurisprudence for Criminal Law Practice.* Durham, NC: Carolina Academic Press.

Wheeler, Stanton, Bliss Cartwright, Robert A. Kagan, and Lawrence M. Friedman. 1987. "Do the Haves Come Out Ahead? Winning and Losing in State Supreme Courts, 1870–1970." *Law & Society Review* 21: 403–445.

Whitaker, Ingrid Phillips, and Victoria Time. 2001. "Devolution and Welfare: The Social and Legal Implications of State Inequalities for Welfare Reform in the United States." *Social Justice* 28: 76–90.

White, G. Edward. 1972. "From Sociological Jurisprudence to Realism: Jurisprudence and Social Change in Early Twentieth Century America." *Virginia Law Review* 58: 999–1028.

———. 1976. *The American Judicial Tradition.* New York: Oxford University Press.

———. 1988. "The Anti-Judge: William O. Douglas and the Ambiguities of Individuality." *Virginia Law Review* 74: 17–86.

———. 2003. *Tort Law in America: An Intellectual History,* expanded ed. New York : Oxford University Press.

White, James Boyd. [1973] 1985. *The Legal Imagination, abridged ed.* Chicago: University of Chicago Press.

———. 1984. *When Words Lose Their Meaning: Constitutions and Reconstitutions of Language, Character, and Community.* Chicago: University of Chicago Press.

White, Mark D., ed. 2009. *Theoretical Foundations of Law and Economics.* New York: Cambridge University Press.

White, Welsh S. 2001. *Miranda's Warning Protections: Police Interrogation Practices After Dickerson.* Ann Arbor: Michigan University Press.

White, Welsh S. 2005. *Litigating in the Shadow of Death: Defense Attorneys in Capital Cases.* Ann Arbor, MI: University of Michigan Press.

Whitehead, John T. and Steven P. Lab. 2009. *Juvenile Justice: An Introduction. Sixth edition.* Cincinnati: Anderson Publishing Co.

Whitman, James Q. 2007. "Honor." Pp. 211–213, in David S. Clark, ed. *Encyclopedia of Law and Society.* Los Angeles: Sage.

Wickham, Gary, and George Pavlich, eds. 2001. *Rethinking Law, Society, and Governance: Foucault's Bequest.* Portland, OR: Hart.

Wilbanks, William, and Coramae Richey Mann. 1996. "Racism in the Criminal Justice System: Two Sides of a Controversy" Pp. 54–64, in Chris W. Eskridge, ed. *Criminal Justice: Concepts and Issues, 2nd ed.* Los Angeles: Roxbury.

Wiley, Deane C. 2004. "Black and White Differences in the Perception of Justice." Pp. 39–43, in Chris W. Eskridge, ed. *Criminal Justice-Concepts and Issues. 4th ed.* Los Angeles, CA: Roxbury.

Wilkins, David E., and K. Tsianina Lomawaima. 2001. *Uneven Ground: American Indian Sovereignty and Federal Law.* Norman: University of Oklahoma Press.

Willems, Jan C. M., ed. 2010. *Children's Rights and Human Development: A Multidisciplinary Reader.* Mortsel, Belgium: Intersentia Publishers.

Williams, Alex. 2008. "The Falling-Down Professions." *New York Times* (January 6): Styles 1.

Williams, Christopher R. and Bruce Arrigo. 2007. "Psychology, Use in Courts." Pp. 1234–1236, in David S. Clark, ed. *Encyclopedia of Law & Society.* Los Angeles: Sage.

Williams, James L., Daniel G. Rodeheaver, and Denise W. Huggins. 2003. "Crime and Punishment in Russia and the United States: 1990–1998." *International Journal of Comparative and Applied Criminal Justice* 27: 39–68.

Williams, Robert A., Jr. 1990. *The American Indian in Western Legal Thought: The Discourses of Conquest.* New York: Oxford University Press.

Williams, Robert A., Jr. 2005. *Like a Loaded Weapon: The Rehnquist Court, Indian Rights, and the Legal History of Racism in America.* Minneapolis: University of Minnesota Press.

Williams, Verna L. 1999. "A New Harassment Ruling: Implications for Colleges." *The Chronicle of Higher Education* (June 14): A56.

Williams, Jan C. M., ed. 2010. *Children's Rights and Human Development: A Multidisciplinary Reader.* Mortsel, Belgium: Intersentia Publishers.

Willing, Richard. 2004. "Lawsuits Target Alcohol Industry." *USA Today* (May 14): 3A.

Willis, Clint, and Suzanne Barlyn. 2007. "Bringing the Law to Life." *NYU Law Bulletin* (Autumn): 21–31.

Willison, Janeen Buck, Daniel P. Mears, and Jeffrey A. Butts. 2011. "The U.S. Juvenile Justice Policy Landscape." Pp. 211–242, in K. Ismaili, ed. *U.S. Criminal Justice Policy: A Contemporary Reader.* Sudbury, MA: Jones & Bartlett Learning.

Wills, Garry. 2004. "Negro President": Jefferson and the Slave Power. Boston: Houghton Mifflin. Wills, Garry. 2010. *Bomb Power: The Modern Presidency and the National Security State.* New York: The Penguin Press.

Wilson, James G. 2002. *The Imperial Republic: A Structural History of American Constitutionalism from the Colonial Era to the Beginning of the Twentieth Century.* Burlington, VT: Ashgate.

Wilson, James Q. 1968. *Varieties of Police Behavior.* Cambridge, MA: Harvard University Press.

———. 1997. *Moral Judgment: Does the Abuse Excuse Threaten Our Legal System?* New York: Basic Books.

Wilson, Robin Fretwell, ed. 2006. *Reconceiving the Family: Critique on the American Law Institute's Principles of the Law of Family Dissolution.* New York: Cambridge University Press.

Wines, Michael. 2003. "Justice in Russia Is No Longer Swift or Sure." *New York Times* (February 23): A3.

Wing, Adrien Katherine, ed. 2000. *Critical Race Feminism: A Reader.* New York: New York University Press.

Wing, Adrien Katherine. 2007. "Critical Race Feminist Theory." Pp. 350–353, in David S. Clark, ed. *Encyclopedia of Law & Society.* Los Angeles: Sage.

Winter, Greg. 2002. "Law Schools Urge Graduates to Start Small and Think Local." *New York Times* (December 16): 131.

Wise, Steven M. 2001. "Why Animals Deserve Legal Rights." Chronicle of Higher Education (February 2): 1313.

Wishman, Seymour. 1981. *Confessions of a Criminal Lawyer*. New York: Times Books.

Witte, John, Jr. 1996. "Law, Religion, and Human Rights." *Columbia Human Rights Law Review* 28: 1–31.

Witte, John, Jr. 2009. *The Sins of the Fathers: The Law and Theology of Illegitimacy Reconsidered*. New York: Cambridge University Press.

Wittes, Benjamin. 2008. *Law and the Long War: The Future of Justice in the Age of Terror*. New York: The Penguin Press.

Wolfson, Nicholas. 1997. *Hate Speech, Sex Speech, Free Speech*. Westport, CT: Praeger.

Woliver, Laura R. 2002. *The Political Geographies of Pregnancy*. Urbana: University of Illinois Press.

Woliver, Laura R. 2007. "Abortion." Pp. 10–13, in David S. Clark, ed. *Encyclopedia of Law & Society*. Los Angeles: Sage.

Wong, Edward. 2004a. "Top Commanders Face Questioning on Prison Abuse." New York Times (June 22): A1.

Wong, Kam C. 2009. *Chinese Policing: History and Reform*. New York: Peter Lang Publishing, Inc.

———. 2004b. "New Law in Iraq Gives Premier Martial Powers to Fight Uprising." *New York Times* (July 7): A1

Wong, Kam C. 2009. *Chinese Policing: History and Reform*. New York: Peter Lang Publishing, Inc.

Wood, Arthur Lewis. 1967. *Criminal Lawyer*. New Haven, CT: College and University Press.

Woodhouse, Barbara Bennett. 2008. *Hidden in Plain Sight: The Tragedy of Children's Rights from Ben Franklin to Lionel Tate*. Princeton, NJ: Princeton University Press.

Woodward, C. Vann. 1957. *The Strange Career of Jim Crow*. New York: Oxford University Press.

Woolford, Andrew, and R. S. Ratner. 2008. *Informal Reckonings: Conflict Resolution in Mediation, Restorative Justice and Reparations*. New York: Routledge-Cavendish.

Worden, Robert E. 1989. "Situational and Attitudinal Explanations of Police Behavior: A Theoretical Appraisal and Empirical Assessment." *Law & Society Review* 23: 667–711.

Wotipka, Christine Min and Kiyoteru Tsutsui. 2008. "Global Human Rights and State Sovereignty: State Ratification of International Human Rights Treaties, 1965–2001." *Sociological Forum* 23: 724–753.

Wright, Lawrence. 2011. "The Apostate." *The New Yorker* (February 14 & 21): 84–111.

Wright, Margaret M. 2007. *Judicial Decision Making in Child Sexual Abuse Cases*. Vancouver, BC: UBC Press.

Wu, Bohsiu. 2000. "Determinants of Public Opinion Toward Juvenile Waiver Decisions." *Juvenile and Family Court Journal* 51: 9–20.

Wueste, Daniel E. 1986. "Fuller's Processual Philosophy of Law." *Cornell Law Review* 71: 1205–1230.

Wunder, John R., ed. 1996. *Recent Legal Issues for American Indians, 1968 to the Present*. New York: Garland.

Xu, Xiaoqun. 2008. *Trial of Modernity: Judicial Reform in Early Twentieth –Century China, 1901–1937*. Stanford, CA: Stanford University Press.

Xu, Xinyi. 1995. "The Impact of Western Forms of Social Control on China: A Preliminary Evaluation." *Crime, Law, and Social Change* 23: 67–87.

Yardley, Jim. 2010. "India, Cases, Honor and Killings Intertwine." *New York Times* (July 10): A1.

Yilmaz, Ihsan. 2005. *Muslim Laws, Politics in Modern Nation States: Dynamic Legal Pluralism in England, Turkey and Pakistan*. Aldershot, UK: Ashgate.

Yngvesson, Barbara. 1993. *Virtuous Citizens, Disruptive Subjects: Order and Complaint in a New England Court*. New York: Routledge.

Yoo, John. 2010. *Crisis and Command: The History of Executive Power from George Washington to George W. Bush*. New York; Kaplan Publishing.

Yorke, Jon, ed. 2008. *Against the Death Penalty: International Initiatives and Implications*. Burlington, VT: Ashgate Publishing Co.

Yoshino, Kenji. 2002. "Can the Supreme Court Change Its Mind?" *New York Times* (December 5): Op Ed Page.

Young, Jeffrey R. 2010. "New Regulations on Campus Piracy Don't Mean New Antipiracy Actions." *Chronicle of Higher Education* (April 23): A14.

Zaibert, Leo. 2006. *Punishment and Retribution*. Burlington, VT: Ashgate Publishing Co.

Zalman, Marvin. 2011. *Criminal Procedure – Constitution and Society. Sixth edition*. Boston. Prentice Hall.

Zamboni, Mauro. 2007. *The Policy of Law: A Legal Theoretical Framework*. Oxford: Hart Publishing.

Zamboni, Mauro. 2008. *Law and Politics: A Dilemma For Contemporary Legal Theory.* New York: Springer.

Zasloff, Jonathan. 1998. "Children, Families, and Bureaucrats: A Prehistory of Welfare Reform." *Journal of Law and Politics* 14: 225–317.

Zatz, Marjorie S. 1994. *Producing Legality: Law and Socialism in Cuba.* New York: Routledge.

Zeder, Jeri. 2008. "At Home in the World." *Harvard Law Bulletin* (Winter): 32–37.

Zelizer, Viviana. 2005. *The Purchase of Intimacy.* Princeton, NJ: Princeton University Press.

Zellner, William W. 1995. *Counter Cultures: A Sociological Analysis.* New York: St. Martin's Press.

Zerai, Assata, and Rae Banks. 2002. *Dehumanizing Discourse, Anti-Drug Law, and Policy in America: A "Crack Mother's" Nightmare.* Burlington, VT: Ashgate.

Zernike, Kate. 2003. "Students Shall Not Download. Yeah, Sure." *New York Times* (September 20): A6.

Zhang, Lening. 2001. "White-Collar Crime: Bribery and Corruption in China." Pp. 23–36, in Jianhoung Liu, Lening Zhang, and Steven F. Messner, eds. *Crime and Social Control in a Changing China.* Westport, CT: Greenwood Press.

Zhang, Lening, Steven F. Messner, and Jianhong Liu. 2008. "A Critical Review of Recent Literature on Crime and Criminal Justice in China: Research Findings, Challenges, and Prospects." *Crime, Law & Social Change* 50: 125–130.

Zick, Timothy. 2008. *Speech Out of Doors: Preserving First Amendment Liberties in Public Places.* Cambridge: Cambridge University Press.

Zieharth, Amy. 2003. "Solving the Diversity Dilemma." *New York Tunes* (June 9): Op Ed. Zimmerman, Richard. 1998. "Law Reviews: A Foray Through a Strange World." *Emory Law Review* 47: 660–695.

Zilney, Lisa Anne, and Laura J. Zilney. 2009. *Reconsidering Sex Crimes and Offenders: Prosecution or Persecution?* Santa Barbara, CA: ABC-CLIO.

Zimbardo, Philip. 2007. *The Lucifer Effect.* New York: Random House.

Zippel, Kathrin S. 2006. *The Politics of Sexual Harassment: A Comparative Study of the United States, the European Union, and Germany.* New York: Cambridge University Press.

Zittrain, Jonathan. 2000. "Balancing Control and Anarchy on the Internet." *Chronicle of Higher Education* (October 13): B20

Zivi, Karen D. 2000. "Who Is the Guilty Party? Rights, Motherhood, and the Problem of Prenatal Drug Exposure." *Law & Society Review* 34: 237–258

Zoepf, Katherine. 2007. "A Dishonorable Affair." *New York Times Magazine* (September 23): 22–29.

NAME INDEX

SUBJECT INDEX

socioeconomic status and, 235
victim's rights and, 238
See also specific courts
Court of Military Appeals, 253
Courtroom workgroup, 206, 235
Covenant marriage law, 25
Crime
defining, 231–232
drugs and, 321
legal culture and, 265
of obedience, 282–283
See also specific crimes
Crime control
due process and, 55, 230
political science and, 131
Crime-fighter, 232
Criminal justice system, 25–27
administrative/regulatory justice system and, 251
correctional system and, 238–239
courts and, 235–238
declining crime and, 231
justice and, 78–79
law and, 230–231
police and, 232–235
for sexual misconduct, 77
Criminal law, 43
vs. civil law, 54–55
Criminal Prosecution Clinic, 225
Critical legal studies (CLS), 115–116
Critical Race Feminist Theory, 117
Critical Race Realism, 117
Critical race theory
feminism and, 117
jurisprudence and, 116–117
narrative jurisprudence and, 121
Critique of law, 7–8
conservative, 8–9
internal, 9–10
radical, 8
unfulfilled promises and, 9
Cujus maxim, 326
Cultural defenses, 268
Cultural relativity, 82
The Cyberlaw Clinic, 225

Damages, 245–247
Danwei (Chinese mediation units), 169–173

Daubert v. Merrill Down Pharmaceuticals, Inc., 329
Davis v. Monroe County Board of Education, 316
Death panels, 29
Death penalty. *See* Capital punishment
Debs, In re, 303
Debtors prisons, 305
Decision-making
by juries, 236
by police, 232–233
Declaration of Independence
lawyers and, 195
natural law and, 101
Deepwater oil spill, 298
Defamation of character, 41
Defendant rights, 164
Democratic model, 96
Democratization
of jurisprudence, 99
natural law and, 46
Department of Justice, 251
Desegregation, 299–300, 301
legal culture and, 262
See also Brown v. Board of Education
Determinism, 130
Deterrence, 96
administrative/regulatory justice system and, 250
legal behavior and, 283–284
Deviance, 89–90
Dialectical perspective on lawmaking, 302
Digital Millennium Copyright Act of 1998, 28
Disbarment, 219–220
Discipline
for lawyers, 219–220
military justice system and, 253
Discretion, 280–281
Discretionary decision making, by police, 232–233
Discrimination
age and, 18–19
cultural pluralism and, 269
equal opportunity and, 310–312
legal culture and, 262, 265
obesity and, 19, 312
by police, 233
unattractiveness and, 19
Disorderly conduct, 43
Distributive principle of justice, 74

Reproductive technology, 16–17
Republic of choice, 265
Responsibility
   legalism and, 84–85
   third-parties, 85
Restitution, 96
   Islam and, 175
Restorative justice, 79
   community justice and, 257
Retributive principle of justice, 74
Riggs v. Palmer, 114
Rights
   of animals, 20
   of homosexuals, 89, 315–318
   of juveniles, 241
   social change and, 325
   of women, 308–310
   See also specific kinds of rights
Rights consciousness, 17–18
   Law and Society Movement and, 127
Right-to-privacy. *See* Privacy
Roe v. Wade, 14, 67, 89, 92, 299–300
Rome
   legal profession and, 193
   Twelve Tables of, 163
Rough justice, 235
Rule of law, 43, 44, 45
   realities of law and, 148–149
   war on terror and, 189
Rule of precedent, 66–68
Russia
   communism in, 169
   jurisprudence of terror in, 168
   presumption of innocence in, 168
   show trials in, 168
   socialist law and, 167–169

Sacred law, 173–177
Same sex marriage, 300, 317
Sanctity-of-life issues, 14–17
Sarbanes-Oxley Act, 31
Satanists, 87
School prayer, 94
Science
   law and, 328–329
   See also Technology

Scopes, 328
SEC. *See* Securities and Exchange Commission
Securities and Exchange Commission (SEC), 250
Selective literalism, 274
Self-incrimination, in China, 171
Self-regulation, 324
Semiotics, 276
Sentencing
   guidelines for, 237–238
   legal culture and, 265
Separation of church and state, 93–94
Sexting, 24
Sexual harassment, 19
   of children, 316
   on college campuses, 21, 316
   feminism and, 316
   law and, 316
   military justice system and, 253
   organizational law and, 40
Sexual misconduct, 77
Sexual molestation
   of children, 13–14, 26
   statue of limitations and, 26
Sexual offenders registration, 234
Sex work, 322
Shadow of the law, 244
Shariah (Islamic law), 174–176
Show trials, 168
Skepticism, 109–110
Skinheads, 87
Sky, 326
Slavery
   African-Americans and, 180–185
   Catholic Church and, 181
Small claims court, 244, 247, 258
Small town justice, 258
Social and cultural anthropology, 152
Social change
   conservatives and, 294
   due process and, 324 325
   globalization and, 302, 330–332
   immigration and, 300
   law and, 293–333
   liberals and, 294
   politics and, 327–328
   regulatory law and, 324

CPSIA information can be obtained
at www.ICGtesting.com
Printed in the USA
BVHW020802040523
663483BV00002B/1